# Advance Praise

The authors have compiled a comprehensive, up-to-date book on inkblot tests as the most important projective techniques for assessing personality. I am greatly impressed by the extent to which psychology has matured in India during the past several decades; the current book is much overdue as a significant contribution to the study of personality, psychodiagnosis and mental health. It certainly should stimulate new research throughout the world.

**Wayne H. Holtzman, PhD**
Hogg Professor Emeritus of Psychology,
Past President, Hogg Foundation for Mental Health,
The University of Texas, Austin

Readers of the *Inkblot Personality Test: Understanding the Unconscious Mind* will gain a meaningful classical perspective and understanding of the three clinical instruments of projective psychology that have benefitted many mental health and psychotherapy practitioners and clients.

**Robert B. Williams, PhD, MA CPsychol CSci NCSP**
Department of Psychology,
Crandall University, Moncton, NB, Canada

The book is like a good workshop explaining the history, development and the progress in the field of projective techniques. It should be of great interest not only to the scholars, researchers and teachers of psychology but even more useful to clinical psychologists as well, due to its application in diagnosing and treating the patients. I believe the reader will find the book to be a valuable companion to the DSM-IV because of vignettes, easy-to-understand language and its clinical application to develop a road map for navigating through the differential diagnosis and formulating treatment plans. Handbook's conciseness and excellent organization, and yet sufficiently broad coverage will have special appeal to the psychology students. This is the kind of textbook that will find a place on the clinicians' desk rather than on a bookshelf.

**Greesh C. Sharma, PhD**
Founder, Director and Clinical Psychologist,
Lower Bucks Institute of Behavior Modification,
Morrisville, PA, USA

Flowing from a lifelong experience on research and clinical work on projective techniques, this book synthesizes theoretical and clinical guidelines about classical inkblot tests, Rorschach and Holtzman, and presents to a wider readership the Somatic Inkblot Series, created by one of the authors. It is also a mirror of an Occident–Orient collaboration. So much in the meeting between the occidental unconscious theory and Indian spirituality, supporting both a deeper insight in human psychology and a holistic perspective of psychic disorders. But it is also the result of a long work done together by all the authors in an international context.

Much more than a technical manual—it reports scoring systems and the Indian normative work on SIS—it is also a pleasant reading, open to imagination in historical reconstruction of a dialogue with Rorschach and to reflections about projection theory and its fundaments. A broad section is devoted to a detailed case discussion in many situations that modern clinician must often face. A section about longitudinal studies highlights a constant attention to patients undergoing psychotherapy and to the ability to document profound psychological changes in this course.

Therefore, the book is also a useful tool for students and clinicians learning and performing psychodiagnosis and psychotherapy.

**Silvia Daini, MD**
Aggregate Professor of Psychiatry,
Catholic University, Rome

This book gives me an excellent overview of three important projective psychological techniques and their theoretical backgrounds. As a European psychologist, I gladly learn about the SIS, originated in USA and widely used in India. I found it helpful to compare the SIS with the other two methods, all this in a single book. Correspondingly, I warmly recommend the book not only to researchers and professionals in India but also to psychologists internationally. So the book also contributes to the common concept system between clinicians. I have listened to Dr Professor Dubey on several congresses in the USA and India, and I am sure that his presence as one of the authors of this book is a guarantee of its high quality.

**Ailo Uhinki, PhD**
Psychologist,
Synteesi, Linnankatu,
Turku, Finland

For the authors, projective psychology is not just a science and a theoretical framework for psychological assessment, but is always a way of life, a true philosophy and a means to an end: to know and reach the most in-depth self. Responses to inkblot projective methods can in fact be seen 'as a mirror of inner world'. These methods are solid and well-validated forms of assessment. A useful tool for clinicians and researchers, this book presents historical, theoretical, empirical and clinical information about the three inkblot projective methods, Rorschach Test, Holtzman Inkblot Technique and Somatic Inkblot Series. Let the deepest memories, fantasies and feelings emerge, of our patients and clients, as well as our own....

**Rui C. Campos, PhD**
Professor of Psychological Assessment,
University of Évora, Portugal

The authors must be congratulated to produce a book of the Somatic Inkblot Series, all be it that this book is long overdue. The handbook of inkblot technique is one of those manuals every clinician should have on their bookshelf. It covers the area of projective testing in a very comprehensive, clear, crisp and readable way. One of the most valuable sections of the manual is the one that deals with the administration, scoring and interpretation of the Somatic Inkblot Series. This section is dealt with in great detail, and yet is so easy to understand that any clinician with just a rudimentary knowledge of the use of projective tests will be able to administer, score and interpret the series with great confidence. As an adjunct to therapy, this tool is second to none. Every therapist knows the frustration when they are confronted with a block of information, knowing that there is something somewhere in the client's mind but being unable to tap it. This is where this manual comes into use, giving the therapist all the skills and methodology to deal with just that kind of situation. This book and Test can be recommended with the greatest of confidence.

**George Savage, MSc, DTech. (Edu)**
Clinical Psychologist in Private Practice,
Ladysmith, South Africa

This is one of the few books that examines and evaluates in detail three major associative projective techniques. For this reason, it can be considered as a valuable contribution to the field of psychological assessment and projective assessment.

More particularly, it presents the reader with extensive information on the theoretical and historical background of the administration, scoring and evaluation principles of the Rorschach, Holtzman and Somatic Inkblot Series instruments. Evaluation is enriched by numerous examples of clinical cases.

A particularly interesting feature of the book is the application of the Holtzman and the SIS in India. The uniqueness of the Indian culture affects the personality and the psychopathology of its people in such a way that makes the application of projective techniques particularly useful and offers the opportunity for interesting cross-cultural comparisons.

**Carina Coulacoglou, PhD**
Director Fairy Tale Test,
Psychologist, University of La Verne,
Athens, Greece

# INKBLOT
## PERSONALITY TEST

# Understanding the Unconscious Mind

**BANKEY LAL DUBEY**
**PADMAKALI BANERJEE**
**ANAND DUBEY**

Los Angeles | London | New Delhi
Singapore | Washington DC | Melbourne

*First published in 2019 by*

**SAGE Publications India Pvt Ltd**
B1/I-1 Mohan Cooperative Industrial Area
Mathura Road, New Delhi 110 044, India
*www.sagepub.in*

**SAGE Publications Inc**
2455 Teller Road
Thousand Oaks, California 91320, USA

**SAGE Publications Ltd**
1 Oliver's Yard, 55 City Road
London EC1Y 1SP, United Kingdom

**SAGE Publications Asia-Pacific Pte Ltd**
18 Cross Street #10-10/11/12
China Square Central
Singapore 048423

Published by Vivek Mehra for SAGE Publications India Pvt Ltd. Typeset in 10/12.5 pt ITC Stone Serif by Zaza Eunice, Hosur, Tamil Nadu, India.

**Library of Congress Cataloging-in-Publication Data Available**

**ISBN:** 978-93-532-8461-9 (HB)

**SAGE Team:** Rajesh Dey, Vandana Gupta, Sonam Rana and Rajinder Kaur

*This book is dedicated to the outstanding research and contribution of*
*Hermann Rorschach, Wayne H. Holtzman and Wilfred A. Cassell,*
*and all those professionals and practitioners who are working in this field.*

Thank you for choosing a SAGE product!
If you have any comment, observation or feedback,
I would like to personally hear from you.

*Please write to me at* **contactceo@sagepub.in**

**Vivek Mehra,** Managing Director and CEO, SAGE India.

# Contents

## PART I: THEORETICAL BASE OF INKBLOT TESTS

# PART II: TESTS' RESULTS AND GUIDELINES

# PART III: APPLICATION OF INKBLOT TESTS
# IN INDUSTRIES AND CLINICAL SET-UPS

# List of Tables

# List of Abbreviations

| | |
|---|---|
| AA | Alopecia areata |
| Affr | Affective ratio |
| BAD | Bipolar affective disorders |
| CBT | Cognitive behavioural therapy |
| CDI | Coping deficits index |
| CS | Comprehensive system |
| CSS | Comprehensive scoring system |
| DEPI | Depression index |
| DSM | *Diagnostic and Statistical Manual of Mental Disorders* |
| ESS | Extended scoring system |
| FNE | Fear of negative evaluation |
| HAS | Hostility and Aggression Scale |
| HGMAT | Hundal General Mental Ability Test |
| HIT | Holtzman Inkblot Technique |
| HPG | High Productivity Group |
| HSPQ | High school personality questionnaire |
| ICD | International Classification of Diseases |
| IMHH | Institute of Mental Health and Hospital |
| LPG | Low Productivity Group |
| MMPI | Minnesota Multiphasic Personality Inventory |
| NIMHANS | National Institute of Mental Health and Neurosciences |
| OAM | Optimism attitude model |
| OI | Optimism Index |
| PAS | Pathological Anatomy Scale |
| PET | Positron emission tomography |

| | |
|---|---|
| PMR | Progressive muscular relaxation |
| PSD | Psycho sexual disorder |
| PT | Projective techniques |
| PTI | Perceptual-thinking Index |
| PTSD | Post-traumatic stress disorder |
| RINPAS | Ranchi Institute of Neuro-Psychiatry and Allied Sciences |
| SAD | Social avoidance and distress |
| SCZI | Schizophrenia Index |
| SIS | Somatic Inkblot Series |
| SIT | Somatic Imagery Test |
| SSCT | Sack's sentence completion test |
| TAT | Thematic Apperception Test |
| WHO | World Health Organization |
| WISC | Wechsler Intelligence Scale for Children |

# Foreword

The authors have compiled a comprehensive, up-to-date book on inkblot tests as the most important projective technique for assessing personality. Three inkblot tests are featured in the book: the Rorschach, the Holtzman Inkblot Technique (HIT) and the Somatic Inkblot Series (SIS). The current direction of studies, mostly by Indian psychologists under the authors' guidance, highlighted in the Foreword by Wilfred A. Cassell, shows worthy advances Rorschach would like.

Part I in the book begins with an excellent, detailed history of Hermann Rorschach and his early experiments with inkblots to diagnose mentally ill patients. The final set of 10 inkblots has been used extensively throughout the world, resulting in thousands of publications that continue to grow in number. Special attention is given to the administration and scoring of the Rorschach tests with special sections detailing the systems developed by Klopfer and Exner.

The HIT is reviewed in detail, emphasizing its excellent psychometric qualities resulting from two parallel forms, each containing 45 rich, colourful inkblots selected from thousands of inkblots originally produced by Holtzman and his colleagues. Unlike the Rorschach test with only 10 inkblots, the HIT test has 22 scores for which the reliability and validity for personality assessment can be more easily determined.

In addition to HIT's psychometric value, when administered in a standard manner, a wealth of information is available on responses to each of the 90 inkblots from the original standardization on several thousand individuals. Special subsets of inkblots that elicit body image or sexual ideation can be assembled for experimental studies of qualitative nature involving free associations much like those described in detail in the 15 case studies based mainly on the Rorschach test and the SIS in Part III of this book. Future research involving HIT inkblots will probably go in three directions: (a) computer-based testing and analysis using configural scoring for efficient, valid psychodiagnosis of mental disorders and personality, (b) special subsets of HIT inkblots for which two responses are requested rather than just one and (c) qualitative use of selected subsets for free association and therapist–patient interaction, much like the interesting and informative case studies presented in Chapter 12.

SIS-I and II are reviewed in detail, which will be of special interest to Western clinicians who have not had a chance to learn much about the test. Many of the most recent SIS studies have been published in the *SIS Journal of Projective Psychology and Mental Health* or in Indian journals, none of which has wide circulation in Western countries, unfortunately. SIS deserves much greater attention from clinicians and researchers everywhere, and this book will help to acquaint them with the attractive features and both research and clinical possibilities of the SIS-I and II.

I am greatly impressed by the extent to which psychology has matured in India during past several decades, much of it under the leadership of Bankey Dubey and his colleagues in clinical psychology, with strong guidance from Wilfred Cassell. This book is much overdue as a significant contribution to the study of personality, psychodiagnosis and mental health. It certainly should stimulate new research throughout the world.

**Wayne H. Holtzman, PhD**
Hogg Professor Emeritus of Psychology
Past President, Hogg Foundation for Mental Health,
The University of Texas, Austin, TX

# Foreword

I wish to express my appreciation to the inspirational spirits of Herman Rorschach and Wayne Holtzman for their original contributions during the 20th century to inkblot design and projective technique—theirs is a 'hard act to follow'. As the creator of SIS, it is with humility that I accepted the invitation of the authors of this book to write this foreword.

This book is an innovative scientific pursuit of the authors in the arena of synthesizing and exploring the genesis, evolution and implications of the vast scientific pursuits related to complex psycho-dimensional personality dimensions of people across the world. An integral component of this work relates to the rigorous inkblot methodological interpretation that is ingrained in determining personality traits and behavioural attributes. It helps to prepare for an intellectual adventure into the methodologically illusive, inner realms of the 'mind/body'. The authors challenge young people to pursue a career, involving a fascinating inner world exploration. At this stage in the 21st century, there are a vast number of scientific fields, undreamed of in the days of Rorschach. These provide advanced technology, facilitating the exploration of inner dimensions of body–mind–spiritual space.

Any prospective explorer, hoping to develop background introspective skills for eventual work in the field of psychological projective techniques, should consider viewing the Rorschach, Holtzman and SIS inkblots procedures initially and documenting what is seen and felt in relation to each visual array. This is analogous to establishing a personal 'diary', which can later serve as a baseline point of personal reference. In no other field of science is there such an intimate reliance on the interaction between the professional's cultural/religious early memories and that of the client/patient's background. Since there is a strong relationship between inkblot visual experiences and that of affect-charged dream imagery, first complete this preliminary exercise while feeling relaxed prior to bedtime. Consider first freeing your mind of the stressful day residual by walking quietly in a beautiful garden, by looking at calming nature pictures or preferably by a potent form of meditation, if so trained in, for example, yoga and mindful meditation. This will set the perceptual stage for the subsequent projection of deeply personal symbolic material.

This exercise establishes a 'blank body–mind–spiritual screen' which documents in a phenonomenological scientific conceptual model your uncontaminated subjective inner world as physiologically based in your genetic colored 'virgin brain'. This establishes a subjective scientific record to subsequently compare your projective viewing experiences. Because of the limitations of written language, it is strongly recommended that you first free yourself from your cognitive inhibitions concerning 'artistic ability' and spontaneously draw (with colours if you are so inclined) upon completing each of the three test procedures, always elaborate on the 'three most liked' and the 'three least liked' blots. Now record your visual stream of cognitions and label their associated emotions. This document serves as a baseline with which to compare your personal experiences with the normative data presented in the later section of the book. This comparison may be considered as a new way of self-examination to enhance your insights into the deeper aspect of your body–mind–spirit functioning. Readers trained in yoga and meditation may use this 'virgin' brain-based document as a blank page for self-reflection and spiritual enhancement during meditation.

Eons ago, long before the modern era, master practitioners of yoga and mindful meditation, courageously explored intangible inner world seas, seeking their mystical destination—*Brahman*, the universal consciousness. Their courageous explorations of Nature's secrets enabled them to expand volitional control over basic physiological functions. To their credit, they did so without the aid of inkblot projective procedures or modern neurophysiologic monitoring technology. Practising SIS-guided yoga and meditation daily can nourish yet unknown underlying body–mind neural networks. As a matter of fact, scientific pursuits and tests related to inkblot procedures and projective techniques that were further propelled by the relentless efforts of Rorschach and Holtzman have been analysed in detail in this book.

The in-depth inkblot memory releasing approach, which can bring to projective awareness long-forgotten memories, has benefited from the rich intellectual history in India. By contrast, in many Western countries there is a bias against the notion that childhood events, such as the unexpressed grief from the death of a parent needs processing later in adulthood, this needs to be therapeutically processed through exploring inkblot and dream imagery symbolically depicting age regressive nature. An example of the latter follows which involves a highly intelligent professional American man who had been repeatedly subjected to ridicule for both practising yoga daily and keeping a dream diary:

> I had a dream about my Dad dying. I did not see him or talk to him; it was more about the fact that he was dead, and I was grieving over it. Some family members were there. I turned to Grace and said—my dad died last night. She looked at me with a puzzled look on her face and I said—wait a minute, my dad died forty years ago. Then I started to cry. I cried so hard I fell on the ground and rolled on to my back and pulled my knees up toward my chest and screamed. I was crying and screaming as hard as I possibly could. Then some part of the dream involved someone finding my dream notebook and was making fun of me because I wrote down my dreams and journals.

> In the dream I felt grief ... profound grief and loss ... intense, profound grief, nothing more. The symbolism in the dream was about grieving the death of my father. It was powerful but quite simple. I think Grace was there because she was part of our lives when Dad died. Maybe I wanted her to understand how profound my grief was after losing my Dad.

This book may serve to expand the consciousness of serious students, researchers and practioners. It presents otherwise abstract information on complex mental processes, including the ambiguous nature of symbol interpretation. Those who are new to the field are advised to supplement this work with reading from the modern literature in the health sciences of diet, exercise and the need for positive human relationships, etc. A holistic approach is recommended. Next, begin formal education in the basic sciences of medicine and psychology. This needs to be enriched by additional reading material in philosophy and religion. Finally, it is suggested to review recent studies indicating that regarding affective disorders yoga and meditation give positive results—comparable to potent psychotropic medication (especially for women who may benefit from its anti-anxiety effects).

Look forward to expanding your knowledge in the field of introspective projective technology. If you eventually become an administrator of a projective procedure, you should gain understanding not only in to the inner world of a patient/client more intimately but also to introspection. In this interactive subjective world, kindly feel empathetic humility towards your inner self as well as towards that of others. In this psychic journey into inner spiritual space, look forward to leaving behind the mundane modern world with all its 'craziness', inhumanity and suffering. Imagine for a few moments about entering a wonderful 'heavenly' mysterious uncharted world, not guided by the laws of present-day science.

During such meditation, actively identify with the original consciousness of the blessed pioneers of yoga. Subjectively, sense the beauty and the healing power of this ancient bridge to healing body–mind–spiritual streams. Realize that no human mind can ever ultimately understand itself, let alone totally comprehend, scientifically, that of another. Consider, as well, reviewing, if you have not already, some basic information on the nature of primitive human spiritual symbols across various cultures, as reflected in the 3,200-year-old cave drawings. Look forward to acquiring skills that should enable you to be more able to empathetically feel reverence for your own as well as for another person's suffering soul.

The authors adopt a spiritual hypothesis and then expand on it. Dream-like imagery and visual hallucinations of a psychological origin when projected onto the ambiguous inkblot stimuli, similarly, mystically represent a psychic bridge of spiritual communication. Of course, this right brain thesis crosses the intellectual boundary from science-based logic to what critics would immediately call irrationality. While we do not understand the underlining mechanism, the authors are aware of many, many scientific studies that document the healing power of participation in spiritual activities and the emotional linkage to such symbols.

More exploratory work needs to be envisioned to explore the relationship between dream imagery and that projected onto inkblots. One promising approach is to administer the inkblot series, prior to sleep, and then analyse the 'day residual' of this stimulation in dreams. Another is to administer SIS soon after waking up, prior to the natural fading of the dream imagery and the linked affect.

This is a highly complex and sometimes illogical-appearing homeostatic body–mind–spirit phenomenon. After a stressful event, 'Mother Nature' activates a restorative healing process by replaying images of the external event, either in real or in disguised symbolic forms with the linked anxiety affect. This establishes a homeostatic-type process, comparable to behaviour therapy, since initially the dreamer is in a relatively relaxed level of arousal. The repetition of this over days, weeks, months and even years removes some of the image-bound anxiety affect. Separation in time from the original stressor in dreams (or inkblot-triggered memories) enables the individual to rethink the stressful events and cognitively correct misperceptions of the past external reality.

Yet, because dream symbols are meant to protect sleep, due to psychological defence mechanisms, most dreamers are partially blind to their meaning. Consequently, even professionals trained in dream interpretation may sometimes require assistance in interpreting their own symbolism. An interpreter with a religious background, trained within a specific culture to decode the projected inkblot responses, is most helpful when dream imagery depicting deceased loved ones has documented spiritual connections.

Unfortunately, many present-day clinicians and religious leaders fail to recognize the importance of such 'beacon' dreams. Also, many critics reject such communication approaches, accusing projective practitioners and dream analysts of heresy.

Overall, from the macro standpoint, various analyses and scientific exploration of inkblot procedures and projective techniques, one can discern that the science of understanding psycho-dimensional and behavioural attributes of individuals is a constantly evolving and metamorphosing knowledge domain. There are significant convergences and divergences on transnational and intercultural spheres regarding personality traits. The multidimensional consequences of such personality and behaviour attributes of individuals in turn influence the government machinery, industry bodies, academia and civil society at large. The more inkblot procedures and projective techniques can be applied with accuracy and precision, the better the quality of life will be across transcontinental dimensions. I hope this book will play a major role in making readers aware and provide them with necessary information about how to deal with complex psycho-dimensional mindset.

I congratulate the authors for their great effort in compiling this valuable book for professionals and practitioners.

**Wilfred A. Cassell, MD, FAPA**
Editor Emeritus,
*SIS Journal of Projective Psychology and Mental Health,*
Anchorage, AK, USA

# Acknowledgements

The book is dedicated to the spirit of the Hermann Rorschach. We wish to acknowledge our great debt to Professor Wayne Holtzman, whose interest, comments and encouragement inspired us to complete the work.

We are grateful to Silvia Daini, MD, Aggregate Professor of Psychiatry, Catholic University, Rome, and Robert B. Williams, PhD, Department of Psychology, Crandall University, Moncton, New Brunswick, Canada, for their valuable suggestions for adding intellectual directions to the expanding SIS stream of body–mind–spirit knowledge.

We wish to express our gratitude to Rui C. Campos, PhD, Professor, Psychological Assessment, University of Évora, Portugal; Greesh C. Sharma, PhD, Director, Lower Bucks Institute of Behavior Modification, PA, USA; George Savage, DTech (Private Practice), Ladysmith, South Africa; Carina Coulacoglou, PhD, Director, Fairy Tale Test, University of La Verne, Athens; and Rakesh Kumar, PhD, Institute of Mental Health and Hospital, Agra, for their critical suggestions.

We also express our thanks to Late Maj. Gen. K. R. Banerjee, Professor of Psychiatry and Former Director, Ranchi Institute of Neuro Psychiatry & Allied Sciences (RINPAS), Ranchi; Professor Amool Ranjan Singh, RINPAS, Ranchi; Professor Rakesh Pandey, Banaras Hindu University, Varanasi; Professor Naveen Gupta, Director, Hindustan Institute of Management and Computer Studies, Farah, Mathura; Professor Umed Singh, Kurukshetra University; Professor L. S. Sam Manickam, Professor, JSS Medical College, JSS University, Mysore; Professors Nilanjana Sanyal,

Jayanti Basu; and Manisha Dasgupta of University of Calcutta, Kolkata, for their critical comments and valuable suggestions.

We are also grateful to Asheem Dubey and Padma Dwivedi as well as to many more colleagues and friends whose encouragement enriched the flow of concepts.

We are very thankful to the many clients who shared their pain and inner world with us. Finally, a special thanks to all the unnamed clinicians and researchers in India and the USA for their help and support.

# Theoretical Base of Inkblot Tests

# Introduction Theoretical Base of Inkblot Tests

# Introduction

As we are marching forward in the 21st century, people all over the world on a transcontinental level are facing newer challenges in every walk of life. Many of these challenges have been carried forward from the 20th century. Out of these, one of the biggest and perhaps the most formidable problems relates to mental health disorders and associated complex psycho-dimensional attributes that essentially in turn affect the body, mind and soul of every individual globally. Additionally, depression and anxiety have risen to their highest levels and have literally become a menace all over the world. The World Health Organization (WHO) has issued a red alert on this front and advised the need to make path-breaking interventions to tackle such menace. It is in this context that the current psycho-dimensional interpretations ingrained in this book will provide an elixir of various scientific ideas and innovations to effectively confront the complex psycho-dimensional constraints that mankind is experiencing every day.

Positive emotions and the spirit of optimism are significant psychological and mental attributes that are extremely important for superior consequences in one's life. In the current era of stupendous competition and challenging situations, balanced and amicable mental predisposition is of paramount importance for success and self-actualization. In this context, yoga and meditation provide individuals, especially those suffering from anxiety and depression, a healing touch. Fortunately, a majority of mental health professionals are relatively 'normal' and can cope effectively with projective released stressful scenes. Yet, like most people, even for professionals, focusing on either the 'mind' or the 'body' may evoke some degree of anxiety. There are critics who disapprove yoga, meditation and other projective techniques. In general, one may expect adverse comments from critics untrained in yoga, depth psychology, art of meditation, symbolism and projective theory. In this clinical age, many modern psychiatrists lack such education. In Western countries, there are convoluting economic factors as well, which restraint such belief from taking place.

Importantly, personality traits and attitudinal attributes are vital in shaping the psycho-dimensional syndromes of individuals. A sense of positivity in the personality dimensions can overcome mundane personal and professional obstacles in an amicable manner in order to result in a desirable outcome. On the contrary, negative personality inhibits progress and is detrimental in the long run. Here it is important to analyse the role that personality plays as an enabling factor for progress and well-being.

The term 'personality' has been in existence since the 4th century. Hippocrates was the first one to describe what personality is. According to him, personality comprises two temperaments which results in four humours, that is, yellow bile, black bile, blood and phlegm. Largely, the field of psychology was influenced by this theory for the times to come, as it was medical in nature. The personality was influenced by humoral imbalances. The aspect of 'humoralism' spanned from the days of Hippocrates in 450 BC down to 1858 AD when Rudolf Virchow discovered the cell responsible for humoral attributes. Another scholar who came up with his theory was Plato. According to his theory, there were four groups of people: artistic, sensible, intuitive and reasoning. Aristotle gave a similar grouping, which was iconic (i.e., artistic), pistic (i.e., common sense), noetic (i.e., intuition) and dianoetic (i.e., logic) and hypothesized that these factors could affect one's place in the society. He was the first one to identify a relationship between the human body and behaviour, which many people neglected as they were driven by the medical sciences and not philosophy. Plato and Aristotle were philosophers who knew that the human body is just physical and is controlled by the human brain which is quite complex in nature and has a major impact on the behaviour. It is hidden from the world but is quite influential. Their successors developed their own theories based on their predecessors' idea.

Another major shift came in the field of personality psychology with the advent of Sigmund Freud in 1923. He proposed that human psyche is divided into id, ego and superego, which directly control our conscious and subconscious, which in turn control our behaviour. Id is based on the pleasure principle, ego is based on the reality principle and superego is based on the moral principle. Carl Jung, the student of Freud, proposed that the individuals could be segregated into different dichotomous personality categories. He was the first one to propose a type theory. In the later part of the 1950s, Carl Rogers further developed the ideas of Maslow who said that humans drive to attain the final goal of self-actualization. He claimed that humans strive for self-actualization but through different ways.

## Elements Affecting Personality Development

In particular, factors that influence identity can be, for the most part, classified into two categories: individual and environmental. Singular factors affecting personality development define individual variables that influence individual's personality traits. These variables might not include heredity, physique, biological attributes, nervous system and intelligence. Heredity is something that transfers from generation to generation. It is because of the hereditary exchange from parents to children, that is, the aptitudes and qualities are transferred from parents to children. The physical make-up of a person by persevering his/her body with the use of organic cosmetics influences his/her identity. The body types are short and forceful, tall and thin, solid and proportional and are considered a factor of identity. Regarding biological factors, the endocrine organs such as thyroid, parathyroid, pituitary organ, adrenal organ and gonads influence the identity of an individual. These factors empower one to form the social condition as indicated by his/her prerequisites. The nature of nervous sensory system additionally influences the identity improvement of a person. About intelligence, people who are extremely astute can improve alteration in social condition.

Other than the individual factors, some natural and social variables influence the identity of an individual too. These factors are a result of the social components that encompass an individual. Some social components that influence the identity of an individual are family, school, maturation, early experience, success and failures; cultural dimensions, and physical and social aspects. First and the pre-eminent factor that impacts the identity improvement of a man is his family. Parents' conduct, their frame of mind, their expectations from children and training and consideration regarding them impact their identity when they grow young. The child's encounters with the different situations within his/her family in early days play an essential role in the advancement of his/her identity. Likewise, the monetary and social status of the family impact a child's identity. The next social factor that influences the youngster's self-improvement is school. The school environment and control influence the identity improvement of a kid. The educator's identity and character, peers' demeanour and character, all impact the identity improvement of a child. About maturity, development enhances the coordination of various connections. Early experience also affects the identity of an individual. Both severe and constructive experiences endured by an individual from the get-go phase of life also influence the identity of a person. Additionally, achievements/successes and failures in one's life play a key role in creating the identity of an individual. Regarding social and cultural aspects, values acknowledged in a specific culture are the social condition. These variables impact the advancement of a youngster's identity. Physical, social and cultural conditions of a nation also influence the advancement of a child's identity.

From a holistic standpoint, the personality aspect and attitudinal perspective depend much on positive emotions, that is, optimism, often interpreted in the form of emotional intelligence and a sense of engagement. Essentially, optimism is the innate belief system that drives an individual towards success. An optimist would always look for the best and is positive that good things will certainly happen. Optimism, as a major dimension of emotional intelligence, which, if properly inculcated and developed, may lead to the enhanced quality of life of an individual. In fact, the degree of correlation between optimism and positive emotions is very high, and this inter-linkage has a positive cascading effect on the general well-being of an individual.

Another significant dimension of optimism is its causal impact on enhancing happiness in individuals in all spheres of life. Empirical evidence suggests that happy people exuberate positive emotions most of the time, that is, optimism in other words, and that in turn generally leads to a successful outcome. The positive valence of moods and emotions not only increases happiness but also makes people think, feel and act in such a manner that enables resource building and an acute sense of involvement with attainable goals. In fact, happy people become successful because they experience frequent positive moods, which in turn have a greater likelihood of working proactively and with endurance even in challenging situations. The positive psychological effects of optimism in happy people transcend the adversities and help them accomplish new goals successfully. The analysis of optimism index (OI), a projective technique to measure optimism, helps in determining the attributes that promote the likelihood of success, thereby making some prediction about a successful outcome. In this context, it is also important to state that optimism can act as a realistic intervention in the form of optimism attitude model (OAM) and enables people to integrate optimistic attitude in their personal and professional lives for achieving happiness and success (Banerjee 2018).

One should take a note of the fact that the sense of optimism and personality development are intertwined and they reinforce each other. Together they form a robust framework that ascertains the implications of positive emotions, levels of engagement, relationship network, meaningfulness and purpose, and achievements in defining the success story. All these powerful positive attributes are essential building blocks of psychological capital that is essentially conceptualized as a positive core construct with which various human attributes such as self-efficacy, hope, resiliency and endurance are integrated synergistically. An analysis of how optimism, as a powerful attribute, determines the core competency of human resources in multifarious dimensions and eventually unleashes the power that every person possesses is of paramount relevance in the contemporary world that is characterized by chaotic cut-throat competition.

Having said that, let us turn towards some analysis of theories that affect personality development. There are numerous different elements such as dialect, entomb individual connections, social job and a capacity to watch or see or think which will likewise influence the advancement of identity.

## Type and Trait Theories of Personality

The following theories are based on assumptions that individual personalities can be described in terms of a limited number of dimensions.

### Dynamic Personality Theory

*Assumption:* This theory assumes that much of human motivation is unconscious and must be inferred indirectly from behaviour. This theory emphasizes stages of development, a conflict between pleasure seeking and reality demands. It also suggests that sexuality is the source for conflict and human growth.

### Learning and Behavioural Theory of Personality

*Assumption:* This theory assumes that personality differences result from variations in learning experiences. Responses may be learned through observation without reinforcement; however, reinforcement is important in determining whether the learned responses will be performed.

Emphasis in this theory is on situation-specific behaviour rather than on broad characterizations of personality across diverse situations.

### Humanistic Theory: Personality as the Self

*Assumption:* This theory is concerned with the individual's personal view of the world, his self-concept and his push towards growth or self-actualization.

Related to the assumptions as stated above there are certain hypotheses that drive the academic and analytical exploration of personality development. They are briefly explained below.

## Psychoanalytical Hypothesis

This hypothesis depends on a couple of essential standards. One of these is mystic determinism, the possibility that humans do not conduct arbitrarily but their conduct is rather based on the understanding of intra-clairvoyant causes, which may not generally be clear to an outside eyewitness or, indeed, even to an individual showing that conduct. The idea that most of our conduct 'signifies' something, regardless of whether we know about its importance or not, is one of the most broadly known highlights of Sigmund Freud's hypothesis. Freud says the piece of mental working that is out of our mindfulness and to which we cannot obtain entrance the oblivious. Musings, sentiments, feelings and thoughts of which we are unconscious but that we can bring into the cognizant part of the psyche are called preconscious. For instance, we can without much of a stretch end up mindful of the sentiments of our tongue, even though, until the point that we read this sentence, we were most likely not contemplating it. Such reasoning is preconscious, paradoxically, as indicated by Freud if we harbour oblivious scorn towards a dear companion, we would guarantee that no such sentiments exist since we do not encounter them intentionally. Freud's another central presumption was that human identity is framed out of the non-stop battle between the person's endeavours to fulfil characteristic impulses (essentially including sex and hostility) while in the meantime adapting to a condition that will not endure totally uninhibited lead. In Freud's view, all individuals are brought into the world with instinctual sexual and forceful driving forces, which request quick delight; however, which people cannot in every case specifically express without causing themselves hurt or facing other negative outcomes. In this way, it turns into each person's deep-rooted assignment some way or another to fulfil instinctual most youthful while considering the requests, principles and substances of the earth. For instance, a man may want to have sexual relations with a specific lady, but since he has been associated with his folks and different operators of society, he realizes that he cannot simply stroll up to her as an idle outsider and endeavour to accomplish his objective straightforwardly. Therefore, he may try to meet her socially, build up a cozy association with her over some time and eventually achieve his unique goal. This answer for the man's concern is unquestionably more socially proper than an immediate articulation of sexual driving forces and in this manner mirrors a bargain between impulse and reality. For Freud, at that point, identity is a sort of field in which what people need to do (sense) clashes with what they have learned they ought to or can do (profound quality and reason) and where some trade-off is worked craftsmanship. Freud ordered his identity hypothesis as per structure and elements Rogers (1980) underscored that every one of us translates a similar arrangement of boosts in an unexpected way, so there are the same number of various 'genuine words' as there are individuals on this planet.

## Self-Actualization

Rogers utilized the word self-completion to catch the hidden nature towards the inclination of people to push ahead and satisfy their actual potential. Rogers contended that individuals endeavour towards development even in a positive environment.

### *Personality Development*

Carl Rogers recommends that even youthful youngsters should be exceptionally respected by other individuals. Youngsters require positive self-reward to be regarded without anyone else's input. Rogers trusted that everyone ought to be given unlimited positive reward. This is non-judgemental and certified love with no strings appended.

## Albert Bandura (Social Learning)

Albert Bandura and Richard Walters (1963) suggested an inventive way to deal with identity through their social learning hypothesis. They propounded the view that what an individual presents to the world as his identity is obtained through a constant procedure of organizing and rebuilding of encounters, accumulated by methods for social learning and later imitated in comparable circumstances.

## Learning through Imitation (Social Learning Hypothesis)

As per Bandura, a noteworthy piece of human learning comprises observational learning, that is, learning through watching the conduct of someone else called a model. As indicated by him, social learning occurs in the following four steps:

1. Paying consideration and seeing the most basic highlights of someone else's conduct.
2. Remembering the conduct.
3. Reproducing the activity.
4. Being spurred to learn and conduct.

## Evaluation of Personality

The importance of evaluation is to assess one's identity. Techniques for evaluating identity are vital because

- They provide a way to examine identity.
- It is frequently exceptionally accommodating, for instance, to have the capacity to survey identity for the motivation behind a business or choice for instruction and so on.
- It is additionally useful for a person to survey his/her very own identity so that he/she can more likely comprehend himself/herself as well as other people, pick a vocation shrewdly and, what is more, in this manner, find more prominent satisfaction for everyday life. As identity is perplexing and changes from individual to individual, it is extremely hard to gauge one's identity by a single strategy or a system. There are various methodologies and systems that are utilized for the legitimate assessment of the identity attributes of an individual. The following techniques are usually utilized for the assessment and estimation of identity attributes.

## Methods of Measurement of Identity Attributes

### Interview Method

An interview or a meeting can be characterized as an eye-to-eye discussion continued with some fundamental objectives. Two expansive kinds of interviews are: structured interview and unstructured interview. In an organized meeting, foreordained enquiries are requested to which answers are very explicit. An unstructured meeting is an open cross-examination. Here the questioner questions or gives the individual a chance to talk openly to get an unmistakable image of the person. From what he/she says, the questioner thinks about his/her advantages, issues, resources and impediments. Meeting is a very adaptable apparatus and can be utilized with a wide assortment of populace. The individual can be watched for non-verbal communication in addition to what is said. However, the meeting strategy is often criticized for being exceptionally emotional. The outcome can get impacted by the individual characteristics of the person asking questions. It is tedious and exorbitant. This technique requires a much prepared and equipped individual to lead the meeting. A meeting must be long enough and complete to gauge the image of a person's identity.

## Observation Method

In this strategy, an individual is seen in different circumstances for a few days and a few ends are planned. There are two sorts of perceptions: (a) direct and (b) indirect. Perception is most precise if the spectators are all around prepared in this action. One of the hindrances of perception is the likelihood of partiality in the onlooker. Assessment by watching can be made more accurate and ensure if the observer utilizes a rundown of conduct characteristics as a guide and rates the individual on a given scale. Having more than one onlooker serves to enhance exactness of the observation and forestalls the inclination in making evaluations.

## Personality Inventories

Personality inventories are printed from proclamations, questions or modifiers which apply to human conduct. In this method of assessment, subjects respond to different things and after that the test is scored and assessed. In comparison to other appraisal systems, inventories and surveys are less tedious and simple to regulate, yet now and again the subject can make a false impression about himself/herself on the off chance that he/she wishes to do as such. A standout among the most regularly utilized identity tests is the 'Minnesota Multiphasic Personality Inventory', also called MMPI. This test enquires for the reply 'genuine' or 'false' or 'cannot state' to 550 proclamations about various identity qualities, for example, frames of mind, passionate responses, physical and mental indications. The responses are quantitatively estimated and identity evaluation is done depending on the score. Identity polls are utilized in brain science for guidance and investigation. They are utilized in the determination process for business or advancement.

## Projective Techniques

Projective strategies depend on the rule that reactions to unstructured upgrades uncover a subject's basic thought processes, dispositions, fears and yearnings. In projective tests, an individual is given a generally unstructured or vague item like a picture, an inkblot or a fragmented sentence, which allows a wide assortment of elucidations from the subjects. The premise of presumption under lying projective tests is that a person's elucidation of the errand will extend his/her trademark method of reactions, his/her own thought processes, feelings and wants, which consequently empower the inspector to see the more inconspicuous parts of his/her identity. The most commonly utilized projective systems are the Rorschach Inkblot Test, Holtzman Inkblot Test (HIT), Somatic Inkblot Series (SIS), Thematic Apperception Test (TAT), the word relationship of Free Association Test and the Sentence Completion Test (SCT).

## Situational Test

Situational tests comprise certain genuine circumstances in which the subject needs to play out certain given exercises. The subject's execution and conduct concerning such circumstances allow us to comprehend his/her identity. In these tests, the subject's conduct is assessed by some prepared judges.

Related to the projective techniques, some of the resistances are about the fact that in the mental health field, a significant percentage of practitioners have their own reservations. These reservations originally had motivated them to enter the field. Such professionals hide their 'inner cry' behind their professional persona. Often in social situations, many so-called 'normal' people become defensive when they meet a mental health professional. To hide their anxiety, they may cover it with humorous comments such as 'If I told you what is on my mind, you probably would think that I am crazy!' When introspecting, most psychologically mature individuals are aware that they have some degree of hidden idiosyncratic anxieties, feelings of inadequacy, socially unacceptable basic sexual/aggressive impulses, body parts functioning like those of primates, guilt, jealousies, obsessive thoughts, complex moods, repulsive smelling body parts that function outside volition and ultimately, our bodies will stop functioning at death.

An individual's relative awareness for such affect charged images fluctuates in the background of awareness. Of course, such fluctuating imagery streams flow in the minds of all subjects during their introspection into the inner world including test administrators. Despite any previously acquired resistances to introspection and projective techniques, it is important for individuals to analyse the depths of human consciousness more clearly for a life-satisfying experience. If one can apply what he/she sees more effectively in an educational or healing profession, then its goals will have been achieved. While there are secondary empathetic risks, expect to eventually acquire more understanding as well as insight of oneself, about minimizing counter-transference issues. If the reader's work is outside the health professions, what is presented here may also be helpful. For example, if your occupational role involves selecting leaders for having introspective empathetic traits, a concern for others, etc., you might also find this book worthwhile. In terms of the history of human knowledge, the physical scientists have far surpassed in measurement technology than those trained in psychological assessment.

While the vast array of standardized psychological questionnaires and rating scales may be revealing, they have definite limitations. Consequently, they may be considered primarily as instruments for the initial enquiry of surface psychological phenomenon. Often responders tend only to reveal what they know about themselves, and then secondarily screen, based on social acceptability, to share. When test administrators utilize the fundamental principles of projection, they more readily penetrate below the surface or outer defensive social facades of the individual.

Moreover, when projective techniques are empowered with hypnotic trance, either with traditional induction procedures or with electronic mesmerizing floral scenes in the electronic forms of the Somatic Inkblot Series (SIS), then resistances tend to melt away. The reader will learn about how this second level of enquiry can technically facilitate the exploration of the depths of body–mind–spirit functioning to open innovative paths to treatment. Such new 'inkblot' therapies now demand more attention for less severe mental disorders. The emerging scientific literature indicates that the side-effect-prone psychopharmacological interventions often are not much more efficacious than placebo.

## The Rorschach Test

The Rorschach test is a mental test in which a subject's impression of inkblots is recorded and after that it is investigated utilizing mental elucidation, complex calculations or both. A few clinicians utilize this test to look at a man's identity qualities and passionate working. It has been utilized to identify a fundamental idea, particularly in situations where patients are hesitant to depict their reasoning procedures openly. The test is named after its developer Swiss psychiatrist Hermann Rorschach. During the 1960s, the Rorschach test was the most broadly utilized projective test.

Since the days of Hermann Rorschach, remarkable technological advances have expanded knowledge in all major scientific disciplines. Several of these have indirectly impacted an introspective human's perspectives. These sometimes show up during projective testing with the inkblot techniques under review. As mentioned earlier, advanced instrumentation has enabled astronomers to look back in a vast ever-changing cosmos to the origin of the universe at the time of the 'Big Bang'.

In an analogous fashion, the imagery projected onto inkblots enables the practitioners to view stressful events from the subject's past life more clearly. The critical images that are projected may reflect, either directly or in disguised symbolic form, real-life historical events. Interpreting these is a much more challenging task than faced by an astronomer whose concepts relate to time, space and energy. In addition to the above, the projected symbolism may be traceable to highly subjective phenomena such as inkblot responses, body imagery, dreams and visual hallucinations.

Let us analyse the implications in a practical domain. For instance, for an astrophysics scientist who has just used modern telescopic technology to enable astronomers to conceptualize 'black hole' cosmic conditions, there are instances of 'psychic blindness' or not seeing the obvious content in SIS inkblots. Moreover, their astronomical theories predict an ultimate dire consequence to our planet. There is a consensus that the source of energy in our solar system will ultimately blow up in a massive ball of fire. However, most astronomers are religiously 'blind' since they cannot conceive cognitively bound scientists of what preceded this monumental event.

This philosophical void can trigger various mood disorders such as 'existential anxiety'. Then in combination with real-life socio-economic stressors, genetically susceptible atheist individuals may experience stress-triggered somatic symptoms such as 'chest pain' and 'palpitations'. Such susceptible people are more likely to project heart responses or perceptually inhibit cardiac-like inkblot structure. In seemingly irrational faith-based spiritual psychotherapy, processing their death anxiety can be facilitated by certain SIS-II inkblots, like B22, which depicts 'a dying person's spirit departing the body'.

Alternatively, like those mentally threatened by the Darwinian evolution theory, cosmic theory can cognitively force others into the comforting balm of explicit, yet irrational, primitive superstitious religious dogma. Characteristically, such uneducated individuals are open to exploitation by authoritarian leaders. Consequently, they regress in social judgement to intellectually restricted or 'brainwashed' victims.

Universities may be administrated by 'mind police' such as retired military generals having connections to dogmatic religious groups, who spy on the social sciences professors to find out those who might dare to challenge their students to think realistically. Teachers, in schools, may sense that children are being neglected or abused but dare not ask about either their social environment or their inner world of fantasies and 'nightmares'. Any professional who questioned the significance of real or symbolic traumatic inkblot responses living in such repressive environments would be similarly censored.

In such countries, there could never be an honest medical science of epidemiology regarding the prevalence of body–mind–spirit disorders. Nor could there be a comprehensive community mental health programme blending introspective inkblot projective techniques with yoga-based therapies supplemented using closely monitored psychotropic medication (when clinically indicated). Unfortunately, this is idealistic, since most nations lack political leaders trained in public health systems, which require adequate taxation-based funding.

Fortunately, after Rorschach, a great number of psychologists took up the challenge. They have made extensive contributions not only in clinical diagnostic settings, but also in many other test assessment applications. Examples of widely used scoring systems that they have developed are presented in this book. As compared to the projective procedures, these may be conceptualized primarily as instruments for the initial enquiry of surface phenomenon. Often responders tend only to reveal what they know about themselves and choose for reasons of social acceptability to share with a test administrator. In contrast, a deeper level of data is accessed when the test administrators utilize procedures based upon the fundamental principles of projection. These more readily penetrate below surface outer defensive social facades of the individual's 'persona', and can symbolically open windows of the mind.

## Thematic Apperception Test

The TAT is an outwardly instructional story technique where the subject is given a demonstration of a progression of pictures that have an obscure similarity to genuine articles and is then requested to create a story connecting every one of the pictures and utilizing them as contribution to the story. This technique is utilized to figure a man's capacity at elucidation and development of the real world. These stories are then tried against institutionalized scoring frameworks and this target quantitative information is then created dependent on the individual's translation and development which is regularly utilized as a technique for further understanding personal conduct standards. TAT is likewise prominently known as the 'image interpretation technique', the reason being that in this technique, the subjects are storytellers of their own problems. It is their words themselves that provides some insight into their point of view. The pictures utilized in these tests are generally interesting because they are not true imitations of individuals and things; however, they are vague portrayals of items spinning around an explicit topic. By and large, the subject is urged to tell as sensational an account they can make utilizing the pictorial portrayals as key contributions to the story and utilizing them to present components of assortment, amazement and an end. TAT can give a point by point understanding into a man's subliminal conduct; what's more, when connected auspicious and accurately, can distinguish inclinations idle mental issues, that might go on and lead to an unfortunate social and individual life.

## Somatic Inkblot Series

The SIS is a structured, projective, diagnostic procedure and is an adjunct to psychotherapy. It is structured as a sequential presentation of intentionally designed and field-tested inkblot-like images. These stimuli demonstrate both typical and atypical response potentials. This technique is based on spontaneous and individually generated responses to semi-ambiguous figures, which elicit intra-psychic associations specific to the person presented with them.

The test is an aid to treatment since the responses can be additionally investigated to make a more successful treatment plan and can be re-tended to in later sessions, giving an opportunity to evoke profoundly guarded material. Amid the organization of the SIS system, customers, patients and understudies may abreact enthusiastic clash raised to cognizance by the pictures, which can be a remedial involvement.

When individuals are empowered with hypnotic trance related to projective techniques, either with traditional induction procedures or with the electronic mesmerizing floral scenes in the electronic forms of the SIS, the resistance tends to melt away. It will be beneficial to learn about how this second level of enquiry can technically facilitate exploring the depths of body–mind–spirit functioning to open innovative paths to treatment. Such new 'Inkblot' therapy now demands more attention. In many clients/patients suffering from the less severe mental disorders, the emerging scientific literature indicates that side effect prone psychopharmacological interventions are not much better than placebo.

As an aide to psychotherapy, the imagery projected onto inkblots enables the examiner to view stressful events from the subject's past life. The critical images that are projected may reflect, either directly or in disguised symbolic form, real-life historical events. Interpreting these is much more challenging task, than faced by an astronomer whose concepts relate to time, space and energy. In addition to the above, the projected symbolism may be traceable to highly subjective body-mind–spirit phenomena such as body imagery, dreams, visual hallucinations, etc.

Just as it has taken modern telescopic technology to enable astronomers to conceptualize invisible 'Black hole' cosmic conditions, there are instances of perceptual blindness, or not seeing the obvious suggestive structure in SIS inkblots. Their theories predict an ultimate dire ending. For example, they inform us that the source of energy in our solar system will ultimately blow up in a massive ball of fire, destroying all life on our planet. Yet, there are unanswered philosophical/religious questions that go unanswered. One critical one is that astronomers cannot conceive of what preceded the 'Big Bang' origin of the universe.

This philosophical void in introspective individuals can trigger various mood disorders such as 'existential anxiety'. In combination with real life socioeconomic stressors, genetically susceptible individuals may experience stressful somatic symptoms such as, 'chest pain', 'palpitations' etc. Such susceptible people are more likely to project heart responses or perceptually inhibit cardiac like inkblot structure.

In the 21st century, many countries have societies that are not open to uncovering the depths of suffering and releasing the 'inner cry'. In these countries, professionals who utilize the mind–spirit enhancing aspects of poetry, dream analysis and projective testing tend to be restricted. In this context, the significance of democratic principles practised in Indian culture is regarded in high esteem worldwide towards mind–body–soul synergy that enhances social well-being.

In general, socially repressed people are not suitable to be open in psychometric testing, especially in projective inkblot assessment. If they do participate, they will give responses denoting religious symbols (e.g., 'angels', 'the devil', etc.). Defensive symbolism may be projected onto the SIS somatic structure suggesting sexuality, death, etc. Those preoccupied with modern warfare tend to project images depicting 'nuclear destruction'. Likewise, those clinically obsessed with threatening astronomical theory are more likely to visualize space hazards (e.g., 'planets colliding', 'dark hole phenomenon', etc.).

Inkblot-evoked images can highlight otherwise hidden aspects of the inner emotional world of humans. These may reveal to the professional past traumatic events and unexpressed distressing emotions, which might otherwise only surface in disguised symbolic dreams. A clinically effective variation of SIS procedures involves administering these at bedtime to stimulate dreams revealing material otherwise unreported in traditional clinical interviews. Other innovative approaches involve viewing inkblots during memory-enhancing aspect of hypnotic trance.

Such innovative work has flourished in India. This country has long been revered for its rich contributions to depth psychology, meditation and healing. People from around the world have traditionally travelled here to acquire skills as practitioners of yoga. Image-focusing exercises have long been effectively taught by the Indian experts. Practising the traditional techniques can eventually lead to positive body–mind–spirit effects. However, acquiring yoga skills takes considerable time and mental discipline. Unfortunately, many succumb to the 'easy road' in this age of widely available mind-altering chemical substances. Consequently, many people mistakenly fail to choose the chemical-free 'road less travelled'.

Such addiction-prone, vulnerable citizens are easily manipulated by mesmerizing modern media technology and are narcotized by drugs. Now, there is a widespread financial linkage internationally between those in political/religious power and organized crime. It is incredibly tragic to think about the wasted lives, the international corruption involved and the never-ending wars.

In this connection, apparently 'ethical' pharmaceutical companies have begun using their vast financial resources to directly advertise a class of drugs called 'antidepressants'. Typically, the advertisements tend to perpetually expand the clinical 'indications' or clinical conditions that would justify administering potentially toxic chemicals. They do so without informing the public that the medication's efficacy as compared to placebo may be low.

In Western countries, in recent years, the sex roles of mental health professionals have changed dramatically. A fundamental one involves the transfer from the male-care provider to female. In addition, at least in the USA, psychiatrists are not trained in administering projective techniques and, in many cases, nor in-depth psychology, dream analysis, psychotherapy, etc. The financial supports from the pharmaceutical industry through grants to medical schools have tended to eliminate such training. In such educational settings, a medical model of aetiology, diagnosis and treatment prevails. Many graduates primarily only practise what is called 'medication management'.

In this book, the reader will have an opportunity to learn about the extensive psychometric background work already completed by Bankey L. Dubey and his colleagues. The normative data and scales that they published for SIS-I, SIS-II booklet and video forms represent important preliminary steps in mathematical quantification of the process.

With the availability of standardized, non-projective psychological tests, there has been a methodological move away from emphasizing the utility of the projective technique in the 21st-century psychopharmacologic-based medical models of 'diagnosis'. Clinical plans now emphasize configuring technological modes for developing new conditioning treatment strategies for addressing psychological and behavioural issues of individuals. Those introspection-based projective procedures such as Somatic Imagery Test (SIT) online version readily lend themselves to electronic image-stimulating procedures mediated through computer monitors and accessible internationally through the Internet.

## Future Roadmap

In the future, the following psychic steps may be initiated once the *Brahman* consciousness is entered: imagery is to be conjured up in conscious awareness, by recalling memories of the modern mesmerizing astronomical photographs of remote galaxies (such as taken by the Hubble telescope and available on the Internet). Once these mental pictures are recalled from memory storage, it becomes subjectively possible during yoga to fantasize travelling on a mystical spaceship, to visit the deceased, located in the spiritual dimension of the 'afterlife'.

This destination can be realized by fantasizing one's spirit first leaving the body (as portrayed in SIS-II B22) and then travelling back in time to the beginning of the universe by passing through the cosmic space to ultimately arrive beyond the original site of the 'Big Bang'. Such a psychic voyage could clear the consciousness from negative existential personal loneliness/grief and restore positive bonds. Simultaneously, it could neutralize/heal extraneous contaminating stressful memories as well as distressing input from the modern media. If accomplished through daily repeated yoga and meditation, this would enrich those having the determination to grow towards positive healing.

After sharing this positive meditation experience with others, we feel that spiritually we had Herman's spiritual support to publish this book.

## Application

This book portrays the analysis of important theoretical interpretations and related techniques in a lucid and candid manner for making readers understand and apply in their professional lives the various aspects of the personality dimensions and how to use them effectively. It is envisaged that the interpretations and analyses ingrained in this handbook will be assimilated and duly applied by professionals across all domains, practitioners, universities, research institutions and students. The uniqueness of this book lies in the relentless effort to explain complex ideas in simple form for better comprehension by all readers.

# 2

# Hermann Rorschach

## *The Artist and Creator of the Inkblot Test*

The users of the Rorschach technique would be interested to know about the pioneer of the inkblot test: Hermann Rorschach. The technique that he developed in a relatively very short time has become an important instrument. The Rorschach psychodiagnostic technique involves a person's perception being projected on 10 inkblots. He believed that his inkblot method would help in assessing various characteristics of a person such as introversion, extroversion, intelligence, emotional stability and problem-solving abilities. The test is being used in clinical settings, army, business organizations and prisons worldwide.

Hermann Rorschach was born on 8 November 1884, in Zurich, Switzerland. He was the oldest of the three children of Ulrich Rorschach, an artist in Zurich. He had a sister named Anna and a brother named Paul. His father's artistic interests may have been behind the young Rorschach's fascination with inkblots in his childhood. The boy's preoccupation with these random designs earned him the nickname 'Klex', meaning inkblots in German, from his classmates at school. Rorschach lost his mother when he was 12, and his father died when he was 18. A year after his father's death, he graduated from the local high school with honours and obtained top marks in all disciplines. He took great interest in drawing, being an artist of some merit. Towards the end of his schooling in Schaffhausen, he wrote to Ernst Haeckel (1834–1919)— the famous advocate of Darwin's evolutionary theory—asking him whether he should go into further studies of art or natural sciences. Haeckel advised the latter, so in 1904, he entered a medical school in Zurich. He spent time at several medical schools—in Neufchatel, Zurich and Bern in Switzerland and Berlin in Germany—completing his studies in Zurich after five years. While in the medical school in Zurich, he was a top student. Eventually, he became close to Eugene Bleuler who influenced his views on 'schizophrenia' while working with him in a psychiatric ward of the university hospital. He graduated in medicine in 1909. Rorschach earned his Doctor of Medicine degree from the University of Zurich in 1912. From 1909 to 1913, Hermann worked as an assistant in the psychiatric hospital in Münsterlingen, Switzerland, and prepared his doctoral thesis on 'Reflex-Hallucinations and Kindred Manifestations'. He conducted some early experiments on children and adults in which he compared verbal associations with associations aroused by inkblots. He developed an interest in psychoanalysis in about 1911, the date of his first publication. He contributed short articles, reports and book reviews to the *Zentralblatt für Psychoanalyse* from 1912 to 1914.

In 1910, he married Olga Stempelin, a Russian woman living in Switzerland. Rorschach's first child, Elizabeth, was born in 1917 and the second child, Wadin, in 1919. The following year, he and his wife accepted posts at a mental institution in Moscow, Russia, where they remained for one year. In 1914, Rorschach secured a job as a resident physician at the Waldau Mental Hospital in Bern, Switzerland. Towards the end of 1915, he was appointed associate director of the asylum at Herisau, Switzerland. He remained here until his last days. In 1919, when the Swiss Society of Psychoanalysis was founded by Oskar Pfister, and Emil and Mira Oberholzer, Hermann was one of the eight members and served as its vice-president. He practised psychoanalysis with a small number of patients. A selection of Rorschach's articles was published in Germany in 1965.

## Development of the Rorschach Inkblot Test

In 1911, Rorschach had begun experimenting on potential clinical uses of inkblots in determining personality traits. This expanded on his earlier studies using schoolchildren as subjects during his medical training at the University of Zurich. He had also benefited from having read about the inkblot research of Justinus Kerner and Alfred Binet. He noted that they had not developed a consistent method of administering and evaluating the inkblot test. Consequently, he started collecting data on inkblots on patients in the mental hospitals where he was employed as well as on healthy normal people. Based on the information he gathered, he was able to devise a system of inkblot testing that he hoped would provide more systematic way of understanding a person's personality traits.

He developed more interest in the inkblot test when he saw that Hens in 1917 published a doctoral thesis on an inkblot test he had devised with Eugen Bleuler. Hens' technique was to study the fantasies of his subjects using inkblot cards, like the one applied by Rorschach in 1911. This led Rorschach to resume his own experiments in 1918. He used altogether 40 cards, but 15 of them more often than the rest. He collected responses from 305 persons (117 non-patients and 188 schizophrenics). He showed them inkblot cards and asked the question: 'What might this be?' Their responses enabled him to distinguish among his patients based on their perceptive abilities, intelligence and emotional characteristics.

Several of Rorschach's colleagues seem to have been very positive to his work and encouraged him to publish his findings. His manuscript containing the original version of the test, consisting of 15 cards, was sent to six publishers—who all refused it. Eventually, Rorschach found a publisher in Bern who was willing to print the book—on the condition that the number of cards was reduced to 10. In June 1921, the book was finally printed, but the printing quality of the inkblot cards was anything but satisfying. They had been reduced in size, the colours had been altered and the original patches of uniform colour density had been reproduced with a varying degree of saturation. In this way, a very important variable was included in the text, the so-called shading qualities of the pattern. It is these 10 cards that are presently being used and are known as the Rorschach test.

By 1922, the ideas presented in Rorschach's book *Psychodiagnostik* had become the subject of some discussion. However, most psychiatrists remained wary of his new methods. They did not believe that the inkblot procedure could yield useful results. Although they acknowledged the potential value for the free-association thought that the inkblots generated. Yet, eventually, to later psychologists, his book represented a masterpiece. During Rorschach's life, the publication was a total disaster, since the entire edition remained unsold. And those few who showed some interest were hostile in their criticisms. The publisher, Bircher, went bankrupt shortly afterwards.

As might be expected, this was quite stressful to Rorschach and he became somewhat depressed. However, despite that he continued his work, which he reported in a lecture to the Swiss Psychoanalytic Society in February 1922. Rorschach outlined his plans to improve upon his inkblot system, but this work was never completed. He did not live to see the great success that his testing methods would enjoy. On 1 April 1922, Hermann Rorschach was hospitalized after a week of abdominal pains, probably caused by a ruptured appendix that he initially ignored. An explorative laparotomy was performed, but the condition proved to be inoperable, and Rorschach died of peritonitis at the age of 37 the following day.

Five years after his death, another publisher, Hans Huber, decided to publish *Psychodiagnostik*. Even today, each reprinting of the plates themselves requires great attention in virtually identical reproduction of the originals. Rorschach cards have a different symmetrical inkblot pattern. Five cards are black and white, two are primarily black and white with some colour and the remaining three are coloured. The subject is instructed to describe what he or she sees in the inkblot. The responses are analysed according to different factors such as the reaction time, content, originality and the subject's attention to colour, shading and form. Rorschach considered the inkblot test a kind of mirror, in which the inkblots constituted optical stimuli which mentally activated kinaesthetic pictures which are then projected back as verbal responses to cognitively processed inkblots. The principles underlying the technique are based upon the viewer's tendency to project idiosyncratic interpretations/emotions when viewing ambiguous visual stimuli. From these keys, trained observers may be able to pinpoint the responder's inner impulses and personality traits.

After his death, the Rorschach test won acceptance gradually. By 1930, it was known in the USA. It gradually gained popularity internationally. The Rorschach Institute was founded in New York in 1939. In the USA, although the test was widely criticized from the 1950s and remained a controversial assessment tool, a research publication by Reynolds and Sundberg (1976) ranked the Rorschach test as number one. They based their findings on *Buros Mental Measure Year Book*. Though there is no dearth of those who have criticized it based on validity and reliability issues, it still occupies a prominent position as a diagnostic procedure in clinical settings. Some clinicians found helpful the computer scoring of data. However, such approaches mathematically fail to evaluate the enriching symbolic responses which often surface during content analysis.

# 3

# Historical Development of Inkblot Techniques

## History of Inkblot Procedures

The history of the inkblot procedure is traceable only through Rorschach's own writing and through the writings of Emil Oberholzer, Walter Morgenthaler and George Roemer. Zubin, Eron and Schumer (1965) indicated that the concept of formless stimuli, used in inkblot techniques to stimulate the imagination, could be traced back to Leonardo da Vinci and Botticelli in the 15th century.

Among the present-day projective tests, the inkblot technique is the oldest one with the earliest published work on inkblot and other vague or formless stimuli for imagination in the 15th century by da Vinci (1982). In the last decade of the 19th century, Binet and Henry (1895) also followed the suggestions of da Vinci about inkblots. They used this projective technique as a means of tapping imagination as well as assessing intelligence. Such studies were concerned primarily with the traditional subject matter of psychology at that time, rather than being used to describe the personality of the individual (Zubin et al. 1965). Later, inkblots were also used for the study of symptom-related 'mental content'.

The concept of projection is generally credited to Freud who used this term in as early as 1896 (Freud 1950). He defined it as a defensive process in which impulses, wishes and ideas of aggressive and sexual nature externalize. During projective testing, the subject matter serves as a lens of projection and the recorded material of elicited behaviour is the screen with the picture projected on it (Rapaport, Gill and Schafer 1968). Before the publication of Rorschach's *Psychodiagnostik* in 1921, many scientists (Bartlett 1916; Kirkpatrick 1900; Parsons 1917; Pyle 1913; Whipple 1910) had used their own versions of inkblots in earlier exploration of the mind.

The real beginning of a concept-based technique started with Hermann Rorschach when he began to experiment with inkblots in as early as 1911. While he was fully aware of the earlier experiments with inkblots, he was stimulated further by Konard Gehring. As a teacher, Gehring had discovered that certain children gave very similar responses to a variety of inkblots, even though the figures were quite different in their form and/or colour. Apparently, initially Rorschach had no intention of constructing a psychodiagnostic test (Roemer 1967). His first purpose was to investigate 'reflex hallucinations'. These likely were visual forms of hallucination. If this speculation is true, he needs to be given credit for studying how Swiss psychotic disturbances may be projected on to inkblots. In any case, it was not until much later when he started collecting material in a systematic manner for diagnostic purposes (Roemer 1967).

Roemer also indicated that Rorschach discovered the diagnostic possibilities of the inkblot technique somewhat accidentally, while working at Herisau in Switzerland. His interest in inkblots may have also been enhanced by his association with Hens (1917), who published a report concerning the use of inkblots with children, normal adults and mentally ill subjects studied at Bleuler's clinic. Rorschach criticized Hens' work because of the limited analysis of his results. Probably, the failure of Hens' approach as perceived by Rorschach stimulated him to deal more directly with the perceptual aspects of the blots.

Rorschach was eagerly gathering material concerning the psychopathological features of certain sects of the Canton of Barn and their founder during 1914–1911 (Bash 1965). His inkblots were being used in contemporary experimentation and he was also encouraged by his friends to experiment. He had a very enquiring mind and consequently was dissatisfied with the contemporary techniques of personality investigations. We now know that he clearly accomplished a major work in a very short time.

Exner (1969) wrote that 'during the later half of the nineteenth century, and the early part of the twentieth century, in Europe, there was much public interest in inkblots, more as a game. It was very common for these to be used in a popular parlor game called "Blotto", where the challenge was to associate an image to a design'. The design might well have been created right there or taken from the many similar designs appearing in contemporary books.

Aside from Rorschach's studies,

Krugman (1942) wrote that Binet and Henri suggested the use of inkblots for studying various personality traits, especially visual imagination in 1985. Dearborn, while working at Harvard University, published an article in 1897 and discussed the potentials of employing inkblot techniques in experimental psychology. As Tulchin mentions, in 1848 Dearborn published the results of applying an inkblot technique to a group of sixteen subjects, wherein he used twelve sets of inkblots, each having ten blots similar in nature. Tulchin also cites the pre-Rorschach work of Sharp, Kirkpatrick, Whipple, Pyle, Bartlette and Parsons, all of whom published material between 1900 and 1917 concerning inkblot methodology in the United States and England. (Exner 1974)

Baumgarten and Tramer (1942) mentioned that in 1910 in Moscow, Theodere Rybakow, a tutor at Moscow University, was using a test consisting of eight inkblots. All these inkblots were asymmetrical. Rybakow indicated that he got interested to work with inkblots by the observations of Konard Gehring, a teacher at an Intermediate school, close to Munsterlingen Asylum where Rorschach was working. Gehring discovered, that certain children gave very similar responses to a variety of inkblots, even though the images were different in their form and color.

Zubin and Eron (1966) described three periods in the history of inkblot's use in projective testing. The first period was started by the artists who painted 'indeterminate forms to simulate creative imagination' known as pre-experimental period in the 19th century. The second was introduced by Binet, known as 'psychological experimental period' in 1895 with his assessment techniques, which measured imagination as an index of cognitive ability (Binet and Henry 1895) and the third period began in 1911 with Herman Rorschach's innovative research on 'the interpretation of accidental forms'. Roemer (1967) mentioned that Rorschach's purpose was to investigate the subject's reflex hallucination through viewing inkblots.

Emil Oberholzer was a close associate of Hermann, and through him Rorschach's ideas and work were made available. He made the test alive after the untimely death of Rorschach. Oberholzer supported

Rorschach's work and taught David Levy, an American Psychiatrist in Switzerland. Levy returned to New York with the Rorschach test. Samuel J. Beck, a student of Levy's at Columbia University, wrote a dissertation on Rorschach and collected norms for children. Marguerite Hertz, another student at Columbia, also used the Rorschach and collected sample of children. Samuel J. Beck, Bruno Klopfer, Zigmunt A. Piotrowski and Marguerite Hertz all attributed great significance to David Levy's enthusiasm for the Rorschach. He organized the first Rorschach seminar in Chicago in 1925.

Bruno Klopfer was a German psychologist, who stayed in Zurich during 1934 and then moved to Columbia (USA) to escape Nazism. He was influenced by Carl Jung and by psychoanalysis, and his general approach has been described as 'phenomenological' and 'qualitative'. Samuel Beck, on the contrary, had a more behaviourist training and put more emphasis on quantitative and 'objective' data. Beck had also been trained in Rorschach methodology under Oberholzer in Switzerland. Both Bruno Klopfer and Samuel Beck did not agree with each other, particularly on the scoring of location, movement and colours, and the difference brought about two prominent Rorschach systems. Beck's Rorschach was summarized in Rorschach's test (1949) and Klopfer's system in the Rorschach Technique (Klopfer and Kelley 1942).

Bruno Klopfer continued at Columbia and Beck went to Harvard. They led discussion groups on the Rorschach Test. Beck was more faithful to Rorschach's ideas, whereas Klopfer added more stuff to the scoring system. They started a paper debating the test, its merits and scoring, which became the *Journal of Personality Assessment* in 1936. However, they started showing disagreement on various issues and Hertz tried to bring them together with no results. Bruno Klopfer taught Zygmunt Piotrowski in New York, and in 1939 he was separated from others with his own scoring system. He conducted research with the Rorschach on brain-injured patients. Samuel Beck and David Levy moved to Michael Reese Hospital and Medical Center, Chicago, and continued working on Rorschach for rest of their life. David Rapaport created a new scoring system at the Menninger Foundation in Kansas with the help of Merton M. Gill and Roy Schaefer in 1940. They were interested in using a battery of tests rather than a single test. This is how the five distinct Rorschach scoring systems emerged and none was consistent with the original 15 main scores of Rorschach.

Exner conducted a survey on psychologists for the use of Rorschach in 1972 and found 'that 3 out of 5 psychologists were trained in

Klopfer's system, 1 out of 2 in Beck's system, 1 out of 5 in Piotrowski's system and 1 out of 10 in Hertz or Rapaport's systems'. A total of 22 per cent did not score Rorschach at all and 75 per cent did not stick to a system for administration, scoring and norms. They did not even follow the similar seating arrangements and instructions.

A research publication by Reynolds and Sundberg (1976) ranked the Rorschach test as number one. They based their findings on Buros' *Mental Measurements Yearbook*. The Rorschach test had been the most widely used projective test during the 1960s (L. J. Chapman and J. Chapman 1982). In a national survey in the USA, the Rorschach test was ranked eighth among psychological tests used in outpatient mental health facilities (Gacano and Meloy 1994). It is the second most widely used test by members of the Society for Personality Assessment, and it is requested by psychiatrists in 25 per cent of cases for forensic assessment, usually in a battery of tests that often include MMPI-2 and MCMI-II (Gacono et al. 2007). In surveys, the use of the Rorschach test ranges from a low 20 per cent by correctional psychologists (Raynor and McIvor 2008) to a high 80 per cent by clinical psychologists engaged in assessment services, and 80 per cent teach it during psychology graduate programmes (Weiner and Greene 2007). A survey conducted on the members of the American Psychological Association Division-12 and the Indian Association of Clinical Psychologists showed concern from respondents about the limitations of the test (Dubey 1982; Manickam and Dubey 2005; Sharma, Ojha and Vagrecha 1975; Wade et al. 1978). The most commonly used systems, Klopfer and Beck, are followed in India. Both the major training institutes National Institute of Mental Health and Neurosciences (NIMHANS), Bangalore, and Ranchi Institute of Neuro-Psychiatry and Allied Sciences (RINPAS), Ranchi, use Klopfer and Beck system, respectively.

## Criticisms of the Rorschach Technique

Although the Rorschach test represented a major step forward in the inkblot projective technique, as might be expected, eventually its limitations were gradually exposed. Bartol (1983) commented that '[n]obody agrees how to score Rorschach responses objectively. There is nothing to show what any response means to the person who gives it. And, there is nothing to show what it means if several people give the same response. The inkblots are scientifically useless.'

Anastasi (1982) had also made an adverse remark in his book *Psychological Testing* and commented:

Even when objective scoring systems have been developed, the final steps in the evaluation and integration of the raw data usually depend on the skill and clinical experience of the examiner. Such a situation has several implications.... [T]he most disturbing implication is that the interpretation of scores is often as projective of the examiner as the test stimuli are for the examinee. In other words, the final interpretation of projective test responses may reveal more about the theoretical orientation, favorite hypothesis, and personality idiosyncrasies of the examiner than they do about the examinee's personality dynamics. (p. 582)

Professor Eysenck has even criticized his own questionnaires after creating a different version of the four questionnaires such as MPI, EPI, EPQ and PEN, though almost half of the questions were taken from the earlier version in each questionnaire. Despite these criticisms, the Rorschach test remains the most popular test internationally (Manickam and Dubey 2005).

Zubin et al. (1965) has listed seven major failures as follows:

1. Failure to provide an objective system, free of arbitrary conventions and showing high inter-scorer agreement.
2. Lack of satisfactory internal consistency, or test–retest reliability.
3. Failure to provide cogent evidence for clinical validity.
4. Failure of the individual Rorschach scoring categories to relate to diagnosis.
5. Lack of prognostic or predictive validity with respect to the outcome of treatment, or later behaviour.
6. Individual differences between groups of normal subjects.
7. Failure to find any significant relationships between Rorschach scores and intelligence, or creative ability.

Fiske and Baughman (1953) reported that practitioners feel that the variation in the total number of responses is too much to allow the ratio scores to be interpreted adequately. Also, the meaning of the index changes depending upon the length of the protocol, because the relationship between Rorschach scores and the total number of responses is complex and curvilinear (1953). Many researchers compute the percentage ratio to control the length of the protocol. Holtzman (1956) pointed out that such procedures were very unsatisfactory not only because of the non-linear relationships between R and other Rorschach's scores but also because of the crude, unstable and metric qualities of most Rorschach variables.

Dubey (1982), in a study on 300 army personell, found that most of the Rorschach indices are dependent upon the number of responses. When the groups of normal, neurotics and schizophrenics were divided, based on number of responses, into high productivity and low productivity, many indices, which were found to be significant earlier, lost their significance. It further strengthened the findings of Fiske and Baughman and supported the intention of Holtzman.

Holtzman and Swartz (1956) pointed out that much of the controversy over the Rorschach test arises from the failure to distinguish between the Rorschach test as a projective technique in the hands of a skilled clinician and the Rorschach test as a psychometric device that yields scores which has a relevance for personality assessment. The analysis of responses to inkblots has ranged all the way from one extreme to the other of the projective psychometric continuum.

## History of Holtzman Inkblot Technique

Wayne Holtzman developed 'Holtzman Inkblot Technique' (HIT) in 1956 to overcome the limitations of the Rorschach test. The main limitation of the Rorschach test, as experientially determined, was the problem of variation in the length of the protocol (Dubey, Pershad and Verma 1979; Dubey, 1978, 1979, 1989a; Fiske and Baughman 1953; Holtzman 1956). Consequently, the usual effect of R linear regression methods for removing the confounding effect of R will generally fail (Dubey 1982; Fiske and Baughman 1953).

In the development and standardization of his inkblot technique, Holtzman (1988) emphasized:

For many of us, despite these negative finding with the Rorschach, the fundamental idea underlying were still intuitively attractive and could not easily be set aside. I was convinced by my own preliminary research on perception and personality that the major limitation in the Rorschach could best be overcome by developing a completely new technique using more inkblots with simplified procedures for administration. How could one develop psychometrically sound scoring procedures for responses to inkblots while preserving the rich, qualitative projective material of the Rorschach? Blake and Wilson

(1950) demonstrated that the first response of a person to each ink-blot had all the necessary ingredients for the standard Rorschach scoring system. Why not limit the subject to one response per card and increase the number of inkblots? Despite its cumbersome nature, Zubin's elaborate rating system demonstrated that several variables could be scored for a given inkblot response demonstrated that number of variables could be scored for a given inkblot response. His system required that a simple inquiry be conducted immediately after the response, while it was still fresh in the mind of the subject, rather than going back to it at a later time in the inquiry phase of the standard Rorschach.

Keeping these ideas in mind, Holtzman collected data on a small number of cases, asking for a single response and following it with a very simple twofold question: *Where was the percept represented in the blot, and what about the blot suggested the percept?*

Holtzman was convinced right from the beginning that the new inkblot technique that he had visualized would have several distinct advantages over the standard Rorschach test. First, the number of responses per individual could be held to a relatively constant value. Second, because each response would be to an independent stimulus, the resulting protocol would be much more amenable to psychometric treatment. Third, a fresh start in the production of stimulus materials could result in a richer variety of stimuli capable of eliciting far more information than the original 10 Rorschach plates. Fourth, two parallel forms of the inkblots to use in the test–retest studies of personality change could be constructed easily from item analysis data in the experimental phase for development. And fifth, adequate estimates of reliability based on internal consistency and parallel test–retest correlations could be obtained independently for each major variable (Holtzman 1988).

With the help of a professional artist and after preliminary experimentation with many different inks and types of paper, each member of the research group constructed many hundreds of inkblots. Clinical experience with the Rorschach sensitized them to the properties of colour, shading, symmetry and form that would be most likely to elicit diverse, rich associations useful in qualitative analysis as well as in quantitative ones. Blots were critically judged by a team of clinicians as to their likely value in a new inkblot test. Only 1 inkblot in 50 survived this initial screening. After many months, enough promising inkblots had been developed to construct three preliminary forms containing 45 inkblots each. Initial studies were completed using a sample drawn from two populations: undergraduate college students and patients in a local mental hospital. The primary purpose of these initial studies was to select the best inkblots for printing and use in two final parallel forms and to develop a comprehensive scoring system. Construction of the final versions of Form A and Form B completed the first stage of long research programme aimed at producing a standardized instrument. Holtzman acknowledged the help of his colleagues (Thorpe, Swartz and Herron) in developing the technique. He further approached several friends around the country who collaborated in the project and helped in collecting nearly 2,000 individual protocols on samples ranging from 5-year-olds to mature adults and from chronic schizophrenic and psychotic depressed patients to mentally retarded children and adults (Holtzman et al. 1961b).

The development of the HIT and its standardization lasted from 1955 to 1962. It involved over a dozen well-known collaborators throughout the USA, who collected data on well-defined clinical populations. Containing 45 inkblots in each of two parallel forms, HIT (Holtzman 1961b) was published by the Psychological Corporation. The accompanying book, *Inkblot Perception and Personality* (Holtzman et al. 1961b), authored jointly with three of Holtzman's graduate research assistants, Jon Swartz, Joseph Thorpe and Wayne Herron, was awarded the Helen D. Sargent Memorial Prize by the Menninger Foundation in 1962 (Holtzman 1963). Subsequently, HIT was translated into other languages and used as research tool and for clinical assessment in many countries. Suitable versions for group administration using projected images of inkblots were also developed and published (Holtzman, Moseley, Reinehr and Abbott 1963; Swartz and Holtzman, 1963).

Donald Gorham, a long-time colleague of Holtzman in the Veterans Administration, developed a computer-based scoring system that was used in cross-culture studies of college students in 17 different countries who were given the group-administrated version of HIT (Gorham 1967). The inkblots were displayed on a screen before a group of participants who wrote their responses in spaces provided on the answer sheet, circling the area of the inkblot used on an outline of each blot. Computer-scored group HIT norms for these participants as well as for high school students, US Navy enlistees, schizophrenics, depressives, psychoneurotic, alcoholics and chronic brain-syndrome patients, a total of over 5,000 participants, were published in Gorham, Moseley and Holtzman (1968). The computer-scored version compared favourably with subsets of hand-scored protocols on most of the inkblot scores. Unfortunately, the computer system developed by the Veterans Administration Hospital at Perry Point, Maryland, was written in machine language and did not prove sufficiently popular to justify later conversion for use by modern computers. *Holtzman is the pioneer in computer-based scoring and group-administered versions of inkblot procedure.*

In 1988, Holtzman was honoured with the Bruno Klopfer Distinguished Contribution Award by the Society for Personality Assessment in recognition of his work on HIT that is summarized in an address to the Society (Holtzman 1988). An annotated bibliography and research guide containing summaries of over 800 articles, books and reviews of HIT through 1998 was published by the Hogg Foundation for Mental Health (Swartz, Reinehr and Holtzman 1999).

Holtzman's interest in cross-cultural studies of personality was sharpened by a year at the Center for Advanced Study in the Behavioral Sciences at Stanford in 1962–1963. He was in the process of designing a longitudinal study of personality development among school children supported by the National Institute of Mental Health when Rogelio Diaz-Guerrero visited him at the Center for Advanced Study and suggested to include a similar sample in Mexico. Rogelio Diaz-Guerrero and Holtzman designed a major international project on child development in Mexico and the USA, with a team of psychologists working in Mexico City under Diaz-Guerrero and a similar group in Austin under the direction of Holtzman. Over 800 children were tested annually for six years in an overlapping, longitudinal, cross-cultural design, using a variety of personality, cognitive and perceptual tests, including HIT. Published simultaneously in both Spanish and English, *Personality Development in Two Cultures* (Holtzman, Diaz-Guerrero and Swartz 1975) contains a wealth of information concerning both similarities and differences in Mexican and North American sociocultural premises and culturally determined personality characteristics. Several journal articles on various specific findings were also published (Holtzman 1965, 1982; Holtzman et al. 1968).

## History of SIS

In developing the SIS, Wilfred A. Cassell had the benefit of insights traceable from the contributions of Hermann Rorschach and Wayne Holtzman. Projective techniques are especially helpful in evaluating those having limited language and verbal skills such as children, foreign born or new immigrants, native people, the learning disabled or the mentally subnormal. There is enough structure in many of the SIS inkblots to provide a sense of security and a measure of self-confidence. Those with limited language and verbal skills usually rely more on visualization and adapt better to projective technique than verbal interviews or testing that requires language skills.

Such images use the language of dreams, visual imagery and symbolic thought, the most basic forms of thinking and expression. It is also the language of repression and brings whatever is buried in the mind closure to consciousness, accessible for processing. Expression stimulated by ambiguous or partially ambiguous visual input can be used in therapy to test insight and to help measure treatment progress. Wilfred A. Cassell initially recognized in 1959 the need for developing a measure of 'body image', as psychiatric resident conducting a collaborative study on hirsutism, with a psychoanalyst Marc Hollender (Hollender and Cassell 1972). Subsequently Hollender, who was the Chairman of the Department of Psychiatry at the Upstate Medical Center in Syracuse, New York, brought Seymour Fisher, a colleague of Wayne Holtzman, to join the research group.

This enabled Cassell the opportunity to train in projective assessment under the guidance of Fisher. He had constructed two inkblot content scales derived from studying patients suffering from rheumatoid arthritis: the barrier and penetration. The former was based upon a summation of responses depicting the periphery of the objects. It was created to assess the degree of definiteness experienced by an individual regarding self-perception of body boundaries. Regarding the latter, this was conceptualized as a mixed measure denoting both the notion of body boundary 'indefiniteness' (e.g., references to opening such as windows, broken containers, etc.) and 'interior body awareness' (e.g., responses representing projections of internal organs). It was for this reason that Cassell learned the index called 'body interior awareness', which scored only 'internal anatomical responses'. Background work had been presented in a book titled *Body Image and Personality* (Fisher and Cleveland 1958).

Apart from the studies involving rheumatoid arthritis patients, they extended their investigative research to work with other groups. Their premise was that levels of physiologic reactivity in skin and skeletal muscle would be significantly elevated in individuals with high Barrier scores. Penetration scores were considered to assess indefinite body boundaries in those with high interior reactivity. Their physiological model has not stood up well, but, at the time, provided a stimulating intellectual basis for envisioning SIS.

After learning Rorschach content analysis theory, Cassell explored the test validity of Fisher and Cleveland's Penetration index as an operational measure of internal body awareness. He investigated what in the post-World War II period were classified in a now invalid diagnostic category as 'psychosomatic' conditions. However, no relationship was found between the channelling of stress-induced physiologic activity to internal organs, such as heart and stomach and the scores on this index.

This failure led him to independently reappraise the content constructs underlying the Penetration score. This revealed that regarding somatic orientation within the body gestalt, this index was spatially mixed and summed separate conceptual categories (e.g., 'apples' versus 'oranges'). The second scoring category of Fisher and Cleveland included responses theorized to symbolize 'indefinite exterior body boundaries', erroneously added with those concretely depicting internal organs. As a follow-up to this analysis, Cassell constructed a new index based solely upon interior anatomy content. This was called the 'Projective Index of Body Interior Awareness' (Cassell 1964).

As a new theory for guiding further clinical studies (Cassell 1965), a comparatively simplistic feedback conceptual model was gradually envisioned by Cassell. During this stage in the history of medical knowledge of SIS, many clinicians believed that each psychologically stressed person had a style for channelling stress-induced arousal to an organ system. Chronic psychological stress was then postulated to subsequently stimulate pathological physical processes. In this early speculative period, it was even claimed that these could be reversed by psychoanalysis.

Originally during his residency, Cassell was strongly influenced by such speculative, overly optimistic thinking of his professors. He hoped that designing inkblots with various degrees of resemblance to the human heart might provide an operational measure of 'heart awareness'. After field testing the newly designed SIS, studies were initiated to assess subjects with medical histories of stress induced somatic symptoms (Cassell 1965).

Apart from their adaptability to psychophysiological research, his selection of heart-like images was also determined by certain personal factors involving his health which augmented his 'death anxiety'. As an active adolescent boy in Canada, his playing hockey was immediately stopped by an old family physician. During routine chest examination for a chest cold, the doctor detected a heart murmur and warned him that he would soon die, if he did not immediately restrict all active sports. Since he was experiencing no cardiovascular symptoms, he only followed his physician's ominous advice for a limited period. Yet subsequently, when actively competing in various sports, he constantly feared dying of a heart attack.

Later during his medical training after volunteering to be a normal control subject in a cardiac function study, the cardiologist reassured him that the family doctor had made an erroneous diagnosis. While his medical reassurance was helpful, his underlying heart/death-related hypochondriacal anxieties were not totally erased. Hence, he projected his body image anxiety in designing his initial SIS inkblots.

Ultimately, several versions of SIS were created. These provided a potentially powerful projective electronic system promising to provide new research and clinical diagnostic/therapeutic applications (Cassell 1977C, 1979, 1980b) including behavioural therapy (Cassell 1977C). The electronic and Internet application of SIS-I and SIS-II technique has advantage over Cards and Booklet forms, and it can also be used as group-administered test.

## Features of the Rorschach, Holtzman and SIS

### Rorschach Inkblot Test

A pioneer among the existing inkblot tests is the Rorschach test which was published in 1921. This projective procedure was developed to explore the basic personality structure and psychopathology of the subject. It consists of 10 cards. Five cards are in varying shades of black and grey and known as Achromatic Cards (Card Numbers I, IV, V, VI, VII). The other five cards are known as Chromatic Cards. Two of them are printed in black and red (Card Numbers II, III) and the remaining three are in different colours (Card Numbers VIII, IX, X). These 10 cards are shown in order. The subject is instructed to report as many responses as are perceived on each card. There are five main scoring categories: location (W, D, d, S, DS, WS, dd, ds, dr, etc.), determinants (form, colour, shape, shading, texture, movement, etc.), contents (human, animal, sex, anatomical, natural, geography, etc.), popular/original and form level. Most practitioners of the Rorschach system (Klopfer, Beck, Piotrowski, Roy Schafer, Hertz and Exner) follow numerical/indices-based interpretations. Most studies suggest that these scoring systems have high degree of reliability and validity. Moreover, in the recent years, computer scoring system has had disappointing results since these lose the charm of projective testing.

## Holtzman Inkblot Test

### Development of the Holtzman Inkblot Technique

Unlike the Rorschach test, which has only 10 inkblots in a single form, HIT consists of two parallel forms, A and B, each of which contains 45 inkblots constituting the test series and two practice blots, X and Y, that are identical in both forms. The inkblots were drawn from a large pool of several thousand samples, many of which were created by an artist working with special papers and inks that produced brilliant colours and rich shading.

Construction and testing of these initial inkblots were divided into three cycles for the purpose of gathering data, each cycle containing a set of 45 untried inkblots. Shading, colour, form, symmetry or asymmetry of the inkblot and white space for figure-ground reversals were used as the primary characteristics of the blots in the selection process. These stimulus qualities were chosen to ensure enough variation of response to yield reliable scores. Earlier work had indicated that somewhere between 40 and 50 inkblots with one response per blot elicited from the subject could be completed in less than an hour by most individuals.

The three experimental sets of the blots were given to some patients in a mental hospital as well as to some college students, since these two groups represented opposite extremes on several important variables from earlier Rorschach studies. The main goal was to select from among these 135 inkblots the 90 best ones for the final two forms. Criteria for choosing each blot were based upon analyses of six major scoring variables: location, colour, shading, movement, form definiteness and form appropriateness. Of equal importance in this item analysis was a new score called pathognomic verbalization, a score designed to capture bizarre and disordered through processes as they are manifest in responding to inkblots.

Other samples in the initial standardization data consisted 80 firemen representative of lower middle class semi-skilled workmen; 140 adult women selected by a random house-to-house canvassing in two Texas communities; 143 college students from the University of Texas, who were given both Form A and Form B with an interval of one week between testing periods; 92 students at the University of Texas; 66 freshmen from the Waco VA Hospital; 51 schizophrenics from the Montrose VA Hospital; 50 mentally retarded students from Woodward State School and Hospital in Iowa; 50 mentally retarded adults from Austin State School; and, finally, 90 depressed patients from 11 VA hospitals participating in a national chemotherapy project. A total of

1,384 individuals responded to one or both forms of the HIT, providing a firm basis for determining the means, standard deviations and inter correlations as well as percentile norms for 22 scores that had been developed.

## Description of the Test Materials

Standard materials for HIT consist of two parallel series, Form A and Form B, the accompanying printed record forms and summary sheets, and the Guide for Administration and Scoring (Holtzman et al. 1961). Sets of 35-mm slides are available for use with the group method of administration as developed by Swartz and Holtzman (1963). A computer-based scoring programme for the group method, as developed by Gorham (1967), is also available. A handbook (Hill 1972) for clinical application of HIT and a workbook (Hill and Piexotto 1973) have been published as guides for clinicians. The original monograph and the scoring guide have been translated into several languages. Since 1977, a programmed test and other HIT materials have been available in a multivolume series in German (Hartmann and Rosenstiel 1977).

The Holtzman Inkblot Test is second in the history of inkblot tests and has attracted many psychologists and researchers in India. It has been taught to graduate psychology students and has created a place for itself in India. The test has only 22 scoring categories and is found to have more psychometric value.

The test–retest stability over time using parallel forms has been found to be high, ranging from 0.36 for popular to 0.81 for location. These results are like reliability coefficients frequently obtained for subtest scores that measure mental abilities. For most HIT scores, as well as patterns of HIT scores, the reliability of measurement and the stability across time are sufficiently high to justify its clinical use in the assessment of individuals. The validity of HIT for personality assessment is of special interest. Much of the earlier work pertaining to the validity and clinical use of HIT has been compiled in a useful handbook by Hill (1972). A comprehensive annotated bibliography containing over 800 known references to HIT through 1998 (Swartz et al. 1999) contains abstracts of these articles. Several hundred studies have been published bearing on the relationships between scores on HIT variables and independent measures of personality. HIT was found to be a valid instrument for the assessment of personality.

The scoring system developed for the HIT includes 22 different variables, covering many aspects of an individual's response to an inkblot.

These variables were derived from the more important systems for scoring the Rorschach test. These are as follows: reaction time, rejection, location, space, form definiteness, form appropriateness, colour, shading, movement, pathognomic verbalization, integration, human, animal, anatomy, sex, abstract, anxiety, hostility, barrier, penetration, balance and popular. When well-trained scorers are employed in the administration of HIT, inter-scorer agreement is exceptionally high. Only penetration and integration fall below correlations of 0.95, and in many cases, the inter-scorer agreement approaches between scores are also generally high. In the initial standardization work, median values for 50 different samples were generally in the 0.70s and 0.80s. Only anxiety, penetration and popular fell below this level, whereas reaction time, rejection and location had average reliability coefficients above 0.90. These initial results for internal consistency have been repeatedly confirmed in more recent studies both in the USA and elsewhere.

## Somatic Inkblot Series

The initial SIS was developed as a research projective technique to facilitate the study of stress-induced psychophysiological cardiac symptoms. Since envisioned in 1959, the concept has formed the basis of a series of projective procedures having wide range of research and clinical investigation. SIS-I provided a structured, projective, diagnostic procedure as an adjunct to psychotherapy. It is structured by a sequential presentation of intentionally designed and field-tested inkblot-like images. These stimuli demonstrate typical and atypical response potentials. The technique is based on spontaneous, individually generated responses to semi-ambiguous figures, which elicit intrapsychic associations specific to the person presented with them.

SIS is a diagnostic procedure because of the interaction of structure and stimuli. These stimuli evoke symbolism and meanings unique to the responding individual, such as are present in somatic delusions and affect-charged dreams. The test stimuli can be differentiated from typical and atypical peer norms and can be analysed according to internationally recognized diagnostic criteria. The procedure is an adjunct to therapy because responses can be further explored to create a more effective treatment plan and can be readdressed in later discussions, providing opportunities to elicit deeply defended material. During administration of the SIS procedure, clients, patients and students may abreact emotional conflict raised to consciousness by the images, which can be a therapeutic experience.

The viewer writes responses on an answer sheet. Most of what is included in the ambiguous structure relates to specific life situations and post-traumatic dream content that has been found to have clinical significance. Viewing the SIS images has both diagnostic and therapeutic applications.

The SIS procedures have been used internationally on different normal and clinical population. Various researchers have reported high reliability and validity and usability of the test (Cassell 1969, 1971, 1972, 1977, 1980, 1988; Cassell and Dubey 2003, 2009b; Dubey and Cassell 1991; Dubey et al. 1993b, 1995a; Goel et al. 1990; Kaur and Verma 1998; Kumar 2000, 2009, 2010; Kumar, Kandhari and Dubey 2008; Kumar, Khess and Kumar 2005; Kumar, Singh and Mohanty 2004; Nicolini 2002; Pandey et al. 1999; Pershad and Dubey 1994; Rathee, Pardal and John 1998; Singh and Banerjee 1996; Verma and Kaur 1999). Sanyal (2016) has called projective techniques as true 'mirror' of self.

There are three subtests in SIS which are discussed further.

1. **SIS-I (Cards/Video of 20 images)**

   The SIS-I consists of 20 inkblot images printed on white cards, each measuring 16.5 cm × 20.5 cm. The images are printed in black, red and grey (screened black). Eight of them are black and red (serial numbers 1, 2, 3, 4, 5, 6, 7 and 8); three are exclusively red (serial numbers 10, 11 and 12); and nine are achromatic (serial numbers 9, 13, 14, 15, 16, 17, 18, 19 and 20). Images provide enough obvious anatomical structure to evoke spontaneous verbalization, but not enough to limit the responses solely to the naming of body parts or colours. In this way, obvious anatomical structure provides a feeling of security, which makes deeper and more symbolic repressed material more accessible to the person taking the procedure.

   The SIS provides clinicians and researchers with a new diagnostic aid for body percept assessment. It can be used to assess the depth and significance of somatic symptoms, conversion reactions, somatic delusions and sexual dysfunction. Analysis of mutilated or distorted anatomy responses can assess the possibility or level of castration anxiety (Cassell 1980). Responses depicting themes of body assault may further clarify the extent of aggressive impulses (Cassell 1977). As a diagnostic tool, the series can help to evaluate undetected affective disorders such as 'masked depression', where depressive feelings are denied during the interview and in non-projective psychological tests. The flow of cognition might reveal early defects of schizophrenic disorder. 'Death anxiety' in those facing major surgery or those with a terminal illness may be signalled by excessive anatomical responses (Cassell 1979). The SIS can be used to help design a treatment programme which might include body awareness exercises such as physical therapy. It also may be used in other therapies such as sensory feedback training, behavioural therapy and desensitization for psychophysiological symptoms associated with pathological anatomy responses (Cassell 1977). This technique has been described in the book *Body Symbolism and the Somatic Inkblot Technique* (Cassell 1980), which has been translated into Italian and Russian.

The video version of the test is designed for a supervised self-administration. It can also be used as group administered test.

2. **SIS-II Booklet Form and Video (62 Images)**

In 1980, after initial success with SIS-I, the development for SIS-II in a booklet form was initiated. It consists of A Series and B Series, each with 31 images, for the combined series total of 62 images. There is also a sample image in the beginning. The stimulus images are printed in rectangles measuring about 5 cm × 6 cm, each with a space provided below the image for writing the response. All images are contained in an eight-page booklet. The first seven pages consist of the stimulus images and the space for responses. The last page is printed with instructions for self-administration and a place for a brief health history and personal data. Unlike SIS-I, it consists of images printed with blue ink on grey paper.

The printed instructions on the back of the booklet are as follows:

> Most people find this test fun and relaxing. First relax, take a few deep breaths, and prepare to enjoy. Please turn this booklet over and read the sample response. Notice that you may write on the picture or the space below it. Label each in terms of what they resemble or look like to you. Please include everything that you see, even if it reminds you of something, remote, vague, dreamlike, highly personal or even potentially embarrassing. Please include every thing that you see with as much detail as possible. Also include any outstanding emotional reactions that you might experience in responding to these pictures. Please begin on the first page, study the sample, and continue until completed. Enjoy! (Cassell and Dubey, 2003).

The SIS-II can be used in a variety of ways but it was essentially designed for self-administration after supervised instruction. Some clinicians use the booklet with a patient to unobtrusively observe self-administration for reaction times and significant verbal and non-verbal responses for each inkblot (delays, overreaction and content shock). Others prefer to allow the patient to take the booklet home and write in responses whenever they have the time to relax and review the figures (intermittent administration) or, if they prefer, in one sitting (continuous administration). Some have found it useful to have the patient complete the test booklet before going to bed, to stimulate the unconscious to process repressed materials in dream during sleep. None of the existing inkblot tests is designed to be self-administered. Projective testing accesses information about the individual not readily available from history-taking, interview, mental status examination or from other forms of testing. It also elicits information, which is not consciously known to the patient or reported as a problem. Usually, clinically significant blocked material will override typical normative responses directly (manifest) or it will appear in symbolized imagery, like dream work (latent).

Because there is no time limit, 'test anxiety' is reduced, and the individual is free to react in his own time, often exhibiting significant verbal and non-verbal clues to each of the inkblots. Since there is no text to read, SIS does not require a high reading skill and therefore it is applicable to all age groups and in a wide variety of cultures. In SIS-II, the subject is asked to rate three inkblot images that he 'most liked' and three images that he 'least liked'. This enquiry invites positive or negative affectual discharge. The subject's emotional investment provides valuable diagnostic clues to his/her psychological function. SIS-II can successfully identify various groups of clinical subjects and can be used to screen out abnormal subjects from normal subjects.

SIS-Video (video version of the 62 images booklet form) was launched after the success of SIS-II booklet form. It provides diagnostic and therapeutic aid. SIS-Video is a self-administered test, which has also been used for group administration test during personality assessment in business organizations. Now this is also available in a computerized version, which has enabled its digital application.

SIS video is highly innovative and, in a sense, a 'time machine'. It takes the viewer away from the present reality. If there is some unresolved painful material in the past memory storage, through the magic of electronic television, the projected responses will tend to be shaped by this material. What emerges in projective awareness is the deep-seated material, even though the viewer may have long forgotten the buried traumatic imagery and associated affect. It facilitates the expression of feelings and forgotten life events underlying many forms of mental illness and conversion pain.

When the viewer rates those images which are the most threatening, the examiner gets a quick psychological overview of the subject's state of mind. The technique enables the professional to more readily empathize. The hypnotic-like administration of SIS is designed to maximize the pulling power of inkblot projection. The subject is given an answer sheet, the first section of which includes a health questionnaire. The process of filling out the health questionnaire creates an immediate perceptual set to project images related to medical and psychiatric problems for themselves or for loved ones. The space–time dimensions of the viewing situation are subtly altered by a video presentation of mesmerizing flowers. These are electronically transformed so the viewer experiences a magical feeling of travelling through a garden of beautiful flowers. This draws the subject away from the present reality, back in time, to the episodes of previous illness or trauma. Following this sequence, a photograph of a beautiful mountain, followed by an artist's rendition of the same scene, heightens the hypnotic effect.

The example of a person responding to a typical inkblot is cited to show the viewer how to fill out the answer booklet. After this presentation, audio suggestions to relax set the stage for slipping further back in time and re-experiencing images of illness or post-traumatic dreams. During the initial viewing, the subject is entirely alone just as in dreaming. This eliminates the inhibiting effect of another's presence.

By writing responses, rather than verbalizing them, just like in hypnotic writing, the subject may more readily access and release painful material. In addition to the cathartic therapeutic response, the person may gain some insight and sense of mastery of the traumatic material by the act of drawing and labelling the images. Also, when the procedure is administered repetitively over time, the experience of watching the flowers, in association with the threatening, anxiety-laden images may serve to desensitize the viewer.

In many instances, there is enough richness of material elicited by interviewing the subject concerning the 'threatening' images, so that little more history needs to be delved into. In this sense, for the busy clinician or interviewer, the procedure readily serves as what has been referred to as a 'quick and dirty' test. Occasionally, an insightful subject may, after having completed the procedure, or having experienced previously repressed post-traumatic dreams, open the interview with a statement about how helpful it was. This person may simply wish to elaborate on memories of past upsetting experiences such as an emotionally unresolved abortion, a miscarriage, past psychological, physical or sexual abuse or the witnessing of an accident. Given the power of the technique, it is rarely necessary to review associations to all 62 images. However, the administrator, who becomes sophisticated concerning content analysis and symbolic interpretation, may glean much additional information from an overall scrutiny of the responses.

Applications of this procedure have proven to be far-reaching and international. The use of graphic images, rather than words, allows SIS video/computer version to cross both cultural and language boundaries. The number of uses in medical diagnosis, psychological assessment and psychotherapy is rapidly growing. It is anticipated that in the 21st century, all students of the healing arts and psychology will have the opportunity to be introduced to this technique during their training. Currently, a complete data bank is being developed where individuals from various SIS centres around the world may submit data and access information via modem or facsimile communication. This could truly be a comprehensive artificial intelligence system to be employed for good in a world beset by evil.

3. **Somatic Imagery Test (SIT)**
   This is a short version of 30 somatic images for quick assessment. It is designed for self-administration after supervised instruction. Please go to http://dubayhealingcenter.com and follow the instructions to take the test. The subject is asked to read the instructions first. Most people find this test fun and interesting. First, please relax, take a few deep breaths, and prepare to enjoy. Label each image in terms of what they resemble or look like to you. Please include everything you see even if it reminds you of something remote, vague, dreamlike, highly personal or even potentially embarrassing. Please include everything you see with as much detail as possible. Also, include any outstanding emotional reaction that you might feel in responding to these images. It takes about 20 minutes to complete the test.

The administration, scoring and interpretation is similar in all three versions. There are only 11 common scoring indices. However, the number of most typical responses varies in all three versions because of the variation in number of images included. SIT has 15 most typical responses. Content analysis and symbolic interpretation is given more emphasis than indices-based quantitative interpretation.

# 4

# Theoretical Postulates of Inkblot Tests

Hermann Rorschach did not postulate a specific theory about his inkblot technique either for personality evaluation in general or for clinical diagnosis (Exner 1969). His observations concerning the responses led him to a variety of conclusions concerning their specific perceptual determinants of responses, that is, colour, movement and form. However, he did not formulate a theory to his test. His introduction to *Psychodiagnostik* points to the simplicity and intent of his experiment:

> The following pages describe the technique of and the results thus far achieved in a psychological experiment which, despite its simplicity, has proved to be of value in research and in general testing. At the outset it must be pointed out that all the results are predominantly empirical. The questions which gave rise to the original experiments of this sort in 1911 were of a different type from those which slowly developed as work progressed. The conclusion drawn therefore are to be regarded more as observations than as theoretical deductions. The theoretical foundation for the experiment is, for the most part, still quite incomplete.... It must also be noted that there has been constant checking of the observations on normal subjects against the observations of patients and vice versa. (Rorschach 1951)

Despite its limitations in terms of theoretical postulations, the Rorschach technique offers a procedure through which the subject is induced to reveal his 'private world' by telling what he 'sees' in the 10 cards upon which he may project his meanings, significance and feelings. This is because they are not socially standardized objects or situations to which must be given culturally prescribed responses. Frank (1939) and many others (Beck 1937; Klopfer 1939) also believe that the Rorschach technique is essentially a procedure for revealing the personality of the individual but certain clinically relevant material. It is just because a subject is not aware of what he is telling and has no cultural norms behind which to hide himself.

As the principal author of the Rorschach test died in 1922 at the age of 37 years, new investigators attempted to extend his basic work in their own ways. This has led to the development of a variety of Rorschach systems. The word 'system' is used here as contrasted with theories in that each system represents an approach to the Rorschach technique.

Currently there are six such systems, none of which is completely different from the others, or from Rorschach's original conceptions. The differences that exist in the present-day Rorschach systems seem to have been precipitated by two factors. First, none of the authors of the six systems, Beck, Klopfer, Hertz, Piotrowski, Rapaport with his colleague Schafer and Exner, had any direct contact with Hermann Rorschach. The second and much more fundamental reason appears to be the general training and background to which each were exposed.

Although there are major differences, there are major agreements too. For example, all those who developed scoring system tended to endorse some form of psychoanalytical theory and accepted many of Rorschach's original interpretative hypotheses (Exner 1969). All these persons developed different systems for Rorschach's scoring and interpretations. The systems, however, have been heavily drawn from the basic procedure suggested by Hermann Rorschach based on his empirical findings. Among these systems, Beck, Klopfer and Exner's systems are used most frequently depending upon the training the user has received.

Zygmut A. Piotrowski (1957) has postulated a theory of Rorschach test known as percept analysis which is described further.

## The Theory of Percept Analysis

Piotrowski (1957) proposed that two different processes require a theoretical explanation: the growth and change of personality on the one hand and the basic concepts and principles of interpreting percept analytic responses on the other.

The theory of percept analysis is logically different from and independent of the theory of personality. Percept analysis does not throw light on the theory of personality. However, the usefulness of percept analysis can be enhanced by the application of sound personality theories to Rorschach data. Percept analysis can ascertain whether a trait is present and how strong it is, but it cannot, with its own methods, determine the origin of the traits, ascertain to what degree, if any, the trait is congenital or acquired, organic or psychogenic, etc. On the other hand, it can be reliably stated that, for example, a person with human movement responses well above the average of their age group felt in their early childhood emotionally rejected by their parents, especially their mothers, but were not physically abused and received adequate care, food and shelter (Piotrowski 1957). This, like other postulates, widens the comprehensiveness of the Rorschach technique, but it does not explain why the human movement responses reveal the traits they do disclose. (Piotrowski 1957)

The theory of percept analysis aims to answer questions like these:

Why are human movement responses signs of a basic and not easily modifiable conception of role in life (Piotrowski and Schreiber, 1952), why are positive interpretations of the black color or dark shading associated with intermittent depressive moods, why do responses cover whole blots measure readiness for a prolonged and difficult personal achievement? These and similar other questions are largely unanswered. The large number of concepts involved in Rorschach, however, creates the difficulty in finding adequate empirical referents for complex personality traits. (Piotrowski 1957)

## Dimension to the Evolving Conceptual Model of SIS

The puzzle was first faced in testing psychiatric patients who were diagnosed as suffering from one or other form of stress-triggered disorders. Those whose medical histories included focal conversion somatic symptoms would at the early viewing stage project a regionally specific anatomical response. Yet moments later, when they are responding to the remaining SIS images, they show avoidance or 'projective repression' of structure, suggestive of the same region (Cassell 1972).

Thus, it was then recognized that the 'time dimension' of region-specific somatic imagery under stress may be highly fluid in consciousness. Psychological defence mechanisms can cause stress-linked pathologic images to fluctuate rather rapidly in the intensity with which they are forced in and out of projective awareness. Formulating the role of psychic defences in the production of a response to inkblots and their fluctuating influence in shaping emergent imagery sometimes may be particularly problematic. This can sometimes obscure interpretation, especially if only one answer for every card is registered. Consequently, in originally modelling the SIS after Wayne Holtzman's test, Cassell decided not to use his scoring approach.

In clinical studies using the SIS, he originally observed that for mentally distressed individuals, often the first projected response merely represented an affect-neutral defensive symbol. In such symbolically defended cases, deeper exploration was conducted with the aid of depth-probing techniques such as post-traumatic stress disorders (PTSD) dream analysis, the study of daytime 'flashbacks', hypnotherapy and barbiturate-induced relaxation. These techniques ultimately uncovered more stress-related aetiological affect-charged memories previously hidden by symbolic defences. Thus, studying the overall chain of free associations and projected responses was found to establish more promising aetiological clues for psychotherapy.

Apart from the somatic symptoms, the stress-triggered disorders have other clinical features involving SIS-observed disturbances in imagery (Cassell 1977). There may be a projection of photographic realistic representation of stressful past events or their symbolic representations, as reported in descriptions of threatening dreams, daytime visual hallucinations, flashbacks, etc. Moreover, regarding understanding the significance of visual hallucinations, unrelated to physical toxicity or disease states, stressful scenes projected may arise from the same psychological or spiritual symbolic mental image stream as projected inkblot responses. Wilfred A. Cassell has postulated three theories of SIS known as Somatic Imagery Theory, Theory of Body Symbolism and Theory of Inner Cry. These have fulfilled the theoretical gap of the Rorschach test. The proposed theories have been illustrated as follows (Cassell and Dubey 2003):

1. **Somatic Imagery Theory**
   Somatic imagery theory proposes that everyone has a unique and highly personalized system of attitudes, both conscious and unconscious, which are projected onto the body concept as a special entity.

These interact with external environmental feedback sources and internal sensations. Relatively discrete mental representations exist for somatic regions, which constantly compete for full registration in consciousness. Somatic awareness transiently increases in states of hunger, physical exertion, emotional arousal and sexual excitement. Subsequently, the mental representations in the body fade into the background of consciousness.

Alterations in body perception also occur in physical illness. In the diseased body, pathologic physiologic processes give rise to percepts from the diseased area, which directly or indirectly enter awareness. The patient's sensitivity to these depends partially on the pre-existing body concept. Sensations that arise from regions of high priority in the body gestalt are more likely to register than those from more perceptually silent areas. If the sensations are subjectively considered aberrant, the individual must then cognitively evaluate their potential abnormal significance. At this stage, the medical patient experiencing somatic symptoms then makes a kind of lay 'diagnosis'. Intense pain or gross changes in body function are readily distinguished from normal body processes. However, other alterations like early stages of disease formation pose problems for subjective interpretation.

The cognitive appraisal of the altered body state is influenced by factors such as age, sex, socio-economic status and past medical and family history of disease experience. There may be a strong motive, conscious or unconscious, to adopt a sick role to obtain disability compensation. There may also be a stress-induced wish to regress to an infantile, dependent position and be taken care of by parental figures such as spouse, grown children, physicians, nurses or nursing home staff.

Interaction between these multiple mind–body (psychosomatic) determinants will influence whether an individual decides to consult a physician to report subjective experiences. Such 'symptoms' reported in the early stages of an initial visit represent verbal communication, containing localized reference to specific organ images within the body gestalt. Their cognitive content reflects altered anatomical awareness associated with the patient's belief that the given region has impaired functionality. Once professional consultation is obtained, the physician formulates a series of diagnostic hypotheses based on 'presenting symptoms', on the nature of the underlying disease processes. Then a former structured medical interview is conducted, with questions designed to uncover the pathological significance of the somatic symptoms. In most instances, an insightful physician will be in a relatively strong position to establish a working diagnosis upon completion of the history.

In this situation, there is no strong need for additional aids in diagnostic interviewing, like anatomical projective test techniques. There are, however, some cases when the diagnosis is not clear. Patients may present symptoms which do not fit into recognizable disease patterns or there may be major obstacles in communication with the individual. Some patients minimize or deny physical illnesses, whereas others exaggerate them.

Clinical experience, upon which the SIS procedure builds, indicates that persons suffering from stress-induced physical disturbances or (hypochondriac) conversion reactions, malingering, etc., will report/perceive abnormal anatomical structure on SIS blots. There may be sensitization with anatomy (increase in the number of anatomical responses) or repression with avoidance of somatic content. This clinical use of content analysis follows the interpretation principles described by Schafer (Schafer 1954, 1960).

When the responder projects the response 'sick stomach', it may indicate a concern about individual's own health or that of the loved one. Alternatively, in a more physiologic fashion, it may signify a deeper level of body awareness involving the stomach. This is consistent with Hermann Rorschach's belief that certain anatomical responses may be a projection of kinaesthetic sensations in the musculature.

There are a variety of techniques which can be used to bring psychological conflicts to the surface. One example is dream analysis. Other approaches involve art work, or sand tray analysis with children. Although 'normal' perceptions reflect good reality contact, an individual's perception is never 100 per cent congruent with the objective reality or conceptually subjective meanings. Both the memory of visualization of the real world and dreams are contaminated by personal, cognitive and affective percepts. Such internalized imagery may often elude both traditional structured interviews and standardized psychological tests. SIS moves into these hard-to-tap areas using the hypnotic electronic technique. It provides a window for examining interpersonal and psychic space in a way previously not possible.

By assessing an individual's responses and associations to them, much can be learned about the person's innermost thoughts and feelings. What is seen or imagined in semi-ambiguous inkblots reveals his/her deeper layer of self-perception. It is hoped that these evolving techniques may be applied by investigators of the inner psychic space, leading to the creation of new body–mind–spiritual theory. At its present stage, the various forms of SIS have been found helpful as an aid to enable professional to empathize more sensitively with the suffering individual's 'inner cry'. Previously, their suffering was more likely hidden because of defensive mental mechanisms. Many existing techniques employed today are highly time consuming and not particularly cost-effective. Perhaps most important of all, they do not readily provide a transparent window into the inner world.

## 2. **Theory of Body Symbolism**
Interest in the symbolic significance of the human body can be traced back to the very dawn of civilization (Wentinck 1972). Indeed, ancient wall paintings and stone carvings evidence preoccupation with this subject. These distinguish *Homo sapiens* from symbolically less able species. Throughout history, pictorial representations of the body have been a central theme of the artistic expression of humanity's search for identity. Philosophically, such representations are an attempt to integrate mental and physical phenomena rather than to isolate or reduce them, as in Cartesian mind–body dualism.

When someone projects the response like 'sick stomach', it may indicate a concern or focus on that organ in one-self or another person. It also might indicate some association or deeper symbolization involving the stomach. Freud, and later Alexander and French, described how gastrointestinal dysfunction or distress can be a manifestation of underlying psychological conflict.

Projective techniques geared specifically towards body imagery and organ function assess both organic and functional disorders, real or imagined. Roy Schafer, a psychoanalyst, advocated a content analysis approach (Schafer 1954, 1960). More recently, content analysis has been reviewed in Aronow and Reznikoff's book *Rorschach Content Interpretation* (Aronow and Reznikoff 1973).

Qualitative content analysis assesses the individual's imaginable mode of information processing. It taps the same inner perceptual field as dream imagery. This occurs on a continuum from pictorial recall to pictorial metaphor. Pictorial recall is a visualized objective reality, rational and realistic. Pictorial metaphor is a complex concept which is highly individualized, consisting of subjective associations of past experiences, interpretation of present realities and future expectations along with their meaning. While 'normal' perception matches reality, it is never 100 per cent congruent with the objective fact. An example is the relative unreliability of some eyewitness accounts. Memory and dreams are contaminated by personal cognitive and affective percepts. These dynamics often elude both structured inter-view and a battery of standardized psychological tests. They are more readily understood through extensive symbolic analysis.

3. **Theory of Inner Cry**

Clinicians worldwide have heard the cry for help in a variety of ways. These range from abused children who escape stress through dissociative disorders to victims of a catastrophe or war, who suffer from PTSD. Other manifestations include ongoing frustrations in life situations and in affective disorders or abnormal behaviour.

Some cry for help through their bodies, with somatoform disor-ders. All these are diagnosable by *Diagnostic and Statistical Manual of Mental Disorders* (DSM) or International Classification of Diseases (ICD) criteria through use of definition and symptom checklists. Underlying conflicts can also be manifested in subtle, more complex and less dramatic ways. Physical symptoms such as functional dis-orders, hypersensitivity of an organ system or pain all in themselves may represent a form of a cry for help. There are common examples of this somato-psychic interaction in such expressions as 'it's a real pain in the neck' (or elsewhere), 'my heart was pounding' (broken, bleeding or heavy), 'what a headache', 'he's a hothead', etc.

For physicians, therapists and researchers, the body, its organ systems and its perceived functions are 'doorways to the mind'. By observing and assessing how people perceive or misperceive body and organ function, much can be learned about their innermost thoughts and feelings. What they see in ambiguous and semi-ambiguous inkblots shows how they see themselves, the quality of their life and lifestyle, their adjustment to conflict, their coping skills and their view of the reality of life.

SIS can help therapists more sensitively to 'hear' a suffering indi-vidual's cry for help, the 'inner cry' that is not only hidden from others, but is often hidden from one's own conscious awareness as well. This is the 'magic'; the unique and distinguishing feature of projective testing.

While SIS uses somatic inkblots that involve body and organ imagery, they have identified a variety of personal problems and mental disorders also. As stated above, everyday conversations are replete with examples of the mind–body connection, such as 'broken heart' for depression or grief; 'stuck in my craw', 'eating at my gut', 'pain in the neck', or 'what a headache' for anger or frustration; 'butterflies in my stomach' or 'scared shitless' for fear or panic, to name just a few.

Since projective tests are not based on verbal communication, they more effectively penetrate a person's 'outer shell' of defences and surface behaviours. Unlike personality and intelligence tests, projective tests do not require reading questions or manuals, so they more directly access mental processes. They use the language of dreams, visual imagery and symbolic thought, the most basic forms of thinking and expression. Projective tests speak the language of repression and bring whatever is buried in the mind closer to consciousness, so it is accessible for processing.

By developing a practised eye and ear for this imagery, therapists can more directly share the perceptual world of their patients with less interference, and fewer variables than in structured interviews or so-called 'paper and pencil tests'. If, as the saying goes, 'a picture is worth a thousand words', inkblots are picture recognition tests, and therefore are potentially more powerful than verbal interviews and tests. Therapists willing to more directly know and experience the patient's psychic pain will be rewarded with clearer understanding of the psychodynamics involved, and therefore be able to provide more effective therapy.

## Applications of Cassell's Theory

In the early 1980s, Cassell developed a new Rorschach content-based interview for psychotherapy growing out of clinical work involving various diagnostic categories. The theoretical background for this was especially brought into sharp focus in working with those suffering from mental disorders triggered by stressful life events, which had stimulated high neurophysiologic arousal.

Originally, because of the practical feasibility of concurrently monitoring heart rate during projective testing and the relative ease of designing anatomical inkblots symbolically resembling the heart, the initial SIS included inkblot structure symbolizing the heart (Cassell 1969). In the original studies, it was found that subjects with somatic symptoms such as 'palpitations' or 'heart discomfort' fell statistically at the extremes. They either projected more cardiac responses or avoided identifying the suggestive embedded anatomical content.

In the early years, similar studies were being conducted using as an index of cardiac awareness, a subject's ability to recognize visual stimuli during tachistoscopic presentation (Cassell and Duboczy 1967). The experimental series presented brief exposures of medical textbook illustrations depicting the heart. Analysis of the data revealed a similar statistical pattern as in the SIS project. What is anticipated in this century are studies in which an individual views a (threatening) somatic inkblot and simultaneously has brain function monitored by 21st-century technology. Until this occurs, we will not have a solid scientific basis for our theory.

## The Role of Familiarity and Sensory Feedback in Anatomy Projection

Familiarity with anatomy is a strong determinant regarding the recognition and subsequent projection of anatomical responses. In SIS studies, it is important for the investigator to eliminate this factor as much as possible. Anatomically sophisticated people, such as those in the health professions, need to be assessed separately in data analysis. However, if an individual who is highly familiar with anatomy fails to recognize such content in a highly structured SIS inkblot, it may be inferred that some mental defence system is actively blocking the process.

Another example in connection with the 'familiarity' factor relates to the individual's current physical state apart from stress-linked somatic symptoms. If the individual is in a state of neurophysiological arousal, either from physical activity or from psychological stress, then sensory feedback mechanisms become operational.

Two studies concerning this are worth mentioning. The first, involving arousal induced by exercise included the assessment of the immediate feedback of cardiovascular sensations. In this project, healthy college students were assigned randomly to one of two matching groups. One was tested with SIS, while sitting on a bicycle without pedalling. The other exercised to the cardiovascular arousal stage of advanced heart rate. It was found that significantly more heart responses were projected by the exercising group.

The second study involved psychophysiologic arousal experienced by patients suffering from schizophrenic disorder during admission to a psychiatric hospital. It was found that those with higher heart rates not only projected more heart responses but in drawing internal organs, they tended to represent the cardiac region as larger. Thus, not only were they more focused on the heart, the increased sensory feedback made it feel larger.

In clinical populations, two additional influences can alter the regional somatic awareness. In those suffering from a severe mental disorder, like the schizophrenic group mentioned above, there may be psychotropic drug induced side effects. For example, some antipsychotic medications can produce extra pyramidal muscle symptoms, thereby altering the focusing of attention within the body gestalt. Similar regional distortions in awareness may be present in patients with medical illness. For example, increased cardiovascular feedback from congestive heart failure and untreated hyperthyroidism individuals with tachycardia can project more anatomical symbolic heart responses in viewing the inkblot stimuli.

When the implications of these overall influences were considered conceptually, an initial step was taken to formulate a theoretical model. It was postulated that an individual's subjective mental representation of the heart had two fundamental psychological dimensions: one involving cognitive characteristics, such as physical shape, size and the individual's hypochondriacal health perspective, and the other, the subjective affect linkage of such somatic imagery. It was also postulated that such affect was partly controlled by psychological defences influencing opposing mental forces of 'sensitization repression' and consequently the extent that the organ image impinged upon projective awareness. In terms of evolution, the most primitive underlying principle affecting regional body awareness concerned sensory feedback mechanisms. Relative to these genetically determined biological factors, the greater the feedback of introceptive sensations from an organ system, the more attention would be drawn to that region's symbolic mental representation within the body gestalt. Finally, regarding extending this conceptual model, it was expected that similar mechanisms might apply to perception of the total exterior 'body image' or 'human' inkblot responses.

## Sex Differences in Inkblot Psychophysiology

The degree that somatic imagery impinges upon projective awareness is influenced by the relative extent to which the degree of physiologic activity in the organ system produces peripheral nervous system sensory feedback. Input from this is then subjectively perceived in the aroused sensory cortical centres as 'sensations'. Related to this 'fight or flight' reactions, a psychopharmacological study using a stimulating dose of caffeine found that in males, but not in females, arousal is associated with a shift in body awareness to the right side (Cassell and Hemingway 1970). This unpredicted finding also needed to be incorporated into the evolving theory. For example, it was expected that this sex-based mechanism would also operate during projective responding to inkblot stimuli. In viewing anxiety affect linked blots, physiologically aroused males likely have as a result a similarly based shift to right focusing.

The subsequent literature in this field is relevant. Rhawn Joseph, in a series of scientific articles in the 1980s, theorized about the existence of sex differences in human brain function. Consistent with this line of thought, in 2006, Larry Cahill and Lisa Kilpatrick at the University of California in Irvine using positron emission tomography (PET) scans found that the amygdala behaves very differently in males and females. In men, the right amygdala is more active and show more connections with other regions of the brain, even when there is no outside stimulation. Conversely, in women, the left amygdala is more connected with different regions of the brain. In addition, the regions of the brain with which the amygdala communicates, while a subject is at rest, are different in men and women. Thus, not only was there a difference as to which hemisphere's amygdala was more active, but also that the regions that the amygdala 'talked' with were quite different.

There are certain general implications to these findings, some of which may be incorporated into a conceptual model of SIS inkblot perception. Many brain regions communicating with the amygdala in men are engaged with and respond to the external environment. For example, the visual cortex is responsible for visualization of the outer world, including inkblot stimuli, while the striatum coordinates motor actions. Conversely, many regions connected to the left hemisphere in women (e.g., the insular cortex and the hypothalamus) receive strong input from the sensors from the body interior and control psychophysiologic internal processes, only alterable consciously by yoga experts.

## SIS Imagery and Dreams

During psychophysiological arousal, this feedback process can give rise to real and symbolic somatic imagery during dreaming. A dreamer with a full bladder sending sensations to the brain will often experience scenes related to the need to urinate. Similarly, tensions in the reproductive structures can stimulate sexual imagery and related physical responses. If these feedback mechanisms were activated under laboratory-controlled experimental conditions in associations with projective testing, it might be expected that similar somatic responses would be projected.

Against this conceptual background, apart from cognitive 'familiarity', affect linkage influences the intensity that heart percepts compete for registration in body gestalt awareness. Affect-linked processes can then either heighten awareness or, through neural inhibition, block organ-specific imagery from registering in full consciousness. Evidence of this emotion-based phenomenon is observed clinically in the mental disorders by 'thought blocking', 'amnesic episodes', 'conversion reactions', etc. There are two clinical approaches that examine this theoretical consideration. One involved the creation of a reduced state of viewing arousal, by inducing hypnotic relaxation; the other involved the use of sedating medication (intravenous barbiturates). These approaches led to the observation that reducing anxiety/threat can free up the release of previously inhibited somatic imagery. Such clinical insights played an important role when SIS-II Video version was designed.

## PTSD Imagery Fluctuates Rapidly

Subsequently, based on the puzzling SIS projective test results, a decision was made to add a temporal dimension to the evolving conceptual model. The puzzle was first found in testing psychiatric patients who were diagnosed as suffering from one or other form of stress-triggered disorders. Those, whose medical histories included focal conversion somatic symptoms, would at the early viewing stage project a regionally specific anatomical response. Yet, moments later, when they are responding to the remaining SIS images, they show avoidance or 'Projective Repression' of structure, suggestive of the same region (Cassell 1972).

Thus, it was then recognized that the 'time dimension' of regional specific somatic imagery under stress may be highly fluid in consciousness. Psychological defence mechanisms can cause stress-linked pathologic images to fluctuate rather rapidly in the intensity with which they are forced in and out of projective awareness.

One practical application of this conceptual model focuses on the cognitive content of projected images as well as their relative affective charge. The second incorporates the responder's own subjective rating of the responses affect arising from the brain's more primitive neural circuitry. This additional information is obtained by asking the responder to select three 'most liked' images and then three 'least liked' ones.

In theory, the former is considered to reflect positive emotional linkage of imagery. As indicated earlier, in the detailed enquiry, the subject matter of these responses is initially introduced to reduce test anxiety. As will be illustrated in subsequent case histories in this book, the later are more likely to relate to unresolved stressful memories.

Sometimes this symbolically hidden material is outside the subject's immediate recollection but when it is noted in the detailed enquiry by the examiner, it can assist the psychotherapist in treatment planning.

Another application, which was previously mentioned for psychologically more stable individuals, is to permit them to view the SIS-II electronic version at home, prior to bedtime. It has been found that the evening residual from this viewing procedure can stimulate dreams, which reflect previously hidden issues that need psychotherapeutic resolution. When this variation technique is used, it is essential for the therapist to interview the first thing in the following morning when the imagery and affect of SIS-stimulated dream are clear in memory.

## Genetic Determinants of SIS Projection

A 21st-century scientist, conceptualizing the neuropsychological mechanisms underlying projection, has more sophisticated scientific studies available than in the past. This information is available to those building on SIS body–mind–spirit concepts envisioned in the preceding century involving visual and auditory sensory input. Now, more advanced systems based on evolving projective theory can incorporate additional sources of ambiguous multidimensional sensory input (Cassell 2010b).

Smell has a potency as a trigger for the release of deep-seated memories, including olfactory stimuli, and warrants consideration. Such inclusion should prove promising, especially in certain disorders triggered by stressful life events. In futuristic thinking, look forward to scientific breakthroughs by innovative developers of projective procedures. It is predicted that many will concurrently monitor and/or stimulate various physiological and psychological dimensions (Cassell 2010b).

Advanced research centres using sophisticated computer-controlled electronic technology has methodologically moved beyond clarifying diagnostic considerations and focus more on therapeutic applications. As an illustration, the US investigators are now actively exploring the use of 'vestigial reality' inducing technology in combat-induced PTSD. Of course, such work is not without its hazards. (It may be recalled that in 2009, a psychiatrist in the US military that was occupationally exposed to secondary or empathetic PTSD ended up homicidal. Of course, because he was a Muslim, many asserted that his true motivation for homicide really was terrorism.)

Overall, there has been an explosion in both the professional literature and the public media related to PTSD. One promising area of scientific research involves pharmacologic attempts to reduce symptoms triggered by severely stressful events. For example, morphine has been found to have this effect in civilian victims of road accidents, children suffering from major burns and injured US combat soldiers. The Somatic images have such therapeutic healing effects in blocking the consolidation of PTSD memories (Cassell 2010b).

There are similar unknowns with SIS research. While there is considerable clinical evidence based upon individual case histories describing the therapeutic value of the technique, there have been no controlled studies attempted. Caution is indicated. Evidence is emerging that for some PTSD victims triggering stressful memories can aggravate their symptoms.

The current literature is controversial due to the inherent complexity of mental disorders. Yet, many of our original published clinical cases showed dramatic improvement after emotionally painful imagery was triggered by a traumatic scene reactivating SIS 'inkblot'. Such a stimulus clearly can have the pulling power to bring back to the victim's mind confused cognitions/emotions. In a detailed enquiry, cognitively reprocessing these in a secure empathetic therapeutic environment, away from the original stressful situation, seemed to be helpful (Cassell 2010b).

Also, the repetition of the key triggering stimulus that effectively brought into projective awareness traumatic imagery, followed by relaxing nature scenes, may have added a behavioural therapy like effect. This aspect of SIS viewing may activate the high frequency waves associated with attention and introspection during meditation. Such repetitive reconditioning of the brain's memory neurons mimics nature's homeostatic healing process. Since this may occur during REM sleep in less intelligent animals, it may not require much in the way of conscious cognitions (Cassell 2010b). However, with humans, SIS therapy, in addition to neural conditioning, can be worthwhile for the victim to learn to interpret symbolic imagery linked to PTSD dreams. Over time, these change from photograph-like traumatic scene reproductions to less stressful disguised dream symbols. With successful SIS therapy, ultimately these become affect neutral, and the individual's sleep is no longer disturbed (Cassell 2010b).

Also, when the victim observes or senses that the therapist concurrently suffers secondary empathetic emotional discomfort during repeated sessions, the intimacy and bonding is enhanced. Severe pain, either from physical or psychological injury, is invariably associated with an observable degree of age regression. Clinical manifestations of this phenomenon may emerge in such a way as immature voice or profuse crying out to an imagined parental figure (Cassell 2010b).

When the therapist empathetically plays this role, no longer does the individual have to feel childlike and alone in suffering subjective torment. Facilitating this dysphoric affect transfer (i.e., 'dumping on the therapist') can play a supportive role. Over time, it can also enable the sufferer to conceptualize the misperceived original stressful circumstances more maturely in a reality-based fashion. If the original stressors involved abuse by a perpetrator, witnessing the therapist experience a degree of anger towards that individual can enable the victim to do the same. This can assist in removing self-blame and irrational guilt. In addition, it can augment insight when the victim realizes that the human imagery projected onto SIS figures depicting past abusive figures may also erroneously distort the current social perceptions—including false transference impressions of the psychotherapist.

Next, for illustration purposes, consideration will be given to instances of protracted severe childhood stress. In vulnerable children this can theoretically result in ego splitting, such as observed in dissociative disorders. Consider an identity disorder condition, which was formerly called 'multiple personality disorder'. Here, a part of the victim's identity may have been linked with the aggressor, so the empathetic transfer therapeutic process outlined above may be especially critical. Otherwise, the victim may be prone to acting out patterns mimicking the original abuser (Cassell 2010b).

The history of knowledge is rapidly expanding regarding stress-related disorders. There is more recognition, in this age, being given to the fact that managing cases of PTSD expose mental health workers to occupationally induced secondary empathic dramatization. SIS therapists face a relatively greater risk because of this projective technique's great pulling power to evoke emotionally charged horrible scenes. In jointly viewing a triggering SIS stimulus pattern, the professional's visual apparatus and its related emotional/cognitive brain centres involving higher function are activated, albeit at a lower intensity but still in an analogous way to the victim's nervous system (Cassell 2010b).

Similarly, professionals working in other fields concerned with human suffering are also at risk. For medical providers, emergency room physicians have a much higher 'burnout' rate and shorter life span than those in other medical specialties. In a like fashion, those who provide emergency care in war-torn countries expose their own dream REM states to secondary empathetic PTSD imagery. Normally, such professionals tend to minimize this risk in verbal reports, so it is hard to obtain objective data (Cassell 2010b).

An exception exists in a book published in 2009 by James Orbinski titled *An Incomplete Offering*. In the book, he documented the reality of his traumatic experiences in Rwanda. These included treating physically/psychologically brutalized adults and children during the period of genocide. (A traumatic memory shared with him by a girl included recollection of hiding in a latrine filled with human waste and then peering out and witnessing her mother's torture and bleeding to death after amputation. Throughout the period, perpetrators cut off children's body parts and sent them to care providers as a warning.) His documentary provides examples of his sleep disturbing dreams related to these experiences and 'flashbacks' suffered years later (Cassell 2010b).

In considering the importance of empathy during SIS clinical work, this phenomenon has been studied by investigators in several scientific disciplines. Relative to this discussion, the ability to empathize is impaired in psychiatric/neurological conditions. On the positive side, some individuals can be taught empathetic skills, and this may prove to be one helpful function of psychotherapy. Experiencing the therapist's empathetic suffering may allow the intact portion of such a 'split personality' to identify with the professional's corrective empathetic affect towards the disturbing SIS-released PTSD imagery. In this way, the individual with a fractured sense of self during therapy may learn to identify less with a powerful past perpetrator. Concurrently, the healthy portion of the ego may become more empathetically compassionate to its own long forgotten 'inner cry'.

Clearly, future attention needs to be given to the investigation of such intimate psychophysiologic phenomenology of two-person interaction during SIS detailed enquiry. For example, an investigator might use a standard illustrative recorded SIS PTSD interview, involving a traumatic accident scene as a test stimulus and then monitor the empathetic reactions of various subjects.

Against this background, it might be helpful to add to existing SIS projective theory by incorporating in the conceptual model genetic factors. Some vulnerable individuals may be genetically predisposed, under stressful conditions, to develop PTSD. Some may believe that contemplating such research requires a great leap in conceptualization.

Still, it may provide guidelines to keep in mind the various published related studies. It may be recalled that many of these illustrate how SIS response patterns that have anatomical/human content relate to socialization and empathy.

In the basic sciences, studies relative to an organism's interest in social interaction indicate that an organism's DNA content can shape this basic process. For example, flat worms that possess a predominance of a gene have been observed to isolate themselves. In contrast, those at the opposite genetic pole have been found to seek out groups. In primates, neuroscientists have also studied basic biological mechanisms, shaping socialization and empathy. Work completed on the so-called 'mirror neurons' in the brains of monkeys is an example. As more is learned about the genetic determinants in humans, researchers may eventually determine the extent to which comparable genetic influences might shape avoidance or seek out the human content in SIS.

Of theoretical relevance are clinical studies involving the autism spectrum. If one of the identical twins suffers from autism, the likelihood is approximately 90 per cent that his or her twin would also be autistic. Children with this disorder (like the flat worms loaded with social isolation gene) also prefer being alone. Consistent with this, eye movement studies indicate that when viewing a picture of the face, they characteristically avoid looking at the person's eyes. It would be helpful to ascertain if this same autistic avoidance would show up with SIS facial stimuli.

Many modern geneticists think that in the overall population various degrees of the genetic defect exist on a spectrum. Projective studies could be designed, using advanced technologically supported multidimensional input, to statistically sort out the degree to which empathy relates to social learning versus genetics.

SIS scores assessing projected human imagery might provide useful aids in pursuing future scientific knowledge concerning this positive aspect of human identity (Cassell 2010b).

## Applying This Model to the Rorschach and Holtzman Procedures

This theory enabled Dr Wilfred A. Cassell to rethink test administration in the early 1980s for both Rorschach and Holtzman tests. The testing interview room is specifically staged. The administrator has a table on which all the cards are placed face up. When the subject enters the consultation room, these are initially viewed as a total gestalt.

Then the subject is asked to rate his/her responses, first for the 'three most liked plates'. Next, the interviewer asks questions to determine the reasons for the choice as well as what emotions are aroused by the viewing process. After completing each, the card is then placed face down on the table. Upon completion of this test anxiety-reducing phase, the process is then repeated with the 'three most disliked ones'. Finally, the examiner completes the test using the standard numerical order of the remaining inkblots while constantly monitoring the verbal and non-verbal affect linkage of all the rest.

Afterwards, all cards are placed face up for a review as a gestalt and the examiner asks: 'Does any of these remind you of your dreams?' This is an important question since SIS has been found in many stress-triggered clinical situations to tap into the same memory stream as affect-charged 'nightmares'. Moreover, in retest situations, if progress is made in treatment, there is a parallel improvement in the patient's direct and symbolic content of the projected inkblot responses.

Sometimes, examiners may choose to first administer the Rorschach and Holtzman tests in a standardized traditional fashion, before using the above inkblot structured psychotherapeutic interview process.

## Influence of Culture on Inkblot Perception

Dana (2000) compared Exner's normative data of North Americans with European and South American subjects and found marked differences on some important variables. For example, texture response is typically zero in European subjects (a European would express it only when it reaches the level of a *craving* for closeness) and there are fewer 'good form' responses in comparison to the North American norms. Form is most often the only determinant perceived by European subjects, while colour is less frequent than in American subjects. The European subjects see more of colour–form responses than form–colour responses in comparison to North American subjects.

The differences in form quality are attributable to purely cultural aspects: different cultures will exhibit different 'common' objects (e.g., French subjects often see a chameleon on Card VIII, which is normally considered as an 'unusual' response, as opposed to cats and dogs by Scandinavians). Christmas elves on Card II and musical instrument on Card VI is a popular response for Japanese subjects (Weiner 2003).

Form quality, popular content responses and locations are the only coded variables in the Exner system that are based on frequency of occurrence and thus immediately subject to cultural influences; therefore, culture-dependent interpretation of test data may not necessarily need to extend beyond these components (Weiner 2003). Similarly, total numbers of responses are comparatively low among Indian subjects than among North Americans. Army personnel give significantly low number of responses in comparison of other Indian norms (Dubey 1982).

Similarly, we have noticed different responses on somatic inkblot images by North American subjects and Indian subjects. A dancing lady and an apple are popular responses for Image A7 in North Americans, whereas two snakes along with a dancing lady and an apple are commonly perceived by subjects in India. Alaskan subjects rarely project a snake response in Alaska. About the projection of sexual responses for A25, A27 and B18, North American subjects gave a higher number of responses than those living in India. It might be inferred that Indian subjects gave less responses because of cultural impact and religious practices. Eve with an apple is the common response for Image A7 in North Americans. Similarly, it is often similarly perceived by Indians educated in Christian/English schools in contrast with other Indian subjects. Similar findings have also been reported in various case studies published in several issues of *SIS Journal of Projective Psychology and Mental Health*.

Weiner (2003) has also advised to administer projective testing, when possible, in the subject's native language. Test responses should also not be translated into another language prior to analysis, except possibly by a clinician fluent in both languages. It is hoped that an anthropologist will follow up on these observations.

# 5

# Studies on Rorschach, Holtzman and Somatic Inkblot Tests

## Inkblot Test in India

### The Rorschach Inkblot Test

The Rorschach test is the oldest and a popular projective test which still is widely used in clinical settings (Dubey 1981a, 1982). Diagnostic testing based upon this instrument remains the most requested function of clinical psychologists (Arora 1982; Dubey et al. 1981a, 1982; Verma 1980; Verma and Misra 2002).

Initially, during the 1950s and 1960s, research papers related to the Rorschach test were published mainly in the *Indian Journal of Psychology* and *Indian Journal of Psychiatry*. At present, there are three journals published from India—*Indian Journal of Clinical Psychology* (since 1974), *Journal of Personality and Clinical Studies* (since 1985) and *SIS Journal of Projective Psychology and Mental Health* (since 1994)—which publish articles related to the Rorschach test and projective psychology. In these three journals, the number of articles published using the Rorschach test as a research tool showed a decreasing trend in the last decade of publication. After the introduction of SIS (Cassell 1980b, 1984b, 1990; Cassell and Dubey 2003; Dubey 2003) and the publication of the *SIS Journal of Projective Psychology and Mental Health* from 1994, publication of research related to projective psychology has increased significantly in India. Although still widely used, like internationally, in India the Rorschach test appears to be diminishing based on the percentage of published articles on the Rorschach test over the last 10 years.

Though publication in these three journals can be considered as a pointer to the trend in research with the Rorschach test, there are several research studies that are conducted in different centres of training that go unpublished. This could be due to the paucity of the appropriate journals, accessibility of the journals and/or the lack of enthusiasm on the part of the concerned research students to complete the process of publication. Moreover, in India there is no funding agency that promotes research exclusively in the areas of clinical psychology or psychology, and lack of financial funding has thwarted the zeal in researchers for getting their work published (Manickam 2003).

The earliest published work on the Rorschach test in India can be traced back to 1947 by Prasad and Asthana. The study by Prasad and Asthana (1947) was an experimental one from a 'general psychology perspective' wherein they investigated the meaning of indices on the Rorschach test. However, H. S. Asthana continued his research with the Rorschach test and published papers in scientific journals and presented papers both in India and abroad in the 1950s, 1960s and 1970s (Asthana 1950a, 1950b, 1956, 1963, 1965, 1966, 1971; Asthana and Mohan 1977). Asthana's work spanned about three decades and he administered the test to diverse groups, developed norms for the Indian population (Asthana 1950a, 1950b, 1971) and described the personality of social organization of Indians using the tool (Asthana 1956). His work on the perceptual development of children (Asthana 1965, 1966) led to the publication of a report that investigated the scope of the Rorschach test as a research tool to study the perceptual framework of children (Asthana and Mohan 1977). Another early research that went unnoticed by earlier reviewers is the work of Ray (1955) who used the test with tribal population. Along with Dosajh (1956) and Jain (1956), Bagh (1955) had also used the test with adolescent school children, almost a half century ago. Dubey (1972, 1975b, 1976, 1977a, 1977b) used the Rorschach test to study hearing problems, tuberculosis patients and management students. Other earlier publications include Gupta (1959), Julka 1963, Raychaudhari and Maitra (1965a). All these studies were conducted on diverse student population.

Asthana (1963) was probably the first Indian researcher to use the Rorschach test for research in clinical settings and brought out its clinical utility in assessing different aspects of personality (Bhargava and Saxena 1995). Since then, clinicians in hospitals and clinical settings had been using the test. With the introduction of the Diploma in Medical Psychology (DMP; later titled as DM & SP and MM & SP; currently MPhil in Clinical Psychology) at the All India Institute of Mental Health (presently National Institute of Mental Health and Neuro Sciences, NIMHANS), Bangalore, India, in 1955, and later at the RINPAS, Kanke, Ranchi, the Rorschach test was introduced to the students of clinical psychology. And now the test forms part of the curriculum of the clinical psychology trainees at the six major training centres in India. Moreover, the master level students who select a course in clinical psychology are also given training in administration and interpretation of the test.

In the history of the use of the test in India, at different periods of time, one or two researchers persisted with their interest and piloted administering the test as a research tool. While H. S. Asthana, starting from 1947, led the scene in the 1950s, 1960s and 1970s, Raychaudhari and Kumar carried the baton in the 1960s and early 1970s. It was taken over by B. L. Dubey in the 1970s and continued for four decades (Dubey 1972, 1975a, 1976, 1977b, 1978; Dubey et al. 2018; Dubey and Sharma 1973). D. Pershad contributed in keeping the test active in research for more than two decades (Pershad and Dubey 1977; Pershad et al. 1979; Pershad and Pareekh 2001). However, in the late 1990s and in the beginning of the 21st century, research interest in the Rorschach test appears to have decreased though a number of clinicians continue to use the tool for the purpose of assessment and psychotherapy (Dubey et al. 2018). Shukla (1977) reviewed the test from a wider perspective of the projective techniques (PTs) in India and Dubey (1977a, 1978, 1981a, 1982) appraised the status of the test in the 1980s in an earlier review. Manickam and Suhani (2003; Manickam and Dubey 2005) and Manickam, Suhani and Jasseer (2004) are doing excellent work and have reviewed in detail the work on Rorschach in India. Sanyal, Dasgupta and Chatterjee (2005) have reviewed theoretical evidence in the Indian scenario and pinpointed to a peculiar and alarming trend of Rorschach avoidance.

Manickam and Dubey (2005) have found that the Rorschach test has been in use in India since 1947 on diverse population and the volume of research speaks its popularity. However, there was no major and in-depth study undertaken on its adaptation or improvising the scoring pattern or comparison of different scoring methods. With the introduction of SIS, there is increased research on SIS as compared to the Rorschach test. Though the studies suggested the usefulness of the test in aiding diagnosis, understanding psychopathology and helping in therapy, the declining research interest on the Rorschach test impels to revitalize the training and research of the test in India.

Piotrowski (2015) has emphasized that academic training with projective methods has been an enduring and enigmatic feature of the assessment curriculum in professional and clinical psychology since the 1940s. However, the past two decades have witnessed a steady stream of rather disparaging commentary directed largely at the lack of psychometric credibility of individual projective methods, particularly from the academic community in the USA.

Piotrowski (2017) presented the results of an exploratory biblio-metric 'topical' analysis about mainly primary research regarding the Rorschach test published as journal articles during 2000–2016. The database PsycINFO was selected to obtain the pool of references. The most prevalent researched topics were (in rank order): norms, psychotic states, eating disorders, historical aspects, psychosomatic factors, treatment planning/outcome, aggression/hostility, personality, psychodynamic issues, depression and personality disorders. The neglected areas of research included assessment training, differential diagnosis, anxiety states, racial/ethnic differences and social desirability. The focus on norms/normative comparisons was quite apparent. The potential impact of editorial preference/bias was also discussed and the limitations of the study were noted in the paper. Based on this analysis, it appears that recent Rorschach scholarship is (a) not cohesive in character and (b) reflects diverse research domains representing disparate research interests. Hence, despite an extensive repository of literature, the Rorschach test remains an emerging area of study with an opaque sense of direction for future research.

Piotrowski (2017a) indicated that projective methods/techniques have been popular clinical tests and have relied upon assessment tools in the field of mental health in the USA. However, the same cannot be said for clinical/professional academic programmes where the professional views of training faculty towards PT have been somewhat contentious, particularly during the past decade. The intention here is to summarize recent survey-based findings on the use of PT, which should provide a candid perspective on what the status of PT may be in the next 10 years. There is very recent evidence that projective assessment is currently a rather neglected evaluation approach by professional psychologists, except for the Rorschach test; however, these data were based on a very low response rate (i.e., 17%; see Wright et al. 2017). At the same time, survey data from South America point to the central role of PT in the assessment process in countries such as Brazil and Bolivia (Piotrowski 2017a). The same can be said for Japan but not Australia. Interestingly, despite a strong psychoanalytic bent, historically, PT are rather ignored in most European countries. Thus, the emerging picture is that PT have pockets of enthusiastic proponents worldwide, with the caveat that support for PT appears to be gradually diminishing, particularly with the recent surge in the interest in evidence-based assessment climate that has permeated the general field of psychological assessment (Bornstein 2017). Another key factor in the diminutive status of some PT has been the proliferation of abbreviated personality tests and brief symptom-focused scales, evident in the contemporary scholarly literature on assessment. Despite these strong headwinds, it is also quite apparent that the death knell for PT has been rather premature, largely reflected in the continued research attention directed towards PT by a small minority of devoted followers and proponents who claim that performance-based testing imparts both clinical and ecological value to the assessment process. Thus, the present status of PT has fallen from the apex of popularity of the mid-1900s, but strong remnants of that former heyday remain.

Martin and Frackowiak (2017) conducted a survey to find out the value of projective/performance based techniques in therapeutic assessment and found that the psychological assessment and projective/performance-based assessment in particular, has seen a decline in recent years, both in training and clinical use. This trend is alarming and raises concerns about the loss of important clinical tools and its effect on the field of psychological assessment. In this survey, they discuss two ways in which this shift affects the practice of psychological assessment: (a) loss of clinically important information accessed only with projective/performance-based methods and (b) loss of an opportunity to connect with clients and help them see aspects of their lives through therapeutic and collaborative use of projective/performance-based measures, as practised in therapeutic assessment.

Schulmeyer and Piotrowski (2017) reported a structured survey, conducted on 44 psychologists working in the mental health system in Bolivia, regarding tests used in the areas of projective and objective (self-report) personality and behavioural assessment. The top instruments were drawing techniques, TAT, Rorschach, Minnesota Multiphasic Personality Inventory (MMPI) and Beck Inventories. In addition, there was a strong emphasis on assessment using DSM diagnostic criteria.

Moreover, our sample felt that these instruments would continue to be popular in the future. These findings corroborate scholarly reports on the continued reliance on both projective and self-report assessment practices worldwide (Piotrowski 2015). Future studies, across nations in South America, should focus on graduate-level educational and training emphasis in mental health assessment to gain a perspective on emerging trends, internationally, in psychological testing.

Piotrowski (2018) opined that PTs have left an impressive, yet contentious, footprint worldwide (Groth-Marnat 2009; Handler and Thomas 2014; Musewicz et al. 2009; Piotrowski 2015; Piotrowski, Keller and Ogawa 1993; Teglasi 2010; Wood et al. 2011). Interestingly, survey data from recent 'test use' studies point to a rather bleak view regarding the status of PTs. Ready and Veague (2014) reported that no projective tests ranked among the top 10 tests being taught in clinical psychology programmes. Wright et al. (2017), in a national sample of professional psychologists, found that the Rorschach test was the only projective method used frequently (ranked in top 13 tests) among a myriad of psychological assessment domains. But do these reports provide an accurate portrait regarding the extent of clinical emphasis devoted to PTs in both training and practice? Undoubtedly, there is a perennial need to empirically address the clinical breadth and status of specific projective methods and their place in contemporary assessment practices. Dubey et al. (2018) emphasized the popularity of SIS test in India and indicated that it has emerged as an extension of the Rorschach Inkblot Test. This unique assessment method relies heavily on content analysis to understand the inner cry of a person and penetrates the deeper layers of the unconscious to elicit underlying conflicts and intra-psychic processes which contribute to emotional and interpersonal issues in one's life.

Piotrowski (2018a) indicated that the status of the Rorschach test and its role in neurophysiological assessment have had a rather erratic and not-so-cherished historical journey. Seminal research in this area largely focused on the Rorschach 'sign' approach in the study of organic brain disorders, while later research investigated mediating factors such as IQ and affective states. At times, research efforts in this area lay dormant or encountered tepid scholarly reviews. Interestingly, there has been a flurry of enthusiasm and research activity recently on the potential of Rorschach analysis in the study of neurocognitive dysfunction. The current investigation provides a historical review of key research findings in this area, based on 58 studies identified via a bibliometric analysis of the extant mental health literature. The presentation traces the key milestones and findings reported in the scholarly research over the past 80 years. The author offers tentative conclusions, based on this provocative body of literature.

Piotrowski (2018b) contends that the fate of PTs will be linked to the precarious status of personality assessment in clinical training settings. Moreover, since 1990, PTs, as a class, have been the target of extensive criticism in the scholarly literature (e.g., Lilienfeld et al. 2000). Thus, the intent of the current study is to determine whether recent shifts in testing practices and research attention in the field of assessment have had a deleterious impact on the popularity of SCTs in graduate training programmes and professional usage worldwide. To that end, the author identified, through an extensive literature review, published survey research about SCTs that reported on assessment training and test usage patterns from 1989 to 2015. The 70 identified survey-based or records-based studies served as the data pool in the current review (training = 16; practice = 54). This analysis indicated that from a historical perspective, sentence completion methods have been popular assessment tools, evident in that 35 of the 70 studies (50%) reported that SCTs have been relied upon to at least a 'moderate' degree. However, reliance on SCTs has been more prominent in academic assessment training (69% of the studies) than in practice settings (44% of the studies). Quite apparent in this review was the obvious diminution of SCT usage since 2003 in both professional clinical academic programmes and in applied settings. One noteworthy exception is that several very recent (since 2014) surveys of internship settings confirm continued emphasis on SCTs. Regardless, supplemental data point to the reality that coursework and training emphasis with SCTs have been rather cursory and unstructured. In addition, these vast survey-based findings suggest that SCTs are embraced more by child clinicians and school psychologists than in mental health assessment of adults. However, based on the evidence in this exhaustive review, it appears that current usage of SCTs is waning. Thus, the future status of SCTs in the assessment enterprise appears rather limited, but certainly not moribund.

Stedman, Essery and McGeary (2018) have provided an overview and discussion of past and present trends in training related to projective personality assessment. The authors summarize the historical use of projective testing (particularly the Rorschach test) and emerging research examining the use of projective tests in both graduate and internship training programmes. The current state of the research suggests a decrease in emphasis on training with PTs across both graduate and internship training programmes.

## Holtzman Inkblot Test

The HIT was developed to partially overcome psychometric limitations of the Rorschach test by constructing completely new sets of inkblots. During the 10-year period following the Second World War, major interest in the Rorschach test was expressed by graduate students, many of whom had learned a little about the Rorschach test while serving in the armed services. Hundreds of studies during this period piled up a wave of criticism from which the Rorschach movement never fully recovered. While much of this early research was either irrelevant or poorly conceived, an impressive number of well-designed validity studies generally yielded negative results. The growing realization that the Rorschach test had inherent psychometric weakness came to a head in a symposium on failures of the Rorschach test that was sponsored by the Society for Projective Techniques (Zubin 1954).

### Studies on the Holtzman Technique in India

Darolia and Joshi (2004) tried to find empirical evidence for the effectiveness of Herron's short (30 inkblots) form of HIT. The data demonstrated high internal consistency and temporal stability of most of the HIT variables. The internal consistency and temporal stability coefficient for most of the HIT indices were found to be larger than 0.60 and 0.70, respectively. Factor analysis of the 22 HIT variables yielded eight significant factors (eigen values > 1). The observed factor structure replicated five of the Holtzman's second-order factors with some minor variations. Overall, the findings suggest that the short form of HIT has psychometric invariance with the standard 45-inkblot form of HIT as far as the factor structure of the two forms is concerned. However, since the 45-inkblot form of HIT has not been used in the present study, further empirical evidence is needed to demonstrate the psychometric compatibility of these two forms of HIT.

Singh (2006b) examined the relationship between two contexts of creativity, that is, novelty and meaning. Psychometric measures of creativity are considered to index novelty context, whereas projective tests, particularly inkblot tests, are considered to tap the meaning context. To realize the main objective of the study, 202 high school male students were randomly drawn from various schools in the Kurukshetra district, Haryana. The selected subjects were administered with HIT and Torrance Tests of Creative Thinking (both verbal and figural). The data obtained were analysed by applying Pearson's method of product moment correlation and inter-battery factor analysis. Both correlational analyses clearly revealed a strong positive overlap between verbal and figural measures of creativity assumed to be indexing novelty context. Analyses have demonstrated weak association between psychometric and projective indices of creativity. Projective tests like HIT are taken as indexing meaning context of creativity.

Singh (2006a) further studied the relationship of novelty and meaning contexts of creativity with Jensen's level I and level II. Psychometric measures of creativity like Torrance Tests of Creative Thinking are considered to measure novelty context of creativity, whereas projective indices, particularly inkblot techniques, are taken to index the meaning context of creativity. Likewise, measures of learning/memory, namely Forward Digit Span, Backward Digit Span and Serial Rote Learning are the indices of level I ability. Raven's Progressive Matrices and Verbal Measures of general mental ability like Hundal's General Mental Ability Test are considered to tap Jensen's level II ability. To obtain the main objective of the study, 202 high school male students were randomly drawn from Kurukshetra District of Haryana. The selected subjects were administered HIT, Torrance Tests of Creative Thinking (both verbal and figural), Forward Digit Span, Backward Digit Span, Serial Rote Learning, Raven's Progressive Matrices and Hundal's General Mental Ability Test. The obtained data were analysed by applying descriptive statistics, Pearson's correlations and principal component factor analysis. Analyses have clearly established the two contexts of creativity, that is, novelty and meaning, and differential relationships with Jensen's level I and level II abilities. Analysis also supports Jensen's hypothesis of factorial distinction between level I and level II abilities. Weak associations have been obtained between psychometric measures of creativity (novelty context) and the indices of level II ability. Overall, findings of the present study highlight the complexity of relationship between creativity and intelligence. Thus, clear-cut distinction has been found between the two contexts.

Kamlesh (1979), in her study on projective (HIT) and psychometric measures of creativity, found verbal originality having positive relationship with location, movement and anxiety variables of HIT; fluency with location, movement and penetration; and elaboration with penetration. The results showed that projective and non-verbal measures of creativity shared only a small portion of their variance. The projective and verbal measures of creativity were found to be independent with negligible overlap. This clearly shows that novelty and meaning contexts of creativity are conceptually different.

Sharma and Singh (1990) investigated the projective and psychometric personality correlates of attribution styles on a sample of 200 male students ranging in age from 16 to 18 years. They were administered high school personality questionnaire (HSPQ), HIT and attribution styles questionnaire. The data were analysed with Pearson's correlations and principal component factor analysis. Factor analysis yielded 14 rotated factors above 1.00 eigenvalue, accounting for 78.48 per cent of the total variance. Of these 14 factors, five mainly loaded on HIT variables, which were almost in agreement with the orthogonal factors reported by Holtzman et al. (1961b).

Lata and Singh (1990) administered HSPQ, Torrance Test of Creative Thinking (verbal) and HIT on 200 female subjects ranging in age between 14 and 16 years for the exploration of projective and psychometric personality correlates of creativity. Obtained data were analysed by applying product moment method of correlation and principal component factor analysis. In total, 14 factors were extracted greater than the eigenvalue of 1.00 accounting for 65.73 per cent of total variance. Four of the HIT factors (Holtzman et al. 1961b) were replicated. The first factor had significant loadings on hostility, anxiety, barrier, reaction time, anatomy, sex, space and integration, depicting psychopathology of thoughts and emotional disturbances like factor III of Holtzman et al. (1961b). Factor II, named as verbal creativity, had significant loadings on all the four variables of creativity (originality, fluency, flexibility and elaboration) plus some HIT variables, namely popular, penetration, human and movement depicting some overlap between verbal creativity and projective creativity. The third factor bore significant loadings on form appropriateness. The Form definiteness, space, animal and human variables were interpreted as factor of perceptual maturity, almost comparable with the findings reported by Holtzman et al. (1961b). The fourth factor mainly loaded on HIT variables, that is, animal, human, sex, anatomy and popular along with factor B of HSPQ labelled as mental capacity, depicted some structured overlap between the aforementioned HIT variables and crystallized intelligence. Another factor which brought together HIT variables of location, shade and space, depicting some structure comparable with factor IV of six orthogonal factors located by Holtzman et al. (1961b). One more factor emerged loading significantly on colour, sex and animal, depicting that the chromatic sensitivity in fantasy production did not match structurally with any of the factors reported by Holtzman et al. (1961b), maybe because of cultural differences.

Rishi and Singh (1995) investigated hostility in relation to personality and motivation. For this, a sample of 170 female college students was administered 16 personality factor (PF), HIT, MAT and hostility scale.

Obtained data were subjected to correlational analysis, particularly Pearson's correlations and principal component factor analysis. Factor analysis yielded 17 factors accounting for 76.42 per cent of the total variance. HIT variables scattered over 10 factors. Factor I loading mainly on integration balance, human, movement and popular replicated one of the six orthogonal factors, that is, perceptual maturity reported by Holtzman et al. (1961b). Factor IV mainly loaded on anxiety and hostility along with factors G and M of 16PF depicting the fantasized anxious hostility. Factor VI was defined as depicting chromatic sensitivity in terms of positive loadings of colour and shading and negative of FD, FA and animal. It almost replicated one of the six factors reported by Holtzman et al. (1961b). Factor VII being loaded on barrier, human and animal variables along with Factor F and Q of 16PF depicts the index of body boundary and ego identity. Factor XI bearing high loadings on pathognomic verbalization and sex along with mating and home parental sentiment of MAT and factor I and Q4 of 16PF depict psychopathology and sexual disturbances. It is also somewhat comparable to one of the factors III reported by Holtzman et al. (1961b). Factor XIII depicted the emotional immaturity being loaded significantly on anatomy, sex, hostility and RT along with factor M of 16PF and fear of MAT. It also resembles with one of the factors reported by Holtzman et al. (1961b). The specific finding of this study is the construct differentiation of the conscious hostility (indexed by HIT) and self-attributed hostility (indexed by the questionnaire).

Singh (1995) administered a large battery of tests consisting of GMAT, Raven's Standard Progressive Matrices, Memory for Numbers Test, HIT and Torrance Tests of Creative Thinking on 202 male school students. The study was conducted to investigate the relationship between intelligence and creativity by taking HIT variables as projective measures of creativity. Two factors of projective creativity were located which resembled with those reported by Clark et al. (1965). The first factor had higher loadings on the variables hostility, anxiety and movement. The second factor had loadings on the variables colour and locations.

Renu and Singh (1996) investigated the projective and psychometric personality correlates of altruism. For these, 100 adult married females ranging in age between 40 and 70 years were administered 16PF, HIT and altruism scale. Obtained data were analysed with the product moment method of correlation and principal component factor analysis. Factor analysis yielded 14 varimaxely rotated factors greater than eigenvalue of 1.00, accounting for 72.22 per cent of the total variance. HIT variables scattered over 10 factors depicting structured overlap with psychometric measures of personality and altruism. Six factors were mainly defined by HIT variables. Factor I of the present solution mainly loaded on abstract, pathognomic verbalization, anxiety, barrier, hostility and animal depicting distorted thinking and almost replicated one of the six orthogonal factors (factor III) reported by Holtzman et al. (1961b). Factor II of this solution, loaded significantly on balance, integration, form definiteness, animal, movement and space, was named as perceptual maturity which resembles substantially with one of the factors (I) located and reported by Holtzman et al. (1961b). This factor is indicative of organized and balanced perception, ideational activity, good imaginative capacity, differentiated ego boundaries and perceptual maturity. Factor IV of this solution has depicted popular, reaction time and colour as significant HIT correlates of altruism. Factor V has brought together four HIT variables, namely shading, colour, form definiteness and animal, and Factors E and Q2 of 16PF depicting chromatic perceptual sensitivity. It has, to some extent, replicated one of the factors (II) reported by Holtzman et al. (1961b). Factor VIII of the present solution emerged as a bipolar factor, loading negatively on location, rejection, reaction time, and positively on form definiteness and space depicting the organized perception. It, to some extent, resembles with factor IV of solution reported by Holtzman et al. (1961). Factor IX mainly defined by anatomy and penetration with factor B of 16PF depicts emotional immaturity and hypochondriac sensitivity. Factor XIII brought together hostility, movement, penetration, form appropriateness, barrier, animal and rejection, all with negative loadings depicting affective disturbance.

Kaur and Singh (1998) conducted a study on the novelty and meaning contexts of creativity in relation to fluid and crystallized intelligence. For this, a sample of 100 male school students of 9th and 10th grades was administered with Hundal General Mental Ability Test (HGMAT), Raven's Standardized Progressive Matrices, HIT and Torrance Test of Creative Thinking with pictures. HGMAT and RPM were used to index gc and gf, respectively. HIT and TTCT were used to represent meaning and novelty contexts of creativity. HIT was scored only for six variables, namely location, colour, movement, anxiety, hostility and penetration, which are considered as the indices of projective creativity (meaning context). Obtained data were factor-analysed, which yielded five factors. Factor I was labelled as crystallized intelligence, on which none of the HIT variables marked significant loading. Factor II was figural creativity (novelty context) on which HIT variables did not load significantly, depicting the construct independence between meaning and novelty contexts of creativity. Five of HIT variables appeared on factor III, that is, hostility, anxiety, movement, location and penetration, which was labelled projective creativity (meaning context). Penetration, location and colour have marked some structured association with RPM, a measure of fluid intelligence.

Kumar and Darolia (2003) examined the compatibility of full and short versions of HIT. For this, both the full and short versions of HIT were administered on 175 postgraduate students of Kurukshetra University, Kurukshetra, with age ranging from 20 to 27 years. Principal component factor analysis was applied on both the data. Eight factors were extracted in data from full scale named as hostile fantasy, perceptual maturity, creative thinking, conventional percepts, body image boundaries and unnamed. In the case of short version also, eight factors were obtained labelled as perceptual differentiation, perceptual maturity, unconscious anxiety, creative thinking, conventional percepts and unnamed. Obtained factor patterns from both full scale and short versions agreed with each other to some extent. Obtained factors in both also replicated some of the orthogonal factors reported by Holtzman et al. (1961b). Thus, full and short form of HIT did not differ much in terms of psychometric properties.

Joshi and Darolia (2004) developed norms of HIT for Indian high school students. The standard 45-card HIT was administered to 372 male students of 9th to 12th grade drawn from various schools of Haryana in the age range of 13–18.5 years. The results indicated that inter-scorer reliability coefficients ranged between 0.68 and 0.98; most of the split-half reliability coefficients ranged between 0.55 and 0.93 except the variables of anxiety, barrier, abstract, popular and pathognomic verbalization, which had relatively lower estimates. The percentile norms were developed for all 22 HIT variables. Seven orthogonal factors were extracted. Three of the rotated factors proved to be good match for Holtzman's factors I, III and V, whereas factors II and VI were replicated with little variations. Seven factors were extracted. The first factor showed high loadings on hostility, animal, anxiety, barrier and human. Higher loadings on the variables of popular, location, balance, human, form definiteness and anatomy constituted the second factor. The third factor had high loadings on rejection, reaction time, form appropriateness and form definiteness (reverse). The fourth factor comprised of variables of integration, movement and penetration along with negative loadings on reaction time, space and form definiteness. Fifth factor had high loadings on shading, space and form appropriateness with negative loading on colour. Factor VI had high loadings on pathognomic verbalization, colour, abstract and penetration. The seventh factor comprised of sex, anatomy, form appropriateness and human variables.

Darolia and Joshi (2004) conducted a study to present empirical evidence for the effectiveness of Herron's short form (30 inkblots) of HIT. The data demonstrated high internal consistency and temporal stability of most of the HIT variables. The internal consistency and temporal stability coefficient for most of the HIT indices were found to be higher than 0.60 and 0.70, respectively. Factor analysis of the 22 HIT variables yielded eight significant factors (eigenvalue > 1.00). The observed factor structure replicated five of the Holtzman's second-order factors with some variations. Overall, the findings suggest that the short form of HIT has psychometric invariance with the standard 45-inkblot form of HIT as far as the factor structures of the two forms are concerned. However, since the 45-inkblot form of HIT has not been used in the present study, further empirical evidences are needed to demonstrate the psychometric compatibility of the two forms of HIT.

Urmila (2005) examined relationship between indices of HIT and their psychometric measures. HIT along with psychometric tests tapping 21 normal and pathological traits of which eight derived from NEO-I scale, two from 16PF scales, four from CAQ scales, two from MAT scales, trait–state anxiety inventory, hostility scale, empathy scale and aggression scale were administered to a randomly drawn sample of 218 adult females. HIT anxiety correlated significantly with psychometric measures of trait anxiety, state anxiety, fantasy, depression and pathognomic deviation. HIT variable of hostility was found to be significantly correlated with psychometric measure of hostility, trait anxiety, state anxiety impulsiveness and aggression. Sex of HIT showed positive correlation with MAT subtest sex/mating. Colour correlated with trait anxiety, paranoia and impulsiveness. Three of the six Holtzman's factors were replicated. One factor yielded high loading on anxiety, hostility, abstract and penetration along with psychometric measure of trait and state anxiety. The second factor had high loadings on location, colour, integration and reaction time along with psychometric measure of empathy and hostility. The third factor had loadings on movement, anatomy, integration and penetration. Another factor had significant loadings on form definiteness, animal, balance and form appropriateness. One more factor having loadings on human, popular, animal (reverse) and form appropriateness also emerged.

Kanupriya and Singh (2005) studied projective and psychometric personality correlates of emotional intelligence on 106 female students with age ranging from 16 to 18 years. The selected students were administered with 16PF, HIT and multidimensional emotional intelligence scale. Obtained data were analysed with Pearson's correlations and principal component factor analysis. Factor analysis with built-in-eigenvalues criterion yielded 16 factors accounting for 70.34 per cent of the total variance. HIT variables loadings scattered over seven factors. Factor I of the present study mainly loaded on some HIT variables, namely space, rejection, sex, location, form appropriateness and shading, depicting perceptual immaturity, almost replicating one of six orthogonal factors (factor I) located and reported by Holtzman et al. (1961). Factor III being defined mainly by barrier, balance, form definiteness, movement, form appropriateness and reaction time was labelled as factor of balanced ego identity. Factor IV bore out significant or near-significant loadings on pathognomic verbalization, abstract, anxiety, reaction time and movement, providing the caricature of a cautious thinking person. Factor V depicted bodily preoccupation in terms of significant loadings on penetration, anatomy, hostility and anxiety, and substantial replication of one of the six orthogonal factors reported by Holtzman et al. (1961b). Factor VI loaded mainly on hostility, anxiety, animal, form definiteness, reaction time, location and colour, so defined as a factor of anxious fantasized hostility. It resembled, to some extent, with factor III of the solution reported by Holtzman et al. (1961). Factor VIII of the present solution loaded significantly on integration, shading, reaction time, location and hostility, depicting the perceptual maturity substantially resembled with one of the factors reported by Holtzman et al. (1961). Factor IX of the present study marked significant loadings on popular, colour, form definiteness and anxiety coupled with factors Q1, E, and O of 16PF depicting the conventional awareness in inkblot percepts. Meenakshi (2011) has tried to see the 'Compatibility of SIS – II and HIT in terms of single response method and multiple response method' for her doctoral work on 400 college male and female students which will be reported soon.

## Somatic Inkblot Test

SIS is an addition to the family of inkblot tests. SIS can be administered both individually and in group; it also can be used through video/computer technology in testing. It has attracted researchers worldwide and is getting popular in India, Italy, South Africa and Russia. SIS is a structured, projective, diagnostic procedure and is an adjunct to psychotherapy. SIS is structured by a sequential presentation of intentionally designed and field-tested inkblot-like images. These images demonstrate typical and atypical response potentials. The SIS procedure is projective because it is based on spontaneous, individually generated responses to semi-ambiguous figures, which elicit intra-psychic associations specific to the person presented with them. SIS was originally conceived in 1959 as a projective test for assessing the significance of physiologic heart symptoms. After years of research and field testing in 1980, a book on a 20-card version of the projective procedure called SIS-I was published. SIS-II (62-image booklet form) was developed in 1984. Encouraged by the tremendous success of the booklet form (SIS-II), the SIS-Video (video version of the 62-image booklet form) was also launched. It provides diagnostic and therapeutic aid. SIS-II and SIS-Video is a self-administered as well as group-administered test.

SIS is a diagnostic procedure because of the interaction of structure and stimuli. These stimuli evoke symbolism and meanings unique to the responding individual. These can be differentiated from typical and atypical peer norms and can be analysed according to internationally recognized diagnostic criteria. The procedure is an adjunct to therapy because responses can be further explored to create a more effective treatment plan, and can be readdressed in later discussions, providing opportunities to elicit deeply defended material. During administration of the SIS procedure, clients, patients and students may abreact emotional conflict raised to consciousness by the images, which can be a therapeutic experience.

Volumes of the *SIS Journal of Projective Psychology and Mental Health* (1994–to date) have continued covering a wide range of clinical, industrial, educational and research applications. Thanks to the technical contributions of Anand Dubey and Rakesh Jain abstracts of all volumes are now available on the web at http://www.somaticinkblots.com, as a free contribution to the worldwide mind–body–spirit knowledge. We expect this to grow in the future as those Indian students who have obtained doctoral degrees continue in their efforts to advance SIS knowledge. The manual of SIS-II/Video *Interpreting Inner World through Somatic Imagery* (Cassell and Dubey 2003) has also cited research contribution of several clinicians.

Singh (2007) emphasized the journey of the Somatic Inkblots Test (SIS) from assessment to treatment. SIS has both diagnostic and therapeutic properties. Besides diagnostics, it provides a useful aid to therapy, which has been proved by several innovative clinicians and researchers. As more clinicians avail themselves of SIS technology, they will become more effective at developing in-depth and sophisticated treatment plans. One can envision and apply optimal blending of information from the medical and psychological aspects of human existence for therapeutic strategy. Cassell (2009) emphasized that SIS projective technology harnesses the projective pulling power of hypnotically presented ambiguous visual colour–form stimuli. The viewer is uninhibited by social acceptability restrictions of the test administrator's presence. What is projected onto the SIS answer sheet flows from mental depths. The released responses represent recollections of the real outer world subjectively blended with hidden inner world imaginations, fantasies, dreams and psychophysiological body percepts.

Cassell (2010a) emphasized 'the pulling power of SIS Test and how it is facilitated by SIS memory releasing electronic viewing technology. This evolving psychological testing system and structured interview aid has far-reaching applications in the 21st century. These extend far beyond mind/body research and clinical diagnostic/treatment into the spiritual realm of existence. Inkblot projective procedures, such as the Rorschach tests were originally conceived for traditional applications by clinicians. Subsequently, their use was extended to other populations, such as testing applicants for military service or roles in industry. Unfortunately, sometimes such extension disregarded basic standards of validity and reliability, resulting in flagrant abuses. As an extreme example, at one time in California, the Rorschach results sometimes determined a prisoner's fate regarding execution! We need to be careful not to repeat such overly optimistic expectations in extending SIS assessment work and the evolving technologies therapeutic applications. Cautions are indicated in an age when basic brain research points out the important role of genetic factors as well as the importance of psychopharmacological-based treatments. To date, all positive therapeutic claims have been based upon individual case history studies. It is humbling to realize, that yet, not even one statistically based outcome study has been attempted. I challenge dedicated SIS workers to contemplate this important line of future therapeutic investigation. Moreover, it may prove to be worthwhile, when recognized treatments fail to relieve suffering, that SIS therapists create new ways to more effectively communicate utilizing the language of spiritual symbols that are consistent with the sufferers own religious doctrine.'

'We now have a growing body of evidence permitting investigation into the mental mechanisms by means of which imagery projected onto such spiritually charged SIS stimuli can mentally displace PTSD memories and relieve discomforting emotions. Focusing on these conjured-up visions readily displaces pathological material that would otherwise flood conscious awareness dragging along discomforting affect. This reflects the brain's basic biological neural inhibiting mechanisms that normally (unless there is a Dissociative splitting) only allow one stimulus to peak into consciousness at a time. This principle is utilized in yoga. Focusing on specific body regions can obliterate negative memories and affect. In some yet inexplicable psycho-soma manner, this can establish optimal neurophysiologic conditions for the body's natural healing processes.'

Clinicians treating individuals suffering from definable mental conditions are encouraged to first introduce SIS-evoked imagery consistent with guidelines established by traditional scientifically based professional disciplines within this society. Yet, standard present-day therapies take time. Frankly, for many victims of PTSD, they are not always as effective as their adherents claim. Moreover, many clinical research studies suggest that the 'personality' of the therapist is more important than the technique. In any case, when these do not entirely resolve symptoms, it is reasonable to envision supplementing them by scientifically exploring concepts and symbolic language in therapy related to spirituality. Eventually, as SIS colour/form/movement stimuli are created with content related to other religions than Christianity, they will have a wider range of spiritual releasing power to augment existing PTSD treatment methods.

> Investigators exploring the boundaries of our scientific knowledge in a relatively intangible spiritual realm are advised to keep in mind a sound scientific basis for their pioneering endeavours. None of what has been discussed above needs be based upon accepting or adhering to the alleged validity of a religious doctrine. We are mere mortals functioning as mind-body scientists in envisioning new techniques for healing—without subscribing to any particular religious belief system which purports to explain the multiple mysteries of Cosmic reality. Cassell (2010)

## Reliability and Validity of Tests

Mathur and Pais (1963) correlated the 'extratensive' and 'introversive' balance experience' as measured by the Rorschach test with that of the scores on Sack's Sentence Completion Test (SSCT). Raychaudhuri and Maitra (1965b) attempted to validate the test using the development stages and Rorschach indices. Raychaudhuri and Mukherjee (1969) also tried to validate movement responses based on expression of agitated impulsivity. Mukherjee and Raychaudhuri (1970) evaluated the correlation between the Rorschach indices and structured measures of personality with clinical rating. Pratap and Filella (1966), in an early attempt, explored the correlation between the test indices and the scores on manifest anxiety scale. Dubey et al. (1994a) administered the Rorschach test to a client before and after six months' period and reported consistency of four responses on two cards, Card IV and VI, and a slight change in two other cards. Banerjee, Mukhopadhyaya and Singh (1998) investigated the significance of the salient features of SIS measure with that of the subtle and common indices of the Rorschach test. Pasari and Paul (2005) administered Rorschach and 16PF on 30 patients of Central Institute of Psychiatry, Ranchi. The results indicated that 10 traits of 16PF were correlated with 22 variables of the Rorschach test. Thus, both the tests validated each other. Manickam et al. (2013) also established the reliability of the Rorschach test. Dewangan and Roy (2015) studied the effect of social desirability on the Rorschach test.

Extensive work was done to establish the reliability and validity of the SIS-II test. The correlation for the content categories over a period of four weeks, on repeat testing, was found to be in the range of 0.69–0.88. The split-half reliability of SIS-II and SIS-Video was established by split-ting the test into two equal halves. These equal halves are the natural divisions of the test that consist of two series, A and B. Therefore, it can be assumed that it is possible that Cassell might have had something in mind to develop two parallel forms. However, in view of rigorous field testing, he chose to combine both sets into one single test. Except most typical and human responses, correlation for R, animal, anatomical, sex, movement and rejection of images was found to be in the range of 0.66–0.89. Inter-scorer reliability for the indices was scored separately by a trained and experienced clinical psychologist, experienced in SIS, and by a fresh psychologist who was provided with a set of definitions for the variables. It was discovered that there was no difference between their independent scorings. It can be argued that it was not a scoring but merely a counting of the responses under different categories (total number of responses: human responses, animal responses, anatomical responses, sex responses, movement responses, most typical responses and rejection of images).

The validity of a psychological test is an essential characteristic that must be demonstrated beyond any doubt. Its validity can be based on theoretical assumptions, clinical experiences and its utility in the field. The division of tests into objective and projective requires different standards for measuring validity. The projective tests, such as the SIS, cannot be tested for validity, like objective tests. The SIS is a method of observation and appraisal. With regards to a test that measures some aspects of personality, it is legitimate to ask, 'Is it valid?' However, regarding a method of observation, the appropriate questions are: 'Is it useful?', 'Is it productive?' and 'Does it conform to some construct?'

The SIS is an objective procedure for observation; therefore, validity in psychometric terms cannot be determined. The question then arises: Can we still call it a valid procedure? The clinical interview and the diagnostic procedures are based on the information elicited from the patient/client and his observations. Has anyone doubted the validity of such clinical interviews and diagnostic procedures? If not, the validity of the projective test, the SIS, must be recognized since its utility would appear to be established at a clinical case history level. It is therefore, necessary to demonstrate empirically the content and construct validity of the SIS. The other types of validity generally given in textbooks cannot be determined (Cassell and Dubey 2009b).

The content validity of the test can be demonstrated if the patient/client suffering from focal somatic symptoms projects altered patterns of anatomical responses. In several studies, it has been found that relationships exist between an individual's physical disturbances and his/her projected anatomical responses (Adamson, Greengrass and Martin 1977; Cassell 1969, 1971, 1972, 1977a, 1980a, 1990; Dubey and Cassell 1993). In a study on heart patients in India, results suggested that the somatic preoccupation was not verbalized any more than compared with a healthy control. It was interpreted that the body disturbances were consciously denied (Goel et al. 1990).

To have construct validity based on the existing literature on the inkblot technique, it can be assumed that most typical responses and atypical responses must be different in broad psychiatric diagnostic categories compared to healthy controls. This hypothesis was tested on neurotics, schizophrenics and healthy normal subjects. Atypical responses were found to be significantly higher in psychotics than in neurotics and normal. Likewise, most typical responses were significantly higher in normal subjects compared to psychiatric patients (Cassell 1988; Cassell and Dubey 2003; Dubey and Cassell 1993). Several researchers have found SIS test as a highly reliable and valid instrument (Kaur and Verma 1998; Nicolini 2002; Pershad and Dubey 1994; Singh and Banerjee 1996; Verma and Kaur 1999).

Rathee et al. (1998) administered SIS-II on 200 psychopathological cases from armed forces to find out its diagnostic validity. The results revealed that out of 10 common indices of both tests, five variables in schizophrenia, four in affective psychosis, seven in unspecified psychosis, five in anxiety, four in depression and seven in hysteria showed high and positive correlations. The findings indicate high diagnostic validity of SIS-II indices against those of Rorschach's among six psychopathological groups of armed forces.

Pandey et al. (1999) examined the stability of SIS-II response contents on a sample of 30 subjects over time in two ways, that is, it analysed the consistency of responses evoked by individual images in several people as well as the individual's consistency in responding to all 62 images of SIS-II. Besides this, it also attempted to present an appraisal of the test–retest reliability of some commonly used SIS-II quantitative indices and response consistency of personality dimension related SIS-II image clusters as proposed by Dubey and associates (Dubey et al. 1995). Separate analyses of response consistency for unstructured and semi-structured images have also been done to substantiate the speculation regarding unstructured images yielding lower response consistency as compared to semi-structured images.

Meta-analysis of the findings of the studies on SIS-II was carried out to provide combined mean and standard deviation of various groups and to see if SIS-II indices could differentiate the groups statistically. All studies that appeared in the *SIS Journal of Projective Psychology and Mental Health* during 1994–2000 were considered for the purpose. The studies were classified into five groups based on specified criteria: normal, neurotics, psychotics, substance dependents and murderers. Critical ratio was computed on combined mean and standard deviation for inter-group comparisons. The results indicate that SIS-II indices do differentiate the comparison groups (Kumar 2000).

Srivastava (2002) concluded the findings of the studies on SIS-I with the aim to provide normative data by combining mean and standard deviations of existing studies and to see if the SIS-I indices can differentiate various groups. All studies published in *SIS Journal of Projective Psychology and Mental Health* from 1994 to 2001 (January) were considered for the study. The studies were pulled into four groups on specific inclusion criteria: normal, coronary heart disease, generalized anxiety disorder and schizophrenia. Critical ratio was computed on combined mean and standard deviation for inter-group comparison. The results revealed that the SIS-I indices significantly differentiate the comparison groups.

In the USA, Panek et al. (2002) have established that when significant differences exist among the total number of responses (R) in comparing groups on data obtained from PTs, it is advisable to also compute comparisons based on percentages obtained by dividing individual variable scores by their respective R's. The purpose of this study was to determine whether different results would be observed on the projective Hand Test (HT) when comparing raw scores versus percentages, even when the R's. do not significantly differ. The HT was administered to 90 individuals seeking treatment at a pain clinic for three distinct physical maladies: arthritis, fibromyalgia and migraine headaches. The results indicated that there were no significant differences among the three groups for R's. A2 (Gender) × 3 (Pain Groups) ANOVA, with age as a covariate, yielded interpretable groups and two gender effects derived from the raw scores. The same results were obtained for percentage comparisons except for one non-significant finding for the repetition (REP) variable. REP is a reliable indicator of an organic brain syndrome and, therefore, it was important to authenticate the significance of this variable. The lack of corroborative support for the percentage comparison suggested caution in over-interpreting the differences among the raw scores, especially in an exploratory investigation utilizing small samples.

Cassell and Dubey (2009) presented two previously unpublished early statistical studies on SIS content validity. The first was completed in 1978 with SIS-I. It used a content analysis scoring system to quantify projective responses in a group of 13 women suffering from premenstrual dysphoric syndrome. As compared to the control group of 37 women, these subjects projected significantly more responses depicting reproductive and sexual symbols. Based upon chi-squared analysis, statistically significant differences were found for such sex-related anatomical responses, but not for unrelated body parts such as heart and lungs. The second study was completed in 1988 with SIS-II Booklet Version. The data were analysed for 37 of the 62 SIS stimuli. In the comparison, 28 pregnant women were compared with 27 non-pregnant controls. A chi-square analysis revealed that pregnant women projected more response related to reproduction and/or pregnancy.

Kumar (2009) studied factor structure of SIS-I quantitative indices on 100 normal adults. Principal component analysis identified four components with eigenvalue greater than 1. However, only three components were rotated subsequently as only one index loaded significantly on the fourth factor. The first factor loaded significantly on typical, most typical (positive) and atypical responses and was labelled as 'objective thinking'. The second factor loaded positively on movement, human and anatomy responses and negatively on animal responses; this factor was labelled as 'emotional maturity'. The third factor loaded significantly on total number of responses (positive loading) and rejection of images (negative loading); it was labelled as 'reaction to stress'.

Cassell and Dubey (2010) pointed out that some psychologists question the validity of projective test as they do with questionnaires. The authors argue that they forget that the projective tests cannot be verified on the same parameters as questionnaires. We put our perception and feelings into the mind of the subject by asking them to choose their answers as 'Yes' or 'No', 'True' or 'False' 'Agree' or 'Disagree', etc. The true validity of a test should be decided 'if it measures for what it was made'. An inkblot test is a powerful instrument. It brings unprocessed symbolic material through projection, which cannot be measured/ assessed through the so-called objective questionnaires.

Khromov and Dubey (2016) administered Rorschach, SIS-I and SIS-II inkblot tests on 98 normal subjects to find out the mutual empirical validity with MMPI test. The results were ciphered on identical forms containing 54 categories which were correlated with MMPI test. The structure of correlation in each pair matrix of three inkblot tests was calculated and has been compared. Cronbach has commented that PTs give wider range of information and lower reliability in comparison with objective psychometric tests, whereas Cassell (1980) emphasized that increased structure of projective stimulus have raised the level of reliability of projective tests. The present research revealed that psychometric properties of inkblots tests increased after increasing the stimulus from Rorschach to SIS-I (20 images) and from SIS-I to SIS-II (62 images). However, it was not able to increase the ability to differentiate subjects' specific mental disorders. Correlation between ambiguity and projection of properties of the person has non-linear character, and the moderate level of ambiguity gives an optimum variant at displaying.

Banerjee (2017) reported a case study where OI and SIS were administered to a 54-year-old male patient suffering from reactive depression with suicidal ideation. He had developed the symptoms five years earlier after suffering a severe loss in business. He consulted a psychiatrist who treated him with antidepressants. He noticed some relief in depressive thoughts and suicidal ideation, though temporarily. At the initial assessment, he scored lots of depressive responses with low scores on optimism scale. He showed low scores on human responses, interpersonal relations and group conformity (team building). After five weeks of reconstructive psychotherapy and relaxation, he was re-administered SIS-II and optimism scale. Tremendous changes were visible on his profile and the human responses; interpersonal relations and group conformity scores increased along with scores on the optimism scale. The increased scores on both scales along with the patient's statement that 'I am relieved from at least 50 per cent of my symptoms' speak of the power of both tests as valid and successful instruments during therapeutic intervention in clinical setups. Both tests help in assessing and ascertaining interpersonal relationship, aggression, thinking in group conformity, emotional stability and total mental health of the person.

When both tests were compared, the findings were going in one direction, suggestive of positive correlation. It can safely be concluded that both instruments can be used as diagnostic, therapeutic and screening tools in clinical situations and industrial set-ups.

## Different Groups

### Normal Population

Kumar (1962c), Prabhu (1967), Asthana (1963, 1971) and Somasundaram, Mathai and Jesudian (1971b) found that the average number of responses for the normal population was in the range of 18–33. Singh (1975) also found that the number of responses given by tribal population that had 'more culture contact' and 'less culture contact' was below the normal range reported from abroad. Singh (1975) opined that the group he studied was 'not perceptually responsive and not receptive' to the world outside and gave a smaller number of popular responses. Human responses (H) accounted for 9.66 per cent (Singh 1975) and it was contradictory to the findings reported by Prabhu (1967) and Kumar (1962c) but agreed with Asthana (1971) and Somasundaram et al. (1971b), who reported human responses in the range of 7–10 per cent.

Dubey and Dosajh (1979) administered the Rorschach test and found that the average number of responses was about 14 (13.76) among army personnel serving in other ranks. Dubey (1979, 1981a, 1981b) conducted several research studies using the Rorschach test on military personnel, both clinical and normal population (Dubey 1979, 1982; Manickam and Dubey 2005), and reported a low number of responses. Dubey (1982), in a study on 300 subjects, found that most of the Rorschach indices are dependent on the number of responses. When the groups of normal, neurotics and schizophrenics were divided into high productivity and low productivity, based on the number of responses, many indices, which were found to be significant, lost their significance. It further strengthened the findings of Fiske and Baughman (1953) and supported the intention of Holtzman (1956). Ramachandra and Chaturvedi (1995) used the Rorschach test to study body imagery. Mohn (2002) has emphasized the application of SIS images on patients.

The Rorschach test and SIS were compared on nine common indices such as R, H, A, M, FM, anatomical, sex, rejection and most typical/popular, and were found compatible. SIS appraises the same construct as the Rorschach test. However, due to the use of self-administration and video technology, it reaches beyond the Rorschach test (Dubey et al. 1994; Cassell 1994; Cassell and Dubey 1998, 2002; Cassell et al. 1996a, 1996b; Rathee et al. 1998).

Dubey et al. (1995a) administered SIS on 500 subjects including 300 normal and 200 psychiatric patients (neurosis and schizophrenia) and analysed SIS protocols to find out (a) whether the pattern of responses in two forms (SIS-II and SIS-Video) are different, (b) to demonstrate whether series A and series B of SIS-Video can be used independently to curtail the testing time and (c) to find out whether some of the objective scoring criteria be formulated to differentiate the patients of major psychiatric diagnostic categories. The results suggest that SIS-II and SIS-Video can be divided into two short tests consisting of series A and series B separately. The normal and the clinical groups differed on various scoring categories adopted here. SIS can help during selection as a screening instrument. These scoring categories, however, are less informative as far as general psychology of an individual patient is concerned. The profile of anticipated and given responses for the image are more important for thorough understanding of the patient.

Bailey and Murstein (1996) tried to find out relationship between SIS-II and a self-reported paranoia scale on a college students' sample (N = 60). The content of the written responses to SIS-II was analysed for paranoid content. Based on the past research with other projective devices, a content analysis of SIS responses featuring eye references, facial references, atypical references and paranoid ideation was conducted. The result indicated that two of the scoring methods, those for eye content and paranoid ideation, were positively associated (p < 0.05) with self-reported paranoia scale score. The findings lend support to the Cassell (1990) eye paranoia scale for SIS-II and extend these findings to a non-clinical sample. Cassell and Dubey (2002) prepared a new manual for SIS-I (card form of the test). Separate norms are also available on Russian and Italian population. The new scoring system along with interpretation of SIS responses with case studies are presented in the manual.

Mishra and Dwivedi (1997) administered the SIS-II and Rorschach to compare the common diagnostic indices in normal, neurotic and schizophrenics. The sample comprised 50 normal, neurotics and schizophrenics each. The results suggest that the diagnostic evaluation, which is achieved by the SIS-II and the Rorschach test in diagnosing schizophrenics, can be compared with confidence. The study further suggests that both tests provide ample support to the theory that SIS-II provides certain additional diagnostic information which is not available through the Rorschach test. The results also suggest that the SIS-II indices as compared with the Rorschach indices discriminate better the normal subjects and paranoid schizophrenics, whereas the Rorschach indices discriminate better depressive neurotics and undifferentiated schizophrenics.

Cassell and Dubey (1998a) tried SIS on different groups of clinical and normal subjects and found high discriminating ability of the test. It was also found to be a successful screening tool during selection in industry. Its reliability, validity, discriminating diagnostic ability and screening value have been emphasized by many researchers (Cassell and Dubey 2003; Verma et al. 1994, 1995). The test has attracted researchers and clinicians in different parts of the world.

Singh et al. (1999) administered SIS-II on 480 subjects, half of them male and half female, divided into four categories (adolescents, adults, later adults and old). It aimed to find out the effect of age and sex on the projection of total number of responses, that is, human responses, animal responses, anatomical responses, sex responses, movement responses, most typical responses and rejection of images. The total number of responses was found to be within the normal range of 61–65. Significant differences on R, most typical and rejection of images were also found in the normal range. Males and females of this study show high human responses, which indicates their healthy interpersonal relationship. Animal responses were found to be higher in males and females of adolescent and adult groups as compared to later adult and old groups. It was also observed that females gave higher animal responses than males. As has been observed in the Rorschach test, the anatomical responses were higher in later adult and old group; it may be due to increased body consciousness in this age. Male subjects gave more sex responses than female subjects. Similarly, later adult and old subjects showed higher sex responses as compared to adolescents and adults. Females showed higher movement responses than males. Pathological responses were almost negligible in all age groups of males and females. All SIS-II indices were found to be positively correlated except the rejection of images. The most liked and the least liked images were found to be B31 and A29, respectively.

Pandey, Tripathi and Tripathi (2001) examined the effect of age on SIS-II response contents. Three groups of subjects belonging to the rural area of Gopalganj district in the age range of 6–12 (children), 13–20 (adults) and 21–40 years (later adults) were individually administered SIS-II. The responses were scored for nine indices. Analysis of the data revealed an age-related increasing trend for various categories of sex responses as well as for movement, most typical, atypical and rejection responses. A reverse trend (i.e., decrease in score with increasing age) was obtained for human responses. Age-specific changes in other SIS-II indices were also observed. Contrary to earlier findings, subjects of the present study across all age groups showed slightly elevated score on atypical response index of SIS-II. This observation, therefore, brings forth the need to develop norms for rural population.

Singh and Dubey (2002) tried to find out the inter correlation among eight SIS indices, that is, total number of responses (R), human responses (H), animal responses (A), anatomical responses (At), sex responses (Sex), movement responses (M), most typical responses (MT) and rejection of images (Rej.) on 480 males and females belonging to four categories (adolescents: 13 to 15 years; adult: 20 to 22 years; later adults: 50 to 52 years and aged: 60 to 62 years). All eight subgroups consisted of 60 subjects. High and positive correlation was observed among various indices of SIS-II.

Hussain et al. (1976) appraised the profile of unwed mothers and Kumar and Patel (1990) compared the profile of marital high- and low-adjusted women. Hostility and aggression as measured through the Rorschach test was also reported by various researchers (Gupta, Verma and Kulhara 1989; Rangaswami 1982; Shivadasani 1971).

Khromov, Pandey and Dubey (2004) studied problems of students (both conscious and unconscious) related to their various interpersonal and intrapersonal domains of life. Twenty-two university students (18 females and 4 males) were assessed on two projective measures (SIS-I and SSCT) and one questionnaire, measuring the student's attitude and problems. The finding suggests that greater number of animal and move-ment responses is associated with little concern for one's health and activity/passivity. High anxiety over one's own infantilism was found to be related with more typical, human and heart responses. The atypical visual images were more frequently seen on the SIS-I protocols of those who were anxious about their emotional life. The finding reveals that SIS-I can be used successfully to reveal the psychosomatic symptoms, interpersonal problems and broken interpersonal relationship. Khromov (2009) further compared the psychometric characteristics of three PTs (Rorschach, SIS-I and SIS-II) and correlated with 12 standard tests: MMPI, 5FPQ, MBTI, BDHI, Raven's Matrices, 16FP, POI, Leongard's, Jenkins's, Learie's, Rotter's and Thomas's scales. From the psychometric point of view, SIS-II has emerged as an advanced version of the Rorschach Inkblot Test and proved to be a successful diagnostic instrument.

D. K. Singh, A. Singh and A. R. Singh (2005) administered the Rorschach test following Beck's method to 100 normal subjects in the age range of 18–50 years; both male and female subjects with minimum education up to the 12th standard were taken for the study. It was a purposive sampling. The findings of the Rorschach test do not match with Beck's norm. It further emphasizes the need of Indian norms on larger population.

S. N. Dubey and B. L. Dubey (2005) administered SIS test along with progressive muscular relaxation (PMR), *shavasana* and GSR Bio-feedback for 10 days. The results suggest significant increase in most typical (MT) and human responses (H) and decrease in rejection of images (Rej.), atypical (AT) and pathological (Pathological Anatomy Scale [PAS] and Hostility and Aggression Scale [HAS]) responses. SIS-I profile is shown and the effect of intervention through PMR and *shavasana* is discussed in the paper.

Chaudhury et al. (2007b) administered the Rorschach test using Klopfer's method to 442 older Indians aged 65 years or more, comprising normal subjects and patients. The normal sample consisted of 282 subjects. The patient sample consisted of 160 patients with the diagnosis of dementia (n = 66), alcohol dependence syndrome (n = 8), schizophrenia (n = 16), mania (n = 5), depression (n = 50) and anxiety disorders (n = 15). The Rorschach protocols of normal older Indians in different age groups showed significant differences from each other and from the Western norms. The Rorschach profiles of the various groups of patients also showed significant differences between them, from normal older Indian subjects and from the Western norms. An interpretation of the Rorschach protocols of normal older Indians and patients using the Western norms would be fallacious and misleading. The use of the Rorschach test to study the aging trends of normal older adults as well as an aid to clinical diagnosis was strongly supported.

Kumar, Dubey and Kumar (2007) tried to find out the inter-correlations in nine indices of the SIS-I. The test was administered to 50 subjects and the product moment was computed to see the correlations. The results revealed positive correlations in seven indices of SIS-I except rejection of images and most typical responses. No significant correlations were found with most typical responses and other indices. Positive correlations were observed between total numbers of responses, human responses, animal responses, anatomical responses, movement responses, typical responses and atypical responses.

Singh Umed (2007) investigated the pattern of responses on SIS-II in normal high school male and female students. The sample comprised 100 male and 100 female high school students. SIS-II was administered individually. The mean, standard deviation and *t*-ratio were computed to compare the two groups. Principal component factor analysis was carried out to understand the factor structure of SIS responses in two groups. *T*-test and factor structures have revealed significant gender differences in some SIS-response patterns. Females have been found scoring significantly higher on SIS-II scales of animal responses, pathological anatomy and depression and low on anatomy and sex than their male counterparts. Five principal components each have been in the two data, which also differentiate the SIS response patterns of male and female subjects.

Singh et al. (2008) intended to determine whether there are significant differences in personality style, as measured by 16PF Form B (Hindi adaptation), between people who give an adult female as a response to Card VII of the Rorschach test and those who do not. One hundred (N = 100) normal subjects of both sexes, in the age range of 21–45 years and with minimum education up to 10th class, were included in the study. General health questionnaire (12 items), Rorschach Inkblot Test (Beck's system) and 16 PF were administered individually. The findings of the study showed that both groups differed significantly on four factors (factors A, H, N and Q3). It is apparent from the result that the subjects who perceived female content were warm-hearted, participating, socially bold, spontaneous, shrewd, calculative, controlled, socially precise and following self-image. The present research findings also reveal that inability to report female content on Card VII seems to be related to social discomfort, dependency needs, passivity, introversion and social anxiety.

D. Kumar and R. Kumar (2009) compared common indices of SIS-I and Rorschach on a group of 50 normal subjects drawn from the general population. The scores on common indices were converted into percent scores taking total number of responses as denominator and product moment correlations were computed on these transformed scores. Of eight analysed common indices, the correlation coefficients were significant on total number of responses, human, animal, sex, movement, most typical/popular, typical/good form, atypical and rejection of images. Alreja et al. (2009) administered the SIS-II to 30 medical practitioners in the age range of 25–45 years. The profile has revealed that medical practitioners have fair imaginative capacity, functioning intelligence, good interpersonal relationship, psychological maturity, fair ego strength, adaptability and fair social conformity.

Kandhari, Sharma and Kumar (2010b) administered SIS-I and developed a comprehensive scoring system (CSS) for SIS-I on 200 normal subjects. The CSS indices were enumerated and defined operationally for objective scoring. SIS-I protocols of the sample were scored as per the developed CSS. Mean and standard deviation of each scoring indices of the CSS were computed. The study aimed at delineating the pattern of responses on SIS-I in normal population.

Kandhari et al. (2011) compared the pattern of responses on SIS-I in normal males and females. SIS-I was administered to 200 normal persons comprising two groups: males (n = 82) and females (n = 112). The data was analysed through Mann–Whitney $U$-test. The results indicate that males and females differ significantly only on TR and CBA.

Shweta et al. (2010) administered the Rorschach test following Beck's method on 238 subjects, consisting 130 males and 108 females. Chi-square, $t$-test and $U$-test were computed to compare the Rorschach variables. Result does not show significant difference between males and females except on two variables—Dd and sex. The findings are in contrast with the Western norm and to some extent with Indian studies also. In addition, religious responses on the Rorschach test focus on a new dimension of further research.

Kruthi, Mahboubeh and Manickam (2015) administered SIS-II test to 10 Iranian couples, studying in Mysore and living together, with no history of marital discord. The mean age of males was 42 years and of the females was 35.5 years. The mean scores on 11 indices were almost like the scores reported by earlier studies. No cultural variation was noticed in their responses.

## Executives in Industry

Dubey studied executives in different set-ups (Dubey 1975b, 1977a, 1980, 1988, 1989a, 2003) and found that they had high productivity, high imaginative ability, controlled emotionality, high adjustment and high group conformity. They were also found high on team building. They gave a greater number of total responses, most typical and human responses with low number of animal, anatomical and sex responses. The rejection of images and pathological responses were almost absent.

Singh and Dwivedi (1998) administered SIS-II procedure to study 50 managers and 100 students. Findings showed significant differences in total number of responses, animal responses and sex responses, whereas no significant differences were found in other response categories. Pathological responses were negligible in both groups.

Dubey et al. (2001) administered the SIS procedure to evaluate 90 executives of a private organization. The SIS profile reveals that they were supported by good ego strength, healthy interpersonal relationship, no erotic disturbances, controlled hostility and aggression, high team building, good human relationship and keeping touch with reality. Two executives showed unhealthy profile suggesting disturbed sexual relations, poor ego strength and, to an extent, neurotic profile.

Dubey Anand and Dubey, B.L. (2012) used the SIS test in industry during selection and counselling of employees. It has been found as an effective tool to ascertain if the new incumbents possess certain personality traits such as team building, interpersonal relationship and intra-psychic balance. The present paper will provide SIS norms and indices for a successful executive in the business world and the services provided by Dubay Doctorin (2D). 2D enables organizations to transform into learning organizations to effectively compete in the marketplace. It is a very simplistic and pragmatic approach that attempts to understand and capitalize on 'the people', 'processes', 'assets' and 'technologies' in a service delivery environment focused on specific business outcomes. It can be applied in any service industry including government services, hospitality services, transportation and logistics services.

## Creativity

Creativity is another significant area that has been studied. Raychaudhuri and Maitra (1968) examined the level of creativity using the movement responses of the Rorschach test and found a significant association. Raychaudhuri (1971) in another study explored the correlation of creativity and gender.

Ramachandra (1994) studied 30 creative artists and an equal number of neurotics and non-creative group using Klopfer's method. The creative group had average number of responses, quick reaction time and healthy emotional relationship with others and good ego strength. The experimental group of the creative artists had the ability to view their problems objectively and incisively as evidenced by the indices. However, the quality of responses suggested a keen perception and disposition to do things differently from that of the other two groups. Interestingly, even at the beginning phase of introduction of the test, Raychaudhuri (1963) studied the responses of the Indian musicians.

Singh, D.K., Manjhi, G. and Singh, A.R. (2007) administered the Rorschach Inkblot Test to examine creativity on 100 normal subjects of both sexes in the age range of 18–20 years, with education up to 12th standard. As a tool, General Health Questionnaire (Shamsunder et al. 1986), verbal test of creative thinking and the Rorschach test (Beck System) were used. Findings of this study show that both groups (high vs low creativity) differ significantly on total number of response (R), whole response (W) and popular response (P).

Singh Umed et al. (2009) tried to explore indicators of creativity and administered SIS-II and Torrance Test of Creative Thinking with Words on 100 male students of 11th and 12th grades, randomly selected from Senior Secondary Schools of Kurukshetra district of Haryana. The obtained data were analysed by applying descriptive statistics, product moment method of correlation and principal component factor analysis and the inter-correlations and factor structure depicted some structured overlap between the two types of measures. Six of SIS-II scales, that is, Total number of Responses (R), Typical, Most Typical, Human, Movement and Depression have emerged significant projective indicators of creativity.

## Disadvantaged Population

The tool was used with the different groups of population—normal subjects, different diagnostic groups, age groups and other special groups including a tribal group. However, only Shanker (1968) explored the caste factor other than that of the tribal group. He investigated the correlation between the education level and the affective factors on the Rorschach test among Dalits (Harijans). In 'CERALD' population, it would be worth investigating the precepts of different caste groups. Julka (1962), Kundu (1969) and Singh (1975) appraised the profile of tribal population. Kundu (1969) described the response pattern of tribal young offenders and Singh (1975) studied the effect of modernization on the response pattern of the tribal population. Chakraborty, Dasgupta and Sanyal (2015) administered SIS-II on 60 orphan and 60 normal children and found that orphan children gave significantly greater number of total responses, animal and anatomical responses than the normal children.

## Children and Adolescents

Bagh (1955) was probably among the earliest researchers to use the Rorschach test on adolescent school children. Asthana (1965, 1966) evaluated the perceptual development of children and Julka (1962) also conducted research with child population. Using the Rorschach indices of aggression and maladjustment, Raychaudhuri, Mukherjee, and Raychaudhuri (1969) compared normal boys and boys with behavioural problems. Dixit (1964) conducted a developmental study of the response pattern of children and adolescents. Joseph and Pillai (1986) differentiated creative students into high and low creative group using certain Rorschach indices. Prakash (1977) reported the profile of institutionalized orphan children. Shankar (1956) and Raychaudhuri and Maitra (1965a) also examined the Rorschach responses of young offenders. Shanmugam (1959) correlated yet another interesting variable, lunar signs ('stars') and the responses of adolescents. Though there were diverse and exciting experiments with the test on children in the initial phase, there were not many innovative attempts in the later period.

Based on the experience of using the test with different groups of children, Asthana and Mohan (1977) recommended the Rorschach test as a research tool to study the percept of children more than three decades ago but there were not many takers for it. Using the hostility measure on the Rorschach test, Singh and Kapur (1984) administered 150 school children in the age group of 11–14 years and found association with locus of control, intelligence and PEN scores. Bhargava and Saxena (1995) examined the profile of deprived group of adolescents and found that the group differed from the control group on longer RT, RT chromatic and achromatic cards.

Cassell and Dubey (1998b) used the SIS procedure to study two adults who were severely disturbed by the media effects of addictive-type playing of violent electronic games and the third, a 14-year-old male, admitted to a psychiatric hospital for highly dangerous and threatening behaviour. SIS images helped in understanding their aggressive and violent behaviour.

Savage (2003) administered the SIS-I to find out the traumatic effect of parental divorce on children. In many cases, the children are not aware of the intention of the parents to dissolve the marriage. Once the decision to divorce is made, most couples find it difficult to approach life in a positive and constructive way. They experience a range of emotional and psychological consequences and many are very vague about their future. Communication between the couples can range from talking about the impending events to complete non-communication. The self-esteem of both or one parent is negatively affected and they may lose their sense of priority and tend to become problem and circumstance driven (Hoffman and Pincus 1989). The case is presented in detail in this case study.

Jain et al. (2005) tried to find out the diagnostic indicators of ADHD on the Rorschach and SIS-I tests. The study was conducted on a sample of 224 children in the age range of 6–11 years drawn from various schools of Baraut near New Delhi. Participants were categorized into two groups—ADHD (n = 111) and control (n = 113). Rorschach and SIS-I were individually administered on each participant, and the response pattern of ADHD and normal children on two projective measures was compared. Frequency data of the scored indices were transformed into percent scores (taking total number of responses as a denominator) and total and transformed scores of the ADHD and control groups were compared (using $t$-test) for identifying the discriminating indices. The sensitivity of both tests in identifying patients of ADHD was also compared. Several Rorschach indices, such as M, D, FC, F + and A, were found significant in differentiating normal children from ADHD. The SIS-I results revealed that both the tests are sensitive in distinguishing the ADHD children from normal controls. Findings have been discussed in the light of available research evidences.

Kumar and Singh (2007) studied the changes in the quantum at different age levels by administering SIS-I. The test was administered on 100 children and 100 adults. The results revealed significant differences on six out of nine variables: movement, typical, atypical, anatomy, most typical and rejection of images, which confirmed the hypothesis. Sharma, Sharma and Upadhyay (2013) administered the Rorschach test in delinquents and Bhogta et al. (2014) used SIS-II in thalassemia patients.

Chaudhury et al. (2007a) administered the Rorschach test using Klopfer's method to 313 children and adolescent patients with psychiatric disorders, namely schizophrenia (n = 66), mania (n = 10), depression (n = 33), anxiety state (n = 24), hysteria (n = 45), nocturnal enuresis (n = 48), head injury (n = 16), epilepsy (n = 32) and mental retardation (n = 39). The Rorschach profiles of the various groups of patients showed significant differences among the groups and from normal Indian subjects and the Western norms. Interpretation of the Rorschach protocols of Indian children and adolescent with psychiatric disorders using the Western norms would be fallacious and misleading.

Kumar, Kandhari and Dubey (2008) used SIS-I to find out the quantum of contribution of gender in productivity. Two hundred (n = 200) adults from general population were administered SIS-I individually.

The sample consisted of 82 male and 118 female participants. After exploring the fulfilment of the assumptions of parametric statistics, the regression analysis was performed to analyse the quantum of gender contribution. The results indicated significant contribution of gender in productivity with a small effect size.

Singh and Singh (2008) examined the impact of environment on the responses of SIS-II images of two different school systems: government schools and Gurukul in Haryana, India. Two hundred male students (100 from government school and 100 from Gurukul), matched with academic grade, were randomly selected for the study. They were administered SIS-II booklet form individually. The means, standard deviations and *t*-ratios were computed to compare the two groups. Obtained *t*-ratios have revealed significant mean differences in some of the SIS-II response patterns. Gurukul students obtained significantly high score on movement responses, atypical responses, rejection of images, pathological anatomy scale, depression scale and paranoia scale and low on typical responses than the students of government schools. Similarly, Verma and Singh (2014) found the effect of age and education on the responses of Somatic Inkblot Test (SIS-II).

## Psychiatric Disorder

Though the Rorschach test was used initially in India with non-clinical population, later a greater number of studies emerged involving hospitalized psychiatric patients (Mishra and Dwivedi 1997). It has also been widely used in India for clarifying diagnostic issues in OPD settings (Kohli and Kaur 2002). Historically, Pramod Kumar (1960, 1960a, 1961, 1961a, 1962a, 1962b, 1963, 1965) was one of the early clinical investigators who have done extensive work with this procedure in clinical populations. Kumar evaluated the profile of those with different psychiatric disorders and compared it with normal control group. Among psychotic disorders, Kumar (1961b) investigated the profile of patients with schizophrenia and verified the differences with that of a normal control group (Kumar 1963). Bagadia et al. (1971) on a large sample analysed the responses of patients with schizophrenia. Dubey (1977a) and Dubey et al. (1977b) studied the psychiatric population, focusing on schizophrenia and compared it with other disorders. Mujtaba and Mujtaba (1985) and Prasadarao, Verma and Kulhara (1987) also evaluated the groups of patients with schizophrenia and other disorders. Deviating from the common trend, Malaviya (1973) studied the Rorschach signs of suicide on a group of schizophrenic patients who had attempted suicide.

Exclusive research on patients with affective disorder was undertaken by Kumar (1960b) and provided a Rorschach profile of the patients with mania and compared it with a control group (Kumar 1965). Similarly, he analysed the profile of patients with depressive disorder (Kumar 1962b) and compared it with a normal control group (Kumar 1962a). Almost a decade later, Bagadia et al. (1973), using a large sample, described the profile of patients with depressive disorder. Pratap and Kapur (1984) studied patients with mania and later Kumar, Mohanty and Kumar (2003) compared the Rorschach test and SIS-I indices of the manic patients. Kumar (1960a) studied the response profile of the test of patients with different neurotic disorders and compared it with the general population (Kumar 1961a). While Dubey and Dosajh (1979) studied the patients with neurotic disorder, Akhtar, Pershad and Verma (1975) studied the patients with obsessive-compulsive disorder. Ramachandra (1994) used Rorschach to compare the profile of a group of patients with neurotic disorder with that of creative artists and non-creative group.

Kumar and Patel (1990) found that the Rorschach test differentiated high marital adjusted and low marital adjusted women. The highly adjusted group gave more average number of response (28.73), whereas the lower adjusted group gave only 18.60. The RT as well as TR were less for the highly adjusted group. Kaur and Verma (1998) administered the Rorschach test and SIS-II to 32 psychiatric patients to assess the interrelations on selected variables. Both scales showed some degree of overlap with a significant correlation between the two scales on movement, human, animal and popular responses (r = ranging from 0.42 to 0.58) but insignificant correlations for anatomy, sex, F+ and total response. Mishra and Gupta, (2008) and Mishra, Kumar and Prakash (2009) administered the Rorschach test and found varying patterns in various psychiatric conditions. Verma et al. (1996) compared PEN and SIS-II on 32 psychiatric patients to find dependence of SIS variables on certain personality dimensions. The result shows that (a) the number of 'most popular' responses depends upon the education of the subject; (b) psychotics scores tended to influence atypical and pathological responses; (c) neuroticism scores influence the number of typical responses; (d) the lie score was found inversely related to perception of human, movement and pathological response and (e) extraversion was not related to any of the SIS variables.

Pandey, Misra and Dwivedi (1996) analysed the three most liked and the three least liked images on SIS-II as given by neurotics, schizophrenics and normal controls (n = 50 in each group). A differential pattern of preferences emerged, like normal controls showed positive affect for healthy body imagery (Images A5A and A13), whereas neurotics and schizophrenics had poor concept (Images A31 and B5). Image B31 was most liked by all subjects, which supports the contention of Cassell to carry pleasant feelings way back home by the subject at the end of the test. Analysis of disliked images revealed that images pertaining to erotic/sex and insecurity were more disliked by the clinical subjects, whereas the normal controls showed no such pattern.

Pershad, Verma and Bhagat (1997) used SIS-II on 50 normal, 57 neurotic and 70 psychotic patients to find out the extent and type of body image disturbances in psychiatric patients. He compared the body image disturbances in patients with different types of psychiatric illnesses. It was observed that most typical responses and sex responses were lowest in the psychotic group, as compared to normal subjects. This indicated that psychotics tended to deny anatomical structure and their perception was not in conformity with the typical responses. Movement responses and projection of images were high in pathological groups. In the normal group, 26 per cent of the subjects gave their responses like structural theme of the image. In the neurotic group, this number was reduced like structural theme of the image. In the neurotic group, this number was reduced to 23 per cent and in psychotics it was only 18 per cent. However, a significantly high correlation was observed between normal and neurotics, normal and psychotics, and neurotics and psychotics in their perceptual and structural theme on 16 images. The highest concordance was the thematic structure of kidney, spine and foetus.

Kohli and Kaur (2002) administered the Rorschach test and PEN to 125 patients attending a psychiatric OPD of Post Graduate Institute of Medical, Education & Research, Chandigarh, India. Cases were referred to the Psychology Unit for ruling out psychotic illness. The questionnaire variables did not show significant correlation with the Rorschach test. The Rorschach profile showed signs of general disturbance and propensity to psychosis rather than clear-cut pathognomic signs.

Cassell, Schaeck and Mohn (2002) administered the SIS-Video, Rorschach inkblot test and figure drawing tests in a case study of a 15-year-old girl who was admitted to a psychiatric hospital in Boston for treatment of major depression and dissociative reaction. She had a history of suicidal ideation and self-mutilation of her left wrist and forearm. The relaxing instructions in the video and the hypnotically present healing flowers may have facilitated the neural extinction of the terrifying hallucinations intruding upon her consciousness. Figure drawing and content analysis of the SIS and Rorschach tests may provide useful aids to supplement standardized clinical interviewing techniques.

Mishra et al. (2009) investigated the presentation of the Rorschach test special scores in various clinical conditions by using Exner's comprehensive system (CS). Patients aged 18–55 years, with the ICD-10 (World Health Organization 1992) diagnoses of bipolar affective disorder, current episode mania with psychotic features (n = 30), schizophrenia (n = 30), schizoaffective disorder (n = 30), depression (n = 30) and 30 normal subjects from the general population were included in the study. The results indicated that although thought disturbances are present in almost all psychotic conditions, they can be differentiated from each other on careful examination of special scores. Schizophrenia patients have severest type of thought disorder followed by mania and schizoaffective disorders.

Dwivedi (2015) tried to explore if Exner's CSS of the Rorschach test is sensitive enough to tap into and discriminate various kinds of disorders of content of thought, specifically delusion of infidelity in persons with psychotic illness. The sample comprised five patients having delusion of infidelity and five patients having other delusions, drawn from the inpatients of Institute of Mental Health and Hospital (IMHH), Agra. The findings revealed that none of the scoring variables of Exner scoring system could differentiate the groups.

## Schizophrenic Disorder

In a study on 25 active schizophrenics and 25 recovered cases, Sandhu (1978) observed that recovered schizophrenics showed improvement in the form level, reality orientation, emotional control and decline in anatomy content. Pershad, Verma and Dubey (1979) evaluated the profile of 'the difficult to diagnose cases' and found that 26.5 per cent gave at least one of the pathognomic signs that Brar (1970) had suggested, namely loosening of association, tendency to overgeneralize, lack of reality contact and pursuit of one's or personal meaning to common symbols. When taken separately, 20 per cent of the protocols had one or more responses of confabulation, 11 per cent had contamination and 6 per cent had position responses.

Dubey (1977a) also found signs on the Rorschach test that differentiated patients with schizophrenic disorder, neurotic disorder and normal group. Dubey and Sharma (1973) compared the over inclusive thinking patients with different psychiatric disorders. Prasadarao et al. (1987) compared patients with obsessive-compulsive disorder with schizophrenics. Mujtaba and Mujtaba (1985) studied 20 Wheeler signs of homosexuality of paranoid and non-paranoid schizophrenic patients. Though both groups had the homosexuality signs, the paranoid group had significantly more signs. While the paranoid group had 9.4 signs, the non-paranoid had only 4.15 of the signs listed by Wheeler. However, the presence of homosexuality signs, as suggested by Mujtaba and Mujtaba (1985), may not be considered as the 'sign' to diagnose homosexuality because the findings are based on small sample. Prasadarao et al. (1987) compared obsessive-compulsive disorder and schizophrenia, and signs that differentiated the group were W%; D%; P; F+%; R; anatomy; sex and M: C. Similar findings were reported on homosexual subjects by Chaudhury and Jyothi (1996). Dwivedi et al. (1995) administered the Rorschach test and found that schizophrenics gave a smaller number of total responses (R) and more responses with anatomy and sex content.

Chaudhury and Jyothi (1996), and Chaudhary, John and Rohatgi (1998) administered the Rorschach test on homosexuality and schizophrenia and validated Thiesen's pattern, alfa index and Weiner's signs. Chaudhury and Sundari (1996) administered the Rorschach test to 44 adolescent schizophrenics and an equal number of age and sex matched normal adolescents to analyse Thiesen's patterns. Only three of the five Thiesen's patterns associated with schizophrenia, namely patterns A, C and D occurred significantly more frequently in the Rorschach records of adolescent schizophrenic as compared to the normal controls. Dubey et al. (2012) administered SIS-II in homosexual.

Chaudhary and Jyothi (1997) administered the Rorschach test to 100 schizophrenic patients and 100 neurotic patients. The records of 54 schizophrenics and 41 neurotics fulfilled the two requirements for application of Piotrowski's alpha index. The alpha index correctly classified 46 schizophrenics and 29 neurotics. The alpha index had a sensitivity of 85.2 per cent and a specificity of 70.7 per cent, which compares favourably with other diagnostic tests in clinical medicine. Chaudhary and Jyothi (1998) administered the Rorschach test on three groups of 20 schizophrenics, each with mean length of hospitalization 3.2 years, 3.7 years and 11.2 years, respectively. The Rorschach test was scored following Klopfer's method. The conditions for applying Piotrowski's alpha index was present in 29 schizophrenics out of whom 28 (96.6%) were correctly diagnosed. The alpha index was equally valid for all the three groups of schizophrenics.

Chaudhury et al. (1999) administered the Rorschach test on 50 schizophrenia patients and an equal number of age and sex matched neurosis patients and normal control subjects. Colour stress sign was present in 30 schizophrenia patients, five neurosis patients and five normal controls. Deviant tempo sign was positive in 24 schizophrenia patients, nine neurosis patients and seven normal control subjects. The differences were statistically highly significant. Wiener's signs were found a valid diagnostic aid for the diagnosis of schizophrenia. Among the two signs, the colour stress sign was comparatively more useful as compared to the deviant tempo sign for the diagnosis of schizophrenia. SIS was used to study schizophrenics with positive results (Saldanha et al. 2013; Singh et al. 2011).

Kumar et al. (2001) administered SIS-I to identify the prominent indices among 32 hospitalized male chronic schizophrenics in the IMHH, Agra, and 32 normal participants. The analysis of results indicated that the schizophrenic group scored lower on total number of responses, animal responses, anatomical responses, sex responses, most typical responses and typical responses.

Kumar and Khess (2004) studied Exner's Schizophrenia Index (SCZI) to capture thought disorder and inaccurate perception, thereby aiding the diagnosis of schizophrenia. However, earlier studies had pointed to the need to analyse the sensitivity and specificity of these six special scores of CS in various psychotic conditions to overcome diagnostic problems. The intensity of SCZI for the diagnosis of schizophrenia must be ascertained because the thought disorder and inaccurate perception are also found in other psychotic disorders especially in mania. Taking these lacunae into account, the present study examines the differential sensitivity of the special scores of SCZI in discriminating schizophrenia and mania. Patients with the diagnosis of schizophrenia and mania (n = 30 in each diagnostic group) as per the ICD-10 criteria were assessed on the Rorschach test for the six SCZI indices. The results indicated that deviant responses were highly pathognomic of mania, whereas contamination and incongruous responses were found more in schizophrenic patients. Dwivedi (2015) used the Exner system on psychotic patients.

Kumar (2005) tried to extend the scoring system of SIS-I and developed the extended scoring system (ESS) in four categories: (a) blot area, (b) attributes, (c) response category and (d) most common responses. To assess the discriminatory power of the ESS, three groups of subjects were drawn—schizophrenics (n = 30), manics (n = 30) and normal (n = 30). The patient groups were drawn from IMHH, Agra. SIS-I was individually administered. The analysis of the results through one-way analysis of variance with Scheffe's post-hoc comparisons revealed that the added indices could discriminate the groups.

Kumar, Dubey and Kumar (2006) compared the response pattern of SIS-I and Rorschach in schizophrenic patients. The sample comprised 30 schizophrenic patients drawn from the inpatients of IMHH, Agra, and 30 normal subjects. They were administered SIS-I and the Rorschach test individually. The mean, standard deviation, $t$-test and correlation were calculated on percent scores. The schizophrenic patients obtained significantly low scores on total number of responses, anatomical responses, movement responses and typical responses as compared to normal subjects. The schizophrenics scored significantly higher on human and atypical responses. The findings also revealed significant and positive correlation between SIS-I and Rorschach scores on total number of responses, rejection of images, most typical responses and sex responses.

Singh, Manjhi, Jaiprakash and Singh (2008) studied the pattern of changes in Rorschach indices after treatment in a four-month follow-up study based on pre- and post-test design. Fifty patients (schizophrenia and mania), admitted in RINPAS, Ranchi, in the age range of 21–45 years, were taken for the study. Findings showed that after treatment, information processing capacity (W, D, F) as well as ideational aspects of personality (P, F, M) were significantly improved. Findings also revealed that features related to self-perception and interpersonal relationships are less susceptible to change as compared to affective, cognitive and coping features.

Priyamvada et al. (2009) compared the profiles of schizophrenia and depression on the Rorschach test. The study was carried out on 30 schizophrenic and 30 depressive patients from both sexes, aged between 20 and 55 years. The findings reveal that both the groups (schizophrenia and depression) differ significantly on reaction time, major details, minor details, poor form level, movement response, shading response, vista response, human response and popular response.

Mahapatra (2009) administered SIS-I to explore if it can also effectively gauge ego strength in schizophrenic patients. SIS-I was individually administered to 50 schizophrenic patients drawn from the psychiatry OPD ward of Veer Surendra Sai Medical College, Burla, Sambalpur. A matched control group of 50 normal participants was also drawn from the general population. Consistent with the hypotheses of PTs, following SIS-I indices were identified as measures of ego strength—total number of responses (R), most typical responses (MT), typical responses (T) and atypical responses (AT). The results clearly indicated that like other projective tools, SIS-I indices successfully measure ego strength in schizophrenic patients.

Mahapatra et al. (2010) further administered the Rorschach test to explore if it can effectively gauge the ego strength in schizophrenic patients. The Rorschach test was individually administered to 50 schizophrenic patients drawn from the psychiatry OPD ward of Veer Surendra Sai Medical College, Burla, Sambalpur. A matched control group of 50 normal participants was also drawn from general population. The following indices of the Rorschach Inkblot Test were identified as measures of ego strength: total number of responses (R), whole responses (W), rare detail (Dd), white space (S), good form (F+), human movement (M) and popularity (P). It was found that R, F+, M and P responses were significantly lower, and W, Dd and S responses were significantly higher in the schizophrenic group. These results suggest that Rorschach indices may successfully measure ego strength in schizophrenic patients.

Kandhari et al. (2010b) developed a CSS for SIS-I, based on Beck's scoring system for Rorschach. The CSS indices for SIS-I were compared in manic, depressive and schizophrenic patients. A sample of 90 patients in three groups, mania (n = 30), depression (n = 30) and schizophrenia (n = 30), were drawn from a psychiatric institute. SIS-I was administered individually to each patient and scoring was done according to the CSS. The Kruskal Wallis test revealed significant difference amongst various indices of CSS.

Vishwakarma, Dwivedi and Kumar (2016) explored the associations among emotional intelligence and Rorschach's special indices (Exner, 1974) in patients with schizophrenia. A sample of 30 male patients with different types of schizophrenia in the age range of 18–45 years was taken from the inpatient department of the IMHH, Agra. The results revealed that two components of emotional intelligence (a) ability to utilize emotions and (b) managing emotions in oneself were significantly reflected on the following Exner's indices: (a) suicide constellation, (b) depression index (DEPI) and (c) coping deficits index (CDI).

Kumar et al. (2016) compared the SIS profile of non-chronic and chronic schizophrenia patients. The results indicated that both groups differed significantly on Human (H) and sex indices of SIS-II. The non-chronic schizophrenia patients show psychologically more social isolation tendencies with higher sexual anxiety than chronic schizophrenia patients.

Dey and Singh (2019) reported the effectiveness of 'coping deficit index of comprehensive system' on 45 patients in three groups (15 subjects in each), namely schizophrenia, anxiety and normal controls. Each patient was assessed with socio-demographic data sheet, respective clinical ratings, CS of the Rorschach test and coping checklist (CCL-1). Statistical analysis revealed two CDI variables to be significantly different between psychiatric and normal group, whereas six variables of CDI have shown significant association with self-reported measure of coping.

## Affective Disorder

Pratap and Kapur (1984) studied hospitalized patients with manic disorder and found that the group had increased indices such as total number of responses, responses on Cards VIII, IX and X, reaction time to achromatic cards, average response time, location details and determinants compared to a control group of normal subjects. Content responses and popular responses as well as F+ and F– Form level ratings differed significantly in the two groups.

Kumar, D. (2003) administered SIS-l and Rorschach on a group of 30 male manic patients drawn from the IMHH, Agra. Raw scores on common indices of the tests were converted into percentages. Percent scores of the indices on SIS-I for normal subjects were taken from a previous study (Kumar et al. 2001). The critical ratios were computed on SIS-l scores of manic and normal subjects. The results revealed that anatomy, typical and atypical responses were able to differentiate the groups. Pearson's product moment correlation was calculated on the percent scores of Rorschach and SIS-I on common indices in manic patients. The obtained coefficient of correlations was significant on all the indices except for most typical responses. Both the tests, Rorschach and SIS-I, are in card forms with chromatic and achromatic colours. Both the tests bear more similarities than the booklet form of SIS-II, which is in single colour and designed for self-administration. This may imply that SIS-I has a potential for use as a parallel form of the Rorschach test. Index-based present study explored the correlations in one diagnostic entity only. Similar studies are required on normal and other clinical population to delineate a pattern of correlation between the tests.

Kumar et al. (2004) further used SIS-I to study 30 schizophrenics, 30 manic and a matched 30 normal subjects. One-way ANOVA was computed with post hoc comparisons. However, no difference was found in the total number of responses in manic and control groups. Human responses are significantly higher in schizophrenics. The animal responses failed to differentiate the groups. Comparison of anatomical responses across the groups revealed that schizophrenics have given significantly lower anatomy content than the manic and control groups. The manic group did not differ from control group on anatomical responses. Similarly, movement responses were less in schizophrenic group than in the other two groups. No difference was found on movement responses in manic and control groups. Most typical indices were able to differentiate manic and schizophrenic groups. The typical responses turned to be powerful indicators and could differentiate all the three groups. The rejection of images was also turned to be a discriminator in schizophrenia and mania. The results indicated statistically significant differences across the groups.

Kumar et al. (2005) tried to find the Rorschach and SIS-I diagnostic indicators of manic and depressive disorders and the diagnostic compatibility of the two tests. Two clinical groups, manic (n = 50) and depressive (n = 50), along with a normal control group (n = 50), were administered Rorschach and SIS-I individually. The individual protocols on these tests were scored on several common indices and between-group comparisons were done using the *t*-test. Findings revealed that the SIS-I provided important diagnostic information not only for differentiating clinical cases from normal healthy subjects but also for differentiating manic patients from depressives. It was also observed that the diagnostic efficacy of the SIS-I was comparable to that of the Rorschach test. Kumar et al. (2006) further used SIS-I on 50 manic patients (25 males and 25 females) and 50 normal subjects (25 males and 25 females). The manic male patients scored significantly higher number of animal responses and lower number of most typical responses than female manic patient. Except slightly higher rejection of images by normal female subjects, no significant gender differences were noticed in normal group. SIS was found to be an effective diagnostic instrument in suicidal patients (Singh and Rani 2014a, 2014b) and therapeutic procedure in depressive patients (Tiwari et al. 2012).

Kumar and Khess (2005) used Exner's method to study SCZI and Perceptual-Thinking Index (PTI) in differentiating schizophrenia from mania. Thirty actively psychotic patients from each group fulfilling the ICD-10 diagnostic criteria were included in the study. The results revealed significant correlation between the indices (r = 0.97; P = 0.01; d = 7.99). SCZI revealed a hit rate of 73 per cent and 83 per cent with cut-off 4 and 5, respectively. And PTI showed a hit rate of 83 per cent with cut-off 4. Overall performance of the indices and the individual criteria indicate that the PTI is marginally better than SCZI in differentiating schizophrenia from mania.

Kumar et al. (2006) studied the pattern of responses on SIS-I in manic male and female patients. The sample comprised 50 manic patients (25 males and 25 females) and 50 normal subjects (25 males and 25 females). The SIS-I Card form was administered individually. The manic male patients scored significantly higher number of animal responses and lower number of most typical responses than female manic patients. Except slightly higher rejection of images by normal female subjects, no significant gender differences were noticed in normal population. George and Kumar (2008) used the CS of the Rorschach test (Exner 1974) to identify DEPI. Thirty patients (n = 30) with the diagnosis of recurrent depression as per the ICD-10 criteria and 30 normal healthy controls from the general population were assessed on Rorschach. The results indicate that patients with depression scored more on DEPI with high specificity and low sensitivity. Kandhari et al. (2012) used SIS-I on manic patients.

Kumari et al. (2009) compared the responses of schizophrenia and bipolar affective disorders (BAD) currently manic patients on SIS-II. The sample consisted of 30 schizophrenic and 30 BAD currently manic inpatients from the RINPAS, Ranchi, India. Fifteen males and 15 females were included in each group. The results reveal that schizophrenic and BAD manic patients obtained significantly different scores on total number of responses, human responses, sex responses, movement responses, typical responses, atypical responses and rejection of images.

Mishra et al. (2010) used Rorschach following Exner's method to find the response pattern of manic patients. The main objective of this study was to develop a profile of mania patients on Rorschach variables. One hundred and twenty BAD patients having psychotic features, ranging from 18 to 55 years in age, diagnosed as per ICD-10, and 50 randomly selected normal subjects from the general population, matched with respect to age and sex with manic group, were included. The findings of the study indicate that manic patients differ significantly from the normal control on several Rorschach variables.

### Anxiety Disorder (Neuroses)

Kaur and Kapur (1983) administered the Rorschach test, following Klopfer's method, to normal people and to patients with conversion and dissociative disorder. Patients with 'dissociative disorder' gave fewer responses, more reaction time and gave more d (small details) and less S (space) responses. The percentages of Fc, FC', C'F and FC were low compared to the normal group. The content analysis showed that the patients' group gave more responses with mythological human responses, animals, nature, clouds, sex and unusual responses than the normal group.

Gupta (1977) used the Rorschach ranking conformity test and found no correlation between normal subjects and a group of patients with neurotic disorder. However, the study had a small sample size of 25 in each group. Probably, Malaviya's (1973) research is the only contribution towards understanding the signs of suicide on the Rorschach test. Akhtar et al. (1975) administered the Rorschach test using Klopfer's method to 50 patients of obsessive neurosis and found that they were high on movement, animal and human responses, often selection of unusual areas, with lower number of colours, shading and anatomical response.

Mishra and Gupta (2008) administered the Rorschach test to 71 neurotic cases taken from a private psychiatric hospital in Lucknow. They gave low R (between 11 and 20), more F and low number of C, M and shading responses. Gender has no bearing on the Rorschach psychogram.

Dubey and Dwivedi (2015) administered SIS-II to an 18-year-old girl, diagnosed as a case of dissociative convulsion disorder, studying in 12th class. She had complaints of fits (fainting attacks), headache and nausea. The SIS responses projected her poor interpersonal relationship, pent-up aggression and abusive childhood. The SIS imagery was used as a therapeutic intervention tool with positive results and relief from symptoms. Gupta, Singh and Singh (2015) administered SIS-II with encouraging results in treating a female patient who had attempted suicide. The SIS images helped in therapeutic intervention.

Cassell and Dubey (2016) illustrated by using the SIS-II test, the psychological defence system of a 100-year-old woman who at the assessment was 'happy and healthy', 'never thinking about her own death'. People worldwide face their ultimate mortality with a wide range of culturally/emotionally coloured reactions. Yet, ultimately as one ages, death dysphoria tends to surface in daytime conscious awareness as well as sometimes directly or symbolically in affect-charged dreams directly. Cassell (2016) further emphasized the fear of death in older people.

Cassell and Dubey (2018) administered the Rorschach test in three case histories involving individuals suffering from existential death anxiety to illustrate that the responses indicated symbolic death content and death anxiety. The overemphasis on somatic content (many 'anatomical' responses) on inkblot tests might reflect the presence of unconscious anxiety and the anticipated decay of one's physical body and may be the plausible symbolic interpretation and indicator of death anxiety. This is not possible if the responses are interpreted using quantitative analysis.

## Organic Disorder

D'Netto and Kishore (1976) administered the Bender Gestalt Test, Raven's Progressive Matrices, Draw-a-Person Test, memory scale and Rorschach Inkblot Test to 40 brain injury cases. All these tests detected abnormalities from 65 per cent to 75 per cent.

Vagrecha and Majumdar (1974) administered Rorschach and Alexander's Pass along Tests and tried to find the difference in IQ and Piotrowski signs in epileptic patients as compared to normal subjects. The findings revealed significant reduction in the IQ of the epileptics but no such differences were found on Rorschach signs. The study found the use of five or more signs on the Rorschach test to be of lesser relevance for organic group than the Piotrowski's findings.

Mishra et al. (2010) administered SIS-II to 50 epileptic patients attending OPD and community outreach programme of RINPAS, Ranchi, India, and 50 normal participants. The results reveal significant differences between the two groups on most of the SIS indices. Most typical response, depression and rejection of images were found to be most discriminating diagnostic indicators.

## Psychosomatic Disorder

Devi and Kaliappan (1997) administered SIS-II to find out improvement in the inner life of 19 tension headache subjects from the banking industry. Multimode behaviour therapy was applied for treating the tension headache subjects. Findings showed a significant reduction in the atypical responses and an increase in the typical and most typical responses among the tension headache subjects. Sharma et al. (1997) used SIS-II to find out psychological profile of 22 patients suffering from alopecia areata (AA). Psychological disturbances were found in 55 per cent of cases.

Nicolini (2000) used SIS-I to examine corporal perception in subjects with migraine, under treatment in an outpatient center for psychosomatic medicine. The SIS-I test is known to be a suitable test for assessing somatic perceptions and mental processes that form the base of the psychosomatic disorder. A control group of 16 subjects and two groups of subjects with psychosomatic pathology, matched in respect of age, number of subjects (16), level of education and professional activity, were taken for study. The SIS-I test helped in getting important information required for establishing the psychopathology of the patients and the relation existing between each subject under treatment in the center and his own body, thus proving to be of useful diagnostic help.

Chaudhury et al. (2001) studied 50 patients consecutively with AA, and an equal number of age and sex matched control subjects without any physical or psychiatric disorders were evaluated with psychiatric interview and mental status examination, Sinha Anxiety Scale, Carroll Rating Scale for Depression, Toronto Alexithymia Scale, the Presumptive Stressful Life Events Scale and the SIS-II. Analysis revealed that patients with AA were significantly more anxious and depressed, obtained significantly higher alexithymia scores and reported significantly more stressful life events as compared to controls. The SIS-II test revealed psychological disturbances in 52 per cent patients.

Kumar (2010) administered SIS-I to a 28-year-old engineering graduate woman severely depressed and with multiple somatic symptoms. It is evident that many of her SIS responses reflected the severe extent of her depression. SIS responses also projected her poor relationship with her mother-in-law. The therapeutic intervention had begun to restore her self-image as a competent mother to care for her child. Mishra, Jahan and Singh (2010a) used SIS-II to study a 12-year-old girl, studying in seventh grade, with complaints of nervousness, headache and low mood, stiffness in upper limbs and body and fits of occasional unconsciousness. She was diagnosed as a case of 'dissociative convulsion disorder' as per ICD-10. The SIS responses projected her poor interpersonal relationship, pent-up aggression, physical abuse and disturbed family functioning. The SIS imagery projected traumatic feelings, which formed the basis for an effective therapeutic intervention. SIS has been tried by many researchers to treat dissociative disorder patients (Dewangan, Basu and Roy 2014; Manickam, Ghanbary and Kruthi 2013; Pandey, Tiwari and Mishra 2011; Sachacher and Jahan 2014; Sengupta, Mishra and Dwivedi 2012).

## Mental Retardation

The Rorschach test was administered to mentally retarded adults with high and low intelligence (IQ above and below 40) (Ojha 1975; Upadhyaya and Sinha 1974). The lower IQ group showed more descriptive themes, poor verbal productivity, less interaction, perceived environment as more threatening, gave less shading and colour responses, had lower mean range of content and less popular responses on Rorschach. Ojha (1975) administered Godard Form Board, Draw-a-Person Test, Shukla's Test of Intelligence, Bender Gestalt Test, CAT and Rorschach to 25 delinquent children in the age range of 5–14 years. The results showed that the delinquents had short span of attention, poor comprehensive ability with low motor, speech and language development.

Vashistha and Bhardwaj (2007) prepared personality profiles of mentally challenged and severely hearing-impaired children through the Rorschach Inkblot Test. It was also assumed that they do have somewhat similar pattern due to their sensory-motor impairments directly influencing their cognition and learning abilities. The findings revealed that mentally challenged children have extroversive personality, whereas severely hearing-impaired children have introversive personality.

Alreja et al. (2009) administered SIS-II to 30 mentally retarded children attending the OPD of RINPAS, Ranchi, and 30 normal children. The results revealed a significant difference in total number of responses, human responses, animal responses, anatomical responses, movement responses, most typical responses, typical responses, atypical responses, rejection of images, depression scale and pathological anatomy scale.

Singh and Mukhopadhyay (2018) reported the literature indicating that psychopathology of parents of ADHD is a crucial component of failure in the management of ADHD-affected children. They studied 20 children with ADHD symptoms (5–12years) from clinical centres, Lucknow, India. The children were rated by their parents based on ADHD symptoms. The SIS-I test was administered to these parents and the result indicated high animal and anatomical response indicating lack of socialization, frustration and preoccupation with inner body parts, thereby projecting somatic anxiety. Higher percentage of typical responses and human responses denotes a balance between the personality and family pathology of the parents of ADHD children.

## Alcohol, Drugs and Substance Abuse

The Rorschach test could differentiate alcoholics from non-alcoholics. Arora (1982) observed that on six categories, namely, +C > 3, M < C, water responses, fabulized responses > 1, F% < 65% and W% < 20, differentiated alcoholics from non-alcoholics. Similarly, Banerjee et al. (1998) examined seven indices of the test—human, animal (A), anatomical, atypical, popular (P), rejection (R) and sex (S)—and the responses of the heroin addicts using Klopfer's method. Out of these four indices, namely A, P, R and S significantly discriminated heroin addicts from the control group. Verma and Misra (2002) studied Rorschach's response patterns of drug addicts. Giovanna Gaetani et al. (1995) studied corporal perception in HIV positive and negative heroin addicts using SIS-I and found a positive correlation. Mukhopadhyay, Banerjee and Mitra (1996) used SIS-I in preparing a comprehensive profile of personality characteristics of male drug addicts.

Mitra and Mukhopadhyay (1996) administered SIS-I to 40 adult male opiate drug addicts (heroin [n = 19], brown sugar [n = 12], tidigesic [n = 9]). The social anxiety level of the clinical samples was measured in terms of social avoidance and distress (SAD) and fear of negative evaluation (FNE). SIS-I measured the pathological personality components of the drug addicts. Rest of the qualitative components analysed the significance of the result obtained by objective measure. The results revealed that the three groups significantly differ in SAD (p < 0.01) and FNE (p < 0.05) of the social anxiety scale. The tidigesic group reported higher score in social anxiety and distress and lower score in FNE and SAD. SIS pathological indices do not differentiate the groups. Qualitative components also report a predominance of specified components such as anatomical responses (At), atypical responses (AT) and human responses (HR). This suggests uniformity in the personality components among opiate addicts, which may be termed as drug dependency traits.

Singh and Banerjee (1996) administered SIS-II on 38 obsessive-compulsive disorder patients to study the response patterns on chosen variables. The results suggested that SIS-II could be a useful psychodiagnostic tool in clinical set-up. Singh and Dubey (1997) administered SIS-II to 50 drug-dependent and 50 alcohol-dependent individuals. The SIS protocols were compared on R, MT, H, A, At, sex and rejection. Drug-dependents scored low on R and MT responses. SIS-II can be used as a powerful psychodiagnostic tool for discriminating drug and alcohol dependent groups from normal subjects.

Banerjee et al. (1998) administered SIS-I and the Rorschach Inkblot Test to 15 heroin addicts and 15 matched normal subjects. Four indices each proved to be a successful discrimination index between heroin addicts and normal subjects. Ambiguity in Rorschach image reported higher number of responses in MT, AT, rejection, animal and sex indices. Verma and Misra (2002) administered the Rorschach test on drug addicts and found that the drug addicts were anxious, had poor control over emotional situations and had lack of contact with reality.

Mitra and Mukhopadhyay (2000) administered SIS-I and compared three drug abuser groups, namely heroin (n = 98), brown sugar (n = 79) and tidigesic (n = 70) and matched normal subjects (n = 48) in terms of level of depression, social anxiety and social motive components as well as the differences in pathological contents and indices of personality. The follow-up groups, that is, rehabilitated (n = 6) and relapsed (n = 35) were also assessed to find support for the outcome. BDI, SIS-I, social evaluative anxiety scale (SAD and FNE) and AMS were used to explore the socio-psychological differences among the groups. Besides, the investigation also took into account the follow-up data and compared the results with their original data of the same subjects. F-ratio used for the inference of the results obtained through questionnaires on t applied to compare the percentage of the pathological contents and SIS indices. Mann–Whitney U-test explored the authenticity of acceptance and rejection of null hypotheses and subsequently the directional hypothesis. The level of depression and social anxiety (SAD and FNE) were reported to be significantly high among drug addicts and the follow-up relapsed group with low social approval motive when compared with the normal and the follow-up rehabs groups. A pathological component, that is, high PAS, depression (D) and paranoia (P), low HAS along with atypical, anatomy, sex and human responses were able to discriminate the clinical groups.

Basu and Nandy (2004) compared 30 male ganja (cannabis) dependent persons, 30 tobacco dependent persons and 30 non-smoking adults from Kolkata. They were individually administered the General Health Questionnaire-28 and SIS-I. The results indicated that the non-smokers had the least general mental distress as well as the highest scores on the positive indices of SIS-I. Among the negative indices, however, the non-smoking group also scored high in animal, anatomy and sex responses. They scored the lowest in two negative indices of mental health, namely atypical responses and rejection of images. The ganja and tobacco smokers shared some of the somatization responses. However, the tobacco smoking group could utilize the social resources than the ganja smokers.

The results have been explained in terms of the intrinsic nature of the two drugs, as well as with reference to the legal and social acceptability status of ganja and tobacco as agents of dependence.

Ranjan et al. (2008) tried to assess the profile of alcohol dependents. Thirty (n = 30) male alcohol dependent inpatients from RINPAS, Ranchi, and 30 normal subjects were administered SIS-II. The result revealed significant differences in atypical, most typical, typical, sex, anatomy, depression and movement responses of the alcohol dependents and normal subjects. The alcoholic group gave significantly higher anatomy (At), sex and atypical responses (AT), and significantly low on most typical responses (MT) and typical responses (T). Overall, the SIS-II profile of alcohol dependent patients indicates that they have somatic preoccupation, anxiety regarding sexual dysfunction and low ability to keep up with the demands of the society.

Chaudhury et al. (2010) studied 100 male patients with alcohol dependence and an equal number of age, sex, occupation and regional background matched controls with the help of State–Trait Anxiety Inventory, Carroll Rating Scale for Depression, The Multiphasic Questionnaire, Maudsley Personality Inventory, Toronto Alexithymia Scale, AFMC Life Events Scale, Self-esteem Inventory and the SIS-II. The analysis of the results showed that alcoholics obtained higher scores on state and trait anxiety, depression, mania scale, paranoia scale, schizophrenia scale, psychopathic deviance, neuroticism, extroversion and AFMC Life Events Scale. Alcohol dependent individuals had a significantly lower self-esteem as compared to control subjects and in comparison with the normal controls, significantly more alcoholics were identified as alexithymic. The SIS profile of the alcohol dependent patients indicated that they vary on human responses, animal responses, anatomy responses, sex responses, most typical responses, typical responses, atypical responses and depression from the normal population.

Cassell and Dubey (2010b) administered the Somatic Inkblots Video to a person who has been abusing alcohol and other drugs for the last 25 years. The SIS images helped in planning therapeutic intervention leading to a positive attitude towards life. This individual shared the emotional pain he had felt during those years and which had impaired his occupational functioning on his job. To facilitate such treatment, Wilfred Cassell designed an advanced electronic series as an adjunct to therapy. This updated system, like the SIS, initially induces hypnotic conditions to facilitate the release of stressful memories. Then the viewer visualizes ambiguous pictures of stressful scenes which predispose to mind altering substance abuse. This artificial intelligence procedure was created solely as an adjunct technique for use by licensed addiction counsellors during individual and group psychotherapy. It does not require the sophisticated training or understanding of statistical normative data expected of a psychologist formally trained in psychometrics.

Bala, Mishra and Jahan (2010) used SIS in case of a 20-year-old male, educated up to 9th standard, using alcohol, ganja, brown sugar (smack), cigarette and tobacco for last five years. According to ICD-10, he was diagnosed as a case of mental and behavioural disorder. On psychological evaluation it was found that he was guarded and nothing could be elicited except inadequate parenting and family problems. However, on SIS images he could not conceal his personality and antisocial traits. The diagnostic/treatment applications of this projective interview aid are the main objective of the presentation of this case history.

## Sexual Disorder

Probably Kapur and Kapur (1967) pioneered the evaluation of the profile of patients with sexual disorder. Mukherjee and Raychaudhuri (1970) explored the Wheeler and Shafer signs of homosexuality in male prisoners on the Rorschach test. Though Rorschach has diagnostic indicators of sexual dysfunction, Dubey (1977b) later used the tool to assess the signs and evaluated its usefulness in treating cases with impotence. Basu and De (1997) used the Rorschach test on transsexuals and found rejection of the male body, glorification of the female features and difficulty in adequate human relationship.

As indicated in this book's foreword by Wayne Holtzman, the HIT is well suited for the projective assessment of an individual's evolving sexuality. Unlike the Rorschach test, it presents a great number of ambiguous inkblots. These obviously provide the test administrator a much wider range of sexually suggestive stimuli. In fact, in his book, the clinical case which was selected for illustration purposes involved a male college student in psychotherapy whose projective responses did not lead to a clear-cut formal psychiatric diagnosis. Rather, the extreme number of sexual responses apparently reflected a previously unrecognized sexual role confusion, which eventually over time demonstrated a surfacing homosexual preference. Sometimes imagery projected onto inkblot stimuli like the HIT can tap into the same stream of sexual images flowing in dreams which shape sexual orientation.

The test–retest capabilities with a second series of 45 cards are a further methodological plus for choosing Holtzman's instrument for possible sexual issues unreported in face-to-face interviews. It might be noted that the pulling power of both the Rorschach test and HIT may be enhanced by pre-test establishment of artificial intelligence relaxation through initial electronic administration of the SIS hypnotic introduction programme.

Normally, the HIT administrator is not subjected to the same degree of criticism, being accused of administering 'pornographic material disguised as scientific technique'. This erroneous criticism is a potential professional role hazard to SIS professionals, especially by bigoted publically celibate but privately sexually active religiously repressive authorities. On the other hand, those who confine their testing to the more ambiguous blots can never really detect somatic repression as an important pathological defence mechanism in the conversion disorders. Also, HIT does not so readily lend itself to behavioural therapy treatment programmes involving gradually increasing exposure to conditioning like higher affect intensities of SIS-activated sexual imagery.

Because the SIS has a degree of non-pornographic sexual structure, the procedure facilitates sexual studies. Sahay and Srivastava (1994) used SIS to study male transsexuals. Dwivedi et al. (1998) used SIS-Video to a 22-year-old young, unmarried, graduate lady, who had reported history of sexual abuse. The SIS responses revealed her traumatic experiences. Her hatred and aggression along with the feeling of helplessness and craving for protection were brought out. The SIS procedure worked as a time machine and took her back in time, helping in processing the so far unprocessed painful material. After therapeutic intervention, she reflected a lot of positive changes in her total outlook. SIS was also found to be a successful therapeutic tool in treating a homosexual case (Dubey et al. 2012).

Pandey et al. (2003) reported the diagnostic utility of sex responses with extended quantitative scoring criteria. Three groups of psychiatric patients, namely anxiety neurosis, paranoid schizophrenics and undifferentiated schizophrenics (n = 25 in each group) and a group of age matched normal control (n = 25) were individually tested on SIS-II. The obtained protocols were scored for (a) sex responses on sex images, (b) sex responses on non-sex images and (c) non-sex responses on sex images. The analysis revealed that partitioning of sex responses on sex and non-sex images provided diagnostically more rich information as compared to the conventional scoring of total sex responses on all the 62 SIS-II images. Sex responses on non-sex images was found to be diagnostically redundant component and responsible for lowering the diagnostic efficacy of total sex responses.

Dubey et al. (2004) used SIS-II booklet form to assess 30 cases of psycho sexual disorder (PSD). SIS images proved to have the 'pulling power' to bring out the inner cry of the suffering patients, which they were not interested in sharing with others. The PSD subjects showed normal productivity, keeping contact with reality, preoccupation with sexual imagery and more concern with body imagery. Psychotherapy along with sex education and medical intervention helped the patients to lead normal lives again.

Sharma (2018) administered the Rorschach test to four victims of childhood sexual abuse to find out the associations, flashbacks and memories related to the trauma of the sexual abuse. The findings indicated their difficulties from psychological abhorrence or fear of intimacy associated with sexual activity to physiological symptomatology such as veganism and orgasmic disorders.

Dwivedi and Verma (2018) administered SIS-II and cognitive behavioural therapy (CBT) in the treatment of gender identity disorder of an 18-year-old male presented with a complaint of feeling of discomfort with his sex organ for several years. The somatic inkblot images helped to understand the underlying psychopathology and conflict of his gender dystopia, and 12 sessions of CBT along with pharmacological treatment and follow-ups indicated substantial change and improvement in his condition.

### Prison Population

As early as 1956, Shanker (1956) appraised the profile of juvenile delinquents. Raychaudhuri and Maitra (1965b) compared normal convicted and incipient delinquent adolescents. Mukherjee (1965, 1966, 1968) conducted a series of studies on different groups of prison population. Majumdar and Mukherjee (1969) examined some of the ratios of the Rorschach test profile of the prisoners who were convicted and U.D. Sharma (1969) compared the colour pyramid and the responses on the Rorschach test of recidivists. Sethi et al. (1971) appraised the psychopathology of murderers using the test.

Yadav (1977) observed that the Rorschach protocol of criminals convicted for rape, robbery and murder showed low productivity (low R), low intellectual efficacy, rejected more cards, showed casual interest to test situation and gave a few movement, W and P responses.

Rangaswami (1982) studied the hostility measure of the test on three groups of prison population and found that the hostility measure on Rorschach was positively correlated to the hostility measure of the Hospital Hostility Questionnaire. The test could differentiate the three groups of convicts who were diagnosed to be schizophrenics, non-convicts who were schizophrenics and the control group that consisted of persons with no psychiatric disorder.

Singh, Manjhi, Dubey and Banerjee (2001) administered the SIS-II test to 30 professional murderers and the result was compared with normal subjects. The findings suggest that the SIS-II is a powerful psychological test to discriminate murderers from normal population.

### Physical Illness

Though the test was used with people with different physical illness in the initial period, it was not used later with the physically or psychosomatically ill population for research. This could be because the clinicians who worked in the medical or general hospital settings were less in number. Even the low number of professionals who worked in medical set-ups might have other professional functions as their priority that dissuaded them from exploring the worth of the test. Moreover, psychological intervention for patients with different physical illnesses are not given due importance in the medical setting by other specialists. Therefore, there might have been less referrals to psychologists for an evaluation that led to the less output in research with the test from medical settings. Ardhapurkar, Mehta and de Souza (1967) evaluated the profile of patients with ischemic heart disease. Ardhapurkar et al. (1974) in another study appraised the Rorschach test responses of patients with bronchial asthma, and Dutta, Jha and Shukla (1976) investigated patients with peptic ulcer. Pandey (1995) used SIS to study alexithymia and found it an excellent projective measure.

Nehra et al. (1997) administered SIS-II to find out the personality and the inner cry of the patients suffering from speech defects. Eighteen cases with speech problem, in the age range of 15–64 years with the mean age of 27.44 years were administered SIS-II individually. The results showed greater number of R, low rejection of images, disturbed interpersonal relations with somatic preoccupation (higher anatomical but lower sex responses with moderate human and most typical responses). The subjects that rejected more images were also found to give low number of responses and most typical responses.

Cinzia and Ferro (1998) used SIS-I card form and cognitive behavioural assessment on 30 hospitalized female obese patients in the age group of 20–59 years. The results suggest that (a) subjects with high scores of psycho-physiological activation, depression and anxiety gave greater number of anatomical content and typical responses, (b) higher scores on neuroticism and psychoticism were associated with lower number of dehumanized contents, (c) anxiety and fear contents responses were associated with sexual content and (d) lie scores were associated with lower pathological emotional content. Verma, Kaur and Bhargava (2000) studied body distortion reflected through the perception on PTs such as inkblot test and human figure drawings.

Khromov (2001) compared aggressiveness (Buss and Durkee 1957), emotional state (SUPOS-8, Miksic) and projective body images (SIS-I, Cassell, 1980b) on 19 subjects with achondroplasia, 18 with traumatically shortened extremities and 95 healthy subjects in the age range of 17–20 years. The data was analysed both contextually and statistically. The most valuable information was discovered from the projected responses of the SIS-I technique, which represents the ego–body image. No other technique was able to get this. The subjects with achondroplasia gave fewer movement responses. Some responses were replaced by an image that suggested, 'I'm small' (i.e., pussy cat). The correlation of such images was 17–6–3 for each group of 10 subjects. The body image for such subjects was evident only at the subconscious level, which allowed them to maintain a good self-esteem. The main psychological features of dwarves were superseding somatic images, inadequacy and infantilism, increased sensitivity and an attachment to other people. Subjects with an acquired orthopaedic defect had clear images of the deformed body at the conscious level, causing frustration, a high level of physical and verbal aggression, negativism and an extra-punitive reaction.

Nicolini (2002) studied corporeal perception in 41 obese female subjects under diet therapy. A possible organic cause of the weight increase had been excluded. The projective SIS-I and EDI-2 tests had been administered to have a psychodiagnostic evaluation. The main objective of the presentation was to compare the results of the two tests and carry out a thorough qualitative and quantitative analysis of the SIS-I protocols. At the end, a case of 37-year-old female subject using SIS-I and EDI-2 is discussed for the better understanding of the tests. It may be concluded that the dissatisfaction of the obese subjects for their own body can be seen both by EDI-2 and the qualitative and quantitative analyses of the responses of the SIS-I test. As a matter of fact, obese women in the present study find difficulties to integrate parts of their own body and, particularly, to assimilate female traits in a gestalt form. It may be further brought out that obese women perceive a disharmony between the experience of their real body and their ideal body. The low level of impulsiveness that is noticed on EDI-2 is supported by low affective interpersonal relationship indicated on the SIS-I test and in the clinical interview. The subject in question indicates her body anxiety, aggressive attitude, sexual conflict and disturbed interpersonal relationships. It further validates the efficacy of SIS and its pulling power to bring out on the surface deep-rooted problems that need therapeutic intervention.

Cassell and Dubey (2004) studied three subjects using SIS Card form. The first case explored the notion that when the cardiovascular system is activated by exercise or emotional stress, the resultant sensory feedback lowers the perceptual threshold for visualizing SIS cardiac content. The second case introduced the potentially new diagnostic category 'body phobia' and illustrated how during deep relaxation, SIS stimulated imagery can provide an effective cognitive behavioural treatment aid. The third case examined the relationship of body consciousness and heart rate in recently hospitalized patients who experience schizophrenic disorder. It reveals how psychotic patients experiencing high sensory feedback from tachycardia can become unduly conscious of the heart and develop related somatic delusions.

Cassell and Dubey (2004a) emphasized that a SIS consultant can provide rapid and comprehensive diagnostic/therapeutic consultation to clinicians in various parts of the world. Relatively immediate consultative aid is readily available through modern electronic communication technology (e.g., FAX, e-mail, etc.). This chapter outlines certain underlying neural mechanisms underlying inkblot projection in SIS consultation. For illustration purposes, it assesses the SIS-II Booklet responses of a 47-year-old man in treatment at the Clinic for Psychosomatic Medicine and Psychotherapy, University Hospital, Ulm University, Germany. The projective assessment was done 'blind', with no direct access to the overall clinical records. When done in this manner, the interpretations and management recommendations are essentially unbiased. This gives a measure of additional validity to the SIS consultant's 'second opinion'. The man was free of cardiac illness yet was unduly concerned about his heart. In completing the brief health questionnaire on the last page of the Booklet, he indicated that his main concern was 'heart trouble and pain'. Regarding the enquiry about mental problems in the questionnaire, he noted 'depression and thoughts of suicide'.

Lal (2004) used SIS-II to explore the differences in personality characteristics of a group of 25 physically disabled and 25 normal adolescents drawn from a rehabilitation centre for disabled at Jaunpur. The analysis of the data revealed that disabled adolescents have poor interpersonal relationships, they feel socially isolated, psychologically immature, have poor self-image and poor ego strength, depict thought blockage and inability to think properly. The responses given by the disabled on pathological scale reveal excessive concern about physical health, depressed emotional state, more hostility and aggression. They also experience exaggerated sense of self-consciousness in social situations.

Chaudhury et al. (2009) administered SIS-II to evaluate psychological distress and psychiatric morbidity in patients with fractures in upper and lower limb. The study included 100 consecutive patients with fracture of the lower and upper limbs each and an equal number of age and sex matched normal subjects. The analysis of the SIS-II profiles indicates that patients with limb fracture and normal controls did not differ significantly on R. The groups were also found to be similar on animal responses, anatomical responses and movement responses. However, significant differences were found on H responses. Sex responses and atypical responses were more among the patients than among the normal subjects.

## Army Population

Dubey (1982) administered the Rorschach test to 200 psychiatric patients admitted in a military hospital and 100 normal subjects, all male, in the age range of 20–40 years. A number for scoring indices of Rorschach protocol is said to be dependent on the number of responses given by the subjects. Therefore, a procedure for controlling the protocol for the productivity was warranted. Accordingly, all 300 protocols were divided based on their number of responses into two groups, taking the combined median as the cut-off point. The above median group was called 'high productivity group (HPG)' and below median group was known as 'low productivity group (LPG)'. Each of these groups was separately analysed by the chi-square test for each of the Rorschach indices. The mean values for the profiles of normal, schizophrenia and neurosis were calculated for various indices separately for HPG and LPG groups to facilitate comparison with other studies. Rathee and Singh (1996) administered SIS-I to 75 normal army subjects (35 males and 40 females) and found that female subjects gave a greater number of responses and male subjects rejected more cards. Female subjects gave more of animal responses and male subjects gave more sexual responses.

Rathee et al. (2002) further assessed diagnostic value of SIS-II among subgroups of psychotic and neurotic patients. SIS-II was administered on each patient individually, following the standard procedures (Cassell and Dubey 1997). The findings reveal that total number of responses, atypical and pathological responses were able to discriminate among subgroups of psychotics. Likewise, R, MT, atypical, movement, rejection of images, human, animal and sex responses were able to discriminate among subgroups of neurotics. The test comments of both groups of psychotics and neurotics proved to be more useful to understand their underlying psychopathology. The patients with less disturbances liked the test and felt comfortable while reacting upon its images as compared to patients with more disturbances. The SIS profile can provide a lot of help in diagnosis of various categories of psychosis and neurosis.

Saldanha (2002) studied 31 militants through SIS (Cassell 1980, 1984) and personalized interviews and divided them into hard core (67.74%), moderate core (22.58%) and soft core (19.68%) types. They were drawn from eight recognized militant groups operating in the valley. Of these, 74.19 per cent were below 30 years. Hostile and aggressive responses on the SIS test were shown by 61.29 per cent. Concordance rates between psychological (SIS) and intelligence reports were as high as 77.77 per cent. Psychological stress was revealed only in 3.22 per cent, and 67.74 per cent were unlikely to benefit from rehabilitative measures. The usefulness of SIS in understanding militant psychology is discussed.

Roopa and Joseph (2004) used the Rorschach Inkblot Test as a part of the routine psychological evaluation for the aircrew. This test supplements information gained from objective questionnaires. Previous studies in other countries have shown that subgroups of aircrew can be differentiated based on the Rorschach indices. Sixty-one aircrew were studied in three groups: non-clinical, medical and psychiatry. All underwent a clinical interview and were administered the Rorschach test individually with no testing of limits by one of two trained psychologists. Responses were scored following Rapaport's (1970) method in terms of location, determinants and content. 'T-test' was used, and the results indicated significant differences between the groups in content responses and non-significant differences in location and determinant indices.

Cassell and Dubey (2010a) administered the SIS-II Video to a US veteran from Vietnam who was suffering from PTSD and the SIS images helped him in reprocessing the combat-related long-term traumatic material. Cassell and Dubey (2017) reported another case study involving a technician (welder) who worked on the North Slope in Alaska on the oil field. He was in a tank to repair it. He lit the torch, and there was an explosion. He had been in treatment for a few weeks for the major trauma he had just over a year ago. The SIS Card version and Video version was administered to him and the inkblots images brought on the surface unprocessed painful material. The SIS images helped as a therapeutic aid and he showed fast improvement.

## Therapeutic Intervention and Dreams

There are not many studies that investigated the therapeutic usefulness of the Rorschach test, though clinicians tend to make use of symbolic content analysis in psychotherapy. Consistent with this approach, the SIS has been extensively used as an aid to psychotherapy with encouraging results. Rating the projected responses on an anxiety threat hierarchy has been found to facilitate an early detection of the clinically most relevant stressors. In addition, exploring the symbolism permits a therapeutic processing of the deep-seated distorted dream for cognitive correction and reality testing (Cassell 1994, 1995, 1996, 1997, 1998a, 2001, 2002; Cassell and Dubey 1996a, 1997, 1998a, 2000, 2003, 2004, 2006, 2007a, 2012, 2016, 2017, 2018; Dosajh 1995, 1996, 1997, 1998, 1999a, 1999b, 1999c; Dosajh and Dosajh 1999). Cassell reported in many instances that those so helped spontaneously responded, 'I guess you have made this test particularly for me' (Cassell 2004, 2005, 2006, 2007, 2008, 2009, 2010a). Other therapists have observed similar promising results (Dubey 1977, 1983, 1986, 1992, 1993, 1996, 1997, 2000; Kumar 2010). It has been observed in grief work that the procedure opens for an expression of the individual's previously inhibited 'inner cry' (Cassell et al. 1996, 1998, 2001, 2003, 2013a; Cassell, Dubey and Roth 1997).

At this stage, the plan is to investigate with controlled statistical based studies. Reviewing the studies conducted on different groups, it appeared that some of the research was conducted due to an easy accessibility of the sample rather than answering or exploring a pertinent research question. However, the SIS and Rorschach tests continue to be used as a tool for personality assessment and for the diagnosis of different types of mental disorders (Verma and Misra 2002). Dosajh (1995, 1996b, 1997b, 1998) used SIS-II to study the efficacy of the test in the treatment of schizophrenics and found it to be a very sensitive instrument for psychodiagnosis and psychotherapy.

Singh and Dwivedi (1997) administered SIS-II to a 35-year-old, educated, married lady who was suffering from ulcer. SIS brought out her cold feelings for her husband, conflicting family life, broken love affair, affectional deprivation and suicidal ideation. SIS worked as a time machine and helped her in processing a lot of unprocessed unconscious material.

Cassell and Dubey (1997) administered SIS-II Video to an adult woman who was suffering from depression. After viewing the SIS-Video, she dreamt about an early traumatic experience in which she witnessed her 18-month-old brother being killed by sled dog. Due to her limited verbal skill at the age of three years and the emotional unavailability of her parents, who themselves were grief stricken, she could never share this experience with anybody before the administration of this test. This suggests the power of somatic inkblot images not only as a diagnostic tool but also a therapeutic aid and a remarkable time machine.

Cassell (1998a) has emphasized the pulling power of SIS images. SIS enables clinicians to release the 'inner cry' of suffering individuals. Unlike most other projective tests, the SIS asks the subject to rate responses on an anxiety–threat subjective retag scale. It specifically determines in order the three inkblots considered to be the most disturbing. The one ranked highest has subsequent post-traumatic dreams of such events. Using that particular SIS inkblot on the answer sheet as a stimulus object for a projective perception, the therapist has the capability to retest situations of activating post-traumatic imagery for therapeutic reprocessing. Television viewing prior to sleep can be particularly effective in stimulating the emergence in full consciousness of long forgotten post-traumatic dreams (Cassell and Dubey 1997). The latter may then become available for subsequent therapeutic analysis and resolution with the assistance of a trained therapist. Further, the SIS Video has been used to stimulate clinically effective psyche beacons for therapeutically guiding meditation. Some of the theoretical background for this approach has been outlined in the SIS Journal (Cassell et al.

1997). Cassell, Dubey and Dubey (2000) used the SIS-Video to study the effects of psychological trauma in two adolescent females. The first was an adolescent Jewish girl who was traumatized in a German concentration camp at Auschwitz and was interviewed as an adult survivor. The second involved studying a hospitalized adolescent girl suffering from dissociative disorder. In both instances, the SIS technology provided a type of 'time machine' for releasing long forgotten emotionally painful feelings and memories. Cassell (2015) further motivated colleagues to establish a scientific reality-based, cross fertilization theoretical dialogue with scientists exploring the hidden body–mind–spirit dimensions of the mysterious cosmo.

Savage (2001) administered SIS-I to three patients who were not responding to the medical treatment. The SIS was able to identify deep-seated conflicts, which the patients were unable to uncover through conventional therapy. The usefulness of a therapeutic tool of reframing along with hypnotic relaxation is also demonstrated with the help of case studies. Savage (2003) further administered SIS and hypnotic relaxation in a case of a child after he underwent the traumatic experience of the divorce of his parents. This case history illustrates that the SIS is very effective as a psychodiagnostic tool and a therapeutic aid. The therapist was able to help the patient to resolve his underlying conflict of his perceived rejection by his father.

Mishra and Mishra (2001) administered SIS-II to 18-year-old female college student who had lost her mother in early childhood and was living with her uncle who had no children. She had a difficult relationship with her stepmother. Her responses to SIS images were able to bring out her inner cry and depressed feelings.

Cassell et al. (2001) demonstrate the application of SIS-II Booklet. The test Image A3 is in a monochromatic bluish grey colour and the form is suggestive of a cross. For many devoted Christians, this can stimulate a spiritual imagery and affect in consciousness, activating healing. The image significantly contrasts with many traditional artistic representations of Christ's crucifixion, which are highly structured and leave little to the imagination. With abstract symbols, like this SIS inkblot, there is an enhanced potential for the external visual stimulus to tap into the dreamer's deep inner well of divine spirituality. In employing this approach, it must be remembered that different religions have their own unique symbols and rituals. SIS therapists must be open-minded and unbiased to employ these for spiritual healing. It is not our role to change or convert any suffering individual's religious orientation.

Rather, we need to foster healing by optimally activating the person's religious symbols in the therapy process. Those sufferings should be encouraged to have reverence for spirituality arising spontaneously through dream imagery for themselves and their loved ones.

Singh and Mishra (2001) administered the SIS-II to a 20-year-old male graduate student who had a history of masturbation for last three years. Because of this habit, he had developed a guilt feeling and had a fear of failure. He got familiar with a female classmate but never had physical relation with her. He developed symptoms of withdrawal, avoiding meeting people, lack of interest in study, feeling of insecurity and odd thinking to commit suicide. He was given re-educative psychotherapy to channel his energy to academic activities. The result was very positive, and the subject showed significant improvement. His suicidal ideation has gone, and he has developed positive attitude towards life.

Cassell et al. (2003) used SIS in interpreting symbolism in dream and emphasized that every night, we spend several hours in the mysterious inner world of our dreams. Those with an innate sense of curiosity have long been fascinated with the meaning of the images and the effect experienced during this altered state of consciousness. The index case study explores symbolism in a devil dream of a severely depressed adolescent girl hospitalized after experiencing suicidal and homicidal ideation. She was interviewed using the Rorschach and SIS stimuli as the sources for visual stimulation of daytime imagery. In the present study it may be inferred that 'Lucifer' embodies both her mother's abusive nature and that part of the adolescent's personality identified with the mother. Her extreme hatred and homicidal ideation were also symbolized through SIS responses.

Manickam and Suhani (2003) administered SIS-II to a 41-year-old male client who had the diagnosis of somatoform disorder. The SIS-II protocol showed repression of sexual responses and rejection of several images. Giving feedback about his responses helped in breaking the resistance and bring out repressed unconscious material. In the next session he revealed his incestuous sexual experiences and the repressed guilt about it. Resolving the conflicts helped the patient to be free from the symptoms over a short-term integrative psychotherapy. Manickam et al. (2004) used SIS booklet form for assessment and therapeutic intervention of a dissociative convulsive disorder patient of a 24-year-old male, who was successfully treated in three sessions. SIS showed severe repression of sexual impulses by rejecting all those images which are likely to evoke a sexual response. A conscious denial of sexual responses prompted to challenge the patient at the initial and early phase of the therapy without threatening the ego functions. Further interview helped the patient to disclose his unprotected homosexual and heterosexual relationships and his anxiety related to sexually transmitted infections including HIV. A dramatic cessation of the pseudo seizures following the session prompts to make use of the SIS technique at the appropriate time in psychotherapy, to reduce the cost of treatment and care of psychological disorders.

Vimal and Mishra (2003) administered SIS-II to a 44-year-old male contractor who was having uncomfortable and peculiar sensations in stomach, chest, head and heart. He was found normal on different investigations. Responses on SIS revealed his disturbed relationship with his father, maternal deprivations and preoccupation with physical symptoms. Significant responses on SIS are discussed in the case study. Vimal (2004) administered SIS-II to a 19-year-old college student. He had complaints of feelings of sadness, excessive crying, dejection, hopelessness and lethargic behaviour. SIS responses were able to bring out his aggressive attitude towards parents, suicidal ideation and low ego/self. Therapeutic intervention helped him in developing a positive attitude and hope for a better future.

Cassell and Dubey (2004) summarized three cases using the original 12-card form of the SIS. The first case explored the notion that when the cardiovascular system is activated by exercise or emotional stress, the resultant sensory feedback lowers the perceptual threshold for visualizing SIS cardiac content. The second case introduced the potentially new diagnostic category 'body phobia' and illustrated how during deep relaxation, SIS-stimulated imagery can provide an effective cognitive behavioural treatment aid. The third case examined the relationship of body consciousness and heart rate in recently hospitalized patients who experience schizophrenic disorder. It reveals how psychotic patients experiencing high sensory feedback from tachycardia can become unduly conscious of the heart and develop related somatic delusions. Cassell (2005) studied four case histories to illustrate how the SIS can provide important information regarding violent fantasies (Cassell and Dubey 1998b; Cassell et al. 2002). The direct and symbolic imagery projected can provide new insights enriching those obtained with standard clinical interviews. We also must learn how to more effectively incorporate its spiritual applications into clinical practice.

Cassell (2006) used SIS-II Video to examine two clinical case histories of individuals whose erroneous premarital perceptions made them vulnerable to unsuspectingly entering into a highly traumatic marriage. Eventually, each of them experienced psychiatric and medical problems. The first case involves a woman who married a sociopath, who intentionally presented a false positive social image of himself. Ultimately, he became homicidal and she was fortunate to survive. The second involves a successful businessman who married a woman who appeared normal. Unbeknown to him, she had Borderline Personality Disorder. His marriage took him to the edge of bankruptcy and for a while shattered his mental health. The SIS images were helpful in processing the traumatic memory and accepting the reality of life. Cassell and Dubey (2006) administered SIS Video to two persons: The first study examines the case history of a severely traumatized 17-year-old girl whose homicidal behaviour led to psychiatric hospitalization. The second case was a 14-year-old African-American youth with a history of violent behaviour. The somatic images were able to bring out aggressive imagery and relevant unprocessed repressed material helpful during therapeutic intervention.

Cassell (2007a) presented a case history of a man suffering from exhibitionism illustrating his phobic like avoidance of somatic inkblot structure suggestive of sexual content. A follow-up interview using intravenous barbiturate-induced sedation combining psychotherapy and behavioural therapy is described in the paper. Cassell (2007b) further administered the SIS to activate projective awareness and regionally specific anatomical imagery underlying psychophysiologic symptoms. A case history involving premature ejaculation using Jacobson deep muscle relaxation to facilitate desensitization therapy was described. The results suggest that a combination of cognitive and behaviour therapy in association with the use of pharmacologic relaxation was helpful. Cassell and Dubey (2007a) studied a case after administering SIS and Sand Tray technique for an educational television interview with a practising child psychiatrist and Jungian trained analyst.

Radheshyam (2007) administered SIS-II to a 26-year-old medical practitioner. His symptoms at initial psychological evaluation were insomnia, loss of appetite, excessive sweating, restlessness, difficulty in concentration and lack of interest in self and work. The responses on SIS projected his aggression and inner cry. SIS further helped him in expressing himself and in recovering from the financial and emotional trauma. The treatment plan involved eight sessions of rational emotive therapy supplemented by introducing SIS symbolism in the therapeutic process. This combination appeared to have marked therapeutic effects. He reported considerable improvement in mood and cognition and a significant reduction in depressive symptoms. Radheshyam, Cassell and Dubey (2009) further administered SIS-II to a 21-year-old female medical student, initially diagnosed with BD in early teenage. At that time, she was initiated on mood stabilizing medication which enabled her to continue her studies. During later adolescence, there was one stressful episode in her life worthy of comment here. During a depressive phase, because of poor motivation, she received an unusually low grade in fifth standard on a term examination. Prompted by a boy from her class and to avoid her family discovering the low grade, she tore up the report. After learning about this incident, her teacher ordered her to inform her parents. Fearing their angry response, she stayed away from classes for a month in a stressful state of 'terror'. SIS images helped in tapping into rich healing streams of natural spirituality not reachable by non-PTs (Cassell 2012a, 2012b, 2013a, 2013b, 2013c, 2014a, 2014b, 2015; Cassell and Dubey 2012a, 2012b; Cassell et al. 2013a, 2013b).

Cassell (2008b) published a psycho-biographical study which used the power of SIS PT to access adolescent PTSD holocaust memories of a psychologist. Traditional interviews reveal only what a person can recall and then chooses to reveal. While these may be supplemented by information from the tone of the voice, body posture, etc., such non-verbal sources have limitations. In many stressful situations, the mind can play tricks by defensively hiding relevant material. Moreover, verbal communication is limited by the number of words to communicate emotionally coloured perceptions. The SIS-II Video initially uses beautiful floral scenes to artificially induce a trance-like state facilitating the release of memories. In viewing semi-structured, yet ambiguous 'inkblots', the released imagery is then projected. What is seen and felt can represent a rich supplemental source of information in a psychobiological study. Case and Dubey (2008) administered the SIS-II to an obsessive-compulsive disorder patient as an aid in cognitive behavioural psychotherapy. The content analysis of SIS-projected symbolic imagery was able to bring to the surface long forgotten, unresolved stressors. The SIS could stimulate in memory long forgotten post-traumatic dreams and provide clinically relevant information for treatment plan. Therapeutic intervention of SIS can be implemented to undermine affect linked irrational obsessions, and thereby reduce compulsive behaviours. SIS was also used in several cases of PTSD (Brock et al. 2015; Cassell et al. 2014) with positive findings.

Cassell et al. (2009a) administered SIS Living Images Test to a severely depressed woman who was admitted to a psychiatric hospital because of serious suicidal ideation. On the day of admission, a standard psychiatric interview established an initial diagnosis of major depression. The following day, new information was obtained about the release of traumatic memories. The SIS images helped in processing the traumatic material and therapeutic planning. Cassell et al. (2009b) demonstrated 'How to Delete Viruses and Reconfigure the Brain's Hard Drive'. In an analogous fashion to computer viruses, these are verbal messages and externally implanted cognitive/emotional/behavioural codes of a negative nature. The SIS website capitalizes on the power of ambiguous pictures to stimulate imagery ranging from the positive to the negative. The SIS Center has a video titled 'Poppa' illustrating the former. This was designed to programme positive paternal dreams at bedtime. If abused, physically, psychologically or spiritually, the child may incorporate such negative input into self-image. Later in life, a trauma victim may be prone to act out this implanted code on immature subjects or vulnerable adults.

Cassell and Dubey (2010b) administered the SIS-II Video to an American Vietnam veteran suffering from PTSD. Like many such military veterans, he had never sought treatment for his mental symptoms. He had been deeply depressed and suicidal. The SIS images helped as a psychotherapeutic aid in reprocessing combat related long-term traumatic material. Brock et al. (2015) emphasized a major underlying aspect of all medical therapies involving the degree of positive empathetic linkage extending from the clinician to the sufferer. This is especially applied for those tormented by recurrent intrusive childhood traumatic memories—the basis of PTSD. In such situations, the clinician-created supportive empathic bond provides an essential foundation of psychotherapy. Moreover, when the treatment plan encompasses 'body–mind–spirit' theoretical principles, the resultant empathetic bridge optimizes the prognosis. Yet such occupational exposure over time, in vulnerable care providers, may induce empathetic 'secondary traumatization'.

Kumari and Mukhopadhyay (2019) administered the SIS test to 25 high- and 25 low-trauma affected adult (18—45 years) patients, both male and female, selected from various trauma centres in Varanasi. The level of trauma symptoms was assessed with the PTSD checklist civilian version (PCL-C). The results indicated that several indices and pathological contents of SIS-I were able to discriminate the groups and proved to be an effective diagnostic tool.

Mitra and Sanyal (2010) tried to provide an integrated understanding of different theories while understanding the psychopathology of a single case. It has been argued that such an understanding can help in effective treatment process as the therapist can be more flexible, empowered by a more in-depth understanding of the phenomena that arise during the process of psychotherapy. The SIS test has been used to tap the unprocessed unconscious material in treating patients (Cervigni 2013; Dasgupta 2013; Dasgupta, Dasgupta and Dwivedi 2012; Gupta and Singh 2012; Manickam and Suhani 2014) with encouraging results.

Sanyal (2013) used SIS-II to verify the therapeutic bearing of the test as a 'lens' or a 'window' in offering light to the unconscious in a non-threatening way. The responses to the SIS-II seemed to verify the assumption that it serves as a 'therapeutic template' based on which the next line of treatment in terms of psychotherapy may be designed in future.

Cassell et al. (2015) used SIS in interpreting three dreams. The images brought the suppressed unprocessed unconscious material hidden in the store house of unconscious mind to the surface. Its symbolic interpretation helps in understanding the inner world of the dreamer. Symbolic interpretation may further help as an aid in therapeutic management of the patients.

## Norms

Several researchers have attempted to develop 'Indian' norms of the Rorschach responses. The earliest attempt was by Asthana (1950b); he also has provided the norms for groups of population (Asthana 1950a, 1963, 1971). Somasundaram (1964) attempted to develop norms for the population in Kerala. Prabhu (1967) also provided the norms of some of the indices for adult population. Jain and Prakash (1967) explored the linear correlation between Sum R and other indices to establish norms and Kumar (1962c) listed popular responses on Rorschach for different groups of population. Though the Rorschach test stimulus can be considered culture-free, the response pattern is influenced by a particular culture. Singh (1975) reported the difference in the responses of tribal population from two types of culture contact area. He administered the Rorschach test to 100 tribal people of Gadeba living in Karapat, Orissa, in two groups: one with more culture contact and the other with less culture contact. The number of responses given by both groups was observed to be below the average. The content of the responses also showed a significant diversity.

Hence, there is a need for developing norms for different population (Manickam 2004). D'Netto, Kishore and Ruggu (1974), and Dubey (1978, 1982) found that the average response of army personnel to be $16 \pm 6.5$ and it is significantly lower than what Klopfer (1954) (R 20–45) and Prabhu (1967) (28.5 ± 9.71) found. Singh et al. (2005) established Beck's norm of Rorschach on Indian population. They administered Rorschach on 100 normal subjects in the age range of 18–50 years, both male and female, with minimum education up to the 12th standard. The results suggest that the findings of Indian studies do not match with the norms suggested by Samuel Beck. It further emphasizes the need of Indian norms on larger population.

Chaudhury et al. (2005) administered the Rorschach test following Klopfer's method to 450 children and adolescents in the age group of two and half to 16 years. Rorschach protocols of normal Indian children and adolescents at different age groups showed significant differences for each other and for the Western norms. An interpretation of Rorschach protocols of normal Indian children and adolescents using the Western norms would be fallacious and misleading. The use of the Rorschach test to study developmental trends of normal children and adolescents were strongly supported in this study.

Chaudhury et al. (2006) further administered the Rorschach test following Klopfer's method to 1,256 subjects consisting of 300 normal army personnel, 300 normal civilians, 250 schizophrenics, 300 neurotics and 106 patients with organic disorders. The Rorschach protocols of normal Indian army personnel and normal civilians showed significant differences from one another and from the Western norms. These differences are culturally determined and not indicative of low intelligence or psychopathology. Patients with schizophrenia, neurosis, head injury and epilepsy show significant differences from the records of normal subjects. The protocols of army schizophrenics show significant deviations from those of normal army personnel and these changes revert to normal with clinical recovery. The Rorschach test is not a culture-free test as claimed earlier. In view of the differences from Western norms, Rorschach protocols of Indian population should be interpreted using the norms for Indians. In case of army personnel, the norms on army personnel should be used (Dubey 1978, 1982).

Singh Umed (2007) investigated the pattern of responses on SIS-II in normal high school male and female students. The sample comprised 100 male and 100 female high school students. SIS-II was administered individually. The mean, standard deviation and t-ratio were computed to compare the two groups. The mean profile of male subjects was found to be total responses: 59.73, human responses: 12.91, animal responses: 5.63, anatomy: 18.48, sex responses: 1.73, movement responses: 1.42, most typical responses: 11.15, typical responses: 22.99, atypical responses: 2.28, rejection of images: 2.19, PAS: 0.53, depression: 0.17, HAS: 0.92 and paranoia: 0.01. The mean profile of female subjects was found to be total responses: 59.89, human responses: 12.15, animal responses: 7.15, anatomy: 10.52, sex responses: 0.75, movement responses: 1.87, most typical responses: 11.55, typical responses: 21.71, atypical responses: 1.91, rejection of images: 2.05, PAS: 72, depression: 0.56, HAS: 1.13 and paranoia: 0.01. However, the most typical responses were slightly lower than those reported by Cassell and Dubey (2003). They reported a mean of MT as 12+.

## Content Analysis

Though different authors studied the response patterns, indices and profile, systematic research on Rorschach's content analyses is yet to be undertaken. Content-wise, D'Netto et al. (1974) observed that military personnel gave responses related to military environment. In clinical situation, the 'content' of the responses does influence in formulating the differential diagnosis and is of much assistance to predict the outcome of psychotherapy and its prognosis. Noble Laureate Professor Erik Kendel (2005) has mentioned 'psychoanalysis still remains the most intellectually satisfying theory of human mind'. In this contention we need to follow Eagle's (2007) view that psychoanalysis cannot be a self-contained discipline but instead must be open to influence from integration with findings and theory from other disciplines. The responses given on various images should be analysed content-wise and symbolically (psychoanalysis) to understand the personality and psychopathology of the case.

Most of the clinicians in India depend on content analysis provided by the researchers from Western countries. Responses such as Xmas father (Card II), Xmas tree (Card VIII), cross (Card VI), vampire (Card I, IV, V), court of alms (Card VIII) and aftermath of September 11 (Card IX) are given by subjects who are Hindus in faith and hail from urban, multi-religious backgrounds. Subjects from Christian and Islamic faith also gave responses such as temple tower (Card II) and lamp that is used in temples (Card II, Card VII). With computerized scoring system and analysis, it might be much easier to conduct studies on content analysis. A multi-centred study to elicit the content profile of both clinical and non-clinical Indian population may be initiated (Manickam 2004). Cassell and Dubey have published about 60 cases (in *SIS Journal of Projective Psychology and Mental Health*, 1994–2019) using content analysis of Rorschach and SIS responses. They have emphasized that content analysis helps in peeping through the inner depth of unconscious and hear the inner cry of suffering individuals. Without content analysis, inkblot responses carry no meaning.

It may appear paradoxical to observe that the research related to the test flourished until clinical psychologists 'took over' it and after that it showed a declining trend. One of the factors for this phenomenon may be the attraction of the young clinical psychologists towards the emerging science of neuropsychology and behavioural intervention strategies within the ambit of clinical psychology in India. This has led to side-lining of psychodynamic psychology and to the 'unconscious' rejection of the psychodynamic process of the clients. With that the projective tests altogether and the Rorschach test slipped into a dormant phase (Manickam 2004). It is also likely that with the introduction of SIS, clinicians and researchers prefer to use SIS, which is less complicated and found more useful than the Rorschach test, particularly for personality assessment and therapeutic intervention (Cassell and Dubey 1994, 2003).

## Test Improvement

Research on improving the scoring methods or evaluation of studies related to the test has not been undertaken. One exception is the critique of Pershad and Dubey (1977) and Dubey (1982) that was published more than a quarter century ago on the productivity of the test and its scoring. To study the productivity on the Rorschach protocol, they suggested the need to differentiate between low, medium and high number of responses from a homogenous group for research comparison than focus on low and high number of responses. Dubey (1985, 2005) analysed the discriminating capacity of the test by regulating the number of responses and Dubey and Pershad (1978b) controlled the responses of the test to observe the shift in clinical significance.

Apart from these, Cassell has suggested an additional approach for clinical use of the Rorschach test. Initially, the 10 Rorschach plates are administered in the traditional order. However, to establish anxiety threat hierarchy prior to a detailed enquiry, all 10 plates are placed face up on a table. The subject then is asked to select three most-liked plates. Starting then with the most liked the examiner requests the subject to report everything seen and felt emotionally concerning the card. Afterwards, this favoured card is placed face down by the examiner on the table. This process is then repeated for the next favoured card and then for the third card, which the subject selected as 'liked'. This initial enquiry serves to reduce test anxiety.

Next, the examiner asks the subject to select three cards which are 'most disliked'. This enables the examiner to explore the responders' imagination, memories and threatening dreams along with their negative affect valance. Then the examiner places first card face down on the table. Next, the response to the two remaining disliked Rorschach cards is similarly treated. Afterward, the remaining four cards are reviewed in the detailed enquiry.

The same approach to content analysis may be used with the HIT. In fact, it is much more likely to elicit clinically relevant imagery and an affect. Ninety as opposed to ten incorporates many more stimuli which are more likely to trigger the release of responses idiosyncratic to the individual.

## Future Perspectives

Manickam and Dubey (2005) have suggested that keeping the diversity of Indian population in mind, separate norms will be more helpful for different groups. The Indian population is too complex and cumbersome for a psychologist to work with (Manickam 2004). Kumar (2015) has suggested various areas of research by clinical psychologists working on projective inkblot tests.

Dubey (2018) during his presidential address indicated that clinicians employing the somatic imagery procedure will help other clinical psychologists to learn the technique and deviate from the stereotyped numeric interpretation of inkblots tests, which label assessors more as a lab technician than as a clinical psychologist. Challenging the cult-like use of existing psychological instruments and reductionist scoring systems may promote the erroneous view of SIS clinicians as heretic and suffer some degree of professional stigma. The psychological tests, particularly the projective procedures, are administered to obtain data-based information not available from the client, case history and the significant family members. The projected responses provide windows to venture into the inner deep recesses of the person and hear (and appreciate) the inner cry of the client. I hope that the beneficial effects of SIS would be available to the patients residing anywhere on the planet Earth. A therapist while sitting in his clinic in another part of the world can still provide therapeutic aid to clients through modern technology. The ultimate vision is to provide competent mental health care through the creative use and ease-of-availability of the somatic imagery procedure from Dubay Healing Center, Ohio (USA).

# 6

# Administration and Scoring of the Rorschach Test

## Administration

Before the administration of the Rorschach test, the examiner should have items such as: Rorschach cards arranged in alphabetical order (face down on the table), record sheets, a stopwatch, a location chart, a pencil and a ball pen.

He/she should ensure assessing the subject's present physical and mental conditions, reason of referral (if referred by someone) and previous diagnosis, if any. The subject should be relaxed and cooperative and he/she should be explained how the test will help in planning the overall treatment plan.

There are three systems (Klopfer's System, Beck's System and Exner's System) most widely used and have almost the common procedure of administration. There is little difference in their 'instructions', though most of the psychologists follow it interchangeably. The instructions by Klopfer et al. (1942) and Beck (1937) are given as follows.

## Instructions by Klopfer et al.

Klopfer has suggested the following instructions:

'People see all sorts of things in these inkblot pictures; now, tell me what you see, what it might be for you, what it makes you think of' (Klopfer and Kelly 1942, 32).

## Instructions by Beck

Beck has suggested the following instructions:

The test consists of a series of 10 cards and you will be given 10 cards, one by one. The cards have on them designs made up out of inkblots. Look at each card and tell the examiner what you see on each card, or anything that might be represented there. Look at each card as long you like; only be sure to tell the examiner everything that you see on the card as you look at it. When you have finished with a card, give it to the examiner as a sign that you are through it. (1949, 2)

However,

[T]he essence of the Rorschach test procedure is to leave the subject entirely free. He makes his own selection, in each test figure, of the portion to which he reacts; any of several factors may determine what he sees; the content may be anything. In his test, Rorschach has thus combined two sets of conditions: (a) fixed objective stimulus and (b) freedom of subjects. (Beck 1937)

You can mention if asked:

I want you to tell me what you see there, what it means to you. There is no right or wrong answer. It is simply a matter of what it means to you or what you see there. Some people see many things others a few. It is entirely up to you. Please place the card facing it down on the table if you cannot see any thing more. I will give you next card and so on.

Any question asked by the subject should be replied in a non-committable way. For example,

*Subject:* Can I turn the card?

*Examiner:* As you like.

If he does not answer for one minute, you can repeat the question: 'What do you see?' or 'What does it mean to you?'
Even if he does not see anything, tell him, 'Well, let's try the next card'.

## Recording of Responses
1. Write down the response on the record sheet in verbatim.
2. Write down reaction time on each card and the total time taken during testing.
3. Write down the position of the card on each response such as <, >, v, etc.

## Enquiry
Enquiry is the most important part of Rorschach testing. We have to consider each response separately for location and determinants.

1. *Enquiring for location*
   Examiner: 'Well, you perceived... Would you show me exactly where you saw this on this card and describe the parts you can see'.
2. *Enquiring for determinants*
   Examiner: 'You said a... What makes it look like... What's more... (Ensure what makes him/her to determine the form, movement, if any, colour and shading, etc.)

## Example: Card VIII—Two Animals Climbing Up
*Examiner:* Where do you see two animals?

*Subject:* The shape—they have four legs, head and looks as if they are climbing.

*Examiner:* What made it look like climbing?

*Subject:* The movement here looks like it.

*Examiner:* What else?

*Subject:* They might be foxes because of the hairs on their body; it's furry.

**Scoring:** D1 (location); FM' Fc' (determinants); A (content); 2 (form level rating); P (popular).

For details, please see Klopfer et al. (1954, 49–239).

## Testing Limits
It is designed to elicit responses and details in location, determinant, content, etc., that have been omitted, distorted and avoided. The examiner will formulate questions in such a way as to check why the subject is unable to respond.

*Examiner:* Now we come to the final part. You have not given any response to these cards. Most people see human beings in some of the cards, can you find where? The examiner gives all the details (legs, head...) and asks whether the subject can see it now.

## Rejection
If the subject is unable to see anything on the card, it is considered as 'rejected'. A response such as 'inkblot' is not considered a response and is treated as a 'rejection'. Rejection of images may be because of non-cooperation, thought blockage and an inability to think properly. Try to make the subject to hold the card for a minimum of two minutes before permitting rejection.

## Termination
The testing can be terminated after thanking the subject for spending so much time and mentioning the purpose that the response given by the subject will help in the overall planning of treatment.

By and large, all major systems of inkblots (Rorschach inkblots, Holtzman inkblots and Somatic inkblots) follow the above procedure with minor variations in the presentation of cards/images.

## *Procedures of Administration Advised by Exner*

Almost similar in all the three systems (Klopfer, Beck and Exner) as described in this chapter; however, some procedures which are different in Exner's System are given as follows.

## Instructions
'What might this be? And nothing else! (Exner, 1974)'

## Attempted Rejections
When the subject fails to perceive anything(s?), particularly on Cards I and II, it suggests that the examiner has failed to establish a rapport with the subject. In such a situation, the examiner should stop testing

and try to understand the reason of rejection. The test can be started again with Card I after the consent of the subject.

### Problems of Brief Protocols

If the subject has given less than 14 responses, the examiner should not proceed further with the enquiry. He should explain to the subject that he/she has not given enough responses to get anything out of it and that the examiner wants the subject to see him/her again and make sure to give more responses next time. The subject can include the responses already given in the next run, if he/she likes to do so (Exner 1974).

### Problems of Lengthy Protocols

Some subjects give an endless number of responses on each card and, in such a situation, the examiner should consider the first five responses on each card for the interpretation.

### Enquiry

> I want to see the things that you saw and make sure that I see them like you do. We will do them one at a time. I will read what you said and then I want you to show me where it is in the blot and then tell me what is there, that makes it look like that to you, so that I can see it too. Just like you did. (Exner 1974)

### Testing Limits

> Some time it may be important to determine if a person can easily see objects that are commonly reported by most people but have not been reported by the client. Usually, these become an issue when a person has failed to give any popular answers. After the inquiry has been completed the examiner selects two or three blots (typically VIII, III and V) to which the person has not given the popular responses. (Exner 1974)

## Scoring Systems of the Rorschach Test

There are different scoring systems that are in practice across the globe. We will, however, discuss the following three scorning systems of the Rorschach test:

1. Klopfer's method
2. Beck's method
3. Exner's method

Although different scoring systems are practised in other countries, no effort has been made to develop an exclusive scoring system that may be applicable to the Indian population. Also, there is no consensus regarding the scoring system to be followed by the clinicians in India. Probably this reflects the philosophy of clinical training, where focus is more on the clinical application of the Rorschach test rather than on its research utility.

The published research papers indicate that Klopfer's method (Klopfer and Davidson 1962) and Beck's method (Beck and Molish 1967) are being used by most clinicians and researchers in India (Banerjee et al. 1998; Chaudhury et al. 2001, 2007; Kohli and Kaur 2002; Kumar and Patel 1990; Manickam and Dubey 2005). Some use Exner's method. Others use specific signs like Piotrowski's organic signs of epilepsy (Chaudhury and Sundari 1996, 1997, 1998; Vagrecha and Majumdar 1974) or the Theisens' pattern on psychotic disorders (Chaudhury and Sundari 1996). Piotrowski's alpha diagnostic formula is yet another area of clinical investigation (Prabhu 1970).

The scoring system taught at NIMHANS is based on Klopfer's method. The institute has also developed a manual based on Klopfer's system (De Vos 1973). The students who use the test as a research tool get trained in one of the established scoring systems for the analysis of the research data, and Klopfer's method is the preferred method of the scoring system (Kaur and Kapur 1983; Pratap and Kapur 1984; Ramachandra 1994).

The second major training centre of clinical psychology is the Central Institute of Psychiatry, Kanke, Ranchi, where Exner's method (1978, 1995, 2001) is followed. Earlier, this institute was following Beck's method (Beck 1945). Only the clinical psychologists so trained in India are using this technique.

The third major training centre of clinical psychology is RINPAS, Kanke, Ranchi, where the Rorschach test and the SIS form part of the curriculum. The Rorschach scoring method taught at this institute is based on Beck's method (Beck 1945). The scoring and interpretation of SIS are followed as per the manual by Cassell (1980) and Cassell and Dubey (2003, 2005). This projective procedure has been adopted as a major 21st-century psychological tool by two major training centres: RINPAS, Kanke, Ranchi, and IMHH, Agra (Kumar et al. 2001, 2003, 2004, 2005, 2007, 2008; Singh et al. 1996, 1997, 2001, 2002, 2007).

Pershad and Pareekh (2001) prepared a protocol manual for the Rorschach test. Although the authors specified that the objective of the manual was to popularize the test using the 'made it easy manual', the scoring approach it has taken may have confused the students. It does not adhere to any scoring system nor has tried to develop a scoring system based on Indian experience. However, on the positive side, it has taken into consideration the diverse population of India in relation to some of the indices and content.

Exner's system and the HIT have also attracted many academicians and clinical psychologists. The three scoring methods—Klopfer's system (1954), Beck's system (1937, 1949, 1967) and Exner's system (1974, 1995, 2001)—are mentioned further in brief. The HIT has been elaborated in a separate chapter. The scoring categories and their explanation have been taken from the main source to avoid any discrepancy. We have also tried to note all scoring categories and their interpretation with a few exceptions. Readers are invited to follow the primary books of a system for detailed explanation.

## Klopfer's Scoring System

The scoring categories and their explanation have been taken from Klopfer et al. (1954). We have tried to note all scoring categories and their interpretation, but left a few which we consider less significant.

### Description of Main Scoring Categories

1. **LOCATION**
   - W: Whole responses are scored when all or nearly the whole blot is used.
   - DW: The individual tries to perceive whole blot on the basis of one detail, though the concept is a bad match for the blot and the discrepancy does not bother the subject.
   - D: Large usual details are scored when large parts of the blot are marked off by the gestalt qualities of the blot.
   - d: Small usual details are scored when smaller parts of the blot are marked off by the gestalt qualities of the blot.
   - Dd: Unusual details are scored when the part of the blot used is not classifiable as a large or small detail.

- Dd: Tiny details are scored for responses such as insular/peninsular, marked off by space, shading or colour from rest of the blot.
- De: Edge details are scored for locations using only the edge of the blot.
- Di: Inside details are scored when the inside, shaded portion of the blot is used.
- Dr: Rare details are scored where an unusual location is used which cannot be classified as Dd, De or Di.
- S: White space is scored when the white background becomes the figure and the rest of the area becomes the background.

(For details of the location, scoring and location charts, please see Klopfer et al. (1954, 49–94).)

2. **DETERMINANTS**

There are four main classes of determinants which are as follows:

**(I) Form Responses (F)**

The concept is determined by the shape of the blot only, and colour and shading have no contribution.

- Score F where there is no other main determinant.

**(II) Movement Responses**

**M: Figure in human-like action (human, mythological)**

- Score M for human beings seeing in action even if described as caricatures, drawings, statues, etc.
- Score M for human beings seen in any live posture, unless it is qualified as a drawing, statue, etc.
- Score M for human-like movement in animals such as fairy tale creatures, Walt Disney animals, but do not score M for movement in trained animals, for example, a trained dog, ape, seal, etc.
- Score M for movement controlled by an individual (such as a person whirling with a scarf, skirts blowing)
- Score M for parts of human beings seeing in action, human face with an expression.

**FM: Animal movement**

- Score FM for animal in movement even if described as caricatures, drawings, statues, etc.
- Score FM for animal in a life-like posture, provided it is not shown as a drawing, statue, etc.
- Score FM for parts of animals in animal-like action.

## m: Inanimate movement (Fm, mF and m)

- Fm: Score Fm if the object is in movement and has a definite form, for example, a spinning top, flying aircraft.
- mF: Score mF if the object is moving and has an indefinite form, for example, leaping flame, swirling clouds.
- m: Score m if there is no form and only movement.

## (III) Shading Responses (Differentiated and Undifferentiated Shading)

### (III-a) Differentiated shading responses

- Fc: Score Fc where the surface or texture effect is either itself highly differentiated or has a definite form, for example, a fur rug on Card VI-W or a teddy bear—it looks soft and fuzzy (Card VII).
- FK: Score FK where three-dimensional or depth impression is combined with a definite form perception, giving vista or perspective to a landscape (a piece of coral rock looking straight down through the water at it W on Card VIII or a canyon with different shape and entrance in the centre—W on Card VII).
- Fk: Score Fk where the shading gives the impression of a three-dimensional expanse projected on a two-dimensional plane involving a definite shape (such as x-ray of chest showing ribs or a topographical map of India on Card I).

### (III-b) Undifferentiated shading responses

- KF: Score KF where some form enters the depth or diffusion impression, but with a formlessness in the concept (smoke rising in spirals from a chimney—Card VII).
- K: Score K where the response implies depth or diffusion with no form (fog, mist, smoke, cloud).
- kF: Score kF where a three-dimensional expanse is projected on a two-dimensional plane with an object having no shape (coast of a big piece of land—looks irregular with jagged edges and little inlets—Card I or x-ray without any specific body part on Card I).
- k: Score k where a three-dimensional expanse is projected on a two-dimensional plane in a way that implies no form at all. Such responses are very rare.
- cF: Score cF where the object has a vague or indefinite form with a focus on the surface (a bear rug with a hole due to gunshot during hunting, it also looks furry, on Card II).
- c: Score c where the subject focuses interest only on the surface or the texture effect without emphasis on form, for example, animal skin and the texture makes me to see its skin.

## (IV) Colour Responses

### (IV-a) Achromatic colour responses (FC', CF', C')

- FC': Score FC' where the object has a definite form with use of an achromatic colour such as black, white or grey (e.g., as Canadian goose migrating—looks like wings and colour like goose black and grey on Card V).
- C': Score C' where object is perceived due to achromatic colour only without any form (e.g., black smoke—its black smoke—the blot gives impression of smoke on Card VII).
- C'F: Score C'F where an object of vague form is designated due to the impression of achromatic colour—black, white, or grey (a fur rug, the shape is indefinite, but it looks like furry as the skin of a brown bear, Card VI).

### (IV-b) Chromatic colour responses (C, FC, CF)

- FC: The following criteria must be met before FC can be scored
  a. The object (person, animal, plant) must be of a definite form.
  b. The colour must be used in the concept.
  c. The colour used must be the natural colour of the creature in its natural state.
  (A butterfly in the centre on Card III, the shape and the colour, it is flying, wings are spread)
- CF: The following criteria must be met before CF may be scored
  a. The object (cloud, explosions, fire, flames, blood) must be of a definite form.
  b. The colour must be used in the concept.
  c. The colour used must be the natural colour of the object (a flower—whole thing, colour and shape on Card IX, or some beautiful strawberry ice cream with orange water ice on Card VIII).

### (IV-c) Pure colour response (C)

Score C when the emphasis is given on colour without any implication of form, even in a definite form. There are four categories of colour responses:

  a. C: Crude colour, for use of colour with no form (blood on Card II).
  b. Cn: Colour naming (red, green, yellow but what they are I don't know Card X).
  c. Cdes: Colour description (pretty pastel colours on Card VIII).
  d. CSym: Or colour symbolism (child's drawing)

## 3. CONTENTS

- H: Living Human figures (whole/almost whole).
- (H): Human figures portrayed as drawings, sculpture or mythological, for example, Satan, witches, *Vaital* (Jinn), etc.
- HD: Parts of living human figures.
- (Hd): Parts of human figures portrayed in drawings, sculpture or parts of mythological human figures.
- AH: Figures that are part human and part animal such as 'Narsingha Bhagwan' or 'Lord Ganesha'.
- H Obj: Parts of human body (external) such as false teeth.
- At: Parts of human body (internal) or human body in anatomical sense, for example, dissected parts, operations, liver, kidney, anatomical charts, x-rays, etc.
- Sex: Sexual organs, sexual activity, sensuous parts of body invoking sexual feelings such as exposed breast, pelvis and lower part of the body.
- A: Animal figure (whole/almost whole).
- (A): A mythological animal, such as a monster with animal characteristics, a caricature, a fairy tale or *Shesh Nag* (Serpent God) and the like.
- Ad: Parts of a living animal (head, tail or paw).
- (Ad): Part of a mythological animal—tail of Hanuman Jee (on d1—Card IV).
- A Obj: Object connected with the body of an animal, such as fur, decorated skin of deer and horn of deer.
- AAt: Animal anatomy, includes dissections, x-ray and internal parts of living animal, etc.
- Food: Objects prepared as food for eating such as fried eggs, fruit salad, mix vegetables, ice cream, etc.
- N: Nature concept/scenery such as aerial views, sunsets, rivers, lakes, landscapes, etc.
- Geo: Geographical concepts such as maps, islands, gulfs, lakes and rivers not seen in a vista or as a part of a landscape.
- Pl: Plants or part of plants such as flowers, trees, fruit, vegetables, leaf, petal and stamen.
- Bot: Plants seen as botanical specimens or botanical chart.
- Obj: All kinds of man-made objects such as airplane, fan, chair and toys.
- Arch: Architectural concepts such as house, bridge and temple.
- Art: Concepts such as design, drawing and art. A painting of a human figure is scored (H) and painting of landscape is scored as N.

- Abs: Score abstract when there is no specific content (e.g., 'power', 'force', etc.).
  Fire, blood, cloud, smoke, mask, emblem, crown, etc., are scored separately.

4. **POPULAR AND ORIGINAL RESPONSES**

Many responses are neither common enough to be scored as 'popular' nor unusual enough to be scored as 'original'. However, Klopfer et al. (1954) have assigned the following 10 responses to be scored as popular.

### A. Popular Response

- Card I: (W or cut-off W) any creature with the body in the centre D and wings at the side (bat or butterfly).
- Card II: (Black area cut-off W with or without D2 and d1) any animal such as dog, bear, rabbit, bull or rhinoceros (if the upper red D2 and lower red D1 are included).
- Card III: (Entire black area D8) two persons in a bending position (dancing, lifting pitcher or something). Score P if the figure is in action with the side bottom (D5) is seen as legs. The human figure seen upside down cannot be scored as P.
- Card III: (Centre red D1) 'bow tie', 'hair ribbon' or 'butterfly'. Score P for shape alone or shape with colour.
- Card V: (W or W cut) any winged creature with the body in the centre D and wings either side. P can be scored even if the card is held upside down with the body in the centre and wings either side.
- Card VI: (With or without top D2) skin of an animal. P can be scored if shading for impression of furriness or markings on the inside of the skin (Fc or cF) is used.
- Card VIII: (Side D1) any kind of four-legged animal in motion. If the animal is not in action, score it a tedency towards P.
- Card X: (Outer blue D1) any many-legged animal such as crab, spider or octopus.
- Card X: (Centre green D2) (without the light green D between the darker green areas) any greenish animal such as a caterpillar and a garden snake. The use of colour is must to be scored as P.
- Card X: (Light green D7) the head of an animal with long ears or horns such as a rabbit or a goat.

## B. Original Response

An original response is one that does not appear more than once in a hundred records. The scoring of original should not be undertaken by beginners. Usually, it should be scored by the examiners who have broad experience with a variety of patients and have read published protocols/norms extensively.

## 5. FORM LEVEL RATING

There are three considerations to determine form level rating: accuracy, specification and organization.

### A. Accuracy

a. *Accurate responses:* Where the response/concept is of a definite form (such as 'a butterfly' on Card III—Centre red D1)

b. *Semi-definite or indefinite response:* Where the response/concept is so vague that almost any blot or blot area could be said to provide a good fit (such as 'cloud' on Card VII).

c. *Inaccurate response:* Where the concept is of a definite form but is referred to a blot area of a dissimilar form (such as a snake on Card IV—whole blot).

### B. Specification

The accuracy of the response may be improved or spoiled by the elaboration or specifications offered by the subject to the detailed structure of the blot area used. Specifications may be classified as (a) constructive, (b) irrelevant and (c) those that weaken the form level.

a. **Constructive Specifications:** Constructive specifications are elaborations of the concept which themselves match in detail the structure of the blot area. These are of two types:

    i. *Form specification:* It specifies a detailed match of the concept of the outline of a blot area (whiskers on a cat, ears on a dog, facial features or details of clothing of a human figure).

    ii. *Determinants specifications:* It specifies a detailed match of the concept of a blot by the use of colour, shading or movement. Not all determinants are counted as constructive specification (for example, score only M, FM and Fm in movement category [do not score mF or m] and FC, FC', Fc and FK in shading category).

b. **Irrelevant Specifications:** Irrelevant specifications are verbalizations of the subject which neither improve nor detract from the accuracy of the match of the concept to a blot. They may increase or decrease the rating by +0.5 or –0.5 or even more.

## C. Organization

Any procedure used by the subject to organize various parts of the blots into a meaningful concept will increase the form level rating.

### The Rating Scale

The form level is rated on a scale ranging from –2 to +5.0. There are two essential steps in ascertaining the form level rating:

- Assigning a basal rating or basal minus rating.
- Adding a credit of 0.5 for each constructive specification or organization and subtracting a credit of 0.5 for specification or organization that weakens the concept.

### Basal Rating of 1.0

The response that fulfils the minimum requirements of a 'definite' basic accuracy of fit with the blot area is given a rating of 1.0. There are three kinds of response assigned a basal rating of 1.0. Give basal rating 1.0 to all popular responses.

*Popular level responses:* Responses frequently given to obvious blot areas requiring same level of organizational ability as popular responses, such as

- Butterfly: Lower red (D1—Card II).
- Pitcher: Lower centre (D4—Card III).
- Boots: Lower outer (D3—Card IV).
- Woman's leg: Lower side (d1—Card V).
- A butterfly: Top (D2—Card VI).
- Human head: Lower side pink (D4—Card IX).
- Two bugs: Upper centre grey (D in Card X).
- Deer: Outer grey brown (D6—Card X).

Concept that requires little imagination or organizational capacity to make the blot area a good fit is also given a rating of 1.0.

### Basal Rating of 1.5

A basal rating of 1.5 is given to the concepts above the minimum requirements of 'definiteness'.

### Basal Rating of 0.0

The rating 0.0 is given to the concept which is completely indefinite in form, usually determined by C, Cdes, Cn, c, C', K, k, and m. Such rating is very rare.

## MINUS RATING

### Basal Rating of –0.5

The rating –0.5 is given to the concept when the specification has lowered down the accuracy without destroying it.

### Basal Rating of –1.0

The rating –1.0 is given to a response where the subject has made some effort to indicate the parts, but the specifications destroy the basic accuracy of the concept. The confabulatory combination is the example of this rating.

### Basal Rating of –1.5

The rating –1.5 is given to confabulatory responses, scored by DW location. Such response is a generalization from one clearly seen detail to the whole blot, when it is impossible to reconcile the concept.

### Basal Rating of –2.0

The rating –2.0 is given to responses in which the concept does not match the blot area and there is no effort to reconcile the shape of the blot. Such responses are usually perseverations and contamination.

(For details of scoring, please see Klopfer et al, et al. 1954.)


## *Scoring of Beck's System*

Beck's instructions are given in the beginning of this chapter. The preparations of subject, administration of cards, noting the responses and enquiry, rejection of cards, testing the limits and scoring symbols (location, determinants, content, and popular and original responses) are almost common in Klopfer's and Beck's systems. However, deviations of Beck's system from Klopfer's system are given as follows.

## Deviations from the Standard Seating Procedure

The seating arrangement may be different in elderly person, s depressed patients and young children. There is no point in following the instructions strictly. If the child is very young, the usual seating arrangement can be dispensed with. The procedure is to make him/her to feel more comfortable. So any kind of deviations from the formal procedure will depend on the clinical situation and the examiner should decide how to proceed further.

*Age Factor.* Any person who can see and speak can take the test. Normally, it can be administered to people aged five years and above.

*About Text Format.* Record the response verbatim and note down the position of the card; 'ʌ' orientation is always implied when there is no other indication.
The D and most Dd are identified by their appropriate numerals. Since the figures are symmetric, there are two each of nearly all D and Dd. The text does not state whether the D in question is one that is on the right or on the left.

## Scoring and Interpretation

1. **LOCATION**
   - *W (whole response)* is scored when the whole blot instigates the response. It has a direct relationship with the subject's intellectual ability and capacity to organize things in a meaningful way.
   - *D response (major detail)* is scored when the response is based upon the usual detail or part of the blot. It may indicate the subject's ability to perceive and react to usual, distinct characteristics of the world.
   - *Dd response (unusual details)* is scored when unusual detail responses are based on smallest details of the blot.
   - *S response (white space details)* is scored when the white space is used as the basis of response. It may indicate negativism or oppositional features.

## 2. DETERMINANTS

Determinants refer to the features of the blot that have produced the response.

- *Form determinant (F)* is symbolized by the capital letter F and is meant for the response which has occurred purely because of the form or the shape of the blot. F has been divided into F+ and F–, which indicate good form level and poor form level, respectively. It indicates a person's connection with reality and his/her thinking and reasoning. Beck has argued for another method of comparing pure form responses with non-pure form responses. His method provides for the lambda index. One advantage of the lambda index over F% is that it avoids the problems involved in interpreting the percentages, especially when R varies. When the lambda index exceeds 1, it indicates excessive affective constraint and when it falls below 0.50, it indicates affective instability.

- *Movement determinants (M)* are scored only for human movement. It indicates awareness towards the external world and reflects some conflicts or emotions which do not get obvious expression in the world of reality.

- *Colour determinants (C, CF, FC)* are scored for pure colour responses and indicate lack of control over emotional responsiveness. CF is scored for a response in which colour features of the blot are primary and form features are secondary. FC is scored when the form dominates and the subject also makes a secondary reference to the colour for elaboration.

  Beck has given the concept of affective ratio (Affr). Affr below 0.55 indicates withdrawal or passivity towards affective stimulation and Affr above 0.75 indicates that the person has an uncontrolled tendency to be caught up by affective stimulation.

- *Shading determinants (Texture, vista and general diffuse)* Beck suggests that texture response (T) indicates painful affective experience, which is usually related to infantile needs, particularly the erotic needs of the infantile period. The vista response (V, VF and FV) is the shading response based upon dimensionality. It suggests a painful feeling tone in which depression of affect and inferiority feelings are involved. The diffuse shading response (Y, YF and FY) indicates anxiety and withdrawal from the environment or passivity. It also indicates a general withdrawal tendency. Y and YF indicate the experience of an extreme form of withdrawal from the environment leading to a complete inability to respond, whereas FY indicates that the experience is a mild form of passivity.

3. **CONTENTS**
   Higher number of animal responses indicates intellectual constriction and stereotypical thinking. A high number of human responses indicates better cognitive development and potential for good human relations. A low number of human responses indicates disturbed human relations. Anatomy responses indicate excess preoccupation with bodily concerns without any physiological illness. Sex and blood responses tend to indicate sexual or aggressive acts. Nature, cloud and botany contents indicate emotional deprivation. Responses such as fire, landscape, household, art, clothing, etc., tend to indicate various kinds of preoccupations causing interference in affective adjustment.

4. **BECK'S POPULAR INDIAN RESPONSE**
   **Card I**
   Bat or butterfly or moth (W)
   Human form (D3 and D4); D3 is usually seen as a woman

   **Card II**
   Two human figures (W)
   Dog or bear (D1)
   Butterfly or moth (D3)

   **Card III**
   Two humans and representations of humans, for example, dolls, statues, caricatures (D1).

   **Card IV**
   Animal skin (W)
   Animals which are massive, furry (W)
   Human foot or shoe (D2)
   Human leg or boot (D6)

   **Card V**
   Bat, butterfly, moth (W)
   Many human leg and many animal legs (D1)
   Chicken leg (D1)

   **Card VI**
   W or D1 as animal hide, pelt, skin or rug (W or D1)

   **Card VII**
   Human heads or faces of women (D1)

   **Card VIII**
   Bears, mice, rat, beavers (D1)

Skeletal form (D3)
Tree/bush (D4)

**Figure IX**
Civil war veterans, clown, dwarf, fireman, ghost, Santa Claus, witch (D3)

**Figure X**
Crab, lobster, spider (D1)
Dog (D2)
Rabbit's head (D3)

## Scoring of Exner's System

The main features, scoring categories and their significance are given below. Readers interested in detailed information about Exner's system should consult Exner (1974, 2003).

1. **LOCATION**
   Exner has given four types of location, W, D, Dd and S, which are almost like Klopfer's system.

   W: Whole response

   D: Common detail response (frequently identified area of the blot).

   Dd: Detail response (infrequently identified area of the blot).

   S: Space responses (area with white space).

2. **DEVELOPMENTAL QUALITY**
   It refers to the quality of processing involved in perceiving the response.

   **Symbols and criteria used for developmental quality**

   **Symbols**
   **+ (Synthesized response):** Two or more objects though described separately but connected in some way (card VIII: a fox is going towards forest).

   **O (Ordinary response):** Blot area having features that create a natural form (bat on Card V).

   **V/+ (Synthesized response):** Two or more objects though described separately but connected in some way, though none with a specific form demand (clouds with mist around on Card IX).

**V (Vague response):** An object without any specific form demands but uses a specific form demand for the response objects (coloured sky during sunset on Card IX).

## Determinants

Exner's determinants are almost like Klopfer and Beck with a little difference in a few of indices, which are described as follows:

- **Form (F):** It is the most common determinant, and is related to intellectual processes. Colour responses often provide an understanding of emotional life.

  'Form colour' implies more refined control of impulse than 'colour form'. It is from the relation and balance among determinants that personality can be most readily inferred.

- **Movements:** M, FM and m are like Klopfer's system.
  - i. Human movement (M): It is scored for all types of human activity (active movement such as running, jumping, lifting and passive movement such as thinking, sleeping, looking, etc.). M is also scored for human-like figures or animals or inanimate objects in human activity, such as 'two bears talking on Card II).
  - ii. Animal movement (FM)
  - iii. Inanimate movement (m).

  The movement responses are further coded as active or passive.

- **Chromatic colour:** These categories are like Klopfer's system: C, CF and FC.

- **Achromatic colour (black, white or grey):** These categories are similar to Klopfer's system except variation in the coding of symbols (C!, C!F, FC!).

- **Shading**

  These categories are different from Klopfer's system. It has three subcategories, each with three symbols of shading (a) texture (T, TF, FT), (b) depth (V, VF, FV) and (c) diffuse (Y, YF, FY).

  *Shading texture:* Texture (T, TF and FT) is scored when the shading features are used to create a tactile impression (such as furry, soft, rough, smooth, etc.).

  *Shading vista:* Vista symbols (V, VF and FV) are scored when the shading features are used to create the impression of depth or dimensionality (e.g., its aerial view, round shape, etc.) (similar to Beck).

  *Shading diffuse:* Vista symbols (Y, YF, FY) are scored when the shading response is neither texture nor vista (e.g., as light, dark) (similar to Beck).

- **Form dimension:** Form dimension is scored when the impression of depth, distance or dimension is not based on the shading features (e.g., a lady is lying down, on Card V-D). This is a new concept from Exner.
- **Pairs and reflection:** rF or Fr is scored where the person has used the symmetry of the blot to perceive two identical objects (e.g., a fox is seeing its reflection in lake water, on Card VIII D1). This is a new concept from Exner.

**Multiple Determinants—The Blend:** It is scored when the percept has more than one determinant.

3. **FORM QUALITY**

Form quality is scored when the area of the blot is used to conform to the form requirements of the object. This is like F level rating of Klopfer.

4. **CONTENTS**

The scoring of content categories is very simple and except in a few categories it is like Klopfer's system.

H: Human
(H): Mythological or fictional human
Hd: Human detail
(Hd): Mythological or fictional human detail
Hx: Human experience (two aggressive persons looking at each other)
A: Animal
(A): Mythological or fictional animal (Shesh Nag or Ganesh Jee in India)
Ad: Animal detail
(Ad): Mythological or fictional animal detail
An: Anatomy (internal anatomy such as kidney, heart, lungs, etc.)
Art: Art (painting/drawing)
Bl: Blood
Bt: Botany (plants)
Ay: Anthropology (cultural/historical things, e.g., sword of Tipu Sultan)
Cg: Clothing
Cl: Clouds
Ex: Explosion
Fi: Fire

Fd:   Food
Ge:   Geography (map)
Hh:   Household
Ls:   Landscape
Na:   Nature (sun, moon, planet, sky, water)
Sc:   Science (airplanes, buildings, bridges, cars, etc.)
Sx:   Sex
Xy:   X-ray

5. **POPULAR RESPONSES**

The popular responses vary from culture to culture. However, a study on a large sample will help in establishing popular Indian responses. The following popular responses have been reported on the Indian sample.

Card 1, Bat or butterfly
Card 2, D1: Bear, dog, elephant or lamb head or whole animal
Card 3, D1/D9: Human figure
Card 4, W/D7: Human or human-like figure
Card 5, W: Bat or butterfly
Card 6, W/D1: Animal skin, hide, pelt or rug
Card 7, D9, D1, D: Human head or face
Card 8, D1: Animal figure
Card 9, D3: Human or human-like figures
Card 10, D1: Spider or crab

6. **ORGANIZATIONAL ACTIVITY**

This is a new concept from Exner. Organizational activity is scored by Z and provides information to the extent the person tends to organize the response. AZ score is assigned to any response that includes form, and meets at least one of the following criteria:

ZW:   Score ZW to a whole response with coding of +, o, or v/+.

ZA:   (Adjacent detail) is scored when two or more separate objects are identified in adjacent detail areas of the blot in a meaningful relation.

ZD:   (Distant detail) is scored when two or more separate objects are identified in non-adjacent detail of the blot in a meaningful relation.

ZS:   It is scored when response with white space is integrated with other areas.

7. **SPECIAL SCORES**

This is a new concept from Exner. Special scores have lots of clinical significance and serve as diagnostic indicators. He has assigned 15 special scores as follows:

- Unusual verbalization (6)
- Perseveration (1)
- Special features of content (4)
- Differentiate human representation (2)
- Personalized answers (1) and
- Special colour phenomenon (1)

- **Unusual Verbalizations**

  Unusual verbalizations are important in the assessment of cognitive activity, particularly while assessing cognitive dysfunction. This is also called as cognitive slippage and is indicated in the following ways:

  i. **Deviant verbalizations (DV, DR):** Use of inappropriate word (neologism and redundancy).

  ii. **Inappropriate combinations (INCOM, FABCOM and CONTAM)—A:** When the subject perceives unreal feature such as 'a man with the head of a cow'. Sometime, such responses are also considered mythological and perceived by the people in Indian culture, for example, 'GOKARNA' story in Bhagawat Maha Puran.

  iii. **Inappropriate Logic (ALOG)**

- **(One) Perseveration (PSV):** also bring the line up... keep the style uniform

  Perseveration is scored when almost identical response is given to too many cards.

- **(Four) Special Features of Content:** also bring the line up (This is a new concept and different from Klopfer and Beck.) The responses indicate cognitive features or project the image of self. These are identified by four special scores:

  i. *Abstract content (Ab):* Responses with clear symbolic representation (indicating human emotion, like loving heart).

  ii. *Aggressive movement (AG):* Responses with aggressive symbols, for example, two fighting bulls.

  iii. *Cooperative movement (COP):* Movement responses indicating positive or cooperative interaction like 'two ladies performing a dance together'.

iv. *Morbid content (MOR):* MOR is scored when a response/object is identified by two different characteristics—identification of the object as dead, destroyed or broken and another identified by the characteristic such as an unhappy person or a depressed person.

- **(Two) Differentiate human representation:** also bring the line up
  (This is a new concept and different from Klopfer and Beck.)
  i. Good human response (GHR) and
  ii. Poor human response (PHR)
- **(One) Personalized Answers:** also bring the line up
  (This is a new concept and different from Klopfer and Beck.) Responses indicated in personalized manner such as 'I, me or we' like 'I see them all the time in the backyard'.
- **(One) Special colour phenomena:** (This is a new concept and different from Klopfer and Beck).

## 8. COLOUR PROJECTION (CP)
This is scored when the subject identifies achromatic blot area as coloured blot.

## 9. STRUCTURAL SUMMARY
After the scoring of responses for location, determinants, content, popular and special scores, arrange these into quantitative formulas and categorize into core section, ideation section, affect section, mediation, processing, interpersonal, self-perception and special indices.

**Core section** (Mixed like Klopfer and Beck's signs):

1. Lambda (L)

$$L = \frac{F(\text{All responses having only pure F determinants})}{R-F(\text{total R minus pure form response})}$$

2. Experience balance (EB): Relationship between human movement and weighted sum C:

$$EB: W \text{ sum } C = (0.5) \times FC + (1.0) \times CF + (1.5) Xc$$

3. Experience actual (EA): Sum of human movement + weighted sum chromatic colour
4. Experience base (eb): The ratio compares (FM + m) with sum of shading and achromatic colour.

$$eb: sum\ FM + m: Sum\ C' + Sum\ T + Sum\ Y + Sum\ V$$

5. Experiences stimulation (es): It is scored by adding two sides of the experience base ratio:

$$es: sum\ FM + m + Sum\ C' + Sum\ T + Sum\ Y + Sum\ V$$

6. D scores (D): Scored by subtracting es from EA (EA – es).
7. Adjusted es (Adj/D): All but 1 m and 1 Y are subtracted from es:
8. Adjusted D scores (Adj/D): It is calculated by subtracting Adj es from EA (EA – Adj es).

**Ideation section** (Newer concept different from Klopfer and Beck):

1. Active: passive ratio (a: p): is calculated by adding the total number of active movement and comparing with total number of passive movements.

$$Ma + FMa + ma: Mp + FMp + mp$$

2. M active: passive ratio: Ratio of active or passive movement to human movement.
3. The intellectualization index: is calculated by multiplying the total number of abstract (AB) responses by 2 and adding the sum of Art and Ay responses (2AB + [Art + Ay]).

**Affect section** (like Klopfer):

1. Form-Colour Ratio: FC: CF + C
2. Affective ratio: (Afr)

$$Afr = \frac{Total\ number\ of\ R\ to\ Card\ VIII + IX + X}{Total\ R\ in\ Card\ I + II + III + IV + V + VI + VII}$$

**Mediation section** (Newer concept different from Klopfer and Beck):

1. From appropriate extended (XA + %)

$$XA + \% = \frac{\text{Sum of responses that have FQ coding of +, o, u}}{R}$$

2. From appropriate-common areas: (WDA%)

$$WDA\% = \frac{\text{Sum of responses that have FQ coding of +, o, u}}{\text{Sum of } W + D}$$

3. Distorted form quality (X – %)

$$X - \% = \frac{\text{Sum of FQ}}{R}$$

4. Conventional form (F + %):

$$F + \% = \frac{\text{Sum FQx + o}}{R}$$

**Processing section** (New concept different from Klopfer and Beck, except aspirational ratio W: M):

1. Economy index: W: D: Dd
2. Aspirational ratio: W: M
3. Processing efficiency (Zd): (Zd): Z Sum – Zest

**The interpersonal section** (New concept different from Klopfer and Beck):

1. Interpersonal interest (H): H + (H) + Hd + (Hd)
2. Isolation index:

$$\text{Isolation index} = \frac{Bt + 2Cl + Ge + Ls + 2Na}{R}$$

**Self-perception section** (New concept, different from Klopfer and Beck):

This section includes: 1: sum of Fr + Rf

1. Total number of FD (form dimension)
2. Total number of MORBID responses
3. Sum of An + X + Xy
4. Sum of V (Vista)
5. H + (H) + Hd + (Hd)

$$\text{Egocentricity index} = \frac{3 \times (\text{Fr} + \text{Rf}) + \text{sum (2 pair responses)}}{\text{R}}$$

# 7

# Administration, Scoring and Interpretation of the Holtzman Inkblot Test

## Administration

The Holtzman Inkblot Technique (HIT) was developed originally to bridge the gap between the intuitively oriented clinician and the scientifically determined academician. To achieve a higher degree of psychometric reliability and validity, HIT is more demanding for the clinician than the Rorschach test. The accrual of scientific evidence for a clinical application is a slow process with which many practitioners are impatient. Since there are nine times as many inkblots in the combined forms of the HIT as there are in the Rorschach, the basic testing materials are significantly costlier. But the time and effort on the part of the clinician invested in administering, scoring and interpreting the HIT need not be any greater than for the Rorschach, once a clinician has mastered the technique. Those who have learned the method well have been enthusiastic about its value for both clinical and research purposes. Many clinicians find the HIT difficult or cumbersome because of the 45 inkblots instead of Rorschach's 10 or because of only one response per card rather than as many as the subject wishes to give. Yet, these are the very features that produce superior psychometric qualities, making the technique more suitable for rigorous scientific validity as well as for processing with modern computer technology (Holtzman 1986).

Standard procedures have been developed for the administration of the HIT.

> The standard instructions differ from those for the Rorschach ink-blots in several ways. First, the examiner instructs the subject to give only one response to each card. Second, the brief inquiry is given immediately after each response. And third, the permissible question by the examiner during inquiry is limited in scope and is asked rather regularly to avoid inadvertent verbal conditioning of certain determinants or content. (Holtzman 1986)

A record form and a summary sheet are provided to the examiner for recording the responses and scoring. The record form also provides space for personal identification data of the subject. A schematic diagram of location is provided to show the location of the responses. Scores for the 22 variables are recorded on the summary sheet.

After establishing a rapport, the examiner sits next to the subject where he can see the location of the responses and the subject's elaboration may be documented. The stack of 45 inkblots is placed in front of the examiner, face down, in serial order with the first trial blot (X) on the top. The examiner picks up the cards one at a time, handing each one in upright position to the subject. The instructions given to the subject should include the following points: '(a) these inkblots were not made to look like anything in particular; (b) different people see different things in each inkblot; and (c) only one response for each card is desired' (Holtzman 1956). However, the verbatim instructions are as follows:

> I have here a set of inkblots which were made by dropping ink on paper and folding it. I'd like you to look at each inkblot and tell me what it might look like, what it might represent, or what it could be. Since these are only inkblots, there are no right or wrong answers and each blot looks like different things to different people. It's possible for a person to see several things in each inkblot, but I want you to give me only one response for each card. After you see something and tell me about it, I'll ask you some questions, because I want to see it in the same way you do. I'll be writing down what you say and making note of the time, but you may take as long as you wish on each card. Do you have any questions? (Holtzman 1956)

The instructions are very simple and differ from the instructions of the Rorschach in the following ways: (a) The examiner instructs the examinee to give only one response per card; (b) a brief enquiry is given immediately after each response; (c) permissible questions by the examiner during enquiry are limited both in number and in scope and are asked rather routinely to avoid inadvertent verbal conditioning of certain determinants or content. Three kinds of questions are permissible as part of the brief enquiry in the standard administration. The actual wording used can vary a great deal, so that the inquiry becomes a natural part of the conversation between examiner and subject (Holtzman 1986). Typical phrasing would be as follows:

'Where in the blot do you see...?'
'Is there anything else you care to tell me about?'
'What is there about the blot that makes it look like a...?'

In the case of school children and young normal adults, administer the HIT twice using the alternate forms for the second administration. The time between test and retest sessions can be varied from one week to one year for the different samples, permitting rather broad generalizations about the equivalences of the two forms and the stability of inkblot scores over a period.

The subject's reaction time for each actual response is recorded in seconds. The examiner may score certain variables concurrently with the administration without any interruption to the subject. The form appropriateness is easier to score at the time the response is given. Replying to a query of the subject such as 'Can I turn the card?' or 'Should I use the whole inkblot?', the examiner should always answer with a non-committal remark like 'That's entirely up to you.' Immediately after each response, a brief enquiry is made by the examiner to check on certain aspects of the response and to obtain additional information helpful in scoring the location, determinants and if there is anything else. When a subject rejects an inkblot, claiming that he can see nothing in it, it will be considered as 'rejection'. The examiner should make effort to keep the number of rejections to a minimum by giving the subject plenty of time and encouragement like 'Does it now suggest anything to you?' (Holtzman 1986).

## Scoring of HIT

Holtzman developed 22 quantitative variables to cover nearly all important scoring categories and dimensions commonly employed with the Rorschach test.

The 22 variables finally adopted can be divided into several categories along traditional lines. Location and space deal with the parts of the inkblot used by the person in organizing his response and figure–ground relations of these parts. Form definiteness, Form Appropriateness, Color, Shading and Movement constitute those variables often referred to as determinant of the response. The form, color and texture off the inkblot are the major stimulus characteristics that play a determining role in the formulation of the concept. Five variables are used for the classification and scoring of the more important kind of content Human, Animal, Anatomy, Sex and Abstract. The quality of the response content is captured in part by such scores as Anxiety, Hostility, Barrier, Penetration and Pathognomic verbalization. Five additional scores—Integration, Balance, Popular, Reaction Time and Rejection complete the set of 22 variables. (Holtzman 1956)

The examiner scores each variable in turn for each response except for the practice inkblots, X and Y. A summary sheet is used for recording the score on each variable. For detailed information about scoring please consult *Holtzman Manual* (1956). The 22 variables are as follows (Table 7.1).

It is advisable to attach the completed summary sheet with the record form to keep together all the information about the subject.

1. **Reaction Time (RT)**
   Reaction time is recorded in seconds—the time from the presentation of the inkblot to the primary response. If the subject rejects the inkblot, the time at which the card is rejected should be recorded as the reaction time. The average RT is obtained by summing the scores for the 45 inkblots and dividing the total by 45.
2. **Rejection (R)**
   Responses such as 'Just looks like an inkblot to me' or 'I can't make it out', are counted as rejections.
3. **Location (L)**
   The following three-point system is used for scoring location:

   0: Use of the whole blot or at least all except minor portion of the blot (cut-off whole).
   1: Use of large area of the blot, such as one entire side or the entire centre of the blot.
   2: Use of smaller areas of the blot.

The total scores for location are obtained by summing the individuals scoring weights across the 45 cards. The scores can theoretically vary from 0 to 90.

**TABLE 7.1** Scoring Variables, Abbreviation and Theoretical Score Range

| 22 Scoring Variables | Abbreviation | Theoretical Score Range |
|---|---|---|
| Reaction time | RT | – |
| Rejection | R | 45 |
| Location | L | 90 |
| Space | S | 45 |
| Form definiteness | FD | 180 |
| Form appropriateness | FA | 90 |
| Colour | C | 135 |
| Shading | Sh | 90 |
| Movement | M | 180 |
| Pathognomic verbalization | V | 180 |
| Integration | I | 45 |
| Human | H | 90 |
| Animal | A | 90 |
| Anatomy | At | 90 |
| Sex | Sx | 90 |
| Abstract | Ab | 90 |
| Anxiety | Ax | 90 |
| Hostility | Hs | 135 |
| Barrier | Br | 45 |
| Penetration | Pn | 45 |
| Balance | B | 45 |
| Popular | P | 25 |

Source: Author personal communication with Holtzman in 2015.

4. **Space (S)**

   Space is scored when there is true figure background reversal, for example, when the white part of the card is used as the figure in the percept with the inkblot serving as background to delineate the form of the white area.

5. **Form Definiteness (FD)**

   Such a variable is entirely concept centred, though some blots are more likely than others to evoke form definite concepts. The importance of form definiteness is obvious when considered concurrently with form appropriateness, the goodness of the fit of the concept to the form of the inkblot.

6. **Form Appropriateness (FA)**

   It deals with the goodness of fit of the form of the concept to the form of the inkblot.

7. **Colour (C)**

   The scoring of the colour is based upon the importance of colour, including black, grey or white, as a response determinant. In general, giving credit for colour is reserved for responses where it is explicitly mentioned by the subject.

8. **Shading (Sh)**

   The scoring of shading is based solely upon the primacy of the shading as a determinant. Shading is scored when qualitative differences are made between which the shading of the blot is used, such as distinction between surface, texture, vista and depth. All instances of shading as a determinant have been pooled into one score.

9. **Movement (M)**

   Score for movement is given only when the subject voluntarily ascribes movement or potential for movement to the percept. The examiner should not make a direct enquiry to elicit movement.

10. **Pathognomic Verbalization (V)**

    Autistic thinking is usually reflected in the subject's description of the response or the explanation of why he saw such a percept. An important consideration in assessing the degree of pathology is the extent to which the subject lacks insight into the deviant character of his response.

11. **Integration (I)**

    It can be scored when two or more adequately perceived blots are organized into a larger whole response. Three other variables must be taken into account in scoring integration. Following are the types of integration.

    a. *Functional integration*

       Functional integration is based upon an interaction between two or more conceptually independent units.

    b. *Collective integration*

       It is scored when an overall grouping is actively imposed on the blots. The essential feature is evidence of conceptualizing, classifying process as distinct from one of sheer enumeration.

    c. *Positional integration*

       It is scored when there is a spatial relationship between the elements perceived such as 'two natives are dancing around bonfire'.

d. *Structural integration*
It is scored when a single content is arrived at by unifying two or more coloured areas including white space.
12. **Human**
13. **Animal**
14. **Anatomy**
15. **Sex**
16. **Abstract**
17. **Anxiety (Ax)**
Emotions or attitudes expressed or implied which reveal the feelings of fear, unpleasantness, sorrow and pity are scored as anxiety.
18. **Hostility (Hs)**
The scoring is based on symbolic, implicit or explicit signs of hostility shown in the response.
19. **Barrier (Br)**
The concept of barrier refers to any protective covering, membrane, shell or skin related to the perception of body image boundaries. A score of 1 is given to each response where barrier is present and score of 0 when barrier is absent.
20. **Penetration (Pn)**
Any concept which might be symbolic of an individual's feeling that his body exterior is of little protective value and can be easily penetrated is likely to be scored 1 on penetration.
21. **Balance (B)**
One of the blots used in the Holtzman test was deliberately selected because of its asymmetry or lack of perceptual balance. Balance (B) is scored as either present (1) or absent (0) on each response.
22. **Popular (P)**
Popular responses in HIT are more common than those in Klopfer or Beck's systems. It occurs for at least one out of seven protocols. These are about 25 in number.

There are other variables which can be scored for most inkblot protocols and the space has been provided on the summary sheet for inclusion of additional scores. However, the adoption of only 22 scoring variables make the test simpler and less complicated.

The scoring weights for the 22 HIT variables as described by Holtzman (1986) are given as follows:

1. *Reaction Time (RT):* The time in seconds from the presentation of the inkblot to the beginning of the primary response.

2. *Rejection (R):* Score 1 when subject returns inkblot to examiner without giving a scorable response; otherwise, score 0.
3. *Location (L):* Tendency to break down blot into smaller fragments. Score 0 for use of the whole blot, 1 for large area and 2 for smaller area.
4. *Space (S):* Score 1 for true figure–ground reversals; otherwise, score 0.
5. *Form Definiteness (FD):* The definiteness of the form of the concept reported, regardless of the goodness of fit to the inkblot. A 5-point scale with 0 for very vague and 4 for highly specific.
6. *From Appropriateness (FA):* The goodness of fit of the form of the percept to the form of the inkblot. Score 0 for poor, 1 for fair and 2 for good.
7. *Colour (C):* The apparent primacy of colour (including black, grey or white) as a response determinant. Score 0 for no use of colour, 1 for its use as a secondary to the form (like Rorschach FC), 2 when used as the primary determinant but with some form present (like CF) and 3 when used as the primary determinant with no form present (like C).
8. *Shading (Sh):* The apparent primacy of shading as a response determinant (texture, depth or vista). Score 0 for no use of shading, 1 when used as a secondary determinant and 2 when used as the primary determinant with little or no form present.
9. *Movement (M):* The energy level of movement or potential movement ascribed to the percept, regardless of the content. Score 0 for none, 1 for static potential, 2 for casual, 3 for dynamic and 4 for violent movement.
10. *Pathognomic Verbalization (V):* Degree of autistic, bizarre thinking evident in the response, as rated on a 5-point scale. Score 0 where no pathology is present. The nine categories of V and the range of scoring weights for each are as follows: fabulation, 1; fabulized combination, 2, 3, 4; queer response, 1, 2, 3; incoherence, 4; autistic logic, 1, 2, 3, 4; contamination, 2, 3, 4; self-reference, 2, 3, 4; deterioration colour, 2, 3, 4; absurd response, 3.
11. *Anatomy (At):* The degree of 'gut like' quality in the content. Score 0 for none; 1 for bones, x-rays or medical drawings; and 2 for visceral and crude anatomy.
12. *Sex (Sx):* Degree of sexual quality in the content. Score 0 for no sexual reference, 1 for socially accepted sexual activity or expressions (buttocks, bust, kissing) and 2 for blatant sexual content (penis, vagina).

13. *Abstract (Ab):* Degree of abstract quality in the content. Score 0 for none, 1 for abstract elements along with other elements having form and 2 for purely abstract content ('Bright colours remind me of gaiety').

14. *Anxiety (Ax):* Signs of anxiety in the fantasy content, as indicated by emotions and attitudes, expressive behaviour, symbolism or cultural stereotypes of fear. Score 0 for none, 1 for questionable or indirect signs and 2 for an overt or clear-cut evidence.

15. *Hostility (Hs):* Signs of hostility in the fantasy content. Scored on a 4-point scale ranging from 0 for none to 3 for direct, violent, interpersonal destruction.

16. *Barrier (Br):* Score 1 for reference to any protective covering, membrane, shell or skin that might be symbolically related to the perception of body image boundaries; otherwise, score 0.

17. *Penetration (Pn):* Score 1 for concept that might be symbolic of an individual's feeling that his body exterior is of little protective value and can be easily penetrated; otherwise, score 0.

18. *Balance (B):* Score 1 where there is an overt concern for the symmetry–asymmetry feature of the inkblot; otherwise, score 0.

19. *Popular (P):* Each form contains 25 inkblots in which one or more popular percepts occur. 'Popular' in standardization studies means that a percept must occur at least 14 per cent of the time among normal subjects. Score 1 for popular core concepts (or their precision alternatives) as listed in the scoring manual; otherwise, score 0.

20. *Integration (I):* Score 1 for the organization of two or more adequately perceived blot elements into a larger whole; otherwise, score 0.

21. *Human (H):* Degree of human quality in the content of response. Score 0 for none; 1 for parts of humans, distortions or cartoons; and 2 for whole human beings or elaborated human faces.

22. *Animal (A):* Degree of animal quality in the content. Score 0 for none (including animal objects and microscopic life); 1 for animal parts, bugs or insects and 2 for whole animals.

Extensive reviews on HIT (Holtzman 1981; Holtzman and Swartz 1983; Swartz, Reinehr and Holtzman 1983a) have proved the reliability, validity and use of the test in different situations. Factor analysis of intercorrelations among the 22 HIT variables have indicated that these scores tend to cluster into the following three meaningful factors.

## Factor 1. Perceptual Maturity and Integrated Ideational Activity: Movement, Integration, Human and Barrier

High scores on these four variables taken together are indicative of a well-organized ideational activity, good imaginative capacity and well-differentiated ego boundaries. All four variables increase with age among children and are significantly higher among college graduates than average adults, indicating a strong component of cognitive ability and creativity (Swartz et al. 1983b). Studies have shown repeatedly that these variables are indicative of creative potential. They show significant relationships with reading comprehension among children, even after general intelligence has been held constant (Laird, Laosa and Swartz 1973).

The energy level of movement ascribed to the percept, regardless of content, has some other interesting correlates. A high score on movement is associated with a perceived empathy in counsellors, whereas low movement is associated with the reverse (Mueller and Abeles 1964). The degree of eye contact and smiling among psychiatric patients when interviewed is also related to high movement scores (Lefcourt et al. 1972). Movement is correlated with the discharge or inhibition of cognitive energy, according to Covan (1976). Increased perception of movement in inkblots follows experimental inhibition of cognitive responses, while discharge of cognitive processes in a series of free-association tasks leads to a sharp decrease in reported perception of movement in inkblots (Holtzman 1986).

Dream deprivation, whether induced by drugs (Lerner 1966) or prevented by interrupting rapid eye movements (Feldstein 1973), results in higher movement scores. These findings support Rorschach's views on the fundamental similarity between movement and dreams due to the centrality of kinaesthetic experience in both, an outcome that is also consistent with Heinz Werner's (1957) sensory tonic theory of perception.

Movement has a particularly strong cognitive component among young children. In the first year of testing for six-year-olds in the longitudinal study, the complete battery of tests for the Wechsler Intelligence Scale for Children (WISC) was given. Factor analyses of inter-correlations among various cognitive tests were carried out, with movement included as an extra variable. Among the US children, movement was clearly a major part of the first factor defined by the verbal subtests from WISC. Movement did not show up heavily loaded on a similar factor for the Mexicans until the nine-year-olds were analysed. Similar results were found among the US nine- and twelve-year-olds, since they had not been given the complete WISC test battery. Movement deals with the component of verbal ability characterized by a lively, active imagination and the ability to project outward from one's fantasies. In this sense, it deals particularly with the expressive, imaginative aspects of verbal ability rather than with information, word meanings and analytic problem-solving (Holtzman 1986).

Human content also has some special meaning worthy of note. As one would expect from projective theory, a high score on human suggests high social interest, whereas lack of any human content indicates the opposite (Fernald and Linden 1966).

One of the most interesting of the symbolic content scores is barrier developed by Fisher and Cleveland (1958). The score is given for references to any protective covering, membrane, shell or skin that might be symbolically related to the perception of body image boundaries. High barrier is indicative of strong ego identity, whereas low barrier suggests diffusion. High barrier is related to being influential and independent in group processes (Cleveland and Morton 1962), adjusting well to physical disablement (Fisher 1963), being able to tolerate pain (Nichols and Tursky 1967) and having a positive evaluation of one's own body (Conquest 1963). These findings are consistent with others showing that low barrier is related to juvenile delinquency (Megargee 1965).

### Factor 2. Perceptual Sensitivity: Colour, Shading and Form Definiteness (Reversed)

The clustering together of colour and shading with form definiteness (reversed) is inevitable. As with scoring systems for the Rorschach, the greater the predominance of colour or shading over form in a response, the higher the score. Among young children, significant negative loadings on this factor also appear for animal, suggesting that many children tend to use colour and shading as a determinant only when they cannot find a familiar animal form. The positive pole on this factor indicates overreaction to the stimulus determinants, whereas the negative pole shows primary concern for form alone as a response determinant (Holtzman 1986).

Among normal subjects, a high colour score has been found to be related to impulsivity (Holtzman 1950) and to increased expression of affect (Mayfield 1968). In her clinical use of HIT, Hill (1972) recommended paying attention to the quality of the colour responses—particularly those given to inkblots having a high stimulus strength for colour—in making interpretations about the lability of affect (Holtzman 1986).

There is little experimental evidence bearing upon the validity of shading or form definiteness, the other two variables that measure degree of perceptual sensitivity. Nor is there much information from correlational studies with other personality measures that would indicate an independent meaning of these variables for assessment purposes. To be sure, there is a consensus among Rorschach clinicians concerning the use of these scores for personality assessment, but the scientific evidence is too tenuous currently to justify any confident interpretations, particularly among children (Holtzman 1986).

### Factor 3. Psychopathology of Thought: Pathognomic Verbalization, Anxiety and Hostility

Pathognomic verbalization is the best single indicator of psychopathology. Among adolescents and adults, the bizarre perception and autistic logic underlying high scores on this variable are characteristic either of schizophrenia or extreme artistic license in responding to inkblots. Highly creative, successful artists do tend to get much higher scores than average individuals on pathognomic verbalization (Holtzman, Swartz and Thorpe 1971), but the quality of the response is noticeably different. Normal individuals tend to give fabulations with notable affectivity, mildly fabulized combinations of otherwise acceptable percepts or even occasional queer responses that often are described in a playful manner. Schizophrenics, on the other hand, manifest a loss of distance between themselves and the inkblots, often giving extremely fabulized combinations, contaminations, queer responses or special kinds of autistic logic that show faulty, fantastic reasoning as a justification for the response. Embellishing a response with highly personal meaning by self-reference is particularly characteristic of psychotic thinking when manifested repeatedly (Swartz 1970). A predominance of absurd responses is characteristic of mentally retarded individuals, whereas a predominance of deteriorated colour associations is indicative of severe disintegration (Holtzman 1986).

Among young children, moderately high scores on pathognomic verbalization simply may indicate immature thought processes coupled with uncontrolled fantasies and loose imagination rather than serious psychopathology.

Signs of anxiety or hostility in the fantasy content form the basis for the anxiety or hostility score. Moderate-level scores on both symbolic content scales are normal, particularly in young children, but very high scores should be interpreted as having a likely clinical significance. Zero or low positive correlations can be expected between each of these two variables and anxiety or hostility scales based upon self-report inventories. The most important evidence of their validity comes from experimental studies. Subjects who rapidly acquire conditioned eyelid response have higher anxiety scores than those who do not condition easily (Herron 1965). Individuals with high anxiety are less tolerant of pain (Nichols and Tursky 1967). Individuals who show a marked increase in hostility scores after experiencing frustrating situations are those who also show a predisposition to hostility as measured by factor 1 of the Buss–Durkee Inventory (Rosenstiel 1973). Both anxiety and hostility scores are directly related to the observed interpersonal distance characteristic of an individual in an experimental setting; the higher the inkblot scores, the greater the distance (Greenberg, Aronow and Rauchway 1977). These findings are all consistent with the theoretical conception of these symbolic content scores. While the meaning of anxiety and hostility scores may be complex, it is clear that very high scores, even among children, have enough validity to justify clinical interpretation (Holtzman 1986).

## Nosological and Normative Studies with HIT

Closely related to the clinical validity of individual variables within HIT is the use of patterns of scores for differential diagnosis. The original standardization data on 15 different populations are presented in percentile norms for eight major reference groups ranging from five-year-olds to superior adults and including psychiatric patients as well as mental retardates. Chronic schizophrenics differ from normal reference groups on almost all HIT variables. Even without pathognomic verbalization, Moseley (1963) was able to develop an objective approach based upon linear combinations of 16 HIT scores that classified accurately 82 per cent of the normal from schizophrenics, 71 per cent of the normal from depressed patients and 78 per cent of the depressives from schizophrenics. Adding pathognomic verbalization in a two-stage model for use with doubtful cases, the efficiency of this objective approach to differential diagnosis was improved even more. More importantly, when cross-validated, the procedure held up completely. Others have had similar success in differentiating schizophrenics, neurotics, normal or organics by various combinations of HIT scores (Barnes 1964; Hill 1972; Holtzman 1986; Shukla 1976a, 1976b). `

Conners (1965) reported several highly significant differences between emotionally disturbed children seen in an outpatient clinic and normal controls of the same age and background. In Connors' study, disturbed children got higher scores on rejection and anatomy and lower scores on all other variables except pathognomic verbalization style (Holtzman 1986).

## Brief Interpretation of Holtzman Indices

*Movement, integration, human and barrier* repeatedly define a factor indicative of well-organized ideational activity, good imaginative capacity and well-differentiated ego boundaries. Each of the four variables has other correlates from independent studies that make them interesting. For example, dream deprivation results in higher movement scores (Feldstein 1973), and Movement is correlated with the discharge or inhibition of cognitive energy (Covan 1976).

*Pathognomic verbalization* has been shown to be the best single indicator of psychopathology. The bizarre perception and autistic logic underlying high scores on this variable are characteristic either of schizophrenia or extreme artistic license in responding to inkblots. Normal individuals tend to give fabulations with notable affectivity, mildly fabulized combinations of otherwise described in a playful manner. Schizophrenics, on the other hand, manifest fabulized combinations, contaminations, queer responses, or special kinds of autistic logic that show faulty, fantastic reasoning as a justification for the response.

*Sings of anxiety or hostility* in the fantasy content form the basis for the anxiety or hostility score. Moderate-level scores on both symbolic content scales are normal, particularly in young children, but very high scores should be interpreted as having likely clinical significance. The most important evidence of their validity comes from experimental studies. Individuals with high anxiety are less tolerant of pain (Nichols and Tursky 1967) and more rapidly acquire the conditioned eyelid response (Herron 1965). Individuals who show a marked increase in hostility score after a frustrating situation are those who also have a predisposition to hostility.

*A high colour score* has been found to be related to impulsivity and is predictive of poor performance under stressful field conditions (Holtzman and Swartx 1983). In her clinical use of HIT, Hill (1972) recommended paying attention to the quality of the colour responses, particularly those given to inkblots having high stimulus strength for colour, in making interpretations about the lability of affect.

Three scores —sex, anatomy and penetration—deal with bodily preoccupation. Blatant sex responses are relatively rare but significant when they do appear. High anatomy scores have been found closely associated with high degree of somatic preoccupation among hospitalized patients (Endicott and Jortner 1967). Penetration and barrier are the two body image scores developed by Fisher and Cleveland (1958).

*Location, form definiteness and form appropriateness* are interesting to consider together because of the dynamic tension that is created within an individual who is confronted with the task of organizing various percepts into a single response. The high achievement-oriented perceptual style characteristic of many Americans is to use the entire inkblot with percepts that are fairly form definite and form appropriate. Such a combination is difficult on many of the HIT inkblots, forcing some individuals to compromise by using smaller detail, reporting vaguer percepts or ignoring the goodness of fit of the percept to the form of the inkblot.

We can safely conclude that Wayne Holtzman developed HIT to bridge a gap between the intuitively oriented clinician and the scientific determinism of the academician. The HIT has higher degree of psychometric reliability and validity than the Rorschach test. Since it has more stimuli (inkblot cards), chances of manipulation become negligible. Although some have criticized about the test having too many cards to administer, after the experience of using this technique, many have found that it takes less time than many questionnaires. A few clinicians have also criticized the procedure on getting 'only one response per card'. While this restricts the projective value of the test, overall this is a 'positive trade off' since this approach increases the procedure's psychometric value. All in all, when compared to the Rorschach, HIT has proven to be a more valuable research tool and diagnostic instrument.

# 8

# Administration and Scoring of the Somatic Inkblot Test

## Administration and Scoring of SIS-II Test (62-Image Booklet and Video)

### Procedure and Instructions

Over the years, SIS has evolved into four formats (Booklet, Cards, Video and Online test). Although the method of their administration varies, they have a common conceptual basis in scoring and interpretation.

The scoring sheet serves to collect personal information, such as age, gender, education and other relevant health data and it is separated from the pages for personal responses to the images. The reason the subject is asked to complete the health questionnaire immediately before viewing the booklet or electronic version is to recall any physical problem. This momentarily creates a perceptual set for projecting clinically relevant material. As appropriate or necessary, the answer (response) booklet from the inkblots can be used in itself, independent of the electronic application. A unique advantage of the SIS procedure is that it can be 'self-administered' should the therapist, counsellor, psychologist, physician, research scientist or the educator finds it appropriate to application circumstances and goals. The procedure can also be used as 'group administration' during selection of employees in various organizations.

## CD/DVD/Video Procedure

When the SIS video is to be presented in a professional's office, the assessment room needs to be equipped with suitable electronic equipment (TV/VCR/computer). In addition to comfortable seating for two or more persons, it is best to provide a small table or desk to facilitate the writing of observations and responses in the answer booklet. Adequate and adjustable lighting and privacy from interruption and extraneous sounds will enhance the experience of the procedure.

The initial instructions and the assistance provided by the professional will induce a relaxed mood, which is intentionally cultivated. This is accomplished using pictures of flowers, peaceful scenes of natural environments and musical interludes. A calm mind and a semi-hypnotic state will serve to promote the release of deeply repressed and/or painful material that otherwise might never have been recalled. Normally, traumatic material is less likely to be verbalized directly in an interview situation or through non-projective psychometric tests.

The professional will provide full disclosure of the potential benefits and risks associated with the administration of the procedure. For children and adolescents, appropriate informed consent must be obtained from a parent or legal guardian.

The electronic versions are primarily intended for supervised administration by a trained professional as an adjunct to individual counselling, therapy or industrial consultations. When asked to give an opinion about the SIS video procedure in 1990, Professor Wayne Holtzman, internationally respected developer of the Holtzman inkblot series (Holtzman et al. 1956), said,

> Unlike many other methods, it is particularly appealing when used by the clinician and subject in an interactive, interpretive mode as part of the total diagnostic-treatment process. The dynamic nature of the stimulus, when presented electronically in full color, reaches well beyond the limitations of traditional projective techniques.

## Examination Instructions

The viewing procedure is to be administered under the direct supervision of a trained professional who has explained its risks/benefits, clinical relevance and value in better understanding a subject's problems. If, at any time, questions or difficulties should arise during or after administration of the procedure, please feel free to contact your clinician who will be pleased to assist.

Before the clinician administers the SIS procedure, it is important that a reasonable comfort level is established with the person who is to view the SIS images. The professional may begin by going over the following instructions listed on the back page of the answer booklet:

Turn the booklet over and observe how the illustrated inkblot is labelled at the top of the first page. Then write down whatever comes to your mind. Include any emotions that relate to each image. When you have completed the procedure, please note the instructions on the back page regarding rating of inkblots which you 'liked the most' and which you 'liked the least'. Remember to include why you chose those images. First, have the subject fill in the brief health history. Explain to him/her that a series of flowers will be shown to help him/her relax. Next, indicate that there will be video instructions on how to fill in the answer booklet.

### SIS-II Booklet Procedure

The booklet version of SIS-II can be used in a variety of ways but it was designed for self-administration under supervised instruction. The subject is provided an eight-page booklet consisting 62 images in two series A and B, each with 31 images and is asked to read the instructions printed on last page of the booklet:

Most people find this test fun and interesting. First, please relax, take a few deep breaths, and prepare to enjoy. Please turn this booklet over and study the sample response. Notice that you may write on the picture or in the space below it. Label each in terms of what they resemble or look like to you. Please include everything you see even if it reminds you of something remote, vague, dreamlike, highly personal or even potentially embarrassing. Please include everything you see with as much detail as possible. Also include any outstanding emotional reaction that you might feel occur in responding to these images. Please begin on the first page, study the sample and continue until completed.

The subject is asked to complete the identification data and a brief personal health history as instructed in the video procedure. Reassure the subject that there are no right or wrong answers. Different people see different things in the inkblots. It is important to write whatever the inkblot looks like regardless of whether it makes sense or how it might seem to others. The subject is asked to select three images which he/she liked the most and three images which he/she liked the least.

## Scoring

There are only 11 scoring indices common in all forms of SIS (card/booklet/CD/DVD or videotape).

### Definitions of Scoring Indices

Mental health professionals with training and experience in projective techniques will have little difficulty in integrating the scoring and charting conventions used in SIS. *Body Symbolism* (Cassell 1980) can be a resource for increasing one's skill in the interpretation of SIS responses of the original 20 cards. Since the procedure conceptually taps into the same stream of imagery as seen in dreams, daytime fantasies and visual hallucinations, a background in the interpretation of such content, either in a direct or in a latent symbolic way, is helpful. Clinicians experienced in art psychotherapy will readily adapt to this technique (Kwiatkowski 1978; Unman 1965). They will find SIS a useful aid, especially for people who cannot draw. In a sense, SIS uses art as a diagnostic and therapeutic tool for those who cannot engage in the traditional art procedures. Other clinicians with experience in dream interpretation, visualization techniques, guided imagery, active imagination therapies and hypnotherapy will also readily adapt to this procedure.

The 11 categories found to be important in understanding and interpreting protocols are:

1. Total number of responses
2. Human responses
3. Animal responses
4. Anatomical responses
5. Sex responses
6. Movement responses
7. Most typical responses
8. Typical responses
9. Atypical responses
10. Rejection of images
11. Pathological responses:

a. Pathological anatomy scale (PAS)
b. Depression (D)
c. Hostility and aggression scale (HAS)
d. Paranoia (P)

Each category is designed to stimulate consistency among the raters and to afford commonality in acquiring information for research and normative data collection. SIS has a very simple scoring system. It is less complicated than existing inkblot tests, since it emphasizes content analysis. The scoring categories have been described as follows:

1. **Total Number of Responses (R)**
   The total number of responses is arrived at by counting all the responses given by the subject on the 62 images of SIS-II Booklet/DVD/Video. The optimum number of good quality responses suggests imaginative capacity and functioning intelligence of the subject. Psychiatrically ill patients will have a poor imaginative capacity and poor functional intelligence.

2. **Human Responses (H)**
   Human responses include the whole human body or external parts of the human body like face, ear, nose, legs, etc. The category does not include mutilated forms of the whole body or parts of it, such as a crushed human being, broken legs or smashed face. These mutilated responses are included in the anatomical responses. The number of human responses suggests the subject's projection of own self and interpersonal relationships with other human beings. When these responses are low, it might be indicative of a desire to be away from others and indicative of schizoid or social isolation tendencies.

3. **Animal Responses (A)**
   Animal responses include living or dead animals, both wild and pet, such as reptiles, birds and sea animals. This category also includes external parts of animals such as wings, legs, claws and beak, but it does not include mutilated parts of the whole animal such as crushed birds or animals and pulled out wings. Whenever many animal responses are given, interpretation should be that the respondent is either more comfortable with animals than people or psychologically immature.

4. **Anatomical Responses (At)**
   Anatomical responses pertain to internal parts of living beings and their mutilated forms, both of humans and animals. These responses are consistently high in those who have a poor self-image, preoccupation with somatic symptoms in the region they focus on.

5. **Sex Responses (Sex)**
   Sex responses pertain to the internal or external reproductive system and to sensuous parts of the body. These responses include thighs, buttocks, breasts, fallopian tubes, ovaries, etc. Heightened anxiety and pathology may be associated with either heightened projections or impaired recognition of imbedded sexual structure. These may signify sexual anxiety and/or dysfunction.

6. **Movement Responses (M)**
   Movement responses indicate activity and kinaesthetic motor impulses. Examples include 'talking human being', 'flying bird' or 'running tiger'. Dancing and joyful movement may reflect a positive mood and low movement may indicate depression.

7. **Most Typical Responses (MT)**
   Most typical responses are those which are given by more than 75 per cent of normal subjects on an image (Dubey and Cassell 1993). The total number of such responses is limited to 18. A higher number of most typical responses is suggestive of coherent, logical thinking and an ability to keep up with the demands of the society. It may also be interpreted as a measure of ego strength and team concept. The list of most typical responses along with the images eliciting them is given as follows:

## SIS-II, A Series (MT Responses)
A7: Apple/fruit
A7: Dancing lady
A9: Two human beings/ladies
A12: Ear
A13: Raised hand
A20: Kidney/lungs
A27: Breast
A30: Skull
A31: Two faces of persons

## SIS-II B Series (MT Responses)
B4: Two faces of persons
B5: Two persons talking
B9: Kidney/lungs
B22: Man/boy sleeping or resting/dreaming and soul going up
B27: Child/children
B28: Mother and child/standing lady
B29: Running man
B30: Ears
B31: Family—father, mother and two children

8. **Typical Responses (T)**

Typical responses are those which are commonly seen by healthy people on the images.

9. **Atypical Responses (AT)**

Atypical responses are those of poor quality and with vague percept, either in structure or verbalization. A response that markedly departs from the category of typical responses is also scored under atypical category. For example, if the viewer responds 'flower' for Image A20, it should be considered as atypical because this image should elicit body anatomy such as kidney/lungs. The number of atypical responses is proportionate to the degree of psychological or psychiatric disturbance. Perseveration may be a sign of neuropsychological impairment and is usually absent in normal people.

A list of typical and atypical responses on each image is given as follows:

### Typical and Atypical Responses (SIS-II, A)
(Images A1–A31 and B1–B31 are reproduced at the end of the book.)

### Image A1
Typical: Two people; two animals
Atypical: Lungs; diseased lungs; ovaries and fallopian tubes; woman's breast; an x-ray of pelvis

### Image A2
Typical: Floral arrangement; people
Atypical: Heart; eye

### Image A3
Typical: Space needle; cross; tree
Atypical: Bleeding body part; vagina (libidinal cathexis in lesbian women)

### Image A4
Typical: A horse's face; abstract art
Atypical: A mask; an eye looking at me; the Devil; a person (mother grieving loss of son)

### Image A5
Typical: Clown; happy person
Atypical: Woman; heart; mouth

**Image A6**
Typical: Person and teddy bear
Atypical: Egg and teddy bear; two chromosomes; legs; lines and teddy bear (lack of gestalt in concrete thought disorder)

**Image A7**
Typical: Woman dancing; Eve and apple; seductive woman; apple
Atypical: Male; pregnant woman; heart; rivers and island; snakes

**Image A8**
Typical: Man; man showing male parts
Atypical: Woman's vulva; egg and sperm; fat body or face; baby; lines

**Image A9**
Typical: Man and woman dancing; hearts; two men or two women dancing
Atypical: Two sets of lines; face; eyes; two ants; two animals

**Image A10**
Typical: Eyes; eyes out of focus; woman's face in rear-view mirror
Atypical: Hazy face; crying

**Image A11**
Typical: Nose; auto; a sitting person; leaning forward; the Thinker; runner waiting for starting gun
Atypical: Person doubled over in severe pain; person doubled over all the way with head between legs; kidney excreting waste (GI problems)

**Image A12**
Typical: Ear
Atypical: Embryo

**Image A13**
Typical: An upraised hand; a hand reaching for help; palm
Atypical: Suffering, pleading, helpless, desperate or attacking hand; hand in flames or reaching out of concealment to grab someone (rape victim)

**Image A14**
Typical: Oesophagus and stomach; Olympic torch carrier; airport tower

Atypical: Foetus; miscarriage; sacred heart; kidney

### Image A15
Typical: Stomach; bird; foetus
Atypical: Kidney; dead baby

### Image A16
Typical: Two lovebirds; heart
Atypical: Two (starving) birds fighting for food; lungs; an x-ray of chest; leaves

### Image A17
Typical: Chest; ribs; heart; lungs
Atypical: Ugly dog; monster looking out at you; gaping open mouth; two catfish looking at evil; sea horses; heart (afraid it will stop; sign of death anxiety)

### Image A18
Typical: Heart; female genitalia; uterus; animal coming out of heart
Atypical: Creature from outer space; atomic bomb exploding; X-ray of brain

### Image A19
Typical: Intestines; colon
Atypical: Human penis; woman creating foetus

### Image A20
Typical: Kidneys; lungs; thorax
Atypical: Weight lifter (back pain detail); a bush with a spear for roots; brain; ovaries; testicles; eyes; ears

### Image A21
Typical: Turtle; flying bird; babies on sides
Atypical: Stretched animal skin; man fleshing two children; smashed animal showing entrails; spinal disc

### Image A22
Typical: Spinal column; chest; rib cage; pelvis; phallus
Atypical: Male genitals burrowing; funny face with low forehead (lower part); man-eating plant (upper part)

### Image A23
Typical: Spinal column

Atypical: 'Mind block' (rape victim repressing male genital symbolism); pots, pans or plates stacked on one another (neutralizing defence against a phallic symbol by a rape victim)

### Image A24
Typical: Female pelvis; people
Atypical: Demons or devils

### Image A25
Typical: Female sex organ
Atypical: Stained glass window; crucifix (substituting religious symbolism); cave or tunnel; beetle; Indian oil lamp; eyes

### Image A26
Typical: Foetus; embryo
Atypical: Face; reflecting repugnant emotion (pregnant woman unhappy with pregnancy)

### Image A27
Typical: Human female breast; baby sucking at a breast; deer's head
Atypical: Female arm being injured; marked decapitated woman

### Image A28
Typical: Leg; thigh; wrist and hand
Atypical: Hand from a horror film

### Image A29
Typical: None typical, all are 'projective'
Atypical: Scary face; person running; shadow of a gun

### Image A30
Typical: Face; skull; Neanderthal man; monkey's face
Atypical: The rapist's face; evil surrounded by evil; the Devil

### Image A31
Typical: Two human faces, man and woman, or adult and child whispering secrets
Atypical: Man and woman arguing; sad faces

### Typical and Atypical Responses (SIS-II B)

### Image B1
Typical: Camp fire; melting ice cream

Atypical: Rotting tooth; amniotic sac with embryo; bleeding heart

## Image B2
Typical: Fire spreading in forest; rag doll on a stick
Atypical: Ovaries; fallopian tubes and uterus; attacking animal; monster; ultrasound image of vagina

## Image B3
Typical: People talking
Atypical: Throat and tonsils; vagina; rectum; pelvic bones; Darth Vader's head

## Image B4
Typical: Two human faces; adult and child
Atypical: A person projecting an alternative personality (multiple personality disorder); mummies; a person threatening someone

## Image B5
Typical: Two seated human figures throwing balls; people conversing
Atypical: Man and woman arguing; me (referring to self) not able to communicate with doctor

## Image B6
Typical: Upper thighs and lower abdomen; pair of pants
Atypical: Fat thighs; penis in vagina; stomach X-ray; woman's lace panties (eroticism, typical in lesbian woman)

## Image B7
Typical: Ribs; upper chest; hot water bottle
Atypical: Brain; painful back; heart with arrow in or through it; pelvis

## Image B8
Typical: Nose; a man's profile; earth
Atypical: Pregnant woman; cocoon

## Image B9
Typical: Lungs; kidney; penis and testicles
Atypical: Woman's reproductive organs; liver and spinal cord; gall bladder

## Image B10
Typical: Bear's face; dog; seeds

Atypical: Sad dog; pregnancy; female; female reproductive organs; ears

## Image B11
Typical: Lungs; two birds; flowers
Atypical: Lungs distorted, fighting for breath; smoker's lungs

## Image B12
Typical: Face; man squinting hard
Atypical: Evil face; expression of pain; angry face; crying face

## Image B13
Typical: Colon; intestines; a question mark
Atypical: Peephole

## Image B14
Typical: Pure projection, lower back; pelvis; apple
Atypical: Heart; trachea and lungs

## Image B15
Typical: Broken glass; paper airplanes; knives
Atypical: Knives to kill someone; suicidal or homicidal imagery

## Image B16
Typical: Spine; spinal cord; vertebrae
Atypical: Tool for drilling; hypodermic needle; painful vertebrae

## Image B17
Typical: Heart; smoking
Atypical: Open vagina, ready for intercourse; a dark hole

## Image B18
Typical: Spinal cord; male sex organ in action
Atypical: Sperm going through tunnel; two people talking; snake in a pipe

## Image B19
Typical: Cell; ovum; egg; sun; heart
Atypical: Broken heart (post-trauma response of rape victim); egg being fertilized (pregnancy wish); ugly spider

## Image B20
Typical: Brain; exposed brain

Atypical: Foetus; diseased or troubled brain

## Image B21
Typical: A gun; exploding cork; firecracker
Atypical: A gun shooting someone; penis with a band around it (sign of impotence)

## Image B22
Typical: Body resting; soul leaving body; dead person
Atypical: Blood spurting from chest; crime victim bleeding to death

## Image B23
Typical: Spider; rib cage; heart; lung; crab
Atypical: Ribcage with cancer

## Image B24
Typical: Kidneys; hanging lamps
Atypical: Twins (pregnancy wish); sperm; testicles; ovaries

## Image B25
Typical: Pelvis of a woman; hands holding glass; circle
Atypical: Apple; koala bear; pelvis with fire inside;

## Image B26
Typical: Female sex organs (cervix, ovaries, uterus, vagina)
Atypical: Skull; top of hammer; dog with large ears

## Image B27
Typical: Foetus; embryo; child
Atypical: Diseased foetus; dead baby

## Image B28
Typical: Mother and child
Atypical: Woman holding baby close and running away; person in despair hugging self; father and child; Jesus holding and comforting someone

## Image B29
Typical: Running human figure; lame
Atypical: Human figure with one leg running in fear

## Image B30
Typical: Two ears; foetus

Atypical: Split brain (multiple personality disorder); lungs

**Image B31**
Typical: A family of two adults and two children standing together;
father, mother and two children.
Atypical: A family disintegrating; people with penises for head; four
children

10. **Rejection of Images (Rej.)**
    If the subject is unable to give any response on any of the 62
    images, that image is considered as rejected. Verbalizations like
    'spot' or 'inkblot' are not considered as a response and are scored as
    rejections. To determine the percentage of rejection of responses,
    the total number of rejected images is divided by the total number
    of images and multiplied by 100. Rejection of images may show
    low intelligence, thought blockage from psychological inhibition
    or organic brain involvement.
11. **Pathological Scales**
    Four pathological scales have been used (Cassell 1980) for evaluat-
    ing individuals. They are as follows:
    a. Pathologic Anatomy Scale (PAS);
    b. Depression (D);
    c. Hostility and Aggression Scale (HAS); and
    d. Paranoia Scale (P).

Some of these are based on the work of Holtzman (1956). The scales
are as follows:

a. **Pathological anatomy scale (PAS)**
   Subjects who have personal health concerns, or who pathologically
   identify with the health of others, may project responses in which
   the body is seen as diseased. These responses are usually related
   to specific body regions in the subject's body image and can be
   appraised by evaluating the qualitative nature of the somatic material projected. The anatomical imagery is like that described by De
   Vos (1973) in Rorschach responses, involving 'diseased anatomy'.
   Body parts might be reported as red, inflamed, infected or cancerous.
   Organs may be sore, painful or hurting. Passages may be blocked
   or obstructed. Bones may be out of place or broken. It is possible to
   assess pathologic anatomy by summing up all such responses. All
   these responses are scored under PAS. Individuals who project these
   responses should be further evaluated for either hypochondriacal
   or excessive concern about physical health. This material should

be explored, clarified and assessed in the detailed enquiry and the follow-up interview since the subject may still have unresolved anxiety about this alteration in body concept. The total number of such responses is counted to form a score for PAS.

b. **Depression scale (D)**

A depressed subject's emotional state can be viewed as either overt or covert. Subjects with overt feelings of depression readily admit them and are good reporters of their own mental state. They usually exhibit non-verbal behaviours, such as sighing, weeping and downcast eyes, which are consistent with the experienced affect. Subjects in a state of masked depression often conceal or deny their feelings. Frequently, they are preoccupied with their bodies hypochondriacally, and project anatomical responses, which are likely to be pathological. A depressed mood can be assessed by inkblot responses with high morbid or depressive content. The severity of these thoughts and feelings can be assessed by a study of their frequency and content quality.

A four-point scale can be used to score the depressive content of inkblot imagery:

*Score 0:* No depressive content.

*Score 1:* Slight or mild depressive content in the face of humans or animals (i.e., a sad face).

*Score 2:* Moderate depression associated with the 'inkblot's' expression. An expression with a marked, or strong, affect (e.g., a weeping person, a grief-stricken person).

*Score 3:* Sadness or depressed affect associated with an anatomical response. For example, a heavy heart, a breaking heart or a heart with a clamp on it. Something that is suicidal, or hanging from roof or a dead man.

Individuals who are clinically depressed, but fail to recognize it, may have similar difficulty recognizing content in the SIS. In the absence of neurological disorder, a high number of rejection responses may signify masked depression.

c. **Hostility and aggression scale (HAS)**

Hostility and aggression can be reflected in projective responses involving physical assault or body injury (Cassell 1977) and are scored as follows:

*Score 1:* Animals that are predatory or hostile to humans; an implement of aggression in a dormant state; a human or an animal that is seen as fierce, aggressive or dangerous; a hostile attitude seen in humans or animals; references to bowel function or defecation with hostile content; a knife or a snake.

*Score 2:* Animals or humans seen as angry or in aggressive struggle, either verbal or physical; furious snakes; or abstract expressions of direct conflict or oral aggression.

*Score 3:* Homicidal scenes and/or anatomical responses involving body destruction. Subjects with a history of acting out hostile impulses have been found to project anatomical responses with murderous themes.

d. **Paranoia scale (P)**

A cardinal projective feature of paranoid ideation involves a heightened awareness of threatening faces that are 'looking' at the individual. This may be experienced as an exaggerated sense of self-consciousness in social situations. An emphasis on the eyes of people or animals may be present in anxiety-laden dreams. It may be clinically indicated in art therapy, with figure drawings emphasizing 'eyes'. The patient may see hallucinatory images of such staring faces. The paranoid scale quantifies such responses.

## Administration and Scoring of SIS 20 Cards/Video Test

(Method of presentation: Same as the SIS Booklet/DVD form)

### Scoring

Scoring of responses is common in DVD/Video/Booklet and Card Forms except for the most typical, and typical and atypical responses on SIS-I (20 cards), which are given as follows:

### Most Typical Responses (MT)

Most typical responses are those which are given by more than 75 per cent of normal subjects on an image (Dubey and Cassell 1993). The total number of such responses is limited to nine. A higher number of most typical responses are suggestive of coherent, logical thinking and ability to keep up with the demands of the society. It may also be interpreted as a measure of ego strength and team concept.

The following is the list of most typical responses along with the images eliciting them:

| Card | Responses |
|---|---|
| Card 1: | Two birds |
| Card 2: | Heart |
| Card 2: | Bird |
| Card 3: | Two human beings/ladies |
| Card 4: | Apple/fruit |
| Card 4: | Dancing lady |
| Card 9: | Kidney/lungs |
| Card 15: | Spinal column/rib cage |
| Card 17: | Spinal column/pelvis |

## Typical and Atypical Responses

*Typical responses (T):* Typical responses are those which are commonly seen by healthy people on a particular image.

*Atypical responses (AT):* Atypical responses are those of poor quality and with vague percept, either in structure or in verbalization. A response that markedly departs from the category of Typical responses is also scored under Atypical category. For example, if the viewer gives the response 'flower' on Card 9, it should be considered as atypical because this image should elicit body anatomy such as kidney/lungs. The number of Atypical responses is proportionate to the degree of psychological or psychiatric disturbance.

Images 1–20 are shown at the end of the book.

### Card 1
Typical: Two persons
Atypical: Lungs

### Card 2
Typical: Clown; happy person
Atypical: Woman; heart; mouth

### Card 3
Typical: Man and woman dancing; hearts; two men or two women dancing
Atypical: Two sets of lines; face; eyes; two ants; two animals

**Card 4**
Typical: Woman dancing; Eve and apple; seductive woman; apple
Atypical: Male; pregnant woman; heart; rivers and island; snakes

**Card 5**
Typical: Turtle; flying bird; babies on sides
Atypical: Stretched animal skin; man fleshing two children; smashed animal showing entrails; spinal disc

**Card 6**
Typical: Two lovebirds; heart
Atypical: Two (starving) birds fighting for food; lungs; an x-ray of chest; leaves

**Card 7**
Typical: Heart; female genitalia; uterus; animal coming out of heart
Atypical: Creature from outer space; atomic bomb exploding; an x-ray of brain

**Card 8**
Typical: Chest; ribs; heart; lungs
Atypical: Ugly dog; monster looking out at you; gaping open mouth; two catfish looking at evil; sea horses; heart (afraid it will stop; death anxiety in an eight-year-old)

**Card 9**
Typical: Kidneys; lungs; thorax
Atypical: Weight lifter (back pain detail); a bush with a spear for roots; brain; ovaries; testicles; eyes; ears

**Card 10**
Typical: Lips, mouth (upper area) and stomach (lower area)
Atypical: Non-anatomical, animal

**Card 11**
Typical: Intestine
Atypical: An animal

**Card 12**
Typical: Female sex organs (cervix, ovaries, uterus, vagina)
Atypical: Skull; top of hammer; dog with large ears

### Card 13
Typical: Female genitalia, perineal area, buttocks, and heart
Atypical: An animal; creature from other space; leaf

### Card 14
Typical: Vagina
Atypical: Stained glass window; crucifix (substituting religious symbolism); cave or tunnel; beetle; Indian oil lamp; eyes

### Card 15
Typical: Spinal column
Atypical: 'Mind block' (rape victim repressing male genital symbolism); pots, pans or plates stacked on each other (neutralizing defence against phallic symbol by a rape victim)

### Card 16
Typical: Eyes, head, tongue, nose
Atypical: Bushy plant; flower

### Card 17
Typical: Spinal column, rib cage, pelvis, phallus
Atypical: Indian lamp; big hammer

### Card 18
Typical: Oral or facial region; crown
Atypical: Gate of hell; castle

### Card 19
Typical: Two birds; hands
Atypical: Butchered animal; dressed chicken

### Card 20
Typical: Face or part of face, eyes
Atypical: Ghost; fearful face

## Administration and Scoring of SIT

### Procedure and Instructions

This is a short version of 30 somatic images for a quick assessment. The instruction to take the test is almost similar in Booklet/Video or card version. The administration, scoring and interpretation is similar in all three versions. Please go to the http://dubayhealingcenter.com portal.

On the top-right you will see a button called 'Begin Your Journey'. This will take you to a login and registration screen. Follow the instructions.

Most people find this test fun and interesting. First, please relax, and prepare to enjoy. Please write each in terms of what they resemble or look like to you. Different people see different things in the ink-blots. It is important to write whatever the inkblot looks like to you. Please include everything you see even if it reminds you of something remote, vague, highly personal or even potentially embarrassing. Please include everything you see with as much detail as possible. Also include any outstanding emotional reaction that you might feel occur in responding to these images.

The test may take about 30 minutes to complete.

## Scoring

There are only 11 scoring indices, common in all forms of Somatic Inkblot Test. However, the number of most typical responses varies in all three forms because of variation in the number of images.

### Most Typical Responses (MT)

Most Typical responses are those which are given by more than 75 per cent of normal subjects on an image (Dubey and Cassell 1993). The total number of MT responses is limited to 15. A higher number of MT responses are suggestive of coherent, logical thinking and ability to keep up with the demands of the society. It may also be interpreted as a measure of ego strength and team concept. The following is the list of MT responses along with the images eliciting them:

| | |
|---|---|
| Image 5: | Apple/fruit |
| Image 5: | Dancing lady |
| Image 6: | Two human beings/ladies |
| Image 7: | Ear |
| Image 8: | Raised hand |
| Image 12: | Kidney/lungs |
| Image 17: | Breast |
| Image 18: | Two faces of persons |
| Image 19: | Two faces of persons |
| Image 20: | Two persons talking |
| Image 26: | Man/boy sleeping or resting/dreaming and soul going up |

Image 27:    Child/children
Image 28:    Mother and child/standing lady
Image 29:    Running man
Image 30:    Family—father, mother and two children

Below is a list of Typical and Atypical responses on each image:

## Typical and Atypical Responses (30-Image SIT)

### Image 1
Typical: Floral arrangement; people
Atypical: Heart; eye

### Image 2
Typical: Space needle; cross; tree
Atypical: Bleeding body part; vagina (libidinal cathexis in lesbian women)

### Image 3
Typical: Clown; happy person; mouth
Atypical: Woman; heart.

### Image 4
Typical: Person and teddy bear
Atypical: Egg and teddy bear; two chromosomes; legs

### Image 5
Typical: Woman dancing; Eve and apple; seductive woman; apple (snakes in India)
Atypical: Male; pregnant woman; heart; rivers and island

### Image 6
Typical: Man and woman dancing; hearts; two men or two women dancing
Atypical: Two sets of lines; face; eyes; two ants; two animals

### Image 7
Typical: Ear; embryo
Atypical: Internal body part

### Image 8
Typical: An upraised hand; a hand reaching for help; palm

Atypical: Suffering, pleading, helpless, desperate, or attacking hand; hand in flames or reaching out of concealment to grab someone (rape victim)

## Image 9
Typical: Two lovebirds; heart
Atypical: Two (starving) birds fighting for food; lungs; an X-ray of chest; leaves

## Image 10
Typical: Chest; ribs; heart; lungs
Atypical: Ugly dog; monster looking out at you; seahorses; heart (afraid it will stop, death anxiety)

## Image 11
Typical: Heart; female genitalia; uterus; animal coming out of heart
Atypical: Creature from outer space; atomic bomb exploding; an X-ray of brain

## Image 12
Typical: Kidneys; lungs; thorax
Atypical: Weight lifter (back pain detail); a bush with a spear for roots; brain; ovaries; testicles

## Image 13
Typical: Turtle; flying bird; babies on sides
Atypical: Stretched animal skin; man fleshing two children

## Image 14
Typical: Spinal column
Atypical: 'Mind block' (in rape victims and spinal injury cases); pots, pans or plates stacked on each other (neutralizing defence against phallic symbol by a rape victim)

## Image 15
Typical: Vagina
Atypical: Stained glass window; crucifix (substituting religious symbolism); cave/tunnel; Indian oil lamp; eyes

## Image 16
Typical: Foetus; embryo
Atypical: Face; reflecting repugnant emotion (pregnant woman unhappy with pregnancy)

## Image 17
Typical: Human female breast; baby sucking at a breast; deer's head
Atypical: Injured female arm; marked decapitated woman

## Image 18
Typical: Two human faces, man and woman
Atypical: Man and woman arguing; sad faces

## Image 19
Typical: Two human faces; adult and child
Atypical: Mummies; person threatening someone

## Image 20
Typical: Two seated human figures; people conversing
Atypical: Man and woman arguing; not able to communicate with doctor

## Image 21
Typical: Broken glass; paper airplanes; knives
Atypical: Knives to kill someone; suicidal or homicidal imagery

## Image 22
Typical: Heart; smoking
Atypical: Open female genitalia ready for intercourse; a dark hole

## Image 23
Typical: Spinal cord; male sex organ in action
Atypical: Sperm going through tunnel; two people talking; snake in a pipe

## Image 24
Typical: Cell; ovum; egg; sun; heart
Atypical: Broken heart (post-trauma response); egg being fertilized (pregnancy wish); ugly spider

## Image 25
Typical: A gun; exploding cork; firecracker
Atypical: A gun shooting someone

## Image 26
Typical: Body resting; soul leaving body; dead person
Atypical: Blood spurting from chest; crime victim bleeding to death

**Image 27**
Typical: Foetus; embryo; child
Atypical: Diseased foetus; dead baby

**Image 28**
Typical: Mother and child
Atypical: Woman holding baby and running away; person in despair hugging; Jesus comforting someone

**Image 29**
Typical: Running human figure; lame
Atypical: Human figure with one leg running in fear

**Image 30**
Typical: A family of two adults and two children standing together; father, mother and two children
Atypical: A family disintegrating; four children; mushrooms

## Rejection of Images (Rej.)

If the subject is unable to give any response on any of the 30 images, that image is considered as rejected. Verbalizations like 'spot' or 'ink-blot' are not considered as a response and are scored as rejections. To determine the percentage of the Rejection of Responses, the total number of the rejected images is divided by the total number of the images and multiplied by 100. Rejection of images may show low intelligence, thought blockage from psychological inhibition or organic brain involvement.

## Overall Clinical Considerations

Attention should be given to the signs of somatic repression. This is reflected when images with high anatomical structure are left blank or when symbolic responses are projected, disguising the somatic content. An example is the response 'Chinese pagoda' for an image with a structure suggestive of spinal cord. Another would be seeing a bush instead of kidneys or lungs on Card 9. Individuals suffering from psychogenic pain in a conversion disorder are examples of this group of respondents. In the detailed enquiry, depending on the clinical indications, specific questions may be asked to explore certain areas pertaining to the patient. For example, if the examiner wishes to explore the subject's perception of communication with the therapist (i.e., transference material), further responses may be obtained after enquiries.

What may at first seem an abnormal image pattern may prove to be a normal variant under the added scrutiny of detailed enquiry. The response may be a defence against painful reality, a temporarily focused but generalized anxiety or an acquired or learned response from family, job, school, life experience or chronic medical problems. The therapist should withhold judgement and not share it with the patient until the dynamics are clear. In classical analytic therapy, this delay is intentional and is an integral part of the treatment plan. The therapist waits until the patient has the insight, awareness and coping skills and is ready to understand and process the new leanings. A subject's therapeutic readiness involves the ability to process affect-laden, repressed material and unrealistic expectations of him/herself and others. Choosing this moment of truth, that is, the time to share judgement is a test of the therapist's knowledge, understanding and judgement.

Another line of psychotherapeutic line of enquiry concerning the determinants of SIS responses involves determining if the subject's projected material reflects inner psychological experiences not directly recorded from past visual experience. These responses may relate to night-time dreams, daytime fantasies or, in psychotic individuals, visual hallucinations. SIS images are like images used in art therapy in that they enable the individual to see them as an expression of externaliza-tion of the self or the self as perceived by others. For example, there can be a perceived fusion between a child, or the self as child, and an abusive or controlling parent or authority figure.

Several artists have been interested in dreams and have attempted to represent dream imagery in their art. Leonardo da Vinci sometimes slept holding a billiard ball in his hand, poised over a metal pail. As he slept, his grasp on the ball weakened and it would fall into the pail, awakening him. Then, he would sketch what he saw in his dream. This method was used by da Vinci to stimulate and channel his creativity. If a subject does not perceive an anatomical structure on an image that generally elicits one (see the response profile), it may be interpreted that the patient is denying physical discomfort and has low awareness. He might be having deep-rooted problems with that part of the body or organ.

Emphasis or sexual avoidance of a structure may suggest conflict in that area. Emphasis on eyes, ears or hair may suggest paranoid idea-tion. A higher conformity to most typical responses may suggest that the patient or client has group conformity in his/her thought process. High scores on the four pathological scales may suggest pathology in the respective area. The greater the percentage of atypical responses with poor quality, the deeper the pathology it may indicate.

## Rejection of Images

It is equally important to understand why a person is unable to perceive on an image. Each image is created to depict a specific/particular area; hence, rejection of such images has lot of clinical significance. Since these inkblots are highly structured, in the absence of any organic pathology inability to perceive a blot can be highly clinically significant. It may help in understanding his reactions to different situations presented through inkblot imagery. The avoidance of such images may further be probed to understand the unconscious process. Though responses to different images are quite relevant to understand the personality of the subject, the rejection of images may be equally relevant and may help in peeping inside the inner self of the subject. Because of such relevance, rejection of images has been given much importance while interpreting the SIS protocol of a subject.

When a person is unable to perceive images in a concrete form, it can be taken as rejection. It has been noticed that people reject those images which depict certain percepts related to their traumatized experience or underlying painful memory. For example, a person having poor interpersonal relationship may reject SIS-II A7, A9, A31, B4 and B5 because these images project human content. Poor interpersonal relationship with the spouse may also lead to rejection of A9, A31 and B31. Images like A25 and B18 project more of erotic content. Since this area is disturbed because of poor relationship, people may not feel like responding anything on these images. Similarly, it has been noticed on a clinical sample of cardiac cases that persons suffering from heart problems reject images depicting a heart —for example, Cards A5, A17 and B19. A few patients, who have recovered and have accepted their clinical problems, bravely do perceive 'a heart' on these images. It suggests that they have no fear regarding their heart as they have been properly counselled. A person suffering from body ailments, such as Kidney problems, generally reject A20 and B9, which project Kidneys. It has also been noticed that females traumatized sexually find it difficult to perceive A22 and A23, which generally project spinal column. The symbolic meaning of these images may relate to male sex organs. Since these persons have undergone a traumatizing experience and have unpleasant memories of the percept, they may find it difficult to see anything on these images. Even if they perceive something, they often give poor-quality responses and attach a special meaning to it. For example, a patient who experienced sexual harassment perceived 'A deadly android looking more like a creepy insect' on A23. It should be kept in mind that the material needs to be assimilated by the experienced clinician with the overall medical and psychiatric history data. Even certain contents from dreams and visual hallucinations may be included for better understanding of the patient.

# PART II

# Tests' Results and Guidelines

# 9

# Quantitative and Indices-based Interpretation of the Rorschach Test

The quantitative indices-based interpretations of the Rorschach responses of Klopfer, Beck and Exner's systems are almost similar. Klopfer's interpretation is given in detail in this chapter. However, the interpretations of the Beck and Exner's indices are explained in an earlier chapter in brief. Those interested may refer to Klopfer, Beck or Exner's system for detailed information.

## Brief Interpretation of Rorschach Indices

Brief interpretation of Rorschach indices with high or low scores is given further. This is common to almost all systems with little variation in the emphasis on indices.

**High W:** A high number of W responses may relate to a person's ability to synthesize and organize the environment. It also reflects the individual's intellectual activity when quality of W is good. A high W is also related to oral tendencies or regression.

**Low W:** A low number of W responses may suggest low interest in seeking relationships between the separate facts of experience and achieving an organized view of the world (Klopfer et al. 1954). A low

W is also seen in depressive patients. If the quality of W is extremely low, it may indicate serious maladjustment and, at times, brain damage.

**High DW:** DW responses are overgeneralization and a strong indication of schizophrenia. Absence of DW is good sign of normal protocol.

**High D:** A high number of D responses may suggest that the person sacrifices the full use of his intellectual ability by focusing on the safe and obvious rather than probing into the more novel.

**Low D:** A low number of D may signify high level of stress in individuals.

**High Dd:** A high number of Dd responses may indicate an attempt of the individual to narrow their perception of their environment to make what is perceived more congruent with their inner world. This can be an anxiety-reducing mechanism.

**Space (S):** A high number of space responses are consistent with negativism, difficulty in handling anger and oppositional tendencies.

**High pure form (F):** A high F may indicate high defences to control undue affects.

**Low pure form (F):** A low F may suggest that a person's inner turmoil is unduly high and reflects the individual's attempt to screen out affective responses to a stressful situation.

**High M:** A high number of M responses with good form quality are associated with high IQ, fantasy, creativity and good interpersonal relationship. High M is also correlated with introversive style of personality.

**Low M:** A low number of M responses may indicate low creativity and passive interpersonal relationship.

**High FM:** A high number of FM responses may indicate that such individuals are governed by their needs and want immediate gratification.

**Low FM:** A low number of FM responses are generally observed in those who are inhibited and deny their basic needs.

**High m (inanimate movement):** A high number of m responses may warn the presence of tension and unresolved conflicts.

**High C:** A high number of C responses may suggest that such individuals may have problems in handling their emotions and may be impulsive.

**Low C:** A low C may indicate good control over emotions.

**High Cn:** A Cn response may indicate presence of organic impairment.

**High FC:** A high number of FC responses may indicate that such individuals tend to be guided by reality and have control over their emotions.

**Low FC:** A low number of FC responses may indicate that the person is guided more by emotions than reality.

**High C':** A high number of C' responses may indicate constrained emotions from an underlying depression frequently present in anxiety neurotics.

**High T:** A high number of T responses may indicate intense needs for affection and dependency.

**Low T:** A low number of T responses may indicate emotional impoverishment.

**High V:** A high number of vista responses may indicate self-critical introspection as well as feelings of inferiority.

**Low V:** A low number of vista responses may indicate the tendency to introspect.

**High Y:** A high number of shading responses may indicate anxiety and constrained expression of emotion.

**High FD:** A high number of FD responses may indicate ability of good introspection, self-awareness and ability to delay and internalize behaviour.

**High Rf or Fr:** A high number of Rf or Fr responses may indicate feelings of self-absorption and an inflated sense of self-worth.

**High H:** The presence of high number of H responses may indicate interest in people, high self-esteem and is a sign of good interpersonal skills.

**Low H:** A low number of H responses may indicate low level of empathy and poor interpersonal skills.

**High A:** A high number of A responses may indicate that the person has a stereotyped way of approaching the world, immature thinking and aggressive attitude. Individuals who lack closeness to other people may either reject blots or may perceive more of animal contents.

**High An:** A high number of An responses may indicate somatic preoccupation and associated somatic symptoms.

**High P:** A high number of P responses may indicate popular view of world with social standards. Often, such individuals may have a conventional way of thinking and may be associated with human relationships.

**Low P:** A low number of P responses may indicate that the person has non-conformity of social norms, is away from reality and it is a sign of psychosis.

**High morbid response:** It may indicate negative self-imagery and depressive feelings.

**Good form response:** A high number of good form responses (X + %) may indicate reality contact with surrounding.

**Poor form or minus form (X–):** Poor form responses (X–) may indicate that the individual has a distorted perception of reality.

## Klopfer's Method

The theory of projection deals with whatever the person has projected in the form of responses. You cannot ask the subject to give more human or other responses, whatever system of Rorschach administration you are going to follow. Probably, the content analysis or psychoanalytic interpretation of the responses is the only way to handle such fundamental problems (Cassell and Dubey 2003). However, Klopfer's interpretation as described by Klopfer et al. (1954) is given as follows.

## Quantitative Analysis

Rorschach protocol is interpreted mainly in two steps: quantitative analysis and sequence analysis. Quantitative analysis is described further in short. It deals with two things: (I). Interpretation of the Psychogram and (II) Interpretation of the Quantitative Proportions (Klopfer, 1954, 252–316). For sequence analysis, the reader should consult Klopfer (1954, 317–351). It is important to consider the relationship between various scoring indices for the understanding of the personality profile of the subject. The clinical skills of the therapist/psychologist work in integrating various findings of Rorschach with case history information and other psychological tests.

## (I) Interpretation of the Psychogram

The examiner must interpret the psychogram in the light of the meaning of various determinants described by Klopfer (1954, 252–287). It is important to deal with each determinant separately and then to see the psychogram in three main areas: movement, shadings and colours. It is also important to see if the responses are distributed over the three main areas or are bulking over one:

1. If the responses tend to bulk in the left half of the psychogram, it may indicate that the person has high imaginative ability and restructures external reality through his own contribution.
2. If the responses tend to bulk in the right half of the psychogram, it may indicate that the person is responding freely to the external reality and depends more on the external stimuli while perceiving. Those with the bulk loading on the left half are relatively perceiver-determined and loading on the right half of the psychogram might be stimulus-determined; the terms introversive and extroversive are used to describe these two modes of perception in Rorschach.
3. If the responses tend to bulk in the centre (F), it may indicate that the person has a limited kind of perception with a limited view of his world.

## Interpretation of M

M may indicate imaginative ability, empathy with others and well-developed ego functioning. It indicates free access to fantasy, good contact with reality, high level of emotional integration and a source of creative energies. It helps in understanding the functioning of personality.

An additional M indicates potential resources of imaginative and empathetic capacity upon which the individual is hesitant to draw, usually because of the inhibitions resulting from internal conflicts. A few or no M, even as an additional response, may indicate the degree of availability of the unused resources. It is suggested that a well-adjusted adult should have three or more M responses. This is in fact the most controversial concept given by Klopfer et al. (1954) because in clinical practices, many subjects do not perceive three or more M responses and as such these protocols cannot be interpreted. It is impossible to interpret M's without reference to other determinants, especially FM's and m's, and without consideration of contents and form level. The M responses help in assessing the following personality traits:

### 1. **Intelligence**

A high number of M responses with good form level and good quality may reflect the signs of high intellectual capacity. An individual capable of a fairly high level of differentiation and integration in his perceptual and cognitive functions can produce M responses. An inability to see M may indicate lack of intellectual differentiation. Young children, mentally subnormal and deteriorated organics rarely perceive M responses. Some individuals with a high level of intellectual capacity may fail to perceive M responses because the emotional factors interfere with empathy with other people.

### 2. **Imagination**

A high number of M responses may indicate high level of imagination, which is also related to fantasy and creativity. Psychoanalytic usage of the term 'fantasy' refers to 'unconscious fantasy'. An individual may go back in time and project responses which may have relationship with past pleasant or unpleasant experiences and which may take the form of fantasy. Such responses can be interpreted psychoanalytically, though Klopfer's system has not given much importance to psychoanalytic interpretation.

While interpreting the protocol of children, one should not forget that children often see more FM responses than M ones because they feel more comfortable to express their conscious fantasy through animals than human beings. In such situations, FM may not be the true reflection of impulses and inner value.

## 3. Inner Stability
The imaginative processes indicated by M may reflect as an aid to adjustment and stability during stress by channelizing the inner resources to avoid uncontrolled impulses. M with good form level indicates adjustment and stability, whereas M with minus form level indicates a breakdown of the control function, an inability to integrate the inner experience with outer reality. More than five M with good form level in an introversive record and more than three M with good form level in an extroversive record may indicate presence of inner control.

## 4. Self-acceptance
When M appears in optimal relationship with FM and both M and FM are well represented, it may indicate the subject's ability to integrate his long-range value system and impulse life so that both can exist concurrently without feelings of guilt or frustration. The self-accepting individual is more with himself, lacking inner conflict and capable of deferring gratifications without feeling of frustration.

## 5. Empathy
Perception of human figures may indicate the capacity for good empathetic relationships with others. Individuals who have had poor relationships with their parents are unable to see M responses. Individuals with poor relationships with their mother find it difficult to see adult female figures and those with poor relationships with their father find it difficult to see adult male figures. Individuals who lack closeness to other people may either reject the blots projecting human responses or may perceive more of animal content. The content with Hd(H) or (Hd) may indicate hostile and critical tendencies, which obstruct freeflowing empathy.

## 6. The Self-concept
The quality and content of M reflects an individual's self and his social environment. The content analysis of the human figures in different actions such as hostile and aggressive, constructive and cooperative, may help in understanding the individual's self-concept. M responses with minus form level may be indicative of defective ego organization.

## Interpretation of FM

FM responses may indicate an awareness of impulses to immediate gratification rather than realistic goals. The relationship of M to FM is most important for understanding the expression of behaviour.

The presence of FM in great numbers may indicate that the individual is self-aware of the impulses which need immediate gratification. When FM responses are scored as additional, it may indicate that the individual tends to suppress his/her primitive impulses by making a conscious attempt to keep them from awareness. However, a large number of FM should be interpreted in relation to FC:CF balance. High FM in the absence of CF may indicate self-acceptance and frustration.

## Interpretation of m

The presence of one or two m is considered a favourable sign of adjustment. Well-adjusted people tend to give low m responses as they have integrated their impulse life with their self and value system. Presence of more than two m responses may reflect awareness of the forces outside the control of the individual, which threatens the integrity of his personality organization. m may indicate tension and conflict between the impulse life and long-range goals. m may also reflect repressive need and a feeling of helplessness, and serve as a warning signal that threatens the ego structure by breaking up the integration. A fairly large number of m responses are signs of hostile forces and an indication of difficulty in adjustment. However, the ratio of m to M and FM, and FC:CF must be considered while interpreting m responses.

## Interpretation of K and KF

By giving a K or KF response, the person uses shading to give a diffused, unstructured but three-dimensional effect to the blot stimulus. The shading responses may indicate the way in which the individual handles his primary needs of security and derived needs for affection and belongingness. K and KF may indicate anxiety of a diffused and free-floating nature and reflect frustration of affectional satisfaction. However, it will indicate anxiety if there are more than three K responses or if the undifferentiated shading responses exceed the differentiated shading responses.

## Interpretation of FK

By giving FK response, the individual is using shading to give the inkblot stimulus a structured and three-dimensional effect. FK may indicate the individual's attempt to handle his affectiona! anxiety. FK in reasonable numbers indicate good adjustment, although the balance of FK to F and Fc is important to consider this. Over-production of FK indicates affectional anxiety.

## Interpretation of k, kF and Fk

The perceptual activity of the person in giving a k response is somewhat similar to that of FK response. The k indicates affectional anxiety behind a good front of outward control and generally found in persons who cover up their anxiety with an intellectual cloak. Fk and kF are often seen in persons who are trying unsuccessfully to handle their anxiety by intellectual means but who do not have the emotional insight to deal effectively with their problems. Such persons know exactly what is wrong with them, yet they are not able to help themselves. Fk responses also come from very busy persons and serve as a defence mechanism to reduce the awareness about their affectional anxiety from breaking through.

## Interpretation of F

An F response may 'represent a limited or impoverished type of perception, stripped both of the emotional and affectional nuances implied by the color and shading elements and of the imaginal enrichment which the individual himself might have contributed' (Klopfer et al. 1954). Presence of F responses in a reasonable number with shading, colour and movement responses do not indicate a limited or impoverished view of the world but that the individual is capable of handling situations in an impersonal way. When there is a predominance of F responses at the expense of colour and shading responses, this may indicate that the person remains aware of his inner values, needs and impulses. Predominance of F responses at the expense of movement responses, but colour responses appear freely, it may indicate that the person is impoverished in the sense of lack of awareness of his inner impulses, while he/she remains emotionally reactive to the impact of the influences of outer world. However, the relationship of F to M, FC, Fc and FK, F%, and form-level rating, should be examined before making the above interpretation.

## Interpretation of c

A c response may indicate an infantile, undifferentiated, crude need for affection and its presence or absence, and the degree of differentiation (c vs cF vs Fc) is related to the degree of awareness and differentiation of the person's needs from affection and dependency. Crude c responses are rarely seen in normal protocols and it is a sign of serious organic brain damage.

## Interpretation of cF

cF responses indicate an early need for closeness, a need to be held and fondled and a deprivation of infantile dependence. It may also indicate the presence of a craving, an awareness of affectional need. cF responses are given by persons who have serious frustration of affectional need in early childhood. However, the absence of cF responses does not indicate absence of such frustration. The infantile craving for contact is also expressed through sexual relationships. The content of cF such as 'soft' or 'furry' may indicate better satisfaction than cold, rough or hard.

## Interpretation of Fc

Fc responses, like cF responses, reflect an interest in the tactual qualities of the blot material with an ability to use these aspects in a differentiated way. An Fc response may suggest that the individual is aware of his infantile craving for contact and has control over its manifestation. It indicates an awareness and acceptance of affectional needs experienced in terms of desire for approval, belongingness and response from others. More number of Fc may indicate that affectional need plays a disproportionate role in adjustment and there is a kind of dependency on affection from others. The lack of Fc does not imply lack of affectional need and it may be interpreted as a denial and reluctance to accept it. Perception of hard surfaces may indicate somewhat more deprivation than that of soft surfaces.

## Interpretation of C', C'F and FC'

Presence of C' with full of C (colour) responses may indicate a rich and uniform reaction to all kinds of stimuli presented to the person and such combination is often found in an artistically impressionable person. When the subject perceives C' with little use of chromatic colour, it suggests that some kind of traumatic experience is interfering with the perception and resulting in withdrawal. This is also known as the 'burnt child' reaction. This interpretation is applicable if the ratio of C', C'F, FC' + Fc, cF, c:C, CF and FC is 2:1.

## Interpretation of FC

FC has been found as one of the most dependable signs of good adjustment. It may indicate a ready control over emotional impact and that the person is able to make pleasant responses to social situations. When FC outnumbers CF, it may indicate good control over emotionality while preponderance of CF over FC may indicate uncontrolled emotionality. (For detailed interpretation, please see Klopfer et al. [1954, 296–297]).

## Interpretation of CF

CF normally represents an uncontrolled reactivity. The subject produces natural CF response when he is influenced by the colour rather than by the form; an example is, 'looks like blood on Card II'. The natural CF combination indicates uncontrolled but appropriate emotional response to the demands of a social situation. The CF combination, thus, has both positive and negative implications, which can be judged by FC:(CF + C) balance. Even if CF outnumbers FC but there is an adequate balance of M, FK and Fc, CF would indicate good control over emotional reaction. However, the content of CF, M and FM is equally important to see the reactivity of emotions and uncontrolled aggression.

## Interpretation of C Responses

Like CF responses, the subject determines a C response only by colour. C responses are scored in the following four ways with their interpretation.

1. **Pure C or Crude C**
   Crude C is scored for a repeated use of colour without any form. Crude C responses are indicators of a lack of emotional control with explosive emotionality. Crude C is rarely seen except in young children and deteriorated organics and is considered as a pathological indicator.
2. **Colour Naming (Cn)**
   The subject simply identifies the colour without integrating it with any form or meaning. The individuals who give Cn responses is

overwhelmed by emotional impact and are incapable of handling their reaction. It is a rare response in adult subjects and is often seen in psychotic patients.

3. **Colour Description (Cdes)**
The subject describes the colour without integrating it with the form of the blot into a meaningful concept. Colour description indicates that the person is strongly moved by emotional impact but he can control his overt expressions.

4. **Colour Symbolism (Csym)**
The subject attaches meaning to the blot concept through colour symbolism but fails to integrate colour with the form of the blot. Csym indicates that the subject is strongly moved by emotional impact though he has outward control.

## (II) Interpretation of the Quantitative Proportions (Quantitative Analysis)

The interpretation of the indices is based on Klopfer's system. Those who are interested in Beck and Exner's system should consult their respective manuals. A brief interpretation based on Klopfer's system is described here. Readers are requested to see Klopfer's book (Klopfer 1954, 249–375) for detailed interpretation.

Analysis of quantitative data helps in understanding the function of the personality. Various ratios and percentages form the basis of the interpretation. Because of the basic lacuna in the interpretation of quantitative data (such as M is lower than 3), you may not be able to interpret the protocol in some cases. However, an analysis of the contents may be more helpful at this point.

## Proportions Relating to Inner Resources and Impulse Life

As per Klopfer et al. (1954), 'none of the ratios may be interpreted unless there are at least three M responses'. Many researchers have raised questions like why the protocol of an individual should not be interpreted if the subject failed to perceive three human movement responses. When an individual gives a low number of total responses (R), it is likely that a low number of M responses will also be projected. The theory of projection advocates interpreting the responses perceived by the subject, whether it is high or low. No one can ask the subject to give more human responses, whatever system of Rorschach administration is being followed. Probably because of such inherent lacuna in the interpretation of individual protocol, 'content analysis and psychoanalytic interpretation of the responses' have been the only way to handle such fundamental problems (Cassell and Dubey 2003). In any case, the interpretations of the ratios are as follows.

## Ratio of M:FM

1. **FM > 2M**
   When FM responses are more than twice of M, it may suggest that the person is ruled by immediate needs for gratification rather than long-term goals. An impulsive behaviour can be ascertained if the CF responses are also exceeding FC responses. However, such ratio is often seen in children who tend to act on impulses without any social restraint.

2. **M > FM**
   When M exceeds FM, the impulse life is subordinated to the value system. Such individuals possess self-acceptance and are able to defer immediate needs for gratification without frustration and conflict. However, when FM is less than half of M or there are almost no FM responses, it may indicate that the impulse life is suppressed in the interest of values.

3. **M = FM**
   When M is equal to FM, it may indicate that the impulse life is not in conflict with the value system. This may further indicate that the person is mature and has a well-developed value system with control over impulses. Such ratio is usually seen in an easy-going, happy person.

4. **M and FM Both Are Few**
   When both M and FM are few, it may indicate poor ego and low imaginal ability. Such ratio is often found in young children, psychopaths and psychotics. However, if there are few M and FM responses with good form level, this may indicate a possibility of neurotic constriction.

5. **Ratio of M:(FM + m)**
   The normal representation of FM + m should be less than 1½M. More number of FM + m may indicate that a strong tension is forcing the person to utilize inner resources for a constructive solution of his everyday problems. When M is approximately equal to FM + m with not more than one or two m, it indicates that the impulse life is well integrated with the value system and that the person is able to utilize his inner resources.

## Proportions Relating to the Organization of Affectional Need

### Ratio of Differentiated to Undifferentiated Shading Responses

When undifferentiated shading responses (K, KF, k, kF, c and cF) out-number differentiated shading responses (Fc and FK), it may indicate poor integration of affectional needs, leading to serious maladjustment.

### Ratio of F: (FK + Fc)

Generally, Fc responses appear more than FK in a majority of Rorschach protocols. Where Fc out number FK, it seems satisfactory to treat them together. However, When FK is more than Fc, it may indicate that the person is able to have control of affectional anxiety rather than stressing over his affectional need.

1. **(FK + Fc) > ¾F**
   When FK + Fc exceed three-quarters of F responses, the need for affection has developed to such an extent that it threatens to swamp the rest of the personality. A rejection of the affectional needs from early life might lead to such behaviour.
2. **FK + Fc = ¼–¾ of F**
   When differentiated shading responses are between one-fourth and three-fourth of F responses, it may indicate that the need for affection has developed well and is integrated with the rest of the personality organization. Such individuals tend to have good interaction with other people.
3. **(FK + Fc) < ¼ F**
   When differentiated shading responses are less than one-quarter of F responses, it suggests that the person lives in denial and has underdevelopment of the need for affection.

### Ratio of Achromatic to Chromatic Responses

This ratio refers to (Fc + c + C'):(FC + CF + C)

1. **Achromatic = Twice Chromatic**
   When the achromatic are more than twice the chromatic responses, it may indicate that the person has had traumatic experiences which has led to withdrawal. Such individuals avoid interaction with others for fear of being hurt by their responses.

2. **Achromatic = ½ Chromatic**

When shading responses outnumber two to one by colour responses, the affectional need does not unduly influence the natural responsiveness to emotional situations.

3. **Achromatic < ½ Chromatic**

When chromatic responses exceed achromatic responses by two to one or more, the person may act out to emotional situations from the environment. The reactivity to emotional situation is further supported if there are more CF + C than FC responses.


## Proportions Relating to Constrictive Control

### F% (Percentage of Form Responses)

1. **F% = 20–50 per cent**

When F appears in a moderate quantity, it may indicate controlled adjustment. Such persons are able to be impersonal on many occasions but react to their own needs and to strong emotional impact from outside.

2. **F% > 80 per cent**

When F responses are more than 80 per cent, the individual has poor personality organization and low intellectual functioning. An overemphasis on F may be considered as pathological and is often seen in mentally subnormal, psychopathic personalities and organic patients.

3. **F% = 50–80 per cent**

When F% is between 50 and 80 per cent, it may indicate that the person is likely to suffer from 'neurotic constriction'. Such persons are intellectually capable of more differentiated response but inhibit and act to their emotional reactions.

4. **F% < 20 per cent**

When F% is less than 20 per cent it may indicate that the person places little emphasis on maintaining an impersonal relationship with his world.


## Total of F and Differentiated Shading Responses: (FK + F + Fc)%

When the total of F and differentiated shading responses exceeds 75 per cent, it may indicate neurotic constriction. However, if F% is about 50 with a moderate number of FK and Fc, the person may have 'modified constriction' but is able to live effectively without bothering others.

### Proportions Relating to Emotional Reactivity to the Environment

Ratio of FC (CF + C)

1. **FC > (CF + C)**
   When FC is more than CF + C, the person has control over the impulsive expression of emotionality. He is capable of control over his responses to social environment even under strong emotional impact. However, if CF + C are totally absent, it may indicate excessive control and the socialized responses shown tend to be superficial.
2. **FC < (CF + C)**
   When CF + C are more than FC, it may indicate a weak control over emotionality and the person tends to react in overt expressions.

### Sum C

If Sum C is less than three, it may indicate that the person has little influences from the environmental forces. As such, Sum C indicates overt reactivity.

### Percentage of Responses to Cards VIII + IX + X

When there are more than 40 per cent responses to Cards VIII + IX + X (about 20% to Card X alone), it indicates that the productivity of the person is stimulated by environmental impact, which is also known as extratensive balance. If the responses to the last three cards are less than 30 per cent, the individual is inhibited while reacting to environmental impact, which is also known as introversive balance.

## Reaction Time: Chromatic versus Achromatic Cards

If the average RT for chromatic cards exceeds achromatic cards by more than 10 seconds, it may indicate that the person is disturbed by emotional impact from the environment. Contrary to this, if the RT for achromatic cards is more than that of chromatic, it may indicate disturbance when environmental stimuli touches the area of the person's affectional needs.

# Proportions Relating to Intellectual Manner of Approach

The percentages of various locations are related to the intellectual manner of approach and are generally found in the following percentages:

| | |
|---|---|
| W% | 20–30 |
| D% | 45–55 |
| d% | 5–15 |
| (Dd and S)% | 0–10 |

## Interpretation of W%

1. **W% over 30 per cent with high form level**
   When there is an emphasis on W with good quality, it indicates organizational ability and interest. Such individuals are capable to integrate separate facts into a meaningful organization and making sense of their world. This is often found with persons of superior intelligence.
2. **W% over 30 per cent with mediocre form level but with organizational effort**
   When W responses are more than 30 per cent with mediocre form level and there is an effort to organize different parts of the inkblots, it may indicate that the person has a compulsive need to do the big thing in an intellectual sense though in reality he lacks the intellectual capacity to do so.
3. **W% over 30 per cent vague or indefinite form perception**
   When W responses are over 30 per cent with vague form level, it may indicate little effort from the individual to organize experience. Such findings are often found in persons with inferior intellectual capacity.
4. **W% less than 20 per cent**
   When W responses are less than 20 per cent, it may indicate a low degree of interest in seeking relationships between the separate facts of interest and achieving organized view of the world.

## Types of W Response

1. **W Cut Responses**
   W cut responses indicate an interest in organizing different aspects though they may not fit rightly. An overemphasis on W may indicate an overcritical and perfectionist approach.

## 2. DW Responses

DW responses are known as overgeneralization and indicate a very weak association with reality. Among children, DW may be considered normal but in adults, overemphasis on DW may be a strong indicator of schizophrenia.

### W:M Ratio

This ratio may indicate the ability of the person to mobilize his creative energies to back up his interests and ambition and his level of aspiration.

1. **W:M in Proportion 2:1**
   When W is twice of M, it may indicate that the person has organizational interest with enough creative potential for intellectual achievement and he/she has high level of aspiration with supporting resources. This ratio is known as 'optimum', but there should be at least three M and six W responses.
2. **W > 2M**
   When W is greater than twice M, the level of aspiration is too high, and the productive resources might be very low. A ratio of 3:1 or higher would be a negative sign.
3. **W < 2M**
   When W is less than 2M, with a ratio 1:2, it indicates that the person has a creative potential but had no opportunity to utilize it.

## Interpretation of D%

1. **D% > 55 per cent, Form Level Good**
   When D is more than 55 per cent with good form level, it indicates that the individual has the ability to differentiate perceptually with little interest in integration and organization. The person has practical application of intelligence, without much drive to seek relationships between the presented facts of experience. This ratio may indicate insecurity in a person with superior intelligence.
2. **D% > 55 per cent, Form Level Mediocre**
   When there is stress on D' with mediocre or poor form level, it may indicate that the person sticks to the practical, everyday, common-sense view of things because he is not capable of more integrated view.
3. **D% < 45 per cent**
   When D is less than 45 per cent with low form level, it may indicate that the person is unable to differentiate between the facts around

him because he has a defective intellectual capacity or emotional disturbance.

## Interpretation of d%

1. **d% > 15 per cent**
   When d is more than 15 per cent, it may indicate that the person has basic insecurity.
2. **d% < 5 per cent**
   When d is less than 5 per cent, it may indicate that the person has low level of interest in the minutiae of experience.

## Interpretation of (Dd and S)%

If the percentage of Dd and S is 10 or less, this is usual or average protocol. When it exceeds at the expense of D, it may indicate little concern with the practical facts of experience. If both W and D are decreasing, it may indicate departure from reality and is an indicator of psychosis.

1. **Emphasis on dd**
   An emphasis on dd indicates obsessional trends and insecurity.
2. **Emphasis on de**
   de is scored when only the edge area of the blot is selected to make a response. An overemphasis on de may indicate a fear to get involved deeply into anything. Very often, dd responses are found in patients suffering from anxiety states.
3. **Emphasis on di**
   di is scored when the inside shaded portion of the blot is used to make a response. A di response with good form level rating is found with intelligent and artistic subjects and di responses with minus form level rating are characteristic of a schizoid personality.
4. **Emphasis on dr**
   dr is scored where an unusual location, which cannot be classified as dd, de or di, is used. An overemphasis on dr indicates compulsive traits.
5. **Emphasis on S**
   S responses may indicate oppositional tendency in the intellectual sphere. S implies an intellectual kind of opposition, a putting of the self across; it is the self-assertive aspect of intellectuality. It is also considered an indication of ego strength and that the personality has resources to resist inundation by environmental forces.

## Other Proportions Relating to Intellectual Aspects

### Number of Responses (R)

A small number of responses may indicate low productivity and a large number may indicate high productivity. However, the quality of W plays a major role in deciding productivity. The average number of responses reported from the Western population falls within a range of 20–45, and for the Indian population it is in the range of 15–40.

### Average Response Time

Less than 30 seconds is considered as quick and normal reaction time. A reaction time over one minute indicates slow mental processes, low intellectual capacity and sign of depression.

### Proportion of (H + A):(Hd + Ad)

If detail responses are more than 50 per cent of H + A, it may indicate an overcritical attitude, anxiety and obsessive-compulsive characteristics.

### Number of Popular Responses (P)

The average number of popular responses generally found in various studies is five in an average record of 15–45 responses. The average number of popular responses indicates that the person tends to see the world like others and has an adequate contact with reality. Fewer popular responses indicate low contact with reality and that the person is viewing the world differently. It may be considered as a psychotic indicator, particularly if the person is unable to perceive popular response even on the 'testing the limits'. If the person has given eight or more popular responses, it indicates a good contact with reality, seeing the world as others and are strong indicators of 'team building'. Such persons can agree with others or will be able to influence others to agree with their own views/opinions.

## Number of Original Responses (O)

The original response is one that does not appear more than once in a hundred records. The scoring of original should not be undertaken by beginners. Usually, it should be scored by the examiners who have enough experience of administering Rorschach with a variety of patients. Original responses generally indicate a high level of intelligence. A person with superior intelligence may give twice as many originals as popular responses.

## Percentage of Animal Responses (A%)

People easily perceive animal content on inkblots and the optimum number is about 20–35 per cent. The A% over 50 may indicate either low intellectual capacity or disturbed adjustment, and such persons have little interest in their surroundings with a stereotyped view of the world.

Readers are advised to consult Klopfer et al. (1954) for a detailed interpretation of various quantitative ratios.

# 10

# Indian Norms and Diagnostic Indicators

Diagnostic indicators of inkblot responses have been a subject of controversy. Are inkblot tests capable of providing diagnosis? Do the diagnoses based on psychological tests match with those made on the criteria of DSM or ICD?

Inkblot tests are projective instruments which bring to surface unprocessed material from the unconscious mind. These instruments help in hearing the inner cry of an individual who is often unable to recollect the pain of sufferings. Inkblot responses further help in planning the therapeutic intervention and management. These responses are brought out symbolically and need to be interpreted.

Before arriving at any diagnostic conclusion, consider the symptoms, case history, findings of psychological tests and other supporting factors. Many critics of inkblot tests believe that the diagnostic formulation based on inkblots indices must be confirmed by other measures (Dubey and Cassell 2005). However, the profiles of normal and clinical groups collected from the findings of reported studies are given in Tables 10.1–10.9.

**TABLE 10.1** Rorschach Profile/Indices of Normal Groups

| Indices | (n = 200) MF Adults[a] | (n = 140) MF Adults[b] | (n = 450) MF Adults[c] | (n = 100) Male Army[d] | (n = 100) Male Army[e] | (n = 113) MF (Beck) 6–11 Years[f] |
|---|---|---|---|---|---|---|
| R | 22.10 | 28.00 | 33.00 | 16.00 | 13.76 | 20.95 |
| W | 29.46% | 27.00% | 9.33% | 15.00% | 40.20% | 12.99% |
| D | 57.80% | 51.00% | 16.97% | 51.00% | 48.62% | 76.57% |
| d (small d) | NR | 13.00% | NR | 25.00% | 8.42% | NR |
| Dd | 6.21% | 9.00% | 6.70% | 9.00% | 0.03 | 9.99% |
| S | 0.43% | NR | 1.61% | NR | 0.14 | 1.37% |
| F | NR | 11.20 | 20.17 | 42.00% | 4.33 | NR |
| M | 1.00 | 3.70 | 3.83 | 12.00% | 1.34 | 6.34% |
| FM | 1.80 | 2.10 | NR | 15.00% | 5.27 | NR |
| m (small m) | NR | 0.30 | NR | 2.00% | 0.33 | NR |
| FC | NR | 3.70 | 3.08 | 12.0% | 0.57 | 1.86% |
| CF | NR | 0.90 | 1.61 | 2.5% | 0.34 | 2.19% |
| C | NR | 0.20 | NR | NR | 0.18 | 0.46% |
| Fc (F Capital small c) | NR | 0.40 | NR | 3.4% | 0.52 | NP. |
| FK | NR | 2.90 | NR | 4.7% | 0.32 | 3.32%(V) |

(Continued)

**TABLE 10.1** *(Continued)*

| Indices | (n = 200) MF Adults[a] | (n = 140) MF Adults[b] | (n = 450) MF Adults[c] | (n = 100) Male Army[d] | (n = 100) Male Army[e] | (n = 113) MF (Beck) 6–11 Years[f] |
|---|---|---|---|---|---|---|
| C' | NR | 0.90 | NR | 2.8% | 0.50 | 5.49%(Y) |
| H | 12.00% | 17.00% | 2.60 | NR | 9.66% | 15.67% |
| Hd | NR | 10.00% | NR | NR | 0.56 | 2.85% |
| A | 38.70% | 24.00% | 6.18 | NR | 54.57% | NR |
| Ad | NR | 09.00% | NR | NR | 0.54 | NR |
| At | 11.00 | NR | 2.34 | NR | 0.59 | 4.98% |
| Sex | NR | 0.20 | NR | NR | 0.34 | NR |
| P | 5.30 | 4.90 | 5.30 | 6.00 | 6.54 | 13.99 |
| F+ % | 82.00 | NR | 83.14 | NR | 79.00 | 54.75 |
| A% | 38.70 | NR | 36.98 | NR | 58.50 | 51.31 |
| Rejection | 0.16% | 29.00% | NR | 34.00% | 16.00% | 1.31% |

*Sources:* [a] Kumar (1960a); [b] Prabhu (1967); [c] Asthana (1971); [d] D'Netto et al. (1974); [e] Dubey (1979); [f] Jain et al. (2005).

*Notes:*

1. Most of the norms are based on Klopfer's method (which is not specified); otherwise, they are based on the Beck and Exner method, where specified.

2. All indices except the total responses were converted into per cent scores by taking total number of responses as denominator for each index.

TABLE 10.2 *Rorschach Profile/Indices of Normal Groups*

| Indices | (n = 282) Male (65–85 Years)[a] | (n = 238) MF, Edu (10+ Years)[b] | (n = 100) MF (18–50 Years) (Beck)[c] | (n = 50) MF (Exner)[d] | (n = 50) MF (Beck)[e] |
|---|---|---|---|---|---|
| R | 14.71 | 26.81 | 21.46 | 21.98 | 21.34 |
| W | 40.11% | 4.17 | 5.02 | 19.24% | NR |
| D | 52.01% | 18.75 | 13.26 | NR | NR |
| D | 1.97% | 1.88 | NR | NR | NR |
| Dd | 4.96% | 1.01 | 2.02 | 3.85% | NR |
| S | 0.95% | 0.99 | 0.84 | 7.83% | NR |
| F | 7.02 | NR | NR | NR | NR |
| M | 0.98 | 3.21 | 2.02 | 6.65 | 7.90 |
| FM | 3.63 | NR | NR | NR | NR |
| M | 0.03 | NR | NR | NR | NR |
| FC | 1.18 | 1.17 | NR | NR | NR |
| CF | 0.84 | 0.85 | 0.72 | NR | NR |
| C | 0.01 | 0.74 | NR | NR | NR |
| Fc | 0.27 | NR | 0.44 | NR | NR |
| FK | 0.58 | NR | 0.89 | NR | NR |
| C' | 0.12 | NR | NR | NR | NR |
| H | 1.56 | 3.89 | 3.08 | NR | 8.24 |
| Hd | 0.29 | NR | 1.48 | NR | NR |
| A | 8.00 | NR | NR | NR | 26.26 |
| Ad | 0.23 | NR | NR | NR | NR |
| At | 0.53 | 0.96 | 0.79 | NR | 3.92 |
| Sex | 0.07 | 0.63 | NR | NR | NR |
| P | 3.06 | 3.24 | NR | 17.37% | 17.95 |
| F+ % | 55.39 | 59.72 | 40.02 | 75.24 | 63.11 |
| A% | 56.02 | 37.17 | 46.30 | NR | NR |
| Rejection | NR | NR | NR | NR | NR |

*Sources:* [a]Chaudhury et al. (2007); [b]Shweta et al. (2010); [c]Singh et al. (2005); [d]Mahapatra et al. (2010); [e]Kumar et al. (2005).

*Note:* Most of the norms are based on Klopfer's method (which is not specified); otherwise, they are based on the Beck and Exner method, where specified.

# TABLE 10.3 Rorschach Indices of Clinical Groups

| Indices | (n = 180) Schizo. MF[a] | (n = 100) Schizo. M Army OR[b] | (n = 100) Neurosis M Army OR[b] | (n = 111) ADHD, MF (6–11 Years) (Beck) | (n = 50) MF, Manic (Beck) | (n = 120) Manic, Adults MF (Exner) | (n = 50) MF, Schizo. Adults (Exner) |
|---|---|---|---|---|---|---|---|
| R | 14.91 | 12.71 | 11.22 | 21.44 | 14.76 | 18.45 | 15.22 |
| W | 5.06 | 4.67 | 4.43 | 14.41 | NR | 5.73 | 30.77% |
| D | 7.63 | 6.18 | 4.43 | 72.26 | NR | 8.65 | NR |
| d | NR | 1.07 | 0.21 | NR | NR | NR | NR |
| Dd | 2.22 | 0.15 | 0.02 | 13.27 | NR | 4.05 | 14.86% |
| S | 2.30 | 0.20 | 0.13 | 1.64 | NR | 1.95 | 60.16% |
| F | NR | 5.88 | 4.34 | NR | NR | NR | NR |
| M | 1.98 | 1.07 | 0.59 | 3.79 | 3.08 | NR | 1.03 |
| FM | NR | 2.29 | 2.44 | NR | NR | NR | NR |
| m | NR | 0.36 | 0.34 | NR | NR | NR | NR |
| FC | 1.33 | 0.43 | 0.44 | 4.28 | NR | NR | NR |
| CF | 3.66 | 0.62 | 0.50 | 3.29 | NR | NR | NR |
| C | NR | 0.70 | 0.69 | 1.11 | NR | NR | NR |
| Fc | NR | 0.47 | 0.63 | NR | NR | NR | NR |
| FK | NR | 0.15 | 0.29 | 3.98(V) | NR | NR | NR |
| C' | NR | 0.33 | 0.44 | 8.08(Y) | NR | NR | NR |
| H | NR | 1.01 | 0.73 | 15.02 | 9.11 | NR | NR |
| Hd | NR | 0.72 | 0.35 | 3.60 | NR | NR | NR |
| A | 0.08% | 4.47 | 4.51 | NR | 23.47 | NR | NR |
| Ad | NR | 0.41 | 0.37 | NR | NR | NR | NR |
| At | NR | 1.36 | 1.53 | 5.93 | 11.52 | NR | NR |
| Sex | NR | 1.75 | 0.50 | NR | NR | NR | NR |
| P | 5.30 | 2.89 | 4.98 | 11.74 | 14.26 | 1.41 | 8.83 |
| F+% | 58.00 | 32.10 | 62.20 | 44.59 | 50.66 | NR | 43.70 |
| A% | 30.08 | 38.39 | 43.49 | 44.75 | NR | NR | NR |
| Rej | NR | NR | NR | 2.59 | 2.15 | NR | NR |

Sources: [a]Asthana (1963); [b]Dubey (1978); [c]Jain and Kumar (2005); [d]Kumar et al. (2005); [e]Misha et al. (2010); [f]Mahapatra et al. (2010b).

Notes:

1. Most of the norms are based on Klopfer's method (which is not specified); otherwise, they are based on the Beck and Exner method, where specified.
2. All indices except the total responses were converted into per cent scores by taking total number of responses as denominator for each index.

**TABLE 10.4** SIS-II Profile/Indices of Normal Groups

| Indices | (n = 300) MF (22+ Years) Adults, Edu (12+ Years)[a] | (n = 892) MF Executives (25–60 Years)[b] | (n = 400) Exec. Pub Sector, MF (25–60 Years)[b] | (n = 100) MF (20–22 Years) Stu.[c] | (n = 480) MF (13–62 Years)[d] | (n = 700) MF (14–17 years) Stud. Edu. (9–11 Years)[e] |
|---|---|---|---|---|---|---|
| Total responses | 70.25 | 68.00 | 66.50 | 62.92 | 63.75 | 59.40 |
| Human responses | 14.20 (20) | 18.20 | 20.30 (30) | 18.09 | 19.18 (30.09) | 14.97 (25.00) |
| Animal responses | 8.45 (12) | 8.60 | 10.65 (16) | 7.53 | 7.63 (11.97) | 7.89 (13.00) |
| Anatomical responses | 11.40 (16) | 12.80 | 11.80 (16) | 8.10 | 10.27 (16.12) | 13.00 (22.00) |
| Sex responses | 4.20 (6) | 3.15 | 3.30 (4) | 1.35 | 1.78 (2.79) | 1.90 (3.00) |
| Movement responses | 8.35 | 6.30 | 8.35 | 6.24 | 6.82 | 2.89 |
| Most typical responses | 14.55 | 14.80 | 14.55 | 13.95 | 14.36 | 12.96 |
| Typical responses | NR | 32.00 | 40.00 | NR | NR | 21.86 |
| Atypical responses | NR | 9.00 | 9.00 | NR | NR | 4.26 |
| Rejection | 0.75 (1.00) | 0.60 (0.85) | 0.85 (1.00) | 0.43 | 0.42 (0.68) | 2.62 (4.30) |
| Pathological anatomy scale | 0.6 | 0.5 | 0.4 | 0.13 | 0.15 (0.11) | 0.52 (0.8) |
| Depression | 0.4 | 0.6 | 0.6 | 0.14 | 0.12 (0.19) | 1.20 (2.00) |
| Hostility aggression scale | 0.5 | 0.4 | 0.5 | 0.11 | 0.15 (0.24) | 2.03 (4.00) |
| Paranoia | 0.02 | 0.3 | 0.3 | 0.08 | 0.11 (0.17) | 1.16 (2.00) |

*Sources:* [a]Dubey et al. (1995a); [b]Cassell and Dubey (2003); [c]Singh and Dwivedi (1998); [d]Singh et al. (1999); [e]Singh (2008).

*Notes:*

1. Percentage is shown in parenthesis.
2. In Singh (2008), subjects were asked to give only one response on each card of SIS.

**TABLE 10.5** *SIS-II Profile/Indices of Normal Groups*

| Indices | (n = 240) M (13–62 Years)[a] | (n = 240) F (13–62 Years)[b] | (n = 100) Army OR, M[c] | (n = 100) Adult MF[d] | (n = 50) Adult MF (10+ Years)[e] |
|---|---|---|---|---|---|
| Total responses | 63.45 | 64.05 | 62.16 | 64.3 | 63.70 |
| Human responses | 19.08 (30.07) | 19.28 (30.10) | 19.15 (31) | 23.8 | 20.42 |
| Animal responses | 7.02 (11) | 8.25 (12.84) | 7.70 (12) | 7.2 | 7.02 |
| Anatomical responses | 10.49 (16.53) | 10.05 (15.69) | 12.65 (20) | 9.5 | 13.84 |
| Sex responses | 2.44 (3.85) | 1.12 (1.75) | 2.68 (4) | 6.0 | 3.46 |
| Movement responses | 6.23 | 7.41 | 4.12 | 7.3 | 7.10 |
| Most typical responses | 14.49 | 14.24 | 14.17 | 11.5 | 14.50 |
| Typical responses | NR | NR | NR | 25.4 | 30.20 |
| Atypical responses | NR | NR | NR | 13.8 | 19.68 |
| Rejection | 0.41 (0.66) | 0.43 (0.69) | 5.25 (8.00) | 0.4 | 0.90 |
| Pathological anatomy scale | 0.06 (0.9) | 0.07 (0.11) | NR | 0.3 | 0.54 |
| Depression | 0.08 (0.13) | 0.14 (0.29) | NR | 0.1 | 0.30 |
| Hostility aggression scale | 0.12 (0.19) | 0.19 (0.30) | NR | 0.4 | 0.64 |
| Paranoia | 0.09 (0.14) | 0.12 (0.19) | NR | 0.1 | 0.00 |

*Sources:* [a]Singh et al. (1999); [b]Singh et al. (1999); [c]Rathee et al. (1995); [d]Chaudhury et al. (2010); [e]Mishra et al. (2010).

*Note:* Percentage is shown in parenthesis.

**TABLE 10.6** *SIS-II Indices of Clinical Groups*

| Indices | (n = 100) Neurosis Army OR, M[a] | (n = 100) Schizo. Army OR, M[a] | (n = 100) Army OR M, Neurosis[b] | (n = 100) Army OR Schizo., M[b] | (n = 100) M, Alcohol Dependent[c] | (n = 50) Alcoholic, M[d] |
|---|---|---|---|---|---|---|
| Total responses | 58.90 | 56.65 | 55.51 (19) | 58.26 (7) | 64.6 | 72.45 |
| Human responses | 14.55 | 16.45 (29) | 16.34 (29) | 16.90 (29) | 16.5 | 16.50 |
| Animal responses | NR | 11.85 (21) | 7.26 (13) | 7.35 (13) | 10.9 | 11.62 |
| Anatomical responses | 21 | 17.35 (31) | 11.20 (20) | 8.98 (15) | 13.4 | 14.15 |
| Sex responses | 14.55 | 5.60 (10) | 2.02 (4) | 1.62 (3) | 2.7 | NR |
| Movement responses | NR | 8.50 (15) | 3.81 (7) | 4.10 (7) | 8.2 | 12.32 |
| Most typical responses | 10.20 (17) | 7.75 (14) | 11.90 (21) | 10.8 (19) | 9.0 | 13.22 |
| Typical responses | NR | NR | NR | NR | 18.9 | NR |
| Atypical responses | NR | NR | NR | NR | 17.3 | NR |
| Rejection | 21 | 4.30 (8) | 13.5 (22) | 12.53 (20) | 0.6 | 10.50 |
| Pathological anatomy scale | NR | NR | NR | NR | 0.5 | NR |
| Depression | NR | NR | NR | NR | 0.7 | NR |
| Hostility aggression scale | NR | NR | NR | NR | 0.5 | NR |
| Paranoia | NR | NR | NR | NR | 0.2 | NR |

*Sources:* [a]Dubey and Cassell (1993); [b]Rathee (2002); [c]Chaudhury et al. (2010); [d]Singh and Dubey (1997).

*Note:* Percentage is shown in parenthesis.

**TABLE 10.7** *SIS-II Indices of Clinical Groups*

| Indices | (n = 100) M, LL Fracture[a] | (n = 100) M, UL Fracture[a] | (n = 30) Ment. Ret. MF[b] | (n = 50) Epilepsy, MF, Edu (10+ Years)[c] | (n = 50) Drug Dependent Male[d] | (n = 50) MF, Epileptic[c] |
|---|---|---|---|---|---|---|
| Total responses | 63.6 | 62.4 | 47.90 | 55.34 | 64.62 | 55.34 |
| Human responses | 16.1 | 21.5 | 13.00 | 14.10 | 16.31 | 14.10 |
| Animal responses | 6.8 | 9.9 | 19.00 | 6.24 | 12.66 | 6.24 |
| Anatomical responses | 10.2 | 13.6 | 3.20 | 15.74 | 13.85 | 15.74 |
| Sex responses | 2.1 | 1.2 | 0.00 | 1.98 | NR | 1.98 |
| Movement responses | 1.2 | 1.7 | 0.70 | 2.20 | 9.56 | 2.20 |
| Most typical responses | 5.0 | 6.7 | 4.00 | 8.24 | 11.65 | 8.24 |
| Typical responses | 16.3 | 18.4 | 12.33 | 23.12 | NR | 23.12 |
| Atypical responses | 45.2 | 42.7 | 31.73 | 24.82 | NR | 24.82 |
| Rejection | 0.17 | 0.19 | 16.07 | 6.94 | 2.80 | 6.94 |
| Pathological anatomy scale | NR | -NR | 0.47 | 4.56 | NR | 4.56 |
| Depression | NR | NR | 2.30 | 2.08 | NR | 2.08 |
| Hostility aggression scale | NR | NR | 0.40 | 0.90 | NR | 0.90 |
| Paranoia | NR | NR | 0.67 | 0.32 | NR | 0.32 |

*Sources:* [a]Chaudhury et al. (2009); [b]Alreja et al. (2009); [c]Mishra et al. (2010); [d]Singh and Dubey (1997); [e]Mishra et al. (2010).

*Notes:* ULF, upper limb fracture; LLF, lower limb fracture.

**TABLE 10.8** *SIS-I Profile/Indices of Normal Groups*

| Indices | (n = 210) MF (18–45 Years)[a] | (n = 113) MF (6–11 Years)[b] | (n = 100) MF (20–45 Years)[c] | (n = 100) MF (6–12 Years)[c] | (n = 100) MF Adults (18–50 Years)[d] | (n = 50) M, Police[e] |
|---|---|---|---|---|---|---|
| Total responses | 39.00 | 37.41 | 40.01 | 37.24 | 36.11 | 24.58 |
| Human responses | 7.04 | 17.54 | 18.53% | 17.91% | 15.20% | 1.96 |
| Animal responses | 11.53 | 31.15 | 28.25% | 30.74% | 32.55% | 1.32 |
| Anatomical | 6.79 | 12.99 | 17.12% | 13.40% | 15.23% | 2.86 |
| Sex responses | NR | 0.12 | NR | NR | NR | 1.63 |
| Movement responses | 2.21 | 2.74 | 6.25 | 2.59 | 4.93 | 1.30 |
| Most typical responses | 6.02 | 5.58 | 13.88% | 5.69% | 13.10% | 2.60 |
| Typical responses | NR | 59.61 | 72.54% | 61.45% | 62.50% | 4.39 |
| Atypical responses | NR | 34.61 | 15.95% | 32.37% | 24.57% | 1.21 |
| Rejection | 0.24 | 1.65 | 0.28% | 1.86% | 0.60% | 2.12 |
| Pathological anatomy scale | NR | NR | NR | NR | NR | 3.60 |
| Depression | NR | NR | NR | NR | NR | 1.54 |
| Hostility aggression scale | NR | NR | NR | NR | NR | 4.30 |
| Paranoia | NR | NR | NR | NR | NR | 1.41 |

*Sources:* [a]Kandhari et al. (2010); [b]Jain et al. (2005); [c]Kumar et al. (2007); [d]Kumar and Singh (2007); [e]Dubey and Dubey (2005).

*Notes:*

1. All indices except the total responses were converted into percentage scores by taking the total number of responses as denominator for each indices.

2. Kandhari et al. (2010), Kumar (2003) and Mahapatra (2009) PhD data have been pooled together.

**TABLE 10.9** *SIS-I Indices of Clinical Groups*

| Indices | (n = 111) ADHD, MF (6–11 Years)[a] | (n = 98) Heroin, M[b] | (n = 79) Br Sugar, M[b] | (n = 70) Tidigesic, M[b] | (n = 100) MF (18–50 Years) Manic[c] | (n = 100) MF (18–50 Years) Depression[c] | (n = 50) Schiz. MF[d] |
|---|---|---|---|---|---|---|---|
| Total responses | 35.66 | NR | NR | NR | 28.06 | 20.41 | 20.12 |
| Human responses | 16.78 | 4.89% | 4.80% | 5.33% | 17.78% | 11.29% | 19.52 |
| Animal responses | 28.94 | 8.56% | 11.80% | 13.67% | 27.32% | 29.53% | 23.62 |
| Anatomical responses | 16.77 | 23.15% | 23.60% | 24.33% | 21.14% | 21.05% | 20.02 |
| Sex responses | 0.14 | 11.04% | 6.20% | 13.67% | NR | NR | NR |
| Movement responses | 2.15 | NR | NR | NR | 1.45 | 2.34 | 4.18 |
| Most typical responses | 4.91 | 4.89 | 4.80 | 5.33 | 9.82% | 16.69% | 7.17 |
| Typical responses | 46.26 | 14.93% | 18.00% | 13.67% | 53.39% | 50.53% | 46.45 |
| Atypical responses | 47.44 | 18.11% | 20.20% | 18.67% | 36.64% | 32.24% | 48.14 |
| Rejection | 4.18 | 1.59 | 0 | 0 | 5.56% | 14.07% | 18.13 |
| Pathological anatomy scale | NR | 9.91 | 12.25 | 9.42 | NR | NR | NR |
| Hostility aggression scale | NR | 5.16 | 5.48 | 4.50 | NR | NR | NR |
| Depression | NR | 8.02 | 8.65 | 10.14 | NR | NR | NR |
| Paranoia | NR | 2.56 | 2.63 | 2.71 | NR | NR | NR |

*Sources:* [a]Jain and Kumar (2005); [b]Mitra and Mukhopadhay (2000); [c]Kumar et al. (2005); [d]Mahapatra (2009).

*Notes:*

1. All indices except the total responses were converted into percentage scores by taking the total number of responses as a denominator for each index.

# Diagnostic Indicators

Based on the findings of the above studies, the following responses are generally present in the respective diagnoses:

1. **Psychosis**
   - Low total number of responses
   - Low shape appropriate responses (F+ %)
   - Low most frequent/popular responses (MT/P)
   - Confused sequence
   - Colour naming
   - Perseveration
   - Confabulation
   - Contamination
   - Multiple card rejection
   - PO responses
   - Stereotype
   - P failure on Cards II, V and VIII
   - Personal reference
2. **Schizophrenia**
   - Low shape appropriate responses (F+ %)
   - High CF responses
   - Absent or low most frequent/popular responses (MT/P)
   - P failure on Cards II, V and VIII
   - Multiple card rejection
   - Confabulation
   - Contamination
   - Bizarre responses
   - Confused sequence
   - PO responses
   - Card description
   - Colour naming
   - Perseveration
   - Stereotype
   - Personal reference
   - Many sex responses
   - Edging
3. **Paranoid Schizophrenia**
   - High W or Dd
   - Very high human action (M) responses
   - Few chromatic colour responses
   - High white background areas (S%)
   - High human content

- High number of objects like teeth, eyes
- Looking at the back of the card
- Hidden percepts
- Pseudo-human percepts
- Multiple card rejection
- Complete rejection
- Personal reference

4. **Mania**
   - Very high total number of responses
   - High human action (M)
   - Quick RT1
   - High colour responses
   - High black and white (Y) responses
   - Extratensive EB
   - Flower contents
   - Wide content range
   - High religious content
   - More and rapid responses to colour blot areas
   - New and additional responses in enquiry
   - Response replacement

5. **Psychoneurosis**
   - Average or above average F+ %
   - Average P/MT
   - Black and white response
   - Three-dimensional responses
   - Tactual (Fc) responses
   - Colour shock or shading shock

6. **Depression**
   - Delayed RT
   - Low total number of responses
   - Low white background areas (S%)
   - High black and white responses
   - High internal organs
   - Low human action (M)
   - High animal responses (A%)
   - Low total blot area (W)
   - Narrow content range
   - Tendency to reject cards

7. **Dissociative Reaction**
   - Shape inappropriate internal organ (responses high)
   - High sex responses
   - Low total number of responses

- Extratensive EB
- Low human content
- Low human movement (M)
- High colour–form (CF) responses
- Card rejections—VI, VII, IX
- Card descriptions

8. **Obsessive-compulsive Disorder**
   - High total number of responses
   - A Dd dominated approach
   - High human action (M)
   - High white background areas (S%)
   - High F+ %
   - Low C or CF
   - Average or high popular responses (P)

9. **Anxiety Disorder**
   - Low total number of responses
   - High Dd responses
   - Average F+ %
   - Frequent and rapid card turning
   - Shading shock or colour shock
   - Average popular responses (P)
   - Card rejection—IX

Exner (2003) has also suggested the following Index which is helpful in diagnosing various clinical disorders.

The resulting items comprise the following composite indices:

1. **Perceptual Thinking Index (PTI)**
   Rorschach PTI is used to assess the reliability, validity and diagnostic efficiency of the patients with psychotic disorder. It replaces the schizophrenia index.
   - XA% < 0.70 and WDA% < 0.75
   - X–% > 0.29
   - Level 2 > 2 and FAB2 > 0
   - M– > 1 or X– % > 0.40
   - R < 17 WSUM6 > 12 or R > 16 and WSUM6 > 17

   Here, XA% is the ratio of all form quality +, o and u divided by the number of R. WDA% is the sum of all form quality +, o and u for W and D location responses only, divided by total R given to the W and D locations.

   On assessment, different scores indicate the different levels of disorder.

Score 4: disturbed cognitive processes; Score 5: schizophrenic processes; Score 6: strong indicator of schizophrenia.

2. **Depression Index (DEPI)**
   - FV + VF + V > 0 or FD > 2
   - Colour–Shading Blends > 0 or S > 2
   - $3r + (2)/R > 0.44$ and Fr + rF = 0 or $3r + (2)/R < 0.33$
   - Afr < 0.46 or Blends < 4
   - Sum Shading > FM + m or Sum C' > 2
   - MOR< 2 OR $2 \times AB$ + Art + AY > 3
   - COP < C2 OR Bt + $2 \times Cl$ + Ge + Ls + $2 \times Na/R$ > 0.24

The following scores indicate the different levels of depression or affecting problems:

Scores 0–4: low signs of depression; Score 5: some signs of depression; Scores 6–7: strong affective problems.

3. **Coping Deficit Index (CDI)**
   - EA < 6 or AdjD Score < 0
   - COP < 2 and AG < 2
   - Weighted Sum C < 2.5 or Afr. < 0.46
   - Passive > Active + 1 or Pure H < 2
   - Sum T > 1 or Isolation/R > 0.24 or Food > 0

A score of 4 or 5 may indicate that the person is poorly coping with the world.

4. **S-Constellation (Suicide Potential)**
   - FV + VF + V + FD > 2
   - Color–Shading Blends > 0
   - Egocentricity, that is, $3r +(2)/R < 0.31$ or > 0.44
   - MOR > 3
   - Zd > + 3.5 or < –3.5
   - Es > EA
   - CF + C > FC
   - X+ % < 0.70
   - S > 3
   - P < 3 or > 8
   - Pure H < 2
   - R < 17

Score 8: 74 per cent suicide cases, 12 per cent depressives and 6 per cent schizophrenics

Score 7: 84 per cent suicide cases, 31 per cent depressives and 19 per cent schizophrenics.

5. **Hypervigilance Index (HVI)**

Based on the variables associated with paranoia, 85 per cent of paranoids were positive for at least four of the variables.

- $FT + TF + T = 0$
- $Zf > 12$
- $Zd > +3.5$
- $S > 3$
- $H + (H) + Hd + (Hd) > 6$
- $(H) + (A) + (Hd) + (Ad) > 3$
- $H + A{:}Hd + Ad < 4{:}1$
- $Cg > 3$

Check positive if condition 1 is true and at least 4 of the other conditions are true.

6. **OBS (Obsessive Style Index)**

This index taps obsessive, perfectionist, methodical thinking and problem-solving.

- $Dd > 3$
- $Zf > 12$
- $Zd > +3.0$
- $Popular > 7$
- $FQ+ > 1$

The OBS index is positive if all five conditions are true or two or more are true and $FQ+ > 3$ or three or more are true and $X+\% > 0.89$ or $FQ+ > 3$ and $X+\% > 0.89$.

# PART III

# Application of Inkblot Tests in Industries and Clinical Set-ups

# 11

# Application of Inkblot Tests in Business Organization

In employee selection process, pre-employment personality profiles, assessments and tests are becoming popular. There are two schools of psychological testing: objective test and projective test. The 'objective test' is also known as paper–pencil test based on 'questionnaires'. It is easy to establish their reliability and validity. They are convenient in administration and scoring and easier in interpretation. There is no difference whether they are given by a trained psychologist or by an inexperienced assistant. Many of these questionnaires such as 16PF, MBTI, Keirsey temperament sorter and MMPI are available as computer software. Somatic Inkblot Test has a more technologically advanced projective system with multiple industrial applications. The instrument helps in assessing the basic personality of an individual. In various business organizations, it has been found to provide a successful screening tool. It has provided otherwise unavailable data concerning the following: interpersonal relationship, self and ego, team-building, hostility, aggression, depression and suspicious attitude (Dubey and Cassell 1993, 2002, 2003). It is also found to have high test–retest reliability, parallel form reliability and split-half reliability with high content validity (Cassell 1969, 1971, 1972, 1977, 1980, 1990; Dubey and Cassell 1993; Goel et al. 1990).

Application of somatic inkblots empowers the selection processes by more rapidly screening a person with desirable traits such as maturity, confidence, vision and team-building. It also brings to surface the information that the individual fails to report in a standard interview process. Moreover, once a candidate is selected, having the opportunity in follow-up session to retest him/her with the relatively objective computerized instrument can prevent economic losses that occur when this person becomes a full-time employee and then is found to be a mismatch for the job.

In viewing semi-ambiguous stimuli, deep-seated material that was previously forgotten may be brought into awareness. For example, if the individual had poor or traumatic experiences in the past, this unresolved memory could distort and emotionally colour his/her perception of the situation at work. 'TAT' and 'Word Association Test' are still included in the Armed Forces Selection Board in India. HIT and Somatic Inkblot Test have been used successfully as 'group administered' on general population and in industry. In its electronic form, the SIS procedure with accompanying software programmes facilitates an easy and quick interpretation of the scores.

One of the authors (B. L. Dubey) taught the Rorschach and Somatic Inkblot Test to graduate students for about 40 years. He administered SIS for personality assessment during selection processes in various private and public sector organizations for about 20 years. The findings have been very encouraging. SIS has been found to be a dependable test in assessing certain very important traits such as 'team building, interpersonal relationship and healthy mind–body imagery', all of which are much required in successful business executives. A profile of executives has been prepared to help organizational/industrial psychologists and human resource personnel working in various organizations to be used as norms/indices. Major areas being assessed by different images of Somatic Inkblot Test are depicted in Table 11.1.

Dubey (1975b, 1980, 1988, 1989a, 2003) administered inkblot tests (Rorschach and SIS) to executives in different situations. As expected, the data revealed several higher mental functions. These were as follows: productivity, imaginative ability, controlled emotionality, good adjustment and group conformity. Regarding leadership skills, their scores were elevated on team-building. Regarding their personality profile, they gave a greater number of total responses, most typical and human responses. In contrast, they scored low on animal, anatomical and sex responses. The rejection of images and pathological responses were almost absent. In another study, Dubey et al. (2001, 2003)

**TABLE 11.1** *SIS Images Assessing Different Areas*

| Area | Images |
|---|---|
| Interpersonal relationship | A: 9, 21, 24, 31; B: 4, 5, 28, 31 |
| Ego/self-image | A: 5, 6, 7; B: 22, 27, 28, 29 |
| Healthy body–mind imagery | A: 10, 12, 13, 14, 15, 16, 17, 18, 19, 20, 22, 23; B: 9, 11, 16, 17, 20, 30 |
| Erotic imagery | A: 4, 8, 22, 25, 27; B: 18, 25 |
| Hostility/aggression | B: 15, 21 |
| Insecurity | A: 13, 24, 26; B: 19, 22 |
| Thinking in group conformity | A: 7, 9, 12, 13, 20, 27, 30, 31; B: 4, 5, 9, 22, 27, 28, 29, 30, 31 |

*Source:* Cassell and Dubey (2003).

administered SIS test to 90 executives of a private organization. The SIS profile revealed that they were supported by good ego strength, healthy interpersonal relationship, no erotic disturbances, controlled hostility and aggression, high on team-building concept, good human relationship and keeping touch with reality. The personality profile data of the executive groups is shown in Table 11.2.

The data is further presented to illustrate the SIS-II as a screening test during the selection procedure. The subjects who did not reject any images, gave more than 13 most typical responses (out of 18), more than 20 per cent of human responses, less than 15 per cent of animal and anatomical responses and gave no pathological responses were recommended for further consideration regarding possible employment (Dubey and Dubey 2012). However, there were other criteria as well for their acceptance or elimination, and none of them was rejected solely based on psychological test performance. Indices found successful are shown in Table 11.3.

SIT (30 images, web-based [http://dubayhealingcenter.com] short version) is an assessment tool that helps in assessing certain important personality traits found to be very effective for the success of people in industry. These personality traits are: (a) interpersonal relationship, (b) team-building and sharing common view of things, (c) pessimistic attitude and (d) aggressive expression. The instrument measures these traits in high and low scores. The high scores are more desirable in first

**TABLE 11.2** *SIS-II Profile of Public and Private Sector Executives and Indicators of Successful Executives*

| Indices | Cassell & Dubey (2003), Pvt Sec. Exec. (n = 300) MF | Cassell & Dubey (2003), Pub Sec. Exec. (n = 892) MF | Cassell & Dubey (2003), Pub Sec. Exec. (n = 400) MF | Cassell & Dubey (2003), Pvt Sec. Exec. (n = 90) MF | Indicators of Successful Executives |
|---|---|---|---|---|---|
| Total number of response | 70.25 | 68.00 | 66.50 | 65.57 | 61–75 (>62) |
| Human responses | 14.20 (20) | 18.20 | 20.30 (30) | 19.21 (30.96) | 20–25% |
| Animal responses | 8.45 (12) | 8.60 | 10.65 (16) | 7.31 (12.75) | <11% |
| Anatomical responses | 11.40 (16) | 12.80 | 11.80 (16) | 12.38 19.97) | <15% |
| Sex responses | 4.20 (6) | 3.15 | 3.30 (4) | 2.24 (3.62) | About 6% |
| Movement responses | 8.35 | 6.30 | 8.35 | 6.31 (10.18) | <13 |
| Most typical responses | 14.55 | 14.80 | 14.55 | 15.24 (85) | >13 |
| Typical responses | NR | 32.00 | 40.00 | NR | >50% |
| Atypical responses | NR | 9.00 | 9.00 | NR | <12% |
| Rejection of images | 0.75 (1.00) | 0.60 (0.85) | 0.85 (1.00) | 0.35 (0.20) | <1 image |
| Pathological anatomy scale | 0.6 | 0.5 | 0.4 | Almost nil | Almost nil |
| Depression scale | 0.4 | 0.6 | 0.6 | Almost nil | Almost nil |
| Hostility aggression scale | 0.5 | 0.4 | 0.5 | Almost nil | Almost nil |
| Paranoia scale | 0.02 | 0.3 | 0.3 | Almost nil | Almost nil |

*Note:* Percentage is shown in parenthesis.

| Indices | Scores |
|---|---|
| **TABLE 11.3** *Hard Core SIS Indices of Executives* | |
| **Indices** | **Scores** |
| Rejection of images | Less than 1% |
| Most typical responses | More than 13 (out of 18) |
| Human responses | More than 20% |
| Animal responses | Less than 15% |
| Anatomical responses | Less than 15% |
| Pathological responses | Almost absent |

*Source:* Cassell and Dubey (2003).

two traits: interpersonal relationship and team-building, whereas low scores are desirable for pessimistic attitude and aggressive expression. It helps to understand if a person can make a good team and will have smooth interpersonal relationships. It is specially designed for business settings. It is a light weight personality assessment tool that can be used by HR professionals.

The short version consists of a slideshow of 30 inkblot images. The responders are asked to write the responses on each image. At the end of the test, the responder is asked to select the 'most liked' and the 'least liked' images, including the reasons for the selection. The results are interpreted by a software and a report for the responder is generated. The report is used by practitioners in the management of conflict resolution for teams, productivity management for teams, team selection, cost reduction exercises, stress management and employee morale management.

Because basic human characteristics are similar across the world, apart from culture, the normative data though has been established in the Indian industry, it is likely that the data may have general applicability in industrial settings worldwide.

# 12

# Interpretation of Inkblot Responses

## Case Studies

## Applications through Content Analysis

### What Constitutes a Projective Test?

Quantitative inkblot response indices for the Rorschach, Holtzman and SIS tests have a considerable historical research and clinical merit derived from the foundation of normative data. While assigning numerical summation scores to the subjective inner world phenomenon may make such an approach appear 'objective', scientifically, the application of mathematics in this context does not have the same ring of reality as counting physical objects. In recent years, sceptical critics have raised fundamental questions regarding these tests' applicability in the 21st-century clinical settings.

The three categories 'human', 'animal' and 'movement' utilize principles of projection more than those assessing such constructs as 'form' and 'colour', which are more analogous to measurements made use of in neuropsychological tests. The later indices are based more upon the optics of perception of objects in the outer world, as opposed to the subjective inner world of emotion coloured imagery. Consequently, for psychometricians to label such tests as strictly 'projective' tends to be somewhat of a misnomer.

## Applying Projective Principles in Treatment

Content analysis is more of a treatment-oriented approach than diagnostic one. Yet, it must be acknowledged that the cost of controlled, statistics-based therapeutic outcome studies has so far prohibited their completion. However, there are many individual cases that used SIS, highly suggestive of clinically significant positive results.

The revised conceptual model proposes that the content derived from the phenomenon of 'inkblot' projection involves imaginative viewing of the visual input, which is sufficiently ambiguous to stimulate a release from the memory storage of otherwise unavailable deep-seated imagery. What normally is released with content analysis is more akin to fantasy, dreams, PTSD flashbacks, etc., and ultimately the suffering individual's 'inner cry'.

However, it must be acknowledged that content analysis does not readily lend itself to quantification scoring and has been criticized for not being 'objective'. A subject's projective profile tends to be highly unique and idiosyncratic. Often, the deep-seated information surfaces and is projected in a disguised symbolic language, initially interpretable only by a trained professional. Consequently, much of the clinical SIS work has relied on individual case history reports, as will be illustrated later in this chapter.

In clinical settings, the responses can reflect emotionally charged misperceptions of other 'humans', the individual's faulty sense of self as a 'human', distortions in the perception of the individual's own body, as well of those of others, etc. On a temporal scale, the projected imagery tends to be highly fluid; fluctuating rapidly in the level of projective awareness during the period an inkblot series is viewed.

As previously outlined, the visualized imagery may surface at any point in a spectrum, ranging from either a photograph-like representation of past real-life events or their distorted misperceptions. Moreover, the images may be projected as symbolic defensive representations. However, in the more severe mental disorders having an organic neurological basis, the mental material that is projected may primarily reflect an underlying neuropathology and symbolism only secondarily.

Prior to the resultant imagery being recognized by the neurophysiologic processes giving rise to awareness and recognition, the inkblot information from the visual input is reshaped by psychological defence mechanisms. These control the competitive balance between 'sensitization' and 'repression'. The psyche forces attracting an image to the door of conscious awareness and an ultimate recognition are opposed by opposing one's activating neural inhibitory processes.

Whether or not the image passes through the door and is then projected onto ambiguous inkblot stimuli depends upon the interplay between such competitions. When threatening affect causes inhibition to override sensitization, then secondarily activated brain circuitry searches the same brain regions as those which give rise to anxiety arousing dreams. Afterwards, if the affect released is potentially too threatening, what is brought to the responder's projective mind is disguised affect-neutralized symbols. While these may have less disturbing affect linkage than the original stressful memories, the unfelt affect may be converted to a variety of secondary physical and mental symptoms.

Of course, this conceptual model needs to be re-examined in association with concurrent neurological studies, such as those involving functional magnetic resonance imaging (FMRI), which measure metabolically active areas of the brain activated during inkblot viewing.

## Content Analysis: Rorschach and Holtzman Tests

Historically, Hermann Rorschach's assessment of content was relatively limited not only due to his early death, but also due to the limited understanding of the mental mechanisms underlying mental disorders in his lifetime. He assigned content to one of the six categories: animal content, human content, animal detail, human detail, inanimate object and landscape.

Several subsequent scholars such as Beck and Molish (1967) and Klopfer et al. (1954) expanded upon the number of content categories. Holtzman et al. (1961) included five categories in the HIT: human, animal, anatomy, sex and abstract.

The high content of somatic structure in SIS taps into an important psychophysiological dimension. Previously, a book written by Schafer (1960), describing the relevance of anatomical content analysis in psychoanalytic treatment was noted. He outlined the importance of 'body image' concept as follows: 'The blots themselves are equivalent to bodies. Their treatment as stimuli, that is, their use of colours, shadings and forms and their scores reflecting this usage, can be seen to additionally relate awareness of the expression of the subjective experience of bodies.' For a comprehensive overview of the field as it was in 1976, the reader is referred to the book written by Aronow and Reznikoff (1976).

Holtzman included five categories in HIT as follows: human, animal, anatomy, sex and abstract. The one which is least abstract and directly relevant to sexual identity issues is the sex category. In Holtzman's handbook, only one psychotherapeutic case report was presented in detail. With Holtzman's permission, content analysis was completed by reanalysing a case history report originally published in 1961.

Without being acknowledged, in the book, the case indirectly illustrated the importance of content analysis with HIT. The case involved a male university student in psychotherapy, who apparently was experiencing homosexual fantasies provoking anxiety.

When initially tested with Holtzman inkblots form 'A', at A29 he said, 'I don't think that there have been five of these that I haven't seen a phallic symbol'. Here, he directly comments on his sexual perceptual bias.

Now 50 years later, for illustration purposes, a detailed analysis has been given to two of his HIT blots.

## FORM A

**A-24:** Oh Hell! Hell! I say, because some creature is about to stab another. My word he has an erected penis too. On both sides—strange as it might sound—head arm, pitchfork, penis, stabbing himself—threatening a part of his own body.

It is apparent that blot A-24 has brought out threatening imagery with highly charged affect. It projects aggressive feelings initially towards others. After the emergence in projective awareness of to which in 1961 were likely socially unacceptable to himself. This projects homosexual conflicted sexually aroused phallic imagery, with an aggression component secondarily directed inwards to himself. The latter could surface as impulses for self-mutilation or even suicide. A 21st-century clinician trained in symbolism now would have more understanding and perhaps would be able to further explore these potentially dangerous projective clues. It might be noted that the presentation of this clinical case was completed when homosexuality was generally considered a mental illness. Thus, his overall chain of inkblot associations brought to the surface the frequently observed neural connection between the brain's centres for aggression and for sexual arousal.

If interested, the reader might refer to a case in Cassell's book *Body Symbolism* (1980) detailing SIS responses in a hospitalized man who practised same sex behaviour. This individual placed burning cigarettes on his skin to arouse erotic feelings. This concomitantly caused physical pain and neurophysiologic excitation, thereby augmenting his libido induced brain's activity. This for him initially facilitated and then triggered ejaculation. He habitually had learned to self inflict pain by the positive conditioning of sexual pleasure and tension relief.

**A-11:** Oh, no! What I see in these things are unreal (laughing)—they don't look like these, just resemble them. I see a vagina—a woman with legs spread apart. I laughed because these little caterpillar-like creatures look like they are getting the Hell out of there. Very interesting, it suggests that her vagina is in such bad shape, they wouldn't live there. That's why I laughed.

This flow of projective somatic images symbolically reflected his own mental picture of a woman's genitalia. The inkblot stimulated the release of the material that otherwise would be hard to bring out in standard clinical interviews. It was linked with anxiety, which he showed immediately as (Oh no!) and then spontaneously laughed as a further tension relieving mechanism. The 'little caterpillar-like creatures' symbolized his phallic impressions within his sexually conflicted immature body gestalt. Also projected was symbolism reflecting an inherent fear, reflecting a type of phobic reaction regarding visualization of a woman's sexual organs. The latter recalls what psychoanalysts referred to as 'a dentate vagina'. It is understandable how this aversion to woman's body could shift his eroticism to that of a man.

These two Holtzman inkblot examples involving content analysis illustrate the validity and usefulness of the HIT to evoke sexual symbolic responses. In uncovering the complexities of the sexual function, the examination of the imagery projected on inkblots enriches that from other more superficial sources. A reader who is interested in reviewing the remainder of his responses may study these in the HIT book titled *Inkblot Perception and Personality* Holtzman et al. (1961b).

It would have been worthwhile for comparison purposes, to have had an opportunity, to view such a subject's overall Rorschach responses as well. It has been reported that several overt homosexual responses were projected on the Rorschach. Yet, for sexual assessment, the psychotherapist, who obtains free associations to the Holtzman series, has a major advantage as there are many more stimuli cards. For any sexually preoccupied individual viewing this larger series, the probability that some of the ambiguous array might more closely match preconceived sexual fantasies and trigger more relevant responses would be higher.

This is also consistent with Holtzman's mentioning in his Foreword that the value of content analysis in assessing sexual imagery otherwise not disclosed in face-to-face interview.

## Increasing the Number of SIS Stimuli

This projective principle was expanded on with a few of the SIS stimuli, which were purposely designed with subtle sexual structure that was suggestive but not pornographic. Such embedded content provides a useful clinical interview aid for those with sexual and/or reproductive problems.

As an example, a case history report published in the *SIS Journal Projective Psychology & Mental Health* (Cassell and Dubey, 1996) involves an adult woman being treated for major depression. She could complete the Booklet form of SIS-II in the relatively tranquil atmosphere of her home. When she was seen the next day for a review of her responses, she exclaimed cheerfully 'Dr Cassell ... you must have designed the test just for me.... I feel a lot better!'

She explained that as a teenager, she was unsupervised and sexually active. She had had multiple miscarriages, but never told anyone or effectively subjectively processed her fears, guilt and remorse. Yet SIS triggered the release of this highly stressful material. She then was able to independently process, with her now cognitively higher functioning mature brain, the deep-seated PTSD memories.

This was totally unpredicted and, consequently, a surprise. It prompted my deeper appreciation of the potential therapeutic releasing power of the SIS technique, totally independent of the therapist's physical presence or immediate assistance. Many other illustrations of this phenomenon have been observed, especially with the electronic versions of the test. These more readily can incorporate technological advances in computer-based artificial intelligence and robotic treatment.

## Robotic SIS Intervention

Despite the inherent scoring problems involved in the quantification of SIS responses, developmental work is currently underway involving 'artificial intelligence' and 'robotic' cognitive/behavioural treatment. This involves establishing a computerized database for individual types of content, supplemented by quantification of the various categories outlined in an earlier chapter. This will include normative data as well as the data derived from assessing individuals who suffer from discrete clinical syndromes.

Two clinical examples, where PT can be useful to busy practitioners, will be mentioned here. The first involves subjects who suffer from severe mood swings but mask these with a variety of symptoms, symbolically detached from emotions. The second involves subjects with conversion disorders, whose somatic symptoms pose physical diagnostic problems for physicians.

Next, an example will be briefly outlined, illustrating how robotic technology may be incorporated into treating members of law enforcement or military. Such professionals have occupational exposure to stressful situations, which may precipitate PTSD. As a part of their treatment planning, it can be helpful for them to experience at lesser intensity protectively released memories of the original stressors in a supervised therapeutic setting.

One version of SIS under development specifically includes stressful scenes in an ambiguous way. Upon completion of the initial viewing process, the treatment team then can establish with computer programming, a custom-made follow-up programme to desensitize the victim's memories using behaviour treatment principles. This involves a repetitive presentation of the 'most disliked' or the SIS stimulus which recalled PTSD imagery.

In the robotic intervention, this pre-selected visual stimulus is followed immediately by anxiety reducing nature scenes. Thus, theoretically, while the neurotransmitters released by the PTSD 'after imagery' are still present at the nerve endings in the visual cortex, those healing ones released by the relaxing scenes can serve to chemically restore the PTSD memory circuitry to healthy levels. In a robotic fashion, on subsequent reconditioning exposure trials, controlled by computer programmes, the clinician need not be present. For optimum therapeutic results, this brain reconditioning approach should be supplemented with cognitive psychotherapy designed to correct erroneous thinking related to the original stressors.

## Re-examining Rorschach and Holtzman Content Scoring Categories

A theoretical model relative to scoring by simple mathematical 'addition' originally was conceived in the 1960s. It was formulated after summing up the SIS responses denoting heart, after analysing the data derived from subjects with psychophysiological cardiac symptoms. While it was known that their heart imagery was linked to anxiety, no direct mathematical relationship was found by summing up the anatomical responses denoting the heart. Instead, a curvilinear statistical relationship was found. It was then recognized that 'sensitization/repression' opposing factors could render the simple mathematical addition of content identical responses invalid.

This type of contaminating mathematical relationship possibly might account for certain validity problems resulting from Rorschach and Holtzman summation scores. Perhaps, for the subjects experiencing somatic symptoms, the same curvilinear type of relationship as with the SIS might be operating. Conceivably, this could render summation scores meaningless for the comparable category of anatomy. For these people, their anxiety linkage to related painful somatic structures could also affect the relative competitive forces of sensitization/repression affecting image surfacing in projective awareness. Perhaps, as well, the same contaminating principle could relate to the 'human' and 'animal' categories, for people that had been traumatized by abusive people or vicious animals. Clinical investigators who rely on either the Rorschach or the Holtzman projective procedures are challenged to consider this possibility.

## Art Communicates Pictorially Inkblot Imagery

A basic scoring problem concerns the inherent subjectivity of using language. Most cultures are highly limited in emotional descriptive words capable of communicating the affect-loaded imagery evoked by inkblots and therapeutically releasing the stressed subject's 'inner cry'. To access this more effectively in clinical situations, a clinician trained in SIS symbolism may choose to supplement the interview with drawings of the imagery evoked by the inkblots —'a picture is worth a thousand words'.

## Professionals Are Humans Too!

Any professional who clinically studies inkblot imagery in serious mental disorders is empathetically exposing the brain's visual recognition centres to bizarre affect charged imagery. This can predispose empathetic clinicians to occupation-induced secondary PTSD. Sometimes, such external imagery can interact in a negative way with the examiner's own memory storage of stressful past events.

With inkblot projective procedures that trigger the release of inner suffering, this psychologically 'toxic' factor is much more likely to be operational than with the non-projective psychological tests. Moreover, the professional who is blind to certain types of past personal symbolic imagery will tend to avoid recognizing the significance of similar symbolism. This is an occupational problem which partly accounts for the difficulty in the general acceptance of PTs.

Just as psychoanalysts are required to go through personal therapy, the same might well apply to clinicians using projective inkblot techniques. Readers are advised to study the illustrative cases that follow with caution. The authors hope that most will recognize that the benefits far outweigh the risks.

Clearly, the above outlined Rorschach and Holtzman scoring systems have considerable clinical and research merit regarding their normative data based in statistics. However, when they solely employ mathematical scores assessing, for example, 'form, colour and movement', they are not base on fundamental principles of projection. It would be a misnomer to refer to arbitrarily scored category of indices, as 'projective tests'.

Consider the underlying mechanisms when a test subject views an inkblot utilizing the powerful pulling power of projection and then verbally responds when examining an inkblot. Initially, 'light energy' from the physical outer world falls on the viewer's retinas. Within the biological organism, neurochemical excitations arise and then are electrically transmitted by the optic nerves to higher brain centres involved in the yet to be scientifically understood process of 'seeing'. In this conceptual model, this end process involves a flow of visual imagery. Unlike inspecting a highly structured object in the physical world, the ambiguity of inkblots tends to cause a flowing and fluctuating experience in the conscious awareness. To further distinguish the body/mind process of projective 'seeing' in clinical applications, the evoked imagery is more likely to have affect-charged disturbing linkage. Since many higher brain functions involve 'neural inhibition', this disturbing material may be blocked from cognitive recognition. Even if it is not, for the reasons of social acceptability, the viewer may avoid honestly reporting what was seen and felt to the professional examiner in writing the responses.

When the professional reviews what is written systematically utilizing one of the 'objective' scoring systems described earlier, certain fundamental scoring problems can arise in clinical situations. This is particularly the case in certain psychotic situations where there is pressure of speech, incoherence, etc. Another example involves conditions arising from severe trauma. In these, an inkblot may stimulate brain centres recording stressful memories in either a photographic representation of the original stressor or stressors or a symbolic representation as present in PTSD dreams. In all these instances, it may be highly problematic for the examiner to codify the flow of the descriptive words in an 'objective' scientific manner. In other words, the scoring process becomes vague and potentially 'invalid' because of the inherent subjectivity of using language to communicate visual symbols.

Wayne Holtzman tried to overcome such fundamental quantification problems by basing his indices on one response per card. Obviously, this makes mathematical sense for obtaining normative data. However, in many clinical situations such as those mentioned above, it is virtually impossible to do so 'objectively'. How does the examiner determine where the descriptive termination ends, of the initial verbal response based upon the basis of a flow of emotionally linked words describing symbolic imagery?

Our clinical application of content analysis attempts to answer this question while avoiding some of the other problems outlined above. The conceptual model envisioned focuses on the cognitive content of projected images as well as their relative affective charge. The first part of this two-pronged approach has a long history in the psychoanalytic literature. The second incorporates the responder's own subjective rating of the emotional linkage or affect valence of the responses. This additional information is obtained by asking the responder to select the three 'most liked' and then the three 'least liked' inkblots.

In theory, the former is considered to reflect positive emotional linkage of imagery. The subject matter of these responses is initially introduced to reduce test anxiety. As will be illustrated in subsequent case histories, these are more likely to relate to unresolved stressful material. Sometimes this symbolically hidden material is outside the subject's immediate recollection and guides the psychotherapist in treatment planning. While changing the traditional order of detailed enquiry undermines to a degree the comparative validity of normative data, the trade-off in therapeutic power is usually worth it.

Whenever possible, an attempt is made to further clarify the meaning of inkblot stimulated projected responses with clinical data from other rich symbolic sources. These include the symbolism in dreams, non-toxic visual hallucinations, daytime PTSD flashbacks and pathological somatic imagery projected onto the responder's own body image, transference distortions in perception of the psychotherapist, etc.

Inkblot tests (Rorschach, Holtzman and SIS) mainly employ two methods of interpretation—clinical and research. Whenever a protocol is to be interpreted for clinical purposes, interpretation of the responses is essential. If the interpretation is required for research purposes, the total number of responses and percentages of various indices and rejection of images needs to be determined. It mainly follows two types of analyses.

1. **Quantitative Analysis**

   It emphasizes the analysis of various indices such as number of responses (R), number of human, animal, anatomical, sex, popular/MT, movement and various indices in determinants and content categories. These indices are established for evaluating a series of mental constructs in various normal and clinical groups. The prognosis is estimated to be more guarded if the number of rejection of images, along with the pathological responses, becomes elevated.

2. **Content Analysis**

   Content analysis is given more emphasis in interpretation since it frequently helps to bring out the unprocessed unconscious material. What is seen through the response profile, along with the affect linkage, may have direct or symbolic significance either in the present or in the past of the viewer. Assessing such material is analogous to the in-depth study of dreams. While the professional's own theoretical frame of reference will strongly influence the interpretation process, the authors believe that in most clinical therapeutic situations, content analysis for any given individual is a richer approach. Fifteen clinical cases with different diagnoses arrived at by applying content analysis to understand the power of inkblot instrument and the outcome of therapeutic intervention are illustrated further.

## Case 1: Past Pain and Migraine

The case examines how SIS-I, SIS-II and Rorschach imagery project with past painful body events. The three tests were administered, and the interpretation of the tests is discussed at length.

An adult female was referred to an internist for pain management by a physician. She had a history of severe recurrent migraine headaches. The referring physician was concerned about her intake of analgesic medication (Demerol). It was the internist's impression that she was experiencing psychological stress because she had moved to a new state. When initially interviewed, she said that her painful headaches indeed seemed worse ever since she moved to a new place. She, however, denied mental problems. Mental status examination revealed an intelligent, middle-aged woman with some hysterical features but who was essentially intact. She showed no gross evidence of thought disorder and denied auditory hallucinations. Initial diagnostic impression was conversion hysteria with migraine headaches exacerbated by the stress of moving to a new place. The treatment plan specified psychotherapy to improve her coping skills and to reduce stress, and hypnotherapy for pain control.

She avoided the spinal content, instead seeing a 'screw on top of an awl', a disguised phallic symbolism. Moreover, she may have repressed the spine as well. She did not want to be independent and stand on her own. An awl is a tool to make holes in leather or wood. Finally, near the top, she projected another eye, perseverating this theme.

**B17:** She gave a normal response 'a wrench'. Her second association, 'a carnivorous sea creature', reflected symbolically her negative view of phallic imagery. An oral aggressive quality is clear.

**B19:** She saw 'a sunny day or intense passion'. This is a positive response associating the sun with warmth and emotion. She expressed herself as the one who is capable of passion generally but not directly or overtly sexual; love more than sex.

**B20:** Mostly, this is seen as the brain but she saw 'an atomic explosion'. Her defensive symbolism served to repress her brain, an area she associated with her inner turmoil.

An atomic explosion suggests the magnitude of her rage as in A18. Her second level of imagery came closer to reality structure in that she saw 'a wig on a Styrofoam headstand with a rose attached'. She allowed herself to see a head but not a brain. Her dream content suggested some degree of splitting that subjectively noted her anxious brain fixation.

Her response to B4 evidenced a cognitive disorder.

Her response to B21 was consistent with her aggressive feeling and previously detected catharsis of guns.

**B12:** She saw 'a gun that has exploded'.

**B22:** She saw 'a person dead in the middle of the road'. It was consistent with the theme of body destruction and helplessness.

**B23:** Instead of seeing anatomical chest structure, she saw 'a ladybug, she has broken the rifle of a would-be killer'. The response of a diminutive female figure (ladybug) with the power to break an attacker's rifle (phallus?) is a strongly defensive symbolism. It reinforces the optimism and positive orientation of a rifle.

**B24:** She saw 'a curly moustache' initially and secondly 'a two-headed snake'. Her first response to a masculine structure may symbolize her perpetrator. It may also symbolize the male genitalia, the moustache as pubic hair and the nose as penis. This seems likely since the next association was to a snake, a well-established phallic symbol.

**B25:** She saw 'an eagle with a crystal body and snakes at the end of its wings trying to see the future in the crystal. It looks like a baby eagle'. The baby eagle signifies regression. She lived at home and was never separated from her family.

The snake imagery from B24 continues the phallic imagery. Metaphorically, this may be a variation of the *Little Red Riding Hood* theme of the virgin in the forest—a baby bird with the snake near at hand on its very wingtips.

**B27:** Evoked a typical response.

In the first hypnotherapy session, she proved to be an excellent subject. She was able to learn and apply relaxation techniques and imagery to reduce her headaches. Over the next several months, there was a dramatic reduction in her pain and need for emergency room visits. However, as her treatment progressed, her case became much more complex. Following the first hypnotherapy session, she recalled a long and traumatic period in her childhood involving sexual abuse by her father. She also became aware of amnesic episodes when she would suddenly find herself outside a bar dressed in provocative clothing. Eventually, she reported being aware of voices in her head telling her to do socially unacceptable things. At that moment, her voice and behaviour changed, adopting one of several multiple personalities. In one therapy session she suddenly spoke in a deep, threatening masculine voice as she assumed the identity of one of her early male abusers. Eventually, she recalled a history of terrifying child abuse in a religious cult where she said she witnessed human sacrifice, mutilation and burning of babies.

She was administered the Rorschach followed by the 20 cards of SIS-I. Her Rorschach responses were as follows:

**Card I:** 'A face with eyes and nose. Part of this smile is covered by a black mask.' Here content analysis revealed that she has internalized the image of a masked man. Historically, this represented the male leader of the cult who abused her in her childhood.

**Card II:** 'It's a face. Above the eyes are red figures. The head must be hurting. He is shouting out in pain.' The person perceived represented a direct projection of one of her male altar personalities who experienced the painful headaches.

**Card III:** 'It's the figure of a person with long black arms. His head is split in two. The eyes are covered with dark sunshades.' In this response sequence, she continued to project one of her male personalities. Seeing the head split in two was interpreted as a direct reference to the 'splitting' intensity of her headaches at a somatic level. At a psychic level, it reflected ego splitting one of her male personalities.

**Card IV:** 'Just a very dark looking mask.' Here, she was able only to see blackness with weak, undifferentiated mask-like form.

**Card V:** 'A butterfly. Black. Sad to see a butterfly all black.' These are popular response but with added depressive content mirroring her own feelings of sadness and depression.

**Card VI:** 'Two persons sitting with backs turned against each other. Above their heads is another butterfly.'

**Card VII:** 'Two elephant faces not looking at each other. Above their heads is another butterfly.'

**Card VIII:** 'Two pink cats walking down. Blue butterfly with square wings.'

**Card IX:** 'Two narrow eyes being hidden by pink, blue and orange masks. The eyes are sad. He wants out.' The theme of a masked person recurs with added content, suggesting depression and a wish to escape or relieve the depression. It represented one of her repressed personalities that was sad for lack of expression in her behaviour. She responded in a brooding, threatening masculine voice.

**Card X:** 'Every object has a partner, two of everything.' Aspects of the inkblot are personified and split in two.

Her responses to the 20 SIS-I cards are as follows:

**Card 1:** 'A spook with distorted eyes. Face of animal with eyes and horns. Red looks like birds.' The spook represents the face of a past abuser. She was afraid of birds. In a phobic way, she insisted upon the removal of a picture of an eagle from the interviewer's office.

**Card 2:** 'Somebody's head has been cut off. Somebody laughing, a get-even type of laughter.' She viewed a mutilation scene involving the motive of revenge. This is consistent with childhood cult abuse and certain of her murderous personalities.

**Card 3:** 'Two people. A man and a woman. The red blotches represent pain, close to the chest and heart, hurting pain.' Her perception of the red central objects as pain close to the chest and heart represent a direct projection of her own conversion pain, related more to her chest than her head.

**Card 4:** 'A person, probably a male, and a red apple.' She again projected male identification. For her, female body images were to be avoided because of their threatening association to her long childhood history of sexual abuse.

**Card 5:** 'A swimming turtle, two dots, little children and a heart.' These are unremarkable responses.

**Card 6:** 'An animal trapped in an enclosure. It can't get out. A person standing on a heart.' The reference to a trapped animal reflected a statement of how she felt when multiple personalities spoke to her in her head.

**Card 7:** 'An animal sitting with feet. A llama. The heart is red. Some poor animal hurting.' She projected her pain onto the image of the animal hurting.

**Card 8:** 'Seahorses.' 'A ribcage and heart.' A heart split in two instead of one. Her reference to the 'heart split in two' described her own mental splitting.

**Card 9:** 'Two masses, inside, joined by something in common. The bottom looks like a knife.' She repressed the anatomical content because for her urogenital imagery was especially threatening. Her projection of the response 'knife' is clinically significant. Prior to viewing the SIS image, she had awakened from sleep on one occasion with a knife in her hand. She was completely unaware of how or why she picked it up. During this phase, several of her personalities were both suicidal and homicidal.

**Card 10:** 'Lips, red running from lips a snake.'

**Card 11:** 'Red colours.'

**Card 12:** 'Someone trapped in a red mask. Two faces on side, one angry, the other dazed.' Her responses continued the theme of being trapped and masked. She projected anger onto one face and confusion on the other.

**Card 13:** 'A beetle chopping away.'

**Card 14:** 'A dark demon with two eyes (top). A tiny cross at the bottom. A face with no eyes or eyebrows.' Because of the past sexual abuse, she repressed vaginal imagery. Non-anatomical symbolism defended against this aspect of herself and involved negative connotations. The dark demon symbolizes certain of her personalities, which act out sexually. After such episode, she would find herself standing outside a bar 'dressed like a hooker' and be entirely amnesic about her sexual behaviour. Another of her personalities was flirtatious and would attract a large following of men at cocktail parties.

**Card 15:** 'Little faces staring up at each other. Eyes. The base support (bottom).' She repressed the spinal content because of the association of the spine with sexual activity during intercourse. Non-anatomical defensive material represents projecting of the faces of her multiple personalities.

**Card 16:** 'A face with two eyes and a nose.'

**Card 17:** 'A skeleton part. The vertebrae and pelvic area. There is also a face with white eyes and a mouth.' She added the comment: 'I don't like it. It makes me depressed.'

**Card 18:** 'Mountain cliffs and a man looking over people standing.' The people standing reflect her multiple personalities.

**Card 19:** 'Masks, carnival, Halloween.' The mask theme continues. She introduced the concept of Halloween, with implications of monsters, ghosts, frightening costumes and a cult ritual holiday she may have associated with her traumatic ritual abuse as a child.

**Card 20:** 'The Devil himself, eyes and horns, the mouth wide open like he wants to say something or scream at someone.' One of her inner personalities represented the Devil. It was his screaming at her that frequently produced her headaches.

The Rorschach and 20-card SIS were later re-administered. The second administration of Rorschach yielded the following responses

**Card I:** 'Pumpkin face, Halloween type faces. I like it. Feels like I'm being laughed at. A bad feeling of being watched. I see two birds on either side of a pumpkin face.' At this stage of therapy, she was working through her incest trauma.

**Card II:** 'Face of a man. Eyes are red, mouth white as if opened, tongue hanging out—it's red.' Her responses again reflect a threatening man's face. It was reasonable to postulate that it represented the face of the perpetrator of her incest trauma, her father or other adult male cult members.

**Card III:** 'Two female images each holding on to someone's head. Looks as if they're pulling on the head. Looks like a red heart or two hearts joined between the females. On each side of the female's head are red falling objects, falling down.' She avoided male content, possibly defensively because of how males have been threatening to her. 'Pulling on the head' may reflect a past abuse or it could depict the psychic forces splitting her personality and figuratively pulling her head apart.

**Card IV:** 'At first I see a monster face coming towards me, black and scary. Next, I see two boot-type shoes on either side of a common object.' At this stage of her therapy, her multiples were closer to the surface. In the projective test situation, she was unable to view the stimulus objectively. It became animated and moved towards her like in dream imagery. Her ego was less intact and she was moving into a border-line or psychotic state as the terrible extent of her past abuse was beginning to emerge. In retrospect, this reminds of Freud's original comments about analysing a patient with hypochondriacal abdominal pains. When terrible problems come into consciousness, he mused philosophically that it might be more humane not to pursue psychoanalysis and leave the patient with less physical suffering, the lesser of two evils.

**Card V:** 'Black butterfly, but I also see two objects joined in the middle each wanting to pull away.' This represents a direct projection of her early splitting of her terrible past from memory.

**Card VI:** 'The smaller object at top has to pull the two larger objects on the bottom. Both two larger objects are joined in the middle by a common body. The object on top would like to be rid of its companions.' The theme of splitting continued with symbolic representation of the great psychic tension it caused.

**Card VII:** 'Two Indian-type girls looking at each other. They each have one feather on their head. They are balancing on the edge of butterfly wings. They don't want to be together.' The theme of splitting continued.

**Card VIII:** 'I see two pink rats walking over on three sets of objects or bodies. In the bottom object I see a scary yellow gold face.' The 'set of bodies' reflects the early stage of her ego breaking into multiple personalities.

**Card IX:** 'I don't like this picture, it frightens me. It's all messed up like me.' She acquired more insight into the extent of her past trauma and resultant psychopathology.

**Card X:** 'Everything in this picture is connected by some common link. I see different objects like two grey insect-type objects at the top looking angrily at each other. Two blue spiders. Two green seahorses. I see blue in the middle, a pelvic-type skeleton. There is, however, in the middle an orange wishbone-type object. Everything's very scattered.' This response symbolized the anger and conflict between her inner psyche structures.

After taking the Rorschach, she completed the 20-card SIS-I for the second time and these were her responses.

**Card 1:** 'Distorted face, twisted white eyes, crooked, two red hens, and the face is sad.' This response parallels her earlier response.

**Card 2:** 'I see red lips, laughing man at bottom holding his arms wide open. Looks like a bird flapping wings at top of picture.' She failed to make a gestalt of the inkblot configuration. The splitting reflected inner psychic fragmentation. The theme of being laughed at or tormented continued.

**Card 3:** 'Two objects, one man, the other female, red hearts in between the two, sharing.' This response was more positive. The couple was sharing and there was less pain consistent with less conversion pain.

**Card 4:** 'Red apple at top, male figure at bottom, the male is smiling.' She failed to recognize the female figure, consistent with a poor feminine identity and low self-esteem. She was more comfortable talking with men than women. As therapy progressed, it became apparent that her mother knew of the long-standing sexual abuse. She recalled hearing her mother's footsteps near her bedroom door when her father was abusing her.

**Card 5:** 'Looks like a black turtle with red heart, two infants on either side. The one on right is upside down. Two red dots above the turtle look like red eyes.' She continued to euphonize her reaction to red colour. Eyes are consistent with her paranoia.

**Card 6:** 'Bottom is a heart, red, with a red man walking on it. Two doves connected or trapped that can't get out or escape. Two reds on top are eyes looking at me.' These responses projected two of her inner personalities seeking expression. The paranoid theme continued.

**Card 7:** 'Large red heart surrounding in the neck of a llama that's all dark.' This response reflected her clinical improvement. At this stage of her therapy, she experienced less physical pain and wasn't taking analgesic medication as frequently.

**Card 8:** 'Two dark seahorses eating on someone's heart.' This response reflected the degree of suffering from her childhood history of abuse.

**Card 9:** 'Two bodies connected to a lower body with a knife at the end of lower body.' She repressed male imagery because of its threatening qualities. The knife refers to human sacrifice by the religious cult.

**Card 10:** 'Red lips at the top, blood running from lips onto a foreign object.' This represented a more direct association to her emphasis on red.

**Card 11:** 'Looks like lower intestines, red, on fire, pain.' This reflected her long history of lower gastrointestinal symptoms.

**Card 12:** This card evoked no response.

**Card 13:** 'In the centre I see a black scary object looking at me.' This response associated with one of her internalized 'bad' objects.

**Card 14:** 'A little girl in the centre with arms open.' She repressed the female genitalia, the area of her past trauma. It showed age regression to the time of the incestuous abuse.

**Card 15:** 'Looks like stacks of bones, a spine?' She had less anxiety and appropriately identified the spine. Experience with a variety of clinical populations suggests that there is less somatic repression and less conversation pain as a person focuses from body to psychic conflicts.

**Card 16:** 'Two faces, dog faces, sticking their tongues out at each other.' This symbolized aggressive feelings.

**Card 17:** 'Black atomic cloud with a sad face, with white in it.' This response reflected hostility and sadness.

**Card 18:** 'Scary face with mouth wide open.' This symbolizes a threatening internalized object.

**Card 19:** 'I see a face again with long eyebrows, mouth open, coming from behind two human-type objects trying to hide.' Threat theme continued.

**Card 20:** 'This is also a scary, angry face, with mouth wide open. There is a wishbone above the head.' It is more of the threat theme.

Four years later she was again given the SIS-II booklet form. It was apparent that her headaches were not migraines but rather conversion phenomena arising from a conflict between her various personalities and emergence of past traumas to full consciousness. Viewing certain SIS images precipitated and intensified her head pain.

She saw A5 as 'a monster with giant arms, a heart with a cloud above. It makes my head hurt and gives me an uncomfortable feeling.' On A10 she responded: 'It makes my head hurt. It's a face. I see eyes and it leaves me with a painful feeling.' For Image B11, she projected 'a nose with sinus pain'. She repressed the picture of the brain on B23. Onto this painful region, which she perceived as the nerve centre of her mental conflicts, she substituted 'an atomic bomb explosion'. Symbolically, this reflected her terrible past traumatic neurosis. Despite earlier brain repression, on B30 she saw 'a brain divided up', directly associating her multiple personalities. Also, relative to her multiple identities was her response to A13 as 'lots of hands reaching up for help' and A14 as 'monsters fighting over a heart', the effect of her destructive personalities. On A18 she saw 'a skeleton skull with the devil inside, scary'. In a follow-up interview, she recalled this was a direct projection of 'the evil one', one of her more powerful identities. On A24 she saw 'a group of people with arms connected'. In the detailed enquiry, she related these to a group of five inner personalities who had gotten together to fight the evil one.

Some responses related to her trauma and sexual anxiety. Instead of seeing a woman on A7, she saw 'a man with an apple above his head'. On A20, depicting kidneys and male urogenital system, she repressed the male sexual content and saw instead 'two lima beans attached by a hair'. For the spinal picture in A23, she refused to respond and said only that she didn't like what she saw. She related A14 to the ritual abuse by family members and others in the cult: 'The foetus, someone killing the baby'. She saw A27 as 'a cut-off breast'. A partial determinant of her response to A14 was that she tried to abort her youngest child at four months' pregnancy. This occurred after her father, in a jealous rage, told her he didn't want her to be pregnant by anyone else. Some of her responses reflected somatic concerns about areas other than the head. To A28 she responded: 'muscle tendon in pain'. For B13, which depicts the female pelvis, she saw 'three growths on the stomach' referring to colitis. This involved excruciating recurrent abdominal pain with diarrhoea. It felt like her 'insides were on fire'. For B17, which lacks somatic structure, she saw 'a heart' relating to palpitations experienced when she was upset.

Interestingly, the responses to the videotape version of SIS-II images accessed much earlier traumatic memories. B24 elicited memory of a burning baby. She recalled that as a child, she had witnessed cult ritual mutilation, murder and burning of babies. The video evoked more painful somatic symptoms (e.g., headache) and was more psychologically threatening than the SIS-I, the SIS booklet and the Rorschach.

## Case 2: The Use of the Rorschach, SIS-I and SIS-II in Releasing Somatic Grief

SIS (SIS-I and SIS Video) and the Rorschach test were administered to a 42-year-old female patient (named X in the Case discussion). SIS and the Rorschach were able to bring out her inner cry and depressive contents related to her father's death due to cancer and her own recovery after cancer. SIS images have been found to be powerful media to take the person back in time and creating hypnotic-like effect, helping the person in catharsis and finally proving to be an effective therapeutic tool. Responses given by the patient on the Rorschach and the SIS-I and SIS-II Video are interpreted using content analysis and psychoanalytic interpretations.

The subject of death has been explored from several standpoints (Kubler-Ross 1969). When a parent dies, the psychological impact normally is very great (Myers 1986). Sometimes, the grief may be prolonged over the course of several years (Doka 1989), resulting in major depression and various conversion reactions involving the experience of somatic pain.

There are many stages in the grief process. One involves the appearance of the deceased person's body or aspects of the body in the subject's dreams (Von Franz 1984). This is one way for the subject to experience spiritual and psychological contact with that individual and to deny the pain of the loss so that sleep can occur. The dreamer, when awake, realizes that it is 'just a dream', and will then feel the emotional discomfort and continue in the normal grieving process. Occasionally—especially at night—the images of the deceased will spill over into conscious awareness in the form of hallucinations when the deceased person appears as a ghost-like figure and sometimes talks. Lay people refer to these hypnologic phenomena involving images of the departed loved one as 'ghost'.

Images of the deceased person's body may be projected onto inkblots (Cassell 1980) and video stimuli having human and anatomical content. This process will be illustrated by presenting the case history of a woman who had lost her father several years ago resulting in depression and who required antidepressant medication. Psychologically, she closely identified herself with him in her own body gestalt. She had developed painful somatic symptoms in her chest, mimicking those which he had experienced in dying with lung cancer.

## A transcript of a video interview with this grieving person is given as follows:

Dr B:   I appreciate your coming here today and could you tell us a little bit about the extent of your depression and how it relates to your father's death and so on?

X:   Miss him. I could always talk to him. He made me feel good. And even now I sometimes still feel it was my fault that he was sick.

*Dr B:*  What was his sickness? Could you tell us?

*X:*  He had cancer and it went into his bones and then he died shortly after we got back. We were gone when we found out that he had cancer. And we got back to home in Aug 1982, and it just wasn't my father.

*Dr B:*  Yeah.

*X:*  He had changed quite a bit from the chemotherapy and that.

*Dr B:*  What were the changes you saw in your father with this cancer and how did that impact you at the time?

*X:*  Well, when I first saw him, he was sitting in the corner of my mother's kitchen; he was just a little thin old man with hardly any hair. He couldn't talk because he'd had a couple of strokes and he had a hard time with that.

*Dr B:*  How old was he at the time?

*X:*  He was 56.

*Dr B:*  So that must have been hard for you to see that?

*X:*  Especially when I saw him the summer before and he was very weak. We had gotten closer and I guess I could just talk to him.

*Dr B:*  Could you tell us if you had images of your dad in dreams?

*X:*  Yes, he looked like my father and not like this person that I saw when we came back.

*Dr B:*  How would you feel when you saw your father the way he used to be in your dreams?

*X:*  Secure.

*Dr B:*  Yeah, you loved your dad. And then when you'd wake up how would you feel when you realized it was just a dream?

*X:*  I would feel very upset, when I woke up and found that he wasn't there, that was the dream and that the dream I have of being with him was real.

*Dr B:*  Did you ever have visual experiences or sense his presence in the waking state?

*X:*  Yes, sometimes I've walked through the malls and might have gotten a glimpse of someone, a gentleman walking or shopping, and I would have to look again because I thought it was my father.

*Dr B:*  Yes, I appreciate your sharing. I know it's very painful. It will help to continue in getting some of the grief out. One of the things we noticed was when you looked at these inkblots, you saw things resembling your father. And at this time, I am going to have Dr Dubey go over the results of the Rorschach test with certain cards, so I'd appreciate if you would share your experience with him as well. OK, thank you!

*Dr D:* I would like to know little more about the responses on Rorschach cards that you have already seen. On Card #II you saw something like 'cancer cells....'

*X:* It's just.

*Dr D:* Would you like to tell something more about it?

*X:* It just reminds me of the cancer cells eating him up inside and he is having a hard time not being able to speak because of the strokes.

*Dr D:* I'm sorry. Does it remind you of something else?

*X:* Just the cancer and the blood. Wondering where the blood went because my father was cremated.

*Dr D:* On Card VIII you perceived 'there is an arm in the centre and there are two persons grabbing and pulling me down'. Would you please tell little more about this?

*X:* They were my son and my mother, you know it just feels like I try to talk to my mother and I try to do what she wants me to do and I try to please her and to please my son too and I can't do it. I'm having a hard time.

*Dr D:* Yes. Of the two persons, one is your mother and the other one your son, is that so? And are they helping each other?

*X:* Well, my son, he tries sometimes. He sticks up for me when he knows I'm being pushed into a corner. He has this feeling. My mother, I love her, but I have a hard time getting her to stand by me.

*Dr D:* Maybe it reminds you that when you really needed her help she was not that helpful?

*X:* She thinks it's all in my head.

*Dr D:* Take care. On Card IX you saw 'a person hiding behind and feeling ashamed like me'. What makes you feel like ashamed?

*X:* I'm just ashamed of myself because I can't seem to do what everybody wants me to do and like I said before, I feel responsible for my father's death. For being bad when I was younger. And I just don't want anybody to see....

*Dr D:* So you think yourself as a bad girl and your father was being punished for your mistakes.

*X:* You see, I came up here. We were in the States and I came up the summer before for vacation. I was under a doctor's care there and I was having some problems and I didn't spend the time I wanted to with him then. And we were getting closer and closer together and I had to leave. It was recommended by a doctor that I go back to be with my doctor there, so I had to cut my trip short and leave him before we really got a chance to get a lot of things said.

*Dr D:* On Card X you perceived 'this is an explosion. There is some-thing coming out of mind'. What makes you to think like that?

*X:* It makes me think of me. I keep a lot of things inside. I don't yell that much at my son. I just let things that happen to me to myself and then when it reaches a certain point, I just lose it. And I try to talk and explain what's going on and I can't because I'm so nervous and crying and then when it's over I feel ashamed. I feel like I've done something wrong.

*Dr D:* And by seeing 'something is coming out' might be giving a sort of release, release of tension.

*X:* By not keeping it in anymore. By finally saying something to someone. Like I say I have a hard time because I just start crying and shaking and I can't get it out. I just sometimes feel like I want to explode because I can't take any more.

Responses on other cards of the Rorschach were normal and clinically not relevant for interpretation.

*Dr D:* Let us review your response on the SIS-I. You have selected Card 20 as the most threatening image to you. And on this card, you have perceived, 'it's like death coming to me. May hurt me'.

*X:* It's just coming to get me. I think about it a lot and I, like I say, I'm afraid of dying. And it's coming.

*Dr D:* Are you still so much afraid that it might come at any time and it may hurt you?

*X:* I'm afraid that it's gonna come very soon and I worry about my son when it happens and my husband but mainly my son. I don't feel I have done very well as far as health goes this year and I'm scared. I don't want to die right now.

*Dr D:* On Card 12 you have seen 'blood'. May be the card is of red colour and probably this red colour reminds you of blood. Would you like to share your feelings?

*X:* It's mine, my father's; you know everything. All the problems that I've had where I've lost blood and my father losing all his blood somewhere and it's just all together.

*Dr D:* Please take care. On Card 18 you have viewed 'the gate of hell'. Would you like to tell about this gate of hell?

*X:* Well, it just looks like the gate of hell. The teeth are the gates that are opening that you walk through. The eyes are watching you to make sure that you do come. It's like it's waiting for me. That's where I'm going to go because I wasn't good.

*Dr D:* Yeah. Is it the whole image or just the eyes watching you and waiting for you?

*X:* It's the mouth opening and as I go through closing in on me.

*Dr D:* Does it still remind about your father?

*X:* I'm afraid that's where my father is.

*Dr D:* On Card 5, you said 'pain'. What sort of pain?

*X:* It's the pain eating inside. The pain that my father felt. The pain that I feel when I need him and he's not there.

*Dr D:* Can you imagine this red spot inside?

*X:* It's like a disease.

*Dr D:* What disease?

*X:* Cancer.

*Dr D:* Yeah.

*X:* I'm scared of cancer. I had it once before, got over it but it kind of. It's like, first they said the cancer is looking good, that it was getting smaller and then suddenly, he started getting bone pain and it was in his bones.

*Dr D:* It's very painful to think of your father and his disease. This is Card 6. Right here you have perceived 'a child in tension'. Can you tell more about this child?

*X:* Well, the child is used to having just a mother around and now he had to learn that the mother has met someone and that they are going to be husband and wife and that the mother must build her life around the husband and the child doesn't understand it because he had always had the mother's attention.

*Dr D:* Does this child remind you of anything?

*X:* My son.

*Dr D:* Yeah.

*X:* Yeah, it was just him and I for quite a while and then I met my husband and I tried to please, you know my son and my husband. It was hard. My son needed to build his life around us and you know we had problems because I would be upset when my husband would punish him. I would say things in front of my son.

*Dr D:* Just to save him?

*X:* Yeah, and I shouldn't have. I should have known. I just wanted my son to grow up and be loved. You know he deserves that.

*Dr D:* Yeah, and now the last image, Card 19. Here you saw 'something is dying'. What is that?

*X:* It's like the slow death my father had. I mean it was fast, but yet it was slow and painful. A person or thing is just lying there helpless and not being able to move or say anything. Occasionally, he opens his eyes, looks around and sees that the family is there with him. There is nothing he can do, he tries to speak but cannot, and just slowly starts dying.

*Dr D:* Take care. Would you like to review some of your responses on SIS Video? In Image A2 you perceived 'a bad life with lots of uncertainty'. Would you like to tell about this?

*X:* I don't know what's going to happen next. And it has been a bad life, maybe not for me, but I have put my husband through an awful lot and my son. Insecurity had made me afraid that my husband would find someone else. Someone, who is better for him; I give everything I have, but sometimes I don't feel that it's enough.

*Dr D:* On next Image A3 you saw 'it's flower and beautiful' but later you said that it's a flower with roots and an insect is eating the roots.

*X:* That's what it looked like.

*Dr D:* Would you please elaborate little more?

*X:* It's just that there are some things that are beautiful and some people that want to destroy them. And my husband is a very good man and sometimes I feel that I am dragging him down. So I feel like I'm the beetle eating the roots because I kind of affected his career also.

*Dr D:* It is very painful. Let's go ahead on Image A13. You have seen 'man's hand reaching for help'.

*X:* My father reaching from the pits of hell. My father wasn't a bad man, but he had problems and....

*Dr D:* Did he get the help he needed?

*X:* Sometimes.

*Dr D:* On A21 you have seen 'a man is being torn apart by sickness'. Who is that man?

*X:* My father being torn apart with cancer.

*Dr D:* You perceived on A26 'baby trapped in a ball and that baby is not able to come out'. Will you please like to describe about this?

*X:* I had to have a hysterectomy because I had cancer and my sister was pregnant and she didn't want to have any more children and she went and had an abortion.

*Dr D:* Take care. In Image B2 you have seen, 'cancer eating up all good cells'. So again, you are thinking....

*X:* My father.

*Dr D:* Let's proceed to Image B3. You perceive 'two people, man and woman sitting in a house on fire'.

*X:* It's, I don't know, it just looked like that two people were sitting there and they really didn't realize what's going on around them.

*Dr D:* And in Image B9, you have seen 'bad lungs'. What do you mean by bad lungs?

X:       My father had lung cancer and the last chest X-ray that he had didn't look too good and it just scares me.

Dr D:    I am sorry.

X:       'Because I don't want to die of cancer. I don't want to go like my father did.

Dr D:    On B20. You saw 'brain covered with bad cells'. What is that?

X:       Cancer cells in the brain.

Dr D:    Last image on SIS Video B22, you saw 'a man lying down with a bad pain'.

X:       Intense pain. Fire in his stomach. It just looked like that his stomach was on fire.

Dr D:    Can you tell more about this?

X:       It was like fire, you know the smoke and uh the pain and my father were hurting very badly in the hips and around there.

Dr D:    Hope it has helped you in releasing lots of emotions and sad feelings.

X:       Well they are.

Dr D:    How do you feel after taking the test?

X:       Drained. Sometimes better. And then sometimes it just brings up memories of watching my father die in the hospital. Because we didn't leave his side until the end. Because my husband was stationed in the States. And I was in and we found out we were coming back. Just before we left I was in a PI ward in Virginia and they were trying to help me. They were trying to help me to get, I guess, get ready for what I was going to see. It was a really big change and....

Dr D:    It's very painful.

X:       I guess nobody could prepare you for that. But then when he went in the hospital the last time, I stayed there day and night, all his kids did. We slept on the floor and in the hallway. We all stayed there with my mother until it was over.

Dr D:    Thank you for sharing your feelings with me. We'll be meeting again.

Dr B:    Dr D, thank you very much for the sensitive and probing interview with Mrs X. It seems we have a powerful approach with the combination of the Rorschach and the SIS (card form and then the video). As I indicated to you, a sensitive, caring psychologist and a patient with enough ego strength that she can face pain even though the grief goes back several years and is very intense. I wanted to ask you some questions in terms of how you feel the Rorschach and the SIS helped us clinically. And especially as it relates to therapy. As you know I have been very interested in a content analysis approach. I had the

*Interpretation of Inkblot Responses*   283

privilege years ago of working with Professor Seymour Fisher on the Rorschach and SIS anatomical responses presented by people who had somatic symptoms. Ultimately, I realized that we needed projective stimuli with more anatomical content and so on and have been stimulated originally by reviewing some of Dr Schafer's work on the psychoanalytic content analysis and others more recently like Lerner (1991). It was fascinating for me to realize that you had met Piotrowski towards the end of his life and that he himself was interested in psychoanalytic content analysis. Could you share about that please, especially in terms of Mrs X's responses?

Dr D:  I use both the tests, SIS and Rorschach, clinically. The SIS provides more vital information and it is a quick test for diagnosis and screening. The SIS is backed by theories of body symbolism and inner cry (Cassell 1980). The theories are very impressive and exciting. About 40 per cent of cases in hospitals, particularly in psychiatric set-up, have psycho manifestation and the causes are psychological in nature.

Dr B:  Exactly. A lot of people cannot verbalize their emotional issues and tend to somatize. In medical set-up, physicians and nurses who focus on the physical symptoms do not imagine the impact of such emotional issues. Many either do not have time or the training to work on the psychological issues is not adequate.

Dr D:  So the test is very helpful in detecting the psychological problems, the inner cry of the patient as in the case of Mrs X. The medicine (antidepressant) may help her in managing physical symptoms and SIS images will help her in processing deep-rooted emotional trauma. Her problem is probably because of her psychological/emotional attachment with her father, which she is unable to resolve after his death.

Dr B:  The antidepressant medicine helps her to feel better symptomatically. The symptoms are removed and so on, but it doesn't get to the core difficulty, the grieving process and her irrational thoughts.

Dr D:  Exactly. As you have noticed that the SIS images have created hypnotic-like effect and she started verbalizing with her inner cry. It helps in understanding the psychopathology of the case and releases tensions of the person undergoing the test. And you could notice her face; she was feeling released and cheerful.

Dr B:  She got relief. As time goes on, in my own career, I have really moved from an interest in the diagnostic aspects to the therapeutic and I am much more interested in the techniques that help people, which release feelings and help them understand themselves.

Dr D:   Many psychologists working in educational institutions and not really trained in handling patients/clinic population do not believe much in inkblot procedure. They believe more in questionnaires because they do not require any training and sophistication in interpretation.

Dr B:   That's right. It's also true in this country that some of the authorities who give seminars on Rorschach do not see a broad range of patients anymore. They are so removed that they're missing some of the richness of clinical work. I wonder if we could go through at this time and have you comment on some of the specific colour responses. Please begin with her Rorschach responses and then SIS.

Dr D:   All four Rorschach Cards II, VIII, IX and X were very informative and effective in this case.

Dr B:   Yes.

Dr D:   She was very upset while viewing chromatic cards.

Dr B:   They carry the punch in terms of the affect.

Dr D:   She was unable to control her emotions and all through she was sobbing. She was crying like a child during the interview session.

Dr B:   Yes. So she really went back in time to the original loss of the father. So this pulled her back and facilitated release of the pent-up grief.

Dr D:   Right. And it is difficult to score such responses under closed scoring categories. For example, on Rorschach Card VIII, she says 'I feel like as I am in the centre and two persons are pulling me from each other, and that one side is my mother and on the other side my son'. Such responses can be interpreted only by using content analysis.

Dr B:   Correct.

Dr D:   And this is how the clinician can hear the inner cry of the suffering individuals.

Dr B:   It makes it more real when you have a stimulus than just talking in generalities in an interview.

Dr D:   Exactly. And on Rorschach Card IX again she perceived 'a person hiding behind and feeling ashamed like me'. This is true projection, which one can never imagine on questionnaires.

Dr B:   Yes.

Dr D:   And such feeling that 'I have let them down, especially my father'. 'I feel like I am a bad girl and my father is being punished because of me', is common in paranoid schizophrenics.

However, such responses are possible due to excessive unre-leased grief and feelings of guilt.

Dr B: Right.

Dr D: And based on such responses she cannot be categorized with paranoid symptoms.

Dr B: That's right.

Dr D: Such responses can be explained only through psychoanalytic interpretation.

Dr B: Yes.

Dr D: She felt that as a child it was her duty to help her father whom she could not do and because of this she is calling herself a bad child.

Dr B: So it is very important that the therapist ultimately go back and make these interpretations.

Dr D: Exactly, this is what Dr Piotrowski (1985) explained me during my visit to his home at Logan's Square, Philadelphia in July 1985. He explained that do not give more emphasis on indices such as M, FM, C, Popular and Form and try to understand the meaning behind the responses given by the subjects.

Dr B: Yes.

Dr D: Because after all, what is the purpose of psychological tests? It is only to understand the psychopathology of the patient.

Dr B: We want information which is clinically relevant to the therapy process.

Dr D: Exactly, and that is why out of 62 images of SIS, I was interested only in a few images giving more clues.

Dr B: Right. What is your feeling about rating the images for their degree of threat and then starting with those that are most threatening?

Dr D: The images rated as most threatening helped in understanding the psychopathology of the case. Such images depict specific body percept and traumatic situation which the patient has experienced in past. In fact, it is not the 10 cards of Rorschach, or 20 cards of SIS-I or 62 images of SIS-II but the three most threatening images which will provide you signals to peep into the inner self of the subject.

Dr B: Yes.

Dr D: Maybe out of 20 cards you are interested only in five or six cards for depth interview/analysis.

Dr B: Excuse me. In the book *Body Symbolism* (Cassell 1980), the last chapter deals with death anxiety. And characteristically, as you know, people deny death as an issue. And we have a technique here on some of those death-related cards you can introduce it clinically and deal with it.

*Dr D:* Yes, she has projected the fear of death by giving responses such as 'Gate of Hell' on Card 18. Further she said, 'I have to go inside—my father has already gone inside'. One can see the sort of fear and insecurity in her.

*Dr B:* There's a lot of rage associated with this. Part of the problem with her is that she hasn't gotten in grips with her anger for her father for leaving and the way he died and some of the old childhood problems as well.

*Dr D:* And on Card 19 she said, 'I'm going to die, and my father died and may be in the near future something is going to happen to me'.

*Dr B:* Would you be concerned about suicidal ideation with her in view of this death preoccupation?

*Dr D:* Well, she has maintained ego strength and is attached with her son and husband, because of this the chances of suicide are very less.

*Dr B:* Yes.

*Dr D:* She is aware of her medical profile. Her strength is still her consideration and caring attitude towards her family.

*Dr B:* Yes. She has also a positive relationship with her husband and other people who love her.

*Dr D:* And if the person has gone through such traumatic experiences, such responses are but natural.

*Dr B:* Thank you for your most interesting comments. What would you recommend in terms of someone considering the use of the SIS as opposed to existing techniques including non-projective tests?

*Dr D:* While taking the questionnaire, you are forced to choose yes or no, true or false, agree or disagree. Most of the time, these questionnaires have cultural influence. Contrary to this you are free to project your feelings and emotions on inkblot tests. SIS is the latest and most powerful amongst the inkblot tests.

*Dr B:* Yes.

*Dr D:* And in fact, in one of my studies, I tried to find out correlation between Rorschach and SIS, it turned to be quite low, reason being the Rorschach measures the basic personality and is used as diagnostic test. The SIS is a projective instrument and an aid to psychotherapy. It helps in understanding the psychopathology of the case. It further helps to peep into the inner deep and hearing the inner cry of the suffering individuals and you can get more information, which is not possible through other tests. The SIS is not against the Rorschach test, but it is a further extension of the Rorschach test. The SIS was also tried in India

| Dr B: | during selection and was found to be a successful instrument in getting the right man on job. |
|---|---|
| Dr B: | Yes. |
| Dr D: | So the SIS covers both the aspects, diagnostic as well as therapeutic. The best part of SIS-II and video is its self-administration. It can also be administered in group. It reduces test's anxiety because the subject is alone while taking the test. It helps in true projection. The test can be taken even at home or while waiting for your turn in the clinic. And because of these qualities, it is the best projective test. |
| Dr B: | And there are variations in the use of SIS test. For example, currently I am interested in administering the procedure at bedtime and seeking at what extent some of the images are picked up in the individual's dreams by doing the interpretation of dream work the following morning. Well, thank you very much. Dr D, your comments have been most helpful, and I have learned a great deal from you in terms of your own experience with the SIS and sometimes one can get too close to a procedure, but I think it has been very helpful and thank you. |

We've had the opportunity to look at an individual who has lost her father and see how this has affected her responses to the Rorschach and the SIS both in the form of both the card and the video. Hopefully this material, as time goes on, may be brought up in therapy in ways, which will help her express the inner cry and further move ahead in resolving the blocked grief. As an experienced clinician might well imagine, it is not just a matter of prying at the pain to release feelings. In addition, there needs to be definitive cognitive therapy in terms of helping her deal with some irrational thinking that she has relative to her pathological guilt. Similarly, she needs further insight into how the sympathetic identification with her father's deteriorating body image contributed to her converting the diseased anatomical imagery into repressed affect, leading to physical symptoms of chest pain and marked cancer phobia.

## Case 3: Body Consciousness in Exhibitionism through Somatic Imagery

Aside from exhibitionism, the patient—a 28-year-old single painter—appeared to have no other major psychological problems. His past behaviour indicated that he had considerable difficulty in relating to women. He denied himself the release of sexual tension through masturbation—rather, when such feelings reached a peak, he impulsively exposed himself to women. Although he had experienced sexual intercourse on one occasion, he recalled feeling quite ashamed about this. In fact, he distinctly remembered imagining that someone was in the room watching the sexual act. When questioned about this, he indicated that the observer might be God who was there to punish him for having sex outside marriage.

During interviews, marked resistance was encountered in discussing body attitudes. It was learned that he had doubts about the adequacy of his sexual functioning including fears of being sterile. His sexual fantasies involved situations where he and a woman would undress for mutual exhibition. However, at no time was sexual imagery in consciousness permitted to involve mental scenes of genital interaction between his body and that of a woman. Related to this, his past family background was characterized by a puritanical home situation and marked sexual restraint.

## Method of Projective Testing

SIS was conducted in the presence of a second investigator who observed the patient's general reaction to the test situation. The study was conducted under two conditions. The first simply involved administering the anatomical pictures to the patient in a manner analogous to that employed with the TAT. The second concerned the modification of the individual's consciousness using rapid acting intravenous barbiturate sedation. This was administered in enough dose to experimentally induce a state of psychic relaxation to control anxiety, thereby reducing the patient's inhibitions in mentally processing the somatic images stimulated by the pictures.

Prior to viewing the pictures, the patient was given the following instructions: 'I have here a series of pictures that I am going to show you one at a time. As you look at each one, tell me everything that comes to mind. Although different things are seen by various people, I am particularly interested in what it reminds you of in viewing it. Remember that there is a lot of time'.

To obtain accurate records, both interviews were tape recorded and later transcribed for analysis.

## Descriptions of the Pictures and Projective Responses Related by the Patient

In this report, the results will be reviewed in terms of those which were most immediately relevant for evaluating the patient's ability to mentally process sexual imagery.

### Urogenital Card (VIII)

It may be observed that this picture presents visual input which facilitates the evaluation of a male patient's propensity to permit phallic material to register in consciousness. Although statistical parameters are not yet available, our research group with this anatomical picture series has compiled extensive clinical experience. It has been found that in this picture, virtually all patients perceive anatomical content. A common response involves first responding to the upper configuration as 'kidneys' and then perceiving the lower areas as 'bladder and penis'.

Remarkably enough, the patient when shown this picture simply responded, 'It looks like a couple of potato sacks'. Judging from his non-verbal behaviour in inspecting the anatomical 'inkblot', the observer considered that this non-anatomical response represented the only imagery that registered in consciousness. However, it must be acknowledged that it is, of course, impossible to exclude the possibility that the patient saw the sexual content but elected to not report it.

Under the drug-induced hypnotic state, the patient responded as follows:

'That looks like a couple of men ... a couple of men's heads ... there's an eye (black mark on left kidney shaped object) ... they've got no hair ... and this is their noses down here.... I don't know what that thing could be (lower area depicting bladder and penis) ... it looks like another person off in the distance because it is smaller than these two ... another person's head with something on his head ... and these two guys are standing here talking ... they could easily be a couple of potatoes or a couple of people ... (patient inverts card) ... it still looks like two potatoes regardless of the way you hold it.'

It may be observed that the relationship between the pictorial reality (i.e., urogenital system) and the patient's response pattern to this picture was highly remote. It is suggested that the patient's imagery was much more dreamlike because the drug had released psychological inhibitions.

Judging from the patient's response, it may be inferred that the picture's connotations more strongly impinged upon the consciousness than in the non-drugged state. Thus, the imagery was stated to resemble the facial area of 'a couple of men'. However, this interpretation is complicated by the fact that previous research has shown that under barbiturate sedation, body consciousness tends to focus on the head (Cassell and Hemingway 1970). Consequently, it must be recognized that a partial determinant of his response could have been a drug-induced artefact.

Next, one might consider the analogy between the projective response to the lower area—which depicts, in a covert fashion, the bladder and penis—as 'a man with a mask over his eyes', and his apparent failure to 'see' what is represented in that aspect of the picture. It is suggested that at some level of consciousness there was psychic awareness that the visual input provoked anxiety. In this sense the 'mask' may be interpreted to symbolize the patient's reluctance to 'see' the phallic imagery impinging upon consciousness. Lastly, attention might be directed to the response 'candlestick with a light burning at the top'. It is of interest that when the therapist later asked the patient to associate to this word, he responded as follows: 'light bulb ... darkness ... stars ... moon ... lamp ... funny shaped lamp like Aladdin's lamp'. It is tempting to interpret the fact that you rub the last object to obtain magical effects, as symbolically reflecting the patient's masturbation fantasies and unresolved sexual tensions.

The last part of the response sequence indicates the re-emergence of non-anatomical content in awareness. Again, it appears that the patient failed to consciously recognize the phallic material inherent in the picture.

After showing all the pictures to the patient in the drugged state, certain cards were presented for a third time. The urogenital card was the first of these. This phase of the case study was designed to have the therapist work with the patient until the phallic material inherent in the picture registered in consciousness. The patient's anxiety in this situation was constantly evaluated and maintained within a range normally employed in desensitization behaviour therapy techniques.

When this card was presented to the patient, the therapist introduced the anatomical content at a higher level of awareness with the following comment: 'You said that this picture has to do with "potato sacks" or "men"'. Now, let's suppose that it has to do with body: What do you see?' With this suggestion, the patient's anxiety level increased, and he became noticeably perplexed. After a long pause, during which the phallic content more strongly impinged upon his consciousness, he asked the question 'male or female?' He was then informed that it was whatever he saw in the picture. After another long pause, during which he appeared to become even more anxious, the patient reported, 'that looks like a man's penis ... and that looks like his testicles ... and that's all that I can see'.

This deviated from previously observed responses in our research unit. Instead of initially referring to the upper areas as 'kidneys', and then subsequently perceiving the other areas in the male urogenital system, he first responded to the lower areas as 'penis'. However, more unusual is his response 'testicles'. Thus, he substituted more anxiety laden somatic images in consciousness over anatomical content more clearly depicted in the picture.

In a retest examination, six months later, he responded as follows:

> It looks like two red things ... like potatoes ... it could be the shape of a person's head ... the black spot looks like an eye ... the coloured part hanging down looks like a stem or foot joining these together.

After having previously perceived the sexual material inherent in this picture, it is remarkable that six months later he once again failed to report seeing anatomy. Eventually, he was reminded of the anatomical content. In this instance, he projected the following pathological anatomy response:

> It's a man's penis but it has a funny shape the way it hangs down ... it is swollen and there is a big lump on it ... it doesn't hang straight down ... it looks like the after-effects of sexual intercourse ... it's aching and has syphilis or something ... the testicles look swollen too.

This may be interpreted to represent a direct projection of his hypochondriacal concerns about the effects of sexual intercourse.

### Male Figure Card (X)
This picture clearly depicts the outline of a man's body. It permits the patient to project responses related to the hands, the feet, the pelvic area, the limbs, the ribs and the lungs. Initially, viewing this picture the patient appeared to be markedly inhibited in that he only reported the following: 'It resembles the shape of a man ... but he doesn't have a head'. Since normally male subjects do not comment on the missing head, this aspect of the response seemed worthy of note. It may be postulated to reflect an upward displacement of his concern about losing his penis.

Under sedation, he responded as follows:

This looks like the shape of a man ... two arms ... and that's his neck ... and he's still got no head. That's his two legs ... and that could be his ribs ... it looks as though somebody's holding his hand around him because I see three fingers. And this thing ... well, that looks like two potato sacks ... joined together and tied at the top. They're narrow at the top and they're wide at the bottom ... they're tied together. That's an owl or something (referring to the pelvic area) an owl or a ... bird ... or a bat, something like that ... with ... with wings anyway. These little pointed things look ... they're ... horns on an owl ... a horn owl.

Once again it is evident that the sedative-induced hypnotic state was characterized by richer flow of visual images and verbal output. In the opening phase of the response sequence there was further evidence of the patient's concern over the figure's 'missing head'. Next, it may be observed that the imagery stimulated by the rib-like structures in the picture had a bizarre and threatening connotation, in that 'somebody's holding his hand around' the man in the picture. Remarkably enough, the areas, which are normally stated to represent 'lungs', are seen as 'potato sacks'. Thus, to complicate the interpretation, there is evidence not just of perceptual inhibition of phallic imagery but other organ images as well.

Lastly, attention might be directed to his response to the pelvic area in the figure. Since the symbolism is most interesting, the interview will be reported in detail.

Patient (P):   That's an owl or something ... an owl or a bird or a bat ... something like that with wings ... anyway ... these little pointed things look like they're horns on an owl ... a horn owl.

Therapist (T):   Suppose that it all had to do with one man. What do you see now?

P:   Well, that could be a belt buckle on his pants or anything.

T:   What else could it be?

P:   (Long pause) I don't know ... can't think of anything else.

T:   You seem to think of that an awful lot. What is that?

P:   I don't know. I can't figure out what it could possibly be ... what part of a man that represented ... (patient shifts focus of attention from the pelvic area to the lungs) ... this looks like the insides ... but ... that there ... I can't figure out what that could be ... can't figure out why the insides would be that low down ... it's down below his waist or something ... it just doesn't seem as though it's not normal because he is something different than other men ... something that's there and is not supposed to be there and that's why I can't figure out what it is.

*T:* If it's below his waist, what is it likely to be?

*P:* Well, it could be his belly, but I guess it's kind of big.

*T:* Anything else it could be?

*P:* No ... I'm afraid, I can't.

In this aspect of the interview, the patient finally correctly identified the red areas as 'internal tissue', although he never labelled them as 'lungs'. However, at no time did the imagery relate to the male genitalia stimulated by viewing the pelvic area of the figure register in consciousness. Yet, it is suggested that it strongly impinged upon awareness in that he projected concern about his own sexual organs as indicated by the response 'it's not normal, etc.'.

This picture was represented to the patient for a third time after his seeing phallic material in the urogenital card had influenced his perceptual set. The dialogue between the patient and therapist is as follows:

*T:* Is there anything different that you see in this one now?

*P:* No, I can still see the body of a man.

*T:* Which body part would be represented here? (Pointing to the pelvic area)

*P:* Well, it's that part of the man ... in that shape I cannot say what it could be.

*T:* What kind of shape would it look better?

*P:* (Pause with no response).

*T:* Suppose that it was the shape of a candlestick, what would that make you think of?

*P:* Well, there are a number of things that I could name off for a candlestick [*pause*].

*T:* Suppose I told you that the part here is the same as in this picture (pointing to the urogenital card) in representation, what would you think of it?

*P:* This sure looks like a man ... he's going to the bathroom or something ... that looks like a penis (patient's anxiety level high).

*T:* You seemed to have a lot of difficulty thinking that this is a penis. The other thing that you said was that the guy had something wrong with him ... 'Is that what you think about yourself?'

*P:* Yes, that's right.

*T:* There's nothing wrong with you.

*P:* I still think that I do ... I don't know why.

This aspect of the interview shows how this research technique may be used to stimulate somatic imagery more in the context of a relationship having potentially therapeutic as well as diagnostic implications. Under sedation, phallic imagery was activated in the patient's unconsciousness. There was a great deal of resistance in bringing this into full awareness and considerable concomitant anxiety. However, in the state of relaxation induced by the drug, the therapist was able to interpret to the patient his psychopathologic body attitudes and partially desensitize the focal somatic anxiety. Of course, it is difficult to estimate the relative effects of visual input from the picture as opposed to verbal cues from the interviewer—in finally introducing the phallic imagery into conscious awareness.

Six months later, in a retest situation, he responded as follows:

That looks like the outline of a man ... there are two arms and two legs and a neck ... there is no head though ... the red part ... I don't know ... could be the intestines or some part of the body such as the heart or something. This response again avoids reference to the phallic aspects of the figure. It is also of interest that the patient readily recognized the anatomical implications of the internal lung-like structures. However, this visual input was not processed in a normative fashion as 'lungs' but consistent with his regression to an oral theme perceived as 'intestines'.

### Human Figures Card (III)
This picture presents line configurations, which may be seen to represent human figures. The bodies are close and share the same 'body buffer zone' (Horowitz, Donald and Lois 1964). Normally, they are a man (left) and a woman (right) interacting in some way like dancing. The red areas represent 'hearts', which are often stated to symbolize their 'love'. Normally, a few subjects give non-anatomical responses such as 'lights' or 'red balls'.

The patient's initial response was unremarkable in that he saw the picture as representing 'a couple of go-go dancers' with the red depicting 'apples'. However, under drugged condition, much more clinically relevant material emerged. He responded as follows:

That looks like a couple of go-go dancers or something ... this guy (left) looks as though he has a knife in his hand and she has got something too but I don't know what it is ... it looks to me as though they are going to cut those things in half ... they are some kind of food or something ... maybe that's his hand hanging out there ... they found a couple of apples ... he's going to cut one in half and give her one and himself take one.

The fact that the patient perceived the male dancer as having a knife in his hand suggests that the theme represents a direct projection of castration anxiety and/or hostility towards women. There is also evidence of regression to an oral rather than sexual level of interaction. It also might be noted that when the patient's therapist heard this response, the following question was asked: 'What does cut an apple in half and giving it to her make you think of?' In response, the patient identified with the picture in a regressive fashion stating, 'Well, he likes her ... I used to do that when I was a boy'.

In the retest situation six months later, his response was quite different:

'There are two people ... two pairs of legs and an arm ... the red dots could be apples.'

When asked the sex of the figures, he reported that they were two 'men'. Further, each of the two parts in between reminded him of a 'penis'. The one on the left man was seen to be 'long and erect' and the right one as 'short and soft'. When asked what they were doing, he stated they were 'standing there comparing sizes'.

In interpreting this response, it is pertinent to note that in the interim since originally tested, the patient had for the first time in his life become involved on one occasion in exhibitionistic behaviour and genital manipulation with a known homosexual. It is evident that the imagery stimulated in consciousness by this picture is much in line with this deviant behaviour.

### Female Figure Card (VII)
This card was designed to evaluate the extent to which a female patient assimilates the feminine aspects of her body image into a gestalt. For the male patient, it appraises his ability to recognize and mentally process sexually evocative material related to a woman's body.

It presents two main aspects. The one of primary significance concerns the humanoid lower configuration consisting of two lines depicting the outline of the body, the hand and feet. There is a red area between these included to elicit responses related to stomach or genitalia. The upper red area denotes the mouth, and the black, the hair or, if the picture is seen as a man, a moustache. The second aspects refers to the top red object. It presents additional anatomical material relating either to the head area or the heart. Normally, this picture is stated to represent 'a dancing woman' with the upper object being 'an apple'. Thus, a mature response involves assimilating the two lines, which are separated in terms of the right and left axes of the body into a gestalt, and then assigning feminine sexual identification to the figure.

In viewing this picture, the patient responded to the upper configuration in the normal fashion, seeing it as 'an apple'. However, consistent with his history of aversion to women, he simply saw the lower lines as representing 'two animals'. The black area was stated to represent 'a little black seal'. His failure to resolve the line configurations into a gestalt representing the body of a woman provided further evidence of his anxiety in mentally processing sexual imagery. The perceptual defence utilized in this instance, involved a breakdown of gestalt mechanisms of perception.

The patient's response sequence in the retest situation is of considerable interest because it shows how the separate components are eventually resolved into a gestalt as the patient's anxiety is controlled. His associations to the picture were as follows:

This is a fish or an apple or bell or something (top red object) ... and it's a big fish and he's swimming after ... these are a couple of snakes (lower lines) ... this looks like a fish or something here swimming ... this (pelvic area) could be a dead bird lying down or a lake ... (long pause) ... it's something shaped like a person's body ... two legs and that looks like a guy's moustache above the mouth (black area).

The interviewer then said, 'You said before that it looked like a little black seal'. The patient then continued:

Like that's something else in my head that I never thought of before ... it looks like a man's moustache ... this is an apple on the tree and it looks as though he is reaching for it.

Finally, the therapist asked him, 'Is it a man or woman?' He then responded as follows:

Well, it's a woman I'd say ... looks as though she's got lipstick on or something and that's why I think it is a woman.

In the opening phrases of his response the patient clearly substituted non-anatomical symbolic content for the structure depicting the body. Particularly noteworthy regarding his past feelings of sexual inadequacy is the response 'dead bird lying down'. Next, attention might be directed to the fact that when the human figure finally succeeded in registering in consciousness, it was assigned a masculine connotation. This is remarkable since the picture is suggestive of the female rather than the male body.

This avoidance of the feminine imagery is consistent with his past behaviour in relation to women. Finally, he was able to connect this distortion in perception. However, six months later, he saw it as the figure of a man.

### Heart Genitalia Card (VI)
This picture presents anatomical content relative to the heart. More strongly embedded in the figure are cues relative to union of the male and female genitalia.

The patient initially responded as follows: 'This is an animal standing inside a red object which could be a cloud.'

When under the drug, he stated: 'That could be a giraffe with those things sticking out of its head ... they could be horns (central object) ... and it looks as though he sees something coming and is standing on the other side of a bush or something ... he's standing in a bush ... this is a bush (red area) ... and this red thing here I don't know what it is ... I think that it could be a mop of hair hanging down, but giraffes don't have hair, so I don't know what it could be.'

Again, the patient substituted non-anatomical imagery when his consciousness was stimulated with material resembling the body. However, at the termination of the drug session when informed that the picture had anatomical content, he then stated that it looked like the 'vagina'. In this situation, the organ image of the more anxiety-laden female genitalia, rather than the cardiac aspects of the configuration succeeded in registering in consciousness. It suggested that, at this time in the study, he had been partially desensitized to mentally processing sexual imagery.

In the retest situation, six months later, he initially failed to detect the anatomical content but when reminded of it reported once again seeing a 'vagina'. When it was further suggested to him that some people see the central object as a 'penis', he became markedly anxious refusing to accept this possibility. In other words, when confronted with imagery depicting union of male and female genitalia, he totally blocked this from consciousness.

## Body Gestalt Card (II)

This card evaluates an individual's ability to organize separate components of the body into an overall image in the form of a gestalt (e.g., 'a person with a big smile'). It consists of three separate units arranged in such a fashion to depict the human form. The top part was created to elicit projective responses related to the head. The middle part depicts the oral region but is sufficiently ambiguous in outline to present suggestive imagery relative to the heart. The lower black area represents the arm, body and legs.

Initially, the patient responded only to the latter seeing it as 'a person with his hands up in the air'. This failure to respond to the other aspects of the figure suggests that the patient had somatic anxiety in the regions depicted (e.g., 'mouth', 'heart').

Under the drugged state, he responded as follows:

> There is a person ... the top part is an animal ... it's got two heads and it only has one leg ... this looks like a person in a drawing and this is his body, and this is his leg ... and this is somebody's mouth.

It is apparent that in the retest situation, he failed to resolve the separate components of the image into a gestalt. Moreover, his response to the upper black area as depicting an animal with two heads and only one leg is highly unusual. The missing leg in the response may be interpreted to reflect his own undue 'castration anxiety'. Also, it is noteworthy that the drug relaxed his inhibitions to the extent that he could see the 'mouth', although, it was separate from the rest of the picture. It might be noticed that a pattern is forming, whereby the exhibitionist failed to recognize anatomical structure in the pictures. The other feature involves themes related to the oral region.

For comparison purposes, an outline will be given of his responses to two anatomical pictures, which lack direct sexual referents.

## Chest Cavity Card (IX)

This picture illustrates the ribcage and heart to a very high degree and is invariably so recognized by most subjects. Yet, this patient saw 'two people eating', failing to recognize the anatomical content which is so strongly present in the picture. Under drug conditions, he stated that it looked like 'the shape of a person's head ... that's the girl's hair hanging down ... but then it could look like ... oh, it reminds me of a couple of seahorses or something ... and this is their tails ... that's their bodies and that's their heads … and they are eating some kind of food or something … don't know what it is … that's the rippling of the water … oh, these are seahorses.'

This illustrates how the patient inhibited not just phallic material but other somatic imagery as well.

## Discussion

A PT employing a series of newly designed anatomical pictures has been developed to stimulate somatic imagery. This approach has been illustrated in a patient with exhibitionism. A marked resistance was observed in fully registering sexual images in the consciousness. This finding may be appraised in the context of an existing theory partially derived from more traditional psychoanalytic procedures (Fenichel 1945). The extreme perceptual inhibition of the phallic imagery observed in the present study has certain theoretical implications. There is a definite parallel between this and the view that in exhibitionism, the individual unconsciously says: 'Reassure me that I have a penis by reacting to the sight of it.' The subjective feeling that his penis might disappear becomes highly plausible to the outsider if one considers the excessive repression of sexual imagery noted in the exhibitionist studied. It is quite understandable how an observer's response to the exposed penis could well provide a useful external source of reality testing for refuting this pathologic body fantasy. It might be noted that this perceptual defence has also been observed in tachistoscopically exposed illustrations of human anatomy to subjects with focal somatic anxiety secondary to psychophysiologic symptoms (Cassell 1966).

Another theoretical formulation of exhibitionism is that the patient is choosing women as observers of the deviant behaviour and, in a magical sense, is unconsciously saying: 'I show you what I wish you would show me.' This is considered to deny the apparent castration of the female's body, reducing the fear that this might happen to him. It may be recalled that the patient's responses to Cards II, III and VII (retest) were consistent with what is implied in the psychoanalytic construct 'castration anxiety'. His phobia-like aversion to processing imagery related to the female body was observed in Cards VI and VII.

Attention might also be directed to the patient's tendency to project oral rather than genital themes in viewing the pictures. It's consistent with the thesis that the exhibitionist is 'an infantile individual' concerning his sexually deviant behaviour (Karpman 1948b). Along the same lines, perhaps it is pertinent to recall that Kinsey found 20 per cent of pre-adolescent boys who engage in sexual play have exhibition-ism as the limit of the activity (Kinsey, Pomeroy and Martin 1948). It is suggested that this regressive aspect has functional significance in that it avoids the anxiety stimulated by sexual imagery.

Another subject for discussion concerns the observation that—like the present patient—exhibitionists in general are sexually inhibited (Rickless 1950). In this context, brief attention might be given to the psychophysiologic aspects of normal sexual functioning. Sexual arousal in a 'normal' male involves the interaction between a physiologically originating drive and mental imagery relating both to his genitalia and to evocative images pertaining to that of a woman. For the exhi-bitionist under present study, sexual tensions would have to be intense before the resultant union of male and female imagery would register in consciousness and motivate normal heterosexual behaviour. It was suggested that abortive attempts to discharge these occurred when the patient acted out sexually in a state of excitation by impulsively expos-ing his genitalia. As was evident in the retest situation, exhibitionistic behaviour of a homosexual nature was also attempted by the patient to provide a release for his sexual impulses.

Of course, as might be expected with the introduction of a new tech-nique, all results do not fit the previous theoretical frame of reference. The above formulation may be seriously challenged since the patient was remarkably insensitive to detecting all anatomical content in the pictures—sexual or otherwise. Thus, there was evidence of perceptual inhibition of images depicting the lungs, mouth and heart. While it may be contended that the oral region and the heart provide imagery during states of sexual arousal (Schneider 1956, 1957), it might appear that the data do not strongly support a specific defect in the patient's perception of the genitalia. However, since the patient did not show psychosomatic symptoms in other regions of the body schema, this thesis warrants consideration. Moreover, during therapy, he was found to be made more anxious by the discussion of sexual themes—rather than those relating to other aspects of the body. Therefore, probably, the primary disorder involved aversion to the genitalia, which second-arily spread to involve other somatic regions.

The patient's avoidance of female anatomy in the pictures recalls mechanisms operating in phobic disorders (Snaith 1968). While the two conditions differ in that the exhibitionist also avoided material presumably related to his own body rather than an external object, the comparison has heuristic value. Further, it has certain theoreti-cal implications in terms of therapy. For example, it is tempting to consider that just as certain clinicians may treat phobic disorders through desensitization procedures, the same general principles might be applied in reducing anxiety related to conjuring up in consciousness scenes involving union of male and female genital imagery. Indeed, the way the therapist assisted the patient in mentally processing sexual images under narcotic relaxation employed insights borrowed from both behavioural and gestalt therapy procedures (Perls, Hefferline and Goodman 1951). However, to be sure, it did not seem to have much 'lasting' effect since repression still occurred in the follow-up session six month later.

## Case 4: Unmasking the Devil with PT—Rorschach and SIS

Every night, humans spend several hours in the mysterious inner world of dreams. It has been estimated that at any time almost half of the world's population is asleep dreaming. Those with an innate sense of curiosity have long been fascinated with the meaning of the images and affect experienced during the thousands of hours spent in this altered state of consciousness.

This project explores symbolism in a devil dream. A severely depressed adolescent girl (T) reported it. She had been hospitalized after experiencing suicidal and homicidal ideation. She was interviewed using the Rorschach and SIS stimuli as the sources for visual stimulation of daytime imagery. It will be shown how analysing the content and emotional linkage of the projected responses provided information for analysis and interpretation.

For a few illustrative moments, please leave your immediate time and space reality coordinates behind and imagine entering her inner world of dreams:

> I had a dream that me and my brother were having fun and were laughing and having fun as we usually do and then all of a sudden, something swished by me like someone was running real fast by me but with no foot … but no foot … but no running sounds and then all of a sudden, something by … appeared in front of us and the lights were turned out … all the lights went out and this bright thing was in front of us and then it turned out to be Lucifer and he was saying that we were a mistake to this earth, that we were going to ruin his plans and then he threw my brother up against the wall and he made his arms spread out and his legs together. He made a

slash mark from elbow to elbow and then from forehead to waist like a cross and he let him bleed and he said I will do anything just to get rid of you guys. I am over … I am overpowered and he … and I shall take over and then he killed him by … he killed my brother by sending a hole through his forehead all the way to the back and then I remember turning away and just running and there was such long darkness and then I had this feeling of being frightened like I knew something was behind me and not knowing what to do and not knowing what would happen next and all of a sudden something hit me on my back and then I died and I heard this cruel laughter in the background and then I woke up.

Discussion between Therapist (Dr B) and Patient (T) follows:

## The Dream's Affect and Symbolism

Dr B:   How were you feeling throughout this dream?

T:      In the beginning when I was with my brother, I was having so much fun with him [*laughing*]. It's like old times. (The temporal reference of the dream portrays a happier time in her relationship with her brother who was two years older. He had not yet developed his own serious problems with suicidal depression. At that time, they were emotionally close having endured severe psychological and physical abuse by their mother.)

Dr B:   It was good.

T:      Yeah. Yeah.

Dr B:   Okay. And then what happened?

T:      And then I felt really frightened. I felt scared and I felt sad because my brother, he died in my dream and we are close and that's the last thing on earth that I want to happen to him. (She had been very, very alarmed about his safety.)

Dr B:   You love him a lot.

T:      Yeah, and I felt frightened, like … and I felt lost.

Dr B:   Okay. And what's the dream all about? Remember we talked about it a little bit?

T:      Yes. I think that the dream is … my fear of what I have of my brother dying and facing Lucifer because I have done a thing with the Ouija Board (a game allegedly to communicate with spiritual forces) and what that does is it opens a door to what … well, what I've heard is it opens the door to let him come into your body and ever since I have done that, I've had nightmares of him (here she indicates that there have been a long series of devil nightmares and, as will be shown later, because of wanting to forget their painful nature, she later was able to recall only one other devil dream) and I would feel scared alone or in the dark. I always had to have a light and I think it's a fear of mine and to also know the fact that he would kill my brother. But the worst part that I think is fear when he said we're a mistake, too – or we were going to ruin his plans. That's the part I didn't get.

*Dr B:* What's that part all about do you suppose?

*T:* I don't know. I've been thinking about it for a while and I also thought about it yesterday after gym group.

*Dr B:* What thoughts have you had about a....

*T:* I don't know. (Here she is repressing the threatening memories and interpretations made available to her previously in the adolescent dream study group.)

*Dr B:* Please try to remember your thoughts.

*T:* What I thought was that I was confused and not sure.

*Dr B:* What did you think about what the kids in the dream analysis group said about the dream?

*T:* I think I got some really good feedback about my dreams.

*Dr B:* Tell me about the feedback. What was good about it?

*T:* Like, some people shared their views concerning what they thought my dream was about and....

*Dr B:* What were those thoughts, do you remember?

*T:* Not really but... (Again, her mental defence mechanisms block the painful interpretation that she had both good and evil in her personality—the devil representing the latter—made by a peer. None of her peers had recognized that the devil image could also symbolize the demonic qualities of her abusive mother.)

*Dr B:* Remember the one girl who wondered about you and if you felt part of you had Satan?

*T:* Oh, yes.

*Dr B:* Tell us about that.

*T:* What I thought about was like I felt that at some point in my life I did have Satan in me when I assaulted my mother and beat her up badly. She said it wasn't me, it was something else that was controlling me. (In order for her mother to deny the reality of her daughter's hate, she projected onto her daughter's psychological identity a satanic label. The anger part was really 'something else'.)

*Dr B:* She said that?

*T:* Yeah.

*Dr B:* How did you feel when she said that?

T:      I felt like she was right. (Children incorporate into their identi-
        ties negative labels assigned by their parents.)
Dr B:   Uh-huh [*affirmative*]
T:      And that something did get hold of me (she readily accepted
        the concept of having a devilish part to herself) but then I also
        felt hurt because for my mother to say that about me.
Dr B:   What way did that hurt you?
T:      It felt like I wasn't a good enough daughter for her (her self-
        esteem was reduced, thereby setting the stage for severe depres-
        sion) and that I couldn't get a second chance.
Dr B:   Do you sense there is a good part and then a bad part within
        you?
T:      Yes.
Dr B:   What's the good part?
T:      The good part is always closeted and always willing to learn
        and knowing what to do.
Dr B:   And helpful to others. (She frequently gave emotional support
        to her brother and other patients at the hospital.)
T:      Yeah.
Dr B:   And the bad?
T:      The bad part is having thoughts, the urge to hurt myself or to....
Dr B:   Tell us about those thoughts.
T:      Thoughts where I think about throwing a chair through the
        window and grabbing a piece of glass and slitting my wrist or
        carving on myself all over my body. (She had acted upon some
        of these impulses.)
Dr B:   When you came here, you'd done some of that. What made
        you do that, do you know?
T:      I was pretty upset with myself because I let some things get over
        or carried away and I just felt like I had to punish myself.
Dr B:   What else besides hurting yourself the bad side represents?
T:      Of wanting to rebel and just do what I want and having
        thoughts of like just things and meaningful words to other
        people and having some thoughts of wanting to hurt people.
Dr B:   What was your conflict like with your mother?
T:      When I assaulted her or just threw ice at her?
Dr B:   Both.
T:      My conflict with my mom was—when I assaulted her—I felt
        like she was provoking me and so I just finally gave in.
Dr B:   What way was she provoking you?
T:      Like she was laughing at me (like the devil in her dream) and
        saying go ahead and do something so I can call the police, you

just wait and see and laughing at me. (At age eleven, during her first hospitalization, she had learned in therapy not to entirely blame herself for her mother's abusive behaviour. Consequently, she felt less guilty and her self-esteem became greater. However, she still could be provoked into rage and assault by her mother's provocative psychological abuse. By contrast, she was never out of control in school or other settings.)

*Dr B:* It hurts.

*T:* Yeah.

*Dr B:* Yeah. Okay. Anything more you want to say about your dream? Oh....

*T:* No.


## Symbolic Content Analysis: Rorschach

For this interview, it was hypothesized that projective responses are generated from the same stream of consciousness as the imagery in night-time dreams. Initially, she was asked to report what she saw (i.e., real of symbolic content) and felt (i.e., affect associated with the image) in relation to viewing the 10 Rorschach cards.

Historically, Herman Rorschach created these cards originally as a visual basis for structured clinical interviewing. Consistent with these historical roots, the following procedure was carried out. Initially, the cards were presented in the traditional order, using them as a visual source for obtaining free association responses.

In the follow-up detailed enquiry, a different order was employed. All 10 plates were placed on a table face up. She was then asked to indicate the three that she 'liked the most' and the three that she 'liked the least'. This emotional rating procedure gives more priority to the underlying image's affect linkage than the content. Extensive projective work indicates that in clinical populations this approach has more value than simply obtaining projective responses on simply the order decided upon by either Rorschach or the original publisher. It facilitates establishing a subjectively determined hierarchy of positive and negative emotional feelings in assessing the significance of what is seen or avoided. When follow-up content analysis is employed, the clinician has to his disposal a powerful emotionally driven technique for exploring the overt as well as the symbolic meaning of responses.

The following represents a transcription of the Rorschach structured interview:

*Dr B:* Okay. I am going to show you some of these cards today. Have you seen these before?

*T:* Yes. (She had been tested by a psychologist employing traditional administration and scoring techniques six months earlier. In a later section of this chapter, the result of testing will be reported.)

*Dr B:* Okay. This is the first card, what do you see?

*T:* I see two animals that have wings with their feet together like they're climbing up.

*Dr B:* Okay. Do you experience any emotions with it?

*T:* Just... (She begins to experience emotional arousal, but the affect linkage is quickly inhibited.)

*Dr B:* What are they?

*T:* No feelings or emotions about it (see later).

*Dr B:* Okay. The second Card?

*T:* It looks like two people squatting down and having their hands together like they're in prayer.

*Dr B:* Any feelings?

*T:* It makes me feel good about the prayer part, like they're praying.

*Dr B:* Do you pray much?

*T:* Yes.

*Dr B:* Tell us about that.

*T:* I pray every morning and every night to ask for restraint (i.e., acting on her aggressive ideation) or just to talk to Him ... to God and to ask Him to help me understand life more. (Her understanding was facilitated by the projective interviewing herein being outlined.)

*Dr B:* And what's your view of God as compared to the devil now?

*T:* Compared to the devil, I think He is a great person (her concept of spirituality involved the personification of 'God' and 'Satan') and that I believe in his ways and I don't believe in Satan's ways.

*Dr B:* Do you ever pray in your dreams?

*T:* I wouldn't pray in my dreams, but I would say oh, God, please help me out loud, stuff like that. (Her spirituality both in the day and in night-time dreams was important to her.)

*Dr B:* That's a form of prayer, isn't it? And one would just say that in a dream?

*T:* When I'm scared or like when I have fearful dreams or when I have dreams of wanting to hurt myself. (In spite of ongoing psychotherapy and psychotropic medication, she continued to experience occasional depressive episodes with suicidal ideation.)

*Dr B:* Do you have many dreams of those?

| | |
|---|---|
| *T:* | I haven't had many but ... I do get them. (She did not always symbolically disguise her identify in some of her self-destructive dreams.) |
| *Dr B:* | Yeah. Okay. Here's the third one. |
| *T:* | These little parts look like monkeys in upside down and looks like two people holding something. |
| *Dr B:* | Any idea what? |
| *T:* | Like something to hold water in, like a jug. |
| *Dr B:* | Okay. Thank you. And then this one is number four. |
| *T:* | It looks like a dragon ... and then these two parts right here look like shoes. |
| *Dr B:* | Any feelings with that? |
| *T:* | No. |
| *Dr B:* | Okay. Here is the next (Card V). |
| *T:* | This one looks like a bat. And this part looks like an animal face, It's an animal eats ant, |
| *Dr B:* | Okay A6? |
| *T:* | Looks like two men back to back like they're about, yeah, like they're ready to do something. |
| *Dr B:* | Like what? |
| *T:* | Like ... what's that called? Like where you both ... where they both step up 10 feet, not seeing each other and they turn around. |
| *Dr B:* | A duel? |
| *T:* | Yeah, a duel. That's what it looks like. (At the interpersonal level, this symbolized the fighting with her mother. It portrays her conflict between identifying with the positive and demonic image of her mother.) |
| *Dr B:* | Okay. A7? |
| *T:* | Looks like two ladies dancing. |
| *Dr B:* | Any feelings there? |
| *T:* | Fun. |
| *Dr B:* | A8? |
| *T:* | Looks like two bears are climbing up a mountain. |
| *Dr B:* | Any feelings? |
| *T:* | Just peacefulness. |
| *Dr B:* | Mm-hmm [*affirmative*]. A9? |
| *T:* | Well, this orange part looks like they're two mooses and then this is ... the green part looks like there are two people there holding something. |
| *Dr B:* | Like what? |
| *T:* | Like a baby. (Consistent with the fact that her mother was intoxicated and not psychologically supportive through her early years. Unconsciously, she longed for nurturing.) |

| Dr B: | Uh-huh and how do you feel looking at that? |
| T: | Good. I like babies. |
| Dr B: | Last one? |
| T: | These parts right here look like they're two more men. |
| Dr B: | That's the sort of orange parts on the side? |
| T: | Yeah, with the yellow and the.... |
| Dr B: | On the lower left. |
| T: | Yes.... |
| Dr B: | Yeah, and the right. What do they look like? |
| T: | Two women like the yellow part's their hair and their heads are thrown back. Looks like they're spilling something, or it looks like a blanket. |
| Dr B: | Any feelings? |
| T: | It looks like ... something like a native culture (her mother's background). |
| Dr B: | Okay. Thank you. Now, we've got them all ... arranged here (plates are placed in order on interview desk face up). Can you pick out the three you like the most? |
| T: | I like that one (Card II). |
| Dr B: | What do you like about that? |
| T: | Because it looks like they're praying (she identifies with the praying figures). |
| Dr B: | Okay. What is the second one that you like the most? |
| T: | That one (Card VII). |
| Dr B: | What do you like about it? |
| T: | Because they're dancing and having fun. (At this stage of hospitalization she was experiencing occasional positive moods and was able to participate in fun hospital activities with her peers. The response provided projective data to support improvement ratings by the staff.) |
| Dr B: | Right. And the third one? |
| T: | That (pointing to Card III). |
| Dr B: | And what about this one? |
| T: | Because it looks like people and they're doing everyday-like things. |
| Dr B: | Okay. Now tell me the three you like the least, the ones that would bother you or what bothers you most in that? |
| T: | This one because it looks like a bat and I don't like bats (Card V). |
| Dr B: | What is there about bats that bother you? |
| T: | Like I don't know, it's something about them that I don't like. |
| Dr B: | Like what? |
| T: | The way they can just bite you. (She had multiple scars on her arms resulting from self-inflicted injuries. While she did not bite herself but used knives, the 'biting' symbolism is apparent.) |

| Dr B: | Okay. And the second one that bothers you the most? |
| T: | This one (pointing to Plate IV) |
| Dr B: | What bothers you about that? |
| T: | Because it's a dragon (a threatening mythical creature symbolically denoting her abusive mother). |
| Dr B: | A dragon? And what does the dragon recall? |
| T: | Hurtful things. |
| Dr B: | Like what? |
| T: | Like ... I don't know, it looks evil. |
| Dr B: | In what way? |
| T: | Like it's just out there to get you. |
| Dr B: | Okay. And then the third one that bothers you? |
| T: | (Pointing to Plate I) |
| Dr B: | And what is there to fear? |
| T: | Because it also looks like an evil face, like it's laughing at me. |
| Dr B: | What does that remind you of? |
| T: | My mom provoking me. (Here, there is no symbolic defence. What emerged in projective consciousness was a real-life image of her abusive mother.) |
| Dr B: | Uh-huh. That isn't fun when she provokes you, is it? How do you feel? |
| T: | I feel it's hurtful. (This term is the same that she associated with the 'dragon', second most threatening Rorschach Plate. For the preceding two years, her mother had maintained sobriety. She was no longer severely beating her daughter and son. She had gone to an alcohol treatment centre after welfare workers threatened to take custody of her children.) |

## Transcription of SIS-I Structured Interview

| Dr B: | No. Okay. I'm going to have this ... put these away. Now we're going to look at the SIS Cards. Here's your first card. What do you see there? |
| T: | I see a lot of things ... the red parts look like two birds. |
| Dr B: | Uh-huh. |
| T: | And then it looks like two people. They're both ladies. |
| Dr B: | Uh-huh. |
| T: | And looks like they're dancing. |
| Dr B: | And how does it make you feel? |
| T: | Cheerful. (At times she felt joy.) |
| Dr B: | Yeah. Okay. Now what do you see in the second one? |
| T: | That part looks like a heart. And this part looks like a man's head and a whole like his chest— head. |

*Dr B:*  Okay. The third?

*T:*  Looks like a man and a woman. Looks like they're talking.

*Dr B:*  Number four.

*T:*  That top part looks like an apple and the other part looks like a lady ... looks like she's just blackened somewhere.

*Dr B:*  Okay. Five?

*T:*  Looks like a turtle ... and the left part ... looks like parts ... looks like a man's head ... his head and there's his neck and chest.

*Dr B:*  Six?

*T:*  Looks like two seals and that part in the middle looks like a person, stick figure and then on a heart.

*Dr B:*  Number seven?

*T:*  That part looks like a heart full of fun and the back part looks like a dragon. There's his neck and there's his body. (Like on the Rorschach, the 'dragon' emerges again to symbolize the aggressive side of her mother and that portion of herself which had identified with the mother's aggressive behaviour. The associations which follow further provide insight into the meaning of the symbol.)

*Dr B:*  Mm-hmm [*affirmative*].

*T:*  It seems like it's a sign between evil and good. (This 'sign' directly symbolizes her own personality splitting and personality tendencies to dissociate.)

*Dr B:*  What part's evil, what part's good?

*T:*  It's the dragon's evil and the heart's good.

*Dr B:*  Okay. Thank you. Here comes eight.

*T:*  It looks like a ribcage. This is a person's body, and this is like the heart.

*Dr B:*  Yeah. Here is Card 9.

*T:*  It reminds me of, you know, those ultrasounds where they put that down at the belly.

*Dr B:*  Right.

*T:*  That looks like twins ... babies in there ... Every time I see a baby, it's something like someone coming onto me. It makes me feel good.

*Dr B:*  How about Card 10?

*T:*  Looks like a piece of meat, like from a cow or something.

*Dr B:*  Any feelings?

*T:*  I don't like it when people kill cows or animals for their meat. That makes me real angry.

*Dr B:*  Card 11?

*T:*  Looks like a snake.

| | |
|---|---|
| *Dr B:* | And how do you feel looking at that? |
| *T:* | Fear, because I don't like snakes. |
| *Dr B:* | What do you not like about them? |
| *T:* | They can bite you. (Her concerns about being bitten here and in the 'bat' Rorschach response represent projections about her injuries from both her mother and her own self-mutilating behaviours.) |
| *Dr B:* | Okay. Card 12. |
| *T:* | Like a dragon. Like a dragon but a good one. (Here the mythic symbol denotes her 'good' side. This illustrates how the immediate emotional linkage to an image can provide clues as to the symbolism.) |
| *Dr B:* | How do you feel looking at it? |
| *T:* | Happy. |
| *Dr B:* | Card 13. |
| *T:* | It reminds of a heart … going bad emotionally (turns it upside down). |
| *Dr B:* | And … okay. You turn it upside down and it reminds you of a heart going bad and what does it recall? |
| *T:* | Like a person that's heartless, like hateful. Looks like something took control of it. |
| *Dr B:* | Does that remind you of any of your own issues? |
| *T:* | Yeah. |
| *Dr B:* | Right. What? |
| *T:* | My internal depression because when I am injured or depressed. It's like I become heartless, like I don't care. |
| *Dr B:* | And you want to hurt yourself? |
| *T:* | Yeah, or others. |
| *Dr B:* | What way do you want to hurt yourself and what way do you want to hurt others? |
| *T:* | Oh myself, I would hurt myself physically, and others, I'm going to hurt them mentally. |
| *Dr B:* | And do you know why you want to hurt yourself physically? |
| *T:* | Because of all the mistakes I've made in life. |
| *Dr B:* | When you cause physical pain, how does it affect you emotionally? |
| *T:* | It takes my mind off all my worries. (No matter how distressing physical pain is 'out there in the body'. Emotional suffering is much closer to the self-concept, and therefore usually much more disturbing. Inducing somatic pain by self-mutilation can take the focus off mental distress, thereby providing temporary relief.) |

*Dr B:*  And when you hurt others, how do you hurt others?

*T:*  I like to make them do everything to me, I'm happy and so I hurt them emotionally.

*Dr B:*  By doing what or....

*T:*  Giving them the treatment that they give me, like a taste of their own medicine or calling them names.

*Dr B:*  Do you ever hurt people that have never done anything to you?

*T:*  No.

*Dr B:*  No? Okay. Card 14.

*T:*  I would say about an animal's head like it's getting a cat scan or rainbows and makes me feel good because like they're trying to find out about animals and they're helping the animal.

*Dr B:*  You like animals.

*T:*  I love them.

*Dr B:*  Yeah. Number 15?

*T:*  Looks like a crocodile.

*Dr B:*  And how do you feel looking at it?

*T:*  Fearful because I don't like crocodiles.

*Dr B:*  Because?

*T:*  Because they can kill people. (Another highly threatening projection.)

*Dr B:*  Okay Card 16?

*T:*  Looks like two ostriches' heads.

*Dr B:*  Okay. We're getting near the end. Card 17?

*T:*  It looks like a heart with a knife going through it. (Clinical experience indicates that the 'knife in the heart' symbolism can represent extreme hatred and/or homicidal impulses.)

*Dr B:*  And how does that make you feel and what does that recall?

*T:*  It recalls of hate.

*Dr B:*  And when you think of hate, what comes to mind?

*T:*  A person that doesn't care about how other people feel, just does what they want.

*Dr B:*  Do you ever feel hate towards your mother?

*T:*  Yes.

*Dr B:*  In what way? And towards yourself?

*T:*  In a way that it feels like she doesn't care for me.

*Dr B:*  In what way you see yourself?

*T:*  That I'm a burden to others.

*Dr B:*  Card 18?

*T:*  Looks like two angels.

*Dr B:*  Two what?

*T:*  Angels.

| | |
|---|---|
| *Dr B:* | Uh-huh [*affirmative*]. And how does that make you feel? |
| *T:* | Peaceful. |
| *Dr B:* | When you think of angels, what comes to mind? |
| *T:* | Guardian angels that help you.... |
| *Dr B:* | Do you think of your ... do you have a guardian angel? |
| *T:* | Mm-hmm [*affirmative*]. |
| *Dr B:* | Tell me about her or him. |
| *T:* | She's always near me. She's with me right now. She's with me right at the door and.... |
| *Dr B:* | And you feel more secure? |
| *T:* | Yeah, at peace; and she helped me when I needed to put myself back on track. She tells me when I need to do that. (Angels personify positive feminine maternal spirituality. They are imagined to be human-like creatures with wings, able to fly to heaven. This fantasy helps her and partially makes up for the poor nurturing received from her mother.) |
| *Dr B:* | Okay. Card 19? |
| *T:* | Looks like two birds—gooses and they're carrying babies on their necks. |
| *Dr B:* | Okay. And how do you feel looking at that? |
| *T:* | Happy. (Her frequent imaging of 'babies' relates to her own frustrated needs for being nurtured.) |
| *Dr B:* | Right. The last one, Card 20? |
| *T:* | Looks like two swordfish. |
| *Dr B:* | Two what? |
| *T:* | Swordfish. |
| *Dr B:* | Mm-hmm [*affirmative*]. Okay. Can you tell me the three cards that you like the most? (She selected 5, 9 and 18.) |
| *Dr B:* | Now tell me the three that you dislike starting with the one that you dislike the most? |
| *T:* | This one (17). |
| *Dr B:* | What is there about that bothers you the most? |
| *T:* | It reminds me of hatefulness. |
| *Dr B:* | Okay. And then the next one that bothers you the most? |
| *T:* | This one (7). |
| *Dr B:* | And what bothers you there? |
| *T:* | Reminds me of evilness. |
| *Dr B:* | All right and one more. |
| *T:* | This one (13). |
| *Dr B:* | What does that remind you of? |
| *T:* | Evilness and hatefulness. (Her memory storage is flooded with hateful imagery.) |

*Dr B:*   Okay. This one (presenting Plate I of the Rorschach again) reminds you of your mother's face sometimes?

*T:*   Yeah.

*Dr B:*   And do you see your mother in your dreams much or her face?

*T:*   No.

*Dr B:*   Does she appear in your dreams much?

*T:*   No. (Normally, her sleep was protected by symbolic images. While these were highly threatening, apparently, they were less so than experiencing memories of her mother directly.)


## Imagery Released by the SIS-II Video

*Dr B.:*   This is like looking at what you saw in the video (showing her the SIS answer sheet). You indicated that you liked A16 the most and why was that?

*T:*   Because it reminds me of nature and I'm a nature lover. (She had retained some of her Alaskan native spiritual appreciation of beauty in the physical world.)

*Dr B:*   And then B19, what did you see there?

*T:*   I said I'm trying to get hearts because it's—one heart is broken.

*Dr B:*   And what appealed to you about that?

*T:*   It reminded me of myself. (Here, she can identify closely with the imagery released in the form of projective response.)

*Dr B:*   In what way?

*T:*   That I'm trying to grasp for something that I—that's broken inside me.

*Dr B:*   In what way have you felt like your heart's broken?

*T:*   Like I have no hope and some stuff.

*Dr B:*   You've got lots of hope. I know when we feel down, we don't feel that way through, but you do feel you have some hope now, don't you?

*T:*   Mm-hmm [*affirmative*].

*Dr B:*   Good girl. And then B28, you liked that one. It's a nice one. It's one of my favourites. What do you see there?

*T:*   A girl holding a baby. (She could not conjure up the normative response depicting a nurturing mother since she never had one. She could identify somewhat with the 'girl' because she had nurtured her beloved brother.)

*Dr B:*   And why do you like that?

*T:*   I love babies.

*Dr B:*   Next, let's look at those that you liked the least. The one that bothered you the most was B29. You indicated that it reminded you of the devil. (The dream symbol under projective examination!) It may be of significance that it emerged in projective consciousness with the SIS-II Video. This projective procedure involves relaxation instructions, hypnotic floral photographs presented in a dreamlike moving manner. In addition, the light in the video presentation can approximate the visual vividness of dream imagery.

*T:*      Yeah.

*Dr B:*   In what way?

*T:*      And it just seems odd because there's a man there and it's like he's going (the symbolic figure was moving towards her in a threatening fashion—just like in the dream). There is a shadow of his leg.

*Dr B:*   Right. (In a demonic fashion, mother had repeatedly beaten her and her brother with objects such as a belt, a cooking spoon and a coat hanger. She would find some minor excuse for the assault such as they're not completing a domestic chore. She would make them take down their pants and beat them on the bare buttocks. She reported that mother would sometimes smile, during the beatings, apparently enjoying the sadistic power. She had witnessed many beatings of her brother and felt great rage towards her mother as a result. The physical abuse stopped two years previously after her brother showed scars on his buttocks to a social worker. As a result, their mother was warned that she could have the children taken from her.)

*Dr B:*   In your dreams, does the devil remind you of your devil dreams in anyway?

*T:*      Mm-hmm [*affirmative*]. It's like to some extent; he looks like that, like … you really can't see the details of him, but he's sorts of shaded too. That's what he looks like.

*Dr B:*   So that—and that—how does that affect you in your dream and then looking at it now? What emotion does it cause?

*T:*      Oh, hate (her mind is flooded with hatred).

*Dr B:*   Hate? Yeah. Okay. And now B31 reminded you of death. In what way does it?

*T:*      Because it looks like shadows of a family and—but ghost like. (In her devil dream she and her were both killed. She also has had homicidal impulses when witnessing her mother beating her brother. Moreover, she feared for her mother's safety when intoxicated and involved with abusive men.)

*Dr B:*   Right. Do you think about death much in terms of your family?

*T:*      Not as often as I used to. I used to fear death and think of it all the time, scared that something was going to happen. (Her

|        | mother had treatment and had maintained sobriety for two years prior to this hospitalization.) |
|--------|---|
| *Dr B:* | And who were you afraid would be visited by death in your family? |
| *T:* | My family, my mom and my brother. |
| *Dr B:* | How about your own death? Do you think about that much? |
| *T:* | Yes. |
| *Dr B:* | What sort of thoughts? |
| *T:* | Of killing myself. |
| *Dr B:* | And those are thoughts you had in the past or do you still get them occasionally? |
| *T:* | I—in the past. (Here, she denied current suicide ideation. However, in subsequent moments of depression it did transiently return.) |
| *Dr B:* | Right. Okay. And then B15 was the third one and you saw… |
| *T:* | Oh, no, that's wrong. |
| *Dr B:* | Oh. Well…. |
| *T:* | No! No! No! No! (It is threatening to the point of stimulating a perseveration type of denial). Take this off!! (Scratching on scribbles in B15). Because it looks like a drawing a child would draw! |
| *Dr B:* | Uh-huh [*affirmative*]. |
| *T:* | Because of the scribbles and everything and it has knives in there! (Seeing knives here was very threatening. It triggered memories of past suicidal thoughts and plans to murder her mother by stabbing her in the heart. It also provoked recollection of homicidal thoughts towards her mother. Related to the dream in which her brother was killed by 'Lucifer' by cutting cross like wounds, it also tapped into the complexities of the strong love–hate relationship with him. In speaking about their relationship, she emphasized the positive intimacy of their early years. However, in this stage of her life, being two years older than her, he had abandoned her for multiple superficial relationships with older girls. He had also psychologically removed himself by entering a world of impaired consciousness from alcohol and drugs. Moreover, he had been hospitalized for trying to kill himself. While she did not want to lose him, part of hers—the demonic side—wanted to hurt him to make him pay back for her suffering. In her troubled mind, she wondered: What could be more devilish than to murder a brother, that despite his abandonment, she still loved him? She was terrified that she would lose control and the sight of knives in the video overwhelmed her.) |

| Dr B: | Okay. And what were your thoughts sort of like? |
| T: | Because it makes me sad to know that kids draw stuff like that. It means they're troubled (the 'kids' represent a projection of her image). |
| Dr B: | Mm-hmm [*affirmative*]. |
| T: | And I don't —I like kids to be happy. |
| Dr B: | In the dream, the nightmare, the devil cuts your brother or how did he... |
| T: | Mm-hmm [*affirmative*]. |
| Dr B: | And what did he use? |
| T: | Well, using his hand. |
| Dr B: | He didn't have a knife or... |
| T: | Like he—just like he had powers. |
| Dr B: | It was done through magic or evil magic. |
| T: | Mm-hmm [*affirmative*]. |
| Dr B: | Mm-hmm [*affirmative*]. Yeah. When you're cutting on yourself with a knife, how do you know what's it like? |
| T: | It just relieves my emotional pain (witnessing the blood and feeling the physical pain—while intense, it took her mind off the greater suffering that she was tormented with emotionally). |

The analysis of dream imagery can often be of great clinical importance. However, consistent with Einstein's observation, such images are not readily 'countable' for statistical analysis. It may be recalled that there was a significant discrepancy in the number of devil dreams reported. At one stage, she spontaneously referred to many such dreams, but later she could only recall one other.

The nature of the dreaming state has since been extensively studied. This work ranges from studies which focus on the psychological to those whose orientation is primarily biological. In attempting to provide modern theoretical pathways for integrating the two levels, Reiser (2001) recently surveyed the literature in attempting to conceptually bridge these two levels of enquiry. In response to Reiser's review, Zuk and Zuk (2002) cited certain problem areas for investigators.

One concerns communication difficulties since when neuroscientists and psychoanalysts talk about 'the dream', 'affect' or 'emotion', the terms mean different things. They also observed that 'REM, while an interesting phenomenon and the subject of much excitement by neuroscientists, says little or nothing about the meaning of the dream'. Also, they pointed out that Reiser's review clearly indicated that Freud's notion of the dream as wish fulfilment is either incorrect or a gross simplification that fails to consider alternative motives.

To partially consider the conceptual framework for the present case history study, perhaps it might be helpful to cite the conclusions of William Domhoff, a well-published dream investigator, whose research has relied heavily on content analysis approaches (Domhoff 1996, 1999, 2000). He recently summarized certain of his observations as follows:

Based upon solid empirical studies concerning (1) the neural network that makes dreaming possible, (2) the development of dreaming in children and (3) the everyday content of thousands of dream reports, it is unlikely that dreaming is 'necessary' or that any clinical theory of dreams has any value beyond that dreams contain some psychological information.

Recognizing the complexity of the field and the multiple methodological problems, it is hoped that the 'Lucifer' dream under consideration provides in Domhoff's terminology 'some information'. For years, this adolescent girl was severely abused by her Native Alaskan mother. Her culture is disintegrating rapidly. There is a high prevalence of alcoholism and violence-related behaviours. Adolescent males have the highest rate of suicide in America so her fears for her depressed brother were justified.

During childhood development, multiple sources of sensory input from this abuse were recorded neurochemically. However, the secondary recall of such traumatic images apparently had failed to appear in her recurrent 'nightmares'. When asked on several occasions if she ever relived any of the terrible abusive scenes involving herself and her brother, she consistently said: No! Of course, there is no way to really know if this was the case. Perhaps she was aware of such dreams but because of emotional discomfort she did not want to report them. Alternatively, she may have been aware of them shortly after they occurred and then 'forgot' them because of anxiety-induced neural inhibition.

In any case, she was terribly tormented by intrusive memories of the abusive scenes during the day. In sharp contrast, her sleep was protected by symbolic images. One of these was the vision of 'Lucifer'. No matter how terrifying this was, apparently it was less threatening than activating from memory storage real-life images of her mother's abuse.

Apart from the dream under scrutiny, she recalled only one other terrifying dream of the devil. She was able to recall that this occurred at age of 11: 'I was in my closet and the devil appeared. He was small and his brain was exposed, I was twisting a hanger around in his brain'. This disturbed her sleep when she was first attempting to understand her traumatic family life. Prior to therapy, she was confused and mentally preoccupied: 'Why does mother hate me so much? What did I do to deserve the beatings? I must have deserved them. I should hurt myself. I don't deserve to live. I should kill myself, etc.' Her mental preoccupation with these issues caused her to focus on her own brain. She introduced this anatomical awareness into her dream imagery along with an object (the 'hanger') that she just had been beaten with by her mother. This dream preceded her first hospitalization and suicidal behaviour. At the time she was first beginning to get the almost delusional belief that some evil force from the devil was penetrating her nervous system accounting for her own demonic thoughts and murderous fantasies.

Sometimes she would get angry at herself and would punish herself by self-mutilating behaviours with knives. Her extreme arousal in viewing SIS-II Video Image B15 depicting 'Knives' was understandable. This irrational thinking surfaced in the early stages of her fourth hospitalization in the 'Lucifer' dream. It may be recalled that she related the onset of her sense of her body image being penetrated to when she originally played an Ouija game. In association with the fundamental Christian mind distorting dogma that she had been exposed to in a Seventh-day Adventist Church, she erroneously believed that the demonic forces had entered her body.

Apart from the devil symbol, many other threatening symbols flooded her dreams. Examples of such symbolic material spilling over into projective consciousness with the Rorschach in her third hospitalization six months earlier are as follows:

**Card I:** 'A bear trying to escape from a very strong woman, she looks like my mother.' Here, she identified with the 'bear' and the 'very strong woman' symbolized her mother as being very powerful and threatening.

**Card II:** 'Two big animals playing patty cake. One is a bear and he looks like he is wounded because of the red blood.' The bleeding 'bear' symbolized her own injuries from the severe beatings.

**Card IV:** 'A monster, this way it looks like a dragon, here are his eyes, he's got horns and wings'; these two responses could symbolize her abusive mother. It also could have depicted that part of her emerging personality that was identifying with the demonic side of her mother. She also imagined it to be an 'explosion with smoke coming out from everywhere' and gave a similar response to the next card. Both responses symbolized her memory of violent domestic scenes.

In addition and reminiscent of her attempting to hide in the closet from her abusive mother in real life and the symbolism inherent in running from Lucifer in her dream, seeing this card also evoked imagery as follows: 'It could also be a tunnel, something that you could hide in'. On Card VIII, the violent imagery continued to be released in projective consciousness as 'a volcano with lava exploding'. On Card X, this theme continued with the response: 'This is a building, there is water below, in front these are fireworks going off, it is colourful, like fireworks going off, looks explosive here'.

Like many fundamental Christians, she had learned to personify the 'Devil' and referred to him as 'Lucifer'. To such concrete thinking people, it probably would seem pointless—if not heresy in her church—to try to understand what 'Lucifer' symbolized.

This sharply contrasts with clinicians who explore dream symbolism as an integral part of the diagnostic/treatment process. In this analytic quest, those who employ the power of projective methodology are much more likely to unmask the 'Devil'. In the present study, it may be inferred that 'Lucifer' embodies both her mother's abusive nature and that part of the adolescent's personality identified with the mother. About the latter, the responses revealed this side of her. One example was her response to SIS-I when she detailed how she had the capacity not only to hurt herself but others. Her extreme hatred and homicidal ideation were also symbolized in the 'knife in the heart' response.

Apart from the satanic, there are many other forms of symbolic imagery in threatening dreams. For example, children frequently observe dream of grotesque human or animal-like biting apparitions. They commonly label them as 'monsters'. The specific form of these is strongly influenced by the reality of their culture.

However, this earlier primitive oral aggressive imagery is replaced. This is especially true of severely disturbed adolescents with poorly controlled aggressive impulses. Perpetrated by the brainwashing techniques of fundamentalist religious leaders, satanic symbols can emerge in dream imagery.

The concrete thinking implicit in personifying the threatening humanoid figures as the 'Devil' can be extreme. For example, satanic cults have evolved historically which in an organized fashion worship 'Satan'. Personal identities of such members may be closely linked with socially unacceptable sexual and aggressive behaviour. When their actions become day residual for night-time dreams, a cycle of evil imagery and behaviour becomes operational. Its reinforcement by the saturation of violence in the media amplifies the system.

Studies of anxiety-laden dreams employing PTs can provide insights into the origins of violence in children and adolescents. Hopefully, such investigations could provide new approaches for developing more effective methods of early detection and prevention. Young people need to have their threatening dreams taken as a possible early symptom of trauma. They need to be listened to with compassion and serious consideration by members of the healing profession, as well as authority figures in education, religion and politics.

This is especially true for those from dysfunctional families where guilt and ignorance may allow their parents to dismiss their suffering by denial and rationalization. For example, the abusive mother in this case history study argued that: 'I did not abuse my children, they were just getting the punishment they deserved' and regarding her daughter's terrifying dreams 'They mean nothing, all children have nightmares!'

Her rationalization was not challenged. She herself was a victim of childhood family abuse. Such a generational pattern of abuse can only be broken through early intervention therapies—including the use of PTs.

## Case 5: The Adjunctive Use of SIS with Hypnotherapy

SIS-I was administered to three patients who were not responding with medical treatment. The SIS was able to identify deep-seated conflicts which patients were unable to uncover through conventional therapy. The usefulness of therapeutic tool of reframing along with hypnotic relaxation is also demonstrated with the help of three case studies.

'What is learned and remembered is dependent on one's psychological state at the time of the experience' (Rossi 1986). Accessing the state-bound memory or experience creates an opportunity for growth through reframing or reorganizing it to facilitate some resolution. This is achieved through the recreation of the emotions, sounds and thoughts related to the repressed event or experience. Accepting the concept of state-bound memory, the therapist strives to create for the patient an opportunity to access the state-bound sources of the problem. Hypnosis is one way of helping patients to access state-bound memories. All patients, however, can access these memories. This chapter illustrates the use of the SIS as a PT and an adjunct to hypnosis to help patients access the state-bound memory, when conventional therapy is unable to achieve the same result.

A three-stage administration technique is used. The first step is to administer the SIS cards and for the patient to identify the three cards they found least disturbing and the three cards they found most disturbing. The second step is to induce a light trance. Depending on the severity of the condition, the author would either induce a light trance or a deep one. The patient is given suggestions of relaxation and the state of relax is then anchored in the fingers. The third step is to ask the patient to open their eyes, look and concentrate on the card and close their eyes again. The patient is asked to report what emotional responses the card evoked or what images came to mind.

Three vignettes describe the use of the SIS to access state-bound memory. The cases described are of a woman with marital problems, an anorectic child and a woman with chronic anxiety. Once the memory was accessed and reframed, the patients showed a dramatic improvement in their condition.

## Case 1

Mrs E. D. is a 38-year-old married woman who was referred by a colleague because she was not responding to conventional treatment and hypnotherapy for the complaint of marital and sexual problems. She dated the onset of her problem to nine years prior to being seen by the author after having had a Pap smear. She reports that she was embarrassed by the examination and had difficulty opening her legs. The examining doctor made derogatory remarks about her being sexually active as a single woman. She is married for two years to her boyfriend of 12 years and has a 2-year-old son. Her husband had visual problems. After extensive therapy by a colleague, which included hypnotherapy, the patient showed no signs of improvement. She was referred for hypnotherapy (Savage 2001).

At the initial interview, the SIS-II Booklet was administered after taking a partial history. The following is what the author considered were some of the more significant responses.

**A3:** I don't know.

**A4:** Left-hand side looks like a rose bud starting to open.

**A5:** Looks like a small body, length and arms. This is the mouth. Like this person is confused like me.

**A6:** Looks like a teddy bear sitting here could either be legs. Also reminds me almost like sperm going somewhere. Could also be me keeping myself closed?

**A7:** Someone drawing could also look like the fruit being hanged, looks like me moving my body away.

**A8:** [*After a long silence*] looks like a figure as well, like a pregnant tummy. Looks like sperm. Pinocchio's nose growing.

**A12:** An ear could be someone always wants to listen.

**A13:** A hand and it looks like some hand of a plant or something. Saying stop right there. Like its telling you if you go any further it might be dangerous. Could also be a flame or something that is in the sea, something like that?

**A22:** Looks like a head cut apart, some object, two heads that were put together but separate.

**A26:** Looks like a deformed face, I see the eyes, or it could be a scan, a baby, development taking place.

**B1:** Head of a baby, flames, picture depicting the moon from space, whirlwind.

**B10:** Scan of womb showing developing foetus, pregnant stomach.

**B15:** Confusion, a child's scribble, danger, dangerous pointing.

**B30:** Ears, there will always be someone who will listen to you.

By looking at the responses, the author formed the hypothesis that the patient was feeling confused and was asking for someone to listen to her story. The frequent references to babies were difficult to interpret. Because hypnosis was the treatment of choice, the following two sessions were spent clarifying any misconceptions the patient might have about hypnosis and to let her experience what it feels like to be in a state of relaxation and to provide her with an anchor for relaxation. This was done with the full knowledge that the referring colleague had used hypnosis and that the patient was familiar with the technique. The primary objective was to establish a rapport and to introduce her to my way of working.

## SESSION 4

Two options were considered; one was to explore the responses to the booklet in greater detail or to administer the SIS cards. The second option was decided on as a further diagnostic tool. The following are her responses to the cards.

## Card 1

| | |
|---|---|
| *Patient:* | Could be a young girl with ponytails. Could be two birds. Young girl's eyes look a bit sad. |
| *Therapist:* | What is she sad about? |
| *Patient:* | I do not know. Maybe she wanted something she was not allowed to get. |
| *Therapist:* | What do you think it could have been? |
| *Patient:* | My mind goes back to when I was 10 years old. Mother had cancer; I knew she was sick when I was nine. I knew she had pain. I did not realize that she had died. I knew she had to go to a hospital. I knew she was in pain, I insisted that she plait my hair. When I left for school she wanted me to kiss her, I refused to kiss her. |
| *Comment:* | At this point, the patient became very quiet and tears rolled down her face. |
| *Patient:* | At school, the principal called me, I thought it was my uncle who had open heart surgery and I thought uncle Bobby had passed away. When I got home, my grandfather told me, my mother was gone. My grandfather was crying. At the funeral, I refused to look at my mother in the coffin. I feel sad. I often think about her. I am sad; I did not kiss her goodbye. My greatest fear is that I lost my mother; I hope my son does not lose me before he is 18. I think of her quite often. My grandfather had two daughters. |
| *Comment:* | On a further questioning, patient told the therapist she had two photos of her mother displayed in her house and that she was sexually active before the marriage. |

## Card 2

| | |
|---|---|
| *Patient:* | Little boy with a big face, there is a smile on his face. There is a smile but no eyes. I cannot read the expression. I do not know if it is a smile or not or they are just stretching their lips. |

| Therapist: | What does that make you think of? |
|---|---|
| Patient: | A person not saying her true feelings, just smiling, a smile on her face. I am always smiling don't let anyone know. |
| Therapist: | Why did you get married? |
| Patient: | He insisted. After a year I proposed, maybe it was the sexual thing, after a few years he wanted to get married. I made up my mind; no, I did not want a big wedding. I never had my parents. I got pregnant; he said we had to get married, as his uncle did not want another child out of wedlock. I was 35, I was single for a long time, I felt free. At the age of 18, my husband started having problems with his eyes. I accepted his condition, I am proud of what he had achieved. I feel it is too much, I feel if I do not help him he will leave me. I went into this relationship knowing his eyes were bad. He had a drinking problem. He wants another child. |

**Card 3**

| Patient: | Another face, long hair. Person is contented, could be a little bit (could not make out what the patient said) I don't know why I said that. It dawned on me she is asking me a question, do you think she did the right thing I want to say yes, maybe I did not forgive XX (she mentioned her own name) for what she did. |
|---|---|

At this point, the hour was over, and the patient was distressed. The session ended with the patient being relaxed.

**SESSION 5**

Conclusions drawn from session 4 were that the patient had some separation anxiety. There was guilt about her mother's death and her refusal to kiss her goodbye on the day she died, and she had some unresolved conflicts about her premarital sexual activities. The author decided to use hypnosis to help her to work through these conflicts. Routine induction was done with systematic relaxation. Using age regression and visualization, the patient was able to 'talk' to the 10-year-old girl and reassure her that young girls react on impulse sometimes and that she could forgive the 10-year-old girl for what she did.

## SESSIONS 6 AND 7

During these sessions, hypnosis was used to complete the grief work and help her to resolve conflicts related to her mother's death. Some ego strengthening was also done.

## SESSION 8

Patient reported that she was feeling relaxed and had visited her mother's grave and was able to complete her ritual of separation and felt proud of her achievement. She reported that she had applied for a promotion post and requested some assertiveness training to prepare her for the interview. She still had the fear of dying. Basic stress management techniques were discussed.

## SESSION 9

She reported that she was able to make decisions with confidence and only spoke very briefly about her marital problems. She was concerned that her husband was very friendly with a colleague at his work. She promised to phone to confirm the next appointment. The patient defaulted and did not return to therapy.

The case demonstrates the usefulness of the SIS in identifying deep-seated conflicts which patient was unable to uncover through conventional therapy. The usefulness of the therapeutic tool of reframing is also demonstrated. The patient presented with marital problems but did not respond to conventional therapy aimed at the 'problem'. The SIS helped to identify the underlying unresolved grief. Once this was dealt with and reframed, the patient was able to continue with her normal duties. Because the patient terminated therapy, no follow-up appointment was given. It is interesting to note that only three cards were used in this case. An unknown factor is that the author does not know whether any of the other cards would have uncovered some other conflicts. Because of the patient's improvement, the matter was not pursued.

## Case 2

J. P. was an 11-year-old boy who was referred to the author by his mother because he was not responding to previous treatment for an 11-year history of primary enuresis. He was extensively investigated medically and was exposed to various recognized treatments for enuresis. He did not respond to medication which he was on for six months. The parents had a discordant relationship when J. P. was about five years old, but they have a good relationship now. Mother was concerned because J. P. was wetting the bed every night.

## SESSION 1
During the session, a routine history was taken and basic information about hypnosis, the treatment of choice by the author, was explained to the parents.

## SESSION 2
By means of a diagram, the author explained the basic working of the brain with reference to the controlling function it has. Hypnotic induction by means of systematic relaxation was done. While in trance suggestions of control by the brain were given with a post-hypnotic suggestion that whenever he is asleep, and his bladder is full he will wake up to go to the toilet. A two-week follow-up appointment was given. Mother phoned the author to report that J. P. had only wet the bed once during the week but had wet the bed over the weekend.

## SESSION 3
This session was used to reinforce the suggestions given during the first session and a two-week follow-up appointment was given. Mother phoned after a week and a half to report that J. P. was back to wetting the bed daily. A fourth session was arranged.

## SESSION 4
Because of J. P's resistance to treatment, it was decided to administer the SIS-I cards to see if there was any underlying dynamics that was missed. The following are the responses to the cards:

**Card 1:** A sheep, a goat.

**Card 2:** Looks like a person who is smiling.

**Card 3:** Two people who are dancing or something.

**Card 4:** Looks like a person who is doing something.

**Card 5:** Looks like a star.

**Card 6:** Looks like birds.

**Card 7:** Heart.

**Card 8:** Looks like a skeleton of a person.

**Card 9:** Kidneys.

**Card 10:** Looks like a snail.

**Card 11:** Looks like a heart.

**Card 12:** Looks like a body or something.

**Card 13:** I don't know, looks like a heart turned upside down.

**Card 14:** Looks like an eye.

**Card 15:** Spine.

**Card 16:** Eyes and nose.

**Card 17:** Looks like a fish swimming in the sea.

**Card 18:** Looks like a monster's face.

**Card 19:** Looks like a cockroach's head.

**Card 20:** Looks like a face.

He liked cards 20, 4 and 19 and did not like cards 5, 13 and 3.

The technique used by the author is to induce a light trance and to ask the patient to look at the cards and while in a relaxed state to say what it reminds them of. The following are the responses while the patient was in a trance. The responses to the cards he liked were as follows:

**Card 4:** A body moving, that is all.

**Card 19:** No response, the patient just looked at the card and did not respond to any probing question by the author.

**Card 20:** Looks like a monster.
The responses to the cards he did not like were as follows:

**Card 3:** He just looked at the card with no response.

**Card 5:** He just looked at the card with no response.

**Card 13:** He looked at the card and said nothing.

| | |
|---|---|
| *Therapist:* | Does it make you think of anything? |
| *Patient:* | Someone playing around in the park. Person is happy. |
| *Therapist:* | Why is the person happy? |
| *Patient:* | Because he is with his friends. |
| *Therapist:* | Is there anything else? |
| *Patient:* | A person's face, makes me frightened [*silence*]. |
| *Therapist:* | Why are you frightened? |
| *Patient:* | Because I get scared ... silence. |
| *Therapist:* | Are you afraid of someone? |
| *Patient:* | Yes. |
| *Therapist:* | Who made you frightened? |
| *Patient:* | I'm scared of the dark. |

The patient could not recall any incident that could have precipitated his fear of the dark nor could he remember how old he was when he first became aware of this fear.

With the patient still in hypnosis, he was regressed to an earlier age. He identified the age as two years, he was alone and afraid. He did not know why he was afraid and there was no one who made him afraid. Using the reframing technique, the 11-year-old boy reassured the 2-year-old boy that it was normal for a young child to be afraid of the dark. The therapist had the 11-year-old boy 'talk' to the 2-year-old until he was sure that the 2-year-old boy was no longer afraid of the dark. The patient was relaxed and reassured. He was asked to open his eye and look at Card 13 a second time. The following is his response:

| | |
|---|---|
| *Patient:* | People are dancing. |
| *Therapist:* | Why are they dancing? |
| *Patient:* | They are feeling happy. |
| *Therapist:* | What happened to make them so happy? |
| *Patient:* | Someone got married. |
| *Therapist:* | Is everyone happy? |
| *Patient:* | Yes, no one is sad. |
| *Therapist:* | Does the card make you feel unpleasant. |
| *Patient:* | No. |
| *Therapist:* | Does the card remind you of anything you are afraid of? |
| *Patient:* | No. |

The patient was given the suggestion of deep relaxation and a post-hypnotic suggestion that he was not afraid of the dark any longer. The patient's fear of the dark was discussed with the parents and they agreed to place a night light in the room. Two weeks later, the mother phoned the therapist to report that J. P. had been dry up to then. One month after the termination, the patient was still dry.

## Case 3

Mrs J. P. is a 52-year-old married woman with an 18 years history of anxiety and depression. Different general practitioners with various medicines with no symptomatic relief treated her. She has one daughter prior to her marriage and four children born within the marriage. Her husband and daughters have formed an alliance against the patient and she reports, 'I feel very alone'. The symptoms she complained of were suggestive of a diagnosis of chronic free-floating anxiety.

At the age of 10, she started sleepwalking and from the age of 15 she was afraid of going to sleep at night. She married at the age of 25 and reports that she is still afraid to go to sleep at night and suffers from agoraphobia. She has a recurring nightmare of seeing her mother in a coffin and of her asking her mother to open her eyes, as she is not dead. Her mother died when patient was 42 years old. Patient has a pronounced stutter whenever she must speak in public. Because of the severity of the symptoms, the author decided to concentrate on symptomatic relief. The first three sessions were devoted to taking the history and to teaching the patient the technique of self-hypnosis, anxiety management and stress management. At the end of the third session, the patient reported no relief in the severity of the symptoms. The author decided to administer the SIS cards to identify any underlying conflict that the patient was unable to access.

## SESSION 4

The following are her responses to the cards she identified as the most liked and those she did not like: she found Cards 2, 4 and 6 least disturbing and Cards 18, 19 and 20 most disturbing.

**Card 2:** This looks like someone very happy, a smiling person.

**Card 4:** This seems to be another kind of dancing, laughing figure to me.

**Card 6:** Looks like someone kissing, two shapes, there is a feeling one wants to get close to the other one.

**Card 17:** This is a spooky something, scary something with pinches.

**Card 18:** This is another scary thing, looks like a nasty animal ready to fight.

**Card 19:** Oh, mmmm looks like a bad face with a mask on, an evil face.

**Card 20:** Another ... like a vicious dog wanting to pounce.
The exploration of the cards was done at the following session.

## SESSION 5
The method used to explore the cards is to induce a light trance and to get the patient to open her eyes, focus on the cards and report what the card reminded her of. The author decided to start with the cards least liked by the patient.

### Card 18
| | |
|---|---|
| *Patient:* | I see a coffin; my uncle is in the coffin. |
| *Therapist:* | What else do you see? |
| *Patient:* | I am 12 years old. They want me to touch him. I am afraid. |
| *Comment:* | At this point, tears started to roll down her face. The reframing took the form of helping the patient to let the 52-year-old person comfort the 12-year-old girl, in her mind, by telling her that it was normal for a young child to be afraid to touch a dead body. The 52-year-old had to continue comforting the 12-year-old until she was sure that the 12-year-old was no longer afraid. When the patient indicated that the 12-year-old was no longer afraid the following card was shown. |

### Card 19
| | |
|---|---|
| *Patient:* | A man's face, cruel [*a long pause*]. |
| *Therapist:* | Whose face is it? |
| *Patient:* | Vicky, my child's father. I loved him so much and he left me. I could not say goodbye. |
| *Therapist:* | Why could you not say goodbye to him? |
| *Patient:* | He hurt us so much; the two of us [*long pause*]. |
| *Therapist:* | Why did he leave you? |
| *Patient:* | I was too poor, he wanted lots of things. When I told him I was pregnant, he told me he could not marry me. He said he was going to marry (X) and that hurt me. He just left. |

| | |
|---|---|
| *Comment:* | The patient was very distressed at this point and there was a long pause. The therapist has made the patient compose a letter in her mind to her ex-boyfriend. In the letter, she had to tell him how she felt when he left her to marry another person, she also had to say goodbye to him in her own way. When she had 'written' the letter, she had to visualize giving the letter to him and watch while he read it. When he had read the letter, she could if she wished say a verbal goodbye or she could just walk away. She did not share with the therapist what she did. |

## Card 20

| | |
|---|---|
| *Patient:* | (She started to cry loudly and uncontrollably) I am scared, a scary face, someone wants to bite me, I don't know, someone wants to hit me. He looks black, big white eyes. |
| *Therapist:* | How old are you now? |
| *Patient:* | I am 4, I see a man [*pause*]. |
| *Therapist:* | What is the man doing? |
| *Patient:* | He is taking me by the hand, going into the house, on the bed … taking off my panty … he is going to cut me. Not going to cut. He is patting me, on my private. He is saying it is all right. I am not afraid anymore. I get up, walking out of the door; I'm going home (patient is crying aloud freely now). I'm scared to go home. My mommy's going to hit me. I'm outside; I'm not scared anymore. It's OK. its 'Mal Willie' (Mad Willy). He's putting me on the swing. I'm so scared of the swing, I am scared, and why is he pushing me so high. I jump off; I'm falling on the tar. My leg is bleeding. I'm scared. I'm so scared of the man he is so big. I'm going home. I'm at home. It's OK. I'm not scared anymore. My mommy is there in the kitchen. I'm in the park, I see him again, Mal Willie (Mad Willie). I'm not alone; I'm not scared of him anymore. |
| *Comment:* | The patient had settled down by now and became very quiet. The therapist reinforced the suggestion of deep relaxation and reframed the incident by helping the patient to visualize the 52-year-old adult comfort the 4-year-old child. She had to continue to talk to the young child in her mind and to reassure the child that it was normal for a 4-year-old child to be afraid of an adult who does things they are uncomfortable with. |

She had to further reassure the 4-year-old that there was nothing she could have done and that she was not to feel ashamed of what had happened. The patient had to continue talking to the young child in her mind until she was satisfied that the young child felt comforted. After a period of silence, the patient settled down. The session ended with the patient being relaxed and being given a post-hypnotic suggestion that she would remember only those things that were comfortable for her to remember.

Session 5 was held three months after session 4 because it was over the Christmas period. At this session, the patient no longer had free-floating anxiety. She did, however, complain of situational anxiety with relation to her husband. The patient terminated the therapy. She contacted the author again 18 months after terminating for a completely different problem.

These cases demonstrate the usefulness of the SIS in identifying deep-seated conflicts which patients are unable to uncover through conventional therapy. The usefulness of the therapeutic tool of reframing is also demonstrated. In Case 1, the patient presented with marital problems but did not respond to conventional therapy aimed at the 'problem'. The SIS helped to identify the underlying unresolved grief. Once this was dealt with and reframed, the patient was able to continue with her normal duties. Because the patient terminated therapy, no follow-up appointment was given. It is interesting to note that only three cards were used in this case. An unknown factor is that the author does not know whether any of the other cards would have uncovered some other conflicts. Because of the patient's improvement, the matter was not pursued.

In Case 2, the young man did not respond to both therapeutic and medical intervention. The SIS cards helped to identify the very basic problem of a fear of the dark. Once identified, it became obvious that this was a very logical question to ask. Everyone, including the author, was so concerned to treat the enuresis that no one thought of asking the patient if he was afraid of the dark. Once a night light was placed in his room and his fear of the dark was reframed, the enuresis stopped.

Case 3 is an example of the effects of childhood sexual abuse. Eighteen years of treatment did not bring symptomatic relief. With the use of the SIS, the underlying problem was identified, treated and reframed, with the desired symptomatic relief.

It could be argued that the problems would have eventually been identified but at considerable emotional cost to the patients. These case histories have demonstrated the usefulness of the SIS cards to identifying deep-seated conflicts.

## Case 6: A Case of Alopecia Areata

Mr X, 29 years, PhD student, presented in July 1992 with recurrent loss of hair over scalp, arms, legs and trunk for last 23 years. His mother had history of AA and bronchial asthma. In view of alopecia totals, he was treated with prednisolone pulse, 300 mg once a month for four months and had complete loss of hair (Sharma 1996). Subsequently, he presented with relapse of alopecia totals in July 1994 and gave history of stress due to conflict with PhD guide. He was treated with topical sensitize diphencyprone and had complete loss of hair in 6 months and is on maintenance therapy for almost 3 years.

As he narrated, he was frequently given severe beating by his father to the extent of physical abuse. He perceives his father to be very authoritarian, aggressive and dominant, leading to frequent quarrels between his parents. He is aggressive towards his brother and sister. He finds it to be a broken family. He has few friends and very limited contacts. He got familiar with a female university student and soon married her. It is a sort of arranged marriage by his friends, though his parents gave their consent at the end. Initially, he was withdrawn from his wife as he was feeling sexually weak. There was problem of erection, which improved to some extent after medication. Medical treatment and supportive psychotherapy helped in improving his symptoms.

A few significant responses on somatic inkblot test with content analysis are given as follows:

**A5:** He perceived this image as 'a man crying for freedom with his body torn apart'. It brings out his inner cry and desire to get away from his broken family home. He further confirmed this feeling during interview and therapy session. He does not find his home worth living and wants to flee.

**A10:** He has viewed this image as 'the face of a gloomy woman marred by distressful life'. It may depict his projection towards his mother who often suffered physical assault from his father and is depressed. The patient projects that most of the Indian families have such bad atmosphere. This may also bring out his sympathy towards his mother and his inability to help her because of the dominant father.

**A13:** He saw 'the hand/palm of a person caught in a fire as if crying out for help'. Once again, his inner cry has come out on surface indicating that he needs help from others. This may also be indicative of his wishful thinking to get support and help from his physician/ therapist for his physical symptoms in the form of alopecia or even sexual inadequacy.

**A15:** He has seen 'an infant priced/pierced/stabbed by a long knife in womb itself'. This may be indicative of his regressive phenomenon, which takes the person back in time and he feels that it could have been better if he had died as a foetus. It suggests his depressive mood and that the person wants to bring the womb itself may also be indicative of severe pain inflicted by his father during his early childhood. Such information is very important for a therapist as it helps him in therapeutic intervention.

**A22:** He viewed it as a 'scorpion' rather than seeing it as backbone or male genital organ. The plausible explanation could be that because of his 'impotence' he has avoided seeing backbone/male sex organ even on suggestion. Since it is painful to think of impotence to a newly married person, he has projected it as a 'scorpion'—a pain-inducing insect.

**A23:** He has seen 'a baby scorpion'. Once again, the imagery of male genital organ has been suppressed and painful imagination in form of a scorpion is brought out on the surface. The other possible explanation could be his injured 'tailbone' because of which he had endured lot of pain and suffering a few years ago.

**A31:** He perceived 'a couple shares their common woes' on this image. Seeing a couple is the most typical response but 'common woes' may bring out his inner cry particularly because of his sexual weakness and inability to perform the role of a husband.

**B4:** He viewed in this image 'a happy man but a woeful woman', suggesting his projection of seeing his wife under woeful imagery. This may also be the projection of his mother whom he always finds in a miserable situation. Again, the theme of disturbed family life and his own withdrawal from reality as a deference mechanism has been brought out.

**B11:** He has seen 'a wig kept on the head of a person'. This may suggest his fear of becoming 'bald'. The loss of hair due to AA has created in him a lot of tension and he is worried to the extent of becoming bald. Such anxiety is quite expected in a young man.

**B20:** He viewed 'the rear view of a head with long hair' which suggests his wishful thinking to have long hair. He further elaborates that he has seen his own photograph with long hair and wishes to have long hair once again.

**B28:** He has seen 'a distressful passionate person' in this image, which people generally see as 'a lady with her child'. Avoiding seeing a lady may be due to his conflict with his wife and 'passionate person' could be the projection of himself.

**B31:** He has seen 'a family with their children knitted together tightly out of some unknown uncertainty/fear/upheaval or resolution' in this image. Since it is the last mage of the test, the theme of a happy family is projected in this image so that the person could carry positive feeling at the end of the test. Instead of seeing a happy family, he had seen a family with their children knitted together tightly is a painful back in time to help him to process the painful memories of childhood. Physical abuse, lot of uncertainty and strict discipline might be a few of the reasons for such an imagination.

It can be concluded that the SIS had helped the patient in projecting the painful childhood experiences, disturbed family relationship and fear of being bald and disturbed physical/emotional relationship with his wife. The test had further helped in establishing the psychopathology leading to psychosomatic disturbances (AA) and the need for counselling.

AA is known to be associated with emotional factors (Dubey and Das 1977). In recent study from India, emotional factors were clamed in 7 per cent cases (Sharma et al. 1996). It is painful to accept and reveal one's own sufferings in front of a physician, but the patient feels comfortable to project his sufferings through the inkblot images and accepts this during analysis.

## Case 7: Inkblot Responses as an Aid to Therapy—A Longitudinal Case Study

Most clinicians consider the use of inkblot testing like the Rorschach, primarily for its diagnostic applications. In recent years, the widespread use of numerical scoring systems such as those developed by Klopfer and Exner have tended to bypass the therapeutic value of Hermann's inkblots in stimulating imagery for free association and content analysis. This failure partially relates to the fact that most modern therapists are not adequately trained in this approach for recalling painful memories and PTSD dreams. In the past, psychoanalysts such as Roy Schafer did preliminary explorations involving Rorschach content analysis as an aid in treatment. Another reason for the original 10 plates becoming relatively unused as an aid to therapy concerns the fact that the colour–form configurations lack enough structure to routinely stimulate clinically relevant interview themes.

As an attempt to create visual stimuli more consistently capable of stimulating imagery for diagnostic and therapeutic purposes, the SIS was envisioned in 1959. This presentation represents a longitudinal case history study of eight years comparing the diagnostic and therapeutic utility of inkblot images. It may also refresh the memories of clinicians concealing how projective stimuli can facilitate not only diagnosis but also provide a powerful yet underutilized tool in the various present-day psychological treatments.

A male college student aged 19 was selected for the case history study (Dubey and Cassell 2000). He was referred by a psychiatrist and was plagued by incapacitating examination anxiety. When interviewed, he had major problems with stammering. Part of his developmental history involved his having been placed at the age of 7 in a boarding school in another city by his parents. At that time, he experienced considerable abandonment feelings and severe homesickness. In addition, it was noted that until the age of 12 he suffered from enuresis.

As part of assessment and treatment plan development, he was given the Rorschach, SIS-I and SIS-Video images. These procedures were completed initially in March 1991, then repeated in October 1991, then the third time in April 1992 and finally in February 1999. Repeating the visualization processes facilitated evaluating the clinical progress, while at the same time providing an aid for stimulating imagery for therapeutic discussion.

The longitudinal treatment plan involved insight-oriented psychotherapy discussing his abandonment issues, content analysis with him concerning the significance of his inkblot responses, cognitive therapy and hypnotic relaxation. During the initial period of three months, his psychiatrist provided him medication to assist in the control of his anxiety. Fortunately, he made impressive improvement from the biweekly psychological intervention.

After six sessions, since he was able to deal with his anxiety more effectively and consequently, he was able to take and successfully pass examinations. The psychopharmacological approach was no longer necessary. However, therapeutic work on the stammering and interpersonal conflict issues continued at intervals over the observation period. These were on an 'if and when needed basis' for approximately 70 sessions over the eight years. As will be shown, eventually the latter sessions began to focus on stressful interpersonal issues not directly related to the original presenting problems.

## Results of Inkblot Interviewing

At the initial evaluation with the Rorschach, there were signs of both low productivity (R = 12) and imaginative capacity suggestive of his anxiety problem. Despite definite improvement in his clinical symptoms, the Rorschach responses did not reveal much change, nor did they stimulate therapeutically relevant percepts. The total number of human content responses remained only two in all test sessions. Most Klopfer's scores were essentially no different with repeat testing. By contrast, the human content with the SIS-I was observed to increase over time. This matched his reduced examination anxiety and improved social skills. Initially, he gave five human responses on the 20 inkblots and this number doubled on the last testing session. The quality of contents during third and fourth testing improved, which can be observed in the tables presented in this report. This was associated with a greater ability to communicate and interact with people. A few clinically significant responses on Rorschach, SIS-Video and SIS-I are shown below for understanding the pulling power of the test.

With the SIS-Video, there was a similar increase in his ability to recognize human content in the video presentations and their quality improved. For example, initially in Image A1, he responded 'it looks like fungi or algae'. Next, he saw it as 'a hand surrounded by fire', denoting the painful grief stemming from his unresolved abandonment issues. In the third session, he projected a response symbolizing his progress: 'a hand getting out, surrounded by plants'. Finally, he saw it as 'a hand of a person clapping!' This reflected his appreciation for the therapeutic assistance given over the years.

Next consideration will be given to illustrating how the discussion of his SIS-Video responses facilitated treatment. First, regarding the early abandonment issues, exploration with him of the following responses warrant comment:

**A3:** Initially, he saw this as 'a human cell or roots of a plant that has been uprooted'. Here, the significance of the projection of the response 'human cell' symbolizes his traumatic loss at age 7 when psychologically uprooted as denoted in the 'plant uprooted'. After his therapist repeatedly processed the family significance of this imagery to him, he gradually began to resolve his abandonment issues. He learned to accept dependency on people as a necessary part of mature life. In working through his transference to the therapist, he acquired insight into the fact that loss and grief need not always follow trusting in close human relationships.

It was highly significant that he rated this symbolic material denoting as the 'least liked' or most threatening imagery evoked by the 62 SIS-Video presentations. This demonstrates the critical importance of the therapist knowing developmental history concerning early losses and not attempting to do 'blind interpretations'. At last, in the final retest situation eight years later, he imagined seeing 'a lovely flower with colourful roots'. With growth in his self-confidence and esteem, he could readily identify with a 'lovely flower'. The colour signified his enhanced emotional state.

**A14:** Initially, he said that this represented 'a picture on the wall'. The next two responses correctly identified the anatomical structure embedded in the inkblot. This was consistent with his developing a more mature awareness and sensitivity to emotionally tinged body sensations, at the eighth year of therapy, he projected the response 'energy being sent from a person'. This depicted his recognition that he could benefit from establishing interdependent relationships with nurturing people. Since he had a religious support system, the additional value of spiritual meditation as a higher source of human 'energy' was also discussed.

**A18:** He responded to this in the SIS-Video presentations as follows: 'smoke ring', 'lava, smoke, volcano, cloud from volcano and finally bright gases and lava ejected by volcano'. His free associations to these responses in therapy immediately led to his emotional pain, low self-esteem, hurt and anger when originally psychologically abandoned in childhood the fact that he visualized the 'gases' in brighter colours he realized symbolized his more positive self-image and hope.

To complicate interpretation, his therapist realized that some of his angry symbolism was stemming from new conflict with his parents. They recently had proposed a bride for him whom he considered unacceptable. Shortly before the fourth interview, he had established a love relationship with a woman of his choice. Consistent with this, he imagined SIS-Video Image A31 to represent 'two lovers kissing'. Similarly, he envisioned B17 as 'a heart beating on Valentine's Day'. Previously, he had given the following responses: 'volcano crater', 'heart' and 'bright flower with petals'. Also related to his evolving amorous interests, he visualized B22 as 'a man sleeping and thinking of a woman he loves'. This illustrates how the SIS may be used to follow maturing as an individual attempt to move beyond childhood fixations through new life passages. The responses on Rorschach, SIS-I and SIS-II on initial testing and three repeat testing are shown in Tables 12.1, 12.2 and 12.3.

| **TABLE 12.1** | *Comparison of Rorschach Responses on First, Second, Third and Fourth Testing* |
|---|---|

First testing: When sick
Second testing: After 10 sessions of hypnotherapy
Third testing: Six months after termination of psychotherapy
Fourth testing: Eight years after the first therapy

| Card No. | First Testing | Second Testing | Third Testing | Fourth Testing |
|---|---|---|---|---|
| I | Bat | Bat | Bat | Bat |
| II | Faces of two persons clapping like | Two persons clapping | Two kids clapping | Two persons clapping like |
| III | A person | Hand of an animal | Frog head | Two ladies dancing |
| IV | Skin of an animal | Animal-like bat | Bat flying | Bat |
| V | Two deer horns up | Bird-like vulture flying | Bat flying | Bat flying |
| VI | Skin of a lion | Skin of a deer | Skin of an animal | Skin of an animal |
| VII | Squirrel standing on a rock | Two kids playing | Two kids standing on something | Two kids playing |
| VIII | Two animals climbing on a rock | Two animals like wolves going up | Two wolves going up | Two animals climbing |
| IX | Arial view of a valley | Rejected | Web's type | Two animals |
| X | Various animals—spider, peacock, rats | Various animals—spider, peacock, rats | Various animals—peacock, spider, fish | Various animals—spider, peacock, rats |

*Source:* Dubey and Cassell (2000).

| TABLE 12.2 | Comparison of a Few Significant SIS-I Responses on First, Second, Third and Fourth Testing | | | |
|---|---|---|---|---|
| SIS-I Images | First Testing | Second Testing | Third Testing | Fourth Testing |
| 1 | Two hens sitting | 1. Two hens<br>2. Head of a person | 1. Two hens<br>2. Head of a person | 1. Two hens<br>2. Head of a person |
| 5 | 1. Bat<br>2. Two kids playing | As someone has been killed | Mother and two babies | Mother and two babies |
| 6 | Two penguins playing | Two kids playing | Two kids joining hands and playing | Two kids playing |
| 14 | Insect with mouth | Insect-like beatles | Clown | Clown |
| 18 | Face of ghost | 1. Bat<br>2. Eyes, mouth, face of some one | Man's face | Face of a person |
| 20 | Rejected | Face of a person | Face of some thing | Face of a person |

Source: Dubey and Cassell (2000).

This longitudinal case history employing the Rorschach and two versions of the SIS perhaps may be best considered from a historical point of view. The use of inkblots in art and psychology predate Hermann Rorschach by many years. What is of interest is the fact that even though there have been attempts to develop inkblots such as the work of Holtzman and others (references), somehow the great creativity inherent in Hermann's blots have been forgotten by modern professionals who over utilize reductionism scoring in cult-like training seminars. Most educated people associate the name Rorschach to the notion of inkblot testing when the subject is brought up. While scoring systems have added immeasurably to diagnostic application, their very use has tended to obscure the clinical merit of using content analysis. Overlooking the rich symbolism of inkblot responses, such as those illustrated in body symbolism (Cassell 1980), especially as they may readily lend themselves to the therapeutic approaches, does the field of projective testing a great disservice. Although many psychologists

| TABLE 12.3 | Comparison of a Few Significant SIS-Video Responses on First, Second, Third and Fourth Testing | | | |
|---|---|---|---|---|
| SIS Images | First Testing | Second Testing | Third Testing | Fourth Testing |
| A3 | Plant uprooted | Roots of a plant | Roots of a plant with branches | Lovely flower with coloured root |
| A13 | Looking like fungi algae | Hand surrounded by fire | Hand surrounded by plant | Hand of person clapping |
| A14 | Picture on a wall | Liver | Human stomach | Energy being sent from a person |
| A18 | Smoke ring | Lava/smoke volcano | Cloud from volcano | Bright gases ejected by volcano |
| A21 | Looking like a bat | Two small kids with bat | Two kids playing around their mother | Hand of a person who is clapping |
| A24 | Rejected | Forest with tree | Pond in a forest | Mother and baby |
| A31 | Faces of man and woman | Man and woman | Man and woman's face | Two lovers kissing |
| B4 | A girl seeing her face in a mirror | Two faces | Two male and female faces | Girl and boy sitting in a park |
| B17 | Looking like volcano crater | Heart beating | Bright flower with petals | Heart beating on Valentine's Day |
| B18 | Rocket going up in war | Male sex organ | Male sex organ | Graphic artist working on epic |
| B22 | A person sleeping and thinking of something | Dead body soul going up | Person lying down and thinking he is dead and soul is going up | Man sleeping and thinking of Shen Ming |
| B23 | Depression created by a bomb | Spider with legs | Spider with legs | Bright colour in a shop |
| B28 | A girl embracing her mother | Woman embracing her child | A girl clinging her mother | Mother and daughter |
| B31 | Couples with kids | Man and woman with their kids | Couple with their two kids: boy and girl | Happy family |

*Source:* Dubey and Cassell (2000).

refer to the Rorschach data as resulting from 'projective testing', this is a misnomer when standard scales are the sole source of data. What is even more of a tragedy for the field concerns the fact that there has been so little effort to improve in the design and presentation of the existing inkblots.

In this study, it was shown how the rich imagery evoked by the SIS tended to make the Rorschach percepts pale in comparison. Normally, 10 relatively ambiguous blots cannot compare in projective pulling power with the SIS stimuli designed with embedded clinically relevant material. For example, the SIS is much more able to stimulate human percepts. In this case, the clinical improvement with treatment over time was associated with a doubling in the number of human responses observed with the SIS-I but not the Rorschach.

Apart from having 62 more visual stimuli for presentation, the SIS in the video version has more pulling power because of technology. It reduces test anxiety by combining floral relaxation for inducing hypnotic viewing with the opportunity for the viewer to write responses. The subject is alone, and like in hypnotic writing, does not have to hear what is reported. Moreover, it is unnecessary to immediately share potentially threatening imagery with a professional person at the time the projective images and their disturbing emotions enter consciousness. When the subjects rate responses for those that are 'least liked', the interviewer has an opportunity to evaluate their anxiety treat. A busy clinician may simply get free associations to the most anxietyladen SIS image, without taking interview time with the others. For the college students under study, most threatening imagery provided very important information confirming the therapist's suspicion that early abandonment was a major stress. Of course, during the initial assessment, the youth had not yet been provided with this insight. It was only after his therapist made this inkblot interpretation that he was able to begin to resolve this childhood loss. Giving associations in therapy sessions to the response to M 'a human cell or roots of a plant uprooted' quickly led to the imagery's affect linkage and his long-forgotten grief.

While longitudinal case histories such as this point the way for clinicians in the new millennium, it must be recognized that there are many obstacles which need to be overcome. This is particularly true in the USA where problems related to professionalism are formidable. Psychoanalysts are rapidly becoming a vanishing breed. Even though they employ free association in interviews, most do not believe that they should include inkblot analysis in their treatment. Present-day residency training programmes for psychiatrists, since the era of psychopharmacology, have become restricted by overadherence to the medical model. The concept of projection, whether it is onto inkblots, the individual's body, the therapist (i.e., transference), fantasy imagery and dream analysis are often relegated to outdated theoretical models. Many psychologists avoid projective testing because it is not readily quantifiable and suggests mysticism. Also, because in the American private economic sector, insurance companies are resisting paying for their work, many are experiencing drastic limitations in their practices. They are being rapidly replaced by less-trained psychotherapeutic practitioners (e.g., social workers, psychiatric nurses, pastoral counsellors, etc.) in test procedures. Moreover, psychologists in several states have convinced legislators to pass laws limiting test procedures only to licensed psychologists.

Whatever the professional discipline of the clinician, there should be a rich background of depth psychology, psychoanalysis and psychosynthesis in interpreting the direct and symbolic meaning of projected responses. In fact, symbolic interpretation is the basis for deciphering the language of the unconscious. Although these issues of the therapist's socio-economic status and power go far beyond the scope of this report, they must be considered challenges to be dealt with in the 21st century.

## Case 8. SIS-II in a Case of Sex Abuse and Somatic Pain

Miss X, 27 years, unmarried, law graduate, practising as attorney, belonging to high middle-class family, had history of sex abuse at the age of 4 years by a 19-year-old boy, physical relationship with an aged family friend, history of feeling depressed, wish to leave the family and conflicting parental relationship, was given SIS video for understanding her personality and therapeutic intervention. Interpretation of a few responses found to be quite relevant has been given for understanding the psychology of the case.

**A1:** She saw 'A man who looks healthy and majestic but pretty empty inside' is a direct projection of how she feels empty inside, although she looks normal and healthy on the outside. The fact that she conjures up images of a man rather than of a woman may reflect her sexual identification partially identified with that of her perpetuator.

**A3:** Many people while viewing this image introduce spiritual connotation with it. Here, she directly projects her feeling of wanting to be free of her past traumatic memories and inner trauma by seeing 'my soul when will it become free'.

**A5:** She viewed 'a lady who is with all her heart celebrating alone'. It is direct projection of same sex identification to the human form. She focuses on the heart because she is introspective and socially withdrawn because of her pain and depression. It may probably also represent a projection of her mother's image that is critical and non-supporting. Her depression is abnormally high, and she has given lot many responses depicting depression.

**A6:** 'A sad teddy bear' brings back the theme of sadness or depression almost in a perseveratory fashion. In addition, the response has repressive features. She totally avoids reference to the human gestalt and focuses instead in a childlike fashion on a teddy dear.

**A10:** 'Blind woman' is the projection of her psychological blindness associated with her repressing images of her past sexual abuse. She also comments that she is getting impatient and needs therapeutic resolution for her long-standing childhood conflict.

**A11:** She viewed 'a needle through the heart—I want to weep but I won't'. This is a direct projection of an emotional pain and depression, the fact that she conjures up the image of a needle penetrating the heart symbolizes her past sexual penetration and body boundary violation. In commenting on this horrible response, she for the first time acknowledges to the examiner her depression and need for emotional catharsis as well as her inability to do so as without therapeutic assessment.

**A12:** She viewed 'can you hear me with your ears and listen with your heart'. With this question, she directly asks the interviewer if she will be heard with empathy and compassion. Previous attempt to share her pain as a child fell on the deaf ears of the parents.

**A13:** She saw 'a window hazy with fog with the centre clear, a hand outstretched asking me to wait. Maybe I should give up'. Here, she continues the theme of her own reluctance to weep and share her pain with the therapist. She has learned from the failure of past attempt to share, which were met with frustration, and further hurt, that the process of attempting to communicate may itself lead to further hurt and rejection.

**A11:** The hand symbolizes that part of herself that 'I won't allow herself to trust the therapy process'. To remove this resistance in therapy, it would be necessary to interpret the symbolic significant of this response in terms of transference. At last, the reference to 'giving up' continues the depressive feelings of her helpless.

**A14:** She saw 'a dry flower' in this image. Here, rather than recognizing the anatomical structure, she projects herself in the image as being dead inside.

**A18:** She viewed 'a man hanging upside down with smoke bellowing out of his head and waiting to fall through the dark circle into a hole'. Many individuals see anatomical contents here such as the heart or image of sexual intercourse. Because of her sexual trauma and resultant pelvic anxiety, she totally avoided reference of somatic structure in the video image. The defensive material projected symbolizes her severe depressive mood and latent death wishes. At times, she fantasizes running away from her home and escaping from her problems.

**A23:** She saw 'looking like a deadly Android, resembles a creepy centipede [*scary feeling*]'. Here, the response is remarkable because of her failure to correctly identify somatic structure, which so clearly depicts spinal column. There are two possible determinants of somatic repression, one relates to her past medical history of having fallen four years back injuring her tailbone and causing considerable pain. The other relate to phallic connotation of this image. While both hypotheses can lead to heightened body anxiety, symbolic analysis of her defensive imagery suggests that the later determinant is more noticeable that she saw a deadly ardroid resembling creepy centipede which is highly threatening to her. Remember that previously in responding to image, the needle had threatening phallic connotation. A little girl violated by penal penetration will always carry such negative association to phallic imagery.

**A31:** In Image A31, she viewed 'a beautiful woman looking at her hazy reflection. She is not sad yet contemplative [*feeling confused*]'. Here, she avoids reference to central content in A31, which pictorially depicts a man and woman in very close interaction, because this material is highly threatening to her due to her experience with her male perpetuator. The normative content is totally repressed. She defends against this structure by substituting image symbolizing herself in therapy looking at her psychological defence mechanism of denial. The introduction of the idea that the woman is confused symbolized her own confusion and cognitive disarray.

**B3** : 'Two people sitting inside a womb overlooking alter of fire.' Here, fire signifies life [*feeling of wonder*]. Was her response on this image, seeing two people inside the womb continue the regressive theme previously noted on A6, the fire denotes her emotional pain. In this essence, rather than associating depressive aspects she introduces the concept of life and wonder. This was positive prognostic implication to therapy and needs to be interpreted to her context. There is hope for recovery if she is willing to share her pain during therapy.

**B6:** She saw 'a half statue girdle downwards with some infection around the girdle [*feeling of depression*]' in Image B6. Here, she partially picks up the correct anatomical structure referring to the lower abdomen and thigh. However, because of her trauma to related pelvic anxiety, she defends against the specific somatic content by seeing a more abstract image 'that is, statue girdle'. Here, it is noteworthy that she projects a pathological anatomical response. 'Infection' symbolizes her own inhered genitalia. The facts that this image accentuates her feeling of depression in responding to the image indicated that she is grieving the loss of her virginity and body boundary intactness. The assault on a child's body is not just injurious in a sexual way but when a perpetuator is a close family friend, the overall ego becomes distorted and confused just like she indicated in A31. The other explanation could be her repeated infection in her pelvic region for which she has taken treatment.

**B12:** She viewed 'a parrot hanging upside down trying to fly away'. Here again she totally represses the real structure of the image, which dents some man's facial area and nose. Substituting image of a parrot neutralizes the threat in this image. The fact that the bird is seeing upside down trying to fly away directory symbolizes the childhood feeling of vulnerability and helplessness to avoid her perpetuator.

**B16:** She saw 'the centipede is back again. I hate centipede [*feeling of filth and dread*]' in image B16. The significance of this response is previously reviewed with A23.

**B28:** She viewed 'a person hugging a white coloured pet'. Most individuals who have had experience of positive nurturing mother will see as a woman holding the child. Here, she defends against by avoiding reference to the maternal and female connotation of the adult figures seeing only a 'person'. Similarly, she avoids reference of the child introducing the image of a pet. Despite this, it should be recognized that of an image which was loving and affectionate. Frequently, when a child has not received maternal love, they will turn to pets to meet the need for aggression. Such individuals with other inkblot tests such as the Rorschach test and the Holtzman test give higher number of animal responses than the human responses.

**B30:** She saw once again 'two ears—can you hear me?' on B30, here like in A12, she directly asks the therapist if her inner cry will be heard and responded to therapeutic alliance and that she is given reassurance that unlike the past when no one has heard her she will be heard with empathy and compassion now. In this sense, her inner cry will be heard, and she will have the helpful therapeutic relationship. Many male therapists because of trust issue prefer to refer such traumatized female patients to a female therapist.

Here, we have presented two cases of clinical interest. Although the subjects of both cases are females, it is important to point out that the problem of inner cry is not only with males or females but human beings in general. It is not limited to any part of the world, society or culture but is universal in nature. The responses to SIS have been successful in identifying the inner cry of the individual, which itself is the first step of therapeutic intervention.

It is important to remember that the projective tests do not have the so-called objective procedure of interpretation. It is the clinician's acumen, which is necessary to interpret a protocol. In the first case study, it was a denial of the problem initially, but through SIS images and on subsequent enquiry it revealed the roots of the problems, whereas in the second case study, it was the obvious percepts to unstructured stimuli. The Rorschach test was tried in the first case but could not reveal much. It could be since somatic inkblot test is based on the theory of body imagery, whereas Rorschach is largely based on general perception.

## Case 9: Symbolism in Violent Hallucination and Somatic Inkblots Imagery

In this case history study, the SIS Video, Rorschach Inkblot Test and figure drawing tests were administered to a teenage girl who was admitted to a psychiatric hospital in Boston for treatment of major depression and dissociative disorder. She had history of suicidal ideation and self-mutilation of her left wrist and forearm. The relaxing instructions in the video and the hypnotically present healing flowers may have facilitated neural extinction of the terrifying hallucinations intruding upon her consciousness. The figure drawing and content analysis of SIS and Rorschach may provide useful aids to supplement standardized clinical interviewing techniques. The case has been discussed in detail (Cassell, Schaeck and Mohn 2002). The study of hallucinatory phenomenon has been long proven of interest. If there is a common clinical bias in evaluating hallucinations, it is the assumption that these perceptual disturbances are evidence of abnormalities in brain chemistry. There is a great deal of supporting evidence for this viewpoint, especially in those with disease of the central nervous system or toxic conditions involving the brain (e.g., chemical-induced hallucinatory states). This case history presentation explores the notion that when there is no clear evidence of neurological dysfunction, the clinician may glean important diagnostic information and novel therapeutic leads by exploring the symbolism in the hallucinations.

Prior to admission, the patient (her fictitious name S) had experienced severe suicidal ideation with plans involving a variety of suicidal behaviours such as overdosing, slitting her throat and electrocution. Her usual behaviour involved self-mutilation of her left wrist and forearm. While she had experienced suicidal ideation from the time she was severely abused by the violent biological father, her pattern of mutilation had only started after she had been removed from high school seven months back by her mother and stepfather. Even though she had been made to do homeschool, she retained communication with a teacher who had been especially supportive of her interests in drama and writing. When she revealed to him her suicidal thoughts, he contacted mental health services who referred her for hospitalization. Her parents initially refused to accept the fact that she hallucinated and was a danger to herself.

During the initial psychiatric evaluation, she reported that she had previously drawn a coloured representation of a reoccurring violent visual hallucination. This was a threatening man with a knife in his hand. Her representation of the figure revealed that he had cut his wrists. Red blood poured from the wounds. When asked to recall who he reminded her of, she said that it reminded her of her abusive biological father. Upon detailed questioning about her drawing, she told the interviewer that the eyes resemble 'mine'.

She was selected for this illustrative case study because she provided a unique opportunity to examine hallucinatory symbolism prior to psychotropic medication. Because she was quite intelligent, she was an excellent candidate for the illustration purposes. She was intelligent with excellent writing skills in poetry and drama. Previously when enrolled in school, she had demonstrated her ability of effective communication in school drama activities. However, consistent with her long-standing dissociative symptoms, she had extremely limited concern in the expression of personal feelings. Further relevant clinical history will be provided subsequently in connection with her projective test results.

On the second day of hospitalization, she was administered the video version of the SIS. The image that she rated as most threatening was B1. A transcript of the detailed enquiry is as follows:

Dr B:    Now we're going to go to B1. On the answer sheet, you indicated that it frightened you and made you think that something was trying to bring you down. And you saw 'a claw reaching out from the depths to drag you down'. Do you want to say more about that?

S:    No. (This projective response incorporates an image of a 'claw' which in disguised form symbolizes the hallucinatory figure's knife.)

Dr B:    When... when have you felt that way? That something's dragging you down?

S:    A lot of times. Like when I do theatre, and someone isn't so accepting about it. That kind of drags me down (her parents were adamantly against such activities).

Dr B:    Do you think that image—that person in the hallucination brings you down?

S:    Yeah.

Dr B:    Yeah. Tell, tell me about that. In what way does he bring you down?

S:    He shows me the way that—a path that he chose (suicide by cutting his wrists), I suppose, that is also a path that I've—I've considered. And the fact that it scares me kind of brings me down.

Dr B:    And he chose what path?

S:    Suicide.

Dr B:    In what way have you considered suicide?

S:    Slitting my wrist the same—same way he did (it will be shown in her free associations to subsequent SIS images). S had been severely traumatized by her biological father and had partially identified with his violent personality. This identification was reflected in her comments about the eyes in the figure resembling her own. Next, her associations to SIS B21 will be explored for symbolic content. She had rated this image as the third most threatening.

Dr B:   Okay. For B21 you said: 'Anything that hurts nature angers me'. Okay. It angers me too. And you see…

S:      'An oil rig digging into the beautiful earth to suck her dry' (here, the symbolism again relates to self-mutilation with the 'earth' symbolizing her body).

Dr B:   Especially the beauty in Alaska, right?

S:      Yes. Oh. And—and just the fact that something can damage that is upsetting. (Here, she totally avoids the imbedded structure of a handgun and substitutes an image of an oil rig digging into the beautiful earth. Again, this depicts the knife in the hand of the hallucinatory figure. The power of this symbol to emerge in projective consciousness is immense. No recognition of the gun takes place, yet a few minutes earlier in viewing A11, consistent with her violent impulses, she had projected the response 'gun'.) The next response that warrants projective analysis was produced regarding her viewing B22. Here, she envisioned a 'person sleeping with dreams so disturbing it causes them illness'. Consistent with this, in association with the visual hallucinations of a figure with a threatening knife; she had recurrent post-traumatic dreams in which a similar figure slashed his own wrists and then chased her.

In this regard, the violent hallucinations simply reflected a spillover into conscious awareness of the violent night-time imagery and emotions. Sometimes, the violence in dreams was directed at her friends as illustrated in her response to SIS B22.

Dr B:   Then B22. 'A person sleeping with dreams so disturbing it caused an illness'. And what does that recall?

S:      Myself.

Dr B:   What way are your dreams disturbing?

S:      They're horribly violent.

Dr B:   What sort of violent images come to mind?

S:      One I have, I recall a lot, a friend of mine is dying because a bowling ball fell on his head.

Dr B:   What were the images like in the dream?

S:      They were real looking. What do you mean? I'm sorry.

Dr C:   Well, what did you see with it? Did you see the ball hit his head? Was there blood?

S:      Yes, there were bones and blood and…

| Dr B: | And how did it affect you in the dream, emotionally? |
| S: | It hurt. I mean I cried, and I was… |
| Dr B: | It was horrible, wasn't it? |
| S: | Yeah. |
| Dr B: | And you wake up feeling how? |
| S: | 'Helpless'. This brings to mind those theoreticians who conceptualize of certain depressions as resulting from 'learned helplessness'. |
| Dr B: | How long does that feeling last in the morning? |
| S: | It lasts throughout the day. |
| Dr B: | Colours the whole day, right? |
| S: | Yeah. |

(Even though this was a horribly disturbing dream, she still was able to recall it, since it was much less anxiety provoking than her terrifying dreams of the knife threatening hallucinatory figure.)

Next attention will be given to her reaction to B15, the only SIS image that had embedded structure of knife-like sharp objects.

| Dr B: | Okay. B15 'Knives being thrown at someone to cause them more pain'. What does that recall? |
| S: | Me. |
| Dr B: | In what way you? |
| S: | Because sometimes the pain that I feel—it feels like somebody's taking a knife and stabbing me (here, she compares her somatic pain in terms of a knife stabbing her). |
| Dr B: | Where do you feel it in your body? |
| S: | In my stomach and in my ribs and my heart (diagnostic medical studies had not revealed any physical problems to account for her discomfort. Consequently, it was assumed that they represented conversion reaction symptoms related to her dissociative disorder). |
| Dr B: | What does your stomach feel like at that point? |
| S: | Oh, it feels horrible. It's… it's just… burning and it's… I don't know. It's just sharp pain. |
| Dr B: | And then your heart, what does it feel like? |
| S: | Same thing. |

Next, the detailed enquiry regarding SIS Images A10 and A12 will be explored in terms of their related body symbolism.

| Dr B: | Right. And A10? |

| | |
|---|---|
| S: | I don't know. It just looked like somebody who is sad and in pain. |
| Dr B: | Does it remind you of the pain that you have? |
| S: | Yeah. |
| Dr B: | What's the pain like that you have inside? |
| S: | It's hurtful. |
| Dr B: | And where do you feel that? |
| S: | Everywhere. |
| Dr B: | Yeah. More in your chest or just everywhere? |
| S: | Sometimes. |
| Dr B: | What's your chest feel like? |
| S: | It feels like sharp shooting… Well, it feels like somebody's stabbing me. |
| Dr B: | A12 what does this recall? |
| S: | An ear with blood in it. (The blood response projected here is quite consistent with knife bleeding.) |

As will be shown subsequently, S was a victim of severe childhood, psychological, physical and sexual abuse. Associated with the resultant traumatic events, she had blocked from conscious awareness many of the events along with their related painful affects. Consciously, when triggered by current stressful life events, these were experienced as somatic pain.

Next, her response to B27 will be outlined.

| | |
|---|---|
| Dr B: | B27. 'Self-reflection. Evil, but completes half versus a pure, but damaged half'. And what does it recall? |
| S: | It brings to mind myself and… and like the darker half winning over the better half. |
| Dr B: | What is the lighter part of you like? |
| S: | What do you mean? |
| Dr B: | The good part. |
| S: | What is it like? |
| Dr B: | Yeah. |
| S: | Happy. |
| Dr B: | And then the darker part, what it's like? |
| S: | Controlling, dominating, hurtful. |

In interpreting the symbolic significance of human content in visual hallucinations, it may be inferred that the figure represents an aspect of the person's own self. For Stephanie, the male figure of the hallucination symbolized both her father and her violent tendencies. The latter resulted from her learning aggressive behaviour from her abusive father (i.e., mutilating her wrists). Of course, genetic factors may also be determinants.

Next, historical information of childhood trauma follows regarding her associations to A22.

Dr B: A22. 'Someone moving to destroy or damage someone'. What that recalls?

S: The way people are affected by certain things.

Dr B: Hm hm. When you were young, were you exposed to too much violence or hurt?

S: Yeah.

Dr B: What was it like?

S: Hard. It was painful.

Dr B: Who was hurting?

S: My dad for the most part.

Dr B: In what way did he hurt you?

S: He would hit us and throw us against the wall and stuff. (Her mother reported sexual abuse, although at this stage in her psychotherapy with her female therapist she was amnesic to this early trauma.)

Next, her comments about A18 are relevant to understanding how the dissociation process fragmented her personality.

Dr B: Hm. A18. 'Someone captured inside a prison they created for themselves.' What does that make you think of?

S: Me.

Dr B: In what way you?

S: Because I have problems with communication. And it seems that I just have barriers that I put up.

Next her discussion in relation to B4 throws light on her distorted cognition presented in her mutilation poem below:

### My Scars

*These scars upon my wrist*
*Are beautiful to me*
*What the world looks at with shame*
*I view with joy and pride*

*These scars upon my wrist*
*are mine I put them there*

*They are some gift*
*That no one can take away*

*These scars upon my wrist*
*Are my reminders Proof*
*that I can feel happiness*
*Despite all the sorrow that consumes me*

*These scars upon my wrist*
*That you look upon with disgust*
*Could someday be owned by you*
*Could someday bring pride and joy to you*
*Could someday be scars upon your wrist.*

Dr B:  B4.'Are flection of a person's true self without the mask they present' And what does that recall?

S:  Me. (Before exploring further her associations, perhaps it might be helpful to consider two drawings that she made for her female psychotherapist. One drawing was of a flower depicting her exterior self. The other presents a troubled interior with a peace symbol that is burning, above it are tear drops symbolizing her sadness and inner cry.)

Dr B:  What way does that reflect you and your mask?

S:  Because one of the images is a lot uglier than the other one.

Dr B:  Uh-huh. In what way do you have an ugly image?

S:  That would be the image that I don't present. It's distorted over things that have happened.

Dr B:  Such as?

S:  Such as my dad being mean, or something as little as J leaving (one of the losses that precipitated her current depression was J's moving away. They then communicated frequently by e-mail. Eventually, S shared her mutilation secret with J. J, in turn, then sent her the drawing presented in figure, indicating that she too found 'peace through cutting).

Dr B:  Hm. And so that person is a person who's feeling what?

S:  Pain.

Dr B:  Pain. Yeah. And how about hurt and anger too?

S:  Yeah.

Dr B:  What's the anger aspect?

S:  The anger at themselves.

Dr B:  And how does that relate to your wanting to cut on you?

S:      One of the reasons I cut myself is the anger that I feel towards
        myself.
Dr B:   What affect does it have when you see your blood during
        cutting?
S:      It feels like something is being released.
Dr B:   Hm hm.
S:      Something being set free.
Dr B:   Somehow, there's some emotional release with it?

Next, her response to B20 depicting a human brain portrays her distorted cognitions and auditory hallucinations.

Dr B:   B20. 'Someone's brain destroyed in parts.' What does that
        recall?
S:      Me.
Dr B:   In what way do you feel your brain is destroyed at times?
S:      My lack of concentration now. And my inability to recall things
        that happened to me three days ago. In dissociative disorder,
        amnesia is a common symptom relating to overriding attempts
        of her mental defence system to obliterate emotional suffering.
Dr B:   Right. And when you have these visions what—how does that
        feel in your brain?
S:      It feels damaged.
Dr B:   And then the visions you… you see things, and… and do you
        hear things at times as well?
S:      Yeah.
Dr B:   What do you hear?
S:      Jumbled noises.
Dr B:   I see. And how do those affect you emotionally?
S:      They kind of throw me off and upset me for a bit, until I can
        like try and regain myself.
Dr B:   Can you ever make out the voices, whether they are of a man
        or a woman, you know?
S:      It just sounds like everybody is jumbled. (These auditory hal-
        lucinations are of concern. They could indicate that she was
        suffering from the early stages of one of the schizophrenic
        disorders.) Next, her responses to B29 and B30 are of interest
        because they provide an opportunity to assess, through the
        mechanism of projection, how her hallucinations affect her.
        This additional aid in assessment was clinically important.
        Initially, neither her mother nor her stepfather would believe
        her or the hospital staff that she was truly hallucinating.

*Dr B:*  B29. 'Someone is running away from fear.' What does that recall?

*S:*  Me. I run from everything.

*Dr B:*  When do you feel fear and anxiety?

*S:*  A lot of times. Just out of the blue, sometimes, I'll be really scared and—and when I hallucinate, I feel scared and just—yeah.

*Dr B:*  B30. 'Two ears each hearing something differently.' And what does that recall? (This depiction of human ears is particularly useful. It enables those suffering from auditory hallucinations the opportunity to communicate about their suffering. The material which follows more sharply brings into clinical focus her dissociated mental processes).

*S:*  Everybody. Everybody seems to hear something different than everybody else. And sometimes they hear two different things that weren't even intended and...

*Dr B:*  Do you ever hear things like that are confusing in your head?

*S:*  Yeah.

*Dr B:*  Tell us about it.

*S:*  Sometimes I – I – I hear things telling me what a bad job I'm doing, and everything.

*Dr B:*  Put down things?

*S:*  Yeah.

*Dr B:*  How does that affect you?

*S:*  Really bad. It makes me feel weak.

*Dr B:*  Do you ever hear things telling you to hurt yourself?

*S:*  No. (Here she reveals [by elimination of suicidal voices] that it is primarily the visual hallucinations which contribute to her mutilating behaviour.)

*S:*  was tested with Rorschach one week after admission when she was still hallucinating. The report read as follows:

Her responses to the Rorschach cards were scored with the Exner scoring technique. Mostly her responses were scored within normal parameters. At the time of this assessment, she appeared somewhat depressed, but not necessarily suicidal. She did, however, appear susceptible to episodes of affective disturbance that may involve features of worthlessness and confusion. She tends to make decisions based on how she feels rather than on what she thinks, although she tends to be confused and uncertain about how she feels much of the time. She appeared to be experiencing considerable emotional stress that was interfering with pleasure in life and making her susceptible to becoming even more depressed and anxious (Cassell, Schaeck and Mohn 2002).

The contents of her responses were interesting and seemed related to the contents of her hallucinations and dreams. One perception was of a 'horrible, ugly giant with big, mean hands and huge feet'. She described another as something 'rough on the edges like something that's been cut up'. Another was a 'scary face with an evil horrible grin with awful sharp teeth'. These references were consistent with hallucinations featuring a man with a knife, cutting himself and threatening to cut her'. She was subsequently interviewed by Dr B, 30 days after her admission. She was asked the question: 'Did you see anything in any of the cards which reminded you of the figure in your visual hallucinations?'

S:      Yes (selecting Card II), I see his face. There are his eyes (pointing to the blank space under the upper red colours).
Dr B:   Can you say anything more?
S:      Yes, he is frowning.
Dr B:   How does that make you feel?
S:      Lonely.
Dr B:   What does the red on top resemble?
S:      It looks like he is crying. His eyes are red.

Assessing the symbolic significance of hallucinations poses serious methodological challenges. Ideally, the clinical investigator should attempt to obtain valid and reliable data at the time the subject is experiencing a hallucination. These data could be compared with projective responses in the non-hallucinatory state. While this may have appeal to those who champion scientific rigour, like dreams, hallucinatory episodes are constantly in flux. Moreover, because of a variety of complicating factors, not the least of which is the individuals' confused cognitive state and inability to clearly demarcate boundaries between actively psychotic and dormant psychotic conditions, such rigorous comparison is not always practical. In addition, the prime emphasis must always be on therapeutic issues. This case study has many limitations, active psychotherapy was going on over the course of treatment and psychotropic medication levels were being brought up to therapeutic levels.

Despite such limitations, perhaps a general observation can be made which could provide guidelines for future clinical investigators. In the absence of clear-cut neurological illness, it may be hypothesized that direct and/or symbolic information can be gleaned by the assessing hallucinations. In assessment, PTs like figure drawing, and content analysis of the SIS and Rorschach stimuli may provide useful aids to supplement standardized clinical interviewing techniques.

In this case history study, the SIS-II Video was used on the second day of hospitalization when the hallucinations were frequent and intensely threatening. When Stephanie viewed the video, the SIS evidence of their presence was only symbolically inferred from two of the three images that she rated as the most threatening: Images B1 ('a claw reaching from the depths to drag you down') and B21 ('an oil rig reaching into the beautiful earth to suck her dry'). While at the time, these were rated as quite disturbing, it could have been potentially much more disruptive to her fragile cognitive state if her mental processes had not employed symbolic defensive overlays blocking the intruding hallucinatory imagery of 'the man with a knife'. Moreover, the relaxing instructions in the video and the hypnotically present healing flowers may have facilitated neural extinction of the terrifying hallucinations intruding upon her consciousness.

One week later, she was responding well to treatment. Self-mutilation impulses and visual hallucinations were infrequent, yet her 'Rorschach responses' showed content consistent with the face of a threatening man. However, no specific enquiry was done concerning what she recalled from the facial responses. A month later in treatment, when she was given an opportunity to view all Rorschach plates laid out on a table in response to a specific enquiry she spontaneously indicated that the imagery evoked by Card II resembled the hallucinatory man's sad face with reddened eyes. Consistent with her clinical improvement, there was no reference to his cutting behaviour, blood, etc., and he seemed much less threatening.

In psychotherapy the following day, she was asked why she thought that he was sad. She said that she did not know why. When asked if she felt sad, she immediately answered in the affirmative. Two days before, she had been crying profusely and was 'red eyed' herself. As indicated earlier, hallucination represented a composite image of her abusive biological father and her own dark side.

As she got in better touch with her sadness and emoted during therapy sessions, the visual hallucinations stopped. The imagery was replaced by her sensing the psyche presence of the man standing behind her. In a paranoid way, she imagined him to be contemplating and touching her shoulder in what she feared would be in a menacing fashion. However, she envisioned that he no longer had a knife in his hand. Currently, there was a reduction in her suicidal ideation and impulses to mutilate her wrists.

Her improvement was reflected in her writing a poem after a few weeks of therapy. The poem is given below.

> You constantly ask me
> What it is I want
> Well, now I will tell you
> I want more than I deserve
>
> I want to be inspired
> And to cry because I am so truly thrilled to be alive
> A reason to keep up the fight
> To put the knife down
>
> Or the extra pills up
> To actually beg to live another day
> I want to never worry about acceptance
> To know that people love me
>
> And to accept that it is not important to understand why
> You asked me what I want
> But it isn't easy to say
> I want a lot
>
> Though it doesn't always feel like enough
> The only thing that I can tell you
> With absolute certainty
> Is that I want more than I deserve.

Finally, in considering the significance of hallucinations whose etiology is primarily not neurological, it might be useful to consider certain psychological origins of their symbolism. Like many other adolescents who have experienced severe childhood trauma and developed dissociative disorder, Stephanie's mental defence system became disrupted. Thus, she suffered from a breakdown of the usually integrated functions of consciousness, memory, identity and perception.

The latter disturbances involved both the outer world and of her body image. She had been depressed for years and long had experienced suicidal ideation. Death in her fantasies provided her a way out of her painful existence. Her self-mutilation impulses were first acted upon when she was taken out of school. For her, this was a devastating attack on her fragile sense of identity. It shut off her outlet regarding drama and writing—all things that her parents despised. Not being able to express her rage directly to them, she acted out her anger on her body.

When she found the act of bloodletting giving her an emotional release, she developed an almost addictive behaviour to this.

Her Internet friends reinforced this maladaptive self-abusive behaviour—as illustrated by the friend who sent her the 'peace through cutting' drawing the figure. She also had so-called friends in cyberspace with suicidal behaviours that also had eating disorders. Consistent with familiarity to the latter, she responded to A7 as follows: 'someone trying to deal with an eating problem, trying to make healthier choices'. In the initial enquiry, she denied having this problem herself. However, in the second month of therapy, she finally revealed that after listening so much to their fears, she too had become concerned about her body image. Since self-destructive behaviours can sometimes be readily transmitted from one person to the next, her Internet 'chat room' was a highly dangerous place for this suggestible adolescent girl. This case illustrates why the 21st-century clinicians need to enquire into the Internet activities in exploring determinants of violence.

The relaxing instructions in the video and the hypnotically present healing flowers may have facilitated neural extinction of the terrifying hallucinations intruding upon her consciousness. The projective instruments may provide useful aids to supplement standardized clinical interviewing techniques.

## Case 10: Cognitive Behaviour Therapy with the SIS in Body Phobia

Although not formally recognized in any existing diagnostic manual, 'body phobia' represents a clinically definable and treatable condition. In 1976, it first occurred to me that this symptom pattern might possibly be worthy of formal recognition. At that time, a small series of case studies were initiated.

For illustration purposes, one will be outlined. It utilized an early 12-card form of the SIS called 'A Projective Test of Body Awareness'. It involved a 29-year-old professional engineer who had initially been referred by his family physician for treatment of depression. During his evaluation, it was noted that a major stressor was his fear of losing his wife. Their marital relationship was characterized by communication conflicts at all levels.

In rating his responses in a hierarchy of threat, he selected Card 2 as the most threatening. He initially had responded: A woman with a big mouth ... the black is the hair.... When elaborating further, he quickly became angry and felt like tearing up the card. He revealed that it strongly reminded him of his mother's highly critical nature and the verbal abuse he suffered as a child. Eventually, he became tearful as the projective scene activated painful emotions associated with these memories.

Initially, it seemed problematic to determine the mental mechanisms by which this oral imagery got transferred or projected onto the image of his wife's body. It was partially clarified as a result of a subsequent interview with a female member of the treatment team. He reluctantly reported to me that he did not feel comfortable in talking to her. The reason was that he could not take his attention off her mouth. He was embarrassed and puzzled to admit that the therapist's lips resembled his mother's. The treatment team then realized that this distorted transference reaction was partially mediated through symbolic body imagery.

The threatening nature of this symbolism was also evident in his selecting Card 10 as the next most upsetting one. Consistent with the above outlined transference hypothesis, he imagined seeing the following scene: 'Lips and pictures taken by the subject from the air (referring to the lower aspect of the card)'.

Here, it is evident that initially the threatening maternal oral image intruded upon conscious awareness. This triggered psychological defences of spatial withdrawal enabling him to mentally distance from unresolved childhood PTSD memories of verbal abuse. Focusing on the SIS inkblot as 'a photo' taken from a great distance facilitated the repressive perceptual inhibition and resultant threat reduction.

The third most emotionally arousing situation involved his viewing Card 4. Once again, he became quite disturbed in visualizing imagery of a 'woman' with its concomitant traumatic memories. This additional projective clue signified a new evident response pattern.

At this point in the evaluation, it seemed that for him maternal originated female body symbolism can stimulate confused memories of love–eroticism, fear–hate, etc. These had strongly shaped his lifelong perceptions, especially distorting his interaction with females.

As might be expected, some of this confusion had been historically transferred of the developmental years to his perception of his own body. Consistent with this projection onto his own body gestalt, his response to the upper object in Card 4 was 'penis'. This abnormal visualization in close SIS proximity to potentially erotic arousing female imagery reflected his heterosexual phallic dysphoria.

His high degree of ambivalence about genital sexuality was illustrated by his response to an original SIS card which clearly depicted the outline of the human body with reddish lungs-like internal organ and a sexually ambiguous pelvic area.

Clinical trials indicated that it simply had too much structure to effectively serve as a projective stimulus. Most viewers perceived it as 'the outline of a man's body showing lungs'. For historical background interest, it is noteworthy that only a small minority perceptually inhibited the somatic content and projected other than human or anatomical responses. All suffered from severe conversion pain syndromes now categorized in modern diagnostic nomenclature as somatization disorder.

This man responded as follows: 'a man … also the picture of the vagina (pointing to the pelvic region) … and a penis (pointing to the white background between the lung-like objects in the chest)'. Here, it is noteworthy that an image of the vagina first intruded into projective awareness. This response indicated that his negative feelings about a woman's oral region had been displaced downwards to the female pelvic region. It was understandable that vaginal intercourse with his wife was associated with more emotional pain than pleasure.

At last, it might be noted that in a similar fashion as his response to Card 4, visualizing a 'penis' in the white background between the lungs-like organ representations was highly abnormal. It provided additional projective evidence of phallic dysphoria.

Overall in analysing the significance of the above outlined sexually ambivalent imagery, it was hypothesized that he may have primarily identified with his aggressive mother's female body. Thus, it appeared that the characteristics projected onto his own body gestalt during psychosexual development may have been unduly bisexual.

### Treatment Plan

These projective data were helpful in developing a comprehensive multidimensional treatment plan. This necessarily included antidepressant medication, cognitive psychotherapy, couple psychotherapy and sexual counselling. The additional dimension to be presently illustrated was behaviour therapy.

To set the stage for the latter, he received four separate training sessions in Jacobson relaxation. When he demonstrated relative competence with this procedure, desensitization sessions were scheduled. In the initial clinical trial, after inducing Jacobson relaxation, the SIS cards were exposed to him by presenting them in an ascending order of threat. Initially, the viewing time of 5 seconds was used, followed by a relaxation period of 20 seconds.

An attempt at measuring his level of arousal was made by asking him to use a subjective scale as follows: This ranged from 0 representing the psyche condition of feeling free of emotional discomfort to 100—the greatest dysphoria ever remembered. In the initial phase, he rated his feelings as 0. In viewing the 12-card series, his arousal level gradually rose to an estimated rating of 20–25 seconds. However, with the last one (Card 2), his rating jumped to 50.

After a five-minute relaxation period, the procedure was repeated but in a modified fashion by increasing both the exposure time and the relaxation period to 30 seconds. Also, he was given the opportunity of rejecting any card before 30 seconds, if the viewing proved too upsetting. This time his arousal level only reached 20. However, to accomplish this, he rejected Cards 2 and 5, after only brief exposure.

One week later, the above procedure was repeated with a further modification. On this occasion, he was instructed to view each SIS inkblot but only to the degree of sensing some minor degree of arousal. Under these desensitization conditions, he rated all cards as 0 with the exceptions of Card 5 (15–25), Card 4 (10–15) and Card 2 (0–10).

The next week, the procedure was repeated for a final desensitization treatment session. By this time, he was relatively comfortable in viewing all cards.

## Discussion

Clinically, this behavioural therapy was associated with reduction in his anatomical image dysphoria. Moreover, there was a temporal correlation with improvement in his psychological and sexual intimacy with his wife. Consequently, it appeared that he had benefited from this SIS-assisted behavioural therapy. Of course, in such a multidimensional complex treatment programme, it is virtually impossible to sort out efficacy for one modality. Clearly, more sophisticated research designs are required to follow the encouraging clinical leads evolving such pilot studies.

In contemplating future investigations, it might be helpful to conceptualize further about the possible mental mechanisms underlying body phobia disorder. During critical periods of psychosexual development, it appears that childhood exposure to stressful situations can distort anatomical imagery. In this condition, the threat primarily involves exposure to sensations and emotionally charged images of the body, rather than external physical objects. The resultant concomitant affect can strongly shape perception and cognition, as well as ulti-mately behaviour. Depending upon the individual's genetic diathesis, this sequence can play a major underlying psychophysiologic role in symptom formation including sexuality.

An example of this complex process was presented. The subject had a childhood history involving a relatively weak father figure, exposure to a verbally abusive mother and resultant distortions in body imagery. Eventually in his marriage, these played an underlying role in his mul-tiple communication and sexual problems. The presenting problem as labelled by his family physician was 'major depression'—a medically valid symptom, complex and socially acceptable label for seeking therapy. However, it turned out to be much more complex. Apart from being clinically depressed, based on the original SIS assessment, it appeared that problems related to sexuality needed to be resolved.

Consistent with such complexity, evaluators of SIS anatomical responses are advised to keep in mind the following principle. Distorted body image affects and its cognitive misinterpretation, not only can relate to the suffering person's own body gestalt but also that of psy-chologically significant others. This is essentially a 'dehumanizing' conceptual model. During extreme psychological stress in childhood, anxiety reducing dissociative defences become activated. In such situ-ation, the child may sense leaving the body only to view it from an imaginary safer distance. Frequently, victims may perceive their per-petrator's body in a concrete and primitive manner. Such distortions as illustrated in the above case study can underlay a variety of clinical problems. One involves the victim's tendency to sexually identify with the perpetrator's body gestalt.

Historically, conceptualizing about such cases provided my original insights into the importance determining the original somatic focus of projected anatomical responses. These not only can reflect altered awareness levels for the assessed individual's own body but also that of other psychologically significant people. Frequently, the detailed enquiry will throw light on the image's original reference. Sometimes for clarification purposes, other techniques should be employed to clarify the root source. With children, sand tray with figurines and art therapy involving human figure drawings can assist in the interpreta-tive process. Other approaches include verbal association tests with key anatomical words, analysing the body symbolism in dream imagery, and, as an additional example, measuring organ-specific physiologic activity as it relates to sensory feedback awareness.

Finally, from the historical standpoint, it is noteworthy that this early work also established the importance of establishing an operational plan utilizing projective data reflecting the hierarchy of organ dysphoria. This facilitates the introduction of a SIS behavioural therapy programme that may provide additional therapeutic potency.

## Case 11: Assessing Suicidal/Homicidal Impulses with the SIS

I have an obsession with death... Death is very intriguing... It's one of the only great mysteries of man that has never been solved... And it's just my mind travels on a parallel... Well it really doesn't travel on a parallel... But it's like my mind wants to question death... It's like... it's almost like it wants to experience it but yet it doesn't. —JF

After reading about the above quotation describing a suicidal youth's 'obsession' with death, are you beginning to feel a little anxious? As a thinking member of the Homo sapiens species, with a time-limited body, your emotional discomfort is understandable. It means that your optic nerves are transmitting neural impulses containing language symbols to your brain's visual areas. This is presently enabling your central nervous system to interact with your various memory pathways. Remarkably enough, in some mysterious body–mind–spirit realm, you may begin to 'think'. The subject involves SIS material that even experienced mental health professionals may find anxiety provoking. After all, epidemiologic studies have always indicated that our profession has high rates of suicide.

Having the ability and opportunity to think about the subject of death is both good news and bad news for you! The former is that you are in the minority of humans with enough neural endowment and education to cognitively process complex symbolic information. The latter is that you will be visually exposed to potentially emotionally upsetting SIS imagery projected by psychiatrically hospitalized suicidal/homicidal Alaskan native males.

While this should stimulate the cognitive centres in your brain, it can arouse secondary empathetic pain in your heart. Moreover, as you read this article, it may also stimulate you to think about your own mortality. In 1973, an anthropological professor of mine, Ernest Becker, wrote a Pulitzer Prize winning book titled *The Denial of Death*. His thesis was that apart from employing reassuring religious doctrine, most individuals use the mental mechanism of denial in philosophically

contemplating their body's fate by contrast, like the above cited suicidal youth, many mentally disturbed Alaskan natives are preoccupied
with their death.

As a clinically relevant background, perhaps it might prove of interest to briefly review the special historical, cultural and socio-economic
background features of Alaska. It was purchased from Russia in 1857
for approximately seven million dollars. At the time, most Americans
considered this an outlandish price in labelling it as 'Seward's Folly'. It
has turned out to be just the opposite since the state is a major supplier
of natural resources.

Unfortunately, these developments have not always benefited
Alaskan natives. Starting with the Russian occupation, foreigners began
imposing their values and undermining those of the Alaskan natives.
For example, the newly acquired territory was divided up by the various
Christian churches. The authoritarian missionaries, priests and educa-
tors then became the powerful figures in the remote communities.
They taught the children that their native religion was based upon
superstition and 'the work of the devil!'

As the acculturation experience shattered existing related support
systems and the integrity of families, a series of predictable public
health problems resulted. In schools, children were informed by the
outsiders that their difficulties were due to their inferior culture.
Moreover, they were punished for speaking in their native language.
Eventually, the acculturation stress caused them to self-medicate
with alcohol. In some northern villages, upwards of 60 per cent of
infants born show evidence of a fetal's alcohol-induced organic brain
impairment. Adolescent Alaskan native males have the highest rate
of suicide in USA, a country where someone commits suicides every
20 minutes. Four cases with SIS analysis are presented ahead (Cassell
2005).

### Case Studies of Suicide Survivors

### Case I

The first is a 31-year-old Alaskan native who entered marital counselling with his wife. He had been intermittently suicidal since childhood.
When he completed the SIS-II Booklet, a flood of emotionally painful
traumatic memories surfaced.

In rating the SIS responses for anxiety/threat, he selected A4 as the
most threatening. Here, he split the gestalt of the figure. He projected

a childhood memory on the left portion as himself. On the right, he visualized an image of his 'monster dad'.

In the detailed enquiry with great anguish, he indicated that the latter reminded him of his abusive 'birth dad'. He gave the following associations: 'he always beat me up... I was so small, and he was so huge... I really felt inferior!' At the age of seven, he was placed in a foster home to protect him from his biological parents. During this period, he had PTSD dreams reliving the earlier series of traumas. To him, the SIS-stimulated image of the 'monster dad' recalled his childhood PTSD dream symbols.

He selected SIS B15 as the second most upsetting one. He imagined this to represent 'a window that cuts my arm!' This brought memories back of an earlier suicide attempt. Because of extensive blood loss, he had almost succeeded. A large scar on his right wrist was consistent with his story. At that time, he was under the influence of alcohol. He had gone into a jealous rage, triggered by learning that his wife had an affair with a Caucasian oilfield worker. She viewed him with a better economic future and more socially powerful, hence more sexually arousing.

The third most troublesome SIS inkblot was B22. He indicated that this reminded him of 'evil spirits!' It recalled 'the enemy trying to put dirty thoughts into his head at night' and 'dirty pornographic movies that I replay in my mind'. He indicated that when he had trouble finding meaningful employment as a teenager, he got money as a male prostitute from paedophiliac Alaskan tourists.

Next, his responses to the three SIS inkblots that evoked positive feeling will be reviewed. At the top of the list was A6 which he saw as 'a kind boy'. He gave associations which reflected childhood wish fulfilment fantasies and day dreams of having a close relationship with his father. However, in the interview, he quickly reverted to negative memories about his father: 'he never provided me a father image... Sometimes I get sad and cry thinking about him, but I cannot raise him from the dead.'

His next favourite was A10. This brought back fond memories of 'looking through the rear window of my 1976 Chevy Monza'. Initially, his emotions were positive when recalling fun times with the car. However, they soon became negative as he remembered eventually losing the vehicle when he could no longer compete with younger native male prostitutes.

His third favourite SIS-stimulated projective scene was evoked with A9. He imagined it to represent himself happily dancing with his wife.

Certain other responses to the SIS-II booklet provide a projective window for revealing the past mental interplay between his intense suicidal and homicidal impulses:

**A3:** 'The inner man of me.'

**A8:** 'Me standing inside my own eyeball looking over my nose towards my wife.' (This symbolized his jealousy and paranoia-like suspicions.)

**A13:** 'Someone drowning.' (This symbolized him a few years back in an unsuccessful suicide attempt.)

**A15:** 'My kneecap dislocated.' (He had sustained multiple severe injuries from placing himself at high risk self-injurious behaviours.)

**A17:** 'A mad wet cat coming inside out of the rain.' (Here, he projected his inner murderous impulses onto the figure of a cat.)

**A18:** 'My broken heart when my wife forced me to leave.'

**A19:** 'When I am drunk looking through a wine glass and everything is fuzzy.'

**B8:** 'Me looking through a telescope or a gun at the man walking towards my wife.' (Instead of cutting on himself, he almost shot the man!)

**B18:** 'An oriental dagger with blood on it.'

## Case II

The second case involves a seventeen-year-old adolescent (JF) who reported being obsessed with death. He was admitted to a psychiatric hospital because of severe suicidal ideation. Like the older native man discussed above, he too had a history of severe abuse as a child.

In viewing the SIS-II Video, he rated A30 as the most upsetting inkblot. It reminded him of the past: 'my mother when she is pissed at someone'. She suffered from severe mood swings and rage reactions.

The next most threatening was A31. This stimulated memories of stressful scenes of his parents fighting. The third most disturbing imagery was evoked by A13. Here, he saw 'a hand and arm area with a cut on it'. He said that the scene was 'very scary!'. It triggered memories of few years back when he had first tried to kill himself.

His three favourite SIS inkblots were as follows:

**B28:** 'A mother hugging her child.' It reminded him of the few times that his mother was able to act in a loving fashion.

**B31:** 'A happy family.'

**A6:** 'Me at the age of eight.' Here, he envisioned the background figure as 'a teddy bear'. However, his positive emotions quickly left. He soon was speaking about memories of when his mother was highly abusive.

Certain of the other, SIS inkblots evoked material relative to his suicidal history. These were as follows:

**A2:** 'Blood on the floor when I was in the third grade.' In describing this scene, he became very emotionally upset:

'My father called me at night and told me to immediately run and get the police. When I was running downstairs to go outside, I looked and saw my mother with a knife cutting deep wounds into her wrist. Blood was squirting out onto her arms and legs. There was a puddle on the floor. It was very, very frightening.'

Following this, he had recurrent anxiety-laden PTSD dreams reflecting in content and affecting his SIS-triggered imagery.

**A4:** 'A leech crawling over a puddle of blood.'

**A5:** 'My mother when I was six shouting at me.'

**A7:** 'A neon sign for a night club.' Here, he failed to visualize a woman's gestalt because of his PTSD-induced aversion to female body imagery.

**A10:** 'An evil person!' His self-concept of irrationally blaming himself as a child for his mother's mood disorder.

**A16:** 'A crying person.' This depicted him at the age of eight, sad, alone and crying by himself at night.

**A17:** 'A couple of dragons devouring a heart!' A horrible scene consistent with the symbols in his PTSD dreams.

**A20:** 'An upside-down person with huge feet.' Like the older native man, he too had frequently engaged in high-risk suicidal behaviour.

Shortly before hospitalization, driving while intoxicated at a high speed, he had almost been killed.

**A25:** 'A valley and an ugly vagina!'

**A28:** 'A bloody arm... like mine was at the age of 14!'

**B1:** 'All consuming flames that consume everything.' This reminded him how once he had almost set his bedroom on fire.

**B2:** 'A headless person that has been ripped apart!' This reminded him of his violent video and computer games.

**B15:** 'A shattered window.' This recalled the shattered window of the truck that he recently had rolled.

**B19:** 'A heart eating sea urchins.'

**B21:** 'An exploding battery.'

**B22:** 'A person's spirit leaving his body.' This suggested his suicidal overdose of pills that had precipitated his recent hospitalization. He exclaimed 'I didn't want to feel more pain!'

### Case III

The third case involved a youth who had been hospitalized because of serious suicidal ideation. He had a long history of psychological and physical abuse by his stepfather. He suffered from related PTSD nightmares and rage reactions.

While viewing the SIS-II Video, he selected A25 as the most threatening inkblot. Here, he conjured up an image of 'a large predator fish or animal which had the capacity to hurt you!' It recalled traumatic memories of his abusive stepfather.

The second most threatening SIS inkblot was A18. This was simply too anxiety provoking for the traumatic memory to fully register in conscious awareness. The best he could do was report, 'it is the shape that bothers me'. He was clearly quite disturbed in seeing it again in the detailed enquiry.

The third most threatening SIS inkblot was B3. He said that this resembled 'a mask!'. His associations revealed a degree of paranoid ideation: 'I do not like faceless people and not being able to see their eyes!'

Next attention will be directed to certain other responses which appeared to have clinical significance:

**A3:** 'A bomb blowing up... maybe a pipe bomb.' When asked to expand on this, he indicated that it reminded him of 'a terrorist attack'. He appeared to be fascinated by news accounts of terrorism. He claimed that he had just read the biography of the mail bomber Ted Kozinski. He reported that frequently when he felt angry, that he fantasied about blowing up people. He quickly added 'I would never do it!'. His response revealed the close approximation in his mind between suicidal and homicidal impulses. Troubled and angry young people like him could be vulnerable to terrorist propaganda. If they were living in certain war-torn cultures, possibly they could easily be manipulated into becoming 'suicidal bombers'.

**A31:** He saw 'two people yelling at each other with a red haze in the head area'. Here, it is significant that he focused on the 'red'. This was consistent with the rage in his parent's long-term marital battles. When their anger was directed to him, he would feel alternatively fear, rage and then sadness.

**B7:** He saw 'A gas mask'. In speaking about this, he revealed a series of fantasies about being a warrior, soldier, etc., and participating in war. These thoughts were constantly activated when he played electronic war games which can inflame aggressive impulses (Cassell and Dubey 1998).

**B19:** It was 'a broken heart trying to catch the little hearts in tentacles.' Here the symbolism reflects a mixture between his sad suicidal feelings and his violent homicidal aggressive ones. In speaking about this impulse battle, he emphasized that he no longer could cry. The last time that he had this healthy release for his pent-up frustrations was at the age of seven after his stepfather had abused him. Since this traumatic event, he had dissociated himself from his PTSD pain. While this defence mechanism protected him from inner cry, over time it provided the fuel for his destructive fantasy life.

**B27:** It seemed to represent 'twins in their mother's womb—one bad and one good'. Here the symbolism depicted the two aspects of his evolving adolescent personality. Clearly the 'bad' reflected his destructive side.

## Case IV

The last illustrative case involved a man who had several violent features in common with the first case. He had been episodically suicidal and had survived two serious overdoses. He also had intermittent jealous rage reactions related to his wife's infidelity and murderous impulses to kill her.

Certain SIS II Booklet responses captured his suicidal/homicidal ideation:

**A4:** 'A mad cat!' This represented the projection of his own rage onto the image of a cat. Prior to hospitalization, when raging about his wife's unfaithfulness he had killed cats.

**A7:** 'A mad female teacher with an apple!' He claimed that his wife had anger problems and was threatening him.

**A27:** 'A woman's breast being cut by glass!' Here again the symbolism depicts the murderous impulses that he had chosen to deny, when questioned as part of a standard mental status examination.

Unfortunately, after discharge he failed to have follow-up treatment. Eventually he killed her. Three years later when incarcerated for murder, reflecting his anger and regret for having acted on his unreported homicidal impulses, he selected the scene evoked by B15 as the one that bothered him the most. It may be recalled that this stimulus array was designed to evoke violent fantasies. In the retest situation, he imagined this to represent 'knives with broken glass!'

In recent years, American mental health practitioners have seen more violent behaviour. At times, there appears to be almost an infectious and theatrical quality with violence. This applies to both suicidal and homicidal violent behaviours. The former has been studied under the name 'suicide contagion' (Davidson and Gould 1989; Gould and Davidson 1988). This refers to the process by which exposure to the suicide or suicidal behaviour of one or more person influences other to attempt or commit suicide. The effect appears to be strongest in adolescents (Gould et al. 1990; Phillips and Carstenson 1988).

An example of the theatrical quality of violence occurred in one northern village recently when an adolescent Alaskan Native youth set the stage for murdering the school principal. He created an audience by boasting in advance to his peers. He informed them exactly where, when and how he was going to commit the murder. On the specified day, he had an appreciative audience of youths when he shot the victim.

As is frequently the case in the United States of America, his photograph and life story were widely circulated in the media. Since murderers have the highest status in any criminal system, this immediately made him a hero with his peers. No doubt, the publicity had some economic value to the owners of the various media enterprises, though unfortunately, it had the potential for educating others concerning the status value of 'copy cat murder'!

It is amazing how some adolescents can impulsively kill, without an ounce of empathy for their victim. Several years ago, I evaluated such a cold-blooded youth. The crime scene involved him being in the back seat of a taxi with his peers. When the driver wanted to get paid a few dollars for the ride, he put a gun to the back of his head. Reportedly, the terrified victim begged for his life pleading: 'Don't shoot! I'm a married man with a wife and children!' The youth shot him! During psychiatric examination he denied remorse.

Sometimes adolescents murder and then kill themselves. American-Indian adolescents who live on reservations have comparably high rates of violence than their Alaskan counterparts. Recently, such a Minnesota youth went on a school shooting spree. This mass murderer watched a popular movie which provided the format for the 'copy cat' violence. While the hero in this film served as a role model, this also points up to the infectious quality of aggression.

The teenager had communicated significant suicidal/homicidal ideation to certain interested peers through the Internet e-mail. Youths who are experiencing suicidal/homicidal impulses now can share and mutually fuel their violent fantasies through the Internet blog groups as well. The technology has also given rise to a new form of abuse referred to as cyberbullying. Adolescents are particularly vulnerable to this and there are now Web resources for those victimized (e.g., www.bullying.org and www.netbullies.com).

American surveys reveal that a high number of young people report having violent fantasies. Yet, most mass murders are not committed by adolescents of minority groups. If there is a common denominator in epidemiologic terms, they are much more likely to be perpetrated in society by humans with male gonads.

Before digressing much further, a brief review historically will be presented concerning how the SIS conceptually evolved as a PT for assessing violent impulses. The background is presented in Cassell's book *Body Symbolism* (Cassell 1980). The original research began in 1959 with a clinical investigation of the body image problems in women with excessive facial hair (hirsutism). It became apparent that there was a need for alternative assessment techniques, apart from standard interviews. PTs appeared to have promised for investigating the subjective manner, whereby somatic symptoms are experienced in various medical disorders.

This led Cassell to work with Seymour Fisher, who in association with Sidney Cleveland had originally developed two Rorschach measures of body awareness: The Barrier and Penetration Scores (Fisher and Cleveland 1958). In examining Rorschach responses, the possibility presented itself that certain anatomical responses might reflect somatic symptom-related health concerns. As an outgrowth of this, Cassell created the Body Interior Awareness Index (Cassell 1964) and employed this concept in subsequent studies (Cassell 1965, 1969, 1971, 1972).

During this early period of introduction, Cassell observed that many students at Syracuse University projected broken, mutilated and violated anatomical responses. In 1962, he began consulting in the student health infirmary at the university. Consequently, he became familiar with their many stressors, including the ongoing Vietnam conflict. In addition, he had the opportunity to work with George Stern, a social psychologist, in conducting health surveys revealing high rates of psychological morbidity. He realized that it was a mistake to solely relate their pathological anatomical responses to body image disturbances and medical symptoms. It seemed more reasonable to conceptualize certain disturbed Rorschach somatic imagery, as reflecting various forms of mental suffering, including unreported suicidal/homicidal fantasies (Cassell 1977, 1979).

This conceptual model played an important role in the subsequent design of SIS stimuli. For SIS-I, the embedded inkblot material in Card XVIII and XX incorporates structure capable of stimulating the projective release of violent imagery from the viewer's brain memory systems. For SIS-II, the same principle provided the impetus for designing images B15, B21 and B22. Work to date has demonstrated how this added structure has increased the projective pulling power of the SIS. However, they have added more occupational hazard by exposing the examiner to a higher degree of secondary empathetic trauma.

The four case histories in the present study serve to illustrate how the SIS can provide important information regarding violent fantasies (Cassell and Dubey 1998; Cassell et al. 2002). The direct and symbolic imagery projected can provide new insights enriching those obtained with standard clinical interviews. Members of this society are challenged to pursue this promising line of scientific investigation. We also must learn how to more effectively incorporate its spiritual applications into clinical practice (Cassell et al. 1997, 2001). Perhaps, we may improve in therapeutically communicating with suffering individuals like JF.

Clearly his 'obsession' goes far beyond reality-based cognitive psychotherapy and atheistic scientific interpretation. It demands a religious response consistent with his native culture and SIS body–mind–spirit theory. This could provide the support of an empathetic bridge reaching beyond biological death into the realm of eternal spirituality.

## Case 12: Infectious Suicidal Imagery in Combat PTSD

The SIS-II Video/DVD version may be used as a hypnotic-based memory stimulating interview aid for treating PTSD. This psychotherapeutic application differs from standardized psychodiagnostic testing, where traditionally the interviewer primarily acts like a 'blank screen' when enquiring about the psychometric properties of elicited responses introduced during inkblot viewing. In the much more active SIS approach, for aiding memory recall during the detailed enquiry, the psychotherapist may introduce outside relative clinical subjects from historical sources beyond the inkblots themselves. The result is an optimum therapeutic fusion of input from the pulling power of PT and that of clinical interviews. This multidimensional technique will be illustrated in reviewing a transcribed television teaching recording using the SIS-II Video. The case involves an American Vietnam veteran suffering from long-standing PTSD. Like many such military veterans, he had never sought treatment for his own mental symptoms. He had initiated treatment only after the recommendation of his stepson's family therapist. The stepson had been deeply depressed and made a serious suicide attempt mimicking his biological father, who suffered from untreated combat PTSD, and ultimately committed suicide. The youth had never been able to bond emotionally to his PTSD disturbed stepfather, who had superimposed onto him, a guilt-ridden mental picture of a boy he had blown apart in combat.

*Dr B:*    I know you have been working in therapy and that's good. If at this time, we could have you look at some images on the SIS that you have responded, and any emotions you would have, and anything that might remind you of even the real world or your past dreams or fantasies, okay?

*J:*    Okay.

*Dr B:*    At this point we'll look at Image A1.

*J:*    It looks like an x-ray of someone's insides.

*Dr B:*    Any special emotions or anything it recalls? (The interviewer attempts to elicit the cognitive symbolic content and affect linkage of the anatomical response. This hidden material surfaces in projective awareness later in the interview with A10.)

*J:*    No, not really. (Here, the symbolic significance and affect linkage is either simply denied or repressed. Consequently, the interviewer elected to actively bring into the SIS detailed enquiry additional clinical information.)

*Dr B:*    Did you see many people mutilated and cut up and all that stuff? (The family psychotherapist had previously indicated that he still had PTSD dreams related to combat experienced many years back in Vietnam.)

*J:*    Yes, sir, I did.

*Dr B:*    How'd you feel about that?

*J:*    Sick. You... You want to do something, but there's nothing you can do because it's... it's already... (combat situations often place the victim in life situations with little or no control on the traumatic outcome of stressful events.)

*Dr B:*    Did you have any of that sick feeling while looking at Image A1? (The SIS interviewer asks a 'leading question' in order to bring into focus the affect linkage of his anatomical response, 'someone's insides'.

*J:*    Some, yeah. (His affirmative answer suggests that previously there was dysphoria with the anatomical imagery but denied. This is consistent with the culturally based historical fallacy that soldiers are expected to 'bite on the bullet' and not experience either psyche or somatic pain. Of course, they do, making them vulnerable to mind anaesthetizing drugs and alcohol.)

*Dr B:*    Okay. Maybe we'll go to Image A2. What do you see there?

*J:*    It looks like somebody's trying to hold on to something.

*Dr B:*    And how do you feel while looking at that?

*J:*    It's...

*Dr B:*    Brings anything to your mind or anything or?

*J:*    It looked like maybe a child is trying to hold on to something.

*Dr B:* Yeah. Okay. A child who is trying to hold on to something. (In this demonstration recording, the SIS-II Video was running at its usual rate. He had paused long before the image of the 'child' surfaced. Later responses clarify the symbolism.)

*Dr B:* How about this one, A3?

*J:* A lot of different colours... Nothing.

*Dr B:* Any feelings at all?

*J:* No. (His inability to conjure up a response related to the affect valence of the SIS stimulus bright colour and his mental defences inhibiting emotional expression. This is consistent with the 'numbing' experienced by victims following severe stressful events.)

*Dr B:* Where could that child be in Image A2 that was trying to hold on to something?

*J:* Oh, maybe a child in the womb.

*Dr B:* A child back in the womb?

*J:* Uh-hum. (In the rapid-fire context of the recording studio, this response totally surprised and puzzled the interviewer. In later considering its symbolic significance after the interview, it seemed more likely theoretically, to have related to the dramatic mental age regression experienced transiently during the activation of stressful memories. There are many examples consistent with this theory: sometimes a soldier wounded and dying on the battlefield will cry out in an infantile voice for his mother or an adult person recalling early life traumatic events or may suddenly whisper inaudibly in a child-like voice.)

*Dr B:* The boy that you shot was 10 years old, any resemblances to him at all? (Here again, the interviewer introduces outside clinical information in actively pursuing PTSD memories. However, in this instance it likely was an erroneous question reflecting more what the interviewer mistakenly interpreted to be the PTSD memory source.)

*J:* There possibly could be, but it's been 25 years... (since the Vietnam conflict).

*Dr B:* Right. Okay. How about image A4?

*J:* It looks like possibly the face of a person, abstract.

*Dr B:* Just relax and let your mind free itself and feel comfortable as much as you can. (Hypnotic suggestions to reduce test anxiety are repeated by the interviewer to heighten the trance-like state of SIS altered projective awareness). How about this one?

*J:* That reminds me of T. (His severely depressed stepson who recently had made an almost lethal aborted suicide attempt.)

Dr B:   Makes you feel good then?

J:      Yeah.

Dr B:   Yeah, T has a capacity for laughter and joy now that he's in therapy, right? I like that unruly wild hair. (The interviewer actively brought forth his stepson's appearance to make the recollection of positive feelings more vivid. This served the function of reducing test anxiety.)

J:      Yeah. You can't... miss him in a crowd, that's for sure.

Dr B:   Yeah. Thank goodness he's getting some help. How about Image A6?

J:      The teddy bear on the corner, security. A friend. The abstract on the side, I'm... I'm not too sure.

Dr B:   That's fine. It must have been very upsetting for you when T was suicidal? (The time dimensions of the interview flip rapidly, moving from the distant past to the recent stressful situation of his stepson's suicidal behaviour.)

J:      Yes, it was. I'm just glad that there were people like you and Dr F (family psychotherapist) who were there to piece him back together. That looks like somebody. It's abstract of somebody dancing or...

Dr B:   The sex of the person?

J:      Female.

Dr B:   How concerned were you about T's suicidal ideation?

J:      Real concerned!

Dr B:   Yeah. (The interviewer empathetically recognizes the intense level of the more immediate stress involving his stepson.)

J:      Not only as his stepfather but as... as a friend of... of T. (Here, he first reveals his confused perception of a dual role—that of stepfather and as well as friend of his stepson) it you know, it – you really don't know when something like that happens where to turn or what to do. You want to – your – your instinct is to – to grab hold of the child and tell him everything's okay.

Dr B:   How about A9?

J:      It looks like oriental writing.

Dr B:   A10?

J:      That looks like somebody's face its parts aren't there.

Dr B:   What happened to it?

J:      It looks like pieces of it have been blown away or removed. (Here, long-standing PTSD memories are pulled into immediate dysphoric projective SIS consciousness by A10).

Dr B:   Did you ever see that in Vietnam?

J:      Yeah.

| | |
|---|---|
| *Dr B:* | Tell us about it. |
| *J:* | I would see bodies floating down a river—bloated, disfigured. You come up alongside of it to see if it had dog tags. If it didn't have dog tags, you shot it and let it sink. If it had dog tags, you retrieved the body. |
| *Dr B:* | What would the faces look like? |
| *J:* | Distorted, bloated, some of them were there; some of them weren't... pieces of their bodies missing. |
| *Dr B:* | Did you ever see images like that in your dreams? (The interview quickly moved from the real-world combat scenes to that of sleep disrupting PTSD dreams still tormenting the veteran.) |
| *J:* | Yeah, I did. The rivers, the bodies floating in the rivers. |
| *Dr B:* | Could you say something about that? |
| *J:* | It... it wasn't so much the... the body in the river. It was the smell. |
| *Dr B:* | What was the smell like? (It is very important therapeutically to include a discussion of olfactory sensations, which frequently link emotions to PTSD imagery and dysphoric affect.) |
| *J:* | Decayed flesh. Death! |
| *Dr B:* | And what effect would that have on you, the smell? |
| *J:* | Well, the first couple of times it happened, I went to the other side of the vessel and put my stomach in the river. |
| *Dr B:* | You were nauseated? |
| *J:* | Yes, sir. But then after a while it... it, I guess it calloused a person. |
| *Dr B:* | You became numb? (The interviewer brings up again his mention of a classic mental symptom of PTSD.) |
| *J:* | You got numb to the fact. |
| *Dr B:* | Yeah. |
| *J:* | And that happened about 90 days after you were there. |
| *Dr B:* | Yeah. (This emotional blunting normally takes time to set in, depending upon the subject's genetic vulnerability, past life experiences and the intensity of the stressors.) |
| *J:* | You just went numb. The only thing you were worried about was your own survival. |
| *Dr B:* | Did you ever get over that numbness? (The psychological defences blocking out the stressful memories through processes of neural inhibition, also inhibited the psychobiological processes underlying the PTSD imagery affect linkage.) |
| *J:* | No. |
| *Dr B:* | In what ways do you still carry that with you? |
| *J:* | I find myself – I find it's hard for me to get close to people. Relationships. I've had three different relationships or two |

different relationships that have gone completely to pieces. And I feel that a lot of that was of my close off or my numbness effect or the ... (It is common for such veterans to have problems with marriage. Not only did his untreated PTSD numbing block emotional intimacy with women, it also impaired his capacity for a close relationship with his stepson.)

Dr B: One of the problems we have in life J when we turn off, as you must do (in combat) are feelings and seeing something horrible then we turn off other feelings, love and intimacy and so we have some more work to do in your therapy. (The interviewer explains the nature of his symptom and emphasizes the positive value of treatment. It may be recalled, that despite the severity of his PTSD, that he had sought therapy only because of his stepson's needs.) How about Image A11?

J: It's a good abstract drawing of something, but I'm not exactly sure what. A nostril, maybe.

Dr B: The smell is strong at times? (The interviewer points out the association between his SIS heightened nasal awareness and the olfactory sensations in his PTSD dreams.)

J: The stra ... yes, the smell of death and ... and decay. The people in Vietnam were not exactly what the American people would classify as clean. They were by no means dirty, but their facilities, their living conditions weren't what we know of them in the USA. Just the ... I don't know, the sewage systems, their ... their way of throwing things away or their ... their ... their garbage or their waste, it's just wherever it happened to fall. And, of course, in a hot, humid climate that all...

Dr B: Be with you 24 hours a day...

J: Was with you 24 hours a day basically.

Dr B: Yeah. And would have a demoralizing effect on you I would think. What about this Image A12?

J: I don't see anything there.

Dr B: Do smells still get to you? (Even 25 plus years later).

J: Some, yes.

Dr B: Tell us about that.

J: Smells. Rotten eggs will usually do it, they will trigger old smells or old senses.

Dr B: What old smells come back from Vietnam when you smell rotten eggs?

J: The streets. They had a delicacy that they called Nukbaum that was basically a fertilized egg and they would bury it and that was one of the smells that ... that kind of stuck with me and it ... it seemed to be in the areas of the cities or the towns. I don't know if it was so much that or if it was everything else combined, but it was not a very pleasant smell.

Dr B: Years ago, when I was in medical school, we had to do a great deal of dissecting. I remember the smell of the flesh and the formaldehyde and it's very hard to get rid of it and it impacted you. Not in any way, the way your trauma impacted you. (Sharing related personal discomfort can enhance empathetic communication in SIS viewing). How about the next image, A13?

J: It looks like a hand reaching up or out of something.

Dr B: How do you feel looking at it and what does it remind you of?

J: It reminds me of one of the hands that I had grabbed when I was pulling bodies out of the river.

Dr B: Tell us about it.

J: I was on the same patrols. You had to verify the – the body that you see floating in the river. You had to make sure if it was of an American or of a V.C. (Viet Cong). When a body is – when rigor mortis sets in, you roll the body over and the hands and everything are stiff. And that image does...

Dr B: It was ghastly at times, wasn't it? (The interviewer empathizes with his obvious dysphoria.)

J: Yes, sir, it was.

Dr B: How did you feel doing that?

J: Not good. I don't know what the feeling was like ... if you can put a name to it.

Dr B: Sometimes there aren't words for those feelings, believe me! (The interviewer comments on the lack of descriptive language to describe such emotional discomfort). Did you have anyone to share, you know, at the end of a tough day of dealing with a body like that or bodies in the river, I mean, did you...

J: There were no medical people or anything like that. The only ... you know, you didn't talk too much about it between the other groups or people or the ... your other men on the boat because they're basically in the same boat that you were. They wanted to forget about it, too.

Dr B: So the strategy psychologically was to forget about it and at night might be to use drugs or alcohol or ... (Previously, he had indicated that he had used chemical substances extensively out of desperation to induce sleep.)

J: Drugs or alcohol.

Dr B: And what would you fantasize? To get away from there what sort of fantasies you'd think...

J: I would think of home.

*Dr B:*  Yeah. Thank goodness you had fantasies then!

*J:*  Yeah.

*Dr B:*  How about A14? I'm getting sick just listening, I'll tell you, this is … this is upsetting! (As was evident from his appearance and non-verbal presentation, the activation of his nauseating memories was causing him distress. Reflecting the interviewer's empathetic feelings during the interview was supportive to him.)

*J:*  That looks like a stomach.

*Dr B:*  And how do you feel while looking at that?

*J:*  Not good!

*Dr B:*  Tell us about it.

*J:*  Well, when you cut a 10-year-old kid in two with a 12-gauge shotgun there's not much to put back together!

*Dr B:*  What images of that come back as you look at that the image?

*J:*  The kid laying there in two pieces.

*Dr B:*  His guts were exposed?

*J:*  Yes, sir.

*Dr B:*  Tell us about it.

*J:*  It's … it's not a pretty sight. It's just …

*Dr B:*  Blood was all over?

*J:*  Yeah. He came around the corner with an AK-47 in his hands and I had no other … I had no choice. And I didn't realize it was a child until I'd shot. (In this instantaneous life-threatening stress, there was not enough time for his brain to cognitively process the reality-based visual sensory input. His perceptual defences immediately and out of his volitional control super-imposed an image of an adult pointing a lethal AK-47 at him. His military-conditioned central nervous system responded in a reflex-like fashion sending rapid-fire neural impulses to his finger holding the trigger. Since then he had been plagued with guilt. He mistakenly believed that his action was preventable.)

*Dr B:*  When you realized that, what did you feel?

*J:*  I guess maybe I felt like committing suicide at that time. Maybe … maybe I was wrong in saying I've never felt like committing suicide or killing myself because I didn't … I didn't feel good about it. (Here, he recalls suicidal ideation that previously he had denied. It might be noted that he was a close military friend of his stepson's father. After his buddy committed suicide, he married his widow. He was partially linked by similar PTSD imagery including the infectious suicidal ideation.)

*Dr B:*  What did his face look like? What did his face look like?

| J: | I can't remember. |
|---|---|
| Dr B: | It's hard to remember. But the guts and ... J, what are you feeling now? 'Because I can tell you're on the verge of tears (identifying and accepting as a healthy normal grief concomitant of the SIS triggered traumatic memory). Can you share that, please, do you agree? |
| J: | I thought I had this one put away, but I guess I don't [*crying*]. |
| Dr B: | There's still a lot of pain inside, isn't there? What's it like? |
| J: | I wish that I could go back and change it. |
| Dr B: | Are you feeling sad? |
| J: | Guilty. |
| Dr B: | And guilty. What's the guilt like? |
| J: | Taking a child's life. There's... |
| Dr B: | It's hard to live with, isn't it? |
| J: | There's no reason for it. |
| Dr B: | It was a reflex and you didn't have a decision; it just happened. But over the years what ways has this guilt come back on you like now? |
| J: | Every time that I... I've a 20-year-old son. And my hardest time with him is when he was 10 (here, he relates how he also transferred a superimposition of the Vietnam boy's death scene not just on his stepson, but also his own biological son). And hoping that I could get through or get him through the ages of his being 10 and on up into... to manhood without him having to ever go through the military or to ever must put himself in that position. And I do the same thing with T (here, he reported apart from his generalized PTSD numbing of intimate interpersonal affect, the reason why he had trouble relating to T, beginning as the boy approached the 10-year age period... unresolved grief and guilt). According to the referring family psychotherapist, this distancing of his stepfather had played a major role in the stepson's depression and serious suicide attempt. The long-term multiple psychological wounds and their effects on him and his relationships were more potentially impairing and destructive than if he had has suffered severe physical injuries.) |
| Dr B: | Yes. |
| J: | I don't. I don't want to ever have any of my children either foster or adopted or my own to ever must go through this. I've told myself, I've told Betty (his wife) that if the military was to go back to a draft, they would not have any of my children. I'd say just take me. |

*Dr B:* You'd go and suffer again to save them from the pain. That's how loving you are. It's important that you forgive yourself. It's a crazy world. How did you feel about the Vietnam conflict and then as the change in its complexion and all and hear what was happening, are you getting any of the news or...?

*J:* The news ... the news we were getting in country was... was not anything like from what I understand and what I've been told by my father that, you know, at 6 o'clock, they sat down and ate dinner to war... (indiscernible) war. And the war that I was part of.

*Dr B:* It's outrageous, isn't it?

*J:* And the lying on our government's part, you know, after I got back, I didn't realize that what kind of non-support that the American people were giving to the Vietnam conflict. When I first came back, I had a friend of mine, her name was K. L., who picked me up at the airport. She worked at Berkeley College. And she picked me up during her lunch hour, so I had to go back to Berkeley College and sit and wait in her car until she got off work. Well, as I was waiting there, students on the campus spotted me in my camouflage greens as I was stretching out getting some leg exercise and just kind of stretching and whatnot on the side of her car, they called me everything from baby killer to, you name it, they called it (the verbal abuse by the students using the label of 'baby killer' added to his intense guilt). They damn nearly tipped her car over in the process of trying to get to me.

*Dr B:* You're a brave man. You just (attempting to support and restore his self-esteem enjoyed prior to Vietnam conflict).

*J:* No, I jumped in the car and I was looking for a weapon, you know...

*Dr B:* You deserved better. You didn't deserve that. You had enough guilt on your own without having that dumped on you.

*J:* This is true, but I didn't... at that time I didn't realize what was going on the American side of it.

*Dr B:* Let's go on to the next image, A15. I appreciate your sharing J. What do you see here?

*J:* I ... Reminds me of a river entrance on a map.

*Dr B:* Tell me more about it. A river entrance on a map?

*J:* Uh-hum. We lost two boats while going up. I say a display of a river, but it... The river mouth was wide, and it narrowed down into nothing. And once you get a 50-foot boat up a river to where you can touch both banks and then you've got somebody behind you and they open fire and you've got yourself a...

*Dr B:* You're trapped?

*J:* You're trapped. You can't back up because the boat behind is...

*Dr B:* Yeah.

*J:* Getting the holy hell stomped out of them so the only thing you can do is... is call in air and hope everybody comes out all right (indiscernible–simultaneous speech)....

*Dr B:* Do you remember that situation?

*J:* Oh, yes, I lost six men in that situation. (Here, he recalls a combat scene which also played an etiological role in his severe PTSD.)

*Dr B:* Tell us about it.

*J:* We ran up a... We were on normal patrol and we were supposed to... It was on night patrol and we were supposed to set up ambushes. And we saw this entrance and it was a pre-given location where we were all gone over prior to going out on patrol, that we would set up ambush on the mouth of this river, but we had to go back up in it, but nobody else had gone in there during the day to find out exactly how much room a person would have, because Charlie (nickname for Vietcong) was kind of funny. He liked to work at night and did most of his ambushing and whatnot at night. His staff, it was moving medical supplies, ammunitions along the Ho Chi Minh Trail at night. You get yourself into a situation you pulled up that river. And we pulled up and the boat behind me pulled in. They took a B-40 HEAT round in the fuel tanks and we lost that entire boat. And then we ended up in the process of the fire fight and we called in air strikes, called in six Cobras and they came in and just basically cleaned house. We got the men back out. It was, all of them that weren't there no more. And the funny thing about it is I can't remember their names or their faces. I don't know if I've mentally blocked it or what.

*Dr B:* We'll go to the next image, A17.

*J:* It looks like a chest cavity.

*Dr B:* And how do you feel while looking at that?

*J:* It's just a sick feeling.

*Dr B:* And what does it remind you of?

*J:* Just death and destruction itself.

*Dr B:* You saw too much of that. A18?

*J:* That looks like a heart of something and the drawing of a heart with something in the middle of it.

*Dr B:* Okay. How about A19?

*J:* That looks like an intestinal tract. Your lower intestines.

*Dr B:* Yeah. A20?

| | |
|---|---|
| J: | That looks like an abstract of Mickey Mouse, but... |
| Dr B: | A22? What does it recall? |
| J: | It looks like a drawing of something with a kind of a headdress on it or something to this effect. |
| Dr B: | Okay. A23? |
| J: | It looks like the spinal cord. |
| Dr B: | Did you get any injuries during the war? |
| J: | I came out of it without a scratch. |
| Dr B: | Any close calls? |
| J: | Oh, yeah. I had two boats blown out from under me in the process. |
| Dr B: | You had which? |
| J: | Two boats blown out from under me. |
| Dr B: | How did that impact you? |
| J: | I counted my lucky stars. I was stuck on the... on the beach for six days. |
| Dr B: | The guy upstairs wanted you to get through. (The interviewer spoke using spiritual symbols that this veteran had previously reported to the family psychotherapist.) |
| J: | He had something else in store for me that I am for sure. |
| Dr B: | Okay. A25? How about that one? |
| J: | That looks like a wound. |
| Dr B: | And when you look at that wound how do you feel? |
| J: | I don't know about how I feel, but all wounds come in different sizes and shapes. It looked like a knife wound. |
| Dr B: | Can you recall seeing a friend, a buddy with a knife wound and how you felt? |
| J: | I don't know if I can remember any incidents. |
| Dr B: | Aside from the young man that you killed, how about hurting others? Do you... Did that happen much, do you recall the enemy? |
| J: | Oh, yeah. |
| Dr B: | Tell us about that and how you felt about it, wounding the enemy? |
| J: | The enemy was the enemy. I mean they were it was... they would... before you went over there your... your mode of survival was anger. They pumped you up. Like when you went through survival school, they pumped you up the whole time. The only way you're going to stay alive is stay mad. |
| Dr B: | How did you keep that mad going? |
| J: | It was just a drone more than anything. When you were on patrol, you were alert. As soon as you received fire from the |

beach, it was like triggering a mechanism within inside. It was instant anger.

Dr B: And when you wounded someone how did that anger get expressed?

J: It was joy. You've taken... you've taken the enemy out. And usually they don't wound them. It was you killed them, period.

Dr B: Uh-hum. How did you feel when you killed your first man?

J: Sick, but I felt and was trained that it was something that had to be done. It was either him or yourself.

Dr B: Do you ever wish you were back there, when the fighting was going on.

J: Back in Nam?

Dr B: In a regressive mode back in your childhood, happy years or whatever.

J: Yeah, there ... there were times when ... when I wished that I could stop the clock and turn the hands back, yeah, and start again.

Dr B: A27?

J: It looks like a breast.

Dr B: What sort of emotions?

J: Tender.

Dr B: Was it hard being away from women during the Vietnam conflict and all that?

J: Women yes, whore no.

Dr B: What role did the whores play?

J: They were ... they were, you know, female companionship, but it was ... the emotion wasn't there. They were there for one thing, that was the money. There was...

Dr B: There wasn't love of war for.

J: No. It was...

Dr B: You must have missed the love part, the intimacy?

J: Yes.

Dr B: Were you lonely at times?

J: Oh, yeah.

Dr B: Tell us about that?

J: Well, you think about home. I'd think about where I would have been if... if my life would have been different, if my mother hadn't passed away, your mind does... you know, your mind wanders.

Dr B: I'm sure! Anything that gets you out of the horror of your immediate reality!

# Discussion

This educational video illustrates the use of the SIS-II Video as a psychotherapeutic aid in treating military combat induced PTSD. The SIS projective procedure serves as a modern day 'time machine' accessing traumatic memories laid down years back. Past stressful scenes were recalled for cognitive correcting and emotional reprocessing in the relative safety of the professional setting. Subsequently, the veteran's individual psychotherapist then had the opportunity to undermine erroneous cognitions sustained originally, when the victim's judgement was distorted by stress-related combat emotions. This therapeutic process can be amplified by follow-up group psychotherapy discussions. Empathetic veterans can emotionally support their buddies when sharing their corrective insights.

The video also illustrated the infectious nature of stressful PTSD death imagery, especially about suicidal ideation. Death-seeking escapist impulses infected the minds of the veteran under review, his stepson, who made a serious suicide attempt, and the boy's biological father, who after suffering from untreated PTSD, ultimately committed suicide. Not shown in the teaching tape was the extensive follow-up therapeutic work involving family psychotherapy, including this veteran's wife. After her first husband killed himself, his military Vietnam veteran buddy eventually married her. Thus, although she never had been in combat, the Vietnam War had caused her great grief.

Many such veterans and their families are still suffering from the long-term psychological injuries of warfare. Majority of them are untreated. Most are reluctant to seek help from limited treatment resources. There are realistic restrictions concerning the cost-effectiveness of such intensive care that necessarily requires many providers involving multidisciplinary therapeutic strategies.

Since the Vietnam conflict, much has been learned about the nature of PTSD from the military's traumatic experiences in Iraq and now Afghanistan. Although some recruits may be particularly susceptible, in general, the mental health of troops fluctuates with the severity and duration of exposure. For example, as the stressors in Iraq have recently fallen, the suicide rate has levelled off. Consistent with senior members of the military increased awareness, troops are being given more preventative information regarding self-destructive impulses. Also, access to video games or the Internet has been helpful, providing that these outlets do not exceed four hours daily. Moreover, troops who exercise or do other forms of physical activity have a greater resistance to stress.

The case study reveals therapeutic fusion of input from the pulling power of Somatic Inkblot Images (SIS-II Video) and clinical interviews.

## Case 13: SIS Imagery in Depression with Somatization—Therapeutic Intervention

This case illustration involves a 28-year-old engineering graduate severely depressed woman with multiple somatic symptoms. These included a sensation of heaviness in her head, various discomforts throughout her body and a year's duration of 'falling unconscious'. Psychosocial history revealed several significant stressors. The onset of her complaints occurred after her marriage, two years back, when she moved into her in-law's home. She complained that her mother-in-law was too controlling: 'Nobody can do anything without her permission. She used to shout at me for small things; she says that I am nothing except my education. She is very dominating and expects that everybody does things, the way she wants'.

Gradually, she started avoiding her abusive mother-in-law, yet she could not avoid her completely. After several episodes of verbal abuse, she began to subsequently imagine persistently hearing her critical voice and persistently feeling anxious retreating to her room. Gradually, she developed more problems. She began experiencing fainting spells and claimed that she used to be 'unconscious for long periods'. Things got even worse after she gave birth to a child, when her mother-in-law took over total care of her infant. After the first year she could assume some responsibility for the child. Yet, her confidence for providing adequate care was very low, consequently her anxiety increased, so did her fainting.

The SIS-II Booklet was administered to uncover psychopathology and as a basis for developing a language for more effective psychotherapy. The significant responses are analysed and discussed ahead:

**A1:** Looks like an elderly man without head. (This response is a symbolic projection of her weakness and lack of social power in dealing with her mother-in-law's domination.)

**A2:** 1. Puppy pushing a piggy. (Here, the 'puppy' symbolizes herself attempting to overcome and push out of the way her mother-in-law, to assume care of her own child.)

2. Two persons making whirlpool. (This symbolizes her struggle not to be pulled down in a fainting spell by her socially stronger mother-in-law.)

**A3:** Looks like a shroud, a magician trying to do some magic. (This may indicate that someone is trying to dominate her.)

**A4:** 1. Lord Ganesha. (This image of a God-like elephant headed God having a large trunk and big mouth depicts in symbolic form her domineering verbally abusive mother-in-law.)

2. Little birdie saying bye. (A symbolic portrayal of her losing attachment with her child.)

**A5:** A bat flying … Vulture flying… Heart carried by both. (This portrays the vulnerability that she feels. She has a feeling of love for her child in her heart but senses him distancing.)

**A6:** 1. A sweet teddy bear. (This reflects her positive feelings for her child that she is so desperately trying to care for.)

2. Ball hitting a wicket. (Indicates aggressive contents.)

**A7:** 1. Lady dancing. (It is a normal response indicating wishful thinking to lead a happy life.)

2. Two snakes grabbing food. (May indicate erotic conflict and aggression.)

3. Man throwing a big stone. (This suggests her feeling of being a victim. Quite possibly her husband supported his mother in her criticisms.)

**A8:** Something hanging in space is leading to darkness. (Here, the 'darkness' symbolizes her depression.)

**A9:** 1. Two persons drifting apart. (This depicts her feeling of separation, perhaps from her husband.)

2. One picture looking like a dragon. (This is a symbolic representation of her relationship with her dominating mother-in-law.)

**A10:** A picture of a lady with burnished eyes and is crying. (This is a direct projection of her 'inner cry'. This symbolism provides an important interview lead for her psychotherapist in assisting her to express dysphoria and grief.)

**A11:** 1. A crow hanging downwards. (Like in A8, this indicates her sense of isolation and depression.)

2. Liver. (As part of her withdrawal from her stressful social environment, she has focused on her own body as a psychological object. Minor body sensations are now experienced as conversion pain and weakness.)

3. Flying dragon. (This represents a symbol of her mother-in-law.)

**A12:** 1. Small baby. (Her longing for her child is reflected in this response.)

2. Jesus Christ. (Her extreme sense of suffering and betrayal maybe causing her to identify with religious symbolism of being abandoned and crucified. Alternatively, this can reflect her reaching out to God for help.)

**A13:** 1. A hand being surrounded by small insects. (This symbolizes the ever-present stinging criticisms that she is bombarded with on a daily basis.)

2. Human brain. (No doubt her social stressors are flooding her mind, making her more conscious of her thinking. This, plus her headaches, are determinant of this anatomical response.)

**A14:** Water being spilled in a pit through a pipe. (This depicts her perception that everything has gone out of her control.)

**A15:** A baby hanging and being engulfed in darkness. (Her stress has caused her to mentally regress, feel helpless and at times faint. She is engulfed in a psychological sea of dark depressive emotions. Not only does she need psychotropic medication, she also requires psychotherapy, both individual and family involvement is indicated.)

**A16:** 1. Two birds playing. (In spite of her hopelessness, she still clings to the notion that everything will work out in the future in her marriage).

2. Plant growing. (She has benefited from her initial psychotherapy and sense personal growth occurring.)

**A18:** A wolf being surrounded by two big dragons. (This response symbolizes her family situation involving the mother-in-law and one other controlling person. The family psychotherapist needs to ascertain the identity of the other 'dragon'. Perhaps her critics have depicted her as wicked wolf eating their resources.)

**A19:** My head is aching while watching this picture. (While the symbolism described above has served to defend her from facing directly her family stressors, eventually the release of the stressful underlying imagery triggered one of her main somatic symptoms.)

**A21:** A starfish ... Small baby and another baby crawling. (Taking care of her child is on her mind).

**A22:** 1. A monster with heads joined and a horn coming out of it with claws. (This again symbolizes her threatening family situation.)

2. Two baby elephants. (Again, the heightened awareness of 'baby' imagery.)

**A23:** 1. An Alligator. (A threatening image depicting her fear of being harmed and being attacked.)

2. Small birdies sitting one over the other on a pot being balanced on a stick. (Her interest in her child causes her in this response to see 'small birdies'.)

**A24:** 1. A set of babies being held by someone. (Baby imagery continues to flood projective awareness.)

2. A monster with fire in his hand towards left. (Another response like in A22.)

3. A big lizard. (Like A23)

**A25:** 1. Like a candle's flame. (This might indicate her repressed conflict in erotic area.)

2. An owl looking scary. (This indicates her feeling of insecurity and suspicion.)

3. Lizards. (Erotic connotation is projected through this response. The therapist should explore this area during therapy.)

**A26:** An elephant resting. (Normal response)

**A27:** 1. A cave. (This might indicate her conflict in erotic area.)

2. Volcano bursting. (She feels like bursting from the tremendous flood her 'inner cry' attempting to surface.)

3. A cat holding something long like a snake in its mouth. (Disguised sexual feelings.)

**A28:** A wolf standing behind a tree. This again symbolizes her threatening family situation.)

**A29:** 1. A deep groove beside a flat hilltop.

2. A crow in search of food. (This indicates her insecurity.)

**A30:** A human skull. (Normal response)

**A31:** A boy with a cap is running.

**B1:** 1. A cloud of gas looking like an octopus.

2. A man falling with high speed.

**B2:** A monster running after snatching a kid. (A direct portrayal of her mother- in-law taking her child.)

**B3:** Two persons watching horror movie in cinema hall.

**B4:** A dead female (female ghost/witch) with bloody eyes and mouth and no nose. (On the basis of this death symbolism, it is important for the clinicians providing care to check for unreported suicidal ideation.)

**B5:** A man and a woman sitting on chairs in a tent with some hanging lamps.

**B7:** 1. A leaf being eaten by small insects. (Indicates her helplessness.)

2. A flower garland. (Normal response)

**B9:** Human kidney turned upside down with bladder upwards. (Normal response)

**B10:** A kid hiding from a dragon between two big wild leaves.

**B11:** 1. Two men with big nose and wounded forehead. (This depicts in symbolic form conflict at home, possibly between male figures over the child's care. The wound may again relate to her headache, now activated by the stress of the test procedure.)

2. A hat. (Normal response)

**B12:** 1. A cruel magician with a big nose ring.

2. Dragon holding a kid's head. (By now the reader can interpret this symbolic material consistent with the above formulation.)

**B13:** 1. A giant robot. (This may indicate authoritarian figure with aggressive contents.)

2. *Hawan kund.* (This may depict her feeling of being burned or sacrificed by the family.)

3. Lord Ganesha. (This may indicate her spiritual strength while feeling helpless.)

**B15:** 1. Fire crackers. (This may indicate her aggression and hostility.)

2. Many grasshoppers and spade-like knives attacking someone and the person trying to protect himself with his rod. (At this point in the protocol, hopefully the reader has learned to interpret the reoccurring symbols depicting her stressors.)

**B17:** A burning heart and flames coming out of it. (The symbol of a 'burning heart' may be translated by her psychotherapist during therapy to more effectively release her 'inner cry' than traditional language for suffering).

**B18:** A big anaconda-like snake in sea trying to pass through a groove. (This may indicate her insecurity.)

**B19:** 1. Sun being broken into pieces. (This indicates her depressive contents.)

2. Insects trying to enter moon. (The insects may connote her mother-in-law who is intruding in her life.)

**B20:** Human brain, small insects eating it. (Here, the 'insects' symbolize her threatening thoughts and upsetting emotions impinging upon her consciousness.)

**B21:** A leaf. (Normal response)

**B22:** 1. A man sleeping and lost in his dreams. (This may indicate her wishful thinking to have good time.)

2. A man drowning in water but protected by a shield. (Prior to initiating treatment, she had a depressive sense of hopelessness. However, now she is hopeful about the future, now protected by the 'shield' of her psychotherapist.)

**B23:** A big spider falling from the wall with a broken stick in its two legs. (Another threatening symbol. She senses a feeling of having a mental 'breakdown'.)

**B24:** 1. Aladdin's lamps in water. (This may indicate her wishful thinking that some spiritual power may help her in improving her present condition.)

2. A saint standing on a flying carpet. (This indicates her feeling to flee from the present environment.)

**B25:** 1. Future being seen in a magic bowl. (Feeling of insecurity and depressive contents.)

2. Fire burning in a cave. (This might indicate her repressed conflict in erotic area.)

**B26:** Leopard and a ghost. (This may indicate her insecurity and fear of being tortured by her mother-in-law.)

**B27:** A newly born child and another foetus. (Normal response)

**B28:** An old lady thinking and looking scary. (Here, the symbolism again refers to her dominating mother-in-law.)

**B29:** A man running towards light. (In spite of all her stressors, at a deeper level of awareness now that she has initiated treatment, she has hope—symbolized by moving towards 'light'.)

**B30:** 1. Right and left ear closed in a glass bowl. (Normal response)

2. A man coming out of right ear. (While she has no overt psychotic clinical features, this response has a bizarre quality.)

**B31:** A happy family—ma, pa, two kids. (This response, like B29, again points to a positive prognosis.)

It is evident that many of her SIS projective responses reflected the severe extent of her depression. The symbolic imagery revealed in a disguised form her family stressors and her 'inner cry'. Even though she was an adult, her mother-in-law's criticisms greatly undermined her sense of confidence. It is understandable that her extreme vulnerability led her to somatize her feelings and imagine 'fainting'. Yet, her initial response to early psychotherapy had begun to restore her image as being a competent mother who cares for her child. The rich and graphic SIS symbols now need to be effectively translated into the language of psychotherapy making up for the paucity of words to describe emotions.

## Case 14: Dissociative Convulsion Disorder— A Case Study

The SIS was administered to a 16-year-old girl, studying in 10th grade with complaints of fits of unconsciousness, convulsive movements, severe headache, low mood and nausea. She was diagnosed as a case of 'dissociative convulsion disorder' as per ICD-10. The SIS response projected her poor interpersonal relationship, pent-up aggression, physical abuse and disturbed family functioning. The SIS-II images were used as therapeutic intervention tool with positive change in her condition and the responses given by the subject are discussed in this case study.

The patient had been a good, sincere student, praised by her teachers and always secured fourth or fifth position in her class among 40 students. All her birth and developmental milestones were normal, with no past history of any behavioural, psychological and neurological problems. However, her parents were not satisfied with her achievements and compelled her to get first position. None of the parents supported her on any issue except her younger brother, who used to solace her in times of distress.

Her symptoms started four months back when she took admission in class 10th. As reported by her parents, she had frequent fits of unconsciousness with severe headache and restlessness. During her pre-board examination, she became very anxious, and often used to cry. She had a love relationship with a 23-year-old person who got married and left her. When she thinks about her lost love relationship, she becomes more anxious and suffers from severe headache with fits of unconsciousness. She further developed problems in her fingers and could not write the answers in the examination.

She was referred for psychological evaluation and therapeutic intervention. On psychological assessment, it was observed that when she failed to solve a problem, she developed muscular rigidity which improved/disappeared after someone helped her in solving it.

During therapeutic session, she expressed severe concern about the punitive reaction of her parents of not securing the first position in the class. In addition, during therapy, she also indicated the abusive relationship between the parents. She further reported that her father frequently abused her mother verbally as well as physically. He is also an alcoholic and would not pay any attention to his children.

## Current Symptoms

Her present symptoms at initial psychological evaluation included nervousness, shyness, severe headache, convulsive movements, clenching of teeth, low mood, etc. She had poor self-image and lack of self-confidence. She was diagnosed as a case of dissociative convulsion disorder as per ICD-10. Her attacks were pseudo seizures. On EEG and CT scan, no abnormality was found in cerebral activity.

## SIS Responses

### The Three Most Liked Images

**A7:** 'Structure of a girl in dancing position' is a normal response suggesting her ego strength and positive attitude towards life.

**A14:** 'A pretty girl sitting on a lonely beach and is in a sad mood' indicates her pensive mood and feeling of loneliness. In the detailed enquiry, her psychotherapist may ask her do you sometime feel this grief like this girl.

**B29:** 'A girl coming home from school and looking very happy' may indicate her wishful thinking to have a happy home during childhood which she never had. This may also indicate her regression and wish to be a school-going girl to avoid problems. In the detailed enquiry, it should be suggested that if she participates in the therapy, she will become like this happy girl.

### The Three Least Liked Images

**B31:** 'People standing close, arguing with each other, a bad practice' brings out the imagery of 'happy family (father, mother and two children)' but she has avoided seeing a happy family because of the broken/disturbed family relationship. This reminds you of how you feel during an argument in your family.

**B5:** 'A girl pointing a pistol to other person' may indicate her aggressive and hostile attitude towards her boyfriend who cheated her. Who this reminds you of in your real life? Have you ever wished to hurt or to even kill your boyfriend? When did you experience having broken and painful heart?

**A9:** 'A man and a woman in silent mood' may indicate her depressive mood and poor interpersonal relationship either between parents or with her father. What it reminds you of in your real world?

### Analysis of a Few Significant Responses

**A3:** 'A girl running and crying for help.' Her inner cry that she needs help from others has come out on the surface. This may also be indicative of her wishful thinking to get support and help from her family members/therapist. Does this girl remind you of yourself and your inner cry? If you share your emotional feeling, your psychotherapist will be able to help you?

**A5:** 'A broken and painful heart' may indicate her depressive feelings about her lost love relationship.

**A10:** She viewed this image as 'the face of a very sad woman and she is weeping marred by distressful life'. This may depict her projection towards her mother who often experienced physical assault from her husband and felt depressed. This may also bring out her sympathy towards her mother and her inability to help her. In addition, here question maybe asked whether she is able to weep or not, and she needs to be encouraged to express her grief which will reduce her pain and symptoms.

**A13:** 'Helpless hand is approaching' may indicate her pensive feeling towards life. She also needs support and help. Here, she may be asked directly when she feels helpless of herself.

**A29:** 'Looks like an evil thing straight out of a horror film I saw earlier.' The image in A29 is more like TAT's blank card which works as pure projection and the imagery of 'evil thing and horrifying thoughts' suggest her traumatic memories. Here question may be asked directly about any post-traumatic dream which she may be experiencing. It is always important, whenever possible, to link her inkblot responses to her disturbing symbolic 'nightmares'.

**A31:** 'A man and woman talking with each other, something serious.' This may indicate disturbed relationship either with her boyfriend or parents. Question need to be asked in this regard what comes to her mind.

**B3:** 'Hearts once broken never heal.' Once again, the broken heart concept has come back suggesting her pessimistic and depressive feelings of broken love relationship. Her psychotherapist needs to suggest that while she feels hopeless because of her broken heart, psychotherapy may help her.

**B4:** 'I never fulfilled my desires in this atmosphere' may indicate her dissatisfaction, particularly in the family.

**B6:** 'A sad girl in mirror' indicates her own sufferings and grief-ridden unconscious material.

**B15:** 'Please stop this violence for God' suggests that she is fed up with violence in the family. Her repeated instances of being exposed to angry and violent family scenes likely played a role in her muscular skeletal symptoms. Certain vulnerable women inhibit the expression of their own inner rage by psychomotor skeletal muscle inhibition. This mechanism has been referred to as 'character armoured'.

**B19:** 'Burning sun and broken heart, how sad, no one gives protection.' This may suggest her broken love affair and broken home with feelings of hopelessness and helplessness. Her therapist might well question her regarding possible suicidal ideation which she has not reported given the intense feelings of hopelessness and helplessness.

**B28:** 'Woman in distressful situation' may indicate her sympathetic feelings towards her mother as well as her own personal anguish.

### Interpretation of SIS Responses on Readministration (After 14 Sessions of Psychotherapy)

#### Response to the Three Most Liked Images

**A7:** 'A girl in dancing position, trying to pluck an apple' is a good response suggesting her ego strength and positive attitude towards life. The dancing position is improvement of her earlier mood prior to psychotherapy.

**B31:** 'Father, mother and two children, nice picture with whole family' also suggests improvement and positive change after therapy.

**B29:** 'A girl wins in a race competition.' She has moved on from an aggressive and hostile attitude to achieve success in life is a positive change.

Following therapy, a dramatic improvement was observed in the images previously labelled as least liked, for example, see B31 and B5.

### Analysis of Other Significant Responses

**A3:** 'A beautiful fairy with magic stick coming from sky to resolve human problems.' This response indicates her hope and optimistic thoughts towards life. It indicates that the supportive psychotherapy has made positive change.

**A5:** 'Eagle catching a heart.' Although she still retains some heaviness and sadness in her heart, it is being reduced is symbolized by eagle catching her heart and flying upwards out of her past pain.

**A10:** 'A girl sees her face in mirror and smiles at herself.' This response indicates her positive ego strength and changed mood in comparison to her perception on this image at initial testing. It also indicates that the therapy has helped her to solve her problems and developed positive attitude towards life.

**A13:** 'A powerful hand capable of security' indicates her positive strength and self-confidence.

**A29:** 'A picture of a hill station' indicates her happy mood and feeling of enjoyment.

**A31:** 'A girl is smiling and a boy is in a sad mood' projects her improved state of mind in smiling shape and wishful thinking to see her ex-boyfriend in agony and sad mood.

**B3:** 'A girl giving answers of some difficult questions.' This is the direct projection of how certainly her psychotherapist's questions have caused her to face the painful emotional issues involved in grieving the loss of her love relationship.

**B4:** 'A mother and child' is an improved normal response in comparison to earlier projection of depressive response on this image.

**B5:** 'A boy and a girl playing with a ball' is a good response indicating her happy mood.

**B15:** 'A picture of many grasshoppers and spade-like knives' is again an improved response in comparison to earlier aggressive response on this image.

**B19:** 'A bug/sun' is again a normal response though she gave depressive response on initial testing.

**B28:** 'A mother hugging the child' indicates good interpersonal relationship, particularly with the mother.

### Treatment Plan

The long-term treatment plan involved improving coping strategies, family intervention and supportive psychotherapy supplemented by SIS symbolism in the therapeutic process. The combination appeared to have marked therapeutic effects and the family members have also noticed considerable improvement after therapeutic intervention.

## Case 15: Somatic Inkblots Imagery in Trans-sexual—A Case Study

Transgender is a general term applied to a variety of individuals, behaviours and groups involving tendencies to vary from culturally conventional gender roles. Transgender is the state of one's gender identity (self-identification as woman, man, neither or both) not matching one's 'assigned sex' (identification by others as male, female or intersex based on physical characteristics). 'Transgender' does not imply any specific form of sexual orientation and such people may be identified as heterosexual, homosexual, bisexual or asexual (Layton 1966).

The word transsexual, on a scale called the 'Benjamin Scale' defines different levels of intensity of transsexualism, namely 'transsexual (nonsurgical)', 'true transsexual (moderate intensity)' and 'true transsexual (high intensity)'. Many transsexuals believe that to be a true transsexual, a person needs to have a desire for surgery, however, it is notable that Benjamin's moderate intensity 'true transsexual' needs either estrogen or testosterone medication as a 'substitute' for or preliminary to operation (Benjamin 1966).

In addition to the larger categories of transgender and transsexual, there is a wide range of gender expressions and identities which are contrary to the mainstream male–female binary. These include cross-dressers, transvestites, etc. The current definitions of transgender include all transsexual people, although this has been criticized. Intersex people have genitalia and other physical characteristics that do not conform to strict definitions of male and/or female, but they are not necessarily transgender, since they do not disagree with their assigned sex at birth.

## Case Mr X

Mr X, 30 years, male, unmarried, Bengali-speaking, was referred by a physician to a private psychiatric hospital in Calcutta for multiple symptoms. The main complaints of the patient were gender identity crisis, too much interest in sex-changing surgeries, feelings of being harassed by teasing of peers in childhood, attempted suicide (thrice), unpleasant past experiences, disturbed sleep, distress in working conditions, poor job satisfaction, lack of peace/low mood, anger/irritation, worry about future and low self-esteem. He has severe depression, hopelessness and frustration towards future life.

His father died in early childhood and he was brought up by his mother in his maternal uncle's house. He is the only child and has good relationship with his mother. His mother is a working woman and is unable to spend enough time with him. Others in the family are not that much cooperative. Most of the people used to tease him for his sexual orientation by telling him that he looks more like a girl than a boy. He was also teased by his schoolteachers and friends on his sexual orientation. He was abused sexually by a few known friends initially but later he had consensual passive homosexual involvement with them several times. His friendships break up easily causing him to often have relationship crisis.

The SIS-II was administered to him following the standard procedure (Cassell and Dubey 2003) for understanding his personality profile and unprocessed unconscious material needs to be addressed during psychotherapy. He was motivated and cooperative during testing. The clinically significant responses on SIS-II are discussed ahead:

**A1:** He perceived 'butterfly' in this image which is not a common response. The butterfly may indicate feminine outlook and interest in feminine objects.

**A2:** He saw 'heart' in this image which is an atypical response that may depict body imagery and to some extent signs of tension and anxiety.

**A3:** 'Cloud' may indicate his free-floating anxiety.

**A4:** Perceiving 'chocolate' in this image may suggest regression to childhood and feministic attitude.

**A5:** He has viewed 'birds', whereas human figure is the most common response which he has avoided. This probably indicates his disturbed interpersonal relationship with others.

**A6:** Perceiving 'toy' may again bring the theme of Image A4 and his regression to childhood to avoid problems as an adult.

**A7:** 'Apple' is a normal response.

**A8:** He has perceived 'planet' though male sex organ is the most common response on this image. Avoiding male sex organ may indicate his deep-rooted sexual conflict which could be due to faulty gender perception or disturbed sexual role as passive homosexuals.

**A9:** He viewed 'two insects', whereas two human beings—a male and a female—is the common response on this image. Avoiding two persons may again indicate disturbed interpersonal relationships particularly between male and female.

**A10:** 'Eyes' is generally perceived normal response on this image.

**A11:** 'Meat (chicken)' is a passive, aggressive response which may indicate helplessness, frustration and depression. The dead chicken (meat) may also be taken as strong indication of suicidal tendency, which the patient has already tried thrice.

**A12:** Perceiving 'eyes' on this image may indicate his suspicious attitude towards others which needs to be addressed during his therapy sessions to explore the possibilities of paranoid tendency, if any at this stage. He is unable to continue friendship with anyone which might be an early indication of some serious pathology.

**A16:** 'Small sparrows' is a beautiful response though most people perceive it as two birds. 'Small sparrows' may again indicate his regression to childhood where he feels comparatively more secure.

**A17:** 'Cage' may indicate his feeling of helplessness and inability to come out of his present situations.

**A21:** He perceived it to be a 'star fish'. Though a tortoise/a big man with two babies are the common responses on this image, avoiding two babies and big man may indicate his perpetuator who had forced sexual abuse during childhood.

**A22:** 'Star fish, sea fish' might indicate his conflicts with gender role as the common response on this image is spinal column which represents male phallic organ—a conflicting area of the patient.

**A23:** He perceived 'scorpio' which is a painful insect though spinal column is a common response and avoiding this response indicates his conflicts regarding male sexuality which is the main problem of the patient.

**A24:** 'Leg joint' is a normal response on this image.

**A25:** 'Female sex organ' is a normal response on this image. Perceiving female sex organ might indicate his wishful thinking to identify this image as his own body part by taking help of surgery.

**A26:** 'Babies in pregnancy' is a normal response on this image.

**A27:** 'Female breast' is a normal response on this image. It may indicate his good interpersonal relationship and closeness with his mother.

**A31:** 'Two faces' is a normal response on this image though a male and a female have been a better response. Avoiding male and female may also indicate his gender role conflict.

**B3:** He has perceived 'clouds' on this image though people talking is the common perception. The clouds may indicate his tension and free-floating anxiety.

**B8:** He has perceived 'nose' on this image which may be an indicator of homosexuality.

**B14:** He has perceived 'water' on this image though this is a rare response which may represent anxiety and insecurity.

**B16:** He viewed 'scorpion' on this image which may repeat the theme of his perception on Image A23. The spinal cord is a common response on this image and avoiding this probably indicates his conflicts regarding male sexuality.

**B18:** He has perceived 'insect' instead of a 'male phallic organ' which is the most common response on this image. Avoiding perceiving the male sex organ and perceiving it as an insect may indicate his conflict in the male phallic region.

**B19:** 'Sun' is a normal response on this image but avoiding two hearts (either side of the sun) may indicate frustration and his conflicts in interpersonal relationship.

**B22:** He perceived 'frozen man' which is a very depressive response. The therapist must take note of this during therapy session to address severe depressive contents with the help of antidepressant drugs and psychotherapy. This may also indicate severe suicidal ideation.

**B27:** 'Twins' is a normal response on this image.

**B28:** 'Mother with a baby' is a normal response on this image. It further indicates his close relationship with his mother.

**B31:** 'Family' is a normal response on this image.

As all the SIS responses indicate that he has contact with reality, has moderate ego strength and is free from psychotic ailments (no psychotic features). However, he has shown severe suicidal tendency, poor interpersonal relationships, conflict in the sexual area and gender role with marked depression and frustration. He was treated with the help of drugs and psychotherapy with significant improvement.

## Discussion

Most suicidal individuals when asked by a clinician will report their suicide ideation. Yet, while this emphasizes the importance of detailed enquiry, some individuals successfully hide plans to end their lives. These maybe highly impulsive, yet lethal. For example, early in my first year of psychiatric training in a military hospital, involved a Korean combat veteran who was under my care. Eventually, he improved sufficiently as to no longer appear clinically depressed. Since he denied suicide ideation, my supervising treatment team had judged him safe for his first weekend pass. However, according to nursing reports, his wife rejected him in a phone conversation claiming that she was 'too busy' to get him. A few minutes later he impulsively leapt from a hospital window killing himself!

While I was still dealing with his loss, two days later another veteran jumped to his death from the window of a medical ward. Previously in the hospital, it had been many months since such suicides had occurred. In retrospect, it appeared that this second veteran also had been depressed with undetected suicidal intensions. This object lesson suggested that for certain vulnerable suggestive individuals, suicide may sometimes have a psychologically 'infectious copycat' quality. It was for this reason that immediately after the tombstone inscription, student readers were forewarned.

Predicting suicide in an individual clinical case poses challenges. Most screening questionnaires have definite limitations. They tend to rely on some form of self-reporting by the individual being screened for dangerous impulses. For example, a motivated suicidal person who has previously denied such intent in clinical interviews may well recognize what the test administrator is assessing and consequently falsify answers.

While this type of falsification may occur in a deceptive individual when reporting responses on the SIS Booklet answer sheet and during the subsequent detailed enquiry, escaping detection is less likely because of the depth revealing power of symbolic projection. Except for B15 (i.e., sharp objects, knives, etc.), B21 (i.e., a gun) and B22 (a dying person's body and spirit), which were purposely designed to access suicidal/homicidal impulses, the visualization of 'weapons' on the remaining images, or the body of a suicide victim should arouse alarm signals. Such responses signal the need for close observation by the treatment team, as well as concerned family members.

Denial mental mechanisms may be still more effectively circumvented by the revealing significance of highly morbid symbolic responses portraying open wounds, dying, etc. For example, the response 'blood' may indicate otherwise unreported psychotic features. If such pathologic material is seen, the clinician would be well advised to ascertain if the responder had similar 'nightmares' with such symbolic imagery. 'Dream scenes in which the content explicitly portrays suicide of any characters should alert the interviewer to otherwise denied ambivalent suicidal ideations of the dreamer. The person should be considered suicidal if the dream content relates to a suicide scene, only if the individual has not been stressed by such a self-inflicted death of a friend, family member or other psychologically significant individual.' This is because such dreams may reflect a form of loving spiritual communication between the grieving person and the deceased. Otherwise, the individual's involuntary flood of self-directed violent impulses may be conceptualized as quite comparable to perceived violence from other people or life threatening external traumatic events which activate PTSD imagery during sleep.

In all honesty, the clinical cases presented merely outline response patterns for clinical consideration as warning signals. No statistical studies have been completed with the SIS, or any of the other tests purported to effectively identify deep-seated fluctuating suicide impulses. SIS researchers are invited to contemplate the almost impossible task of securing valid data baselines preceding the suicide.

Recall that modern astronomers now scan the mysterious cosmos with multiple technologies. In an analogous fashion, for a reality-based 'picture', SIS students need training to view their projective data within the context of all other relevant scientific methods.

The paper was designed for training students in SIS technology for detecting, otherwise unreported, suicidal/homicidal ideation with the help of responses projected on Somatic Inkblots Images. Four clinical cases were presented in a case study mentioned in this chapter (Case 11. Assessing Suicidal/homicidal impulses with the SIS) to illustrate how SIS technique brings to the surface psychopathology of violent behaviour. A trained SIS psychotherapist can reactivate such imagery under reduced anxiety conditions, thereby enabling psychotherapeutic management and neutralization of dangerous impulses.

## Overview of Clinical Cases

We have tried to emphasize with the help of several international clinical cases, the true universal application of projective testing, particularly inkblots images (the Rorschach, Holtzman and SIS), as a tool for personality assessment, diagnostic evaluation and therapeutic aid. These findings apply to professionals working with suffering souls across a wide spectrum of ages from children, adolescents and throughout the various stormy passages of an adult's life. Most of the psychologists are using inkblot procedure as an 'objective test' and follow a procedure (such as Klopfer, Beck, Exner, Piotrowski and Rapaport) heavily loaded with indices-based interpretation. While these psychological instruments represent a significant step beyond non-projective tests, since emphasis is placed on numerical calculation, they emerged as a protest against the rigid framework and numerical calculation of forced choice questionnaires involving choosing choices such as 'Yes or No, True or False, Agree, Disagree or Can't decide'.

Modern diagnostic classification systems for mental disorders represent a significant step forward regarding facilitating treatment planning. Historically, these evolved from the international scientific teamwork of psychiatrists, psychologists and clinical investigators. As new findings appear, especially about the less scientifically based personality disorders, these data will be incorporated into psychiatric nomenclature.

As might be expected, unravelling nature's complex hidden body–mind–spirit functioning frequently seems like a formidable clinical task. There are many significant variables, which can make what to some diagnosticians seem simple, yet to others, infinitely more complex. Complexity can arise from multiple idiosyncratic case history including genetic factors, age, sex, socio-economic status, cultural differences, etc.

For severe chronic forms of mental illness, for example, the schizophrenic disorders, the medical model has been proven clinically valuable. For these, their biological roots have been explored by a variety of scientifically based evidence studies. Examples include investigations concerning genetics, epidemiological prevalence, neurophysiologic functioning, psychopharmacology, etc.

Normally for such disorders, standardized interview techniques which focus on classical symptoms patterns, family history, mental status examination, etc., enable a trained clinician to rapidly establish a working diagnosis, a meaningful initial treatment plan and the prognosis. Yet, frequently in the early stages of suspected psychosis, psychological testing may be required for diagnostic clarification. Often as well, there may be other indications for such assessment: for example, to assess cognitive improvement from antipsychotic medication, to detect unreported suicidal/homicidal ideation, to make a valid judgement to establish level of care, etc. If somatic delusions are present, the SIS may be particularly helpful in cognitive psychotherapy for reality testing, patient body gestalt education. Moreover, projective testing can facilitate the early detection of recurrence, when paranoid fears of medication side effects lead to unreported non-compliance.

In addition, there are many other mental disorders having psychotic and/or severe affective disturbances. These pose similar diagnostic problems, perhaps often better conceptualized for management purposes utilizing the medical model. One important example that fits well into the above conceptual framework throughout the world is BAD. However, medical interviewing to elicit symptoms/signs in a 'cook book' fashion has definite limitations. Many of these are quite comparable to those associated with 'question and answer' scored non-projective tests.

Clinical interviewing blends the art and science of human interaction. It involves a two-person communication system. The professional questions the other, while monitoring non-verbal clues as to the verbally hidden nature of the suffering individual's body–mind–spiritual status. Normally, this approach works relatively well. However, it only reveals verbally to the clinician what the sufferer consciously can recall from memory storage. Thus, it is subject to limitations, like the limited number of words to describe distraught emotions. Material may be held back and not reported for reasons of social acceptability, fearing 'looking crazy', etc.

Despite these, the traditional clinician's diagnostic interview approach is normally adequate. In comparison with the projective tests under review, it may be compared to a pathologist examining a microscopic slide through a low power microscope. Using this analogy, the various projective procedures presented in this book are analogous to the more powerful electronic microscopes available. Of these, the SIS specially patterned inkblot structure was designed to stimulate imagery pertinent to that experienced by those experiencing tormented mental states. They can access directly, or through symbolism, clinically relevant data inaccessible with interviews.

Several of the clinical cases illustrate how the innovative technology with the electronic mesmerizing forms of the SIS accentuates the pulling power for the clinicians. Historically, it might be recalled that in the early Rorschach day, psychoanalysts explored the use of Rorschach content in therapy (Schaefer 1954). While Wayne Holtzman scoring system focused on 22 indices, remarkably, in his book, a central case history illustrated content analysis. Later, Paul Lerner published a book entitled *Psychoanalytic Theory and the Rorschach* which failed to generate much interest. Perhaps this was because it was based more on index-based scoring than symbolic content. While using mathematical summations on the surface appears more scientifically valid, what emerges resembles the superficial psychological data derived from the use of questionnaires. In his book, *Psychological Testing*, 1982, Anastasi claimed that inkblot projective testing often revealed the subjective world of the examiner more than the subject, without truly appreciating the clinical merit. It should be remembered that projective tests emerged as a protest against the rigid framework of so-called objective tests. It is erroneous in many instances, with the Rorschach and Holtzman to refer to the index data as 'projective' since they reflect primarily the optics/cognition of vision rather than deep-seated memories and subjective perceptions. Perhaps it might be useful for illustration purposes to extend the analogy to modern astronomical technology like the Hubble telescope. This has enabled astronomers to view new aspects of the cosmos to which they were previously blind. Some of their observations have represented enormous steps of scientific value that enabled them to extend the boundaries of existing knowledge. Others have simply been mind-boggling and presented challenges that ultimately involve attempts to scientifically understand the understandable, like what spiritually predated the 'Big Bang'.

With the electronic forms of the SIS, prior presentation of mesmerizing electronic audio/visual stimuli hypnotically bypasses psychological defences, thereby reducing neural inhibitions to memory. Without inhibiting effects of the clinician's presence, this enables the viewer to look back into events from years before, quite analogous to the way modern astronomers view light from ancient cosmic events. When the inkblots containing clinically relevant suggestive structure flow in and out of the viewer's field of vision for recording on an answer sheet, it is much like an inner cosmic experience. Since these are written down on an answer sheet-like hypnotic writing, deeper memories can more readily be documented. After the viewing process, relaxing audio and nature scenes can serve as a robotic technique to desensitize the viewer to those memories linked with disturbing affect prior to travelling out of the inner world into the external reality of the clinician's office.

Like with Hubble, what is seen in the multiple projected responses, as illustrated with the clinical cases outlined in this chapter, normally goes beyond that revealed by clinical interviews. Moreover, they more readily lend themselves to blending diagnostic/psychotherapeutic processes.

Projective procedures are essential for those who have appreciation and reverence for the hidden mysteries of the body–mind–spirit. These techniques can uncover deeper dimensions than non-projective tests. The latter only access the surface of psyche suffering. Their mathematical rating scales are prone to create an intellectualized barrier between clinician and client. All readers interested in the depth revealing power of the Rorschach, Holtzman and SIS will be exposed to the psychologically toxic occupational exposure to secondary empathetic discomfort. It is predicted that most will find the risk/benefits rewarding.

# Appendix*

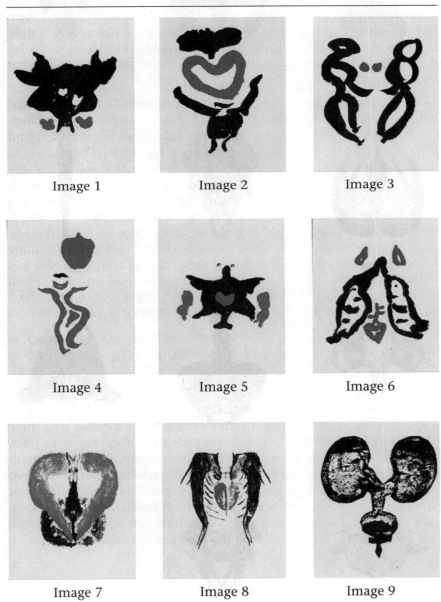

Image 1    Image 2    Image 3

Image 4    Image 5    Image 6

Image 7    Image 8    Image 9

* *Disclaimer:* The images used in the appendix are for representation purpose only.

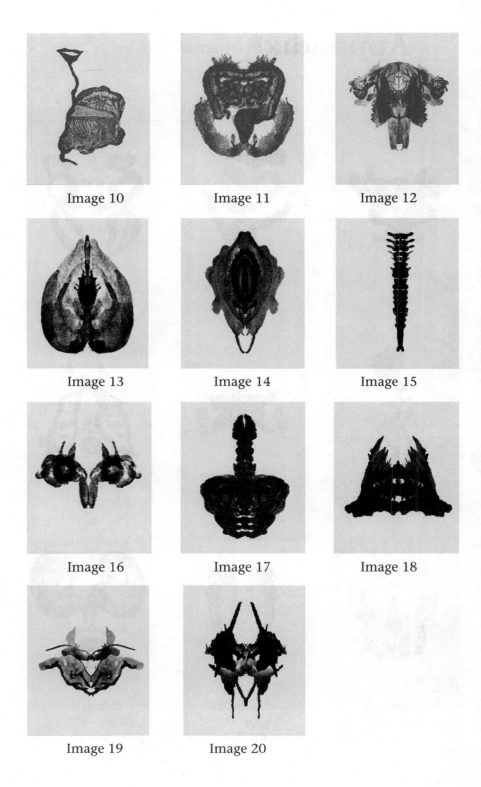

Image 10       Image 11       Image 12

Image 13       Image 14       Image 15

Image 16       Image 17       Image 18

Image 19       Image 20

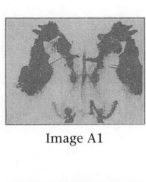

Image A1

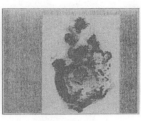

Image A2

Image A3

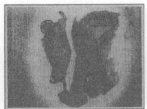

Image A4

Image A5

Image A6

Image A7

Image A8

Image A9

Image A10

Image A11

Image A12

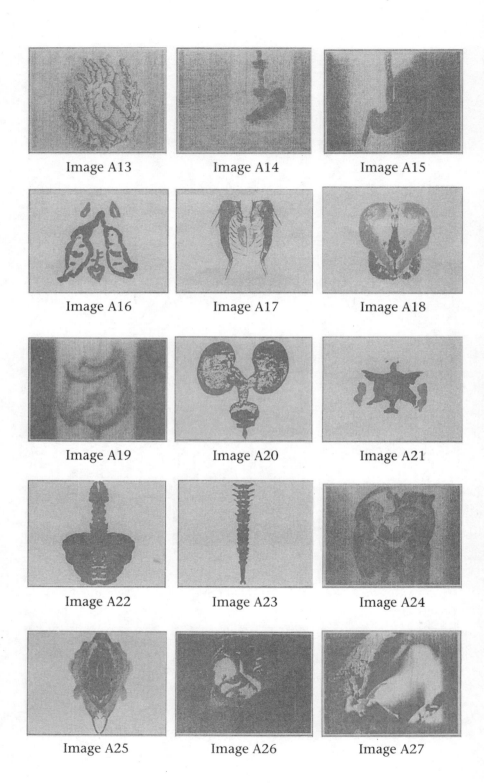

Image A13

Image A14

Image A15

Image A16

Image A17

Image A18

Image A19

Image A20

Image A21

Image A22

Image A23

Image A24

Image A25

Image A26

Image A27

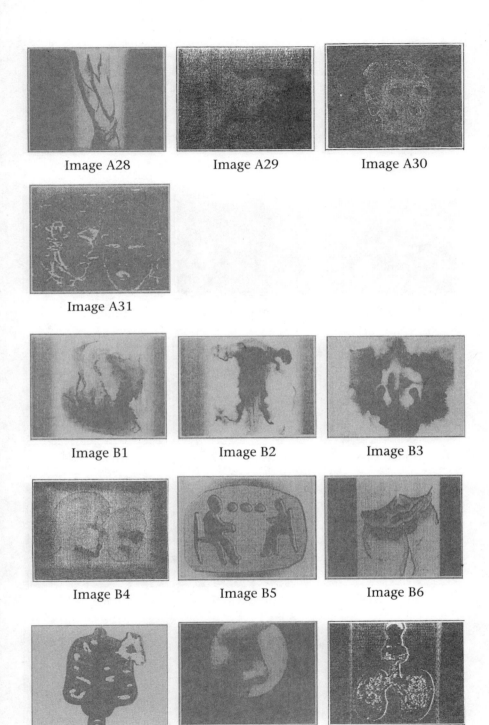

Image A28    Image A29    Image A30

Image A31

Image B1    Image B2    Image B3

Image B4    Image B5    Image B6

Image B7    Image B8    Image B9

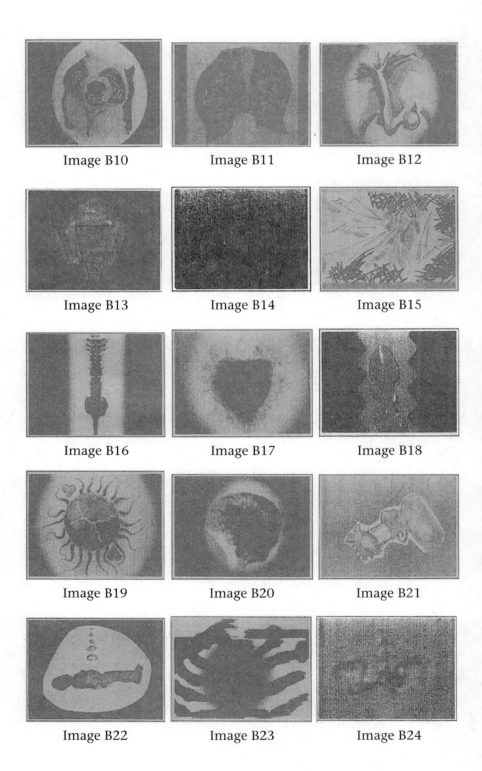

Image B10     Image B11     Image B12

Image B13     Image B14     Image B15

Image B16     Image B17     Image B18

Image B19     Image B20     Image B21

Image B22     Image B23     Image B24

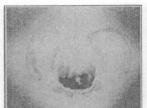

Image B25

Image B26

Image B27

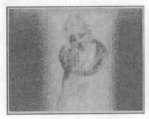

Image B28

Image B29

Image B30

Image B31

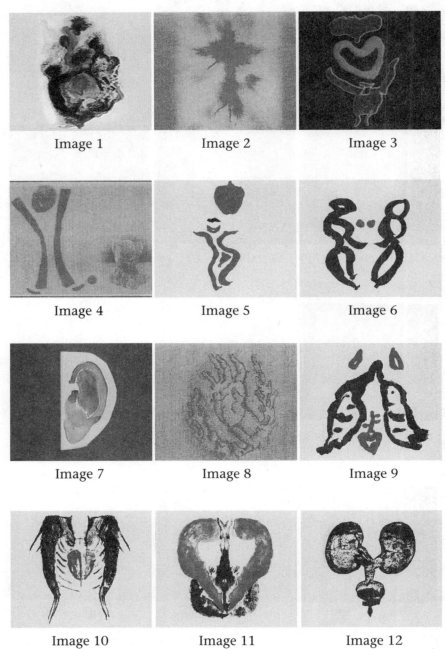

Image 1

Image 2

Image 3

Image 4

Image 5

Image 6

Image 7

Image 8

Image 9

Image 10

Image 11

Image 12

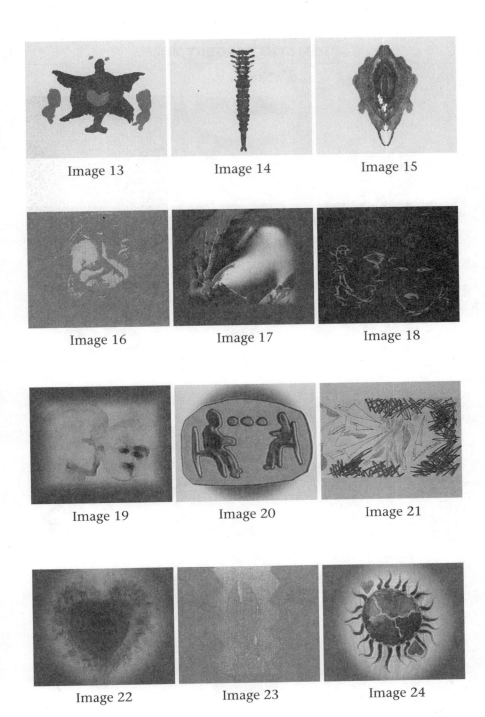

Image 13

Image 14

Image 15

Image 16

Image 17

Image 18

Image 19

Image 20

Image 21

Image 22

Image 23

Image 24

Image 25

Image 26

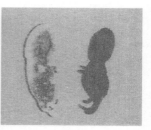

Image 27

Image 28

Image 29

Image 30

# Bibliography

Abbasi, A. 1999. 'Review of Soul on the Couch: Spirituality, Religion, and Morality'. *Contemporary Psychoanalysis* 10: 150–154.

Acklin, M. W., and J. Oliveira-Berry. 1996. 'Return to the Source: Rorschach's Psychodiagnostics'. *Journal of Personality Assessment* 67: 427–433.

Adamson, J. D., R. Greengrass, and R. M. Martin. 1977. 'Cassell's Anatomical Pictures Responses by Groups of Hospitalised Inpatients'. *British Journal of Projective Psychology and Personality Study* 22: 27–35.

Adamson, J., and R. Sterenko. 1977. 'Personality and Cardiac Function'. *British Journal of Projective Technique* 22: 41–47.

Adamson, J. D., and J. Varmose. 1976. 'Somatic Symptoms in Schizophrenia'. *Canadian Psychiatric Association Journal* 21: 1–6.

Ahmad, H., and P. Awootar. 1983. 'Response Pattern of Schizophrenic and Normal Subjects on Holtzman Inkblot Technique'. *Indian Journal of Clinical Psychology* 10 (2): 245–250.

Akhtar, S., D. Pershad, and S. K. Verma. 1975. 'A Rorschach Study of Obsessional Neurosis'. *Indian Journal of Clinical Psychology* 2: 139–143.

Allen, S. 1994. 'Psychological Assessment of Post Traumatic Stress Disorder'. *Psychiatric Clinics of North America* 17: 327–349.

Alreja, S., D. K. Mishra, K. S. Sengar, A. R. Singh, and S. Chaudhury. 2009. 'SIS–II Profile of Medical Practitioners'. *SIS Journal of Projective Psychology & Mental Health* 16: 178–179.

Alreja, S., D. K. Mishra, M. M. Varghese, K. S. Sengar, and A. R. Singh. 2009. 'SIS–II Profile of Mentally Retarded Children'. *SIS Journal of Projective Psychology & Mental Health* 16: 51–54.

Alvia-White, D., A. Schneider, and G. W. Domhof. 1999. 'The Most Recent Dreams of 12–13 Year of Boys and Girls: A Methodological Contribution to the Study of Dream Content in Teenagers'. *Dreaming* 9 (2/3): 163–171.

Ames, L., J. Learned, R. Metraux, and R. N. Walker. 1954. *Rorschach Responses*. New York, NY: Hoeber.

Anastasi, A. 1982. *Psychological Testing*, 5th ed. New York, NY: Macmillan.

Ardhapurkar, I., Z. Mehta, and A. de Souza. 1967. 'Rorschach in Ischemic Heart Disease'. *Indian Journal of Psychiatry* 9: 260–263.

———. 1974. 'Rorschach Protocols in Cases of Bronchial Asthma'. *Clinician* 37: 292–295.

Aronow, E., and M. Reznikoff. 1973. 'Attitude towards the Rorschach Test Expressed in Book Reviews: A Historical Perspective'. *Journal of Personality Assessment* 37: 309–315.

———. 1976. *Rorschach Content Interpretation*. New York, NY: Grune & Stratton.

Arora, U. 1982. 'A Rorschach Study of Alcoholics'. *Indian Journal of Clinical Psychology* 9: 141–145.

Asthana, H. S. 1950a. 'Historical and Experimental Approach to the Problem of Personality'. Unpublished doctoral dissertation submitted to the University of Lucknow, Lucknow.

———. 1950b. 'Indian Norms of Rorschach Responses'. *Indian Journal of Neurology & Psychiatry* 2: 10–18.

———. 1956. 'Some Aspect of Personality Structuring in Indian (Hindu) Social Organization'. *Journal of Social Psychology* 44: 155–163.

———. 1963. 'A Rorschach Study of Indians'. *Rorschachiana* 45: 283–286.

———. 1965. Perceptual Development in the Indian Child: A Rorschach Study. *Comptes Rorschach et des Methodes Projectives*. Paris.

———. 1966. *A Rorschach Study of Child Development in India*. Harvard University Social Relation Colloquium. Cambridge, MA: Harvard University.

———. 1971. 'Normative Data on Rorschach Inkblot for Indian Sample'. Unpublished research report. Sagar: Department of Psychology, Sagar University.

Asthana, H. S., and C. Mohan. 1977. 'Perceptual Development in the Indian Child: A Rorschach Study'. Unpublished Report. Sagar: Sagar University.

Baer, L. 1994. 'Factor Analysis of Symptom Subtypes of Obsessive Compulsive Disorder and Their Relation to Personality and Tic Disorders'. *Journal of Clinical Psychiatry* 55 (3): 18–23.

Bagadia, V. N., S. Anand, K. R. Saroj, and L. P. Shah. 1971. 'Analysis of Rorschach Test of 250 Cases of Schizophrenia'. *Indian Journal of Psychiatry* 13: 248–251.

Bagadia, V. N., D. V. Jeste, K. P. Dave, S. U. Doshi, and L. P. Shah. 1973. 'Depression: A Clinical Study of 250 Cases'. *Indian Journal of Psychiatry* 15: 224–230.

Bagh, D. 1955. 'Use of Rorschach's Inkblot Test among School Adolescents'. *Indian Journal of Psychology* 30: 61–64.

Bailey, C. J., and B. I. Murstein. 1996. 'Paranoia Assessment with the SIS-II: In a College Sample'. *SIS Journal of Projective Psychology & Mental Health* 3: 109–122.

Bala, K., D. K. Mishra, and M. Jahan. 2010. 'SIS-II Profile of Patient with Antisocial Personality: A Case Report'. *SIS Journal of Projective Psychology & Mental Health* 17: 178–179.

Balter, L. 1993. 'Review of Psychoanalysis and Religion, Psychiatry and the Humanities' (Vol. 11). *Psychoanalysis Quarterly* 62: 481–486.

Banerjee, P. 2017. 'Optimism Index: A Screening Tool for Mental Health'. *SIS Journal of Projective Psychology & Mental Health* 24 (2): 133–134.

———. 2018. *The Power of Positivity: Optimism and the 7th Sense*. Thousand Oaks, CA: SAGE Publications.

Banerjee, S., A. Mukhopadhyaya, and U. Singh. 1998. 'An In-depth Study of Somatization in Heroin Addicts through SIS-I & Rorschach Inkblot Test'. *SIS Journal of Projective Psychology & Mental Health* 5: 33–39.

Barnes, C. M. 1964. 'Prediction of Brain Damage Using the Holtzman Inkblot Technique and Other Selected Variables'. *Dissertation Abstracts* 24, 4789 (No.64-3350). Ann Arbor, MI: University Microfilms.

Barnes, R. E., and G. D. Carnes. 1971. 'Rorschach Anatomy Response Correlates in Rehabilitation Failure Subjects'. *Journal of Personality Assessment* 35: 525–531.

Barrett, D., ed. 1996. *Trauma and Dreams*. Cambridge and London: Harvard University Press.

Bartemeier, L. H. 1965. 'Psychoanalysis and Religion'. *Bulletin of Menninger Clinic* 29: 237–244.

Bartlett, F. C. 1916. 'An Experimental Study of Some Problems of Perceiving and Imaging'. *British Journal of Psychology* 8: 222–267.

Bash, K. W. 1965. 'In Memorium Dr. Walter Morgenthaler'. *Journal of Projective Technique* 29: 267–270.

Basu, J., and S. De. 1997. 'Utility of Projective Tests in the Psychological Assessment of Transsexual Patients: A Case Study Approach'. *SIS Journal of Projective Psychology & Mental Health* 4: 41–55.

Basu, J., and R. Nandy. 2004. 'Substance Dependence, General Mental Health and Somatization Responses: A Study of Ganja Smokers, Tobacco Smokers and Non-Smokers'. *SIS Journal of Projective Psychology & Mental Health* 11: 75–84.

Baumgarten, Tramer. 1942. 'Franziska Zur Geschichte des Rorschach Test'. *Archives of Neuropsychiatry* 50: 1–13.

Beck, S. J. (1932). 'The Rorschach Test as Applied to a Feeble-Minded Group. Paper back, Publisher Columbia University Press, (USA)

Beck, S. J. (. 1937). 'Introduction to the Rorschach Method: A Manual of Personality Study'. *American Ortho Psychiatric Association Monograpgh* 1: XV+278.

Beck, S. J. (1949). *Rorschach Test: Basic Process*, 2nd ed. New York, NY: Grune & Stratton.

Beck, S. J., and H. B. Molish. 1967. *Rorschach's Test: A Variety of Personality Pictures*, 2nd ed. New York, NY: Grune & Stratton.

Becker, E. 1973. *The Denial of Death*. New York, NY: The Free Press.

Beit-Hallahmi, B. 1992. 'Review of Psychoanalysis and Religion'. *Psychoanal Books* 3: 256–258.

Bellamy, Elizabeth N. 1995. 'Hospitalized Suicidal Patients and the Somatic Video Procedure: A Descriptive Study'. *SIS Journal Projective Psychology & Mental Health* 2: 85–91.

Benjamin, H. 1966. *The Transsexual Phenomenon* (p. 23). New York, NY: Julian Press.

Benson, P. L., and D. L. Williams. 1987. *Religion on Capitol Hill: Myths and Realities*. Oxford: Oxford University Press.

Benzein, E. G., B. I. Saveman, and A. Norberg. 2000. 'The Meaning of Hope in Healthy, Non-Religious Swedes'. *Western Journal of Nursing Research* 22 (3): 303–319.

Berlin, Heather A., Edmund T. Rolls, and Susan D. Iversen. 2005. 'Borderline Personality Disorder, Impulsivity, and the Orbital Frontal Cortex'. *American Journal of Psychiatry* 162: 2360–2373.

Bhargava, M., and A. Saxena. 1995. 'Rorschach Differentials of Deprived Adolescents'. *Indian Journal of Clinical Psychology* 22: 24–29.

Bhogta, S. K., S. Roy, M. Jahan, K. S. Sengar, and A. R. Singh. 2014. 'SIS-II Profile of Patients with Thalassemia'. *SIS Journal of Projective Psychology & Mental Health* 21 (2): 119–121.

Bilu, Yoram. 2000. 'Oneirobiography and Oneirocommunity in Saint Worship in Israel: A Two-Tier Model for Dream-Inspired Religious Revivals'. *Dreaming: Journal of the Association for the Study of Dreams* 10 (2): 85–102.

Binet, A., and V. Henry. 1895. 'La Psychologic Individualle'. *Annals of Psychology* 2: 411–465.

Bohm, E. 1958. *A Textbook in Rorschach Test Diagnosis*. New York, NY: Grune & Stratton.

Bonnier, P. 1905. 'L'aschematic'. *Review Neurology* 13: 604–609.

Brady, D. 1995. 'A Study of Somatic Inkblot Series: Application in Medical Setting'. *SIS Journal of Projective Psychology & Mental Health* 2: 129–134.

Brar, H. S. 1970. 'Rorschach Content Responses of East Indian Patients'. *Journal of Projective Technique & Personality Development* 34: 88–94.

Brenneis, C. B. 1994. 'Can Early Childhood Trauma Be Reconstructed from Dreams?' *Psychoanalytic Psychology* 11: 429–448.

Brierley, M. 1953. 'Review of Psychoanalysis and Religion'. *International Journal of Psychoanalysis* 34: 338–345.

Brock, D., W. A. Cassell, C. Tyrone, C. Maureen, B. L. Dubey, J. Halia, R. Leigh, and S. Laurel. 2015. 'SIS Symbols of PTSD & the Need for Empathy in Therapy'. *SIS Journal of Projective Psychology & Mental Health* 22 (1): 3–8.

Bulkeley, Kelly. 1993. 'Gods and REMS: The Implications of Recent Dream Research for the Psychology of Religion'. *Pastoral Psychology* 41 (6): 349–358.

———. 1994. *The Wilderness of Dreams: Exploring the Religious Meanings of Dreams in Modern Western Culture*. SUNY Press

Buss, A.H., and A. Durkee. 1957. 'An Inventory for Assessing Different Kinds of Hostility'. *Journal of Consulting Psychology* 21: 343–348.

Byrne, D. 1971. *The Attraction Paradigm*. New York, NY: Academic Press.

Campbell, Joseph. 1988. *Myths, Dreams, and Religion*. Washington, DC: Spring Publications, Inc.

Carstairs, G. M., R. W. Payne, and S. Whittaker. 1960. 'Rorschach Responses of Hindus and Bhils'. *Journal of Social Psychology* 51: 217–227.

Case, W. A., and B. L. Dubey. 2008. 'The Mutilated Breast Syndrome—SIS Augmentation of Psychotherapy in Postpartum Onset OCD'. *SIS Journal of Projective Psychology & Mental Health* 15: 103–112.

———. 2011. 'Childhood PTSD Roots of Borderline Personality Disorder—Emotionally Unstable Personality Disorder (ICU-10)'. *SIS Journal of Projective Psychology & Mental Health* 18: 3–9.

Cassell, M. A., W. A. Cassell, B. L. Dubey, P. Dwivedi, E. Molchanov, A. M. O'Roark, and L. C. Routh. 1999. 'A Video Projective Technique for PTSD in Women'. *SIS Journal of Projective Psychology & Mental Health* 6: 3–28.

Cassell, W. A. 1964. 'A Projective Index of Body Interior Awareness'. *Psychosomatic Medicine* 26: 172–177.

———. 1965. 'Body Perception and Symptom Localization'. *Psychosomatic Medicine* 27: 171–176.

———. 1966. 'A Tachistoscopic Index of Regional Body Awareness: Exterior and Interior Perception'. *Journal of Projective Techniques* 30: 31–36.

———. 1969. 'Responses to Inkblot Configurations Resembling the Heart'. *Journal of Projective Techniques and Personality Assessment* 3: 123–126.

———. 1971. 'Body Consciousness in Exhibitionism'. *British Journal of Projective Technique* 16: 21–31.

———. 1972. 'Individual Differences in Somatic Perception'. *Advances in Psychosomatic Medicine* 8: 86–104.

———. 1977a. 'Aggressive Imagery and Clinical Symptoms in Schizophrenia'. *British Journal of Projective Technique* 16: 21–23.

———. 1977b. 'SIS-I'. In *Eighth Mental Measurements Handbook*, edited by Oscar K. Buros. Highland Park, NJ: The Gryphan Press.

———. 1977c. 'Desensitization Therapy for Body Image Anxiety'. *Canadian Psychiatric Association Journal* 22: 239–242.

———. 1979. 'Anatomical Rorschach Responses and Death Symbolism'. *British Journal of Projective Technique and Personality Study* 24: 7–16.

———. 1980a. 'Body Awareness and Somatic Delusions Involving Sexual Organs'. *American Journal of Psychoanalysis* 40: 125–135.

———. 1980b. *Body Symbolism and the Somatic Inkblot Series*. Anchorage, AK: Aurora Publishing.

———. 1984a. 'Computerized Projective Testing as an Aid in Medical Diagnosis'. *Alaska Medicine* 26 (1): 1–9.

———. 1984b. *Somatic Inkblot Series Video*. Anchorage, AK: SIS Center.

———. 1987. 'The SIS Video Version'. *Proceedings of Annual Meeting of the Society for Personality Assessment*. San Francisco, CA: Society for Personality Assessment.

———. 1988. 'Validity Study of the SIS-II Booklet in Pregnant and Non-Pregnant Women'. Paper presented in the meeting of the International Congress of Psychology, Sydney, Australia.

———. 1989. 'Therapeutic Application of SIS'. *Proceedings of Society for Personality Assessment.* New York, NY: Society for Personality Assessment.

———. 1990. *Somatic Inkblot Series Manual.* Anchorage, AK: SIS Center.

———. 1991. 'Art Therapy Using the SIS-II Video'. *Japanese Bulletin of Arts Therapy* 22: 131–135.

———. 1994. 'The Somatic Inkblot Series: Continuing Rorschach's Conceptualization'. *SIS Journal of Projective Psychology & Mental Health* 1: 3–14.

———. 1995. 'Editorial'. *SIS Journal of Projective Psychology & Mental Health* 2: 93–95.

———. 1996. 'Future Direction of Projective Technique'. *SIS Journal of Projective Psychology & Mental Health* 3: 91–94.

———. 1997. 'Editorial'. *SIS Journal of Projective Psychology & Mental Health* 4: 87–88.

———. 1998a. 'Somatic Inkblot Series: A Therapeutic Tool for 21st Century'. *SIS Journal of Projective Psychology & Mental Health* 4: 1–2.

———. 1998b. 'The Somatic Inkblot Series (SIS) and Eye Movement Desensitization and Reprocessing (EMDR)'. *SIS Journal of Projective Psychology & Mental Health* 4: 69–70.

———. 2001. 'SIS Explorations of Human Consciousness'. *SIS Journal of Projective Psychology & Mental Health* 8: 3–14.

———. 2002. 'Editorial: Intellectual Struggle in Advancing SIS Knowledge'. *SIS Journal of Projective Psychology & Mental Health* 91.

———. 2004. 'Editorial: SIS Lessons'. *SIS Journal of Projective Psychology & Mental Health* 1: 73–74.

———. 2005a. 'Editorial: Evidence Based Medicine and the SIS'. *SIS Journal of Projective Psychology & Mental Health* 12 (2): 85.

———. 2005b. 'Assessing Suicidal/Homicidal Impulses with the SIS'. *SIS Journal of Projective Psychology & Mental Health* 12 (2): 99–106.

———. 2005c. 'Presidential Address: SIS Stimulation of Beacon Imagery'. *SIS Journal of Projective Psychology & Mental Health* 12: 3–8.

———. 2006. 'SIS Cognitive Psychotherapy for Spouse Induced PTSD'. *SIS Journal of Projective Psychology & Mental Health* 13: 25–36.

———. 2007a. 'Body Consciousness in Exhibitionism'. *SIS Journal of Projective Psychology & Mental Health* 14: 3–13.

———. 2007b. 'Desensitization Therapy for Body Image Anxiety'. *SIS Journal of Projective Psychology & Mental Health* 14: 14–19.

———. 2007c. 'Editorial: Historical Periods in SIS Theory and Practice'. *SIS Journal of Projective Psychology & Mental Health* 14: 1–2.

———. 2008a. 'Viewing Holocaust Nightmares through the Lens of SIS Imagery: A Psycho-Biographical Study'. *SIS Journal of Projective Psychology & Mental Health* 15 (1): 3–24.

———. 2008b. 'Editorial: Basing SIS Theory in Psychophysiologic Reality'. *SIS Journal of Projective Psychology & Mental Health* 15: 1–2.

———. 2009. 'Editorial: SIS Portraits of the Inner Mental World Painted by Blog Pooling of Interpretations'. *SIS Journal of Projective Psychology & Mental Health* 16: 1–2.

———. 2010a. 'Editorial: The SIS Journal as a Cyberspace Scientific Meeting Hall for Sharing Scientific Based Truths'. *SIS Journal of Projective Psychology & Mental Health* 17: 1–3.

———. 2010b. 'Editorial: Genetic Determinants of SIS Projection'. *SIS Journal of Projective Psychology & Mental Health* 17: 101–103.

———. 2011a. 'Editorial: Dissolving Death Anxiety with Yoga Empowered'. *SIS Journal of Projective Psychology & Mental Health* 18: 123–128.

———. 2011b. 'Editorial: Changing Personal and Professional SIS Perspectives'. *SIS Journal of Projective Psychology & Mental Health* 18: 1–3.

———. 2012a. 'Editorial: Memory Interaction with SIS Perception versus Projection'. *SIS Journal of Projective Psychology & Mental Health* 19 (2): 77–79.

———. 2012b. 'Editorial: "Wizard of OZ" Empathy Deficient Sociopaths—a Challenge for SIS Unmasking'. *SIS Journal of Projective Psychology & Mental Health* 19 (1): 1–4.

———. 2013a. 'Editorial: A Somatic Inkblot Series "Bucket List" Exercise'. *SIS Journal of Projective Psychology & Mental Health* 20 (2): 75–77.

———. 2013b. 'SIS Illumination of Unreported Violent Impulses'. *SIS Journal of Projective Psychology & Mental Health* 20 (2): 78–80.

———. 2013c. 'Editorial: SIS Psychotherapeutic Applications'. *SIS Journal of Projective Psychology & Mental Health* 20 (1): 1–2.

———. 2014a. 'Editorial: Religious Symbols and Astronomical Projections'. *SIS Journal of Projective Psychology & Mental Health* 21 (2): 65–67.

———. 2014b. 'Editorial: A Spiritual "Afterlife" Death Dream'. *SIS Journal of Projective Psychology & Mental Health* 21 (1): 1–2.

———. 2015. 'Editorial'. *SIS Journal of Projective Psychology & Mental Health* 22 (2): 75–79.

———. 2016. 'Editorial'. *SIS Journal of Projective Psychology & Mental Health* 23 (1): 1–2.

———. 2017. 'Editorial'. *SIS Journal of Projective Psychology & Mental Health* 24 (1): 1–2.

Cassell, W. A., A. Dubey and B. L. Dubey. 2000. 'SIS Projective Responses in PTSD and Dissociative Disorder'. *SIS Journal of Projective Psychology & Mental Health* 7: 93–108.

Cassell, W. A., A. M. Schaeck, and D. Mohn. 2002. 'Symbolism in Violent Hallucinations'. *SIS Journal of Projective Psychology & Mental Health* 9: 81–92.

Cassell, W. A., and B. L. Dubey. 1996a. 'Efficacy of the Booklet and Monochromatic Version of the SIS in a Case of Repeated Miscarriages'. *SIS Journal of Projective Psychology & Mental Health* 3: 131–145.

———. 1996b. 'The Use of the Rorschach and SIS in Releasing Somatised Grief'. *SIS Journal of Projective Psychology & Mental Health* 3: 3–32.

———. 1997. 'Therapeutic Dream Stimulation with SIS-Video'. *SIS Journal of Projective Psychology & Mental Health* 4: 3–23.

———. 1998a. 'Mental Disorders Triggered by Exposure to Violent Imagery in the Media and in Electronic Games'. *SIS Journal of Projective Psychology & Mental Health* 5: 87–104.

———. 1998b. 'Application of Somatic Inkblot Series in Personality Assessment, Screening, Diagnosis and Therapy'. *SIS Journal of Projective Psychology & Mental Health* 5: 3–32.

———. 2000. 'Inkblot Responses as an Aid to Therapy'. *SIS Journal of Projective Psychology & Mental Health* 7: 3–10.

———. 2002. 'Application of Somatic Inkblot Series I: New Scoring System'. *SIS Journal of Projective Psychology & Mental Health* 9: 5–22.

———. 2003. *Interpreting Inner World through Somatic Imagery: Manual of Somatic Inkblot Series*. Anchorage, AK: SIS Center.

———. 2004a. 'A Nervous System Based Model for SIS Inkblot Projection and Consultation'. *SIS Journal of Projective Psychology & Mental Health* 11: 95–104.

———. 2004b. 'Somatic Inkblot Series: Historical Background and Earlier Projects'. *SIS Journal of Projective Psychology & Mental Health* 11: 11–18.

———. 2006. 'Tracing the Roots of Violence by Associating Dream and SIS Images: A Vicarious Visit to an Adolescent's Birthday Party'. *SIS Journal of Projective Psychology & Mental Health* 13 (2): 85–106.

———. 2007a. 'Restructuring Rorschach Pathological Body Symbolism in the Somatoform Disorders with Truth Serum Behavior Therapy'. *SIS Journal of Projective Psychology & Mental Health* 14: 20–29.

———. 2007b. 'SIS and Sand Tray Psychotherapy of Suicidal Adolescents'. *SIS Journal of Projective Psychology & Mental Health* 14 (2): 87–97.

———. 2009. 'Content Validity of SIS-I and SIS-II Booklet Version'. *SIS Journal of Projective Psychology & Mental Health* 16: 58–59.

———. 2010a. 'Infectious Suicidal Imagery in Combat PTSD'. *SIS Journal of Projective Psychology & Mental Health* 17: 27–37.

———. 2010b. 'SIS II-Video and Treatment of Alcoholism'. *SIS Journal of Projective Psychology & Mental Health* 17: 104–119.

———. 2010c. 'Questionable Validity of Projective Technique and SIS Intervention'. *SIS Journal of Projective Psychology & Mental Health* 17: 4–15.

———. 2012a. 'Spiritual Warfare and SIS Spiritual Symbols'. *SIS Journal of Projective Psychology & Mental Health* 19 (2): 80–90.

———. 2012b. 'SIS Screening for Dangerous Impulses—a Blog Based Training Exercise for Students'. *SIS Journal of Projective Psychology & Mental Health* 19 (1): 5–17.

———. 2015. 'Editorial: New Name, Old Game'. *SIS Journal of Projective Psychology & Mental Health* 22 (1): 1–2.

————. 2016. 'A SIS-II Projective Case Study of Becker's Concept Denial of Death'. *SIS Journal of Projective Psychology & Mental Health* 23 (1): 2–11.

————. 2017. 'Efficacy of a Case of Post-traumatic Stress Disorder'. *SIS Journal of Projective Psychology & Mental Health* 24 (2): 74–82.

————. 2018. 'Anatomical Rorschach Responses and Death Symbolism'. *SIS Journal of Projective Psychology & Mental Health* 25 (2): 109–119.

Cassell, W. A., B. L. Dubey, E. Molchanov, and L. C. Routh. 1999. 'Stimulating Beacon Images for Meditation and Projective Psychotherapy'. *SIS Journal of Projective Psychology & Mental Health* 6: 7–30.

Cassell, W. A., B. L. Dubey, and G. J. Roth. 1997. 'Medical, Psychological and Spiritual Application of the SIS Inkblots'. *SIS Journal of Projective Psychology & Mental Health* 4: 89–112.

Cassell, W. A., B. L. Dubey, and Kalyani Menon. 2015. 'What Does It Socially Symbolize When a Woman Dreams of Having a Penis?' *SIS Journal of Projective Psychology & Mental Health* 22 (12): 80–82.

Cassell, W. A., B. L. Dubey, P. Dwivedi, and A. R. Singh. 2009. 'How to Delete Viruses and Reconfigure the Brain's Hard Drive'. *SIS Journal of Projective Psychology & Mental Health* 16: 91–116.

Cassell, W. A., B. L. Dubey, T. Charles, and P. Dwivedi. 2013. 'Perceiving One's Own Dead Body and Death Anxiety Dissolving SIS Spiritual Symbols'. *SIS Journal of Projective Psychology & Mental Health* 20 (1): 3–17.

Cassell, W. A., and D. Fields. 1995. 'Somatic Inkblot Series—Video: Case Report and Discussion'. *SIS Journal of Projective Psychology & Mental Health* 2: 3–18.

Cassell, W. A., D. Mohn, F. J. Ilardi, and B. L. Dubey. 2003. 'Unmasking the Devil with Projective Technique'. *SIS Journal of Projective Psychology & Mental Health* 10: 167–188.

Cassell, W. A., F. J. Illardi, A. Collins, M. Mishra, and B. L. Dubey. 2001. 'Optimizing Spiritual Healing by Assessing Dream and SIS Imagery'. *SIS Journal of Projective Psychology & Mental Health* 8: 75–94.

Cassell, W. A., and J. Duboczy. 1967. 'Cardiac Symptoms and Tachistoscopic Recognition of the Heart Image'. *Canadian Psychiatric Association Journal* 12: 73–76.

Cassell, W. A., P. Dwivedi, and B. L. Dubey. 2009a. 'SIS Living Images and Psychotherapy: A Case Study'. *SIS Journal of Projective Psychology & Mental Health* 16: 60–61.

Cassell, W. A., and P. Hemingway. 1970. 'Body Consciousness in States of Pharmacological Depression and Arousal'. *International Journal of Neuropharmacology* 9: 1–7.

Cassell, W. A., P. Pandey, A. Tiwari, N. Mishra, and B. L. Dubey. 2013. 'SIS Guided Therapy for an Adolescent Girl's Tension Headaches'. *SIS Journal of Projective Psychology & Mental Health* 20 (1): 49–54.

Cassell, W. A., T. Charles, B. L. Dubey, and H. Janssen. 2014. 'SIS Incites Long-term PTSD Combat Memories and Survivor Guilt'. *SIS Journal of Projective Psychology & Mental Health* 21 (2): 68–80.

Cervigni, A. 2013. 'Therapeutic Intervention through SIS Imagery: Two Case Studies'. *SIS Journal of Projective Psychology & Mental Health* 20 (2): 122–127.

Chakraborty, R., M. Dasgupta, and N. Sanyal. 2015. 'A Comparative Psychosocial Study of Aggression, Attachment Style and Personality among Orphans and Normal Children'. *SIS Journal of Projective Psychology & Mental Health* 22: 103–114.

Chapman, Loren J., and Jean Chapman. 1982. 'Test Results Are What You Think They Are'. In *Judgment under Uncertainty: Heuristics and Biases*, edited by Daniel Kahneman, Paul Slovic, and Amos Tversky, 238–248. Cambridge: Cambridge University Press.

Charney, D. S., A. Y. Deutsch, J. H. Krystal, S. M. Southwick, and M. Davis. 1993. 'Psychobiologic Mechanisms of Post-traumatic Stress Disorder'. *Archives of General Psychiatry* 50: 295–305.

Chatters, L. M. 2000. 'Religion and Health: Public Health Research and Practice'. *Annual Review of Public Health* 21: 335–367.

Chaudhury, S., D. Saldanha, K. Srivastava, Jyothi S. G., G. S. Sundari, and M. Augustine. 2007a. 'Rorschach Responses of Indian Children and Adolescents with Psychiatric Disorders'. *SIS Journal of Projective Psychology & Mental Health* 14 (2): 150–161.

Chaudhury, S., and G. S. Sundari. 1996. 'Thiesens' Pattern in Rorschach of Adolescents with Schizophrenia'. *SIS Journal of Projective Psychology & Mental Health* 3: 69–75.

Chaudhury, S., J. Prakash, T. S. Walia, K. Seby, S. Sukumaran, and D. Kumari. 2010. 'Psychological Distress in Alcohol Dependence Syndrome'. *SIS Journal of Projective Psychology & Mental Health* 17: 38–44.

Chaudhury, S., and Jyothi S. G. 1996. 'Relationship between Homosexuality and Paranoid Schizophrenia: A Rorschach Study'. *SIS Journal of Projective Psychology & Mental Health* 3: 147–152.

———. 1997. 'Diagnostic Utility of Piotrowski's Alpha Index'. *SIS Journal of Projective Psychology & Mental Health* 4: 35–40.

———. 1998. 'Piotrowski's Alpha Index Validated with Schizophrenics Varying in Duration of Illness'. *SIS Journal of Projective Psychology & Mental Health* 5: 41–45.

Chaudhury, S., Jyothi S. G., M. Augustine, K. Srivastava, and P. K. Chakraborty. 2005. 'Rorschach Test Norms for Normal Indian Children and Adolescents'. *Indian Journal of Clinical Psychology* 32: 41–53.

Chaudhury, S., and M. Augustine. 1990. 'Rorschach Profile of Normal Army Personnel'. *Medical Journal Armed Forces India* 46: 263–266.

Chaudhury, S., M. Augustine, D. Saldanha, K. Srivastava, S. M. Kundeyawala, A. A. Pawar, and V. S. S. R. Ryali. 2006. 'Norms of the Rorschach Test for Indian Subjects'. *Medical Journal Armed Forces India* 62: 153–160.

Chaudhury, S., M. S. V. K. Raju, B. L. Dubey, T. R. John, S. K. Salujha, and K. Srivastava. 2001. 'Alopacia Areata: Evaluation Using Psychological Tests and the Somatic Inkblot Test'. *SIS Journal of Projective Psychology & Mental Health* 8: 143–148.

Chaudhury, S., P. S. Murthy, A. Banerjee, D. Kumari, and S. Alreja. 2011. 'Poly-Trauma Survivors: Assessment Using Rating Scales and SIS II'. *SIS Journal of Projective Psychology & Mental Health* 18 (1): 39–49.

Chaudhury, S., P. S. Murthy, I. Banerjee, S. Kumari, S. K. Sukumaran, and R. Vikash. 2009. 'Psychological Distress Associated with Fractures of Upper and Lower Limbs'. *SIS Journal of Projective Psychology & Mental Health* 16: 18–23.

Chaudhury, S., S. Sudarsanan, K. Seby, S. K. Salujha, K. Srivastava, S. M. Kundeyawala, and S. P. Rathee. 2007. 'Rorschach Responses of Older Indians'. *SIS Journal of Projective Psychology & Mental Health* 14: 30–43.

Chaudhury, S., T. R. John, H. S. Bhatoe, and S. Rohatgi. 1999. 'Evaluation of Piotrowski's Organic Signs of Head Injury'. *SIS Journal of Projective Psychology & Mental Health* 6: 53–57.

Chaudhury, S., T. R. John, and Jyothi S. G. 1999a. 'Validation of Weiner's Signs in Schizophrenia'. *SIS Journal of Projective Psychology & Mental Health* 6: 38–44.

Chaudhury, S., T. R. John, and S. Rohatgi. 1998. 'Evaluation of Piotrowski's Organic Signs in Epilepsy'. *SIS Journal of Projective Psychology & Mental Health* 5: 127–130.

Chaudhury, U. 1952. 'Psychological Analysis of Personality Structures of Rural Bengal Population on the Basis of Rorschach Test'. PhD thesis. Calcutta University, Calcutta.

Cinzia, S., and R. Ferro. 1998. 'SIS-I and Body Image Evaluation in Subjects Suffering from Series Obesity'. *SIS Journal of Projective Psychology & Mental Health* 5: 105–113.

Cleveland, S. E., and R. B. Morton. 1962. 'Group Behavior and Body Image: A Follow Up Study'. *Human Relations* 15: 77–85.

Conners, C. K. 1965. 'Effects of Brief Psychotherapy, Drugs and Type of Disturbance on Holtzman Inkblot Scores in Children'. *Proceedings of the 73rd Annual Convention of American Psychological Association*, 201–202.

Conquest, R. A. 1963. 'An Investigation of Body Image Variables in Patients with the Diagnosis of Schizophrenic Reaction'. Unpublished doctoral dissertation, Western Reserve University, Cleveland, OH.

Covan, F. L. 1976. 'The Perception of Movement in Inkblots Following Cognitive Inhibition'. Unpublished doctoral dissertation, Yeshiva University, New York, NY.

Dahlenburg, R. Taylor. 1993. 'The Effect of Group Dream Work on Spiritual Well Being'. *Dissertation Abstracts International* 54 (4-A): 1238.

Daini, S., A. Manzo, F. Pisani, and A. Tancredi. 2010. 'Attempted Suicide: Psychopathology and Wartegg Test Indicators'. *SIS Journal of Projective Psychology & Mental Health* 14: 171–177.

Daini, S., and L. Bernardini. 2007. 'Emotional Feelings in Eating Disorders: A Rorschach Test Quantitative Analysis'. *SIS Journal of Projective Psychology & Mental Health* 14: 76–84.

Daini, S., L. Carotti, A. Manzo, C. Minerva, and G. Mancano. 2008. 'A Projective Sight on Male Anorexia: A Rorschach Test Exploration'. *SIS Journal of Projective Psychology & Mental Health* 14: 65–72.

Dana, R. H. 2000. *Handbook of Cross-Cultural and Multicultural Personality Assessment*. Mahwah, NJ: Lawrence Erlbaum.

Darolia, C. R., and H. L. Joshi. 2004. 'Psychometric Evaluation of a Short Form of Holtzman Inkblot Technique'. *SIS Journal of Projective Psychology & Mental Health* 2: 124–132.

Dasgupta, M. 2013. 'The Efficacy of Dance/Movement Therapy as Revealed through the Qualitative Lens of Somatic Inkblot Series (SIS-II)'. *SIS Journal of Projective Psychology & Mental Health* 20 (2): 110–121.

Dasgupta, T., R. Dasgupta, and P. Dwivedi. 2012. 'Somatic Inkblots Imagery in Transsexual: A Case Study'. *Journal of Projective Psychology & Mental Health* 19 (1): 61–65.

Davido, R. D. 1994. *The Childhood Hand That Disturbs Projective Test: A Diagnostic and Therapeutic Drawing Test*. Westport, CT: Greenwood Publishing Group.

Davidson, J., R. Smith, and H. Kudler. 1989. 'The Validity and Reliability of the DSM-III-R Criteria for PTSD'. *Journal of Nervous and Mental Disease* 177: 336–341.

Davidson, L. E., and M. S. Gould. 1989. 'Contagion as a Risk Factor for Youth Suicide'. In *Alcohol, Drug Abuse, and Mental Health Administration Report of the Secretary's Taskforce on Youth Suicide*, Vol. 2., 88–109, Risk Factors for Youth Suicide. Washington, DC: US Department of Health and Human Services, Public Health Service (DHHS publication No. [ADM] 89–1622).

Davis, T. L., and, Hill, C.E. (2001). 'Dream Interpretation from a Spiritual Perspective'. In L. Vande Creek & T. L. Jackson (Eds.) *Innovations* in *Clinical Practice, A Source Book, Vol.19, P 79–94*. Sarasota, FL:

Da Vinci, L. 1982. 'Study of Christ for the last suppur. Nach dem codex vaticanus, 1270'. In *Quellenschriften F. Kunstgeschichte*, Vol. 15. Vienna: W. Braumuller

Day, F. 1944. 'The Future of Psychoanalysis and Religion'. *Psychoanalytic Quarterly* 13: 84–92.

De Angelis, T. (2011). 'Psychologist Suicide Monitor', *Psychology*, 42: 10, 19.

Deslauriers, Daniel. 2000. 'Dream Work in the Light of Emotional and Spiritual Intelligence'. *Advanced Development* 9: 105–122.

Devi, S. G., and K. V. Kaliappan. 1997. 'Improvement of Psychosomatic Disorders among Tension Headache Subjects Using Behavior Therapy and Somatic Inkblot Series'. *SIS Journal of Projective Psychology & Mental Health* 4: 113–120.

De Vos, A. 1973. *An Introduction to Rorschach Technique: Monograph Bangalore*. Karnataka: National Institute of Mental Health and Neuro Sciences, Bangalore (India).

Dewangan, R. L., S. Basu, and P. K. Roy. 2014. 'Rorschach Response in Somatization Problem among College Students'. *SIS Journal of Projective Psychology & Mental Health* 21 (1): 342–348.

Dewangan, R. L., and P. K. Roy. 2015. 'A Study on Social Desirability Biasness in Rorschach Inkblot Test'. *SIS Journal of Projective Psychology & Mental Health* 22 (1): 24–29.

Dey, B., and T. B. Singh. 2019. 'Understanding the Sensitivity of Coping Deficit Index of Comprehensive System of Rorschach in Discriminating Schizophrenia and Anxiety Spectrum Disorder and Association with Self-reported Measure'. *SIS Journal of Projective Psychology & Mental Health* 26 (1): 56–62.

Dharamvir, Pershad D., B. L. Dubey, and S. B. S. Mann. 1994. 'Body Imagery in Vertigo Patients'. *SIS Journal of Projective Psychology & Mental Health* 1: 65–72.

Dixit, G. 1964. 'A Development Study of the Rorschach Response Pattern of Children between 5+ and 10+'. Unpublished doctoral thesis, Allahabad University, Allahabad.

Doka, K. J. 1989. Recognizing Hidden Sorrow (*Difeoretesial Sig*) Lexington Books, Massachusetts.

Domhoff, G. W. 1996. *Finding Meaning in Dreams: A Quantitative Approach.* New York, NY: Plenum Publishing Co.

———. 1999. 'New Directions in the Study of Dream Content Using the Hall and Van de Castle Coding System'. *Dreaming* 9 (2/3): 115–137.

———. 2000. 'Methods and Methods for the Study of Dream Content'. In *Principles and Practice of Sleep Medicine*, 3rd ed., edited by M. Krygere, T. Roth, and W. C. Dement, 463–471. Philadelphia, PA: W.B. Saunders.

Donegan, N. H., C. A. Sanislow, H. P. Blumber, R. K. Fulbright, C. Lacadie, P. Skudlarski, and J. C. Gore. 2003. 'Amygdala Hyperactivity in Borderline Personality Disorder: Implications for Emotional Dysregulation'. *Biological Psychiatry* 54: 1284–1293.

D'Netto, T. B., R. Kishore, and R. K. Ruggu. 1974. 'Analysis of Rorschach Responses of Normal Army Personnel'. *Indian Journal of Clinical Psychology* 2: 87–92.

D'Netto, T. B., and R. Kishore. 1976. 'The Psychometric Assessment of Head Injury'. *Indian Journal Clinical Psychology* 3 (1): 23–28.

Doniger, Wendy, and Kelly Bulkley. 1993. 'Why Study Dreams? A Religious Studies Perspective'. *Dreaming: Journal of the Association for the Study of Dreams* 3 (1): 69–73.

Dosajh, N. L. 1956. 'Imagination and Maturity as Factors Indicative of Success in Teaching'. Unpublished doctoral thesis, Panjab University, Chandigarh.

———. 1995. 'A New Combination of Therapies for the Treatment of Schizophrenia of Less than Five Years Duration'. *SIS Journal of Projective Psychology & Mental Health* 2: 135–138.

———. 1996a. 'Projective Technique with Particular Reference to Inkblot Tests'. *SIS Journal of Projective Psychology & Mental Health* 3: 159–168.

————. 1996b. 'Editorial'. *SIS Journal of Projective Psychology & Mental Health* 3: 89–90.

————. 1997a. 'How a Single Image of SIS-II Leads to Complete Psycho Diagnosis'. *SIS Journal of Projective Psychology & Mental Health* 4: 152–154.

————. 1997b. 'Some Experience with Somatic Inkblot Series II'. *SIS Journal of Projective Psychology & Mental Health* 4: 25–33.

————. 1998a. 'Projective Psychology in India'. *SIS Journal of Projective Psychology & Mental Health* 5: 83–86.

————. 1998b. 'Somatic Inkblot Series—an Excellent Psycho Diagnostic Tool'. *SIS Journal of Projective Psychology & Mental Health* 5: 136–138.

————. 1998c. 'Use of SIS-II and other Projective Tests in the Treatment of a Case of Schizophrenia'. *SIS Journal of Projective Psychology & Mental Health* 5: 46–50.

————. 1999a. 'How Responses of Spiritual Urge Leads to Psychological Troubles'. *SIS Journal of Projective Psychology & Mental Health* 6: 61–64.

————. 1999b. 'New Horizons in Psychotherapy'. *SIS Journal of Projective Psychology & Mental Health* 6 (2): 1–3.

————. 1999c. 'Maintaining Mental Health of the Aged through Psycho Synthesis'. *SIS Journal of Projective Psychology & Mental Health* 6: 58–60.

Dosajh, N. L., and R. Dosajh. 1999. 'A Case of Family Therapy'. *SIS Journal of Projective Psychology & Mental Health* 6 (2): 4–6.

Drevets, W. C., J. L. Price, and J. R. Jr Simpson. 1997. 'Subgenual Prefrontal Cortex Abnormalities in Mood Disorders'. *Nature* 386 (6627): 824–827.

Dubey, Anand. 2010. 'Rethinking Enterprise Resource Planning (ERP)'. *Government Technology* 23 (10): 14–19, 49.

Dubey, A., and B. L. Dubey. 2012. 'Application of SIS in Business Organization'. *SIS Journal of Projective Psychology & Mental Health* 19 (1): 43–47.

Dubey, B. L. 1972. 'A Study of Hearing and Speech Defects in Mentally Retarded Children'. *Indian Journal of Mental Retardation* 5: 84–89.

————. 1975a. 'Personality Profile of DPM Students'. *Prabandhan: Indian Journal of Management*: 2: 15–22.

————. 1975b. 'Psychological Survey of T.B. Patients'. *Indian Journal of Tuberculosis* 22: 83–85.

————. 1976. 'A Comparative Study of Personality, Intelligence and Performance of Neurotics and Psychotics'. *Indian Journal of Clinical Psychology* 3: 153–156.

————. 1977a. 'Rorschach Analysis of Impotence Cases and Their Response to Psychotherapy'. *Indian Journal of Clinical Psychology* 4: 145–149.

————. 1977b. 'Personality Variables and Performance of Management Students'. *Indian Journal of Industrial Relations* 12: 515–518.

————. 1978. 'Rorschach Indicators in Normal and Clinical Groups in Military Population'. Unpublished PhD thesis, Panjab University, Chandigarh.

————. 1979. 'Rorschach Indices of Psychiatric Patients in Army'. *Indian Journal of Clinical Psychology* 6: 175–179.

Dubey, B. L. 1972. 1980. 'A Personality Study of Business Executive'. *PU Management Review* 3: 37–43.

———. 1981a. 'An Evaluation of Rorschach as Clinical Tools'. *Indian Journal of Clinical Psychology* 86: 157–163.

———. 1981b. 'Rorschach Indicators in Normal and Clinical Groups in Military Population'. *ISPT Journal of Research* 5: 54–56.

———. 1982. *A Pragmatic View of Rorschach Inkblot Technique.* Agra: National Psychological Corporation.

———. 1983. 'Management of Sexual Disorders through Psychotherapy'. *Psyche-Care News* 5: 103–104.

———. 1985a. 'Discriminating Capacity of Indices as Affected by the Length of the Number of Responses on Rorschach'. Paper presented in Inter-American Congress of Psychology, Caracas, Venezuela.

———. 1985b. 'Clinical Psychologists in the Community: Presidential Address'. *Indian Journal of Clinical Psychology* 12: 1–8.

———. 1986. 'Making Again Productive—a Therapeutic Intervention'. *Indian Journal of Clinical Psychology* 13: 185–187.

———. 1987. 'Management of Stress and Mental Health of Executives'. *Prabandhan: Indian Journal of Management* 2: 63–69.

———. 1988, September. 'Personality Profile of Indian Executives'. Paper presented in 24th International Congress of Psychology, Sydney.

———. 1989a. 'Rorschach Variables as Affected by the Length of the Protocol'. *Indian Psychological Review* 35 (1): 12–16.

———. 1989b. 'Rorschach Profile of Indian Executives'. *Indian Journal of Clinical Psychology* 16: 74–77.

———. 1991, 11–15 August. 'Some Experiments with Somatic Inkblot Series'. 49th Conference of International Council of Psychologist, San Francisco.

———. 1992. 'Projective Value of Somatic Inkblot Series-II in a Case of Stammering'. *Journal of Personality and Clinical Studies* 8 (2): 173–176.

———. 1993a. 'Somatic Inkblot Technique: Evolution and Current Status'. *The Mind* 2: 22–31.

———. 1993b. 'Personality Assessment through Inkblot Techniques'. In *Management and Business Education*, edited by J. L. Rastogi, and Bidhi Chand pp 297–306. New Delhi: Rawat Publications.

———. 1996. 'SIS as a Projective Psychotherapeutic Tool for the 21st Century'. Presidential Address. *SIS Journal of Projective Psychology & Mental Health* 3 (2): 95–107.

———. 1997a. 'Application of Somatic Inkblot Series in Personality Assessment and Psychotherapy'. *Indian Journal of Psychology* 72: 73–80.

———. 1997b. 'Clinical Utility of Somatic Inkblot Series—Video'. *Perspective in Psychological Researches* 20: 10–15.

———. 2000. 'SIS Technology in Millennium Year'. *SIS Journal of Projective Psychology & Mental Health* 7: 91–92.

———. 2003. 'Editorial: SIS as an Electronic Aide to Assessment and Therapeutic Intervention'. *SIS Journal of Projective Psychology & Mental Health* 10 (2): 165–166.

Dubey, B. L. 1972. 2005a. 'SIS Stimulation of Beacon Imagery'. *SIS Journal of Projective Psychology & Mental Health* 12 (1): 3–8.

———. 2005b. 'Editorial: SIS as an Electronic Aide to Assessment'. *SIS Journal of Projective Psychology & Mental Health* 12 (1): 1–2.

———. 2006. 'Editorial: Somatic Inkblot Series: Assessment and Therapeutic Tool'. *SIS Journal of Projective Psychology & Mental Health* 13 (2): 83–84.

———. 2018. 'Presidential Address: Future Direction of Somatic Inkblot Test as a Projective Psychotherapeutic Technique'. Delivered at 8th International Conference of SIS, Punjab University, Chandigarh (India) on 27–29 April 2018. *SIS Journal of Projective Psychology & Mental Health* 25 (2): 106–108.

Dubey, B. L., A. Agrawal, and R. S. Palia. 2001. 'Personality Profile and HRD Intervention in a Telephone Cables Company'. *SIS Journal of Projective Psychology & Mental Health* 8: 127–134.

Dubey, B. L., C. Ajith, Somesh Gupta, and B. Kumar. 2004. 'Role of Somatic Inkblot Series in Psychosexual Disorder in India'. *SIS Journal of Projective Psychology & Mental Health* 11: 115–120.

Dubey, B. L., and D. Pershad. 1978a. 'Validation of the Proposed Statistical Design for Rorschach'. *Indian Journal Clinical of Psychology* 5: 91.

———. 1978b. 'Shift in the Clinical Significance of Indices of the Rorschach When Controlled for Responses'. *Perspective in Psychological Research* 1: 119–122.

———. 1984. 'Current Status of Rorschach Testing'. In *Recent Advances of Psychological Testing*, (ED) S.P. Kulshresth, pp 50–60. Dehradun: Jugul Kishor & Co.

Dubey, B. L., D. Pershad, and S. K. Verma. 1979. 'Rorschach Responses of Different Types of Neurotics'. *Journal of Rajasthan Psychological Society* 3: 29–32.

———. 1981. 'An Evaluation of Rorschach as a Clinical Tool'. *Indian Journal of Clinical Psychology* 8: 157–163.

Dubey, B. L., and G. C. Sharma. 1973. 'A Comparative Study of Over Inclusive Thinking on Rorschach Test'. *ISPT Journal of Research* 18: 99–102.

Dubey, B. L., and K. D. Das. 1977. 'Personality Patterns of Alopecia Areata'. *Indian Journal of Clinical Psychology* 4: 45–50.

Dubey, B. L., M. Mishra, C. B. Dwivedi, and N. Mishra. 1994. 'Diagnostic and Therapeutic Utility of SIS-II and Rorschach'. *SIS Journal of Projective Psychology & Mental Health* 1: 18–25.

Dubey, B. L., and N. L. Dosajh. 1979. 'Rorschach Responses in Normal Army Personnel'. *Indian Journal of Clinical Psychology* 6: 169–173.

Dubey, B. L., and P. Dwivedi. 1994, July. 'Clinical Utility of Somatic Inkblot Series in Adolescents'. 23rd International Congress of Applied Psychology, Madrid.

———. 2015. 'Therapeutic Intervention through SIS in a Case of Dissociative Convulsion Disorder'. *SIS Journal of Projective Psychology & Mental Health* 22 (2): 99–102.

Dubey, B. L., P. Dwivedi, and W. A. Cassell. 1993, 15–19 August. 'Inner Cry through Somatic Inkblot Series'. *Proceedings of 51st International Council of Psychologists*, Montreal.

———. 1994, 18 July. 'Assessment of Traumatic Life Experience Reaction'. Workshop conducted in 23rd International Congress of Applied Psychology, Madrid.

———. 1996a, 8–12 July. 'Application of Somatic Inkblot Series'. 14th International Congress of Rorschach and Projective Method, Boston.

———. 1996b, 16–21 August. 'Clinical Significance of Somatic Inkblot Series'. 26th International Congress of Psychology, Montreal.

Dubey, B. L., P. Dwivedi, W. A. Cassell, and Anand Dubey. 1998a, 18–22 February. 'Diagnostic Compatibility of Somatic Inkblot Series and the Rorschach with Emphasis on Hearing the Inner Cry of Their Individuals'. Mid-winter Meeting of Society for Personality Assessment, Boston.

———. 1998b, 9–14 August. 'Compatibility of SIS and Rorschach'. 24th Congress of International Association of Applied Psychology, San Francisco, CA.

Dubey, B. L., P. Dwivedi, W. A. Cassell, and M. Sahay. 1993. 'Projective Value of Somatic Inkblot Series-II in a Case of Stammering'. *Journal of Personality and Clinical Studies* 8: 173–176.

Dubey, B. L., P. Pandey, A. Tiwari, and N. Mishra. 2012. 'Assessing Sexuality "Homosexuality"'. *SIS Journal of Projective Psychology & Mental Health* 19 (2): 121–125.

Dubey, B. L., R. Kumar, and Anand Dubey. 2018. 'Somatic Inkblot Series and the *Journal of Projective Psychology & Mental Health*: Inception to Silver Jubilee'. *SIS Journal of Projective Psychology & Mental Health* 25 (1): 5–34.

Dubey, B. L., and S. K. Verma. 1980. 'A Personality Study of Business Executives'. *Management Review* 3 (1): 37–43.

Dubey, B. L., and W. A. Cassell. 1992a, July. 'Diagnostic Utility of Somatic Inkblot Series Video'. *Proceedings of 25th International Congress of Psychology*, Brussels.

———. 1992b, July. 'Clinical Utility of Somatic Inkblot Series Video'. *Proceedings of 50th International Council of Psychologists*, Amsterdam.

———. 1993. 'Some Experiences with Somatic Inkblot Series'. *British Journal of Projective Psychology* 38 (1): 19–41.

———. 2000. 'Inkblot Responses as an Aid to Therapy'. *SIS Journal of Projective Psychology & Mental Health* 7: 3–10.

Dubey, B. L., W. A. Cassell, and Anand Dubey. 2005. 'Impact of Number of Responses on the Interpretation of Rorschach Indices'. *SIS Journal of Projective Psychology & Mental Health* 12: 27–48.

Dubey, B. L., W. A. Cassell, D. Pershad, and P. Dwivedi. 1995a. 'Diagnostic Utility of Somatic Inkblot Series'. *SIS Journal of Projective Psychology & Mental Health* 2: 77–84.

Dubey, B. L., W. A. Cassell, P. Dwivedi, and M. Mishra. 1995b. 'Inner Cry through Somatic Inkblot Series'. *SIS Journal of Projective Psychology & Mental Health* 2: 119–128.

Dubey, S. N., and B. L. Dubey. 2005. 'Effect of Psychological Intervention through SIS-I Images on Police Personnel'. *SIS Journal of Projective Psychology & Mental Health* 12 (2): 153–158.

Dutta, K. S., B. K. Jha, and T. R. Shukla. 1976. 'Rorschach Study of Peptic Ulcer'. *Indian Journal of Clinical Psychology* 3: 149–152.

Dwivedi, C. B., M. Mishra, and B. L. Dubey. 1995. 'Diagnostic Significance of the Indices of the SIS-II and the Rorschach Inkblot Tests'. *SIS Journal of Projective Psychology & Mental Health* 2: 165–170.

Dwivedi, P., B. L. Dubey, W. A. Cassell, and D. Pershad. 1992, July. 'Somatic Inkblot Series Video in Adolescents'. *Proceedings of 25th International Congress of Psychology*, Brussels.

Dwivedi, P., M. Mishra, and N. Mishra. 1998. 'Somatic Inkblot Series on a Sexually Traumatized Female'. *SIS Journal of Projective Psychology & Mental Health* 5: 150–153.

Dwivedi, P., M. Mishra, and W. A. Cassell. 1994. 'SIS-Video in Adolescents'. *SIS Journal of Projective Psychology & Mental Health* 1: 27–32.

Dwivedi, S. D. 2015. 'Sensitivity of Exner's Comprehensive Scoring System in Detecting Specific Delusions in Psychotic Patients: Preliminary Observations'. *SIS Journal of Projective Psychology & Mental Health* 22 (1): 58–61.

Dwivedi, S. D., and R. Verma. 2018. 'Intervention through Somatic Inkblot Series and CBT in a Case of Gender Identity Disorder'. *SIS Journal of Projective Psychology & Mental Health* 25 (2): 178–181.

Eagle, M.N. 2007. 'Psychoanalysis and Its Critics'. *Psychoanalytic Psychology* 24(1): 10–24.

Ellenberger, H. 1954a. 'The Life and Work of Herman Rorschach'. *Bulletin of the Menninger Clinic* 18: 175–218.

———. 1954b. 'Herman Rorschach, M.D. 1884–1922: A Biographical Study'. *Bulletin of the Menninger Clinic* 18 (5): 173–219.

Endicott, N. A., and J. Endicott. 1963. 'Objective Measures of Somatic Preoccupation'. *Journal of Nervous and Mental Disease* 137: 427–435.

Erb, M., E. M. Hodgins, R. Freese, R. Miller-Isberner, and D. Jackel. 2001. 'Homicide and Schizophrenia: May Be Treatment Does Have a Preventative Effect'. *Criminal Behavior Mental Health* 11 (1): 6–26.

Ewing, Katherine P. 1990. 'The Dream of Spiritual Initiation and the Organization of Self Representations among Pakistani Sufis'. *American Ethnologist* 17 (1): 56–74.

Exner, John E. Jr. 1969. 'Rorschach Responses as an Index of Narcissism'. *Journal of Projective Technique and Personality Assessment* 33: 324–330.

———. 1974. 'The Rorschach: A Comprehensive System'. New York, NY: John Wiley.

———. 1989. 'Rorschach Interpretation'. *Proceedings of Annual Meeting of the Society for Personality Assessment*. New York, NY.

Exner, John E. Jr. 1995. *A Rorschach Workbook for the Comprehensive System*, 4th ed. Asheville, NC: Rorschach Workshops.

———. 2001. *A Rorschach Workbook for the Comprehensive System*, 5th ed. Asheville, NC: Rorschach Workshops.

———. 2003. *The Rorschach: A Comprehensive System*, Vol. 1: Basic Foundation, 4th ed. New York, NY: Wiley.

Eysenck, H. J. 1965. 'Tests and Reviews: Character-Projective: The HIT'. In *Mental Measurements Yearbook*, 6th ed., edited by O. K. Buros, 440–441. Highland Park, NJ: Gryphon Press.

Fazel, S., G. Gulati, L. Linsel, J. R. Geddes, and M. Grann. 2009. 'Schizophrenia and Violence: Systematic Review and Met-Analysis'. *Plos Medicine* 6 (8)(e1000120 E. pub 2009 Aug. 11).

Feldstein, S. 1973. 'REM Deprivation: The Effects of Inkblot Perception and Fantasy Processes'. Doctoral Dissertation, the City University of New York, 1972. *Dissertation Abstract International* 33: 3934B–3935B (Order No.73-2835).

Fenichel, O. 1945. *The Psychoanalytical Theory of Neurosis*. New York, NY: W. W. Norton & Company.

Fernald, P. S., and J. D. Linden. 1966. 'The Human Content Response in the Holtzman Inkblot Technique'. *Journal of Projective Technique and Personality Assessment* 30: 441–446.

Feygin, D. l., J. E. Swain, and J. F. Leckman. 2006. 'The Normalcy of Neurosis: Evolutionary Origins of Obsessive-Compulsive Disorder and Related Behaviors'. *Progress in Neuropsychopharmacology and Biological Psychiatry* 30: 854–864.

Fisher, S. 1963. 'A Further Appraisal of the Body Boundary Concept'. *Journal of Consulting Psychology* 27: 62–74.

———. 1970. *Body Experience in Fantasy and Behavior*. New York, NY: Meredith Corporation.

Fisher, S., and S. E. Cleveland. 1958. *Body Image and Personality*. Princeton, NJ: Van Nostrand.

———. 1968. *Body Image and Personality*, 2nd ed. Princeton, NJ: Van Nostrand.

Fiske, D. W., and E. E. Baughman. 1953. 'Relationships between Rorschach Scoring Categories and the Total Number of Responses'. *The Journal of Abnormal and Social Psychology* 48: 25–32.

Foa, E. B., D. S. Riggs, C. V. Dancu, and B. O. Rothbaum. 1993. 'Reliability and Validity of a Brief Instrument for Assessing Post-Traumatic Stress Disorder'. *Journal of Traumatic Stress* 6: 459–473.

Fontenelle, L. F., A. M. Domingues, and W. F. Souza. 2007. 'History of Trauma and Dissociative Disorders among Patients with Obsessive-Compulsive Disorder and Social Anxiety Disorder'. *Psychiatric Quarterly* 78: 241–250.

Fontenelle, L. F., M. V. Mendlowicz, C. Marques, and M. Versiani. 2004. 'Trans-Cultural Aspects of Obsessive-Compulsive Disorder: A Description of a Brazilian Sample and a Systematic Review of

International Clinical Studies'. *Journal of Psychiatric Research* 38: 403–411.

Frank, L. K. 1939. 'Comments on the Proposed Standardization of the Rorschach Method'. *Rorschach Research Exchange* 3: 101–105.

Fremantle, A. 1962. 'Review of Psychoanalysis and Religion'. *Psychoanalysis Quarterly* 31: 551–553.

Freud, S. 1927. *The Ego and the Id*. Standard Edition of the Complete Psychological works of Sigmund Freud. Vol 21. Edited by J. Strachey. London: Hogarth Press.

———. 1950. 'Further Remarks on the Defence Neuro-Psychoses (1896)'. In *Collected Papers*, Edited by J. Strachey Vol. 1, 155–182. London: Hogarth Press.

———. 1953. 'Fragment of an Analysis of a Case of Hysteria'. In *The Standard Edition of the Complete Psychological Works of Sigmund Freud*, Edited by J. Strachey Vol. 7, 7. London: Hogarth Press.

Friedman, P., and J. Goldstein. 1974. 'Phobic Reactions'. In *American Handbook of Psychiatry*, Vol. 3, 2nd ed., Chapter 6, edited by S. Arietti, 10. New York, NY: Basic Books.

Fromm, E. 1951. *Psychoanalysis and Religion*. London: Gollancz.

Fromm, E., and M. Eisen. 1982. 'Self Hypnosis as a Therapeutic Aid in the Mourning Process'. *American Journal of Clinical Hypnosis* 25 (1): 3–14.

Gabbard, Glen A., and Mardi J. Horowitz. 2009. 'Insight, Transference Interpretation, and Therapeutic Change in the Dynamic Psychotherapy of Borderline Personality Disorder'. *American Journal of Psychiatry* 166: 517–521.

Gacono, C. B., F. B. Evans, L. A. Gacono, and N. Kaser-Boyd, eds. 2007. *The Handbook of Forensic Rorschach Psychology*, 80. Mahwah, NJ: Lawrence Erlbaum.

Gacano, Carl B., and J. Reid Meloy. 1994. *The Rorschach Assessment of Aggressive and Psychopathic Personalities*. Hillsdale, NJ and Hove: Lawrence Erlbaum.

Gaynes, B. N., S. L. West, C. A. Ford, P. Frame, J. Klein, and K. N. Lohr. 2004. 'Screening for Suicide Risk in Adults: A Summary of the Evidence for the US Preventative Services Tech Force'. *Annals of Internal Medicine* 140: 822–835.

Geller, B. 2008. 'Prospective Continuity with Adult Bipolar I Disorder: Characteristics of Second and Third Episodes: Predictor of 8 Years Outcome'. *Archieves of General Psychiatry* 65 (10): 1125–1133.

George, L., and R. Kumar. 2008. 'Diagnostic Efficiency of New Rorschach Depression Index (DEPI)'. *SIS Journal of Projective Psychology & Mental Health* 15: 118–127.

Ghaemi, S., M. Bauer, F. Cassidy, G. Malhi, P. Mitchell, and J. Phelps. 2008. 'Diagnostic Guidelines for Bipolar Disorder: A Summary of the International Society for Bipolar Disorders Diagnostic Guidelines Task Force Report'. *Bipolar Disorder* 10: 117–128.

Giovanna Gaetani, G., L. Fiorenzo, A. Lucchini, S. Giovanni, R. Vitali, and R. Ferro. 1995. 'Corporal Perception in HIV Positive and Negative Heorin-Addicts Assessed with SIS-I'. *SIS Journal of Projective Psychology & Mental Health* 2: 96–110.

Goel, D. S., S. P. Rathee, M. Saldanha, A. S. Chawla, and B. L. Dubey. 1990, April. 'SIS-I in Coronary Heart Disease'. *Proceedings of first National Workshop on SIS and Rorschach*, Chandigarh, India.

Gorham, D. R. 1967. 'Computer Use in Psychological Testing'. *Memorias del XIth Congreso Interamericano de Psicologia* 9: 1–7.

Gould, M. S., and L. Davidson. 1988. 'Suicide Contagion among Adolescents'. In A. R. Stiffman & R. A. Feldman (Eds.) *Advances in Adolescent Mental Health*, Vol. 3, pp 29–59, Greenwich, CT: JAI Press.

Gould, M. S., S. Wallenstein, M. H. Kleinman, P. W. O'Carroll, and J. A. Mercy. 1990. 'Suicide Clusters: An Examination of Age-Specific Effects'. *American Journal of Public Health* 80: 211–212.

Gournaris, Michael J., Irene W. Leigh, and Ross E. Mitchell. 2005. 'Consistency of Structural Summary Scores in Computerized Rorschach Programs'. *SIS Journal of Projective Psychology & Mental Health* 12: 20–26.

Graber, D. R., and J. A. Johnson. 2001. 'Spirituality and Healthcare Organizations'. *Journal of Health Care Management* 46 (1): 39–50.

Gray, N. A., R. Zhou, and J. Du. 2003. 'The Use of Mood Stabilizers as Plasticity Enhancers in the Treatment of Neuropsychiatric Disorder'. *Journal of Clinical Psychiatry* 64 (5): 3–17.

Groth-Marnat, G. 2009. *Handbook of Psychological Assessment*, 5th ed. Hoboken, NJ: Wiley.

Guarnaccia, V., C. A. Dill, S. Sabatino, and S. Southwick. 2001. 'Scoring Accuracy Using the Comprehensive System for the Rorschach'. *Journal of Personality Assessment* 77: 464–474.

Gunter, P. Richard. 1983. 'Religious Dreaming: A Viewpoint'. *American Journal of Psychotherapy* 37 (3): 411–427.

Gupta, B. K. 1959. 'An Experimental Investigation into Personality Patterns of Delinquent Adolescents'. Doctoral thesis, Allahabad University, Allahabad.

Gupta, Naveen, and A. Singh. 2012. 'Enhancing Productivity and Culture through SIS Intervention: A Case Study'. *SIS Journal of Projective Psychology & Mental Health* 19 (1): 71–75.

Gupta, Naveen, A. Singh, and R. A. Singh. 2015. 'Management of Depression in India'. *SIS Journal of Projective Psychology & Mental Health* 22 (2): 115–118.

Gupta, P. K. 1977. 'Rorschach Ranking Conformity Test: An Evaluation'. *Indian Journal of Clinical Psychology* 4: 51–53.

Gupta, R., S. K. Verma, and P. Kulhara. 1989. 'Expression of Hostility on Rorschach Cards'. *Journal of Personality & Clinical Studies* 5: 9–13.

Gupta, S. C. 1975. 'A Study of Etiological Factors in Murderers: A Psycho Social Investigation'. PhD thesis, Kanpur University.

Gupta, S. C., and B. B. Sethi. 1974. 'Psychological Aspects and Personality Patterns of Murderers'. *Indian Journal of Psychiatry* 16: 111–120.

Handler, L., and A. D. Thomas, eds. 2014. *Drawings in Assessment and Psychotherapy: Research and Applications*. New York, NY: Routledge.

Hartmann, H. A., and Von Rosenstiel, eds. 1977. *Lehrbuch der Holtzman Inkblot Technique (HIT)*. Bern/Stuttgart/Wien: Hans Huber.

Harris, E. C., and B. Barraclough. 1997. 'Suicide as an Outcome for Mental Disorders: A Meta-Analysis'. *British Journal of Psychiatry* 170: 205–228.

Hasler, G., Pinto A., Greenberg, B.D., Samuels, J., Syer, A.J., Pauls, D., Knowles, J.A., McCracken, J.T., Tini, J., Ridle, M.A., Rauch, S.L., Rasmussen, S.A., Willour, B.L., Gravos, M.A., Cullen, B., Biendenu, O.J., Shuqart, Y.Y., Lind, K.Y., Hoehn-Faric, R., Wang, Y., Ronquillo, J., Nestat, G., and Murphy, D.L. 2007. 'OCD Collaborative Genetics Study: Familiaty of Factor Analysis-Derived Analysis YBOCS Dimensions in OCD Affected Sibling Pairs from the OCD Collaborative Genetic Study'. *Biological Psychiatry* 61: 617–625.

Hens, S. 1917. Fantasy Exa with Shapeless sticks in schoolchildren, Normal Adults and Mentally Ill normal adults and mentally ill. Dissertation, Zurich.

Heron, J., T. G. O'Connor, J. Evans, J. Golding, and V. Glover. 2004. 'The Course of Anxiety and Depression throughout Pregnancy and Postpartum in a Community Sample'. *Journal of Affective Disorders* 80: 65–73.

Herron, E. W. 1965. 'Personality Factors Associated with the Acquisition of the Conditioned Eyelid Response'. *Journal of Personality and Social Psychology* 2 (5): 775–777.

Hertz, M. R. 1934. 'Reliability of Rorschach Inkblot Test'. *Journal of Applied Psychology* 18: 461–474.

Hill, E. F. 1972. *The Holtzman Inkblot Technique: A Handbook for Clinical Application*. San Francisco, CA: Jossey-Bass.

Hill, E. F., and H. E. Piexotto. 1973. *Workbook for the Holtzman Inkblot Technique*. New York, NY: The Psychological Corporation.

Hiltner, S. 1950. 'Religion and Psychoanalysis'. *Psychoanalytic Review* 37: 128–139.

Hinkle, J. E., S. E. Nelson, and D. Miller. 1968. 'Psychological Test Usage by Psychologists in Private Practice'. *Psychotherapy: Theory, Research and Practices* 5: 210–213.

Hintikka, J., K. Koskela, O. Kontula, and H. Viinamaki. 2000. 'Gender Differences in Associations between Religious Attendance and Mental Health in Finland'. *Journal of Nervous & Mental Disease* 188 (11): 772–776.

Hixson, K. A., H. W. Gruchow, and D. W. Morgan. 1998. 'The Relation between Religiosity, Selected Health Behaviors, and Blood Pressure among Adult Females'. *Preventive Medicine* 27 (4): 545–552.

Hoffman, A., and B. K. Pincus. 1989. *The Law of Custody*. London: Butterworths.

Hollander, E., S. Kim, S. Khanna, and S. Pallanti. 2007. 'Obsessive-Compulsive Disorder and Obsessive-Compulsive Spectrum Disorders: Diagnostic and Dimensional Issues'. *CNS Spectrums* 12 (3): 5–13.

Hollender, M. H., and W. A. Cassell. 1972. 'Psychological Problems Associated with Hirsutism'. *International Psychiatry Clinics* 3 (2–6).

Holtzman, W. H. 1950. 'The Rorschach Test in the Assessment of the Normal Superior Adult'. Unpublished doctoral dissertation, Stanford University, Stanford, CA.

————. 1956. *Inkblot Perception and Personality*. Austin, TX: University of Texas Press.

Holtzman, W. H. (1963). Inkblot Perception and Personality. The Meaning of Inkblot Variables. Bulletin of Menninger Clinic, 27: 84–95.

————. 1981. 'Holtzman Inkblot Technique (HIT)'. In *Assessment with Projective Technique: A Concise Introduction*, edited by A. I. Rabin, 47–83. New York, NY: Springer Publishing Co.

————. 1986. 'The Holtzman Inkblot Technique with Children and Adolescents'. In *Projective Technique for Adolescents and Children*, edited by A. I. Rabin, 168–192. New York, NY: Springer Publishing Co.

————. 1988. 'Beyond the Rorschach'. *Journal of Personality Assessment* 52 (4): 578–609.

————. 2002. 'Over Half a Century of Playing with Inkblots and Other Wondrous Pursuits'. *Journal of Personality Assessment* 79 (1): 1–18.

Holtzman, W. H., R. Diaz-Guerrero, and J. D. Swartz. 1975. *Personality Development in Two Cultures: A Cross Cultural Longitudinal Study of School Children in Mexico and United States*. Austin, TX: University of Texas Press.

Holtzman, W. H., and J. D. Swartz. 1956. *Inkblot Perception and Personality*. Austin, TX: University of Texas Press.

————. 1983. 'The Holtzman Inkblot Technique: A Review of 25 Years of Research'. *Zeitschrift fur Differentielle und Diagnostische Psychologie* 4 (3): 241–259.

Holtzman, W. H., J. D. Swartz, and J. S. Thorpe. 1971. 'Artists, Architects and Engineers: Three Contrasting Modes of Visual Experience and Their Psychological Correlates'. *Journal of Personality* 39 (3): 432–449.

Holtzman, W. H., J. S. Thorpe, J. D. Swartz, and E. W. Herron. 1961a. *Administration and Scoring Guide*. Cleveland, OH: The Psychological Corporation.

————. 1961b. *Inkblot Perception and Personality*. Austin, TX: University of Texas Press.

Horowitz, M. J., F. D. Donald, and O. S. Lois. 1964. 'The Body Buffer Zone: An Exploration of Personal Space'. *Archives of General Psychiatry* 11: 651–656.

Hovens, C. M., S. A. Stacker, A. C. Andres, A. G. Harpur, and A. F. Wilks. 1992. 'RYK, A Receptor Tyrosine Kinase-Related Molecule with Unusual Kinase Domain Motifs'. *Proceedings of the National Academy of Sciences of the United States of America* 89: 11818–11822.

Howe, Leroy T. 1986. 'Dream Interpretation in Spiritual Guidance'. *Journal of Pastoral Care* 40 (3): 262–272.

Hussain, S. E., P. V. Gullet, K. P. Singh, and G. S. Mani. 1976. 'Psychological Background of Unwed Motherhood'. *Indian Journal of Clinical Psychology* 3: 183–187.

Jacobson, E. 1938. *Progressive Relaxation*. Chicago, IL: University of Chicago Press.

———. 1964. *Anxiety and Tension Control: A Psychobiologic Approach*. Philadelphia, PA: Lippincott.

Jain, K. 1956. 'Personality Studies of Adolescent Girls with Special Reference to the Subjects in Colleges of Allahabad'. Doctoral thesis, Allahabad University, Allahabad.

Jain, K. S., and B. S. Prakash. 1967. 'Linearity Relation between Sum R and Other Rorschach Score Variables—a Normative Study'. *Journal of General Psychology* 77: 259–261.

Jain, R., B. Singh, S. Mohanty, and R. Kumar. 2005. 'SIS-I and Rorschach Diagnostic Indicators of Attention Deficit and Hyperactivity Disorder'. *SIS Journal of Projective Psychology & Mental Health* 12 (2): 141–152.

Janet, P. 1907. *The Major Symptoms of Hysteria*. New York, NY: MacMillan.

Joseph, A., and A. Pillai. 1986. 'Projective Indices of Creativity'. *Indian Journal of Clinical Psychology* 13: 9–14.

Joshi, H. L., and C. R. Darolia. 2004. 'Standardization of Holtzman Inkblot Technique on Indian High School Students'. *Psychological Studies* 49 (1): 52–58.

Judd, L. L., H. S. Akiskal, and P. J. Schettler. 2002. 'The Long-term Natural History of the Weekly Symptomatic Status of Bipolar Disorder'. *Archives of General Psychiatry* 59 (6): 530–537.

Julka, G. 1962. 'The Rorschach Responses of Bhil Children'. University of Rajasthan Studies (Education) 5: 21–42.

———. 1963. 'Aggression, Fear and Anxiety among Children'. Unpublished doctoral thesis in education, submitted to Rajasthan University, Jaipur.

Kamlesh. 1979. 'Personality and Motivational Correlates of Projective and Psychometric Measures of Creativity'. Unpublished manuscript, Kurukshetra University, Kurukshetra.

Kandhari, S., J. Sharma, D. Kumar, N. Kandhari, and R. Kumar. 2012. 'Efficacy of Comprehensive Scoring System for SIS-I in Discriminating Mania'. *SIS Journal of Projective Psychology & Mental Health* 19 (1): 35–42.

Kandhari, S., J. Sharma, and R. Kumar. 2010. 'Development of a Comprehensive Scoring System for SIS-I'. *SIS Journal of Projective Psychology & Mental Health* 17: 120–125.

Kandhari, S., J. Sharma, R. Kumar, and D. Kumar. 2011. 'Gender Differences in SIS-I Profile of Normal Population'. *SIS Journal of Projective Psychology & Mental Health* 118 (1): 14–21.

Kandhari, S., J. Sharma, D. Kumar, N. Kandhari, and R. Kumar, 2012. 'Efficacy of Comprehensive Scoring System for SIS-I in Discriminating Mania'. *SIS Journal of Projective Psychology & Mental Health* 19: 35–42.

Kanupriya, and U. Singh. 2005. 'A Study of Projective and Psychometric Personality Correlates of Emotional Intelligence'. Unpublished MPhil dissertation, Department of Psychology, Kurukshetra University, Kurukshetra.

Kanzer, M. 1988. 'Early Reviews of "Interpretation of Dreams"'. *The Psychoanalytic Study of the Child* 43: 33–50.

Kaplan, D. M. 1989. 'The Place of the Dream in Psychotherapy'. *Bulletin of the Menninger Clinic* 53: 1–17.

Kapur, M., and R. L. Kapur. 1967. 'Study of Impotence through Projective Tests'. *Indian Journal of Psychiatry* 9: 202–211.

Karpman, B. 1948a. 'The Myth of the Psychopathic Personality'. *American Journal of Psychiatry* 104 (9): 523–534.

———. 1948b. 'The Psychopathology of Exhibitionism'. *Journal of Clinical Psychopathology* 9: 179–225.

Kaur, D., and M. Kapur. 1983. 'Rorschach Study of Hysteria'. *Indian Journal of Clinical Psychology* 10: 97–102.

Kaur, R. P., and S. K. Verma. 1998. 'A Correlational Study of Selected Rorschach and SIS-II Variables in Psychiatric Patients'. *SIS Journal of Projective Psychology & Mental Health* 5: 115–118.

Kaur, S., and U. Singh. 1998. 'A Study of Novelty and Meaning Contexts of Creativity in Relation to Fluid and Crystallized Intelligence'. Unpublished MPhil dissertation, Department of Psychology, Kurukshetra University, Kurukshetra.

———. 2010b. 'Discriminating Power of the Comprehensive Scoring System for SIS-I'. *SIS Journal of Projective Psychology & Mental Health* 17: 16–22.

Kelsoe, J. R. 2000. 'A Genome Survey Indicates a Possible Susceptibility Locus for Bipolar Disorder on Chromosome 22'. Systems Biology Conference, Science Sessions, PNAS Podcasts.

Kendel, E. 2005. *Psychiatry Psychoanalysis and the New Biology of Mind.* Washington, DC: American Psychiatric Publishing.

Kerr, N., J. Scott, and M. Phillips. 2005. 'Patterns of Attention Deficits and Emotional Bias in Bipolar Disorder and Major Depressive Disorder'. *British Journal of Clinical Psychiatry* 44: 343–356.

Khromov, A. B. 2001. 'Psychological Characteristics of Subjects with Achondroplasia and Traumatically Shortened Extremities'. *SIS Journal of Projective Psychology & Mental Health* 8: 53–64.

———. 2009. 'Comparison of Psychometric Characteristics of Rorschach and Cassell's Projective Techniques'. *SIS Journal of Projective Psychology & Mental Health* 16: 32–36.

Khromov, A. B., W. A. Cassell, and B. L. Dubey. 1999a. 'A Comparative Study of Personality Problems of Russian and American Female Adolescents'. *SIS Journal of Projective Psychology & Mental Health* 6: 29–33.

———. 1999b. 'Some Personality Correlates of Selected SIS Variables: Russian Experiments'. *SIS Journal of Projective Psychology & Mental Health* 6: 35–40.

Khromov, A. B., and B. L. Dubey. 2016. 'Comparison of the Correlates' Structure of the Rorschach, SIS-I and SIS-II Projective Techniques with the MMPI Test and Factorial Analysis of the Indicators'. *SIS Journal of Projective Psychology & Mental Health* 23 (1): 12–21.

Khromov, A. B., G. Starbuck, M. Birkedahl, and B. L. Dubey. 2002. 'The Reflective Analysis of the Personality Problems of the Young Female Subjects: A Cross Cultural Approach'. *SIS Journal of Projective Psychology & Mental Health* 9: 49–56.

Khromov, A. B., R. Pandey, and B. L. Dubey. 2004. 'Students Attitude towards the Vital Problems and Somatic Inkblot Images of the SIS-I'. *SIS Journal of Projective Psychology & Mental Health* 11: 4–10.

Kinsey, A. C., W. B. Pomeroy, and C. E. Martin. 1948. *Sexual Behavior in the Human Male*. Philadelphia, PA: W. B. Saunders.

Kirkpatrick, E. A. 1900. 'Individual Test of School Children'. *Psychological Review* 7: 274–280.

Kishore, R., and K. Dutt. 1988. 'Psychometric Assessment in Head Injury Cases'. *Indian Journal of Clinical Psychology* 15 (1): 34–37.

Kleiger, J. H. 1997. 'Rorschach Shading Responses: From a Printer's Error to an Integrated Psychoanalytic Paradigm'. *Journal of Personality Assessment* 69: 342–364.

Klopfer, B. 1939. 'Should the Rorschach Method Be Standardized?' *Rorschach Research Exchange* 3: 45–54.

Klopfer, B., and H. H. Davidson. 1962. *The Rorschach Technique: An Introductory Manual*. New York, NY: Harcourt, Brace & World.

Klopfer, B., M. D. Anisworth, W. G. Klopfer, and R. R. Holt. 1954. *Developments in the Rorschach Technique*, Vol. 1, Technique and Theory. New York, NY: World Book.

Klopfer, Bruno, and Douglas Kelley. 1942. *The Rorschach Technique: A Manual for a Projective Method of Personality Diagnosis*. Chicago, IL: World Book.

Koenig, H. G., K. I. Pargament, and J. Nielsen. 1998. 'Religious Coping and Health Status in Medically Ill Hospitalized Older Adults'. *Journal of Nervous & Mental Disease* 186 (9): 513–521.

Kohli, A., and R. P. Kaur. 2002. 'Rorschach Profile and Its Relationship with PEN Questionnaire in Borderline Psychosis'. *SIS Journal of Projective Psychology & Mental Health* 9: 109–113.

Kramer, H. 1993. *Conversations at Midnight*. New York, NY: Morrow and Co.

Kruthi, M., C. Mahboubeh, and L. S. S. Manickam. 2015. 'Somatic Inkblot Series II Profiles of Iranian Couples: An Exploratory Study'. *SIS Journal of Projective Psychology & Mental Health* 22 (2): 124–129.

Kubler-Ross, E. 1969. *On Death and Dying*. New York, NY: Macmillan.

Kumar, D. 2003. 'Diagnostic Indicators on SIS-I and Rorschach among Manic and Depressive Patients'. Unpublished PhD thesis, Dr B. R. Ambedkar University, Agra.

Kumar, D., B. L. Dubey, and R. Kumar. 2006. 'Gender Differences in SIS-I Profile of Manic Patients'. *SIS Journal of Projective Psychology & Mental Health* 13: 61–64.

Kumar, D., B. L. Dubey, and R. Kumar 2007. 'Inter Correlations of Nine SIS-I Indices'. *SIS Journal of Projective Psychology & Mental Health* 14: 59–63.

Kumar, D., J. Kumar, and R. Kumar. 2005. 'Diagnostic Indicators on SIS-I and Rorschach among Manic and Depressive Patients'. *SIS Journal of Projective Psychology & Mental Health* 12: 53–60.

Kumar, D., and R. Kumar. 2009. 'Correlation between Rorschach and SIS-I Indices in Normal Group'. *SIS Journal of Projective Psychology & Mental Health* 16: 55–57.

Kumar, P. 1960a. 'The Rorschach Test in Manic and Normal Groups'. *Indian Journal of Psychology* 35: 35–38.

———. 1960b. 'Rorschach Test in Some Metal Disorders: Psychoneurotic Groups'. *Indian Journal of Psychiatry* 2: 129–134.

———. 1961a. 'The Rorschach Test in Some Mental Disorders: Schizophrenic Group'. *Psychologia* 4: 36–40.

———. 1961b. 'Rorschach Test in Psychoneurotic and Normal Groups'. *Indian Journal of Psychology* 36: 169–172.

———. 1962a. 'Rorschach Test in Some Mental Disorders: Depressive Groups'. *Indian Journal of Psychiatry* 3: 93–100.

———. 1962b. 'Popular Responses on the Rorschach Test'. *Psychologia* 5: 161–169.

———. 1962c. 'The Rorschach Test in Depressive and Normal Groups'. *Indian Journal of Psychology* 37: 89–92.

———. 1963. 'The Rorschach Test in Schizophrenic and Normal Groups'. *Indian Journal of Psychology* 38: 121–124.

———. 1965. 'The Rorschach Test in Some Mental Disorders: Manic Groups'. *Indian Journal of Psychology* 40: 13–17.

Kumar, P., and S. Patel. 1990. 'Rorschach Study of Women Showing High and Low Adjustment in Marriage'. *Journal of Personality and Clinical Studies* 6 (1): 73–76.

Kumar, R. 2000. 'Meta-Analysis on the Findings of SIS-II'. *SIS Journal of Projective Psychology & Mental Health* 7: 141–147.

———. 2005. 'An Extended Scoring System of SIS-I'. *SIS Journal of Projective Psychology & Mental Health* 12: 123–128.

———. 2009. 'Factor Structure of SIS-I in Adults'. *SIS Journal of Projective Psychology & Mental Health* 16: 124–127.

———. 2010. 'SIS Imagery in Depression with Somatization—Therapeutic Intervention'. *SIS Journal of Projective Psychology & Mental Health* 17: 69–72.

———. 2015. 'Areas of Research in Somatic Inkblot Series'. *SIS Journal of Projective Psychology & Mental Health* 22 (2): 130–138.

Kumar, R., and A. R. Singh. 2007. 'A Comparison of Somatic Inkblot Series-I Indices in Normal Children and Adults'. *SIS Journal of Projective Psychology & Mental Health* 14: 44–47.

Kumar, R., and C. R. J. Khess. 2004. 'Special Scores of Rorschach Comprehensive System in Schizophrenia and Mania: A Comparative Study'. *SIS Journal of Projective Psychology & Mental Health* 11: 85–90.

Kumar, Ranjeet, and Khess, C.R.J. 2005. 'Diagnostic Efficiency of Schizophrenia Index and Perceptual-Thinking Index in Schizophrenia and Mania'. *SIS Journal of Projective Psychology & Mental Health* 12 (2): 115–122.

Kumar, R., 2005. 'An Extended Scoring System of SIS-I'. *SIS Journal of Projective Psychology & Mental Health* 12: 123–128.

Kumar, R., M. Jahan, M. Dutta, and S. K. Deuri. 2016. 'SIS-II Profile of Non-Chronic and Chronic Schizophrenia Patients'. *SIS Journal of Projective Psychology & Mental Health* 23 (2): 102–105.

Kumar, R., S. Kandhari, and B. L. Dubey. 2008. 'Estimation of the Contribution of Gender in Productivity on SIS-I'. *SIS Journal of Projective Psychology & Mental Health* 15 (1): 48–51.

Kumar, S., and C. R. Darolia. 2003. 'Psychometric Study of Full and Quick Version of Holtzman Inkblot Technique'. Unpublished MPhil dissertation, Department of Psychology, Kurukshetra University, Kurukshetra.

Kumar, S., R. Singh, and S. Mohanty. 2001. 'A Study of Somatic Inkblot-I in Hospitalised Male Chronic Schizophrenics'. *SIS Journal of Projective Psychology & Mental Health* 8: 31–34.

———. 2004. 'Comparative Study of SIS-I Indices between Schizophrenic and Manic Patients'. *SIS Journal of Projective Psychology & Mental Health* 11: 91–94.

Kumar, S., R. Singh, S. Mohanty, and R. Kumar. 2006. 'SIS-I and Rorschach in Schizophrenia: A Co-Relational Study'. *SIS Journal of Projective Psychology & Mental Health* 13 (2): 120–124.

Kumar, S., S. Mohanty, and R. Kumar. 2003. 'SIS-1 Profile and its Correlation with Rorschach in Manic Patients'. *SIS Journal of Projective Psychology & Mental Health* 10: 201–204.

Kumari, R., and A. Mukhopadhyay. 2019. 'SIS-I Profile of PTSD Patients'. *SIS Journal of Projective Psychology & Mental Health* 26 (1): 30–36.

Kumari, D., J. Prakash, A. R. Singh, and S. Chaudhury. 2009. 'Personality Profile of Schizophrenia and Bipolar Affective Disorder (Mania) on SIS-II'. *SIS Journal of Projective Psychology & Mental Health* 16: 134–137.

Kundu, C. L. 1969. 'The Inkblot Responses of Some Tribal Delinquents'. *Journal of Educational Research & Extension* 5: 127–135.

———. 1980. *Rorschach Psychodiagnostic: An Indian Case Study*. Kurukshetra: Vishal Publication.

Laird, D. R., L. M. Laosa, and J. D. Swartz. 1973. 'Inkblot Perception and Reading Achievement in Children: A Developmental Analysis'. *British Journal of Projective Psychology and Personality Study* 18 (2): 25–31.

Lal, R. 2004. 'SIS with Physically Disabled Adolescents'. *SIS Journal of Projective Psychology & Mental Health* 11 (2): 121–123.

Lal, R. S. 1956. 'Rorschach Test and Assessment of Intelligence under Indian Conditions'. *British Journal of Educational Psychology* 26: 112–116.

Larson, Cedric A. 1958, October. 'Herman Rorschach and the Ink-Blot Test'. *Science Digest* 44 (October 1958): 84–89.

Larson, D. B., K. A. Sherrill, J. S. Lyons, F. C. Jr. Craigie, S. B. Thielman, M. A. Greenwold, and S. S. Larson. 1992. 'Associations between Dimensions of Religious Commitment and Mental Health'. *American Journal of Psychiatry* 149 (4): 557–559.

Lata, S., and A. Singh. 1990. 'A Study of Projective and Psychometric Personality Correlates of Creativity'. Unpublished MPhil dissertation, Department of Psychology, Kurukshetra University, Kurukshetra.

Layton, L. 1996. 'In Defense of Gender Ambiguity: Jessica Benjamin'. *Gender and Psychoanalysis* 1: 27–43.

Leckman, J. F., D. E. Grice, J. Boardman H. Zhang, A. Vitale, C.Bondi, D.J.Cohen, S.A.Rasmussen, W.K.Goodman, C.J.McDougle and G. L. Pauls 1997. 'Symptoms of Obsessive-Compulsive Disorder'. *American Journal of Psychiatry* 154: 911–917.

LeDoux, J. E. 1997. 'Emotion, Memory, and Pain'. *Pain Forum* 6: 36–37.

Lefcourt, H. M., M. S. Telegdi, D. Willows, and B. Buckspan. 1972. 'Eye Contact and the Human Movement Response'. *Journal of Social Psychology* 88 (2): 303–304.

Lerner, B. 1966. 'Rorschach Movement and Dreams: A Validation Study Using Drug Induced Dream Deprivation'. *Journal of Abnormal Psychology* 71 (2): 75–86.

Lerner, P. 1991. *Psychoanalytic Theory and the Rorschach*. Hillsdale, NJ: The Analytic Press.

Levi, J. 1960. *Rorschach Patterns Predicting Success or Failure in Rehabilitation of the Physically Handicapped*, 168–175. Telangana: Universities Press.

Lilaratne, S. S. 1967. 'Personality Differences in Religious Groups by Means of the Rorschach Test'. PhD thesis, Calcutta University.

Lindorff, David. 1995. 'One Thousand Dreams: The Spiritual Awakening of Wolfgang Pauli'. *Journal of Analytical Psychology* 40 (4): 555–569.

Lipowski, Z. J. 1974. 'Physical Illness and Psychopathology'. *International Journal of Psychiatry in Medicine* 5 (4): 483–497.

Lowen, Alexander. 1975. *Bioenergetics*. New York, NY: Coward-McCann.

Mackenzie, E. R., D. E. Rajagopal, M. Meibohm, and R. Lavizzo-Mourey. 2000. 'Spiritual Support and Psychological Well-Being: Older Adults' Perceptions of the Religion and Health Connection'. *Alternative Therapies in Health & Medicine* 6 (6): 37–45.

Mahapatra, J. 2010. 'A Comparative Study of Schizophrenia and Affective Disorders on SIS-I and Rorschach'. Unpublished PhD thesis, Sambalpur University, Orissa.

Mahapatra, J., D. Sahoo, P. K. Mishra, and R. Kumar. 2009. 'SIS-I Indices as a Measure of Ego Strength in Schizophrenia'. *SIS Journal of Projective Psychology & Mental Health* 16: 152–154.

———. 2010. 'Assessment of Ego-Strength through Rorschach Indices in Schizophrenia'. *SIS Journal of Projective Psychology & Mental Health* 17: 23–26.

———. 2011. 'Evaluating Ego-Strength in Depression on SIS-I Indices'. *SIS Journal of Projective Psychology & Mental Health* 18 (1): 69–76.

Majumdar, A. K., and A. B. Roy. 1962. 'Latent Personality Contents of Juvenile Delinquents'. *Journal of Psychological Researches* 6: 6–8.

Majumdar, P. K., and K. Mukherjee. 1969. 'Examination of Certain Rorschach Ratios: A Factorial Study with Criminal Population'. *Indian Journal of Applied Psychology* 6: 82–87.

Malaviya, P. 1973. 'A Replication of Rorschach Signs with Suicide Attempted Schizophrenics'. *Indian Journal of Psychiatry* 48: 53–58.

Mancia, Mauro. 1988. 'The Dream as Religion of the Mind'. *International Journal of Psycho-Analysis* 69 (3): 419–426.

Manickam, L. S. S. 2003. 'Research Issues in Indian Concepts of Psychology: Obstacles on the Path Traversed and Perspectives for Future Action'. Paper presented in Conference on Indian Concepts of Mental Health, Mysore.

———. 2004. 'Perspectives of Counselling in India'. Research Report, Centre for Applied Psychology Studies, Thiruvananthapuram.

———. 2013. 'Consistency of Response Pattern on Rorschach after an Interval of 14 Years: A Case Report'. *SIS Journal of Projective Psychology & Mental Health* 20 (1): 62–67.

Manickam, L. S. S., and B. L. Dubey. 2005. 'Rorschach Inkblot Test in India: Historical Review and Perspectives for Future Action'. *SIS Journal of Projective Psychology & Mental Health* 11: 61–78.

Manickam, L. S. S., and B. T. Suhani. 2003. 'Psychotherapeutic Usefulness of SIS-II in a Male Client with Somatoform Disorder: Case Illustration'. *SIS Journal of Projective Psychology & Mental Health* 10: 209–218.

———. 2014. 'Marital Conflict: An Exploration of Relationship Issues in Couples through SIS-II'. *SIS Journal of Projective Psychology & Mental Health* 21 (1): 37–41.

Manickam, L. S. S., B. T. Suhani, and J. Jasseer. 2004. 'Psychotherapy of a Male Patient with Dissociative Convulsive Disorder: SIS Breaks the Resistance'. *SIS Journal of Projective Psychology & Mental Health* 11: 36–44.

Manickam, L. S. S., M. Ghanbary, and M. Kruthi. 2013. 'Therapeutic Effectiveness of SIS-II in a Case of Psychogenic Cough'. *SIS Journal of Projective Psychology & Mental Health* 20 (2): 91–97.

Martin, H., and M. Frackowiak. 2017. 'The Value of Projective/Performance-based Techniques in Therapeutic Assessment'. *SIS Journal of Projective Psychology & Mental Health* 24 (2): 91–95.

Masters, W., and J. Johnson. 1970. *Human Sexual Inadequacy*. Boston, MA: Little Brown and Company.

Mataix-Cols, D., M. C. Rosario-Camtos, and J. F. Leckman. 2005. 'A Multidimensional Model of Obsessive-Compulsive Disorder'. *Ameican Journal of Psychiatry* 162: 228–238.

Mataix-Cols, D., S. L. Rauch, P. A. Mando, M. A. Jenike, and L. Baer. 1999. 'Use of Factor-Analyzed Symptoms Dimensions to Predict Outcome with Serotonin Reuptake Inhibitors and Placebo in the Treatment of Obsessive-Compulsive Disorder'. *American Journal of Psychiatry* 16: 1409–1416.

Mathur, S., and C. M. Pais. 1963. 'Extratensive and Introtensive Experience Balance as Tested by Rorschach Test and Sack's Sentence Completion Test'. *Manas* 10: 1–14.

Matsumaga, H., K. Maebayashi, K. Hayashieda, K. Okino, T. Matsui, T. Iketani, N. Kiriike, and D. J. Stein. 2008. 'Symptom Structure in Japanese Patients with Obsessive-Compulsive Disorder'. *American Journal of Psychiatry* 165: 251–253.

Mayfield, D. G. 1968. 'Holtzman Inkblot Technique in Acute Experimental Alcohol Intoxication'. *Journal of Projective Techniques and Personality Assessment* 35 (5): 491–494.

McCloskey, L. C. 2014. 'Construct and Incremental Validity of the Rotter Incomplete Sentences Blank in Adult Psychiatric Outpatients'. *Psychological Reports: Measures & Statistics* 114 (2): 363–375.

McGuffin, P., F. Rijsdijk, M. Andrew, P. Sham, and A. Cardno. 2003. 'The Heritability of Bipolar Affective Disorder and the Genetic Relationship to Univocal Depression'. *Archives of General Psychiatry* 60 (5): 497–502.

McMain, S. F., P. S. Links, W. H. Gnam, T. Guimond, R. J. Cardish, L. Korman, and D. L. Streiner. 2009. 'A Randomized Trial of Dialectical Behavior Therapy versus General Psychiatric Management for Borderline Personality Disorder'. *American Journal of Psychiatry* 166 (12): 1365–1374.

Megargee, E. I. 1965. 'The Relation between Barrier Scores and Aggressive Behavior'. *Journal of Abnormal Psychology* 70 (4): 307–311.

Menon, D. K., T. R. Shukla, and R. Menon. 1974. 'Color Preference and Color Perception on Inkblots'. *Indian Journal of Clinical Psychology* 1 (2): 64–90.

Miklowitz, D. J., M. W. Otto, and E. Frank. 2007. 'Psychosocial Treatments for Bipolar Depression: A One Year Randomized Trial from the Systematic Treatment Enhance Program'. *Archives of General Psychiatry* 64 (4): 419–427.

Milne, L. C., and Philip Greenway. 2000. 'Sexual Content in Rorschach and Perceived Control of Internal States'. *SIS Journal of Projective Psychology & Mental Health* 7 (2): 119–126.

Mishra, D., A. Khalique, and R. Kumar. 2010b. 'Rorschach Profile of Manic Patients'. *SIS Journal of Projective Psychology & Mental Health* 17: 158–164.

Mishra, D. K., M. Jahan, and A. R. Singh. 2010a. 'Dissociative Convulsion Disorder: A Case Study'. *SIS Journal of Projective Psychology & Mental Health* 17: 73–75.

Mishra, D. K., R. Kumar, and J. Prakash. 2009. 'Rorschach Thought Disorders in Various Psychiatric Conditions'. *SIS Journal of Projective Psychology & Mental Health* 16: 8–12.

Mishra, D. K., S. Alreja, M. Jahan, and A. R. Singh. 2010. 'SIS-II Profile of Epileptic Patients'. *SIS Journal of Projective Psychology & Mental Health* 17: 187–191.

Mishra, M. 1996. 'Compatibility of SIS-II and the Rorschach Indices in Normal, Neurotics and Schizophrenics'. Unpublished PhD thesis, Banaras Hindu University, Varanasi.

Mishra, M., and C. B. Dwivedi. 1997. 'Content Scale Based Diagnostic Compatibility of the SIS-II with Rorschach Test in Normal, Neurotics and Schizophrenics'. *SIS Journal of Projective Psychology & Mental Health* 4: 121–140.

Mishra, M., and N. Mishra. 2001. 'Therapeutic Utility of SIS-II'. *SIS Journal of Projective Psychology & Mental Health* 8: 51–52.

Mishra, R. K., M. K. Kharakwal, M. A. Kilroy, and K. Thapa. 1996. *Rorschach Test: Theory and Practice*, New Delhi: SAGE Publications.

Mishra, S., and M. P. Gupta. 2008. 'Rorschach Profile of Neurotic Patients'. *SIS Journal of Projective Psychology & Mental Health* 15: 134–144.

Mitchell, P. B., J. R. Ball, and J. A. Best. 2006. 'The Management of Bipolar Disorder in General Practice'. *Medical Journal of Australia* 184: 566–570.

Mitra, G., and A. Mukhopadhyay. 1996. 'SIS and Social Anxiety—An Assessment of Personality Factors of Drug Addicts'. *SIS Journal of Projective Psychology & Mental Health* 3: 153–164.

———. 2000. 'Psychological Factors in Drug Addicts and Normals: A Comparative Study'. *SIS Journal of Projective Psychology & Mental Health* 7: 53–78.

Mitra, S., and N. Sanyal. 2010. 'A Single Case in Interpretative Wrappings of Multiple Psychological Theories'. *SIS Journal of Projective Psychology & Mental Health* 17 (2): 165–170.

Mohn, D. 2002. 'Application of the SIS Board: Editorial'. *SIS Journal of Projective Psychology & Mental Health* 9: 79–80.

Moreno, C., G. Laje, C. Blanco, H. Jiang, A. B. Schmidt, and M. Offson. 2007. 'National Trends in the Outpatient Diagnosis and Treatment of Bipolar Disorder in Youth'. *Archives of General Psychiatry* 64 (9): 1032–1039.

Morgan, A. B. 1968. 'Some Age Norms Obtained for the Holtzman Inkblot Technique Administered in a Clinical Setting'. *Journal of Projective Technique and Personality Assessment* 32: 165–172.

Mosley, E. C. 1963. 'Psychodiagnosis on the Basis of Holtzman Inkblot Technique'. *Journal of Projective Technique and Personality Assessment* 17: 86–91.

Mujtaba, B., and V. Mujtaba. 1985. 'Homosexuality and Paranoid Schizophrenia: A Study through Rorschach Ink Blots'. *Journal of Personality & Clinical Studies* 1: 27–29.

Mukherjee, K. 1965. 'Personality of Criminals: A Rorschach Study'. *Council of Social & Psychological Research Bulletin* 5: 15–18.

———. 1966. 'Personality of Criminals—a Rorschach Study'. *Council of Social & Psychological Research Bulletin* 6: 5–11.

———. 1968. 'Personality Characteristics of a Group of Male Criminals'. Doctoral thesis, Calcutta University, Calcutta.

Mukherjee, K., and M. Raychaudhuri. 1970. 'Assessment of Equivalence of Clinical Ratings, Structured and Projective Measures of Personality'. *Manas* 17 (2): 67–76.

Mukherjee, M. 1969. 'Parents of Disturbed Children'. *Child Psychiatry Quarterly* 2 (4): 1–5.

Mukhopadhyay, A., S. Banerjee, and G. A. Mitra. 1996. 'Comprehensive Profile of Personality Characteristic of Male Drug Addicts'. *SIS Journal of Projective Psychology & Mental Health* 3: 33–41.

Muller, W. J., and N. Abeles. 1964. 'The Components of Empathy and Their Relationship to the Projection of Human Movement Responses'. *Journal of Projective Technique and Personality Assessment* 28 (3): 322–330.

Murstein, B. I. 1956. 'The Projection of Hostility on the Rorschach'. *Journal of Projective Techniques* 20: 418–428.

———. 1960. 'Factor Analysis of the Rorschach'. *Journal of Consulting Psychology* 24: 262–275.

———. 1965. *Handbook of Projective Techniques*. New York, NY: Basic Books.

———. 1970. 'Empirical Test of the Levels of Hypothesis with Five Projective Techniques'. *Journal of Abnormal Psychology* 75: 38–44.

———. 1995. 'Editorial'. *SIS Journal of Projective Psychology & Mental Health* 2: 1–2.

Musewicz, J., G. Marczyk, L. Knauss, and D. York. 2009. 'Current Assessment Practice, Personality Measurement, and Rorschach Usage by Psychologists'. *Journal of Personality Assessment* 91 (5): 453–461.

Myers, E. 1986. *When Patient Die*. New York, NY: Viking Penguin Inc.

Nehra, A., M. Raghunathan, S. K. Verma, and S. B. S. Mann. 1997. 'Recognition of Psychological Problems in Patients Suffering from Speech Defects with the Help of SIS-II'. *SIS Journal of Projective Psychology & Mental Health* 4: 145–151.

Nichols, D. C., and B. Tursky. 1967. 'Body Image, Anxiety and Tolerance for Experimental Pain'. *Psychosomatic Medicine* 29: 103–110.

Nicolini, P. 2000. 'The Corporeal Perception in Subjects with Psychosomatic Disorders Evaluated with the SIS-I Test'. *SIS Journal of Projective Psychology & Mental Health* 7: 127–132.

———. 2002. 'Diagnostic Value of SIS-I and EDI-2 Tests in the Obese Patients—Presentation of a Clinical Case'. *SIS Journal of Projective Psychology & Mental Health* 9: 133–152.

Nordentoft, M., P. B. Mortensen, and C. B. Pederson. 2011. 'Absolute Risk of Suicide'. *Archives of General Psychiatry* 68 (10): 1058–1064.

Nowakowska, C. 2005. 'Temperamental Commonalities and Differences in Euthymic Mood Disorder Patients, Creative Controls, and Healthy Controls'. *Journal of Affect Disorder* 85 (1–2): 207–215.

O'Hanlon, W. H. 1987. *Taproots: Underlying Principles of Milton Erickson's Therapy and Hypnosis*. New York, NY: W. W. Norton & Company.

Ojha, K. N. 1975. 'Psychological Assessment of Mentally Retarded Children'. *Indian Journal of Clinical Psychology* 2: 45–50.

Osby, U., L. Brandt, N. Correia, A. Eckborn, and P. Sparen. 2001. 'Excess Mortality in Bipolar and Unipolar Disorder in Sweden'. *Archives of General Psychiatry* 58 (9): 844–850.

Ostow, Mortimer. 1986. 'Archetypes of Apocalypse in Dreams and Fantasies and in Religious Scripture'. *American Imago* 43 (4): 307–334.

Pal, S. K. 1969. 'Personality Study of Engineering, Law, Medical and Teacher's Training Students'. PhD thesis, Allahabad University.

Pandey, P., A. Tiwari, and N. Mishra. 2011. 'Dissociative Convulsion Disorder: A Case Study'. *SIS Journal of Projective Psychology & Mental Health* 18 (2): 173–176.

Pandey, R. 1995. 'Projective Measure of Alexithymia and the SIS'. *SIS Journal of Projective Psychology & Mental Health* 2: 145–152.

Pandey, R., M. Misra, and C. B. Dwivedi. 1996. 'A Quantitative Analysis of Liked and Disliked SIS-II Images'. *SIS Journal of Projective Psychology & Mental Health* 3: 123–130.

———. 2003. 'Diagnostic Significance of Sex Responses on SIS-II on Sex and Non-Sex Images'. *SIS Journal of Projective Psychology & Mental Health* 10: 205–208.

Pandey, R., M. Misra, R. Mishra, and C. B. Dwivedi. 1999. 'Stability of SIS-II Response Contents across Time and Predesignated Image Clusters'. *SIS Journal of Projective Psychology & Mental Health* 6: 31–37.

Pandey, R., V. R. M. Tripathi, and S. Tripathi. 2001. 'Age Related Changes in SIS-II Response Contents'. *SIS Journal of Projective Psychology & Mental Health* 8: 35–40.

Panek, P. E. 2001. 'Editorial: Projective Psychology in the New Millennium: Issues and Challenges'. *SIS Journal of Projective Psychology & Mental Health* 8: 73–74.

Panek, P. E., J. S. Skowronski, and E. E. Wagner. 2002. 'The Advisability of Routinely Computing Percentages when Comparing Groups across Projective Test Variables'. *SIS Journal of Projective Psychology & Mental Health* 9: 2–4.

Pardini, D. A., T. G. Plante, A. Sherman, and J. E. Stump. 2000. 'Religious Faith and Spirituality in Substance Abuse Recovery: Determining the Mental Health Benefits'. *Journal of Substance Abuse Treatment* 19 (4): 347–354.

Parsons, C. J. 1917. 'Children's Interpretation of Inkblots'. *British Journal of Psychology* 9: 74–92.

Pasari, S. B., and S. E. Paul. 2005. 'Relation between 16PF and Rorschach Inkblot Test on Patients with Alcohol Dependence'. *Indian Journal of Clinical Psychology* 32: 12–16.

Pati, G. 1963. 'Comparative Study of Socio Cultural and Personality Factors of Delinquents, Adult Criminals and Normal Juveniles of Orissa'. PhD thesis, Utakal University, Orissa.

Paul, G. L. 1969. 'Outcome of Systemic Desensitization in Behavior Therapy'. In *Appraisal and Status*, edited by C. M. Franks, 63–159. New York, NY: McGraw-Hill.

Perls, F. S., R. F. Hefferline, and P. Goodman. 1951. *Gestalt Therapy: Excitement and Growth in the Human Personality*. New York, NY: Julian Press.

Pershad, D., and B. L. Dubey. 1977. 'A Proposed Statistical Design for Rorschach Indices'. *Indian Journal of Clinical Psychology* 4: 191–192.

———. 1994. 'Reliability and Validity of Somatic Inkblot Series in India'. *SIS Journal of Projective Psychology & Mental Health* 1: 33–38.

Pershad, D., and S. C. Pareekh. 2001. *A Protocol Manual for the Rorschach Test*. Agra: H. P. Bhargava Book House.

Pershad, D., and S. K. Verma. 1995. 'Diagnostic Significance of Content Analysis of SIS-II'. *SIS Journal of Projective Psychology & Mental Health* 2: 139–144.

Pershad, D., S. K. Verma, and K. Bhagat. 1997. 'Body Image Disturbances in Psychiatric Cases'. *SIS Journal of Projective Psychology & Mental Health* 4: 75–84.

Pershad, D., S. K. Verma, and B. L. Dubey. 1979. 'Pathognomic Signs on the Rorschach: How Useful Are They?' *British Journal of Projective Psychology* 24: 27–29.

Petrosky, E. M. 2005. 'The Relationship between the Morbid Response of the Rorschach Inkblot Test and Self-Reported Depressive Symptomatology'. *SIS Journal of Projective Psychology & Mental Health* 12 (2): 87–98.

———. 2006. 'The Relationship between Early Memories and the Rorschach Inkblot Test'. *SIS Journal of Projective Psychology & Mental Health* 13: 37–54.

Phillips, D. P., and L. L. Carstenson. 1988. 'The Effect of Suicide Stories on Various Demographic Groups: 1968–1985'. *Suicide Life Threat Behavior* 18: 100–114.

Piotrowski, C. 2015a. 'Projective Techniques Usage Worldwide: A Review of Applied Settings 1995–2015'. *Journal of the Indian Academy of Applied Psychology* 41 (3): 9–19.

———. 2015b. 'Clinical Instruction on Projective Techniques in the USA: A Review of Academic Training Settings 1995–2014'. *SIS Journal of Projective Psychology & Mental Health* 22 (2): 83–92.

———. 2017a. 'The Linchpin on the Future of Projective Techniques: The Precarious Status of Personality Assessment in the (Overcrowded) Professional Psychology Curriculum'. *SIS Journal of Projective Psychology & Mental Health* 24 (2): 71–73.

———. 2017b. 'Rorschach Research through the Lens of Bibliometric Analysis: Mapping Investigatory Domain'. *SIS Journal of Projective Psychology & Mental Health* 24 (1): 34–38.

———. 2018a. 'The Rorschach in Research on Neurocognitive Dysfunction: A Historical Overview, 1936–2016'. *SIS Journal of Projective Psychology & Mental Health* 24 (1): 44–53.

———. 2018b. 'Sentence Completion Methods: A Summary Review of 70 Survey-Based Studies of Training and Professional Settings'. *SIS Journal of Projective Psychology & Mental Health* 25 (1): 60–75.

———. 2018c. 'Editorial: 25 Years in Promoting Projective Assessment: A Silver Jubilee Tribute'. *SIS Journal of Projective Psychology & Mental Health* 25 (1): 1–4.

Piotrowski, C., J. W. Keller, and T. Ogawa. 1993. 'Projective Techniques: An International Perspective'. *Psychological Reports* 72: 179–182.

Piotrowski, Z. 1985. 'Psychoanalytic Interpreting of Rorschach Responses'. *Personal Communication.*

Piotrowski, Z. A. 1957. *Percept Analysis.* New York, NY: MacMillan.

Piotrowski, Z. A. and M. Schreiber. 1952. 'Rorschach Percept Analysis Measurement of Personality Changes during and after Intensive Psychoanalytically Oriented Psychotherapy'. In *Specialised Techniques in Psychotherapy*, edited by B. Bychowski and J. L. Despert. New York, NY: Basic Books Inc.

Pitman, R. K., S. P. Orr, A. Y. Shalev, L. J. Metzger, and T. A. Mellman. 1999. 'Psychophysiological Alterations in Post-Traumatic Stress Disorder'. *Seminars in Clinical Neuropsychiatry* 4: 234–241.

Pokhriyal, R., and H. Ahmad. 1988. 'Response Patterns of Acute Schizophrenics and Endogenous Depressives on the Holtzman Inkblot Technique'. *Journal of Personality and Clinical Studies* 4 (2): 205–207.

Prabhu, G. G. 1967. 'The Rorschach Technique with Normal Adult Indians'. *Indian Psychological Review*: 97–106.

———. 1970. 'Clinical Utility of Piotrowski's Alpha Diagnostic Formula'. *Indian Psychological Review* 6: 110–112.

Prakash, J. 1977. 'A Rorschach Study of the Institutionalized Orphan Children'. *ISPT Journal of Research* 1: 109–112.

Prasad, K., and H. S. Asthana. 1947. 'An Experimental Study of Meaning by Rorschach Method'. *Indian Journal of Psychology* 22: 55–58.

Prasad, M., and T. R. Shukla. 1975. 'A Study of Juvenile Delinquents with the Help of Holtzman Inkblot Technique'. *Indian Journal of Clinical Psychology* 2: 33–37.

Prasadarao, G., S. K. Verma, and P. Kulhara. 1987. 'Rorschach Responses of Obsessive Neurotic and Schizophrenic Patients'. *Journal of Personality and Clinical Studies* 3: 43–47.

Pratap, S., and J. Filella. 1966. 'Rorschach Correlation of Taylor's Manifest Anxiety Scale for a Group of Normal People'. *Indian Journal of Psychological Research* 10: 103–109.

Pratap, S., and M. Kapur. 1984. 'Rorschach Study of Literate Manics'. *Indian Journal of Clinical Psychology* 11: 29–34.

Priyamvada, R., S. Kumari, R. Ranjan, J. Prakash, A. R. Singh, and S. Chaudhury. 2009. 'Rorschach Profile of Schizophrenia and Depression'. *SIS Journal of Projective Psychology & Mental Health* 16: 37–40.

Prossin, A. R., T. M. Love, R. A. Koeppe, J. Zubieta, and K. R. Silk. 2010. 'Dysregulation of Regional Endogeneous Opioid Function in Borderline Personality Disorder'. *American Journal of Psychiatry* 167 (8): 925–933.

Pyle, W. H. 1913. *Examination of School Children.* New York, NY: Macmillan.

Radheshyam. 2007. 'SIS in Paranoid Ideation: A Case Study'. *SIS Journal of Projective Psychology & Mental Health* 14 (2): 145–149.

Radheshyam, W. A. Cassell, and B. L. Dubey. 2009. 'SIS Detection of Invisible Imagery in Bipolar Depression'. *SIS Journal of Projective Psychology & Mental Health* 16: 24–31.

Ramachandra, S. 1994. 'Rorschach and the Creative Artists'. *SIS Journal of Projective Psychology & Mental Health* 1 (1): 39–50.

Ramachandra, S., and S. K. Chaturvedi. 1995. 'Body Imagery in SIS Test'. *SIS Journal of Projective Psychology & Mental Health* 2: 53–60.

Rangaswami, R. 1982. 'Expression of Hostility in Criminal Schizophrenics, Schizophrenics and Normal'. *Indian Journal of Clinical Psychology* 9: 131–135.

Ranjan, J. K., A. Kumari, D. Kumari, J. Prakash, and K. S. Sengar. 2008. 'SIS–II Profile of Alcohol Dependence Patients'. *SIS Journal of Projective Psychology & Mental Health* 15: 157–162.

Rapaport, D., M. M. Gill, and R. Schafer. 1968. *Diagnostic Psychological Testing*, New York, NY: International University Press, Inc.

Rasch, M. A., and E. E. Wagner. 1989. 'Initial Psychological Effects of Sexual Abuse on Female Children as Reflected in the Hand Test'. *Journal of Personality Assessment* 53: 761–769.

Rathee, S. P., D. S. Goel, M. L. Chawla, and D. Saldanha. 1994. 'A Study of Somatic Inkblot Series-I in Coronary Cases'. *SIS Journal of Projective Psychology & Mental Health* 1: 51–64.

Rathee, S. P., V. Pandey, and A. Singh. 1995. 'Diagnostic Efficacy of Somatic Inkblot Series-II amongst Psychiatric Patents of Armed Forces: A Preliminary Study'. *SIS Journal of Projective Psychology & Mental Health* 2 (1): 61–66.

Rathee, S. P., P. K. Pardal, and T. R. John. 1998. 'Diagnostic Validity of SIS-II among Psychpathological Cases of Armed Forces'. *SIS Journal of Projective Psychology & Mental Health* 5: 139–144.

———. 2002. 'Diagnostic Value of SIS-II among Sub-Groups of Psychotic and Neurotic Patients of Armed Forces'. *SIS Journal of Projective Psychology & Mental Health* 9: 38–48.

Rathee, S. P., and A. Singh. 1996. 'A Comparative Study of Male and Female on SIS-I'. *SIS Journal of Projective Psychology & Mental Health* 3: 43–49.

Ray, A. B. 1963. 'Juvenile Delinquency Pattern by Rorschach Inkblots'. *Psychologia* 6: 190–192.

Ray, P. C. 1955. 'The Tensional Feelings among the Abors and Galongs as Indicated by the Rorschach Technique'. *Indian Journal of Psychology* 30: 95–103.

Raychaudhuri, M. 1963. 'Personality of the Indian Musicians'. *Rorschachiana Japonica* 6: 164–214.

———. 1964. 'An Investigation into the Personality Structure of the Musicians'. PhD thesis, Calcutta University, Calcutta.

———. 1971. 'Relation of Creativity and Sex to Rorschach Response'. *Journal of Personality Assessment* 35: 27–31.

Raychaudhuri, M., and A. K. Maitra. 1965a. 'Developmental Parallels in the Rorschach Responses: An Approach to the Test Validation'. Council of Social and Psychological Research Bulletin 5: 1–7.

———. 1965b. 'A Rorschach Study of Normal Convicted and Incipient Delinquent Adolescents'. *Rorschach Japonica* 8: 175–185.

Raychaudhuri, M., and A. K. Maitra 1968. 'Relationship between Level of Creativity and Projection of Movement Responses as Measured by Rorschach M. Welsh Mv and a Drawing Completion Task'. *Indian Journal of Psychology* 43: 30–36.

Raychaudhuri, M., and K. Mukherjee. 1969. 'Effects of Inhibition of Agitated-Aggressive Expression on Rorschach Movement Responses: A Validation Study'. *Rorschach Japonica* 11: 181–188.

———. 1970. 'Rorschach Differentials of Homosexuality in Male Convicts: An Examination of Wheeler and Schafer Signs'. *Journal of Personality Assessment* 35: 22–26.

Raychaudhuri, M., K. Mukherjee, and S. Raychaudhuri. 1969. 'Rorschach Indices of Aggression and Maladjustment—A Comparative Study with Normal and Indisciplined Boys'. *Archives of Child Health* 11: 31–38.

Raynor, Peter, and Gill McIvor. 2008. *Developments in Social Work Offenders (Research Highlights in Social Work)*, 138. London: Jessica Kingsley Publishers.

Ready, R. E., and H. B. Veague. 2014. 'Training in Psychological Assessment: Current Practices of Clinical Psychology Programs'. *Professional Psychology: Research and Practice* 45 (4): 278–282.

Reiser, M. F. 2001. 'The Dream in Contemporary Psychiatry'. *American Journal of Psychiatry* 158 (3): 351–359.

Renu, B., and U. Singh. 1996. 'A Study of Projective and Psychometric Personality Correlates of Altruism'. Unpublished master dissertation, Dept of Psychology, Kurukshetra University, Kurukshetra.

Reynolds, W. M., and N. D. Sundberg. 1976. 'A Survey of Rorschach Teaching in A PA Approved Clinical Graduate Programs'. *Journal of Personality Assessment* 40: 228–233.

Reznikoff, E., M. Aronow, and K. L. Moreland. 1995. 'The Rorschach: Projective Technique or Psychometric Test?' *Journal of Personality Assessment* 64: 213–228.

Rickless, N. K. 1950. *Exhibitionism*. Philadelphia, PA: Lippincott.

Riquelme, J. J., and Erna Perfetti. 2000. 'Rorschach in Women Victims of Rape'. *SIS Journal of Projective Psychology & Mental Health*: 133–140.

Rishi, N., and U. Singh. 1995. 'A Study of Hostility in Relation to Personality and Motivation of Girl Students'. Unpublished MPhil dissertation, Dept of Psychology, Kurukshetra University, Kurukshetra.

Ritzler, B. 1995. 'Putting Your Eggs in the Content Analysis Basket: A Response to Aronow, Reznikoff and Moreland'. *Journal of Personality Assessment* 64: 229–234.

Rizzuoto, A. M. 1991. 'Review of Psychoanalysis and Religion'. *International Review of Psychoanalysis* 18: 576–580.

Robinson, L. H. 1985. 'The Illusion of No Future: Psychoanalysis and Religion'. *Journal of American Academy of Psychoanalysis* 13: 211–228.

Roemer, G. 1967. 'The Rorschach and Roemer Symbol Test Series'. *Journal of Nervous Mental Diseases* 144: 185–197.

Roopa, C. G., and C. Joseph. 2004. 'Rorschach Indices of Personality in Aircrew Referred for Psychological Evaluation'. *Indian Journal of Aerospace Medicine* 48 (1): 1–9.

Rorschach, H. 1921. Psychodiagnostic. Bern: Ernst Bircher.

———. 1942. *Psychodiagnostics: A Diagnostic Test Based on Perception*. New York, NY: Grune & Stratton.

———. 1951. *Psychodiagnostics* (translated by P. Lemkau and B. Kronenberg), 5th ed. New York, NY: Grune & Stratton.

Rorschach, H., and E. Oberholzer. 1923. 'The Application of the Interpretation of Form to Psychoanalysis'. *Journal of Nervous and Mental Diseases* 60: 225–248, 359–379.

Rosenstiel, L. V. 1973. 'Increase in Hostility Responses in the HIT after Frustration'. *Journal of Personality Assessment* 37 (1): 22–24.

Rossi, E. L. 1986. *The Psychobiology of Mind–Body Healing: New Concepts of Therapeutic Hypnosis*, 47. New York, NY: W. W. Norton & Company.

Sachacher, B., and M. Jahan. 2014. 'SIS-II Profile of Patient with Body Dysmorphic Disorder: A Case Report'. *SIS Journal of Projective Psychology & Mental Health* 21 (1): 59–61.

Sachs, G. S., M. E. Thase, and M. W. Otto. 2003. 'Rationale, Design and Methods of the Systematic Treatment Enhancement Program in Bipolar Disorder (STEP-BD)'. *Biological Psychiatry* 53 (11): 1028–1042.

Sahay, M., and P. K. Srivastava. 1994. 'Somatic Inkblot Series-II in Male Transexuals'. *SIS Journal of Projective Psychology & Mental Health* 1: 73–78.

Saldanha, D. 2002. 'Profile of Militants: An Attempt to Study the Mind of Militants'. *SIS Journal of Projective Psychology & Mental Health* 9: 23–32.

Saldanha, D., L. Bhattacharya, K. Srivastava, and B. L. Dubey. 2011. 'SIS-I Profile of Psychosexual Dysfunction'. *SIS Journal of Projective Psychology & Mental Health* 18 (1): 62–68.

Saldanha, D., and B. L. Dubey. 1995. 'Effect of Sodium Pentothal on SIS Video-A Images'. *SIS Journal of Projective Psychology & Mental Health* 2: 19–28.

Saldanha, D., P. Menon, S. Guliani, V. Goyal, M. Garg, A. Tewari, and M. Agrawal. 2013. 'Effect of Therapeutic Intervention in a Case of Schizophrenia through SIS-II and Rorschach'. *SIS Journal of Projective Psychology & Mental Health* 20 (1): 55–61.

Sandhu, J. S. 1978. 'Rorschach Responses in Schizophrenia'. *Indian Journal of Clinical Psychology* 5: 145–153.

Santosa, C. M., C. M. Strong, C. Nowakowska, P. W. Wang, C. M. Rennicke, and T. A. Ketter. 2007. 'Enhanced Creativity in Bipolar Patients: A Controlled Study' (E Publ 28 Nov 2006). *Journal of Affect Disorder* 100 (1–3): 31–39.

Sanyal, N. 2013. 'Somatic Inkblot Series-II: The Therapeutic Window of Emotionally-Withdrawn Children'. *SIS Journal of Projective Psychology & Mental Health* 20 (2): 81–90.

———. 2016. 'Editorial: Projective Techniques True "Mirror" of Self'. *SIS Journal of Projective Psychology & Mental Health* 23 (2): 65.

Sanyal, N., M. Dasgupta, and M. M. Chatterjee. 2005. 'Who is Afraid of Rorschach Inkblots? Projective Studies in India an End Century Assessment'. *SIS Journal of Projective Psychology & Mental Health* 12 (2): 107–114.

Sarkar, P., S. P. Rathee, and N. Neena. 1999. 'Comparative Efficacy of Pharmacotherapy and Bio-Feedback among Cases of Generalized Anxiety Disorder'. *SIS Journal of Projective Psychology & Mental Health* 6: 69–77.

Saul, L. J. 1940. 'Utilization Early Current Dreams Formulation Psychoanalytic Cases'. *Psychoanalysis Quarterly* 9: 453–469.

Savage, G. 1995. 'Bereavement and Hypnosis: A Case Study'. *SIS Journal of Projective Psychology & Mental Health* 2: 29–40.

———. 2001. 'The Adjunctive Use of a Projective Technique with Hypnotherapy'. *SIS Journal of Projective Psychology & Mental Health* 8: 41–50.

———. 2003. 'The Diagnostic Value of the SIS in Treating a Child with Panic Attacks during the Post-Divorce Period: A Clinical Case Study'. *SIS Journal of Projective Psychology & Mental Health* 10: 219–224.

Savary, L. M. 1990. 'Dreams for Personal and Spiritual Growth'. In S. Krippner (Ed.) *Dreamtime and Dream Work: Decoding the Language of the Night*, pp. 6–12. Los Angeles, CA: Jeremy P. Tarcher Inc.

Schaefer, R. 1954. *Psychoanalytic Interpretation in Rorschach Testing*. New York, NY: Grune & Stratton.

———. 1960. 'Bodies in Schizophrenic Rorschach Responses'. *Journal of Projective Technique & Personality Assessment* 24: 267–281.

Schilder, P. 1935. 'The Image and Appearance of the Human Body'. *Psychological Monographs* 4.

Schlossman, H. H. 1966. 'Circumcision as Defense: A Study in Psychoanalysis and Religion'. *Psychoanalysis Quarterly* 35: 340–356.

Schneider, L. 1956. *You and Your Senses*. Boston, MA: Harcourt.

Schulmeyer, M. K., and C. Piotrowski. 2017. 'Assessment Practices of Psychologists in the Mental Health System in Bolivia'. *SIS Journal of Projective Psychology & Mental Health* 24 (2): 109–115.

Segal, H. 1978. *Introduction to the Work of Malanie Klein*. London: The Hogarth Press and the Institute of Psychoanalysis.

Sengupta, A., N. Mishra, and N. Dwivedi. 2012. 'SIS in a Case of Somatised Pain'. *SIS Journal of Projective Psychology & Mental Health* 19 (2): 126–130.

Sethi, B. B., S. C. Gupta, A. S. Raj, and S. S. Nathawat. 1971. 'Rorschach as a Measure of Psychopathology in Murder'. *Indian Journal of Psychiatry* 13: 243–247.

Shanker, P. 1968. 'Education and Rorschach Affective Factors of the Harijans'. *Indian Psychological Review* 4: 95–100.

Shanker, U. 1956. 'Rorschach Responses of a Group of Juvenile Thieves'. *Indian Journal of Psychology* 31: 15–20.

Shanmugam, A. V. 1959. 'A Rorschach Study of Stars and Isolates among High School Students'. *Psychological Studies* 4: 35–49.

Shapiro, D. H. Jr. 1990. 'A Sense of Control, Health, and Illness: Exploring the Mind–Body Relationship and the Socio-Cultural/Spiritual Context: Reflections on Bali'. *International Journal of Psychosomatics* 37 (1–4): 40–49.

Shapiro, F. 1995. *Eye Movement Desensitization and Reprocessing: Basic Principles, Protocols, and Procedures.* New York, NY: Guilford Press.

Sharma, M. G., Vandana Sharma, and A. Upadhyay. 2013. 'Effect of Psychotherapy in Phobic Patients and Their Follow-Up'. *SIS Journal of Projective Psychology & Mental Health* 20 (1): 36–41.

Sharma, Shweta. 2018. 'Impact of Childhood Sexual Abuse on Female Sexuality'. *SIS Journal of Projective Psychology & Mental Health* 25 (2): 173–177.

Sharma, S., D. Mishra, and R. Kumar. 2013. 'Personality Characteristic of Juvenile Delinquents as Compared to Non-Delinquents on Rorschach Test'. *SIS Journal of Projective Psychology & Mental Health* 20 (2): 98–105.

Sharma, S., and A. Singh. 1990. 'A Study of Psychometric and Projective Personality Correlates of Attribution Styles of High School Students'. Unpublished MPhil dissertation, Dept of Psychology, Kurukshetra University, Kurukshetra.

Sharma, U. D. 1969. 'A Comparative Study of Color Pyramid and a Rorschach Inkblot Tests Responses by a Group of Recidivists'. *Council of Social and Psychological Research Bulletin* 12: 26–31.

Sharma, V. K., B. L. Dubey, S. Murlidharan, and B. Kumar. 1997. 'Personality Profile of Alopecia Areata with the Help of SIS-II'. *SIS Journal of Projective Psychology & Mental Health* 4: 161–166.

Sharma, V. P., K. N. Ojha, and V. S. Vagrecha. 1975. 'Clinical Psychology in India'. *Indian Journal Clinical Psychology* 2: 73–76.

Shivadasani, H. K. 1971. 'Rorschach Hostility Content and Its Relationship with Various Forms of Aggression—Hostility'. *Psychological Studies* 16: 15–18.

Shukla, T. R. 1972. 'Perception of Penetration of Body–Image–Boundary in Schizophrenia'. *Psychologia: An International Journal of Psychology in the Orient* 15 (4): 240–242.

————. 1974. 'Split-Half Reliability of HIT Variables'. *Indian Journal of Clinical Psychology* 1: 101–103.

————. 1976a. 'Pathological Verbalization on Inkblot and Psycho Diagnosis'. *Indian Journal of Clinical Psychology* 3: 17–21.

————. 1976b. 'Psychodiagnostic Efficacy of the HIT under Indian Conditions: A Normative Study'. *Indian Journal of Clinical Psychology* 3 (2): 189–198.

————. 1977. 'Projective Techniques in India'. *Indian Journal of Clinical Psychology* 4: 105–107.

Shweta, R. C. Bajpai, K. S. Sengar, A. R. Singh, and N. G. Desai. 2010. 'Rorschach Profile of Indian Adults'. *SIS Journal of Projective Psychology & Mental Health* 17 (2): 180–186.

Singh, A. R. 2007. 'Editorial: SIS: A Journey of Projective Technique from Assessment to Treatment'. *SIS Journal of Projective Psychology & Mental Health* 14 (2): 85–86.

Singh, A. R., and K. R. Banerjee. 1996. 'Efficacy of SIS-II in Discriminating OCD Patients and Normals'. *SIS Journal of Projective Psychology & Mental Health* 3: 165–169.

Singh, A. R., and K. R. Banerjee. 2002. 'Treating Panic Attack with Hypnosis in Combination with Rational Emotive Therapy: A Case Report'. *SIS Journal of Projective Psychology & Mental Health* 9: 105–108.

Singh, A. R., K. R. Banerjee, and S. Chaudhury. 2001. 'Mental Health during War: An Experience and Lesson from the Past'. *SIS Journal of Projective Psychology & Mental Health* 8: 135–140.

Singh, A. R., and B. L. Dubey. 1997. 'Profile of Drug and Alcohol Dependent Cases'. *SIS Journal of Projective Psychology & Mental Health* 4: 69–74.

Singh, A. R., B. L. Dubey, and K. R. Banerjee. 1997. 'Prognostic Utility of SIS-II'. *SIS Journal of Projective Psychology & Mental Health* 4: 141–144.

Singh, A. R., K. C. Manjhi, B. L. Dubey, and K. R. Banerjee. 2001. 'Profiles of Professional Murderers'. *SIS Journal of Projective Psychology & Mental Health* 8: 28–30.

Singh, B., R. Kashyap, and A. K. Srivastava. 2011. 'Diagnostic Indicators of SIS-I among Non-Paranoid Schizophrenics'. *SIS Journal of Projective Psychology & Mental Health* 18 (2): 165–167.

Singh, D. K., G. Majhi, Jai Prakash, and A. R. Singh. 2008. 'Changes in Rorschach Indices: Pre and Post Treatment Assessment'. *SIS Journal of Projective Psychology & Mental Health* 15 (1): 42–47.

Singh, D. K., G. Majhi, and A. R. Singh. 2007. 'Projective Indices of Creativity: A Pilot Study'. *SIS Journal of Projective Psychology & Mental Health* 14 (2): 117–120.

Singh, D. K., A. Singh, and A. R. Singh. 2005. 'Relevance of Beck Norms of Rorschach Inkblot Technique on Indian Population—An Exploratory Pilot Study on Normal Subjects'. *SIS Journal of Projective Psychology & Mental Health* 12: 49–52.

Singh, M. K., and A. Mukhopadhyay. 2018. 'SIS Indices in Parents of Children with ADHD and Intervention Steps'. *SIS Journal of Projective Psychology & Mental Health* 25 (1): 80–85.

Singh, M. P., and B. L. Dubey. 2002. 'Inter Correlation among Various Indices of SIS-II'. *SIS Journal of Projective Psychology & Mental Health* 9 (2): 121–132.

Singh, M. P., and P. Dwivedi. 1997. 'Somatised Pain: A Case Study with the Help of SIS-II'. *SIS Journal of Projective Psychology & Mental Health* 4: 167–171.

———. 1998. 'A Comparative Study of Managers and Students on SIS-II'. *SIS Journal of Projective Psychology & Mental Health* 5: 63–68.

Singh, M. P., and Nalini Mishra. 2001. 'Diagnostic and Therapeutic Value of SIS-II Test'. *SIS Journal of Projective Psychology & Mental Health* 8: 141–142.

Singh, M. P., M. Mishra, and Nalini Mishra. 1999. 'Effect of Age and Sex on the Length of the Protocol of SIS-II Images'. *SIS Journal of Projective Psychology & Mental Health* 6 (1): 50–52.

Singh, M. P., A. Singh, and B. L. Dubey. 1999. 'Effect of Age and Sex on SIS-II Responses'. *SIS Journal of Projective Psychology & Mental Health* 6 (2): 51–76.

Singh, S., and R. Kapur. 1984. 'Psychometric and Behavioral Correlates of Group Rorschach Measure of Hostility'. *Indian Journal of Clinical Psychology* 11: 35–44.

Singh, S. K., R. K. Singh, D. K. Singh, and J. Prakash. 2008. 'Characteristics of Subjects Who Perceive Female Figure on Card VII of Rorschach Test'. *SIS Journal of Projective Psychology & Mental Health* 15: 113–117.

Singh, Umed. 1995. 'A Study of Relationship between Types of Creativity and Types of Intelligence'. Unpublished doctoral dissertation, Dept of Psychology, Kurukshetra University, Kurukshetra.

———. 2006a. 'Novelty and Meaning Contexts of Creativity vis-a-vis Jensen's Level I and Level II Abilities'. *SIS Journal of Projective Psychology & Mental Health* 13 (2): 147–160.

———. 2006b. 'Distinction of Novelty and Meaning Contexts of Creativity'. *SIS Journal of Projective Psychology & Mental Health* 13: 65–79.

———. 2007. 'Gender Differences in Factor Structure of SIS-II Responses'. *SIS Journal of Projective Psychology & Mental Health* 14 (2): 110–116.

Singh, Umed, and N. Singh. 2008. 'Effect of School Environments on SIS-II Percepts'. *SIS Journal of Projective Psychology & Mental Health* 15: 145–151.

Singh, U., and K. Rani. 2014a. 'Gender-Specific Personality Differentials of Suicide Ideation among Adolescents'. *SIS Journal of Projective Psychology & Mental Health* 21 (2): 81–89.

———. 2014b. 'SIS-II Correlates of Suicide Ideation among Adolescents'. *SIS Journal of Projective Psychology & Mental Health* 21 (1): 49–57.

Singh, U., N. Verma, and N. Singh. 2009. 'SIS-II Indicators of Creativity'. *SIS Journal of Projective Psychology & Mental Health* 16: 128–133.

Singh, V. K. 1975. 'Culture-Contact and Personality Adjustment'. *Indian Journal of Clinical Psychology* 2: 129–134.

Smith, J. H., and S. A. Handelman, eds. 1990. *Psychoanalysis and Religion*. Baltimore, MD: Johns Hopkins University.

Snaith, N. H. 1968. *The Book of Job: Its Origin and Purpose*. London: SCM Press.

Somasundaram, C. P. 1964. 'Rorschach Responses of People of Kerala: A Normative Study'. PhD dissertation, University of Kerala.

Somasundaram, C. P., K. V. Mathai, and G. Jesudian. 1971a. 'The Application of the Rorschach Technique in Patients Disabled by Convulsive Disorders'. *Neurology India* 19: 64–72.

———. 1971b. 'The Rorschach Popular Responses in Patients with Epilepsy'. *Neurology India* 19: 73–76.

Spanjaard, J. 1969. 'Manifest Dream Content: Significance in Interpretation of Dreams'. *International Journal of Psychoanalysis* 50: 221–236.

Sperbeck, D. 2000. 'Editorial'. *SIS Journal of Projective Psychology & Mental Health* 7: 1–2.

Spezzano, C., and G. Gargiulo. 1997. *Soul on the Couch: Spirituality, Religion, and Morality in Contemporary Psychoanalysis*. Hillsdale, NJ: Analytic Press.

Spitzer, R. L., J. B. W. Williams, M. Gibbon, and M. B. First. 1990. *User's Guide for the Structured Clinical Interview for DSM-III-R*. Washington, DC: American Psychiatric Association Press.

Srivastava, A. K. 2002. 'Somatic Inkblot Series-I: A Meta Analysis'. *SIS Journal of Projective Psychology & Mental Health* 9: 33–37.

Stanley, B. and L. J. Siever 2010. 'The Interpersonal Dimension of Borderline Personality: Toward a Neuropeptide Model'. *American Journal of Psychiatry* 167 1, 24–39.

Stedman, J. M., J. Essery, and C. A. McGeary. 2018. 'Projective Personality Assessment: Evidence for a Decline in Training Emphasis'. *SIS Journal of Projective Psychology & Mental Health* 25 (1): 54–59.

Stedman, J. M., C. A. McGeary, and J. Essery. 2017. 'Current Patterns of Training in Personality Assessment during Internship'. *Journal of Clinical Psychology* 73.

Stein, M. B., R. Yehuda, C. Koverola, and C. Hanna. 1997. 'Enhanced Dexamethasone Suppression of Plasma Cortisol in Adult Women Traumatized by Childhood Sexual Abuse'. *Biological Psychiatry* 42 (8): 680–686.

Stensland, M. D., J. F. Schultz, and J. R. Frytak. 2008. 'Diagnosis of Unipolar Depression Following Initial Identification of Bipolar Disorder: A Common and Costly Misdiagnosis'. *Journal of Clinical Psychiatry* 69 (5): 749–758.

Stewart, W. A. 1967. 'The Manifest Content of Certain Types of Unusual Dreams'. *Psychoanalysis Quarterly* 36: 329–341.

Sreeramareddy, C. T., P. R. Shankar, V. S. B. Mukhopadhyay, B. Ray, and R. G. Menezes. 2007, August. 'Psychological Morbidity, Sources of Stress and Coping among Undergraduate Medical Students of Nepal'. *BMC Medical Education*. doi:10.1186/1472-6920-7-26.

Summerfeld, L. J., M. A. Richter, M. M. Anthony, and R. P. Swinson. 1999. 'Symptom Structure in Obsessive-Compulsive Disorder: A Confirmatory Factor Analytic Study'. *Behavior Research Therapy* 37: 297–311.

Sundberg, N. D. 1961. 'The Practice of Psychological Testing in Clinical Services in the United States'. *American Psychologist* 16: 79–83.

Swartz, J. D. 1970. 'Pathognomic Verbalizations in Normal, Psychotics and Mental Retardates'. Doctoral dissertation, University of Texas at Austin. *Dissertation Abstracts International* 30: 5703B–5704B (Order No.70-10,872).

Swartz, J. D., and W. H. Holtzman. 1963. 'Group Method of Administration for the Holtzman Inkblot Technique'. *Journal of Clinical Psychology* 19: 433–441.

Swartz, J. D., R. C. Reinehr, and W. H. Holtzman. 1983a. *Holtzman Inkblot Technique, 1956–1982: An Annotated Bibliography*. Austin, TX: Hogg Foundation for Mental Health.

———. 1983b. 'Personality Development through the Lifespan: Assessment by the Means of the Holtzman Inkblot Technique'. In *Advances in Personality Assessment*, edited by C. D. Spielberger, and J. N. Butcher, Vol. 3. Hillsdale, NJ: Lawrence Erlbaum Assoc.

Swartz, J. D., R. C. Reinehr, and W. H. Holtzman 1999. *Holtzman Inkblot Technique: Research Guide and Bibliography*. Austin, TX: Hogg Foundation for Mental Health.

Tait, C. D., and R. C. Ascher. 1955. 'Inside the Body Test'. *Psychosomatic Medicine* 17: 139.

Tatara, Mikihachiro. 1994. 'Belief and Religious Sentiments in Japanese as Revealed in Their Dreams'. *Hiroshima Forum for Psychology* 16: 39–44.

Tedeschi, R. G., C. L. Park, and L. G. Calhoun. (Eds) 1998. The LEA Series in Personality and Clinical Psychology-Posttraumatic Growth: Positive changes in the aftermath of Crisis. Mahwah, NJ: Lawrence Eribaum Associates Publishers.

Teglasi, H. 2010. *Essentials of TAT and other Storytelling Assessments*, 2nd ed. New York, NY: Wiley.

Tewari, M. K., and P. Dwivedi. 1999. 'SIS Video in a Case of Depression'. *SIS Journal of Projective Psychology & Mental Health* 6: 47–49.

Tiwari, A., P. Pandey, N. Mishra, and A. Dubey. 2012. 'SIS-II Profile of Depressive Patients'. *Journal of Projective Psychology & Mental Health* 19 (1): 48–55.

Tripathi, S. N., and G. Julka. 1960. 'Content Analysis of the Rorschach Test'. *University of Rajasthan Studies* 4: 21–24.

Upadhyaya, S., and A. K. Sinha. 1974. 'Some Findings on Psychodiagnostic Tests with Young Retarded Adults'. *Indian Journal of Clinical Psychology* 1: 73–79.

Urmila, S. 2005. 'A Study of Some Indices of HIT in Relation to Their Psychometric Measures'. Unpublished doctoral dissertation, Department of Psychology, Kurukshetra University, Kurukshetra.

Vagrecha, Y. S., and D. P. S. Majumdar. 1974. 'Relevance of Piotrowski's Signs in Relation to Intellectual Deficit in Organic (Epileptic) and Normal Subjects'. *Indian Journal of Clinical Psychology* 1: 64–66.

———. 1975. 'Diagnostic Value of Piotrowski's Sign in Rorschach Responses in Epileptic Patients'. *British Journal of Projective Psychology & Personality Study* 20: 27–32.

Vande Kemp, Hendrika. 1994a. 'Psycho-Spiritual Dreams in the Nineteenth Century, I: Dreams of Death'. *Journal of Psychology & Theology* 22 (2): 97–108.

———. 1994b. 'Psycho-Spiritual Dreams in the Nineteenth Century, II: Metaphysics and Immortality'. *Journal of Psychology & Theology* 22 (2): 109–119.

Van der Kolk, B. A., A. C. McFarlane, and L. Weisaeth. 1996. *Traumatic Stress: The Effects of Overwhelming Experience on Mind, Body, and Society*. New York, NY: Guilford Press.

Van der Kolk, B. A., and O. Van der Hart. 1991. 'The Intrusive Past: The Flexibility of Memory and the Engraving of Trauma'. *American Imago* 48: 425–454.

Vashistha, K. C., and S. Bhardwaj. 2007. 'Rorschach Profiles of Mentally Challenged and Severely Hearing-Impaired Children'. *SIS Journal of Projective Psychology & Mental Health* 14 (2): 121–128.

Verma, M. K., and S. Misra. 2002. 'Rorschach Response Patterns of Drug Addicts'. *SIS Journal of Projective Psychology & Mental Health* 9: 62–64.

Verma, N., and U. Singh. 2014. 'Effect of Age and Education on SIS-II Percepts'. *SIS Journal of Projective Psychology & Mental Health* 21 (2): 113–118.

Verma, S. K. 1980. 'Psychological Referrals in Psychiatry Units of a General Hospital'. *Indian Journal of Clinical Psychology* 7: 157–160.

———. 1995. 'Reliability and Validity of Somatic Inkblot Series Test'. *SIS Journal of Projective Psychology & Mental Health* 2: 67–71.

———. 1996. 'Newer Trends in Inkblot Techniques'. *SIS Journal of Projective Psychology & Mental Health* 3: 1–2.

———. 2001. 'SIS as An Instrument of Change'. *SIS Journal of Projective Psychology & Mental Health* 8: 1–2.

Verma, S. K., and H. Kaur. 1999. 'A Proposed Model for Quantification of Abnormal Somatic Concern on SIS-II'. *SIS Journal of Projective Psychology & Mental Health* 6: 65–68.

Verma, S. K., H. Kaur, and R. Bhargava. 2000. 'Distortions of Body Image on SIS-II and DAP'. *SIS Journal of Projective Psychology & Mental Health* 7: 39–43.

Verma, S. K., D. Pershad, K. Bhagat, and R. Kaur. 1996. 'Interdependence of SIS Variables with Personality Traits in Psychiatric Cases'. *SIS Journal of Projective Psychology & Mental Health* 3: 51–58.

Verma, S. K., D. Pershad, R. Kaur, and R. Nehra. 1995. 'Diagnostic Significance of SIS-II'. *SIS Journal of Projective Psychology & Mental Health* 2: 72–76.

Verma, S. K., D. Pershad, and R. Nehra. 1994. 'Cross-Validation of SIS-II in Psychiatric Population'. *SIS Journal of Projective Psychology & Mental Health* 1: 15–18.

Verma, S. K., and A. Nehra. 1998. 'Projective Psychotherapy'. *SIS Journal of Projective Psychology & Mental Health* 5: 59–62.

Vernon, P. E. 1933. 'The Rorschach Inkblot Test'. *British Journal of Medical Psychology* 13: 179–205.

Vimal, P. 2004. 'SIS in a Case of Depressive Neurosis'. *SIS Journal of Projective Psychology & Mental Health* 11: 45–46.

Vimal, P., and S. Mishra. 2003. 'SIS in a Case of Hypochondriasis'. *SIS Journal of Projective Psychology & Mental Health* 10: 225–226.

Vishwakarma, P., S. D. Dwivedi, and R. Kumar. 2016. 'Emotional Intelligence, Exner's Special Indices on Rorschach in Schizophrenia'. *SIS Journal of Projective Psychology & Mental Health* 23 (2): 66–72.

Von-Franz, M. L. 1984. *On Dreams and Death*. Boston, MA: Shubkala.

Wade, T. C., T. B. Baker, T. L. Morton, and L. T. Baker. 1978. 'The Status of Psychological Testing in Clinical Psychology: Relationship between Test Use and Professional Activities and Orientations'. *Journal of Personality Assessment* 42: 3–10.

Waehler, C. A., L. T. Becky, E. E. Kristin, and M. L. John. 2008. 'Dispositional Tendencies Exhibited through Spontaneous Rorschach Card Rotation'. *SIS Journal of Projective Psychology & Mental Health* 15 (1): 25–34.

Wagner, E. E. 1983. *The Hand Test: Manual*, revised edition. Los Angeles, CA: Western Psychological Services.

Wallace, J. M. Jr., and T. A. Forman. 1998. 'Religion's Role in Promoting Health and Reducing Risk among American Youth'. *Health Education & Behavior* 25 (6): 721–741.

Watson, C. G, M. P. Juba, V. Manifold, T. Kucala, and P. E. D. Anderson. 1991. 'The PTSD Interview: Rationale, Description, Reliability, and Concurrent Validity of a DSM-III-Based Technique'. *Journal of Clinical Psychology* 47: 179–188.

Weathers, F., B. Litz, D. Herman, J. Huska, and T. Keane. 1993, October. 'The PTSD Checklist (PCL): Reliability, Validity, and Diagnostic Utility'. Paper presented at Annual Convention of International Society for Traumatic Stress Studies, San Antonio, TX.

Weiner, I. B. 2003. *Principles of Rorschach Interpretation*. Mahwah, NJ: Lawrence Erlbaum.

Weiner, I. B., and R. L. Greene. 2007. *Handbook of Personality Assessment*. Hoboken, NJ: John Wiley & Sons.

Weiss, A. A., and H. K. Winnik. 1963. 'A Contribution to the Meaning of Anatomy Responses on the Rorschach Test'. Israil Analysis of Psychiatry, 1: 265–276.

Wentinck, C. 1972. *The Human Figure*. Wynnewood, PA: Livingston.

Werner, H. 1957. *Comparative Psychology of Mental Development*. New York, NY: International University Press.

Wickelgren, I. 1989. 'Image of Pain'. *Science News* 136: 136–137.

Williams, K. E., and L. M. Koran. 1997. 'Obsessive-Compulsive Disorder in Pregnancy, the Puerperium, and the Premenstruum'. *Journal of Clinical Psychiatry* 58: 330–334.

Williams, M. T., E. Turkheimer, K. M. Schmidt, and T. F. Oltmans. 2005. 'Ethnic Identification Biases Responses to the Padua Inventory for Obsessive-Compulsive Disorder'. *Assessment* 12: 174–185.

Williams, R. B., J. B. Flagg-Williams, and L. A. French. 2015. 'Children's Drawings, Thematic Apperceptive Technique Questions, and Memory'. *SIS Journal of Projective Psychology & Mental Health* 22 (2): 93–98.

Wolpe, J. 1969. *The Practice of Behavior Therapy*. New York, NY: Pergamon Press.

Wolpe, J., J. P. Brady, M. Serher, S. Auros, and R. P. Liberman. 1973. 'The Current Status of Systematic Desensitization'. *American Journal of Psychiatry* 130 (9): 961–965.

Wood, J. M. 2006. 'Controversy over Exner's Comprehensive System for the Rorschach: The Critics Speak'. *Independent Practitioner*. Available at http://works.bepress.com/james_wood/7J (accessed on 18 March 2019).

Wood, J. M., M. T. Nezworski, S. O. Lilienfeld, and H. N. Garb. 2011. *What's Wrong with the Rorschach: Science Confronts the Controversial Inkblot Test*. New York, NY: Wiley.

Wright, C.V., S.G. Beattie, D.I. Galper, A.S.Church, L.F. Bufka, V.M. Brabender, & B.L.Smith 2017. 'Assessment Practices of Professional Psychologists: Results of a National Survey'. *Professional Psychology: Research and Practice* 48 (2): 73–78.

Yadav, R. A. 1977. 'Rorschach Responses of the Institutionalized Offenders'. *Indian Journal of Clinical Psychology* 4: 151–156.

Yazmajian, R. V. 1964. 'First Dreams Directly Representing the Analyst'. *Psychoanalysis Quarterly* 33: 536–551.

Zilboorg, G. 1962. *Psychoanalysis and Religion*. New York, NY: Farrar, Straus & Cudahy.

Zimmerman, M., C. J. Ruggero, I. Chelminski, and D. Young. 2008. 'Is Bipolar Disorder over Diagnosed?' *Journal of Clinical Psychiatry* 69 (2): 161–174.

Zubieta, J. K., P. Huguelet, R. L. O'Neil, and B. J. Giordani. 2001. 'Cognitive Function in Euthymic Bipolar 1 Disorder'. *Psychiatry Research* 102 (1): 9–20.

Zubin, J. 1954. 'Failure of the Rorschach Technique'. *Journal of Projective Techniques* 18: 303–315.

Zubin, J., and L. D. Eron. 1966. *Experimental Abnormal Psychology*. New York, NY: New York State Psychiatric Institute.

Zubin, J., L. D. Eron, and F. Schumer. 1965. *An Experimental Approach to Projective Techniques*. New York, NY: John Wiley & Sons, Inc.

Zuk, C. V., and G. H. Zuk. 2002. 'Origin of Dreaming'. *American Journal of Psychiatry* 159: 495–496.

# Index

# About the Authors

**Bankey L. Dubey** is the Director of SIS Center, Anchorage, Alaska, USA. He is a clinical psychologist and management consultant. He completed his PhD in 1978 on the Rorschach test and had undergone two years internship in clinical psychology. He has also done postgraduate diploma in personnel management. He was trained by Dr Wilfred Cassell in the application of Somatic Inkblot Series (SIS) at SIS Center, Anchorage, USA. He has been the Editor-in-Chief of *SIS Journal of Projective Psychology and Mental Health* from 1994 to 2006 and continuing as Editor Emeritus since 2006. Dr Dubey is President of the Somatic Inkblot Society and heading the SIS Internet Therapy Division. He has been the President of Clinical Psychology for the years 1984 and 1985. He has published 3 books and about 160 research papers.

He started his career as a clinical psychologist in T. N. Medical College, Mumbai, in 1969 and served the Ministry of Defence (Command Hospital Chandigarh) for eight years before shifting to Panjab University, Chandigarh, in 1980 from where he retired as Professor of Psychology in 2005. He is associated with the Department of Psychology, University of Alaska, Anchorage, as Adjunct Faculty. He has been the visiting faculty in Postgraduate Institute of Medical Education and Research, Chandigarh, for 15 years. He helps people in understanding the personality through SIS tests and practices hypnotic relaxation therapy. SIS is one of the major therapeutic tools which he uses during relaxation therapy.

He is widely travelled and has conducted workshops in various international meetings in Anchorage, New London, Boston, San Francisco,

Columbia, Philadelphia, Chicago, Geneva, Amsterdam, Brussels, Madrid, Singapore, Sydney, Hobart, Macerata and several cities in India.

**Padmakali Banerjee** has over 25 years of experience in research, teaching and training, and academic administration. She has extensive experience as an executive, life coach and psychologist. Dr Banerjee has done her PhD from University of Delhi. She is a consultant in management development programmes and a trainer on HRD issues with various private and public sector organizations. Her areas of expertise include leadership studies, motivation, management communication, entrepreneurship and stress management. She is an international affiliate of American Psychological Association and the academic affiliate of Accreditation Council for Business Schools and Programs. Her professional experience extends across an array of industries including telecom, oil and gas industry, education and training, tourism and hospitality, and FMCG. She is the Executive Editor of *Amity Management Analyst*, a bi-annual referred journal of Amity Business School. She has published research papers in reputed refereed journals and has closely worked with corporate functionaries holding leadership development workshops and training programmes for corporate leaders. She was also actively associated as a founding member with the Bradford University Program, UK, in India right from the inception, including academic delivery, administration and quality audit.

In the current leadership position as the Pro-Vice-Chancellor and Dean Academics and Director of Amity University, Haryana, and Director, Amity Business School, she has been involved in strategic planning and leading the development and implementation of the University's academic and administrative processes. She is spearheading many innovative initiatives such as flexible credit system, industry university integration, internationalization and establishment of centre of excellence including centre for BRICS studies, centre for robotics, centre for stem cell research.

She is Editorial consultant of *SIS Journal of Projective Psychology and Mental Health*, and *International Journal of Hinduism and Philosophy*, UK. She has developed a psychometric test Optimism Index—a predictive tool for success. She has been instrumental in national and international academic tie-ups and collaborations. She has received awards and scholarships for academic excellence. In her professional career, she has exhibited her passion for entrepreneurship by empowering youth and developing leaders in different walks of life. She leads with a collaborative style.

**Anand Dubey**, entrepreneur and business leader, is the Vice President and Chief Information Officer (CIO) of Dubay Business Services, USA. He is also the Editor of *SIS Journal of Projective Psychology and Mental Health*. He started his career in the field of information technology and engineering in 1994. He completed his MBA in telecommunication in 2000 and was appointed to the position of Chief Information Officer, State of Alaska (USA), in 2007.

Mr Dubey has undergone advance training in the application of SIS and has been working with SIS since 1990. He was instrumental in preparing the 'Somatic Inkblot Series-II/Video Manual' in 1997 and the book *Interpreting Inner World through Somatic Imagery* in 2003. He has co-authored research publications with Dr Wilfred A. Cassell and Dr B. L. Dubey. He has been developing software programs for the application of SIS in business organizations and made SIS system popular internationally. He is currently leading the development of Dubay Healing Center, an online mental health treatment portal.